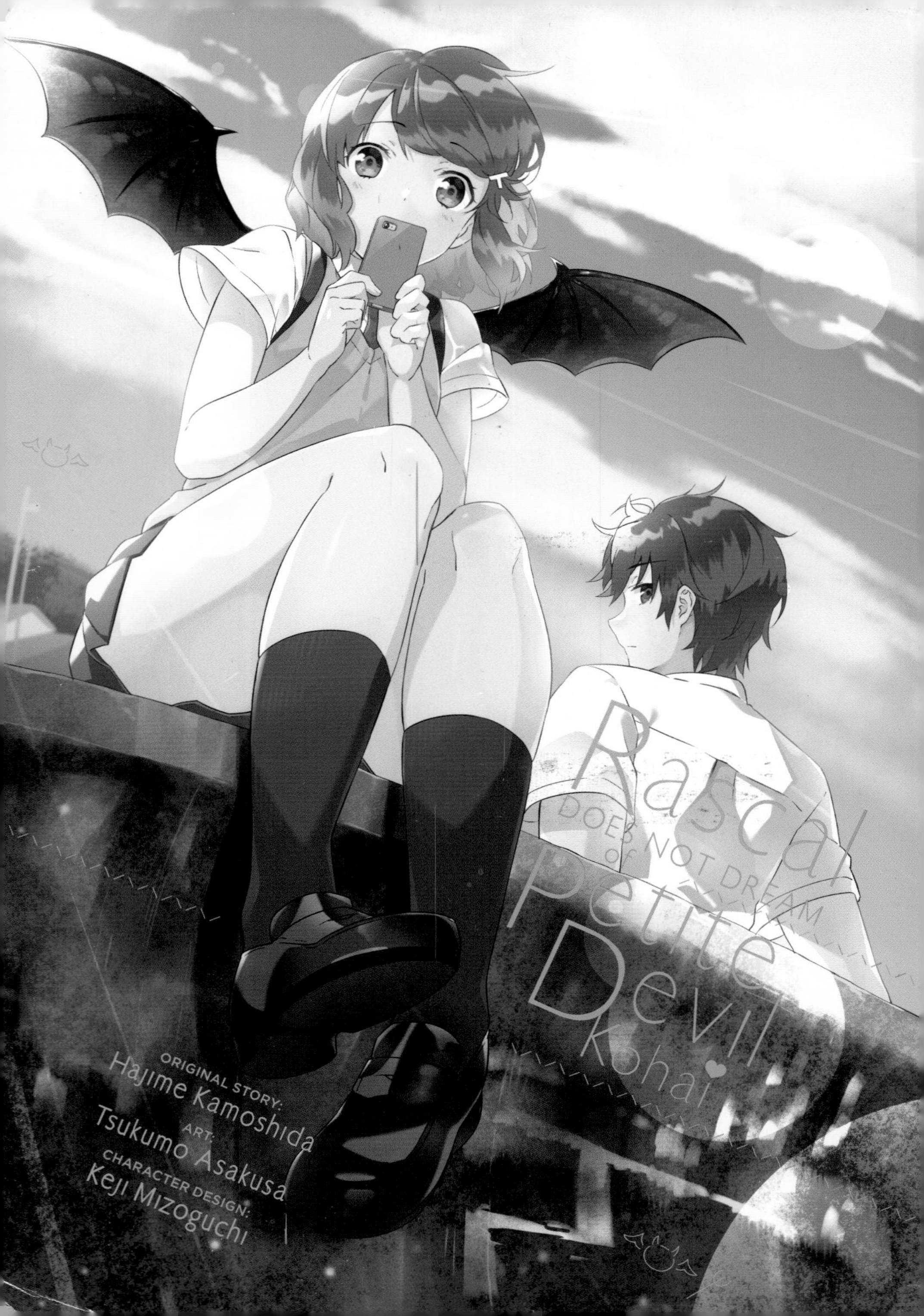

Rascal
DOES NOT DREAM
OF
Petite
Devil
Kohai
ORIGINAL STORY:
Hajime Kamoshida
ART:
Tsukumo Asakusa
CHARACTER DESIGN:
Keji Mizoguchi

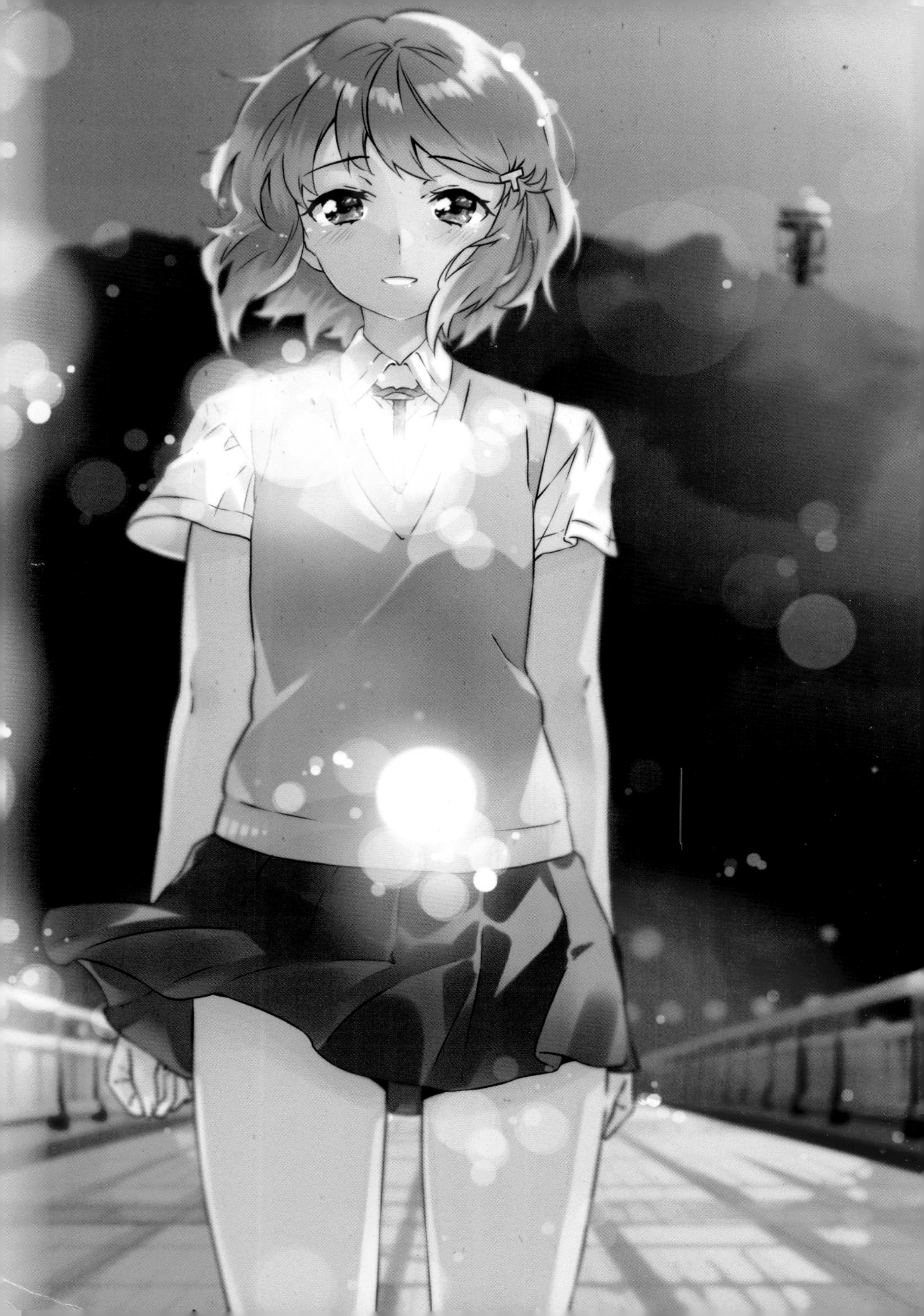

CONTENTS

#001     005

#002     047

#003     089

#004     111

#005     135

#006     153

#007     181

#008     209

#009     241

#010     269

#011     295

#012     321

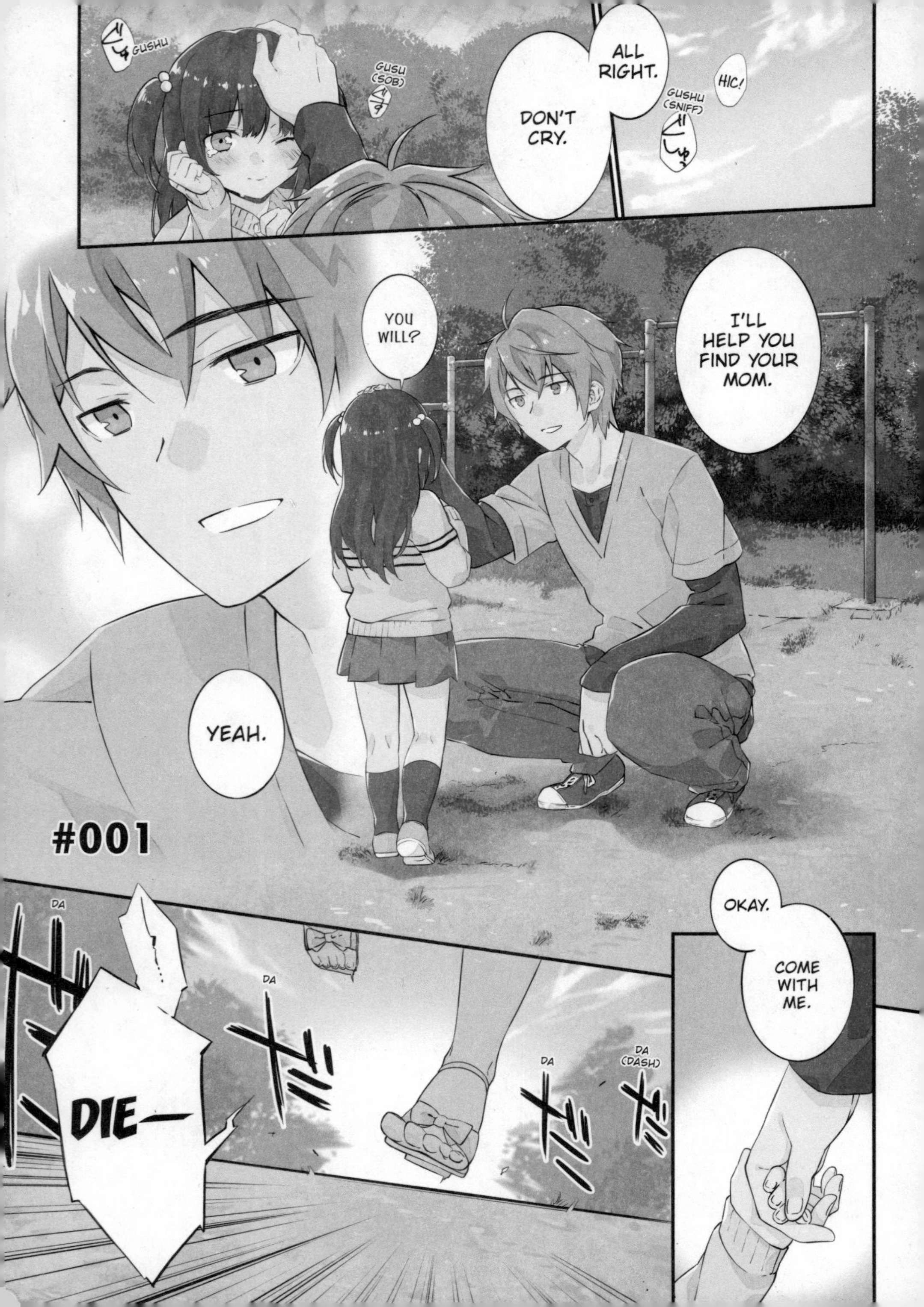
HIC!
GUSHU (SNIFF)
ALL RIGHT.
DON'T CRY.
GUSU (SOB)
GUSHU
I'LL HELP YOU FIND YOUR MOM.
YOU WILL?
YEAH.
#001
OKAY.
COME WITH ME.
DA (DASH)
DA
DA
DA
DIE—

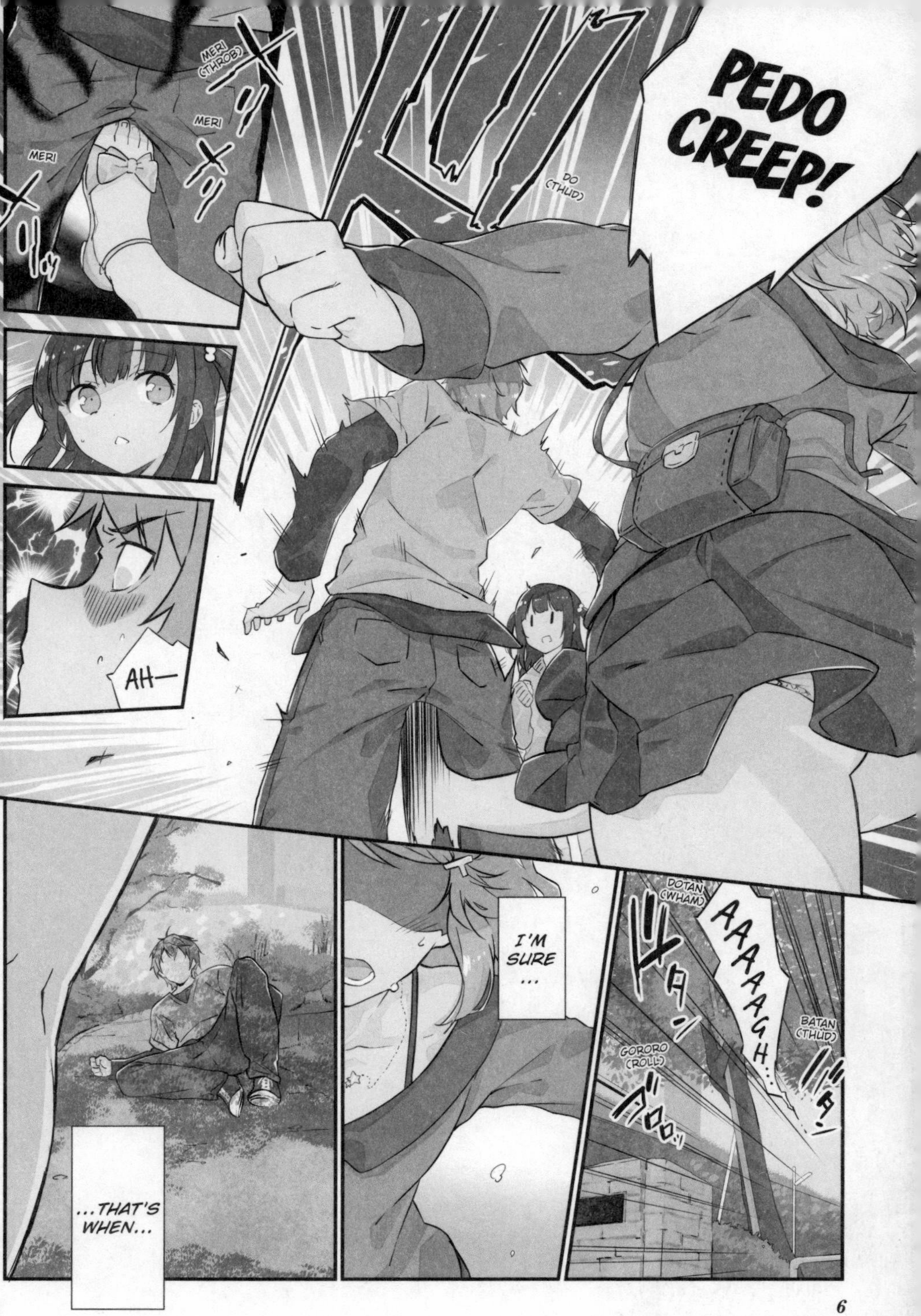
PEDO CREEP!
DO (THUD)
MERI (THROB)
MERI
MERI
AH—
DOTAN (WHAM)
AAAAAGH...
BATAN (THUD)
GORORO (ROLL)
I'M SURE ...
...THAT'S WHEN...

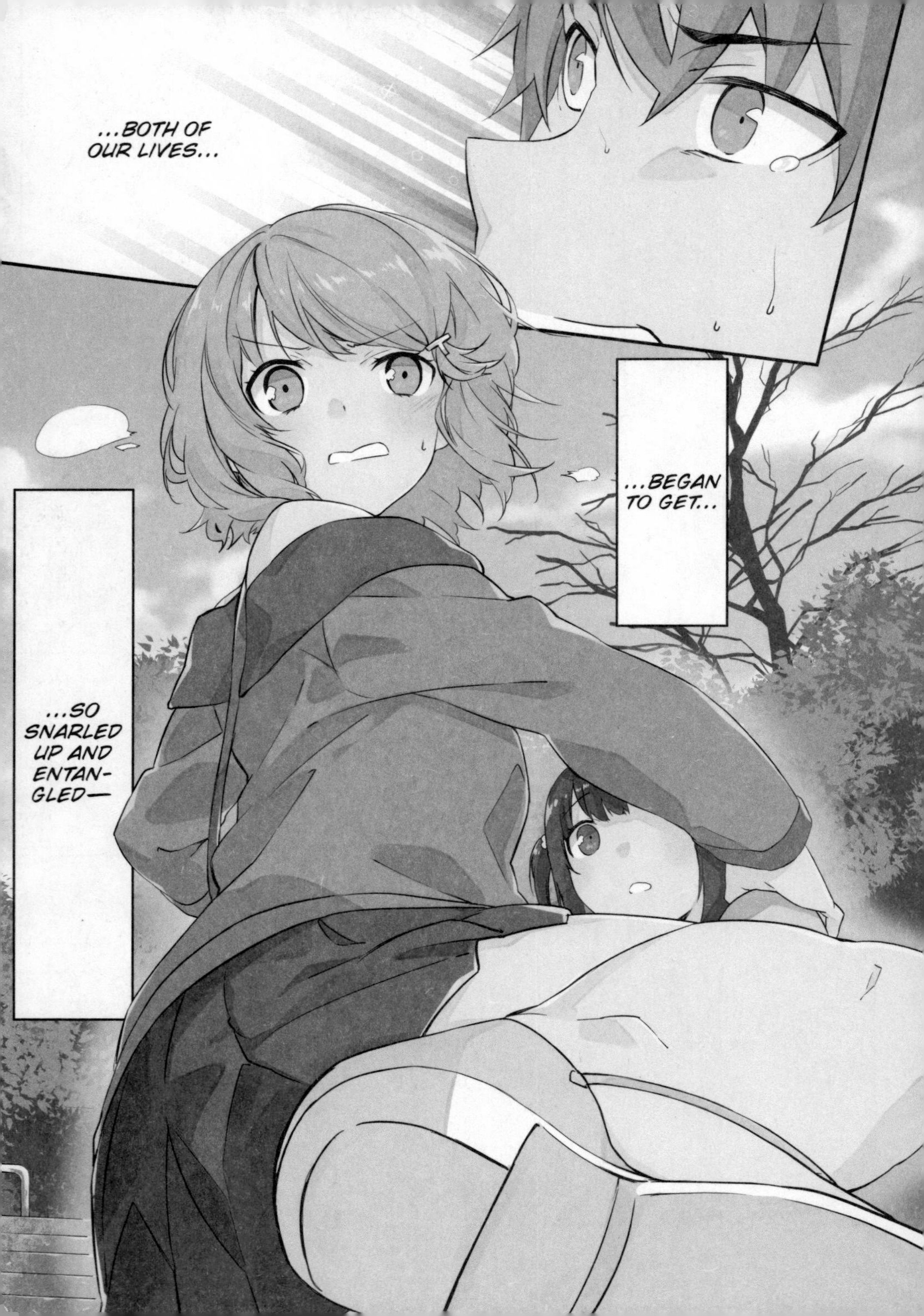
...BOTH OF OUR LIVES...
...BEGAN TO GET...
...SO SNARLED UP AND ENTANGLED—

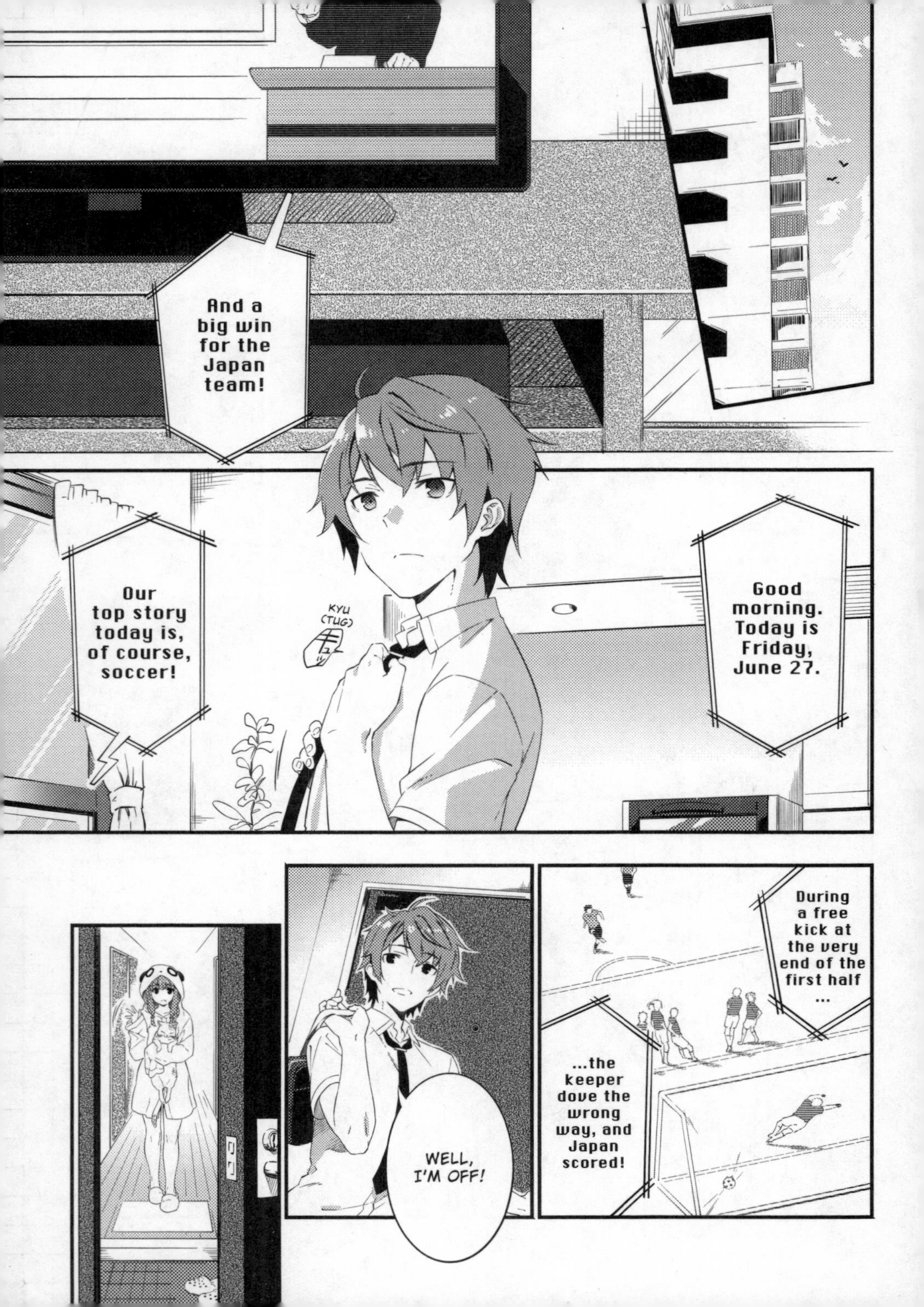
And a big win for the Japan team!
Good morning. Today is Friday, June 27.
KYU (TUG)
Our top story today is, of course, soccer!
During a free kick at the very end of the first half ...
...the keeper dove the wrong way, and Japan scored!
WELL, I'M OFF!

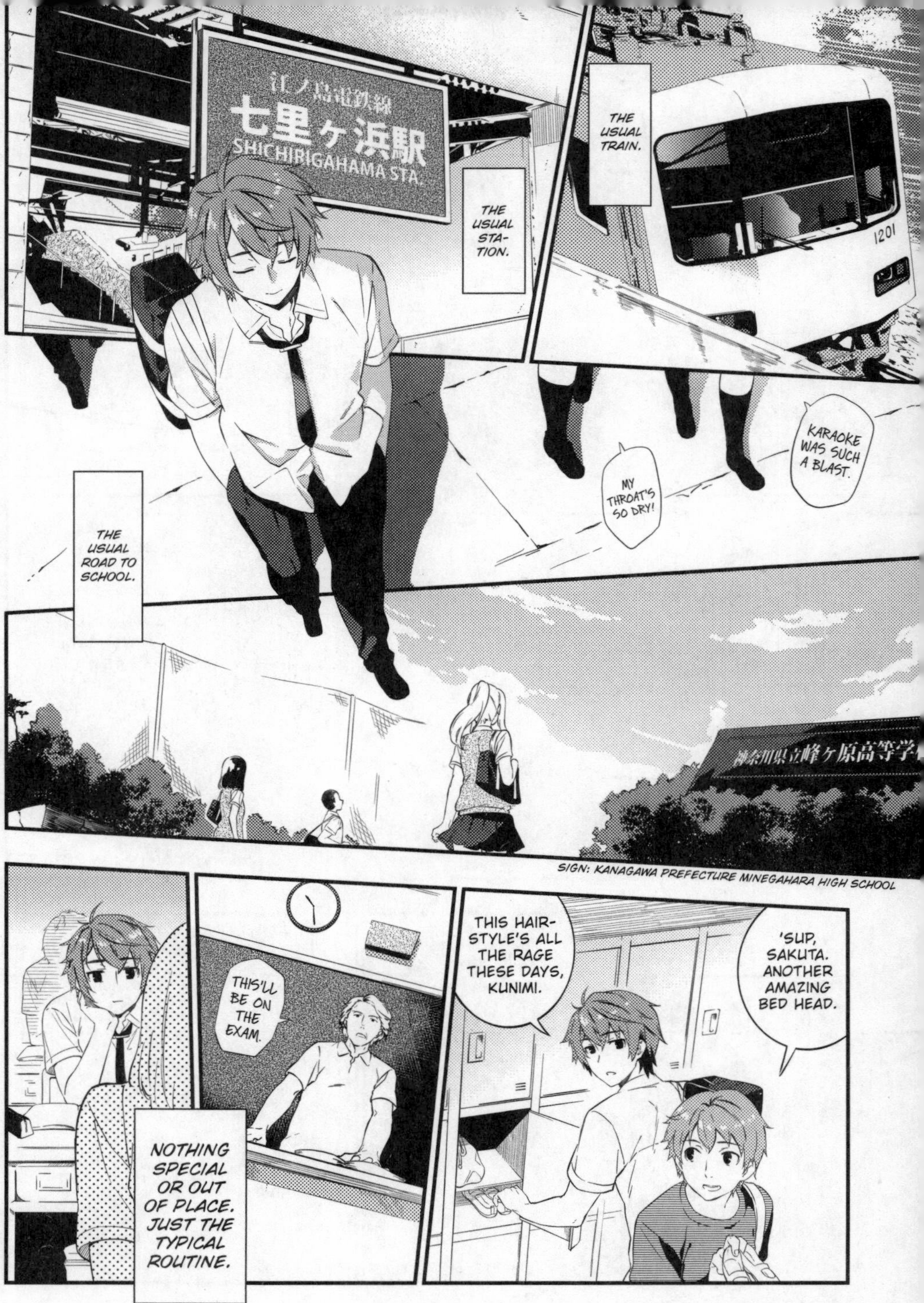
THE USUAL TRAIN.
江ノ島電鉄線
七里ヶ浜駅
SHICHIRIGAHAMA STA.
THE USUAL STATION.
KARAOKE WAS SUCH A BLAST.
MY THROAT'S SO DRY!
THE USUAL ROAD TO SCHOOL.
SIGN: KANAGAWA PREFECTURE MINEGAHARA HIGH SCHOOL
'SUP, SAKUTA. ANOTHER AMAZING BED HEAD.
THIS HAIR-STYLE'S ALL THE RAGE THESE DAYS, KUNIMI.
THIS'LL BE ON THE EXAM.
NOTHING SPECIAL OR OUT OF PLACE. JUST THE TYPICAL ROUTINE.

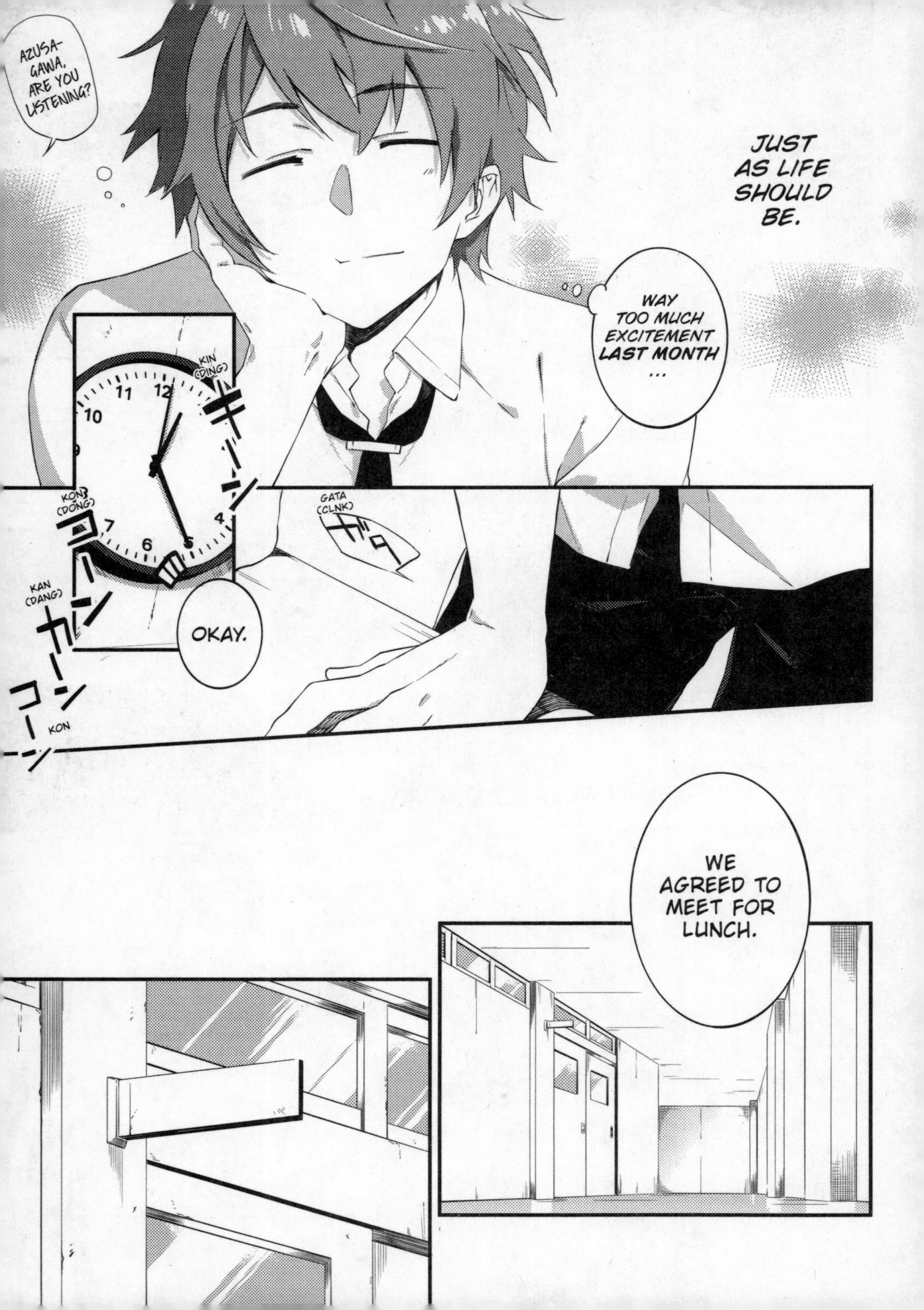
JUST AS LIFE SHOULD BE.
WAY TOO MUCH EXCITEMENT LAST MONTH ...
AZUSAGAWA, ARE YOU LISTENING?
KIN (DING)
GATA (CLNK)
OKAY.
KON (DONG)
KAN (DANG)
KON
WE AGREED TO MEET FOR LUNCH.

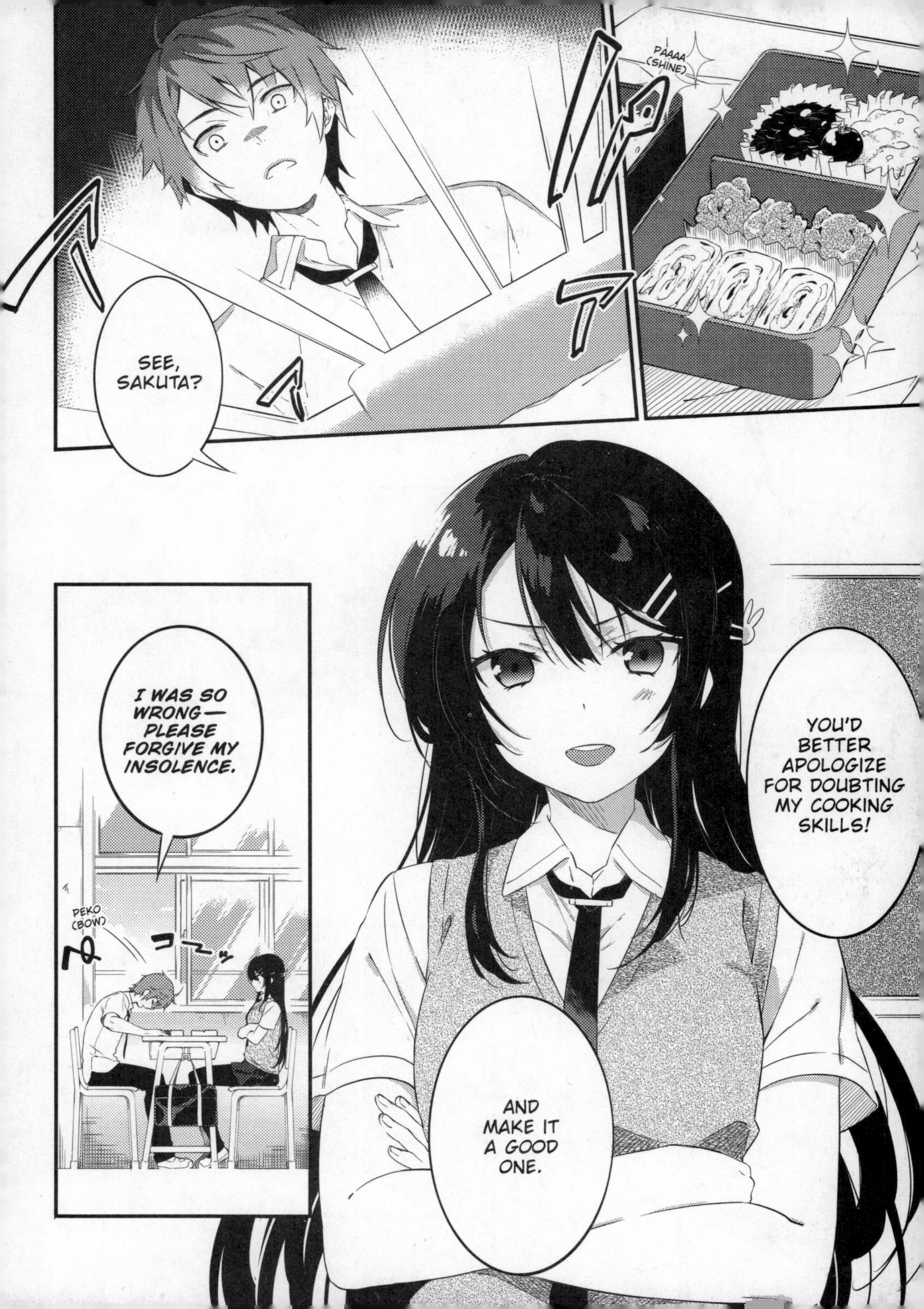
PAAAA (SHINE)
SEE, SAKUTA?
YOU'D BETTER APOLOGIZE FOR DOUBTING MY COOKING SKILLS!
AND MAKE IT A GOOD ONE.
I WAS SO WRONG—PLEASE FORGIVE MY INSOLENCE.
PEKO (BOW)

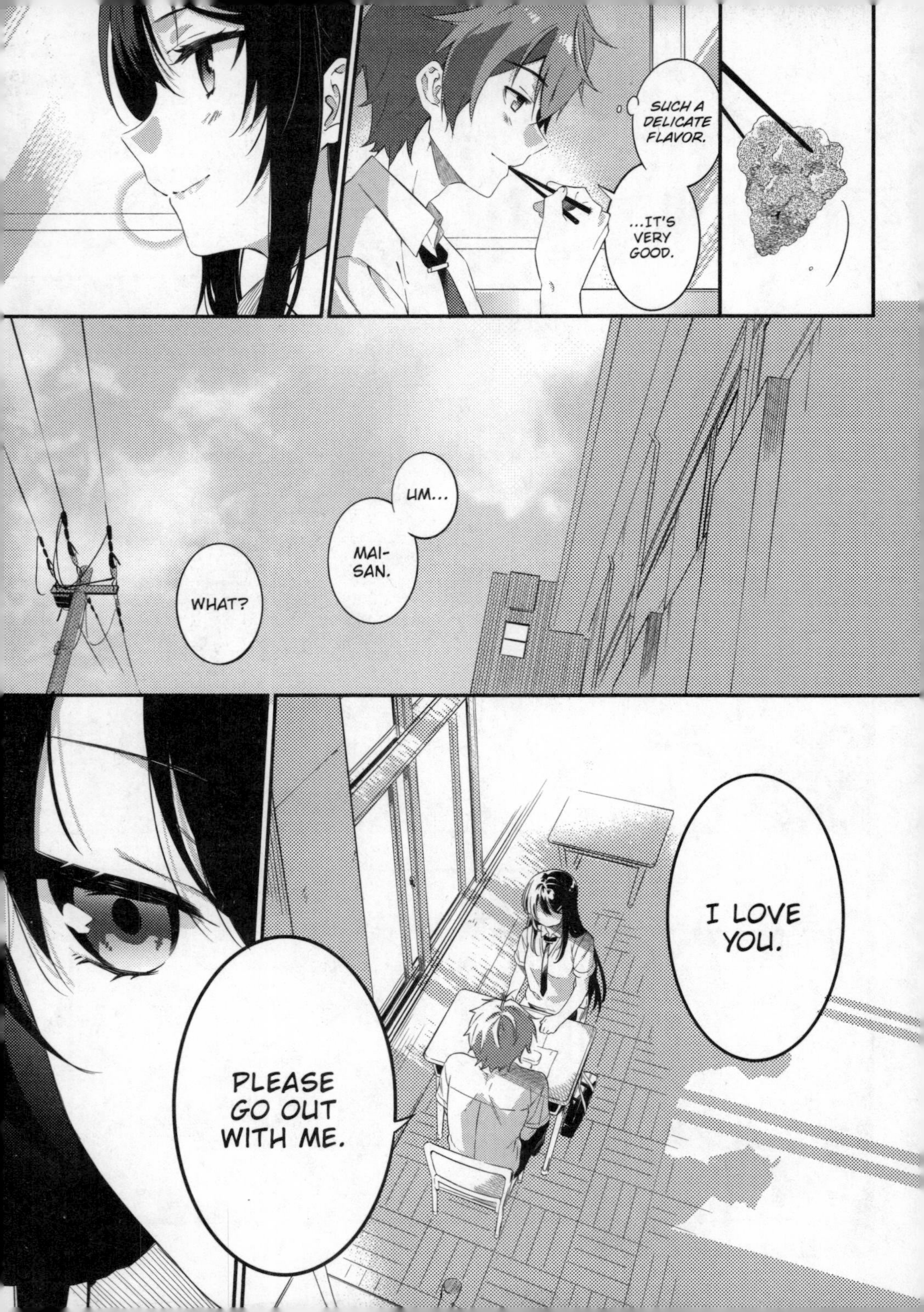
SUCH A DELICATE FLAVOR.
...IT'S VERY GOOD.
UM...
MAI-SAN.
WHAT?
I LOVE YOU.
PLEASE GO OUT WITH ME.

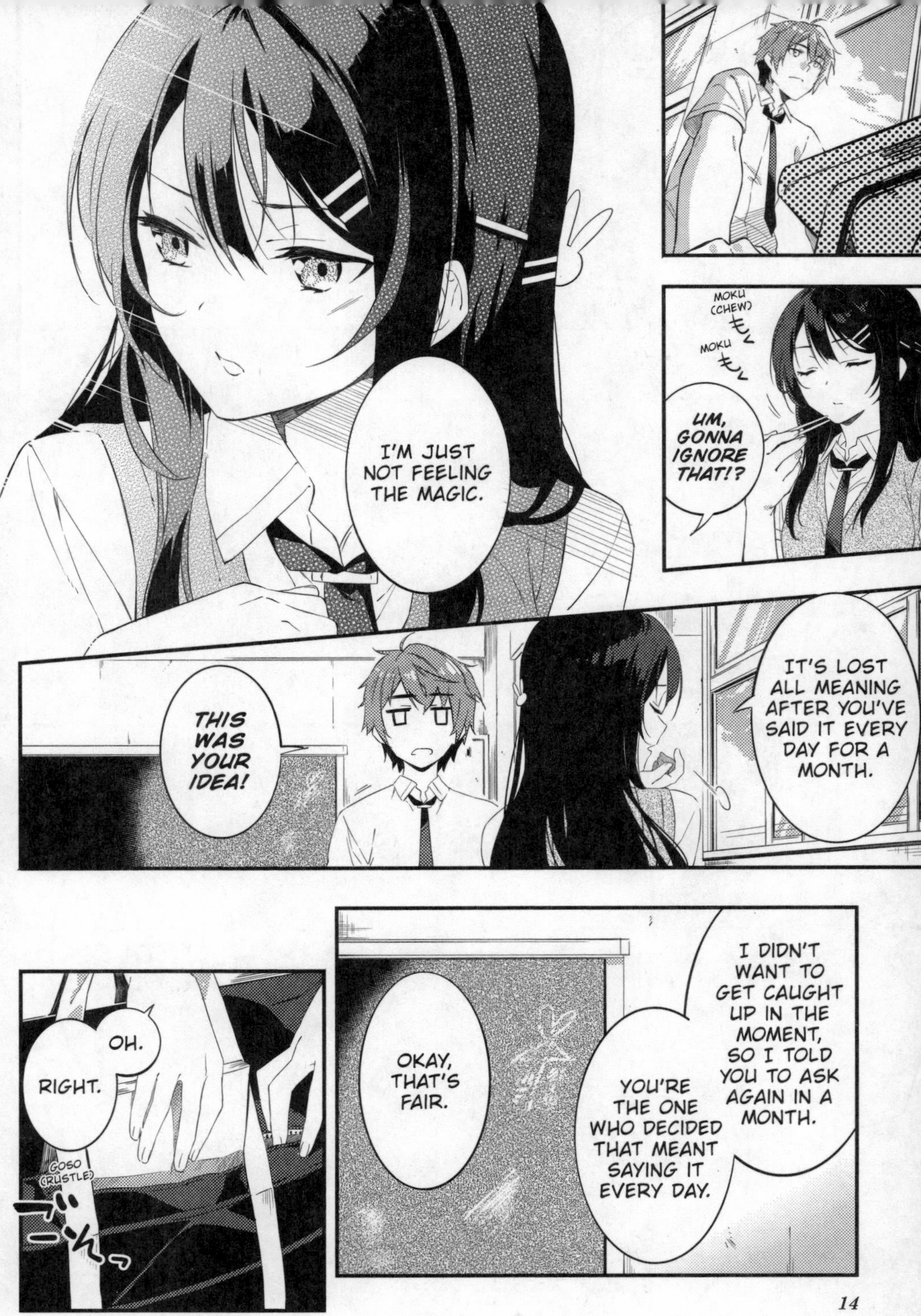
MOKU (CHEW)
もく
MOKU
もく
UM, GONNA IGNORE THAT!?
I'M JUST NOT FEELING THE MAGIC.
IT'S LOST ALL MEANING AFTER YOU'VE SAID IT EVERY DAY FOR A MONTH.
THIS WAS YOUR IDEA!
I DIDN'T WANT TO GET CAUGHT UP IN THE MOMENT, SO I TOLD YOU TO ASK AGAIN IN A MONTH.
YOU'RE THE ONE WHO DECIDED THAT MEANT SAYING IT EVERY DAY.
OKAY, THAT'S FAIR.
OH.
RIGHT.
GOSO (RUSTLE)

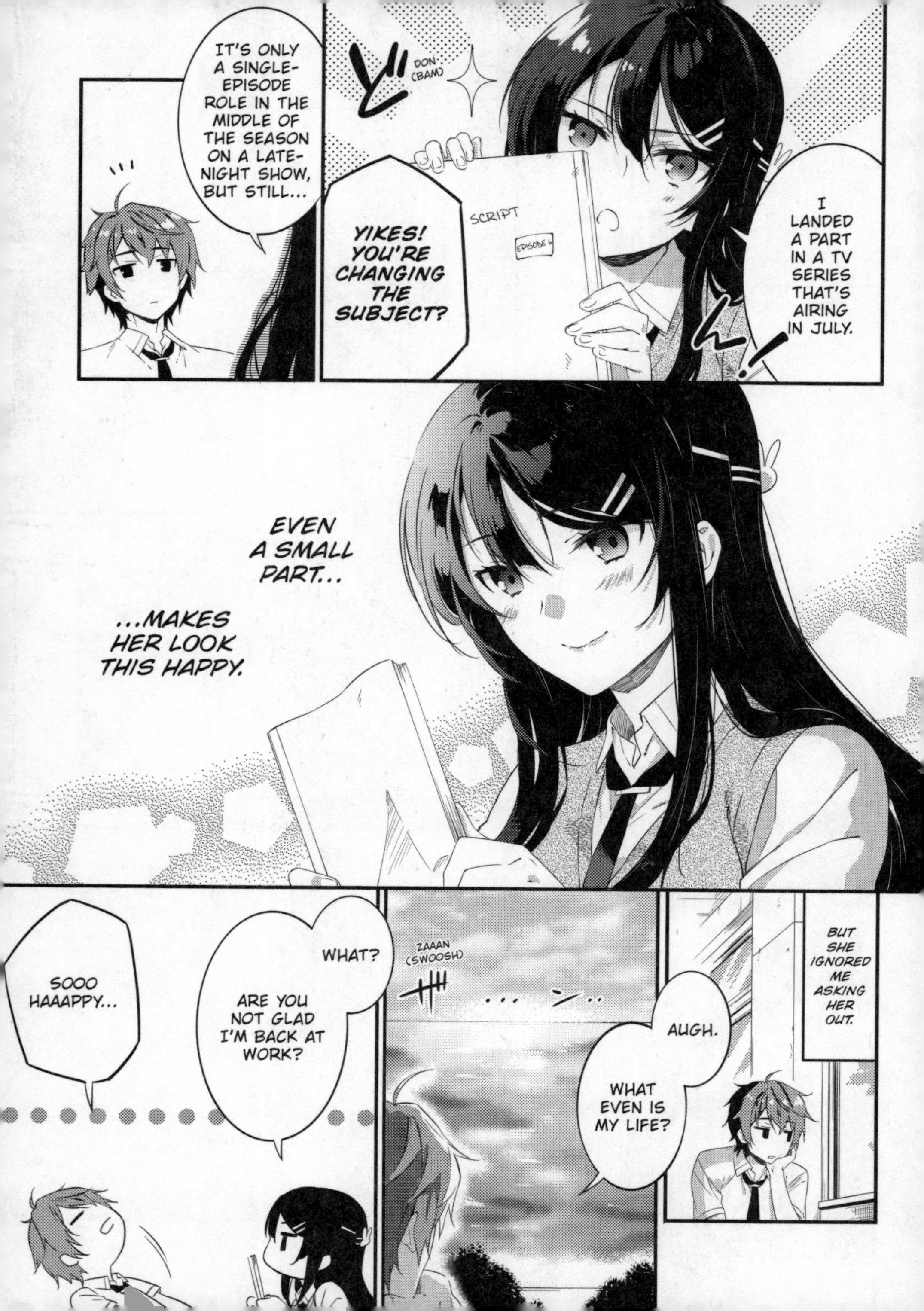
I LANDED A PART IN A TV SERIES THAT'S AIRING IN JULY.
DON (BAM)
SCRIPT
EPISODE 6
YIKES! YOU'RE CHANGING THE SUBJECT?
IT'S ONLY A SINGLE-EPISODE ROLE IN THE MIDDLE OF THE SEASON ON A LATE-NIGHT SHOW, BUT STILL...
EVEN A SMALL PART...
...MAKES HER LOOK THIS HAPPY.
BUT SHE IGNORED ME ASKING HER OUT.
AUGH.
WHAT EVEN IS MY LIFE?
ZAAAN (SWOOSH)
WHAT?
ARE YOU NOT GLAD I'M BACK AT WORK?
SOOO HAAAPPY...

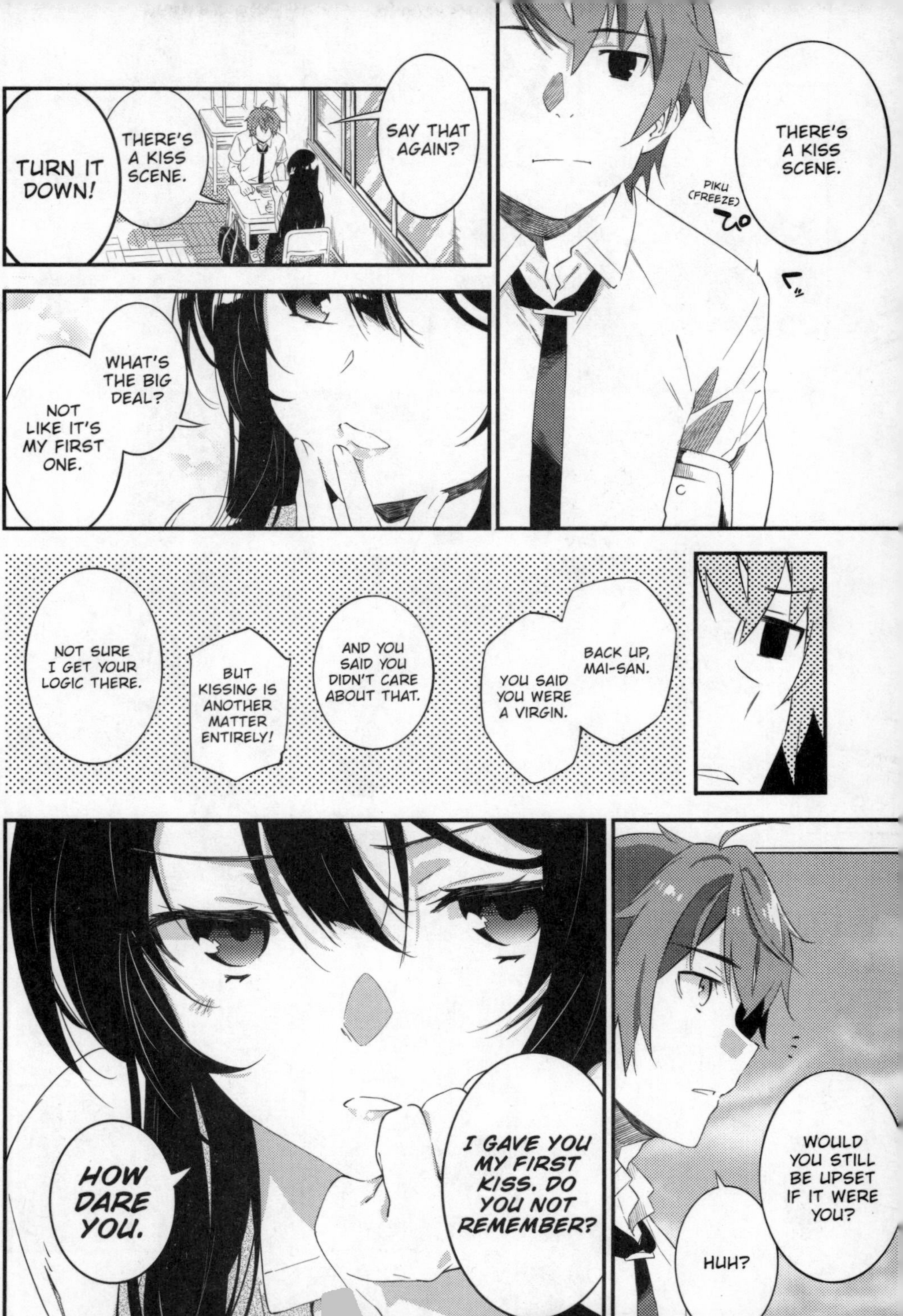
THERE'S A KISS SCENE.
PIKU (FREEZE)
SAY THAT AGAIN?
THERE'S A KISS SCENE.
TURN IT DOWN!
WHAT'S THE BIG DEAL?
NOT LIKE IT'S MY FIRST ONE.
BACK UP, MAI-SAN.
YOU SAID YOU WERE A VIRGIN.
AND YOU SAID YOU DIDN'T CARE ABOUT THAT.
BUT KISSING IS ANOTHER MATTER ENTIRELY!
NOT SURE I GET YOUR LOGIC THERE.
WOULD YOU STILL BE UPSET IF IT WERE YOU?
HUH?
I GAVE YOU MY FIRST KISS. DO YOU NOT REMEMBER?
HOW DARE YOU.

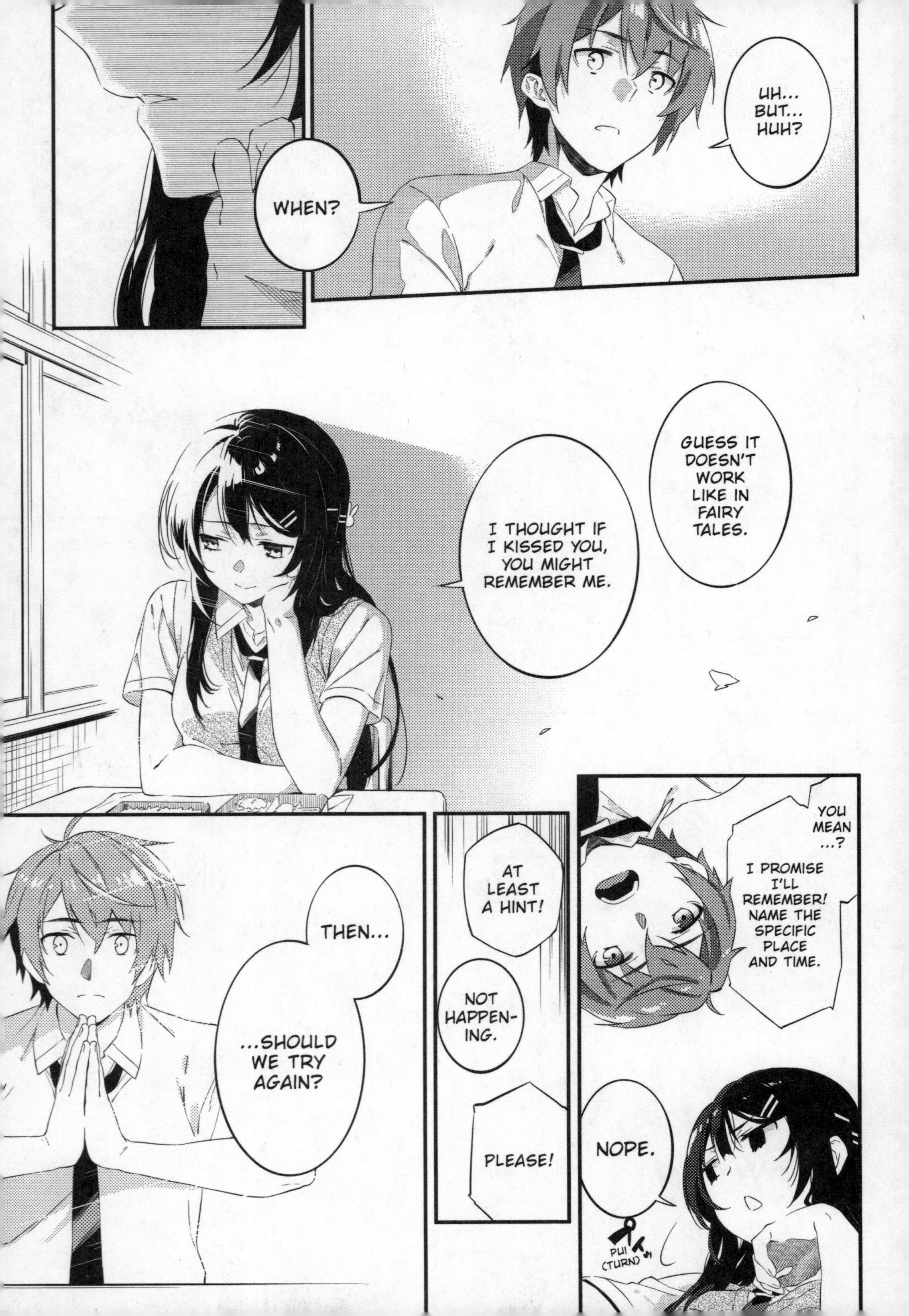
UH... BUT... HUH?
WHEN?
GUESS IT DOESN'T WORK LIKE IN FAIRY TALES.
I THOUGHT IF I KISSED YOU, YOU MIGHT REMEMBER ME.
YOU MEAN ...?
I PROMISE I'LL REMEMBER! NAME THE SPECIFIC PLACE AND TIME.
NOPE.
PUI (TURN)
AT LEAST A HINT!
NOT HAPPEN-ING.
PLEASE!
THEN...
...SHOULD WE TRY AGAIN?

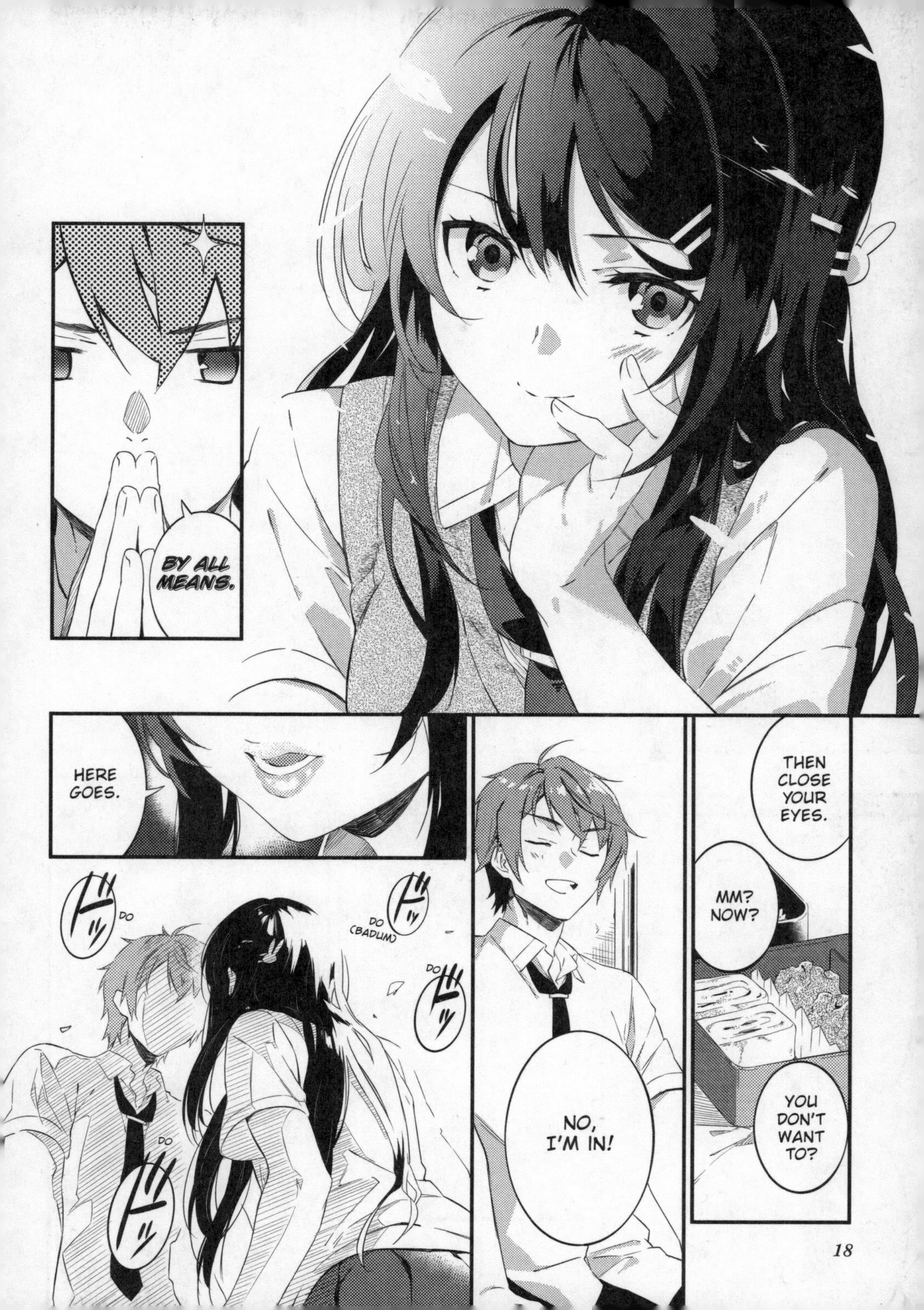
BY ALL MEANS.
THEN CLOSE YOUR EYES.
MM? NOW?
YOU DON'T WANT TO?
NO, I'M IN!
HERE GOES.
DO (BADUM)
DO
DO
DO

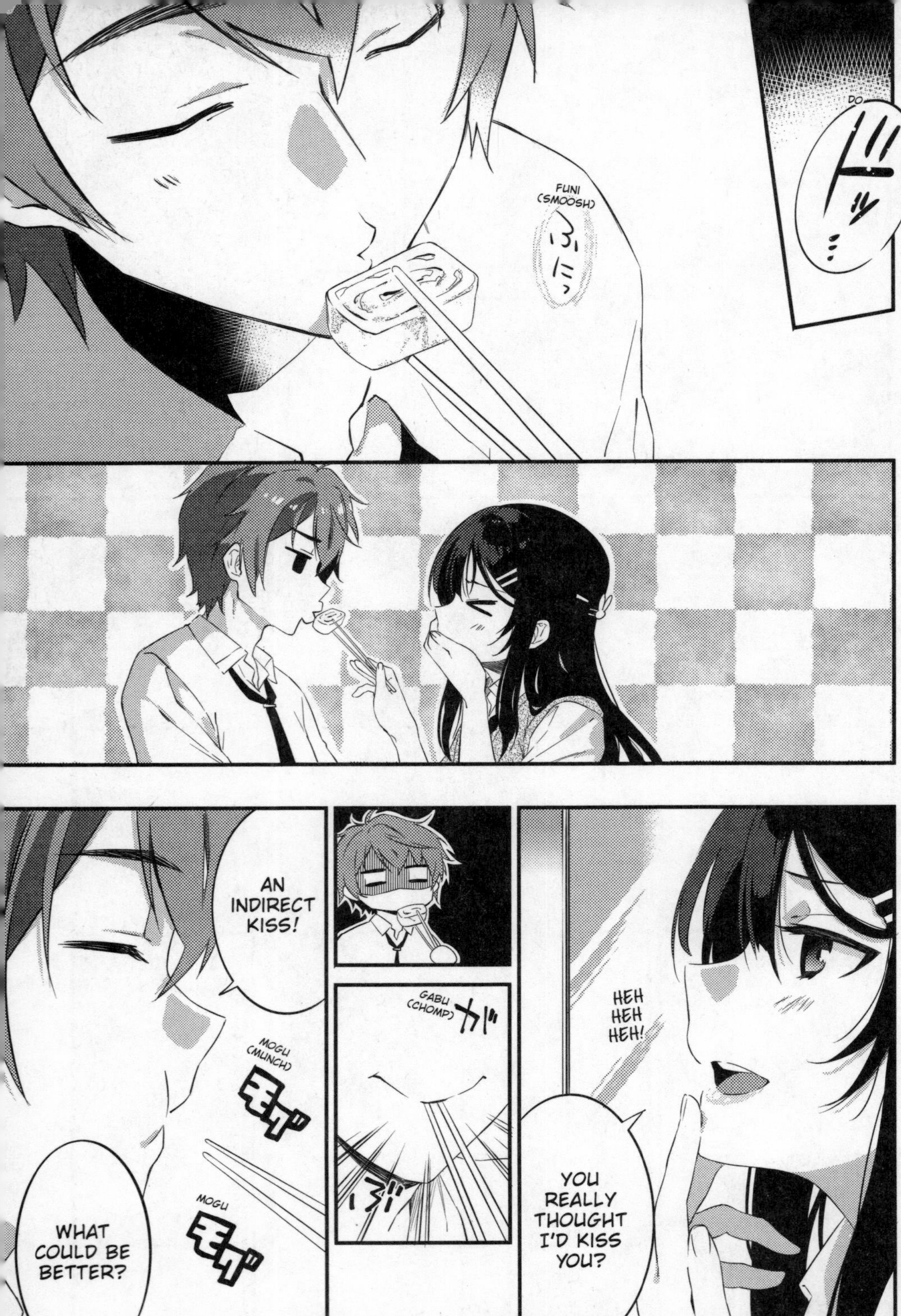
DO
ドッ
FUNI (SMOOSH)
ふに
HEH HEH HEH!
YOU REALLY THOUGHT I'D KISS YOU?
GABU (CHOMP)
ガブ
AN INDIRECT KISS!
MOGU (MUNCH)
モグ
MOGU
モグ
WHAT COULD BE BETTER?

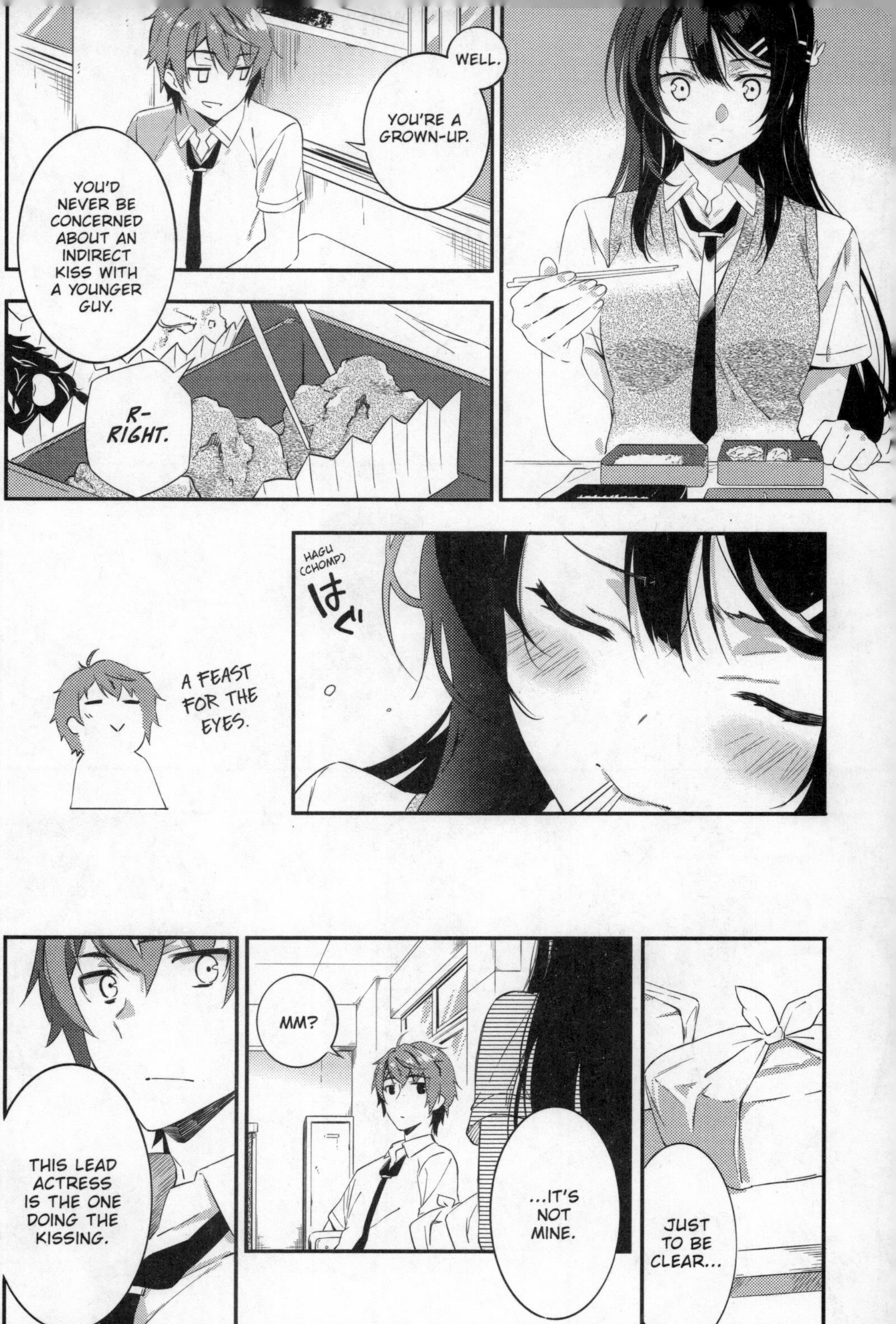
WELL.
YOU'RE A GROWN-UP.
YOU'D NEVER BE CONCERNED ABOUT AN INDIRECT KISS WITH A YOUNGER GUY.
R-RIGHT.
HAGU (CHOMP)
はぐ
A FEAST FOR THE EYES.
JUST TO BE CLEAR...
...IT'S NOT MINE.
MM?
THIS LEAD ACTRESS IS THE ONE DOING THE KISSING.

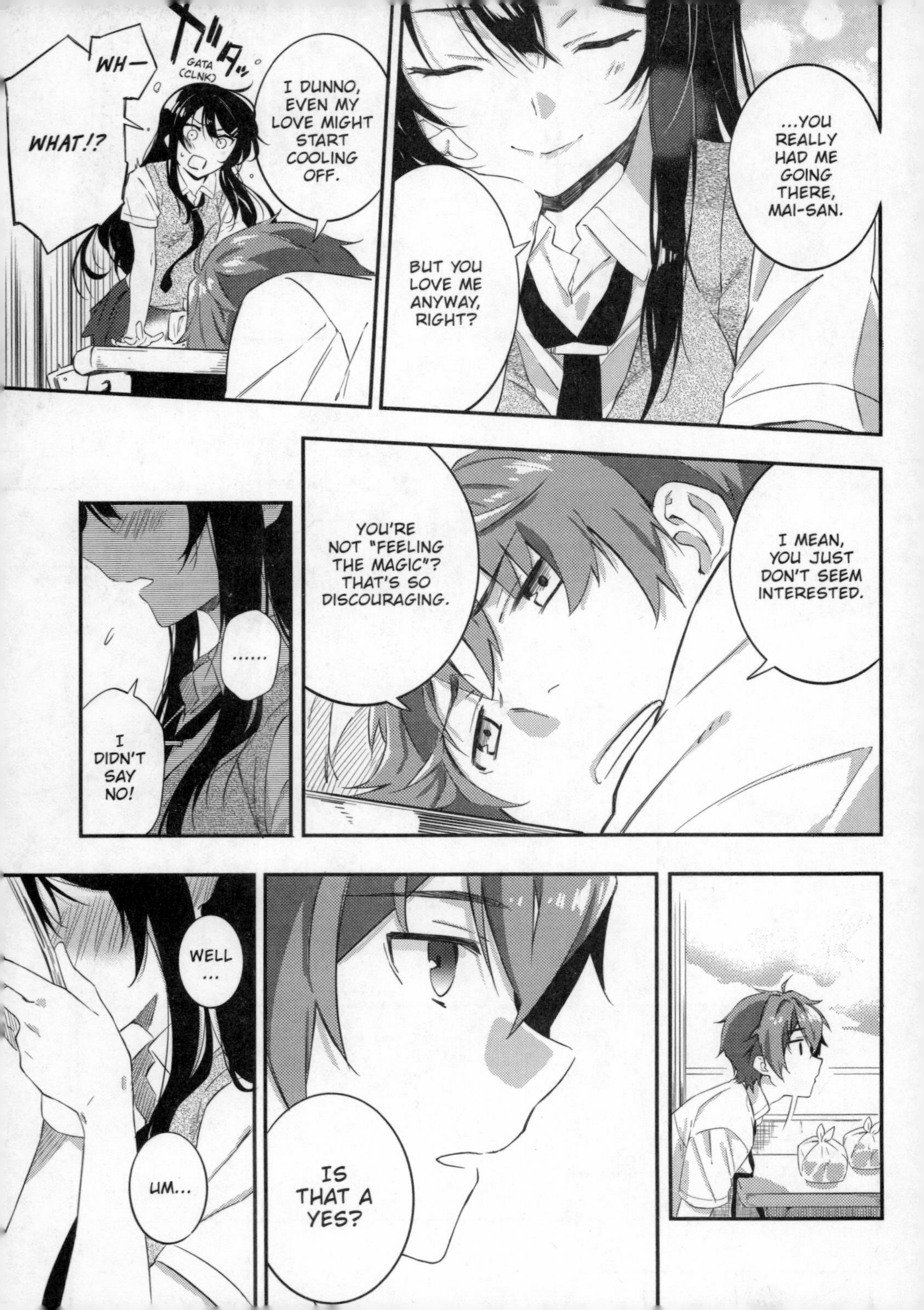
...YOU REALLY HAD ME GOING THERE, MAI-SAN.
BUT YOU LOVE ME ANYWAY, RIGHT?
I DUNNO, EVEN MY LOVE MIGHT START COOLING OFF.
ガタッ
GATA (CLNK)
WH—
WHAT!?
I MEAN, YOU JUST DON'T SEEM INTERESTED.
YOU'RE NOT "FEELING THE MAGIC"? THAT'S SO DISCOURAGING.
......
I DIDN'T SAY NO!
IS THAT A YES?
WELL...
UM...

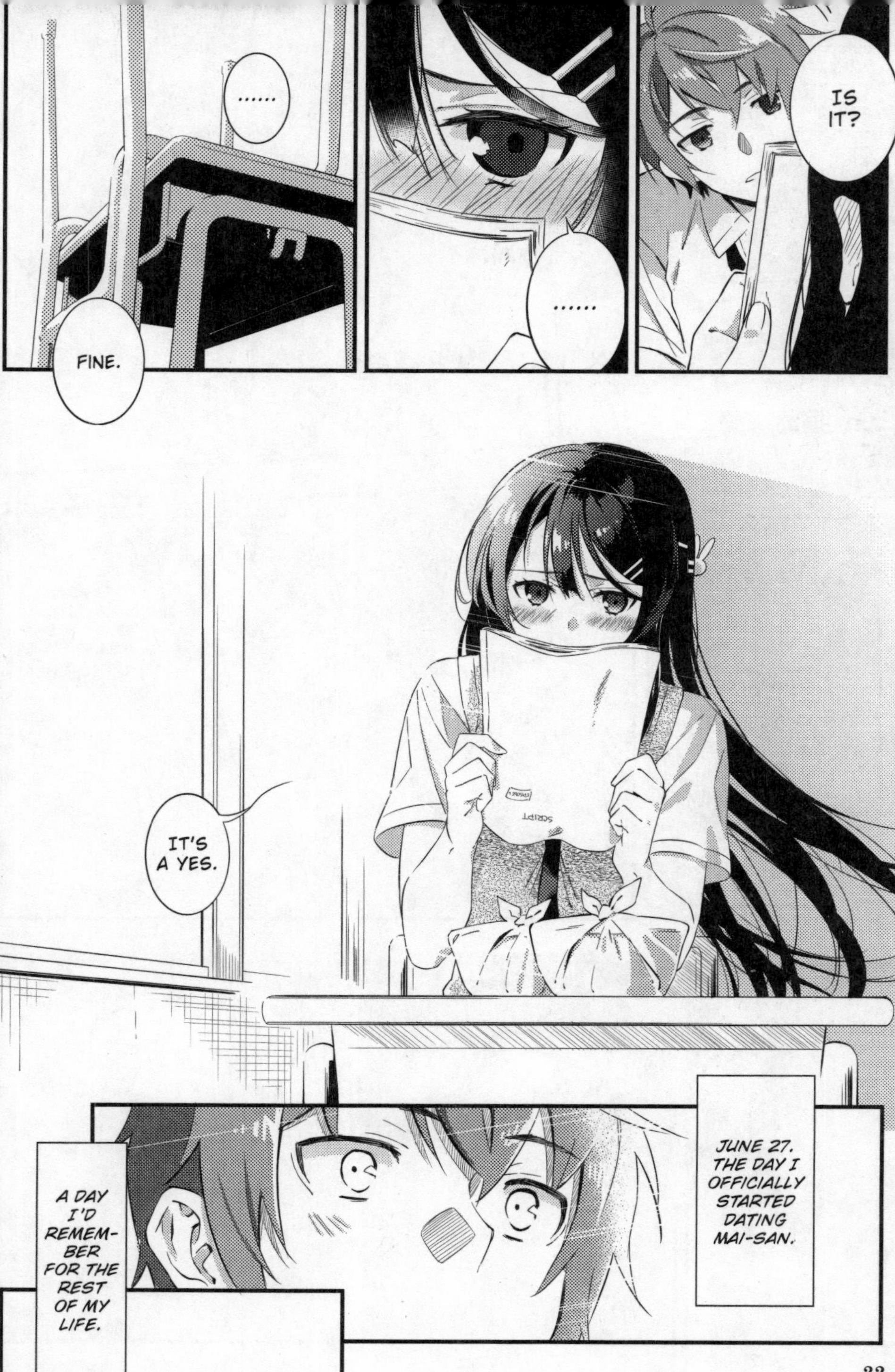
IS IT?
......
......
FINE.
IT'S A YES.
JUNE 27. THE DAY I OFFICIALLY STARTED DATING MAI-SAN.
A DAY I'D REMEMBER FOR THE REST OF MY LIFE.

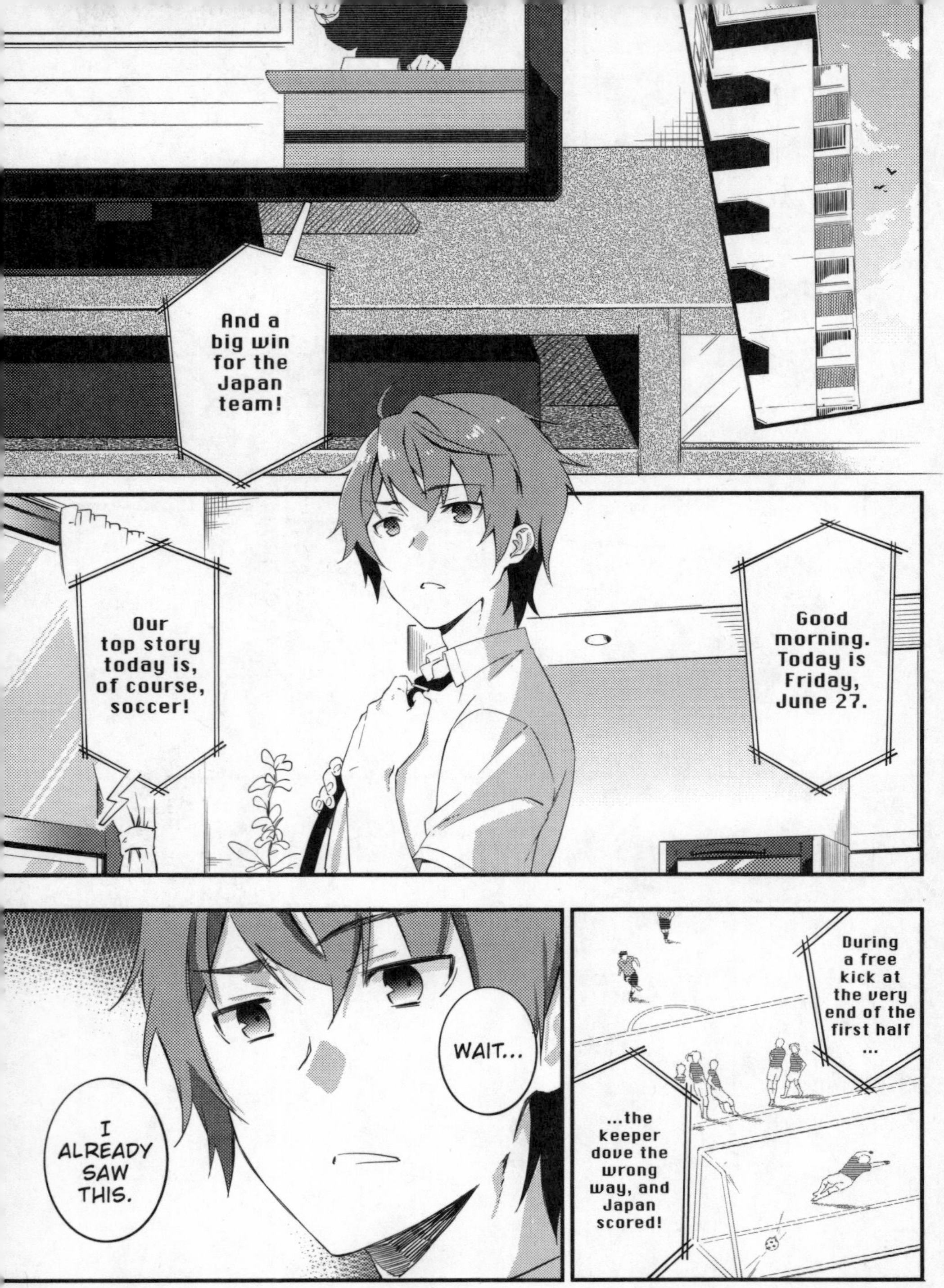
And a big win for the Japan team!
Good morning. Today is Friday, June 27.
Our top story today is, of course, soccer!
During a free kick at the very end of the first half...
...the keeper dove the wrong way, and Japan scored!
WAIT...
I ALREADY SAW THIS.

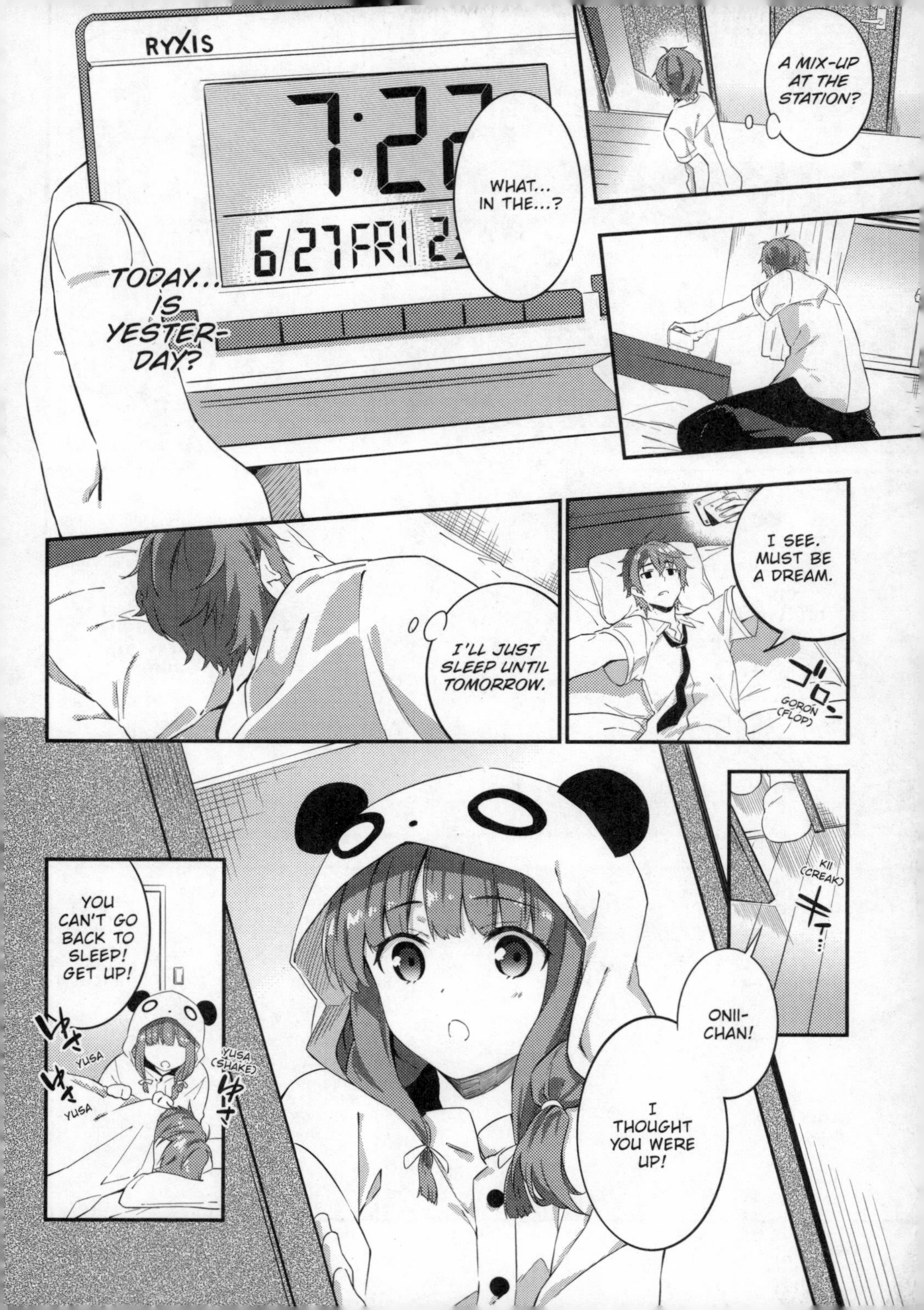

A MIX-UP AT THE STATION?
RYXIS
7:2
6/27FRI
WHAT... IN THE...?
TODAY... IS YESTERDAY?
I SEE. MUST BE A DREAM.
ゴロン
GORON (FLOP)
I'LL JUST SLEEP UNTIL TOMORROW.
キィ…
KII (CREAK)
ONII-CHAN!
I THOUGHT YOU WERE UP!
YOU CAN'T GO BACK TO SLEEP! GET UP!
ゆさ
YUSA (SHAKE)
ゆさ
YUSA
ゆさ
YUSA

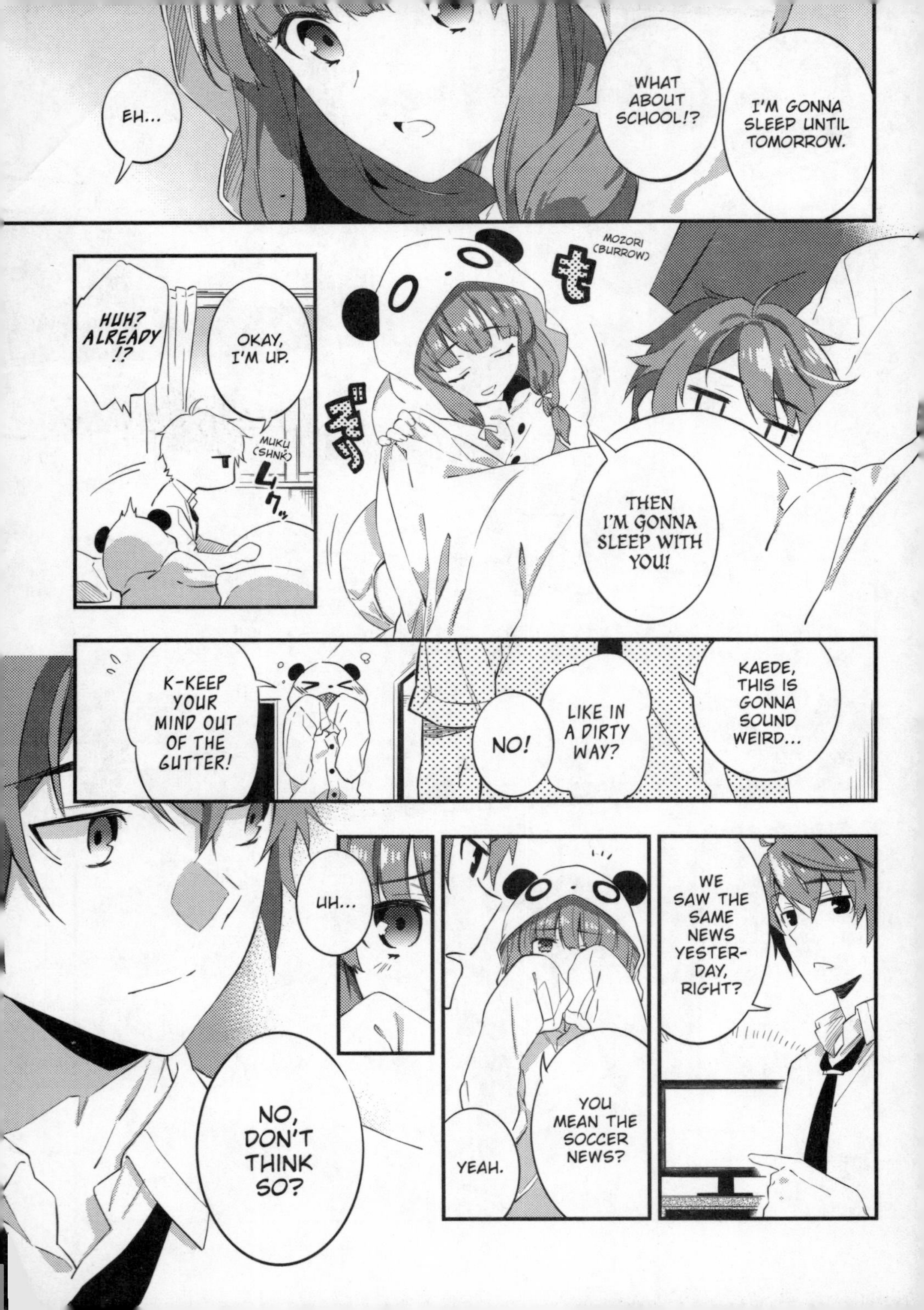
I'M GONNA SLEEP UNTIL TOMORROW.
WHAT ABOUT SCHOOL!?
EH...
MOZORI (BURROW)
THEN I'M GONNA SLEEP WITH YOU!
OKAY, I'M UP.
HUH? ALREADY!?
MUKU (SHNK)
KAEDE, THIS IS GONNA SOUND WEIRD...
LIKE IN A DIRTY WAY?
NO!
K-KEEP YOUR MIND OUT OF THE GUTTER!
WE SAW THE SAME NEWS YESTER-DAY, RIGHT?
YOU MEAN THE SOCCER NEWS?
YEAH.
UH...
NO, DON'T THINK SO?

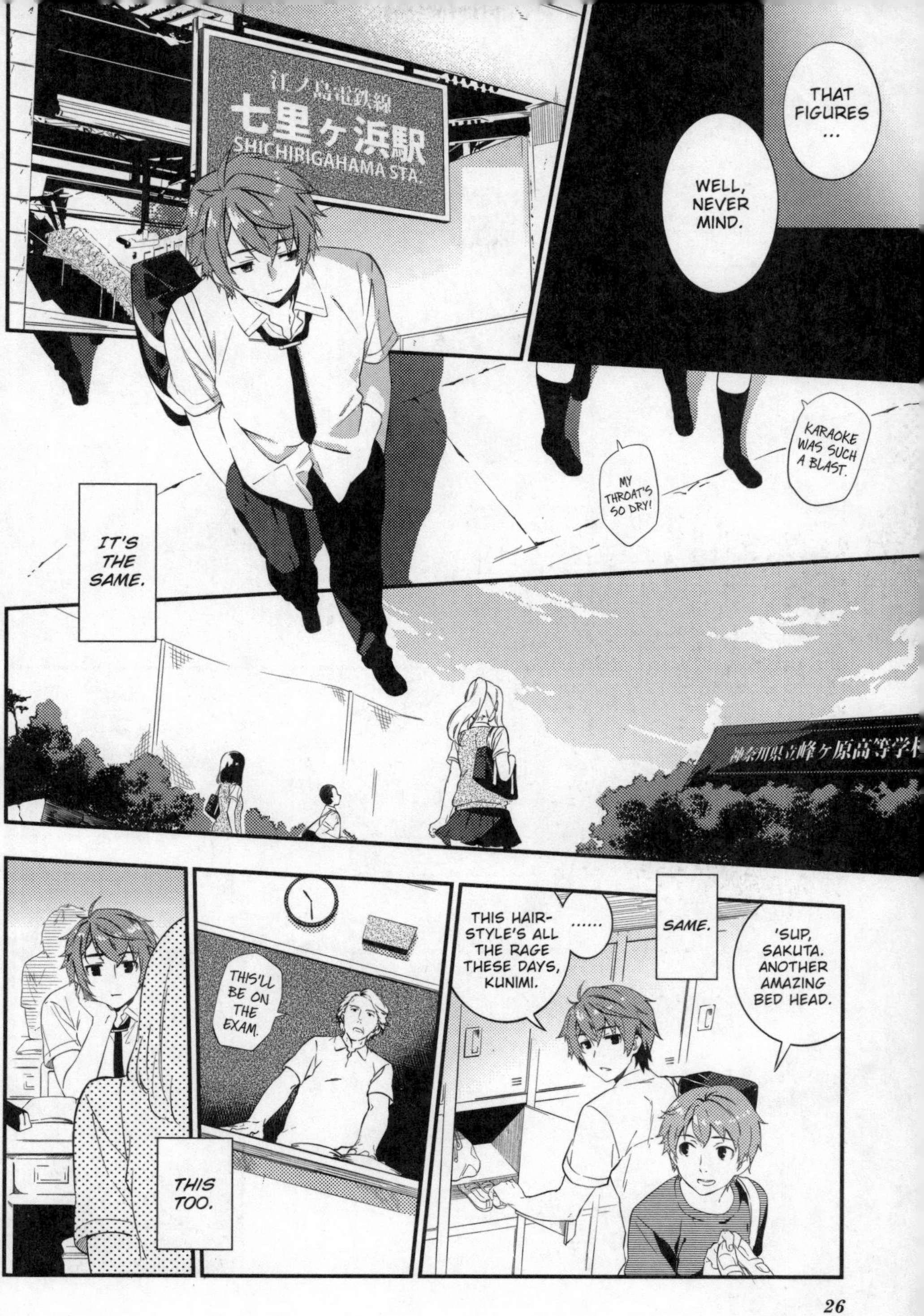
THAT FIGURES...
WELL, NEVER MIND.
江ノ島電鉄線
七里ヶ浜駅
SHICHIRIGAHAMA STA.
KARAOKE WAS SUCH A BLAST.
MY THROAT'S SO DRY!
IT'S THE SAME.
神奈川県立峰ヶ原高等学
'SUP, SAKUTA. ANOTHER AMAZING BED HEAD.
SAME.
......
THIS HAIR-STYLE'S ALL THE RAGE THESE DAYS, KUNIMI.
THIS'LL BE ON THE EXAM.
THIS TOO.

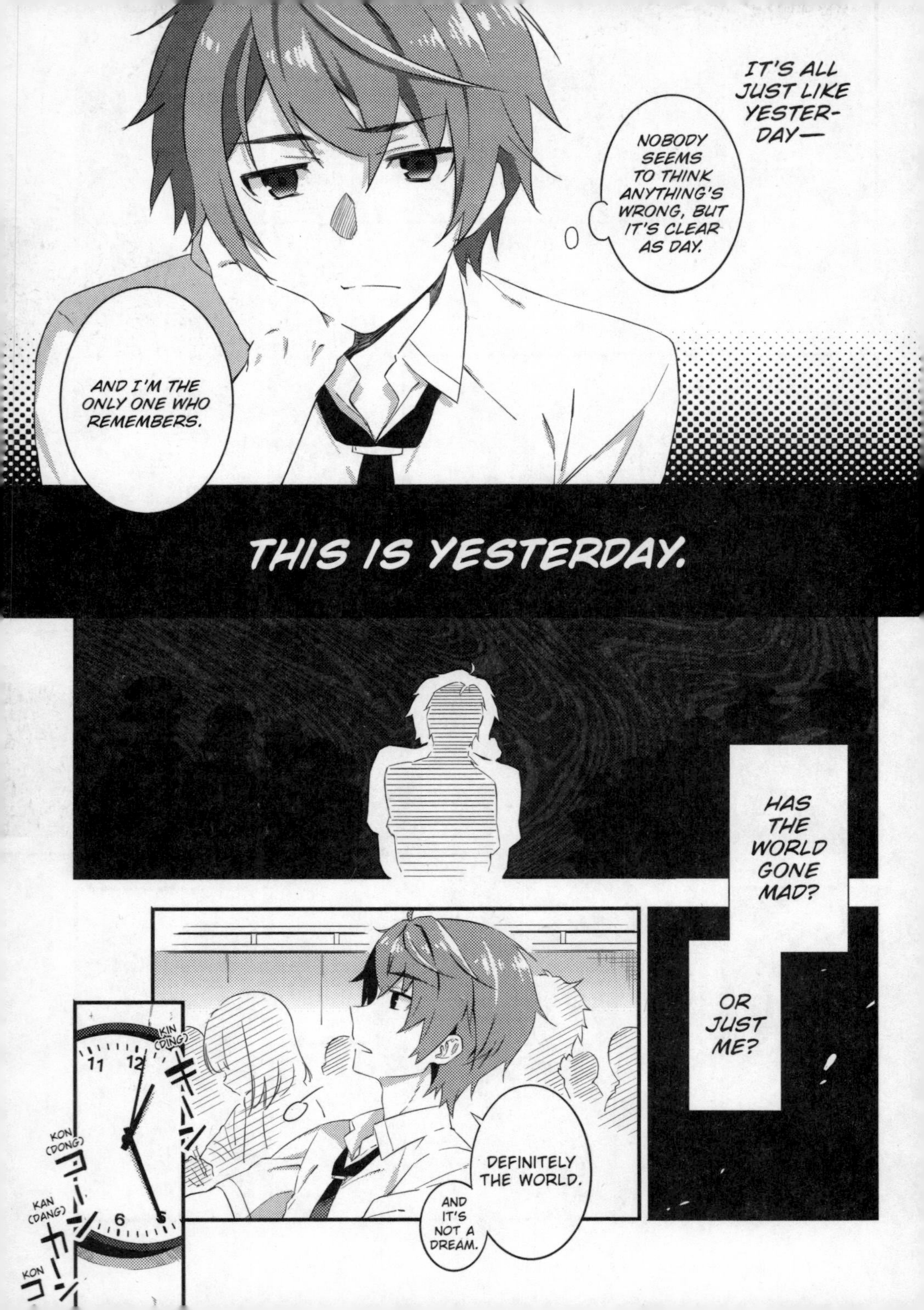
IT'S ALL JUST LIKE YESTER-DAY—
NOBODY SEEMS TO THINK ANYTHING'S WRONG, BUT IT'S CLEAR AS DAY.
AND I'M THE ONLY ONE WHO REMEMBERS.
THIS IS YESTERDAY.
HAS THE WORLD GONE MAD?
OR JUST ME?
DEFINITELY THE WORLD.
AND IT'S NOT A DREAM.
KIN (DING)
KON (DONG)
KAN (DANG)
KON

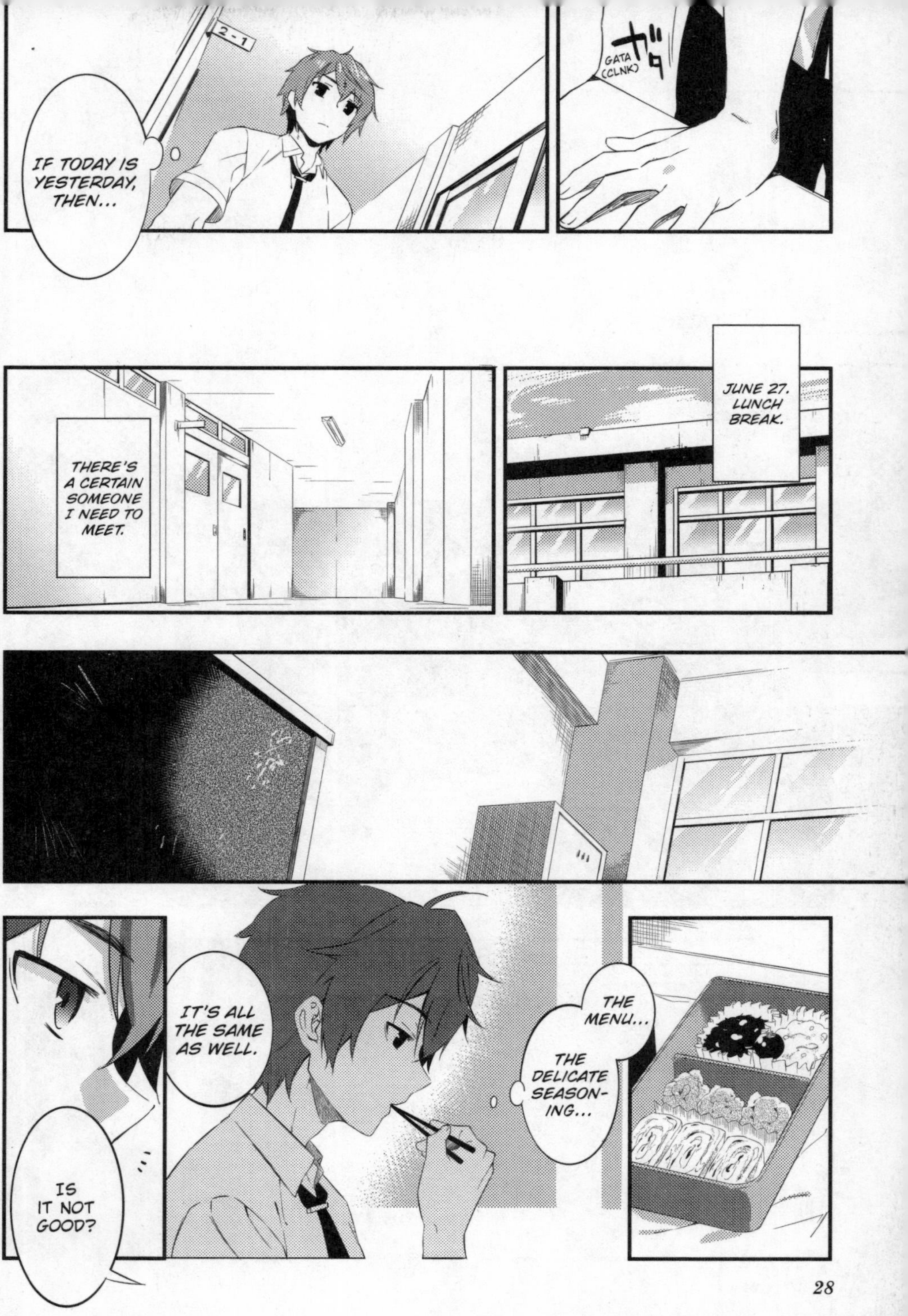
ガタ
GATA (CLNK)
IF TODAY IS YESTERDAY, THEN...
JUNE 27. LUNCH BREAK.
THERE'S A CERTAIN SOMEONE I NEED TO MEET.
THE MENU...
THE DELICATE SEASON-ING...
IT'S ALL THE SAME AS WELL.
...
IS IT NOT GOOD?

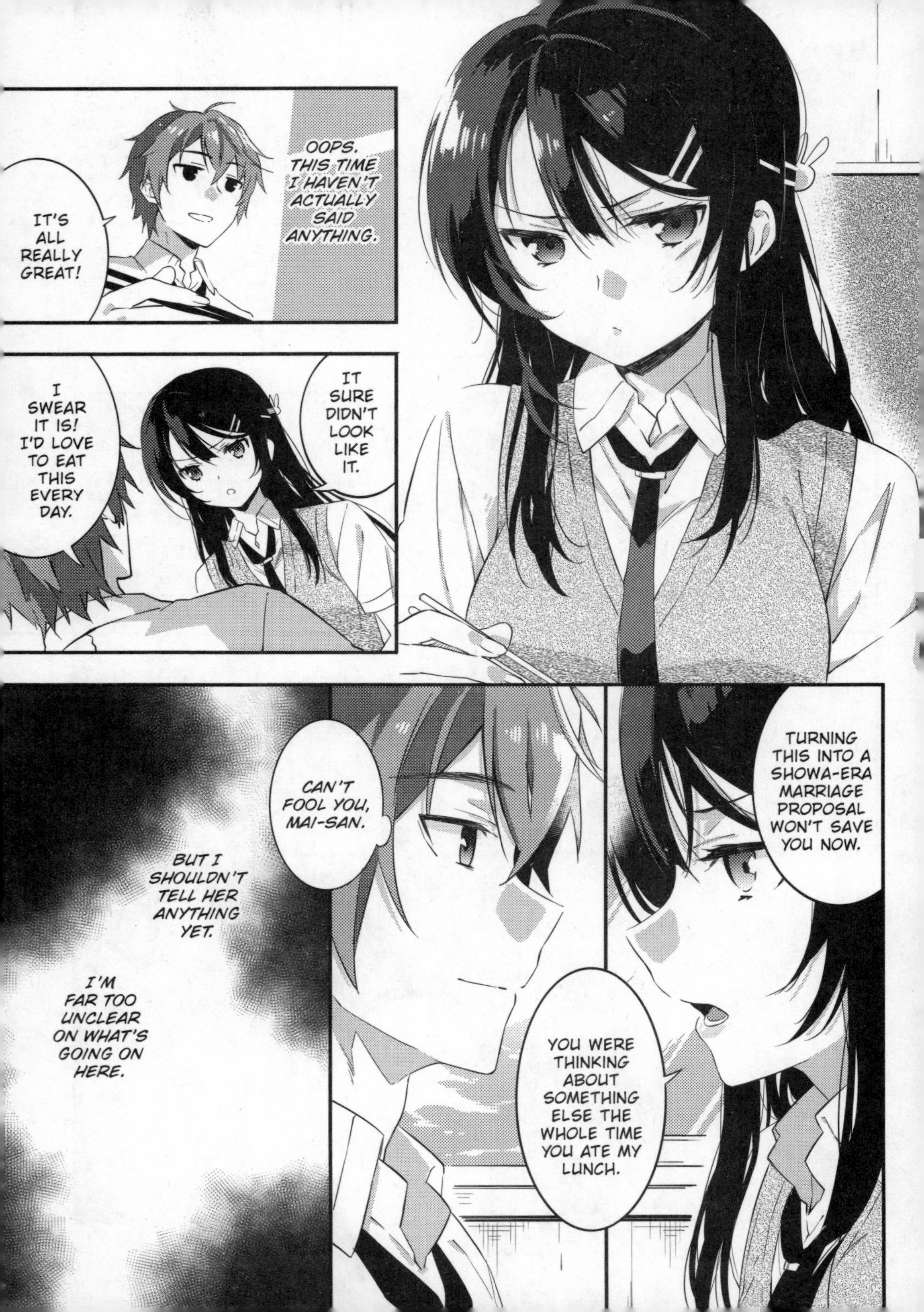
OOPS. THIS TIME I HAVEN'T ACTUALLY SAID ANYTHING.
IT'S ALL REALLY GREAT!
IT SURE DIDN'T LOOK LIKE IT.
I SWEAR IT IS! I'D LOVE TO EAT THIS EVERY DAY.
TURNING THIS INTO A SHOWA-ERA MARRIAGE PROPOSAL WON'T SAVE YOU NOW.
YOU WERE THINKING ABOUT SOMETHING ELSE THE WHOLE TIME YOU ATE MY LUNCH.
CAN'T FOOL YOU, MAI-SAN.
BUT I SHOULDN'T TELL HER ANYTHING YET.
I'M FAR TOO UNCLEAR ON WHAT'S GOING ON HERE.

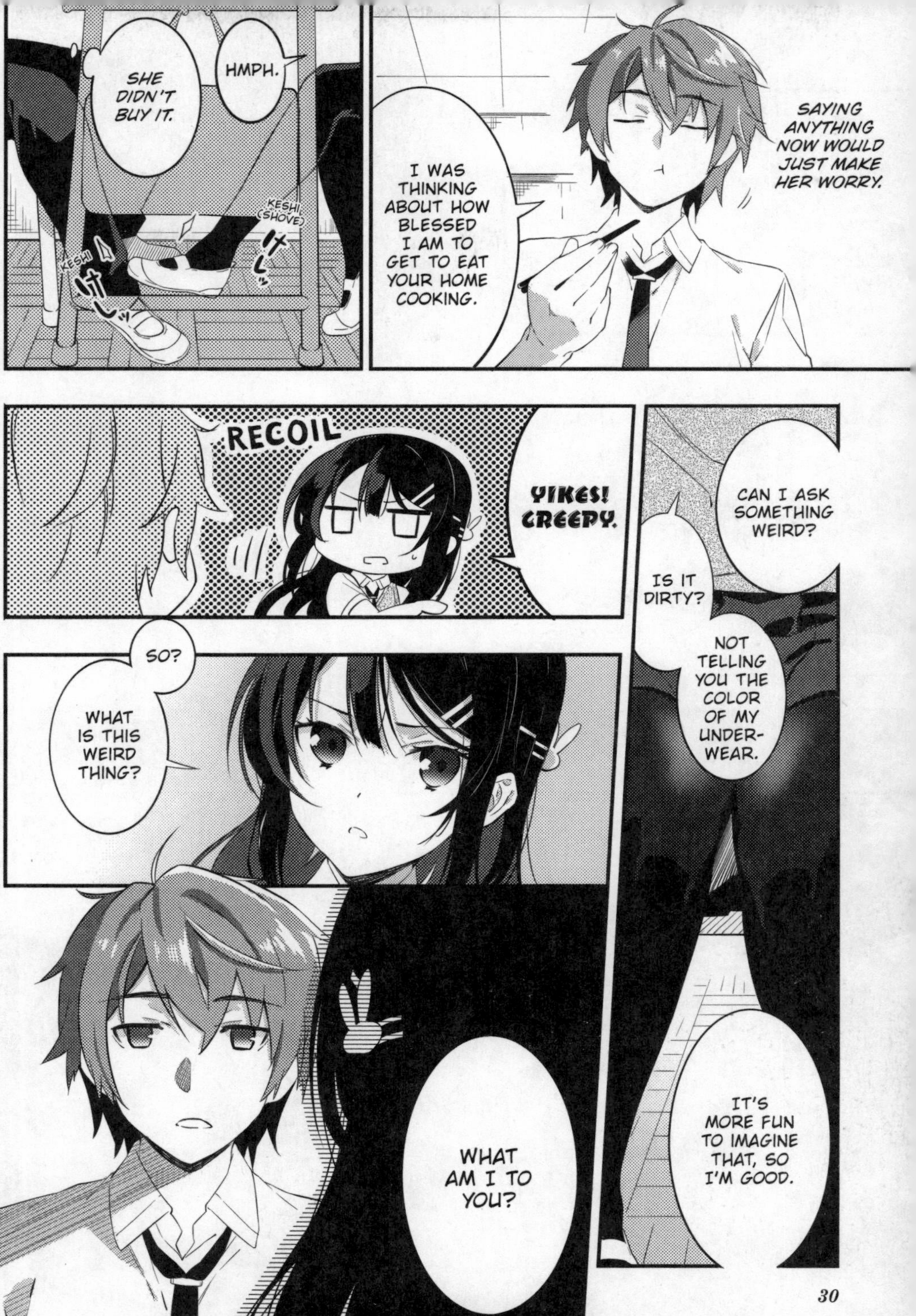
SAYING ANYTHING NOW WOULD JUST MAKE HER WORRY.
I WAS THINKING ABOUT HOW BLESSED I AM TO GET TO EAT YOUR HOME COOKING.
HMPH.
SHE DIDN'T BUY IT.
KESHI (SHOVE)
KESHI
CAN I ASK SOMETHING WEIRD?
IS IT DIRTY?
NOT TELLING YOU THE COLOR OF MY UNDER-WEAR.
IT'S MORE FUN TO IMAGINE THAT, SO I'M GOOD.
YIKES! CREEPY.
RECOIL
SO?
WHAT IS THIS WEIRD THING?
WHAT AM I TO YOU?

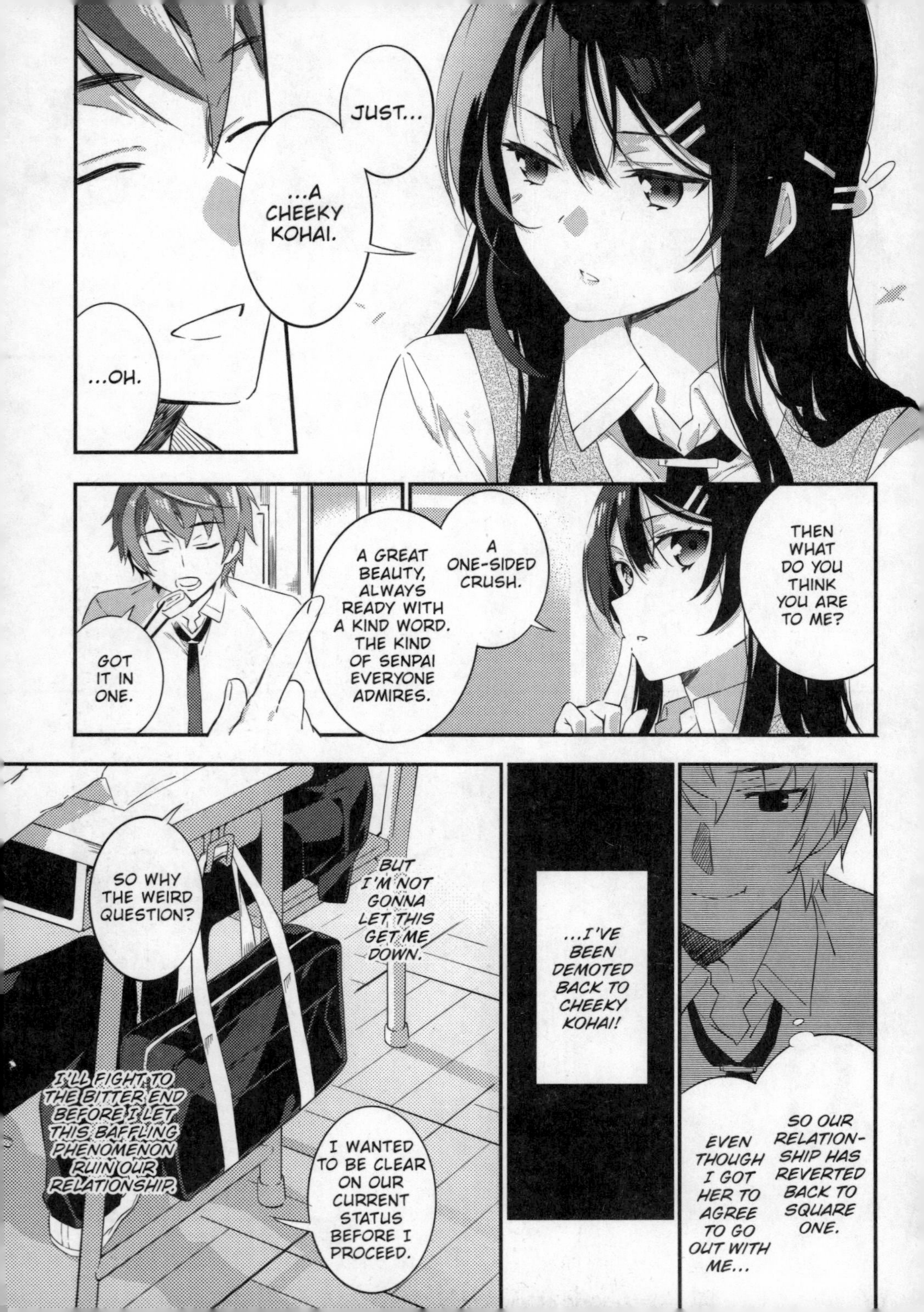
JUST...
...A CHEEKY KOHAI.
...OH.
THEN WHAT DO YOU THINK YOU ARE TO ME?
A ONE-SIDED CRUSH.
A GREAT BEAUTY, ALWAYS READY WITH A KIND WORD. THE KIND OF SENPAI EVERYONE ADMIRES.
GOT IT IN ONE.
SO OUR RELATION-SHIP HAS REVERTED BACK TO SQUARE ONE.
EVEN THOUGH I GOT HER TO AGREE TO GO OUT WITH ME...
...I'VE BEEN DEMOTED BACK TO CHEEKY KOHAI!
BUT I'M NOT GONNA LET THIS GET ME DOWN.
SO WHY THE WEIRD QUESTION?
I WANTED TO BE CLEAR ON OUR CURRENT STATUS BEFORE I PROCEED.
I'LL FIGHT TO THE BITTER END BEFORE I LET THIS BAFFLING PHENOMENON RUIN OUR RELATIONSHIP.

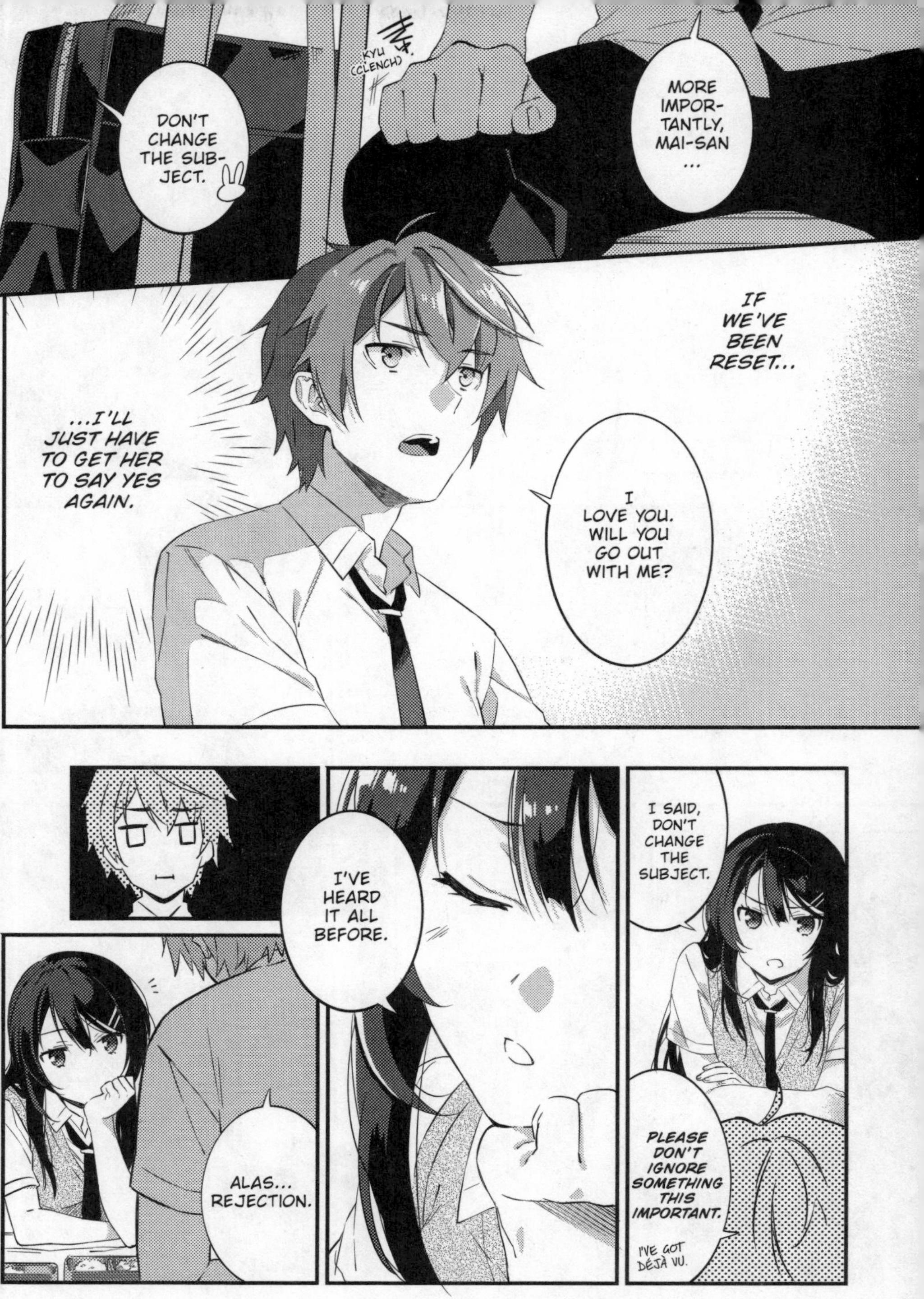
MORE IMPORTANTLY, MAI-SAN ...
KYU (CLENCH)
DON'T CHANGE THE SUBJECT.
IF WE'VE BEEN RESET...
...I'LL JUST HAVE TO GET HER TO SAY YES AGAIN.
I LOVE YOU. WILL YOU GO OUT WITH ME?
I SAID, DON'T CHANGE THE SUBJECT.
PLEASE DON'T IGNORE SOMETHING THIS IMPORTANT.
I'VE GOT DÉJÀ VU.
I'VE HEARD IT ALL BEFORE.
ALAS... REJECTION.

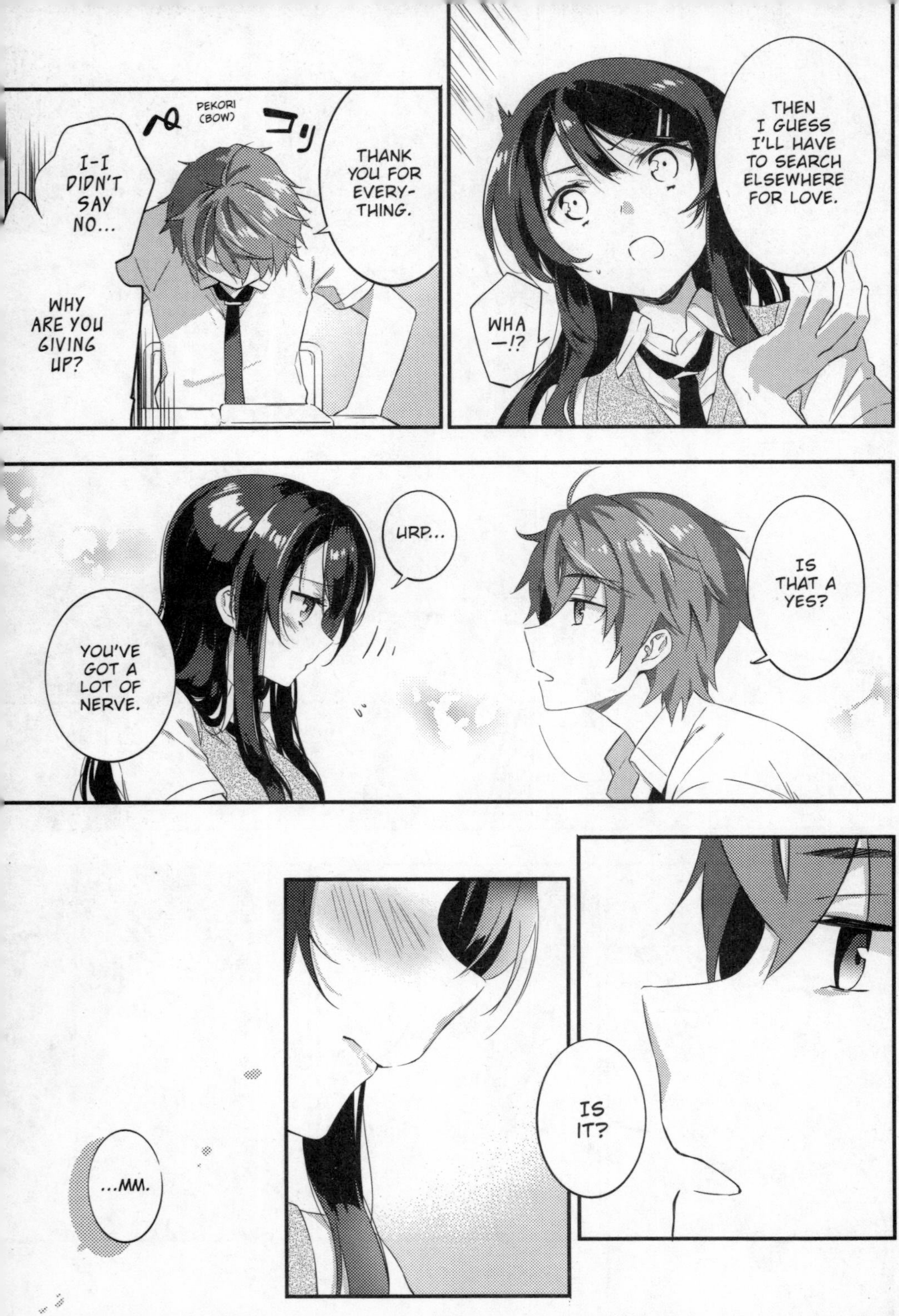
THEN I GUESS I'LL HAVE TO SEARCH ELSEWHERE FOR LOVE.
WHA—!?
THANK YOU FOR EVERYTHING.
PEKORI (BOW)
I-I DIDN'T SAY NO...
WHY ARE YOU GIVING UP?
IS THAT A YES?
URP...
YOU'VE GOT A LOT OF NERVE.
IS IT?
...MM.

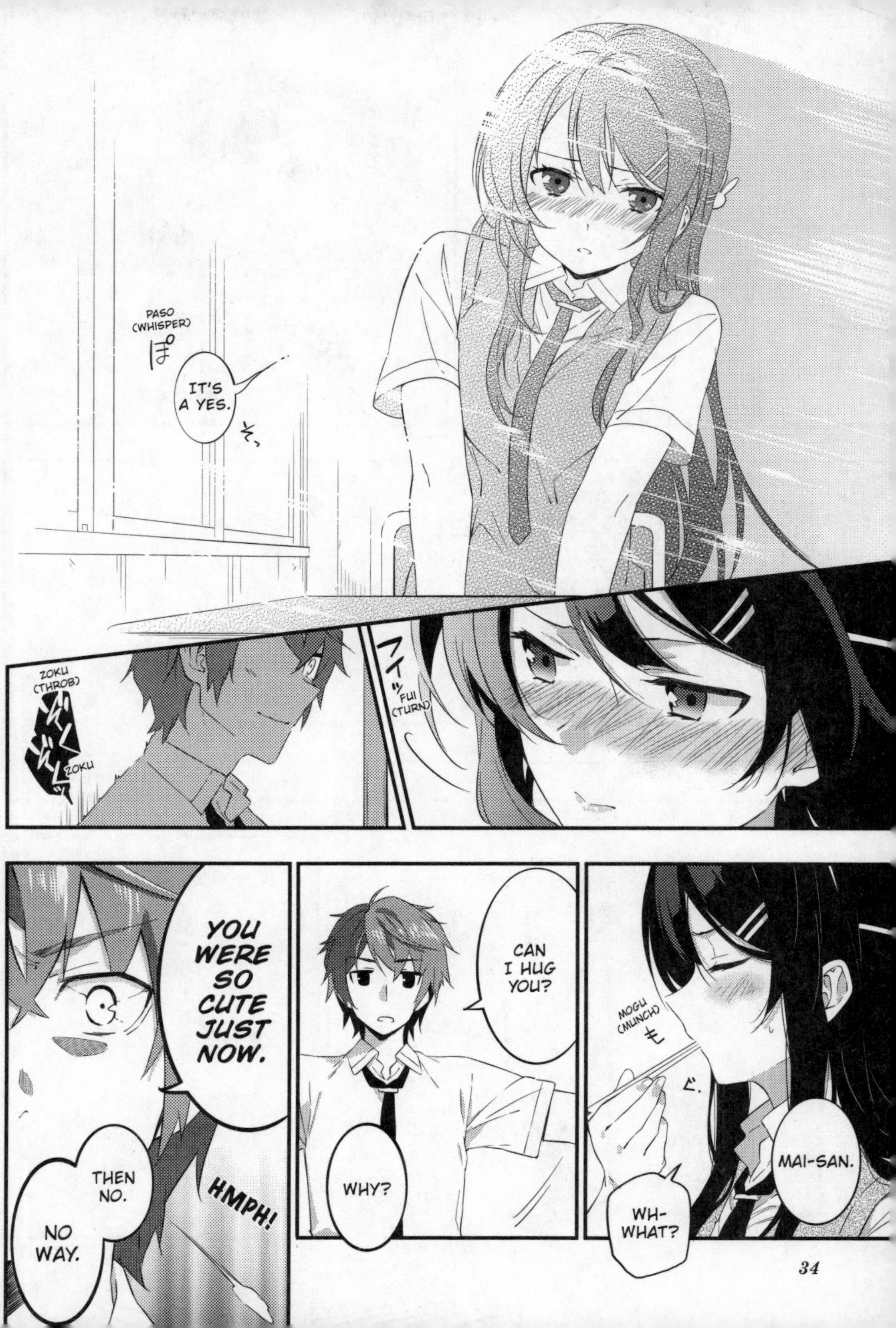
PASO (WHISPER)
ぽ
IT'S A YES.
そっ
フイッ
FUI (TURN)
ZOKU (THROB)
ZOKU
MAI-SAN.
WH- WHAT?
MOGU (MUNCH)
も
ぐ
CAN I HUG YOU?
WHY?
YOU WERE SO CUTE JUST NOW.
HMPH!
THEN NO.
NO WAY.

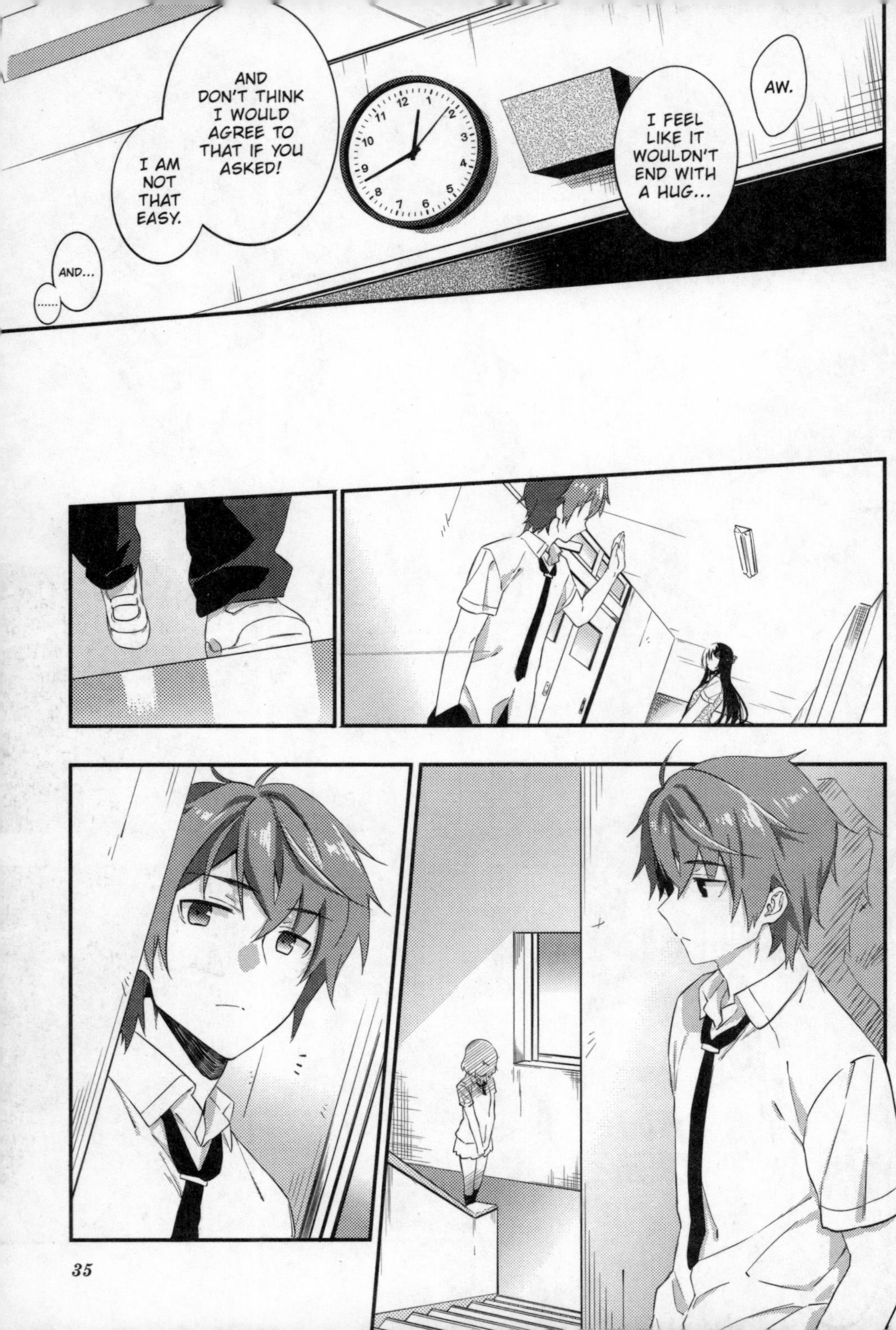
AW.
I FEEL LIKE IT WOULDN'T END WITH A HUG...
AND DON'T THINK I WOULD AGREE TO THAT IF YOU ASKED!
I AM NOT THAT EASY.
AND...
......

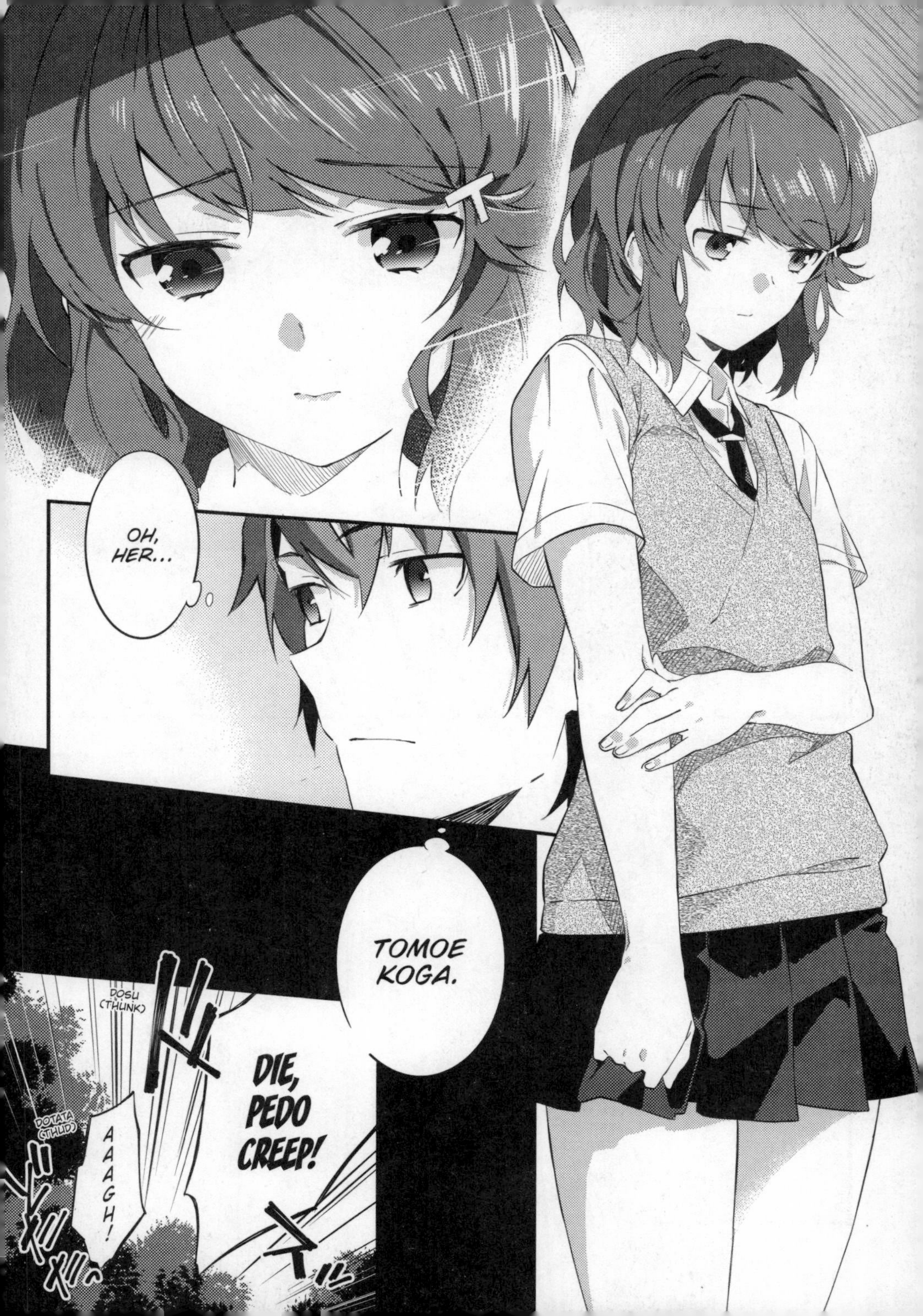
OH, HER...
TOMOE KOGA.
DIE, PEDO CREEP!
DOSU (THUNK)
AAAGH!
DOTATA (THUD)

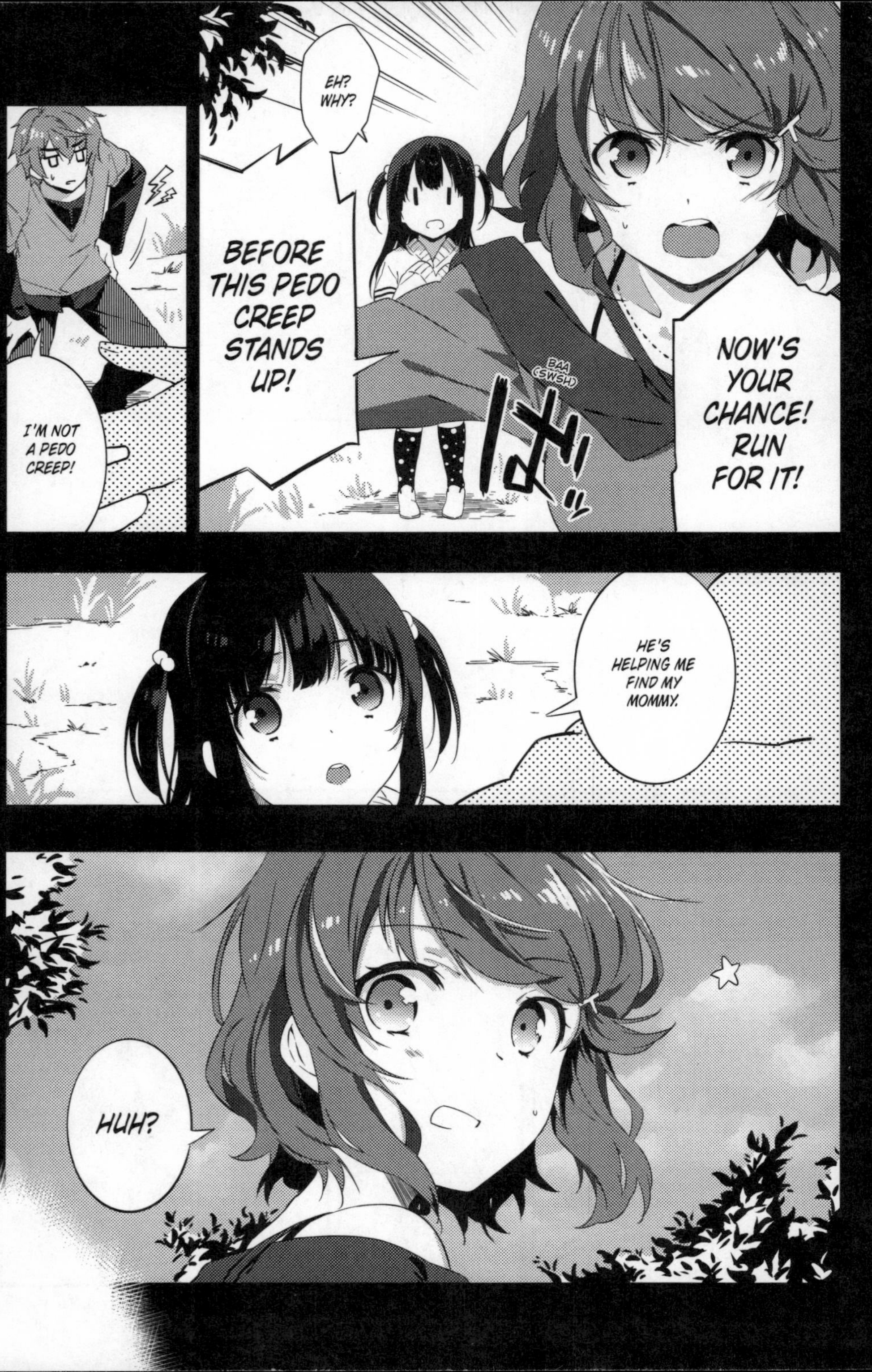
NOW'S YOUR CHANCE! RUN FOR IT!
BAA (SWSH)
BEFORE THIS PEDO CREEP STANDS UP!
EH? WHY?
I'M NOT A PEDO CREEP!
HE'S HELPING ME FIND MY MOMMY.
HUH?

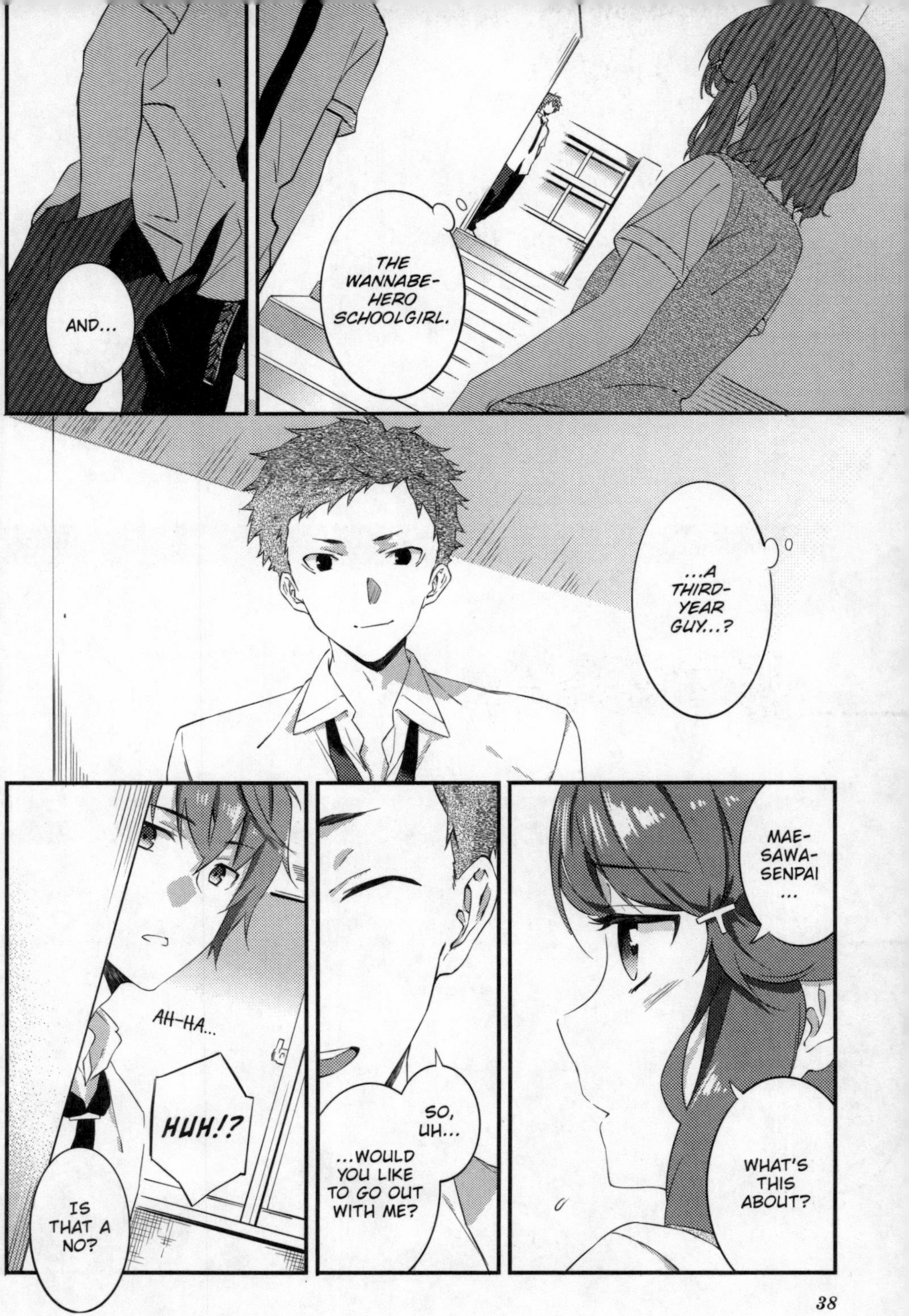
THE WANNABE-HERO SCHOOLGIRL.
AND...
...A THIRD-YEAR GUY...?
MAE-SAWA-SENPAI ...
WHAT'S THIS ABOUT?
SO, UH...
...WOULD YOU LIKE TO GO OUT WITH ME?
AH-HA...
HUH!?
IS THAT A NO?

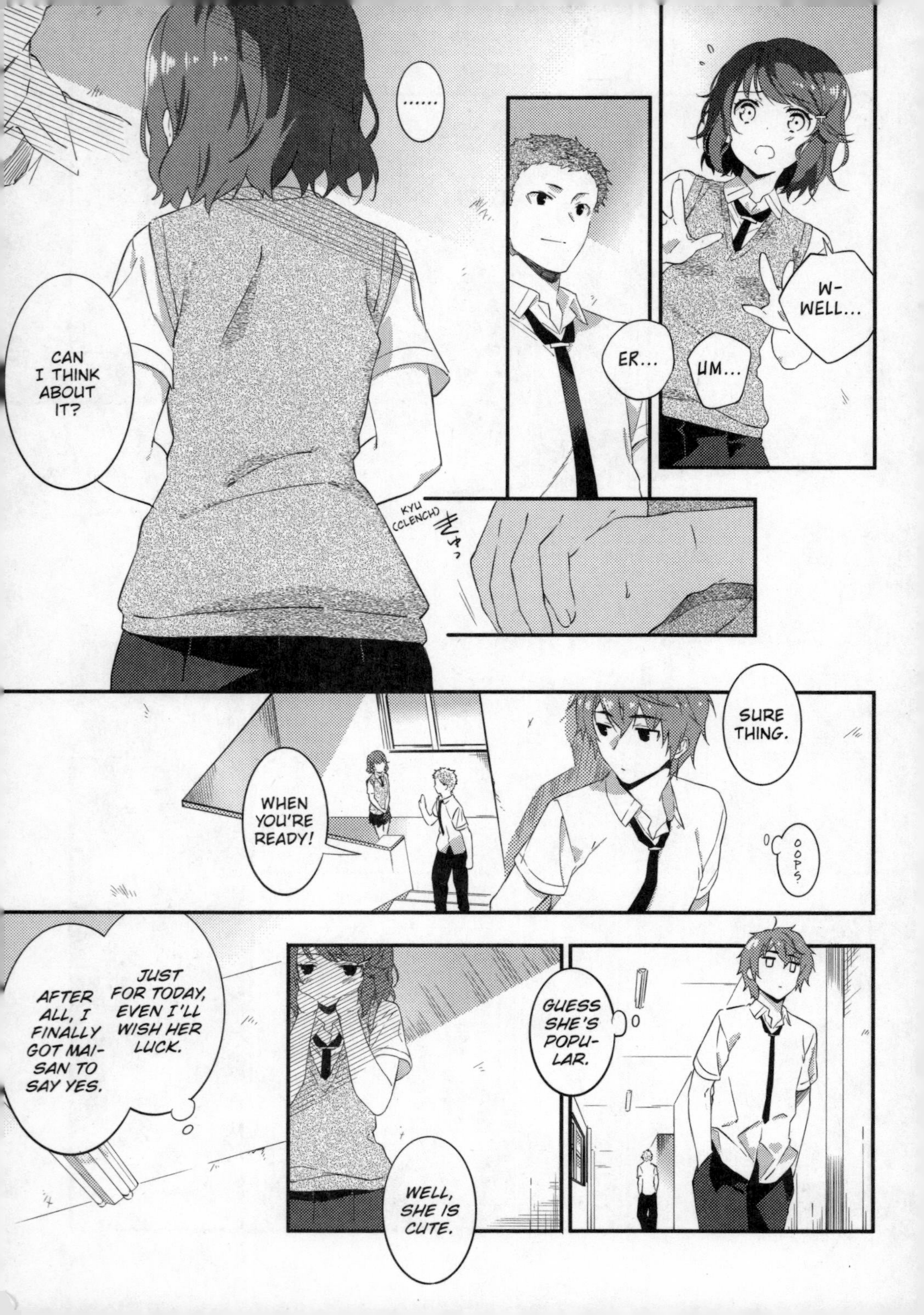
W-WELL...
UM...
ER...
KYU (CLENCH)
......
CAN I THINK ABOUT IT?
SURE THING.
OOPS.
WHEN YOU'RE READY!
GUESS SHE'S POPU-LAR.
WELL, SHE IS CUTE.
JUST FOR TODAY, EVEN I'LL WISH HER LUCK.
AFTER ALL, I FINALLY GOT MAI-SAN TO SAY YES.

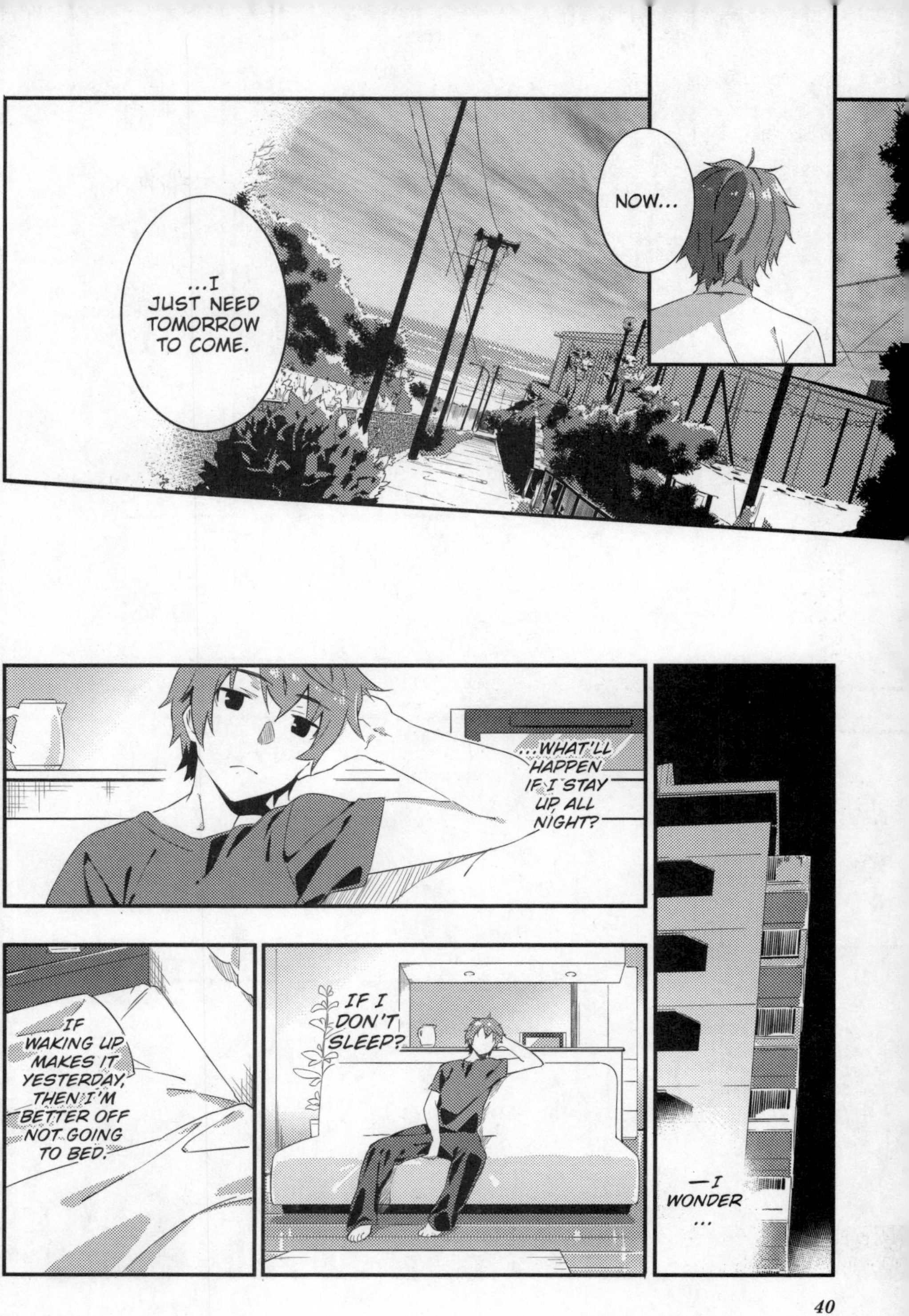
NOW...
...I JUST NEED TOMORROW TO COME.
—I WONDER ...
...WHAT'LL HAPPEN IF I STAY UP, ALL NIGHT?
IF I DON'T SLEEP?
IF WAKING UP MAKES IT YESTERDAY, THEN I'M BETTER OFF NOT GOING TO BED.

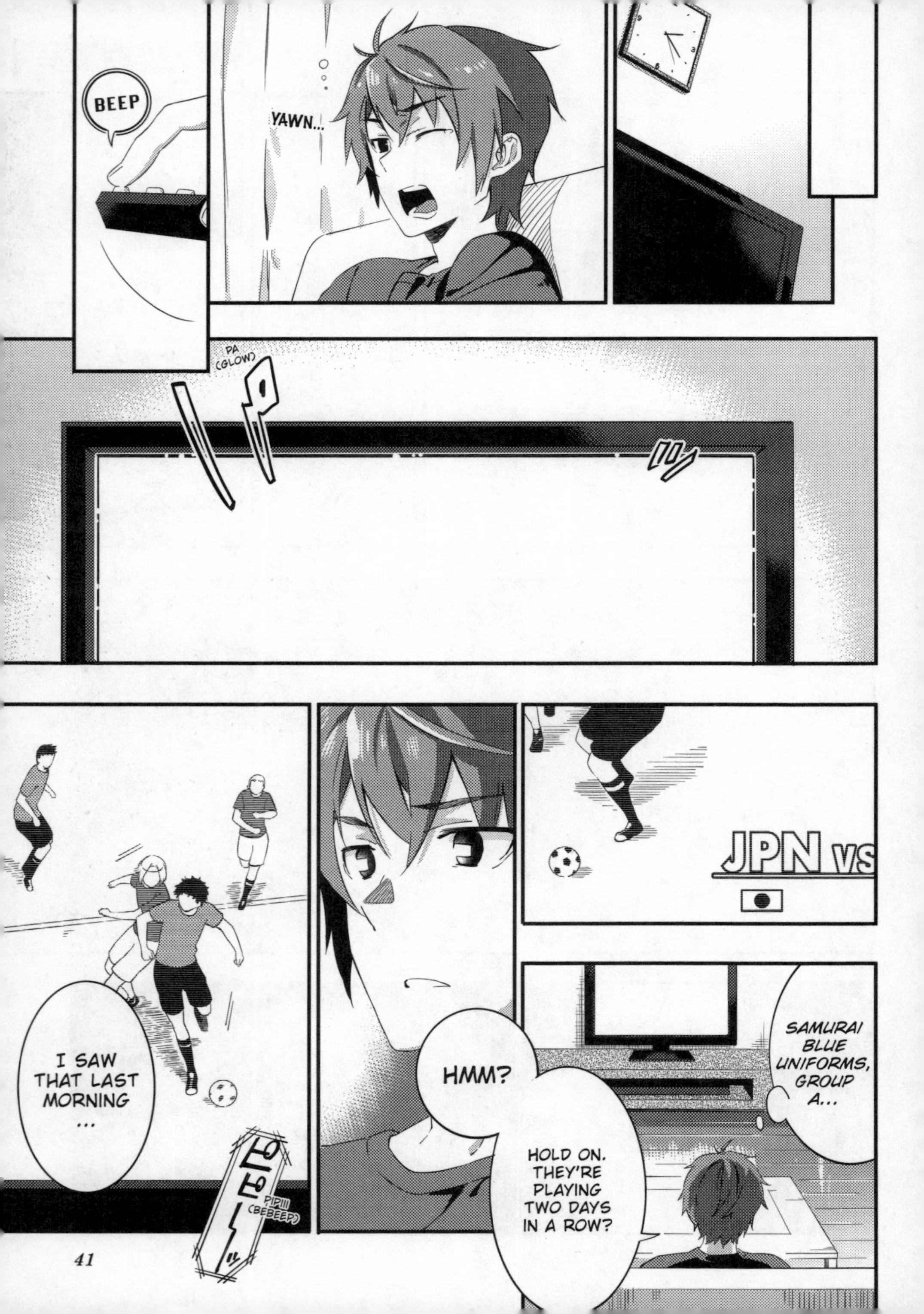
YAWN...
BEEP
PA (GLOW)
JPN vs
SAMURAI BLUE UNIFORMS, GROUP A...
HMM?
HOLD ON. THEY'RE PLAYING TWO DAYS IN A ROW?
I SAW THAT LAST MORNING...
PIPIII (BEBEEP)

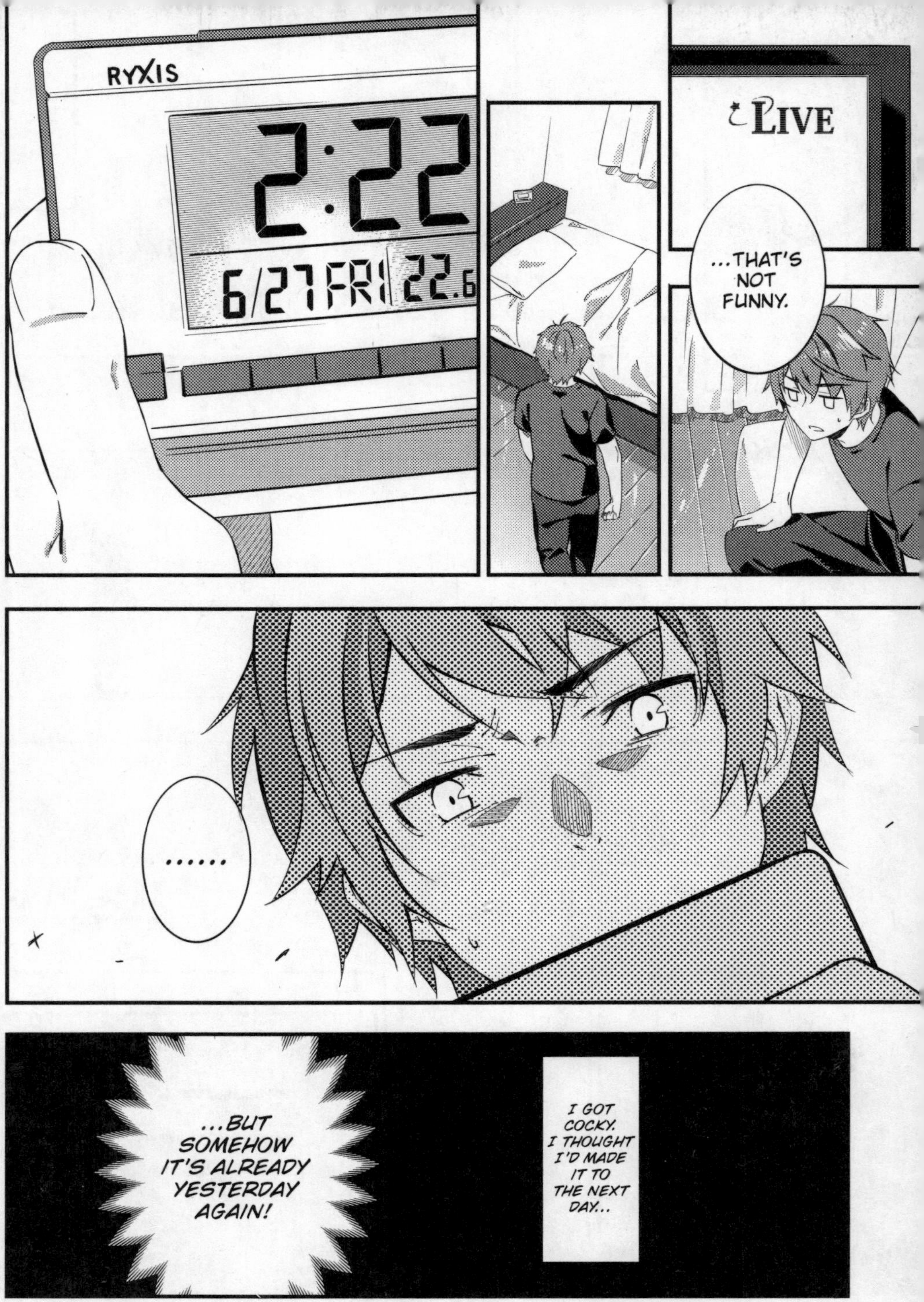
LIVE
...THAT'S NOT FUNNY.
RYXIS
2:22
6/27 FRI 22.6
......
I GOT COCKY. I THOUGHT I'D MADE IT TO THE NEXT DAY...
...BUT SOMEHOW IT'S ALREADY YESTERDAY AGAIN!

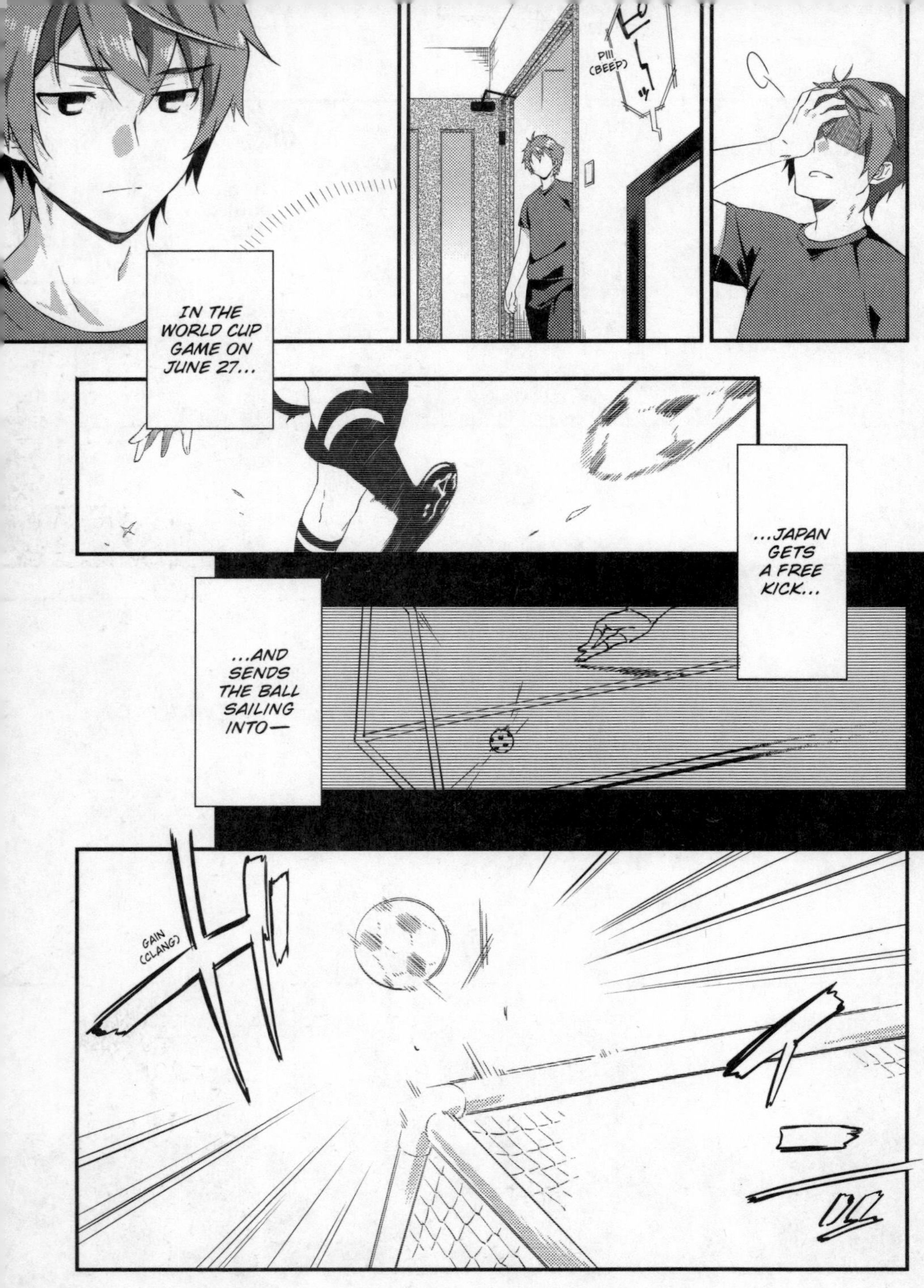
PIII (BEEP)
IN THE WORLD CUP GAME ON JUNE 27...
...JAPAN GETS A FREE KICK...
...AND SENDS THE BALL SAILING INTO—
GAIN (CLANG)

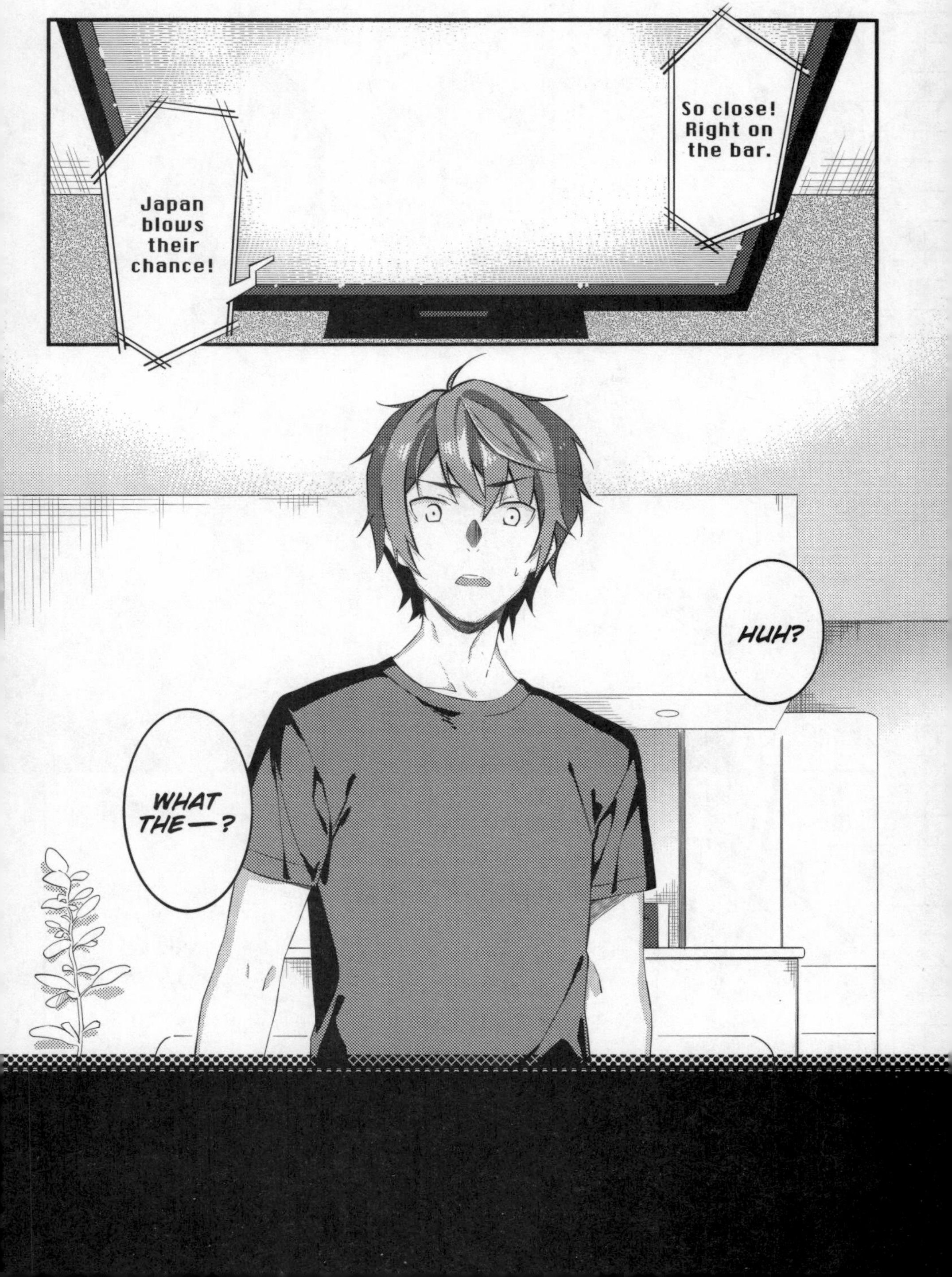
So close! Right on the bar.
Japan blows their chance!
HUH?
WHAT THE—?

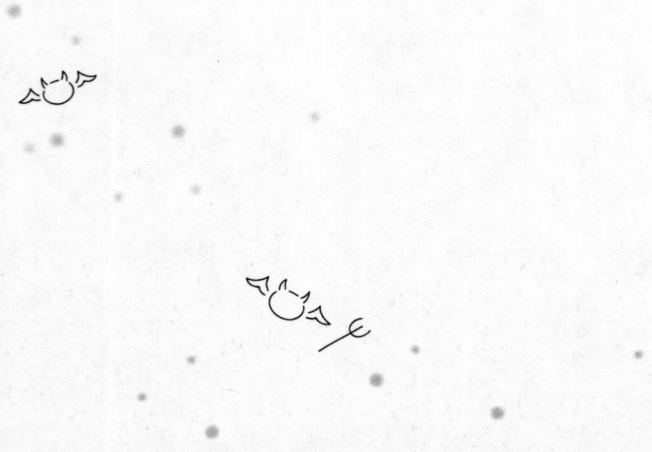

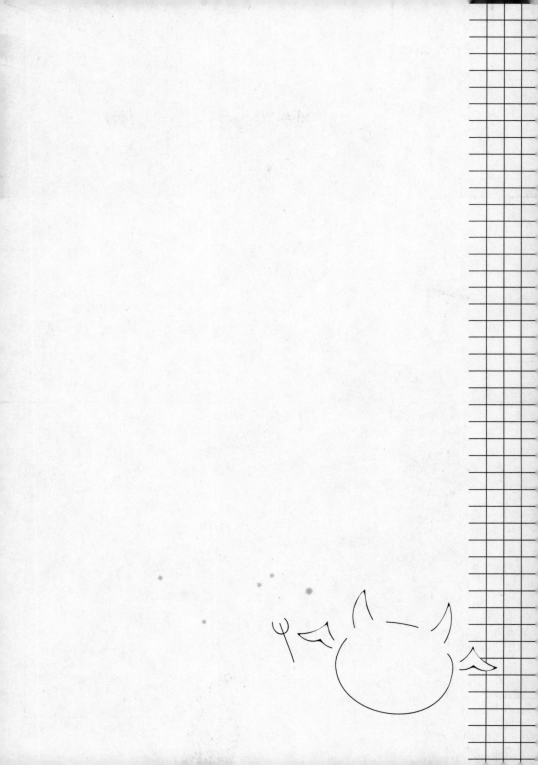

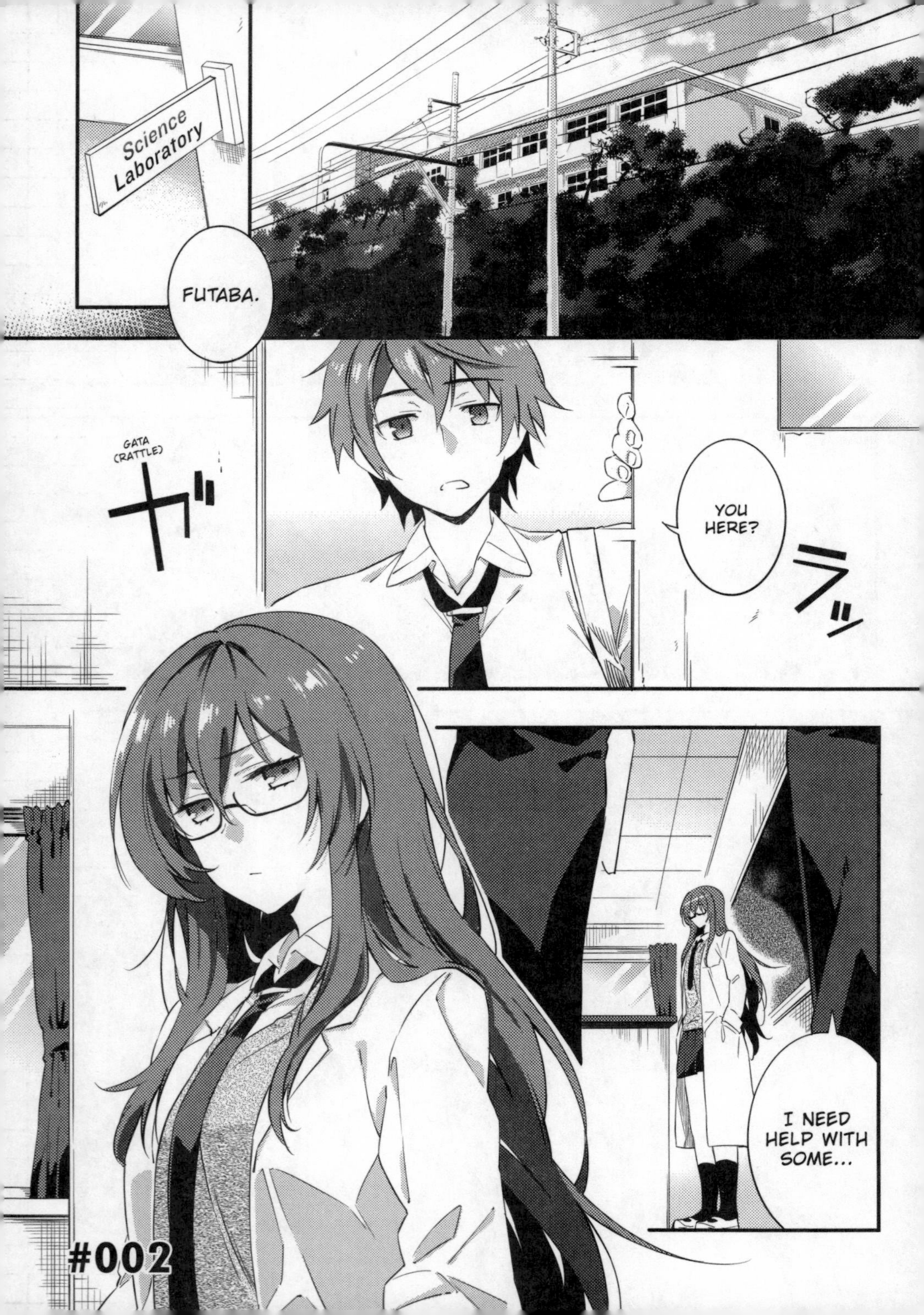

Science Laboratory
FUTABA.
ラッ
YOU HERE?
GATA (RATTLE)
ガ
I NEED HELP WITH SOME...
#002

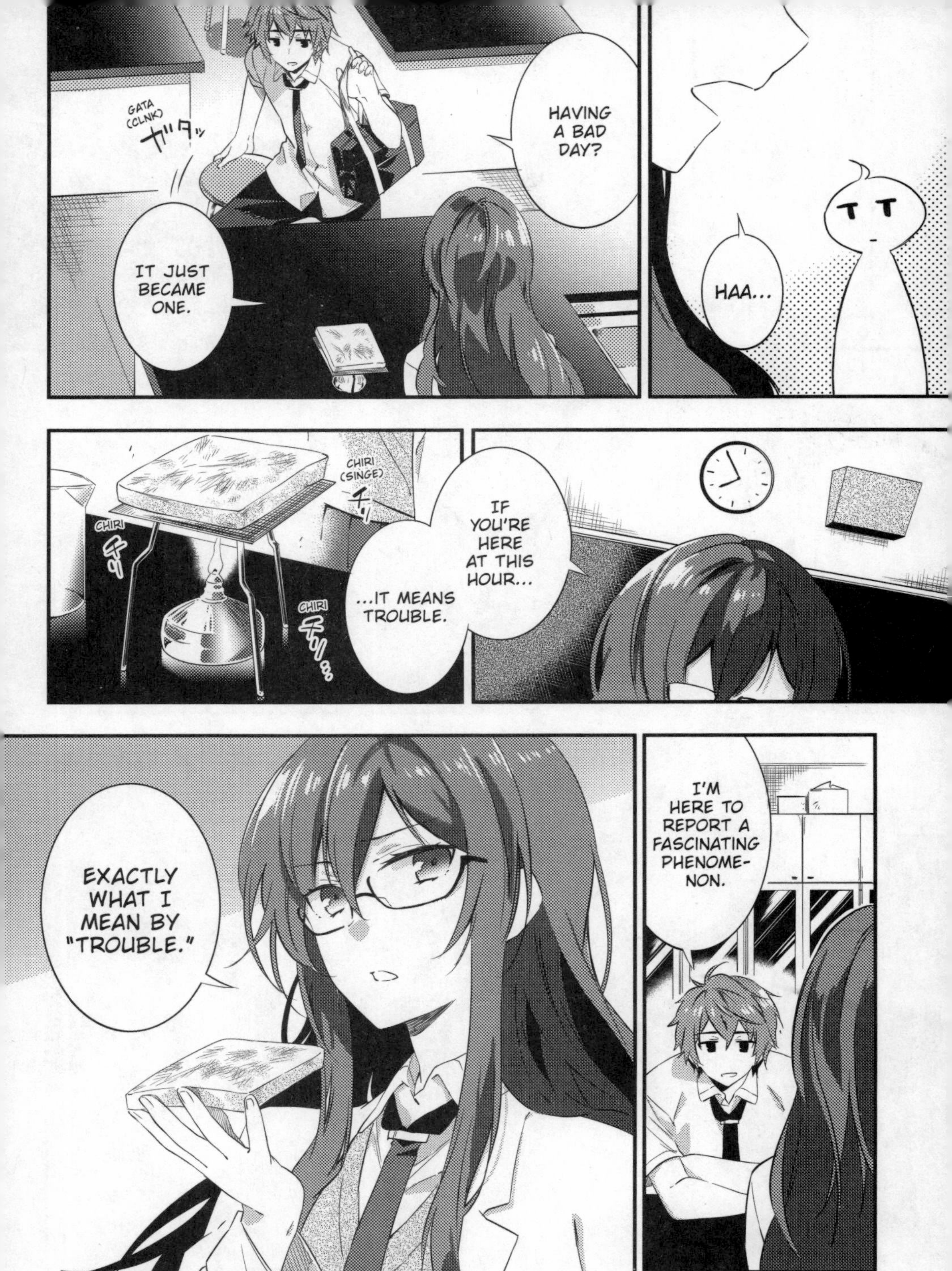
HAA...
HAVING A BAD DAY?
GATA (CLNK)
IT JUST BECAME ONE.
IF YOU'RE HERE AT THIS HOUR...
CHIRI (SINGE)
...IT MEANS TROUBLE.
CHIRI
CHIRI
I'M HERE TO REPORT A FASCINATING PHENOME-NON.
EXACTLY WHAT I MEAN BY "TROUBLE."

# #002

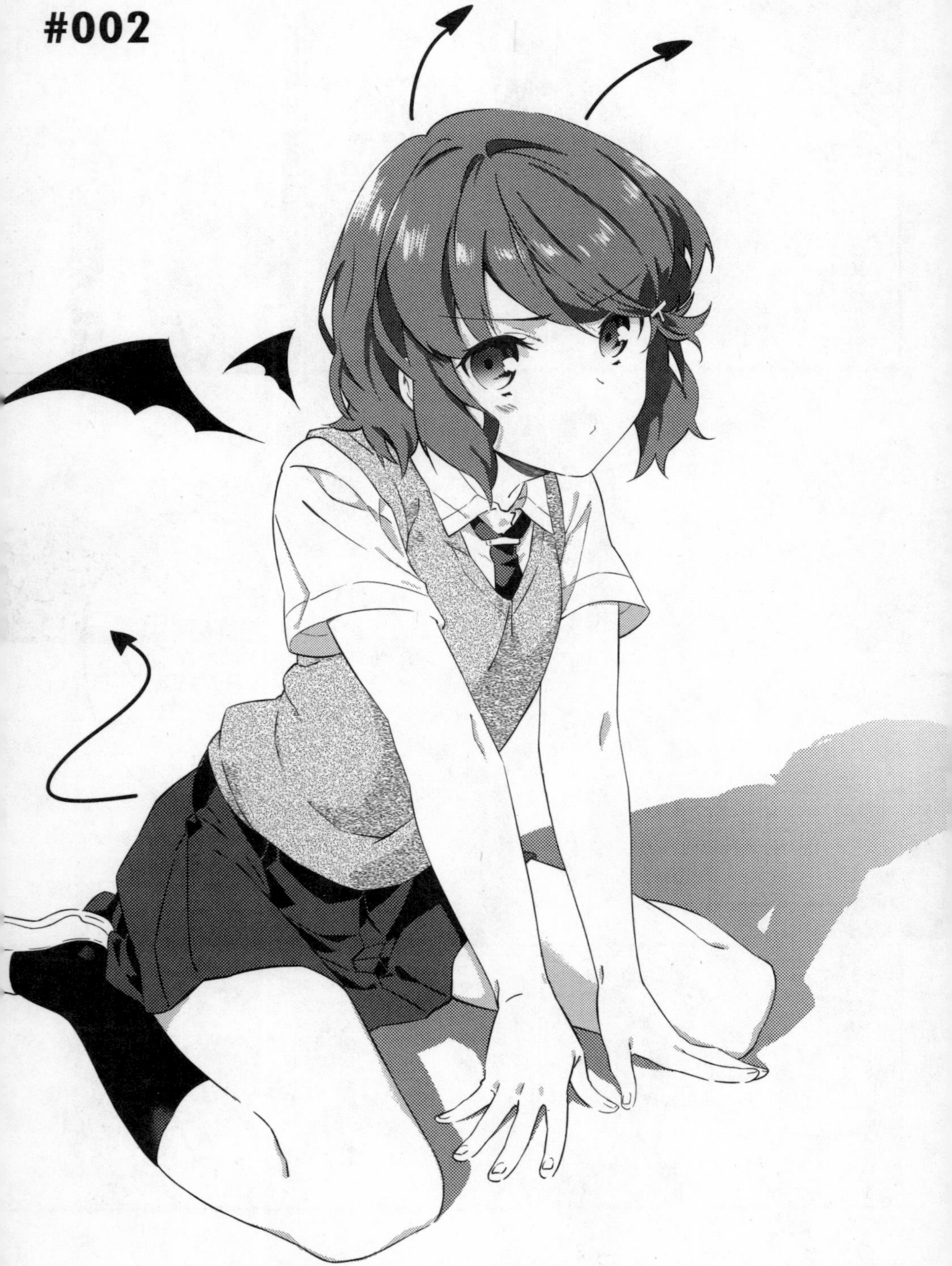

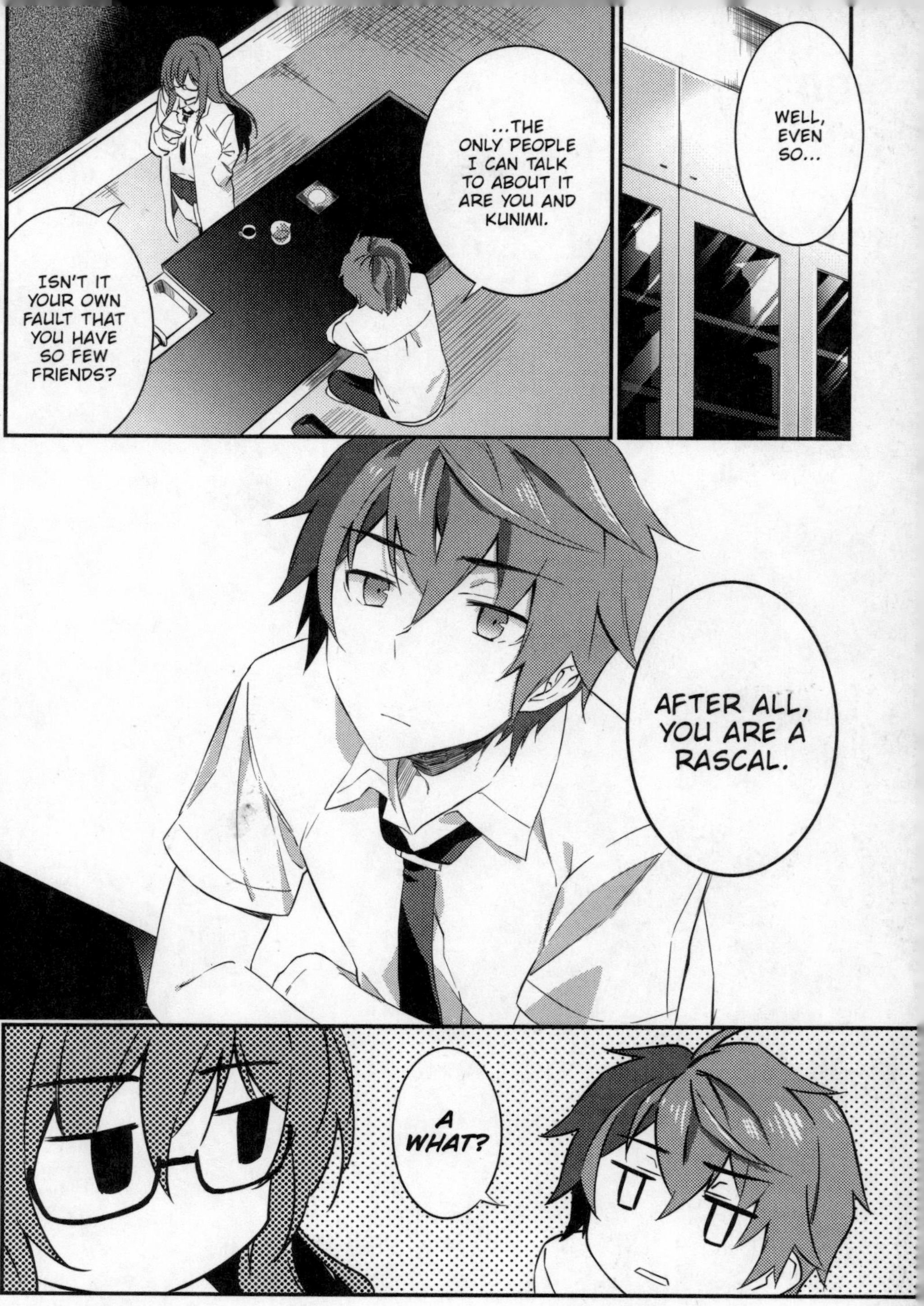
WELL, EVEN SO...
...THE ONLY PEOPLE I CAN TALK TO ABOUT IT ARE YOU AND KUNIMI.
ISN'T IT YOUR OWN FAULT THAT YOU HAVE SO FEW FRIENDS?
AFTER ALL, YOU ARE A RASCAL.
A WHAT?

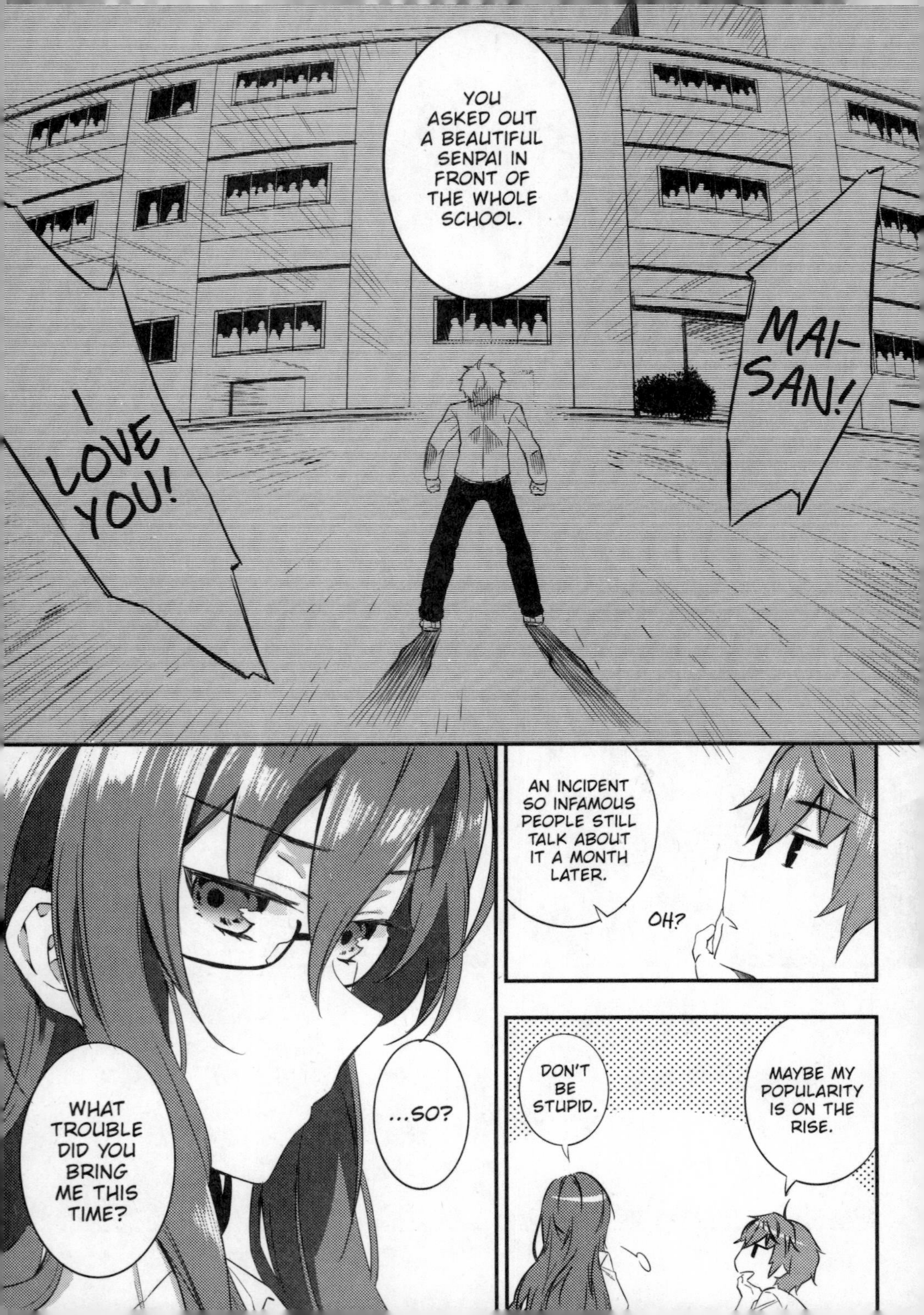
YOU ASKED OUT A BEAUTIFUL SENPAI IN FRONT OF THE WHOLE SCHOOL.
MAI-SAN!
I LOVE YOU!
AN INCIDENT SO INFAMOUS PEOPLE STILL TALK ABOUT IT A MONTH LATER.
OH?
MAYBE MY POPULARITY IS ON THE RISE.
DON'T BE STUPID.
...SO?
WHAT TROUBLE DID YOU BRING ME THIS TIME?

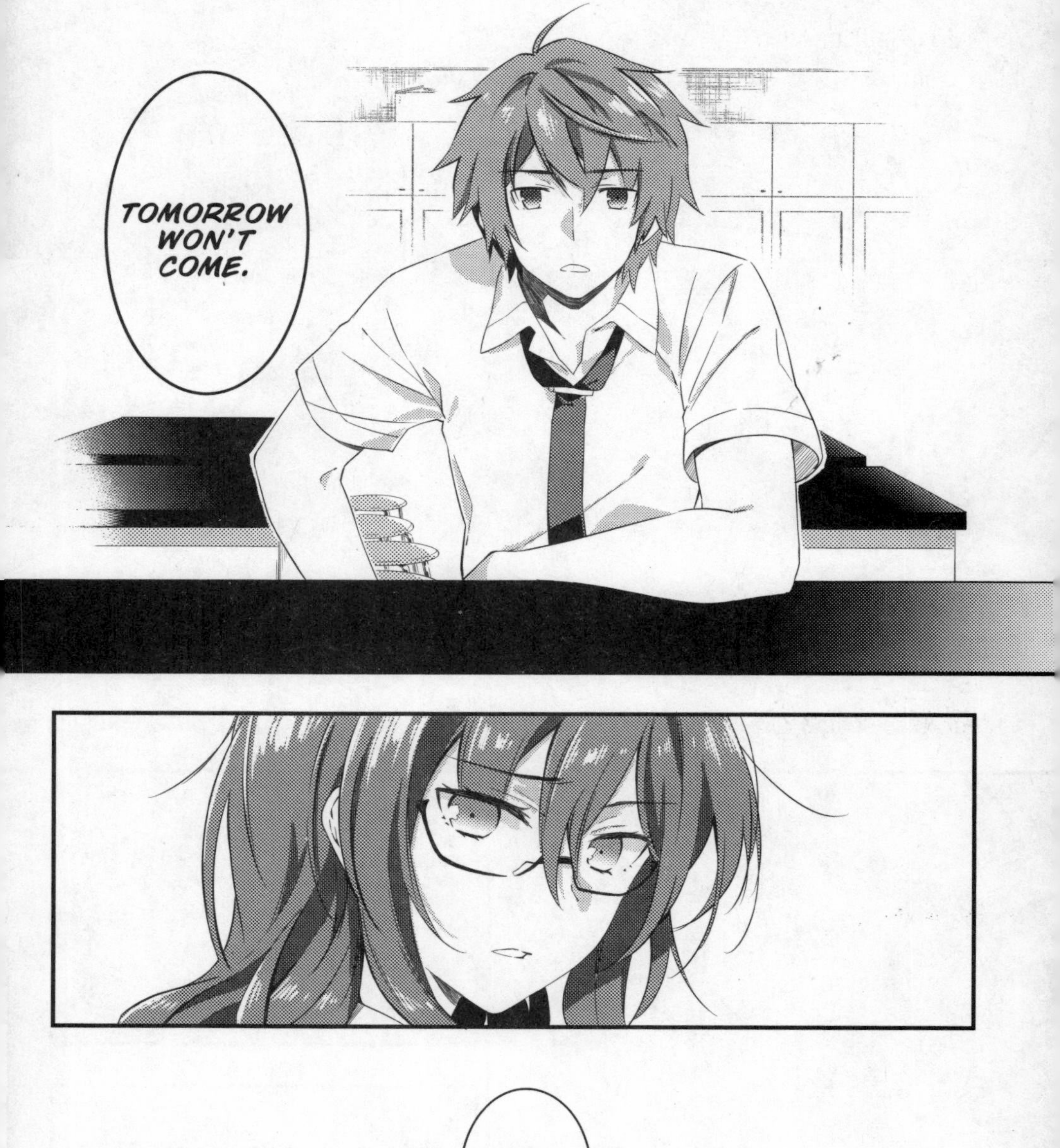
TOMORROW WON'T COME.
HUH?

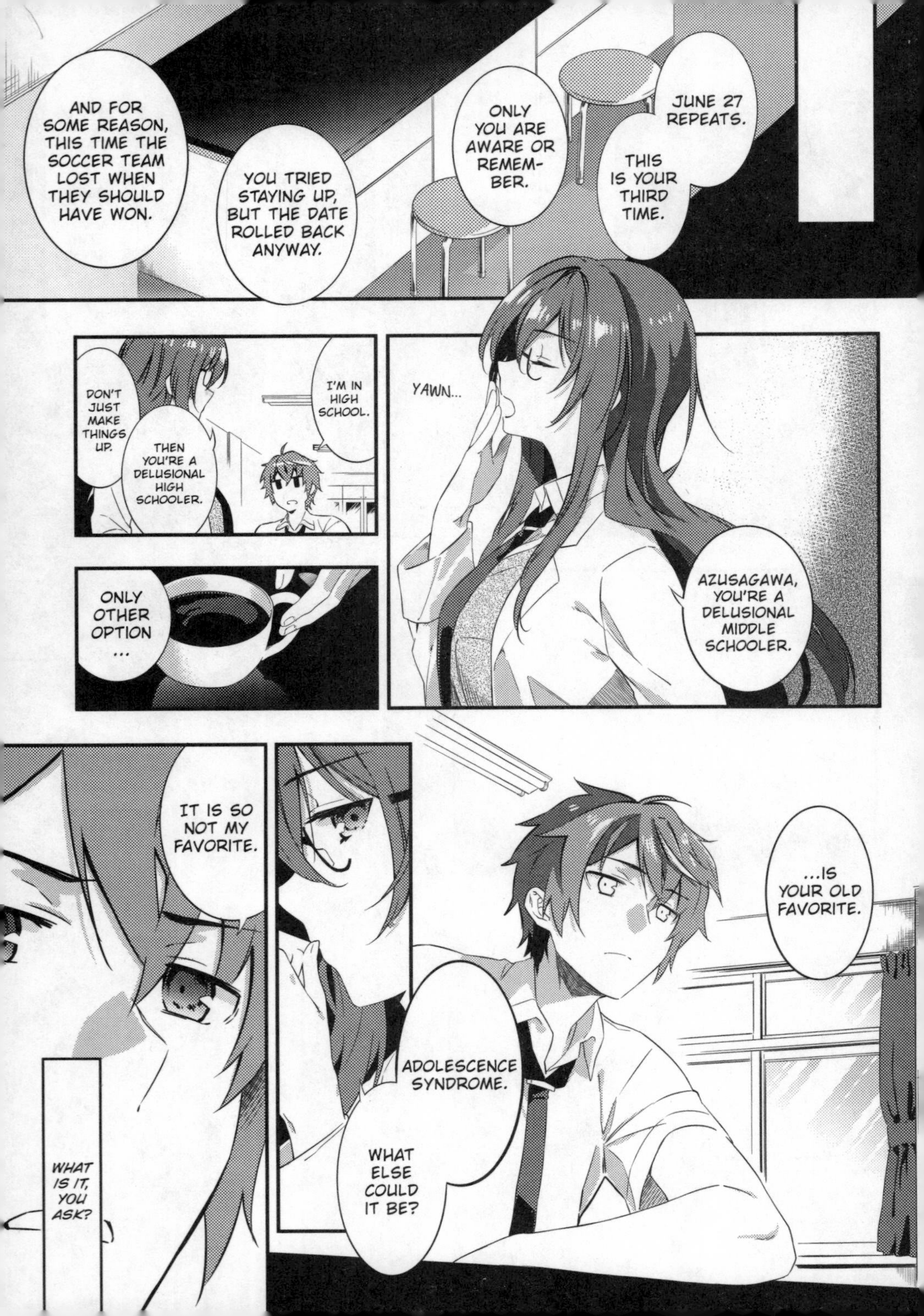
JUNE 27 REPEATS.
THIS IS YOUR THIRD TIME.
ONLY YOU ARE AWARE OR REMEMBER.
YOU TRIED STAYING UP, BUT THE DATE ROLLED BACK ANYWAY.
AND FOR SOME REASON, THIS TIME THE SOCCER TEAM LOST WHEN THEY SHOULD HAVE WON.
YAWN...
AZUSAGAWA, YOU'RE A DELUSIONAL MIDDLE SCHOOLER.
I'M IN HIGH SCHOOL.
THEN YOU'RE A DELUSIONAL HIGH SCHOOLER.
DON'T JUST MAKE THINGS UP.
ONLY OTHER OPTION ...
...IS YOUR OLD FAVORITE.
ADOLESCENCE SYNDROME.
WHAT ELSE COULD IT BE?
IT IS SO NOT MY FAVORITE.
WHAT IS IT, YOU ASK?

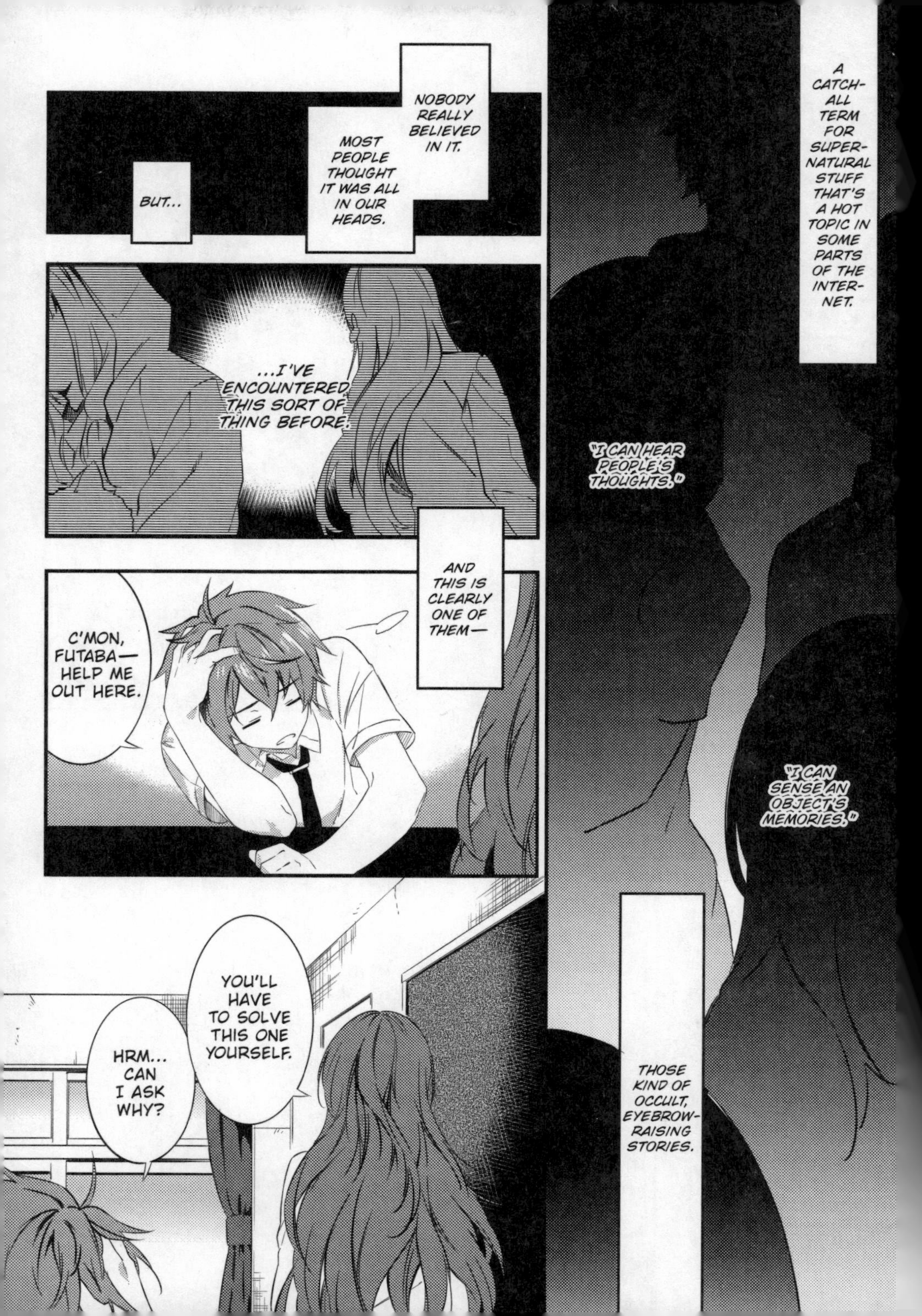
A CATCH-ALL TERM FOR SUPERNATURAL STUFF THAT'S A HOT TOPIC IN SOME PARTS OF THE INTERNET.
"I CAN HEAR PEOPLE'S THOUGHTS."
"I CAN SENSE AN OBJECT'S MEMORIES."
THOSE KIND OF OCCULT, EYEBROW-RAISING STORIES.
NOBODY REALLY BELIEVED IN IT.
MOST PEOPLE THOUGHT IT WAS ALL IN OUR HEADS.
BUT...
...I'VE ENCOUNTERED THIS SORT OF THING BEFORE.
AND THIS IS CLEARLY ONE OF THEM—
C'MON, FUTABA—HELP ME OUT HERE.
YOU'LL HAVE TO SOLVE THIS ONE YOURSELF.
HRM... CAN I ASK WHY?

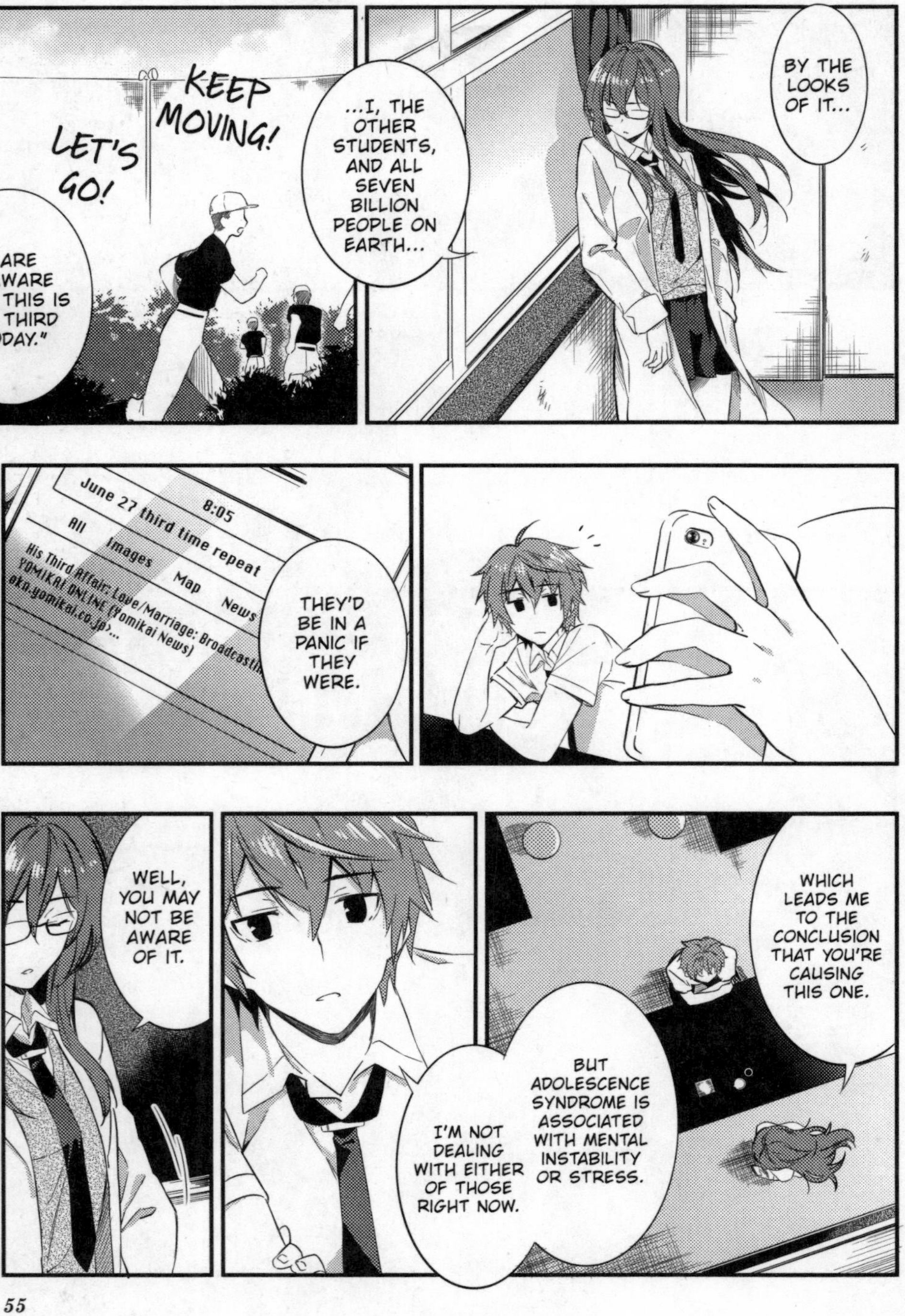
BY THE LOOKS OF IT...
...I, THE OTHER STUDENTS, AND ALL SEVEN BILLION PEOPLE ON EARTH...
KEEP MOVING!
LET'S GO!
...ARE UNAWARE THAT THIS IS THE THIRD "TODAY."
June 27 third time repeat
8:05
All Images Map News
His Third Affair: Love/Marriage: Broadcastin
YOMIKAI ONLINE (Yomikai News)
oko.yomikai.co.jp>...
THEY'D BE IN A PANIC IF THEY WERE.
WHICH LEADS ME TO THE CONCLUSION THAT YOU'RE CAUSING THIS ONE.
BUT ADOLESCENCE SYNDROME IS ASSOCIATED WITH MENTAL INSTABILITY OR STRESS.
I'M NOT DEALING WITH EITHER OF THOSE RIGHT NOW.
WELL, YOU MAY NOT BE AWARE OF IT.

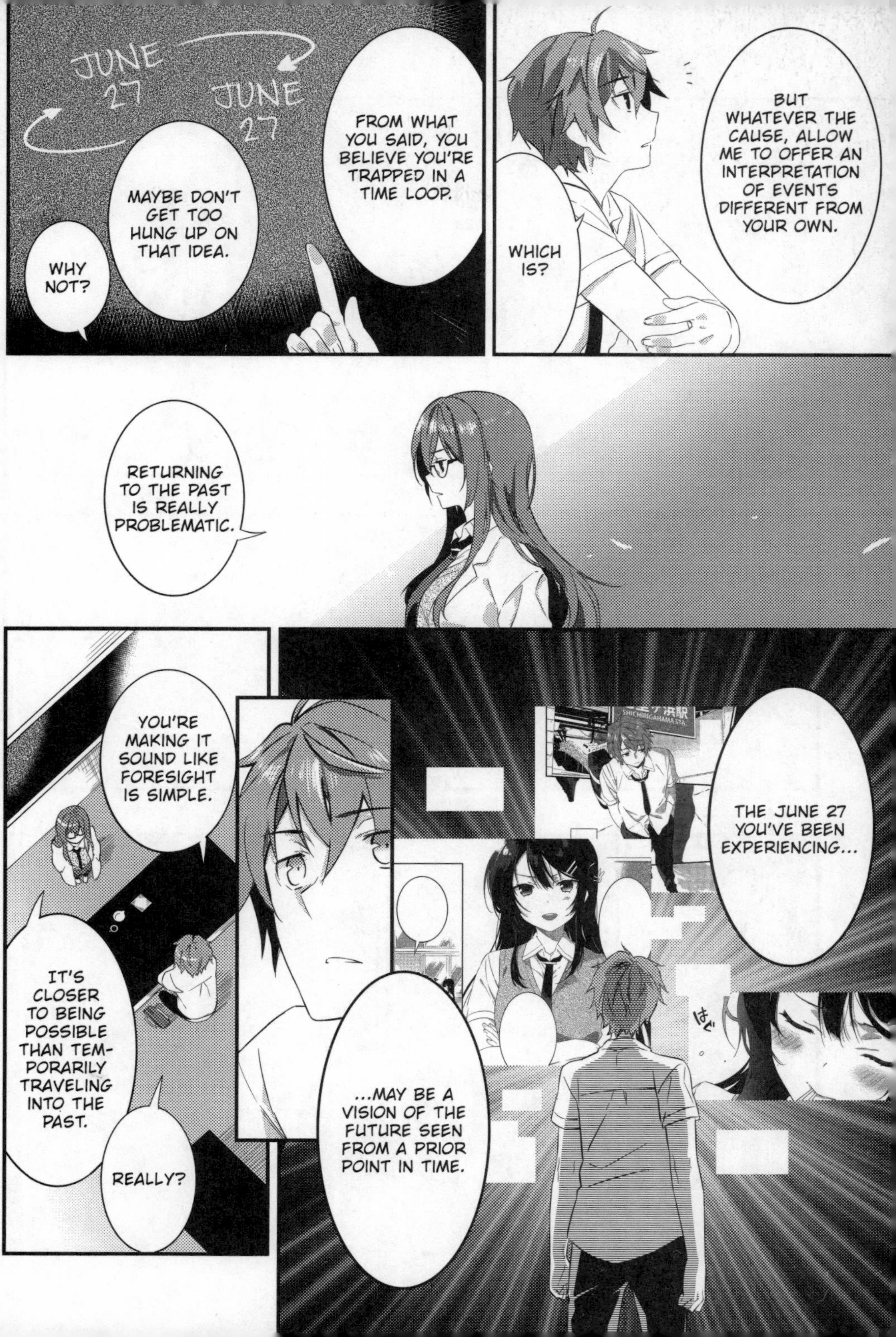
BUT WHATEVER THE CAUSE, ALLOW ME TO OFFER AN INTERPRETATION OF EVENTS DIFFERENT FROM YOUR OWN.
WHICH IS?
JUNE 27
JUNE 27
FROM WHAT YOU SAID, YOU BELIEVE YOU'RE TRAPPED IN A TIME LOOP.
MAYBE DON'T GET TOO HUNG UP ON THAT IDEA.
WHY NOT?
RETURNING TO THE PAST IS REALLY PROBLEMATIC.
THE JUNE 27 YOU'VE BEEN EXPERIENCING...
...MAY BE A VISION OF THE FUTURE SEEN FROM A PRIOR POINT IN TIME.
YOU'RE MAKING IT SOUND LIKE FORESIGHT IS SIMPLE.
IT'S CLOSER TO BEING POSSIBLE THAN TEMPORARILY TRAVELING INTO THE PAST.
REALLY?

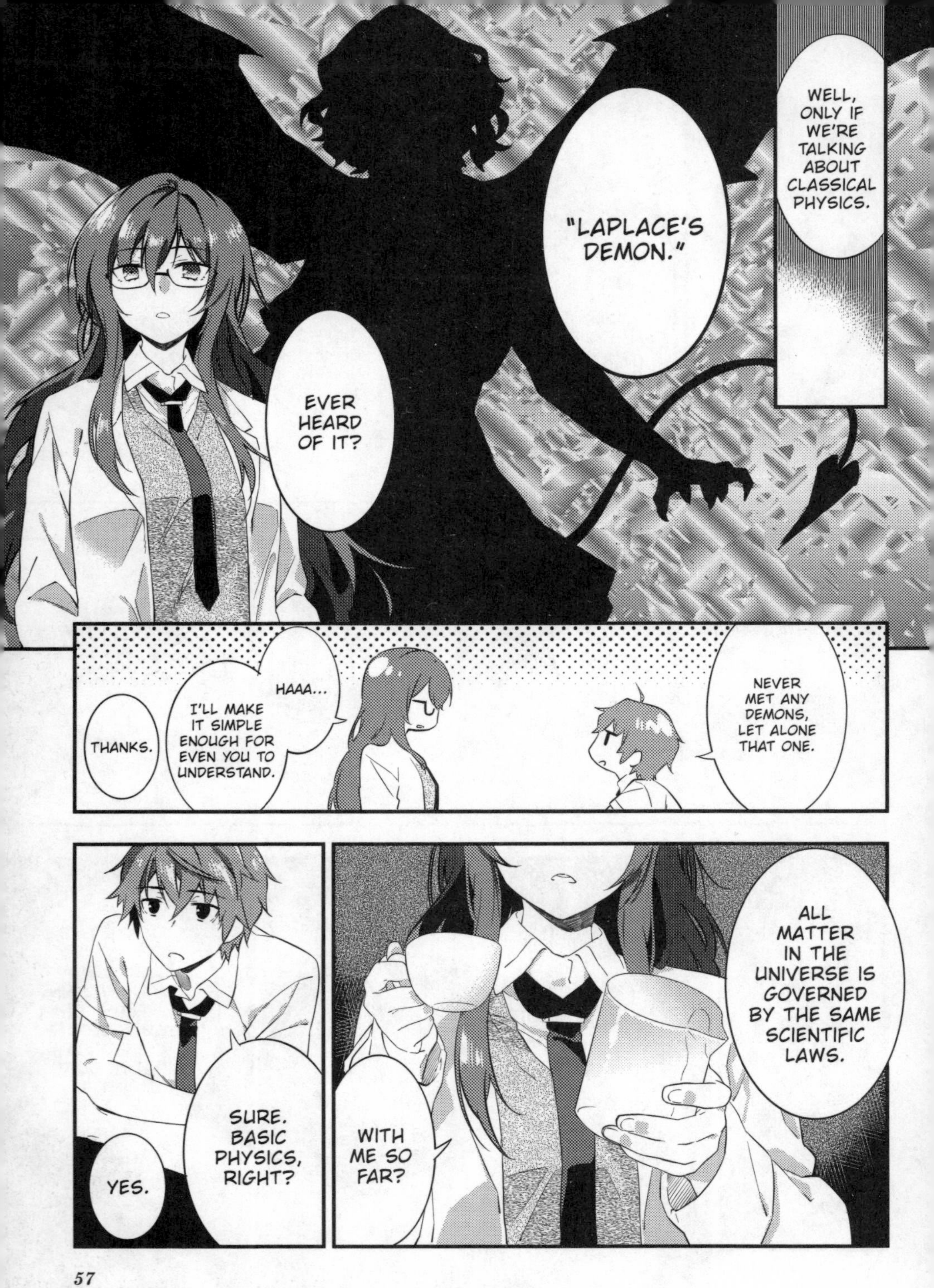
WELL, ONLY IF WE'RE TALKING ABOUT CLASSICAL PHYSICS.
"LAPLACE'S DEMON."
EVER HEARD OF IT?
NEVER MET ANY DEMONS, LET ALONE THAT ONE.
HAAA...
I'LL MAKE IT SIMPLE ENOUGH FOR EVEN YOU TO UNDERSTAND.
THANKS.
ALL MATTER IN THE UNIVERSE IS GOVERNED BY THE SAME SCIENTIFIC LAWS.
WITH ME SO FAR?
SURE. BASIC PHYSICS, RIGHT?
YES.

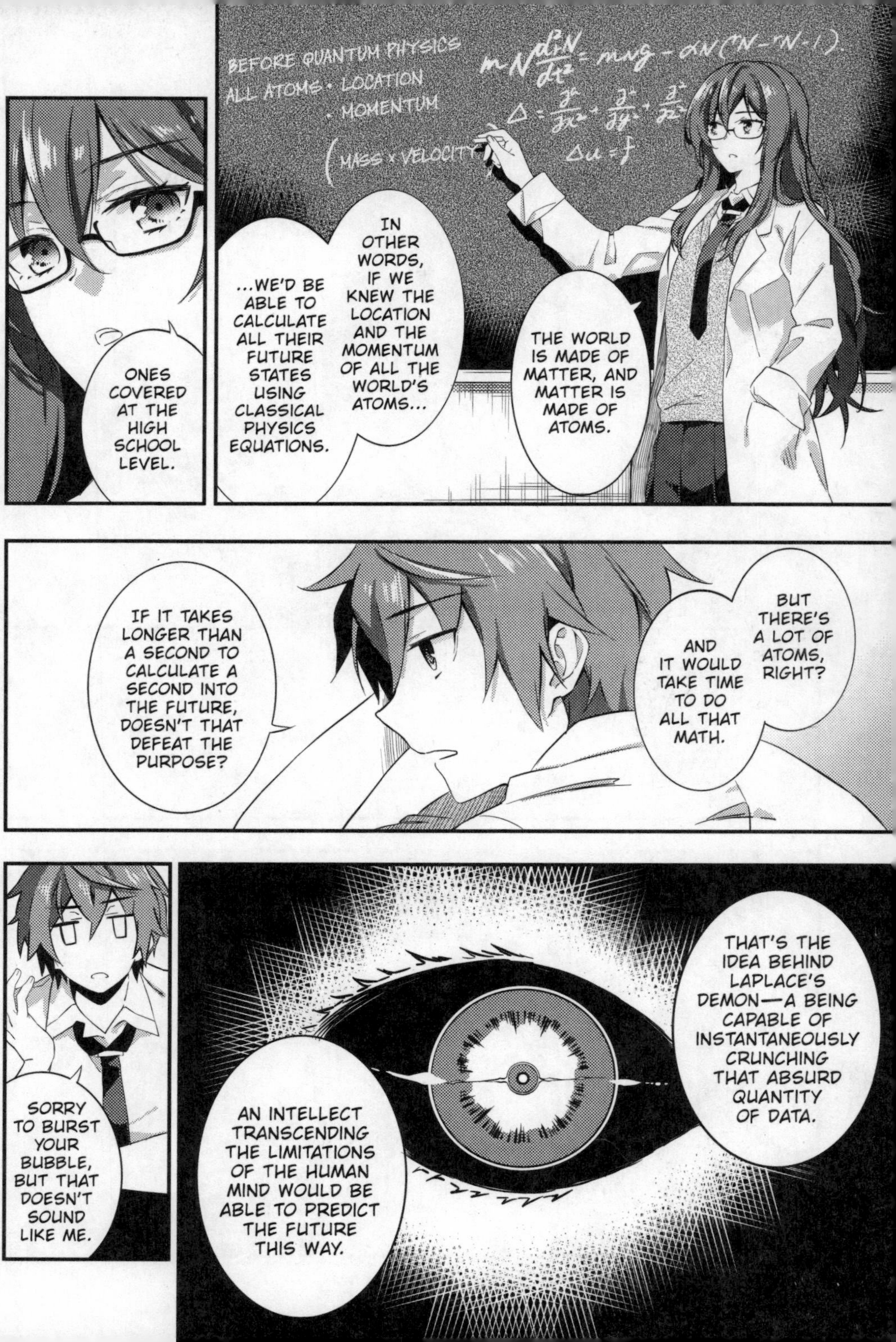
BEFORE QUANTUM PHYSICS
ALL ATOMS • LOCATION
• MOMENTUM
(MASS x VELOCITY
THE WORLD IS MADE OF MATTER, AND MATTER IS MADE OF ATOMS.
IN OTHER WORDS, IF WE KNEW THE LOCATION AND THE MOMENTUM OF ALL THE WORLD'S ATOMS...
...WE'D BE ABLE TO CALCULATE ALL THEIR FUTURE STATES USING CLASSICAL PHYSICS EQUATIONS.
ONES COVERED AT THE HIGH SCHOOL LEVEL.
BUT THERE'S A LOT OF ATOMS, RIGHT?
AND IT WOULD TAKE TIME TO DO ALL THAT MATH.
IF IT TAKES LONGER THAN A SECOND TO CALCULATE A SECOND INTO THE FUTURE, DOESN'T THAT DEFEAT THE PURPOSE?
THAT'S THE IDEA BEHIND LAPLACE'S DEMON—A BEING CAPABLE OF INSTANTANEOUSLY CRUNCHING THAT ABSURD QUANTITY OF DATA.
AN INTELLECT TRANSCENDING THE LIMITATIONS OF THE HUMAN MIND WOULD BE ABLE TO PREDICT THE FUTURE THIS WAY.
SORRY TO BURST YOUR BUBBLE, BUT THAT DOESN'T SOUND LIKE ME.

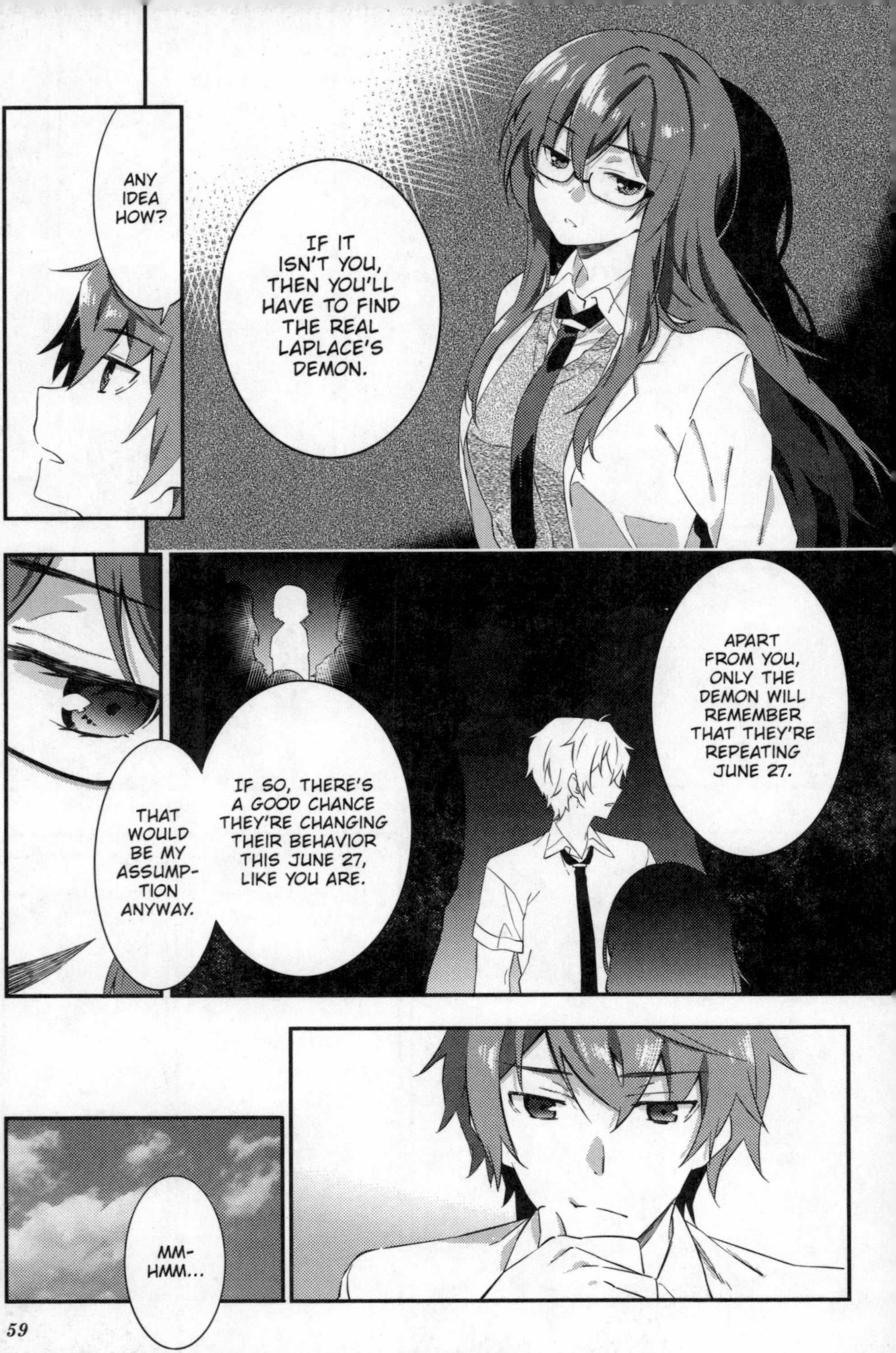
IF IT ISN'T YOU, THEN YOU'LL HAVE TO FIND THE REAL LAPLACE'S DEMON.
ANY IDEA HOW?
APART FROM YOU, ONLY THE DEMON WILL REMEMBER THAT THEY'RE REPEATING JUNE 27.
IF SO, THERE'S A GOOD CHANCE THEY'RE CHANGING THEIR BEHAVIOR THIS JUNE 27, LIKE YOU ARE.
THAT WOULD BE MY ASSUMPTION ANYWAY.
MM-HMM...

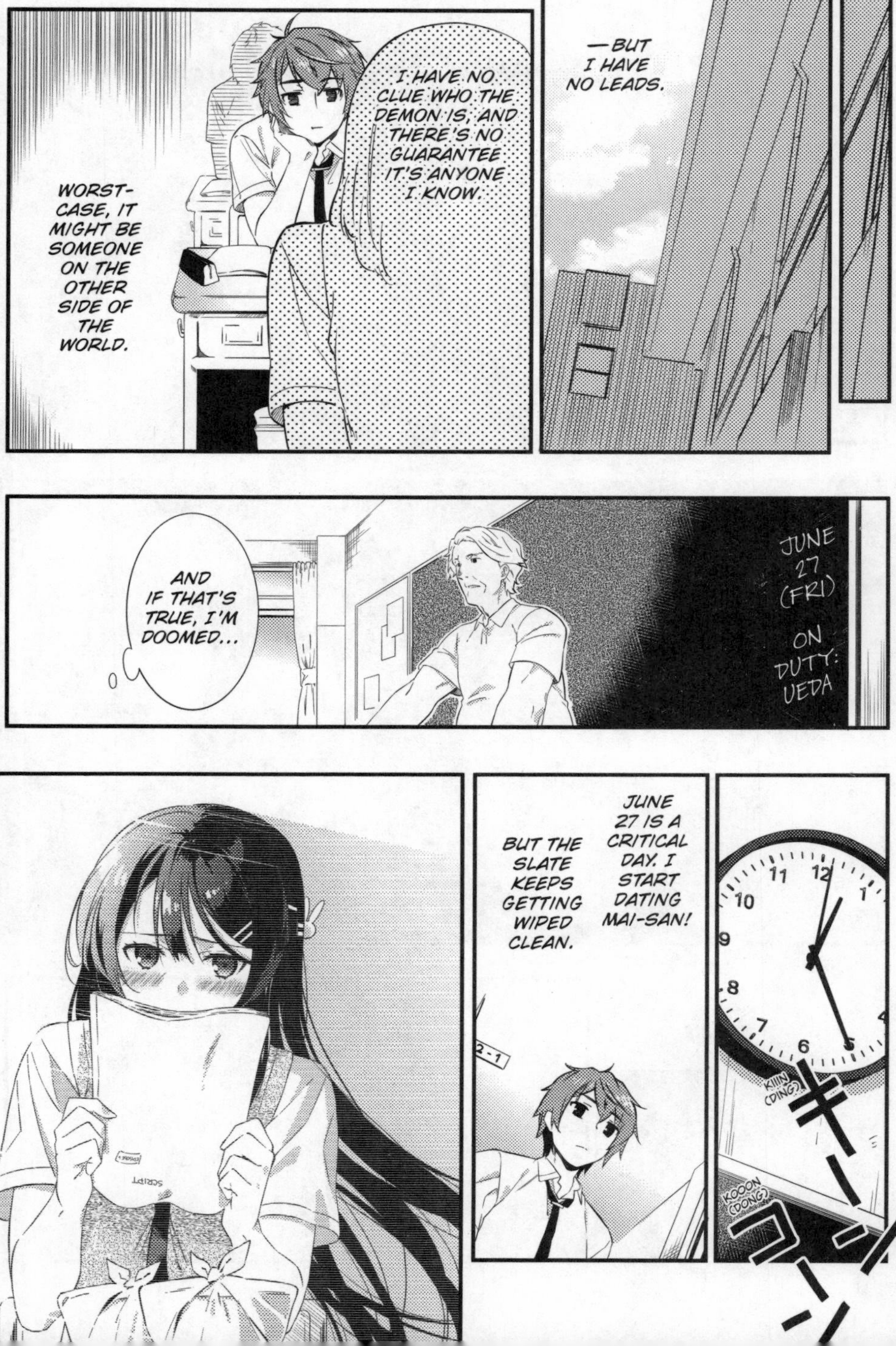
—BUT I HAVE NO LEADS.
I HAVE NO CLUE WHO THE DEMON IS, AND THERE'S NO GUARANTEE IT'S ANYONE I KNOW.
WORST-CASE, IT MIGHT BE SOMEONE ON THE OTHER SIDE OF THE WORLD.
JUNE 27 (FRI) ON DUTY: UEDA
AND IF THAT'S TRUE, I'M DOOMED...
KIIN (DING)
KOOON (DONG)
JUNE 27 IS A CRITICAL DAY. I START DATING MAI-SAN!
BUT THE SLATE KEEPS GETTING WIPED CLEAN.
2-1
SCRIPT

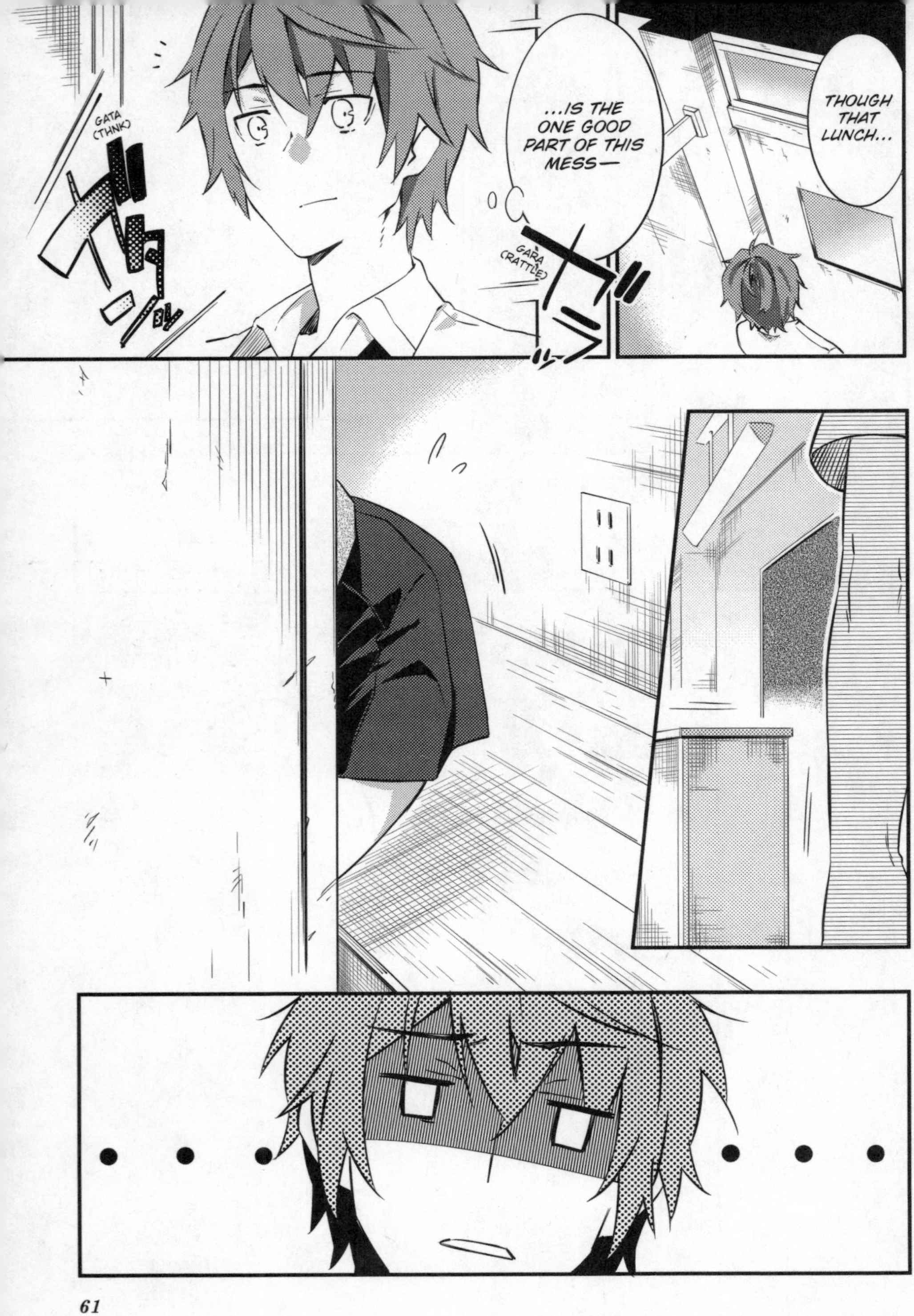
THOUGH THAT LUNCH...
...IS THE ONE GOOD PART OF THIS MESS—
GARA (RATTLE)
GATA (THNK)
• • •
• • •

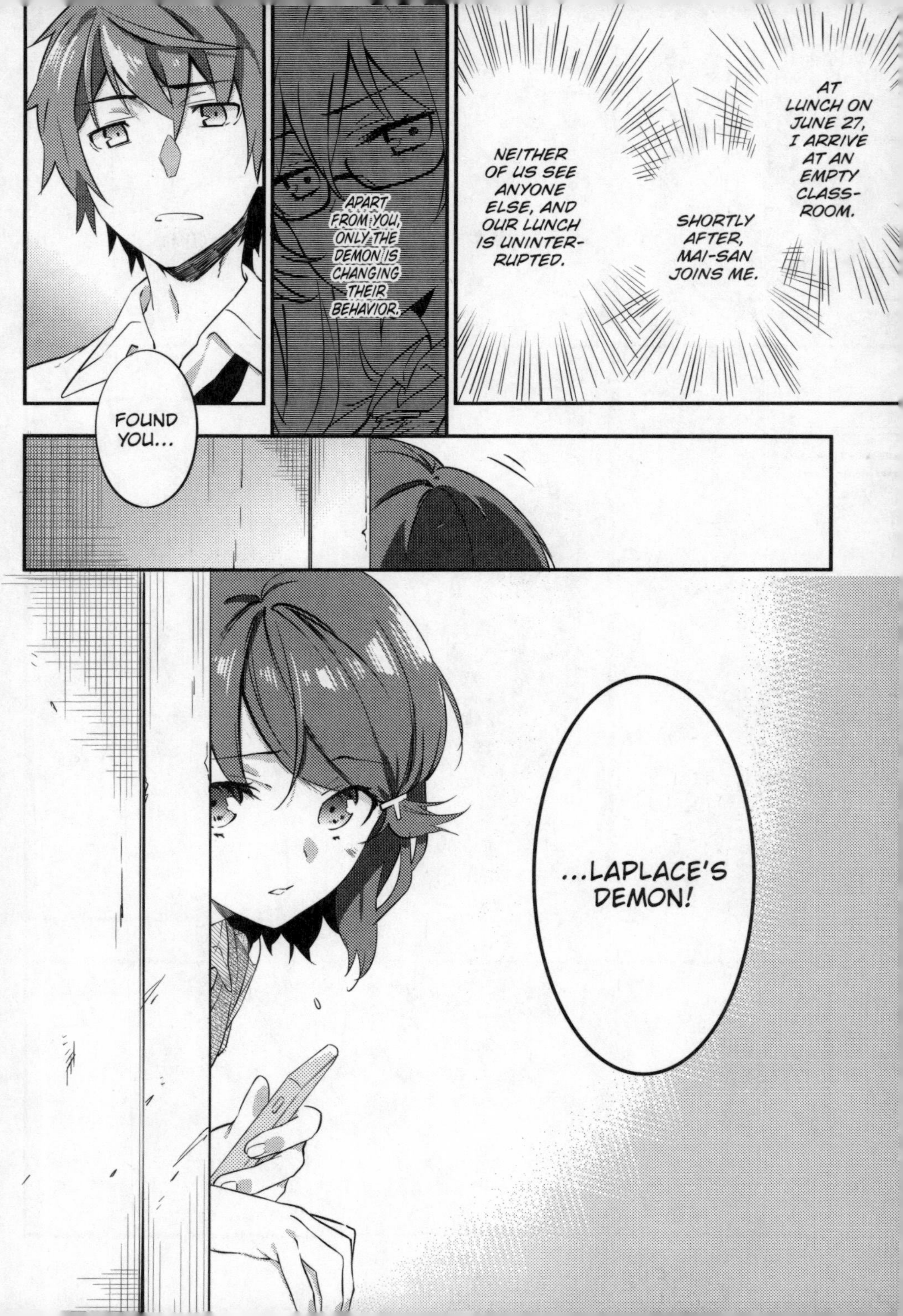
AT LUNCH ON JUNE 27, I ARRIVE AT AN EMPTY CLASSROOM.
SHORTLY AFTER, MAI-SAN JOINS ME.
NEITHER OF US SEE ANYONE ELSE, AND OUR LUNCH IS UNINTERRUPTED.
APART FROM YOU, ONLY THE DEMON IS CHANGING THEIR BEHAVIOR.
FOUND YOU...
...LAPLACE'S DEMON!

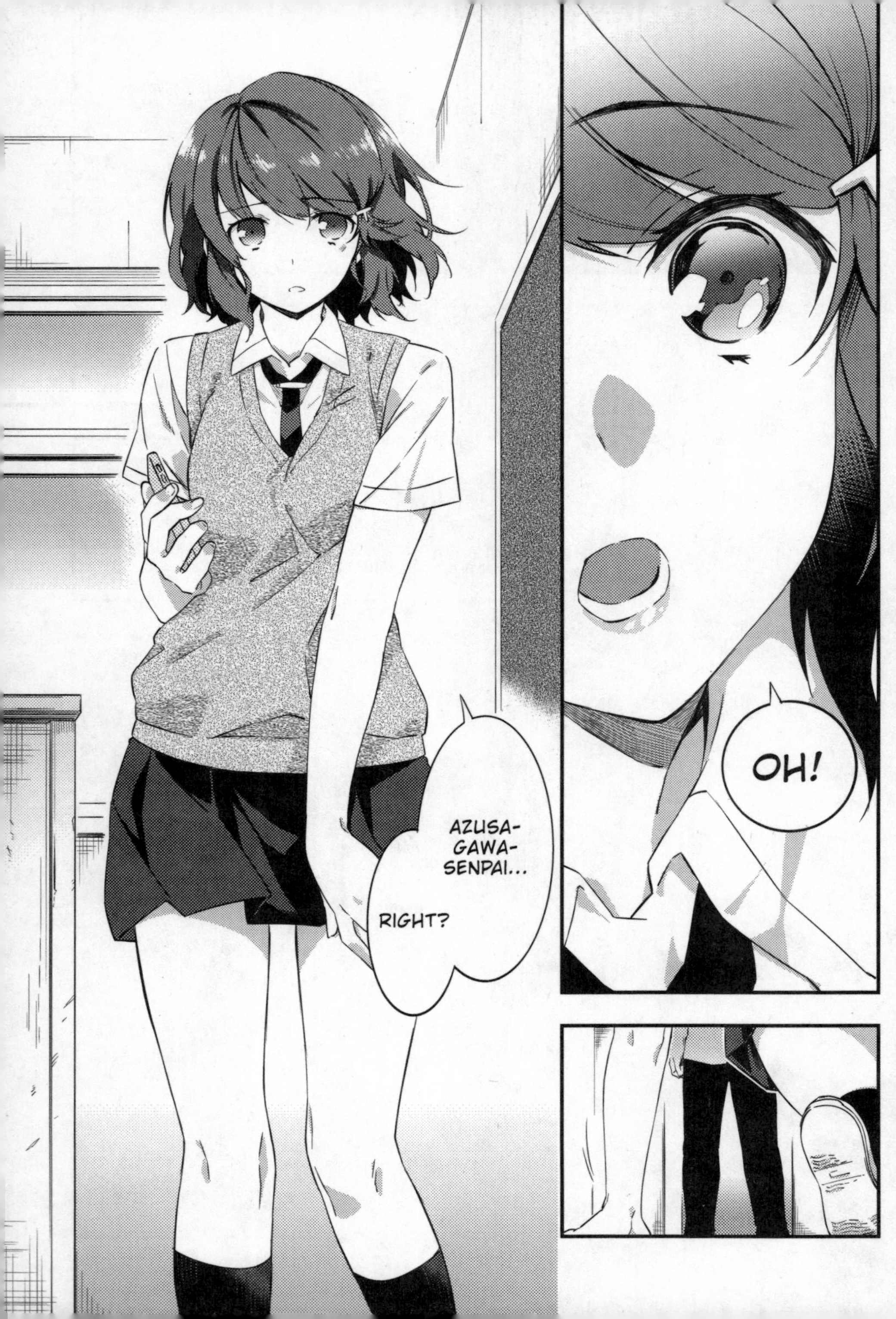
OH!
AZUSA-GAWA-SENPAI... RIGHT?

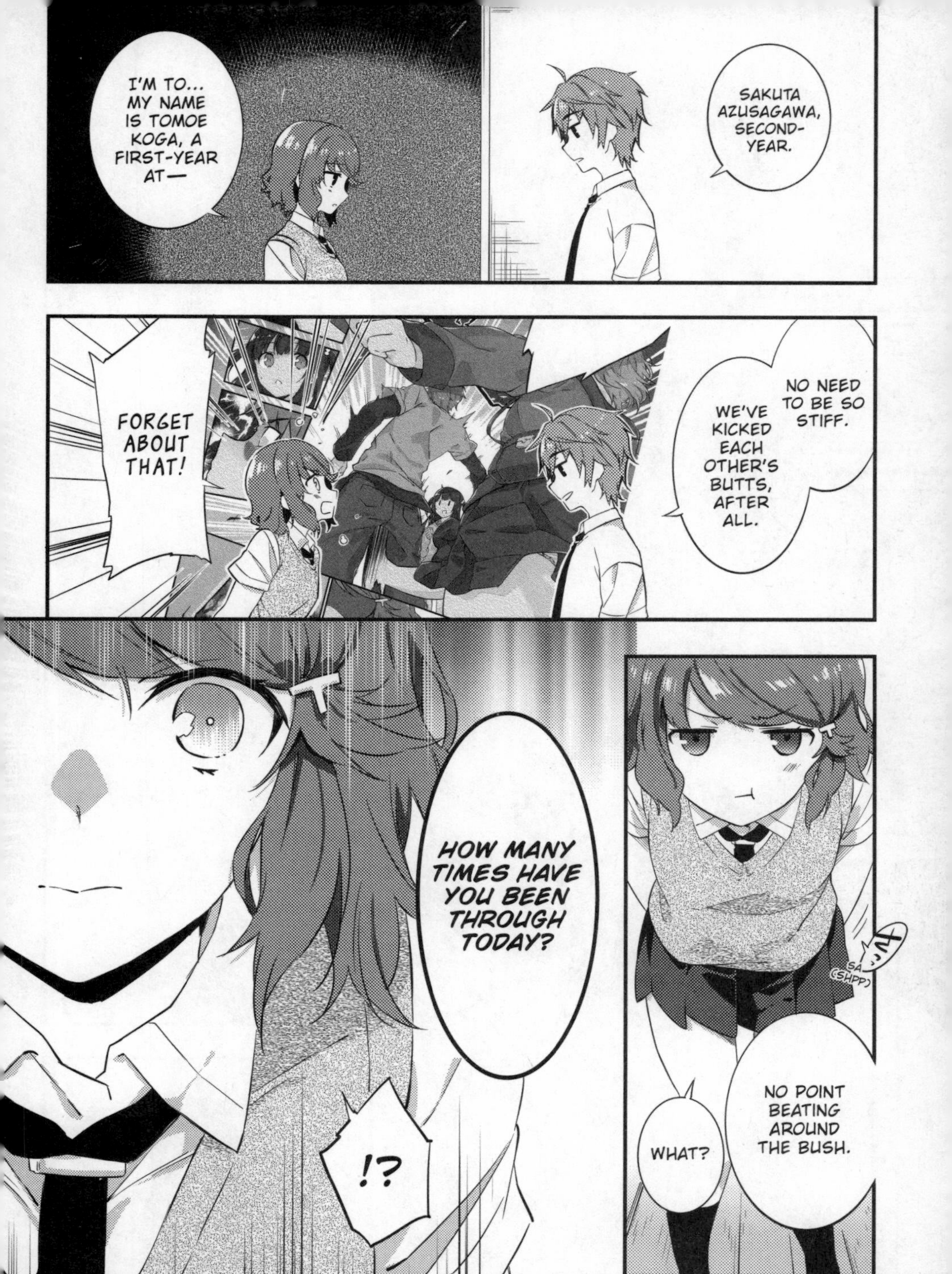
SAKUTA AZUSAGAWA, SECOND-YEAR.
I'M TO... MY NAME IS TOMOE KOGA, A FIRST-YEAR AT—
NO NEED TO BE SO STIFF.
WE'VE KICKED EACH OTHER'S BUTTS, AFTER ALL.
FORGET ABOUT THAT!
SA (SHPP)
NO POINT BEATING AROUND THE BUSH.
WHAT?
HOW MANY TIMES HAVE YOU BEEN THROUGH TODAY?
!?

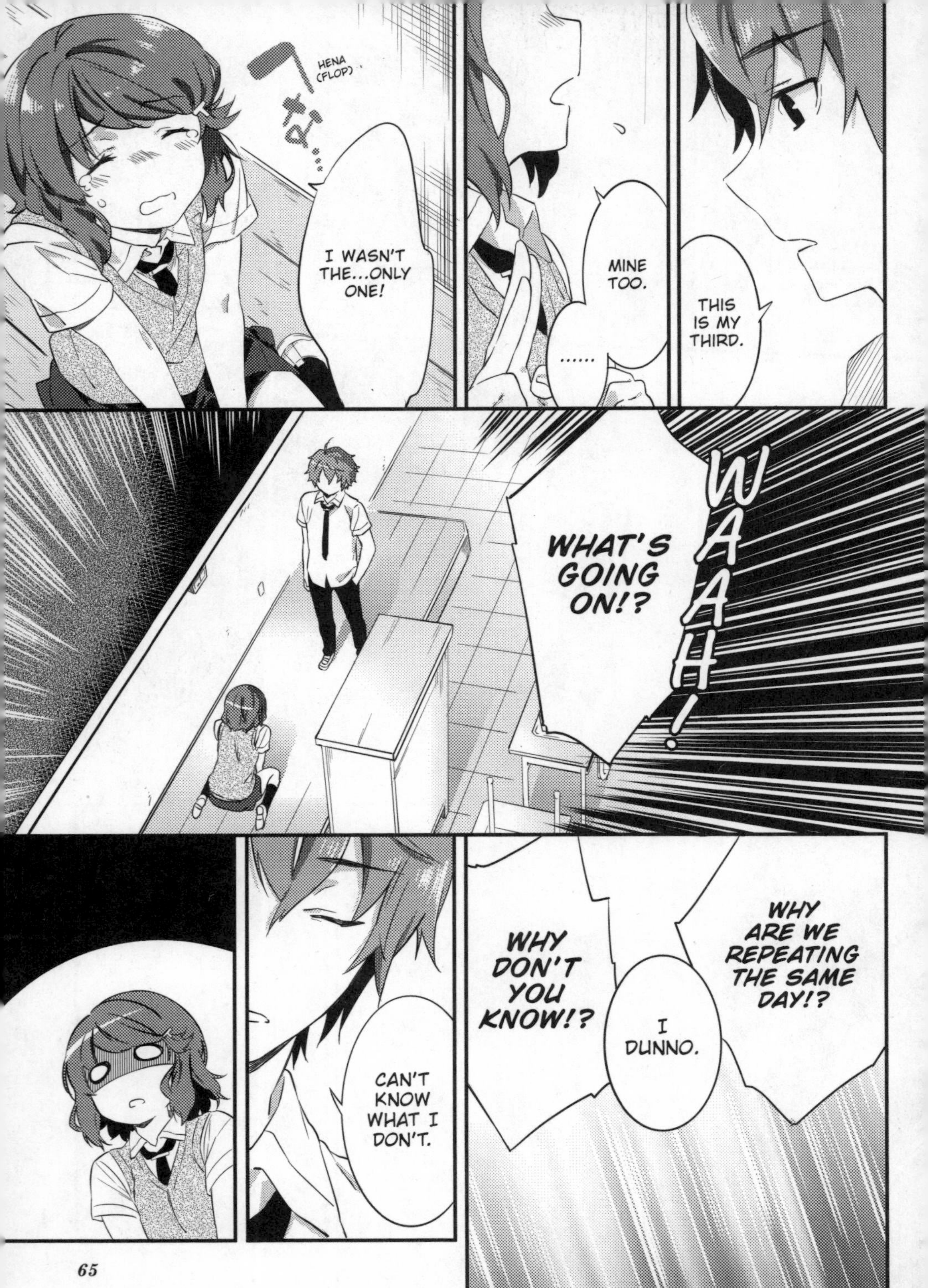
THIS IS MY THIRD.
MINE TOO.
......
I WASN'T THE...ONLY ONE!
へな…
HENA (FLOP)
WAAAH!
WHAT'S GOING ON!?
WHY ARE WE REPEATING THE SAME DAY!?
I DUNNO.
WHY DON'T YOU KNOW!?
CAN'T KNOW WHAT I DON'T.

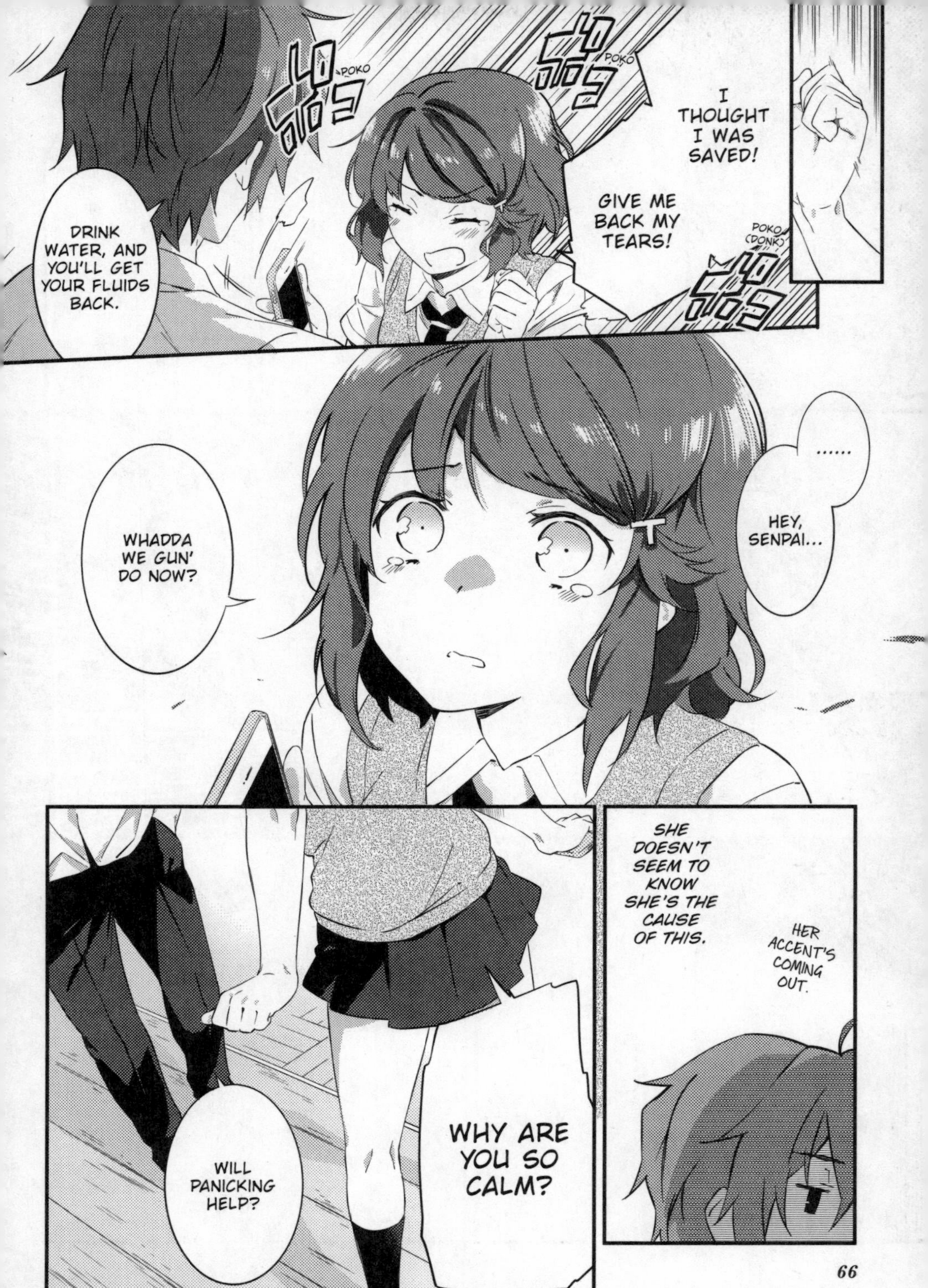
POKO
I THOUGHT I WAS SAVED!
GIVE ME BACK MY TEARS!
POKO (DONK)
POKO
DRINK WATER, AND YOU'LL GET YOUR FLUIDS BACK.
......
HEY, SENPAI...
WHADDA WE GUN' DO NOW?
SHE DOESN'T SEEM TO KNOW SHE'S THE CAUSE OF THIS.
HER ACCENT'S COMING OUT.
WHY ARE YOU SO CALM?
WILL PANICKING HELP?

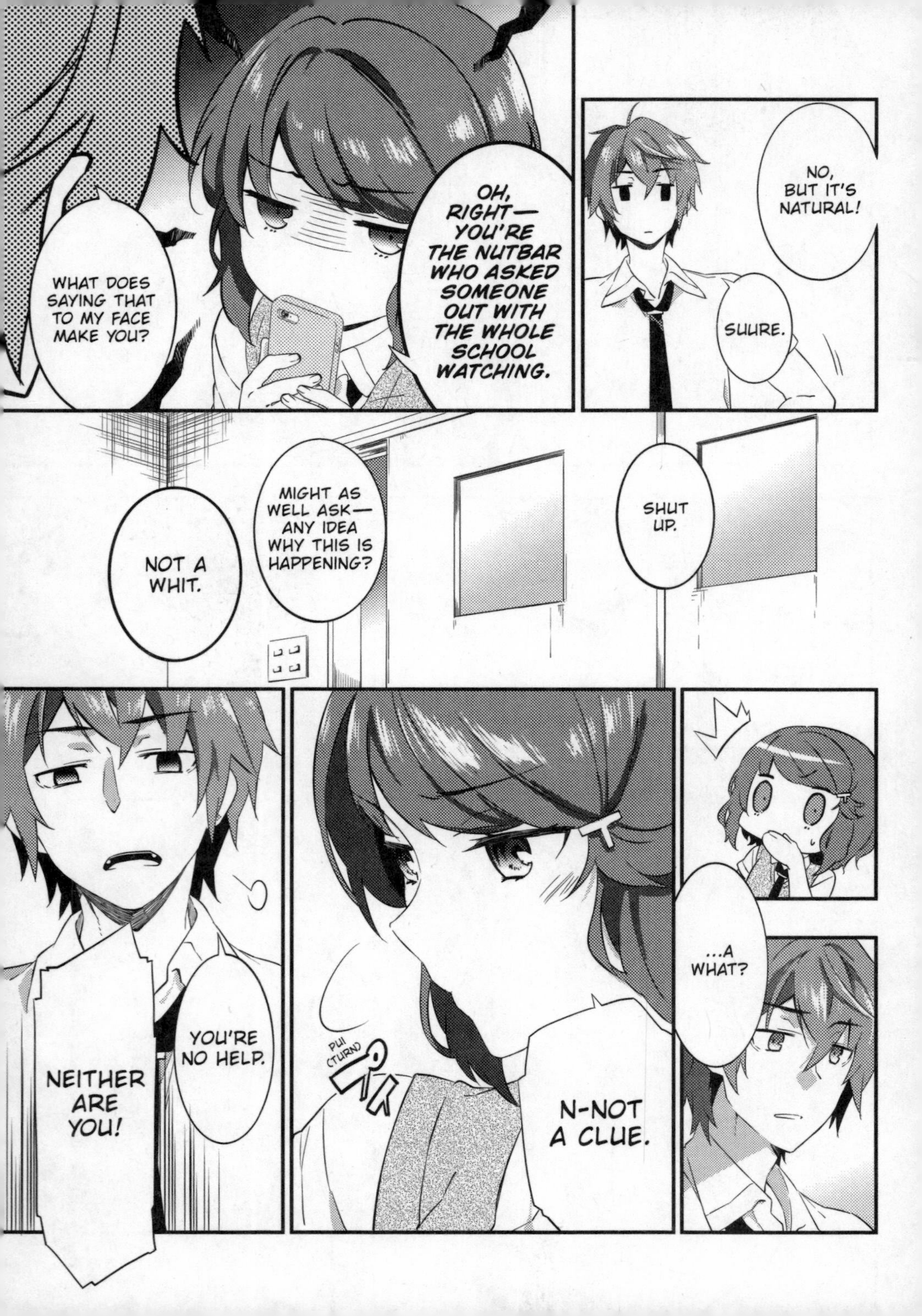
NO, BUT IT'S NATURAL!
SUURE.
OH, RIGHT— YOU'RE THE NUTBAR WHO ASKED SOMEONE OUT WITH THE WHOLE SCHOOL WATCHING.
WHAT DOES SAYING THAT TO MY FACE MAKE YOU?
SHUT UP.
MIGHT AS WELL ASK— ANY IDEA WHY THIS IS HAPPENING?
NOT A WHIT.
...A WHAT?
N-NOT A CLUE.
PUI (TURN)
YOU'RE NO HELP.
NEITHER ARE YOU!

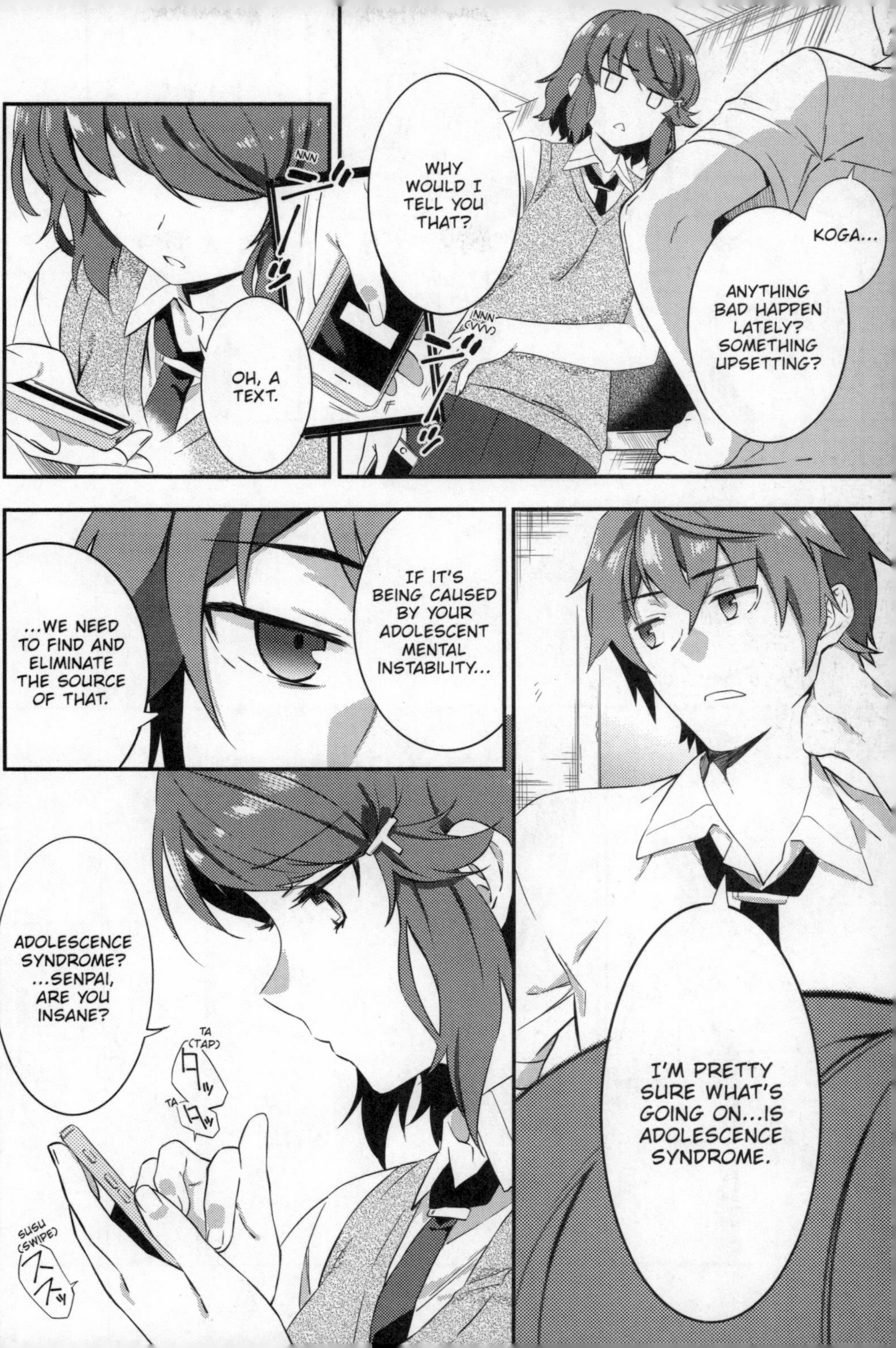
KOGA...
ANYTHING BAD HAPPEN LATELY? SOMETHING UPSETTING?
WHY WOULD I TELL YOU THAT?
NNN
NNN (VVV)
OH, A TEXT.
I'M PRETTY SURE WHAT'S GOING ON...IS ADOLESCENCE SYNDROME.
IF IT'S BEING CAUSED BY YOUR ADOLESCENT MENTAL INSTABILITY...
...WE NEED TO FIND AND ELIMINATE THE SOURCE OF THAT.
ADOLESCENCE SYNDROME? ...SENPAI, ARE YOU INSANE?
TA (TAP)
TA
SUSU (SWIPE)

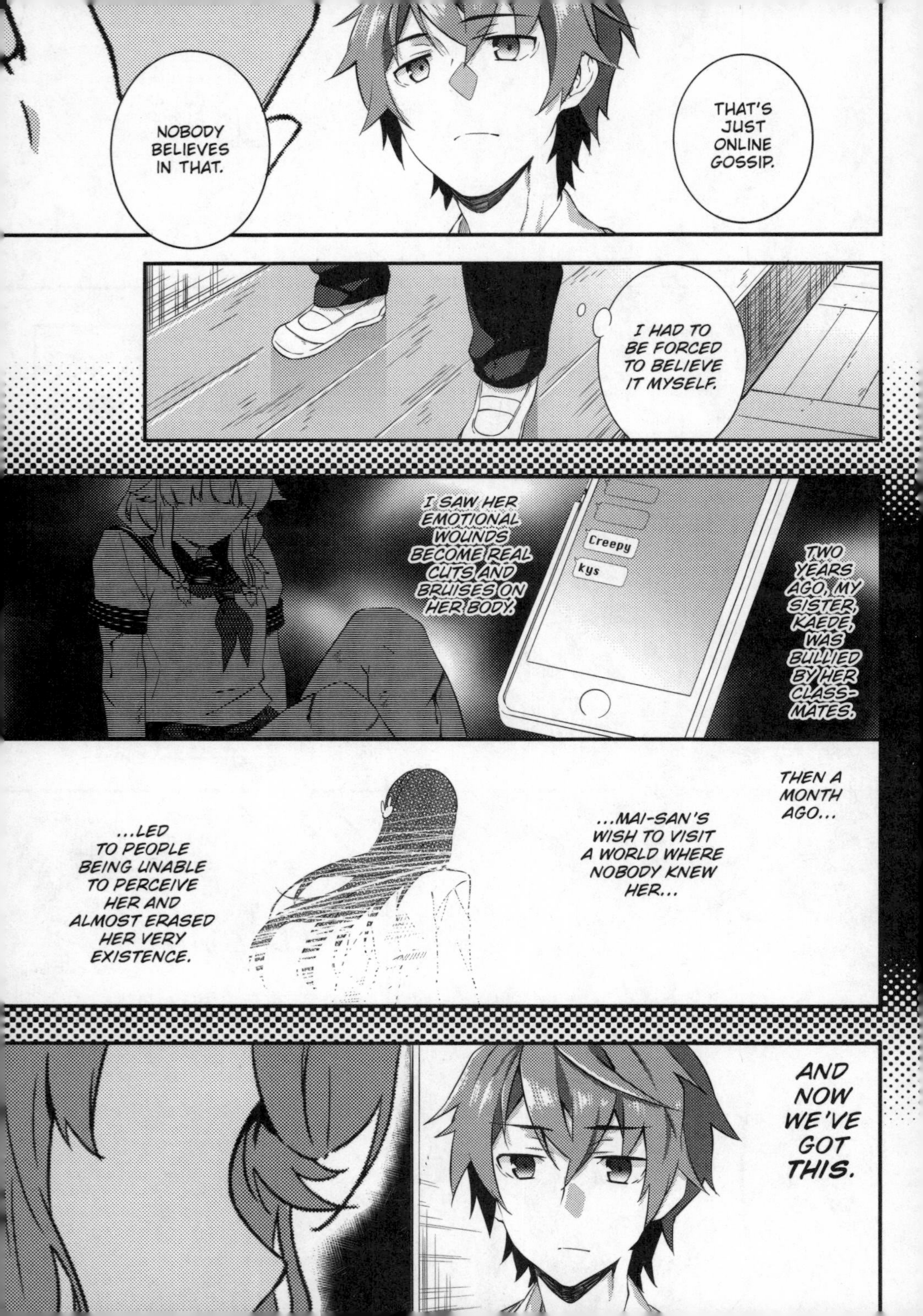
THAT'S JUST ONLINE GOSSIP.
NOBODY BELIEVES IN THAT.
I HAD TO BE FORCED TO BELIEVE IT MYSELF.
TWO YEARS AGO, MY SISTER, KAEDE, WAS BULLIED BY HER CLASSMATES.
Creepy
kys
I SAW HER EMOTIONAL WOUNDS BECOME REAL CUTS AND BRUISES ON HER BODY.
THEN A MONTH AGO...
...MAI-SAN'S WISH TO VISIT A WORLD WHERE NOBODY KNEW HER...
...LED TO PEOPLE BEING UNABLE TO PERCEIVE HER AND ALMOST ERASED HER VERY EXISTENCE.
AND NOW WE'VE GOT THIS.

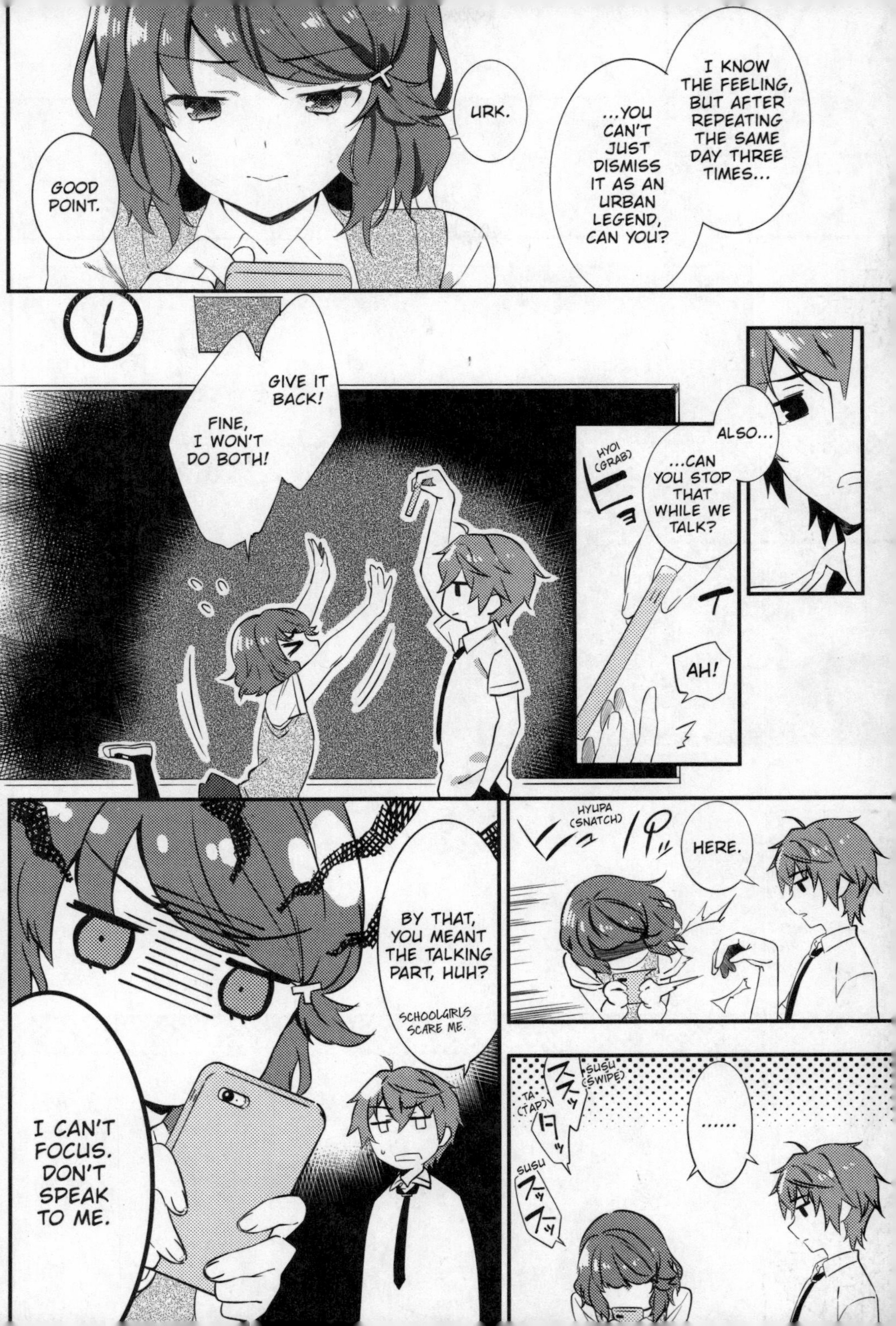
I KNOW THE FEELING, BUT AFTER REPEATING THE SAME DAY THREE TIMES...
...YOU CAN'T JUST DISMISS IT AS AN URBAN LEGEND, CAN YOU?
URK.
GOOD POINT.
ALSO...
...CAN YOU STOP THAT WHILE WE TALK?
HYOI (GRAB)
AH!
GIVE IT BACK!
FINE, I WON'T DO BOTH!
HYUPA (SNATCH)
HERE.
SUSU (SWIPE)
TA (TAP)
SUSU
......
BY THAT, YOU MEANT THE TALKING PART, HUH?
SCHOOLGIRLS SCARE ME.
I CAN'T FOCUS. DON'T SPEAK TO ME.

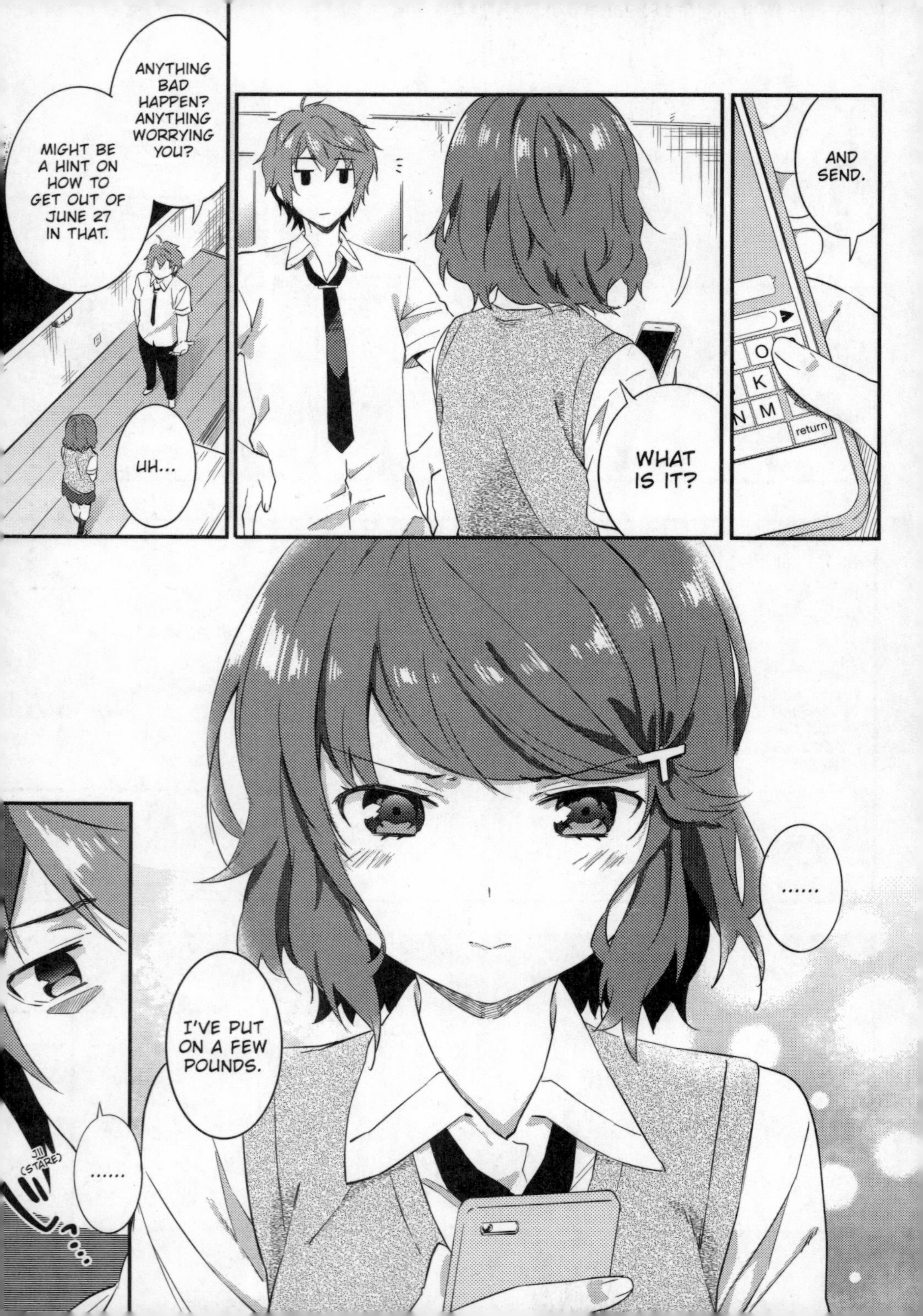
AND SEND.
WHAT IS IT?
ANYTHING BAD HAPPEN? ANYTHING WORRYING YOU?
MIGHT BE A HINT ON HOW TO GET OUT OF JUNE 27 IN THAT.
UH...
......
I'VE PUT ON A FEW POUNDS.
JII (STARE)
......

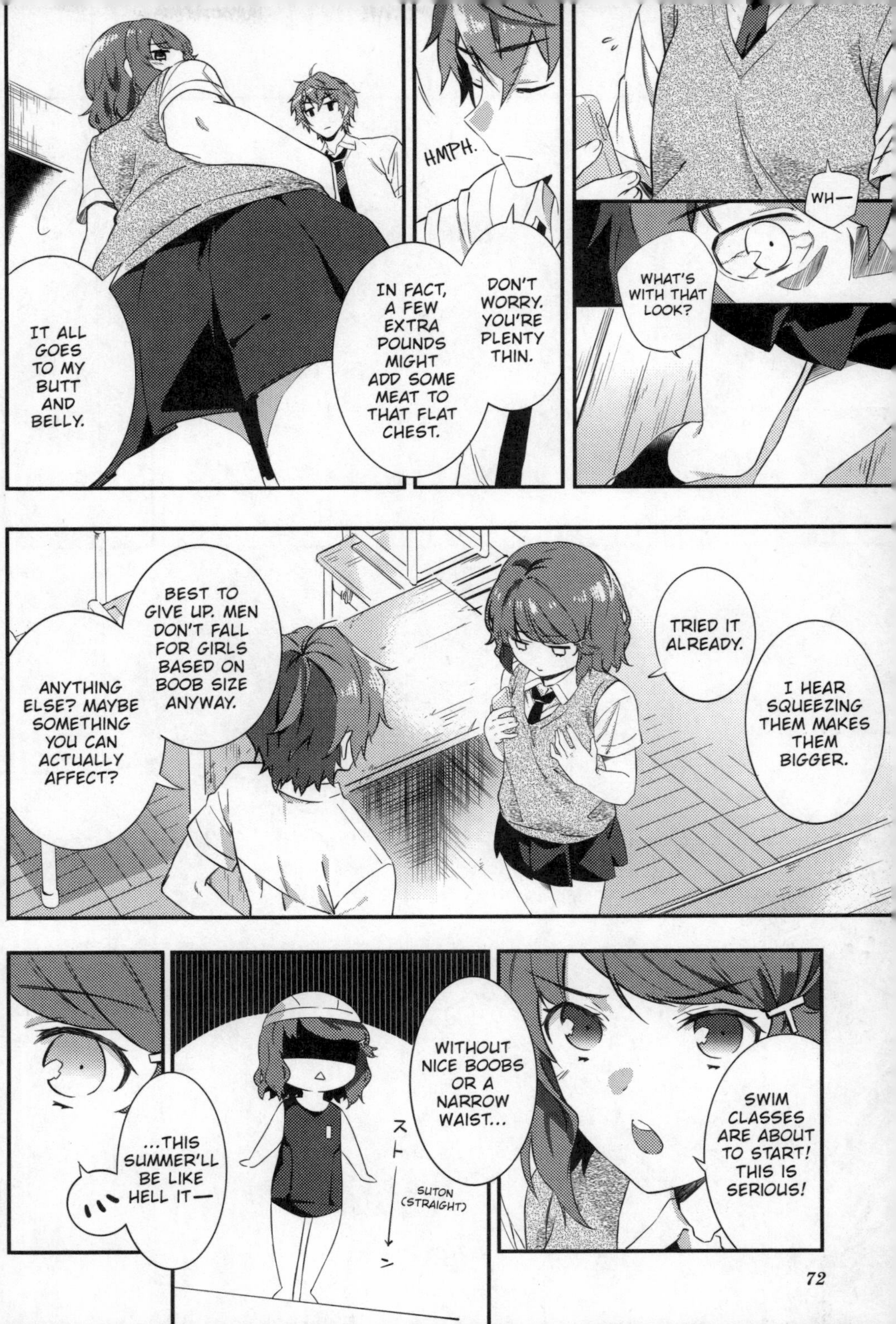

WH—
WHAT'S WITH THAT LOOK?
HMPH.
DON'T WORRY. YOU'RE PLENTY THIN.
IN FACT, A FEW EXTRA POUNDS MIGHT ADD SOME MEAT TO THAT FLAT CHEST.
IT ALL GOES TO MY BUTT AND BELLY.
I HEAR SQUEEZING THEM MAKES THEM BIGGER.
TRIED IT ALREADY.
BEST TO GIVE UP. MEN DON'T FALL FOR GIRLS BASED ON BOOB SIZE ANYWAY.
ANYTHING ELSE? MAYBE SOMETHING YOU CAN ACTUALLY AFFECT?
SWIM CLASSES ARE ABOUT TO START! THIS IS SERIOUS!
WITHOUT NICE BOOBS OR A NARROW WAIST...
ストン
SUTON (STRAIGHT)
...THIS SUMMER'LL BE LIKE HELL IT—

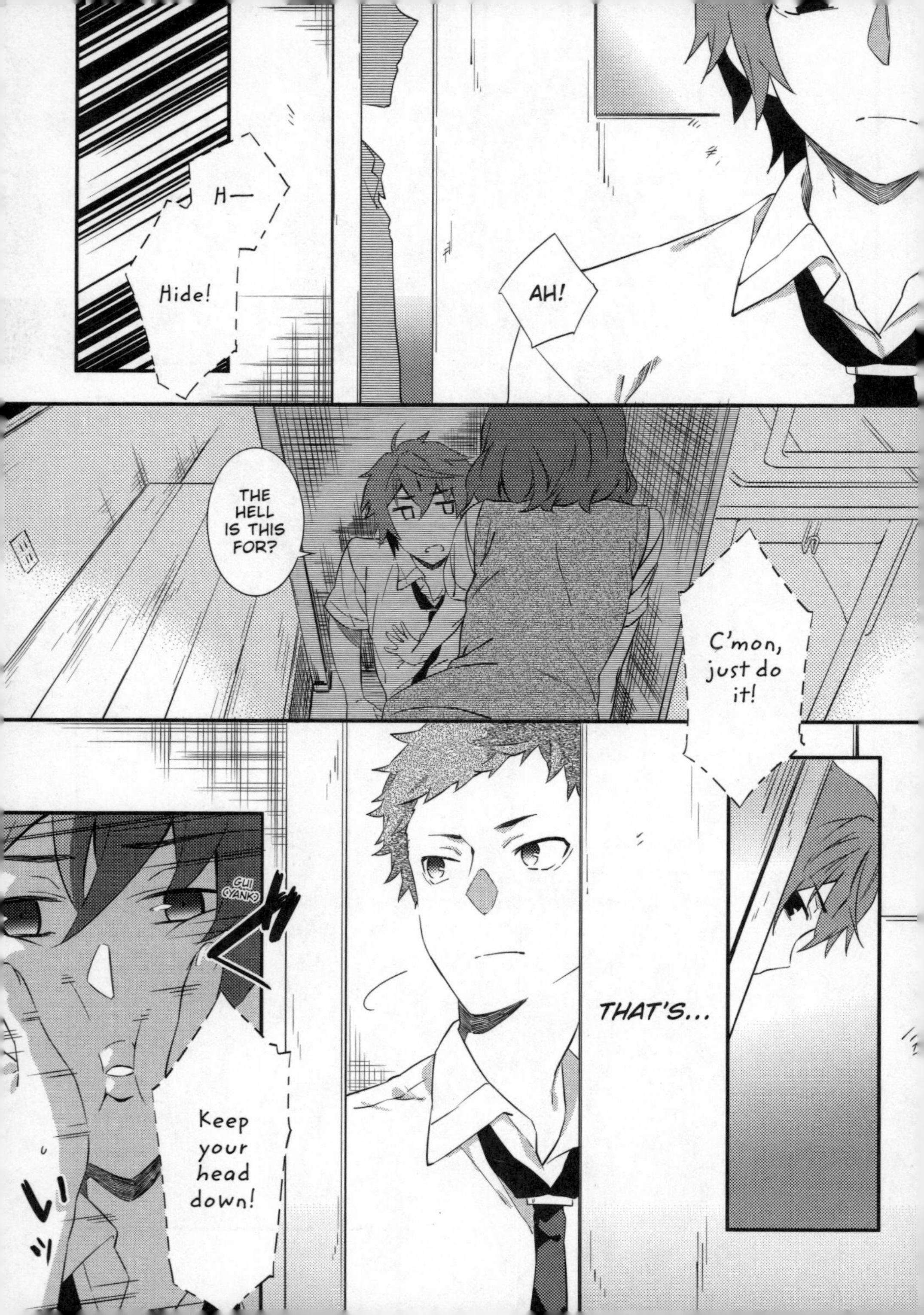
AH!
H—
Hide!
THE HELL IS THIS FOR?
C'mon, just do it!
THAT'S...
GUI (YANK)
Keep your head down!

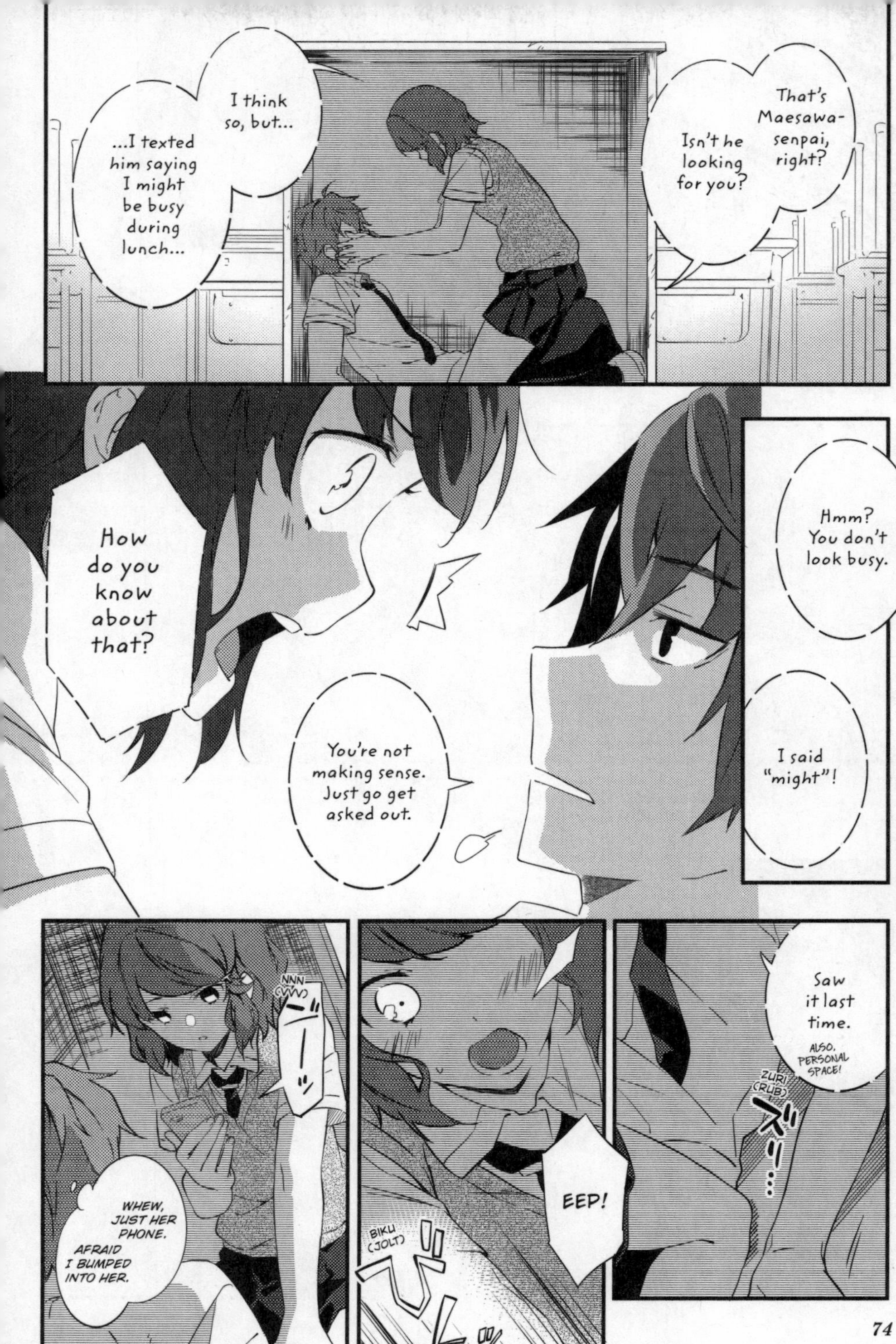
That's Maesawa-senpai, right?
Isn't he looking for you?
I think so, but...
...I texted him saying I might be busy during lunch...
Hmm? You don't look busy.
How do you know about that?
I said "might"!
You're not making sense. Just go get asked out.
Saw it last time.
ALSO, PERSONAL SPACE!
ZURI (RUB)
ズー…
EEP!
BIKU (JOLT)
NNN (VVVV)
WHEW, JUST HER PHONE. AFRAID I BUMPED INTO HER.

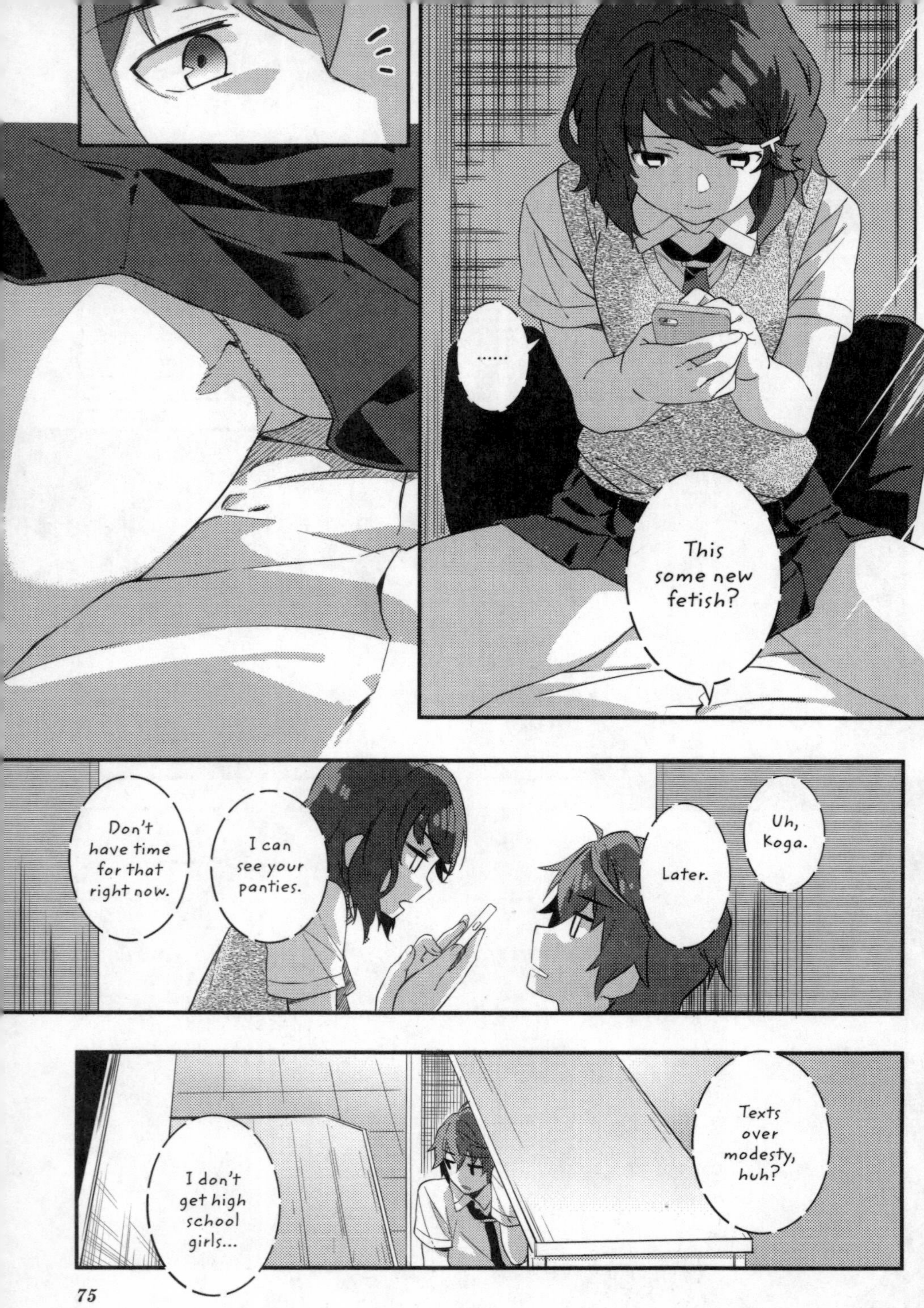
......
This some new fetish?
Uh, Koga.
Later.
I can see your panties.
Don't have time for that right now.
Texts over modesty, huh?
I don't get high school girls...

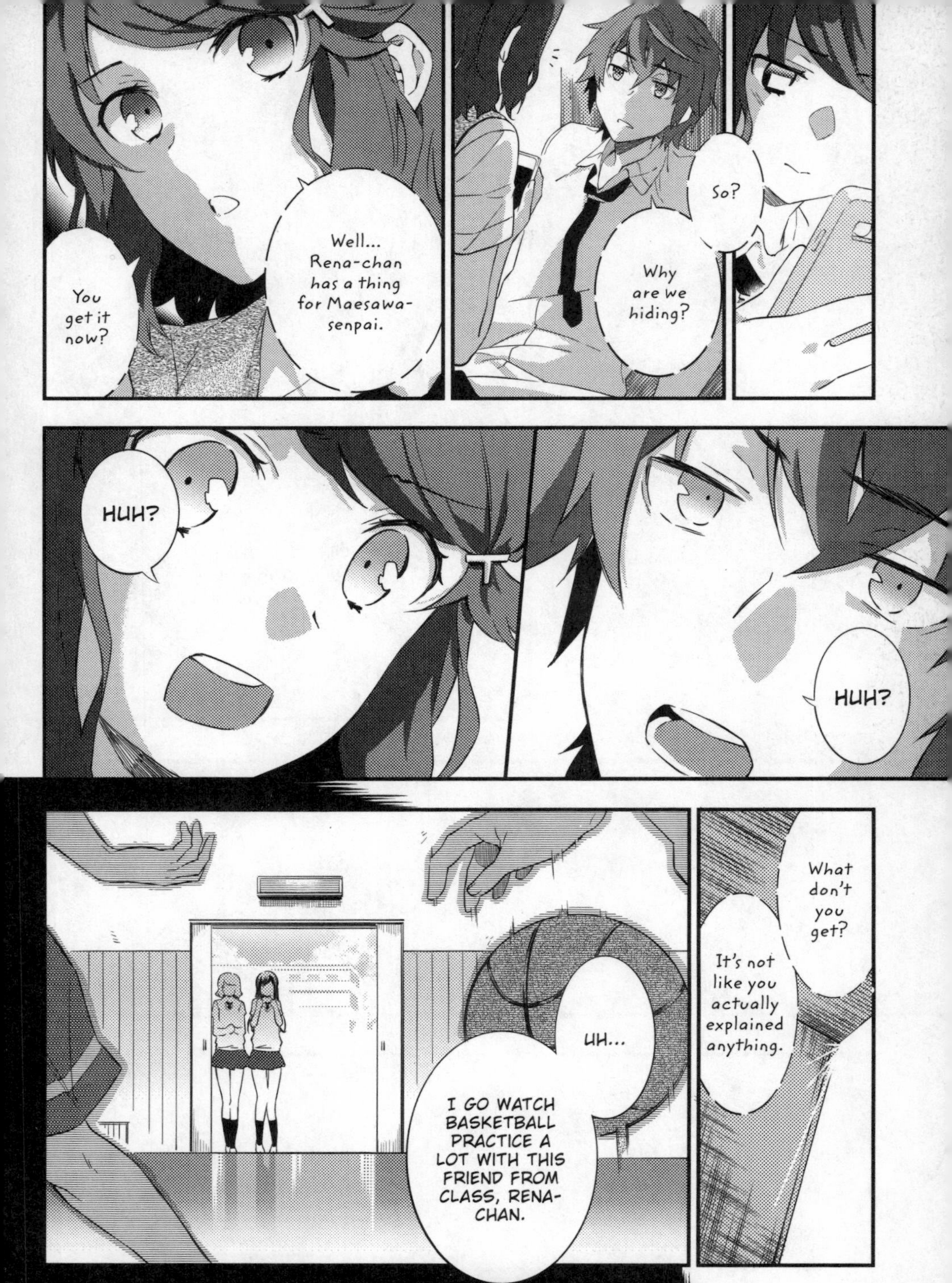
So?
Why are we hiding?
Well... Rena-chan has a thing for Maesawa-senpai.
You get it now?
HUH?
HUH?
What don't you get?
It's not like you actually explained anything.
UH...
I GO WATCH BASKETBALL PRACTICE A LOT WITH THIS FRIEND FROM CLASS, RENA-CHAN.

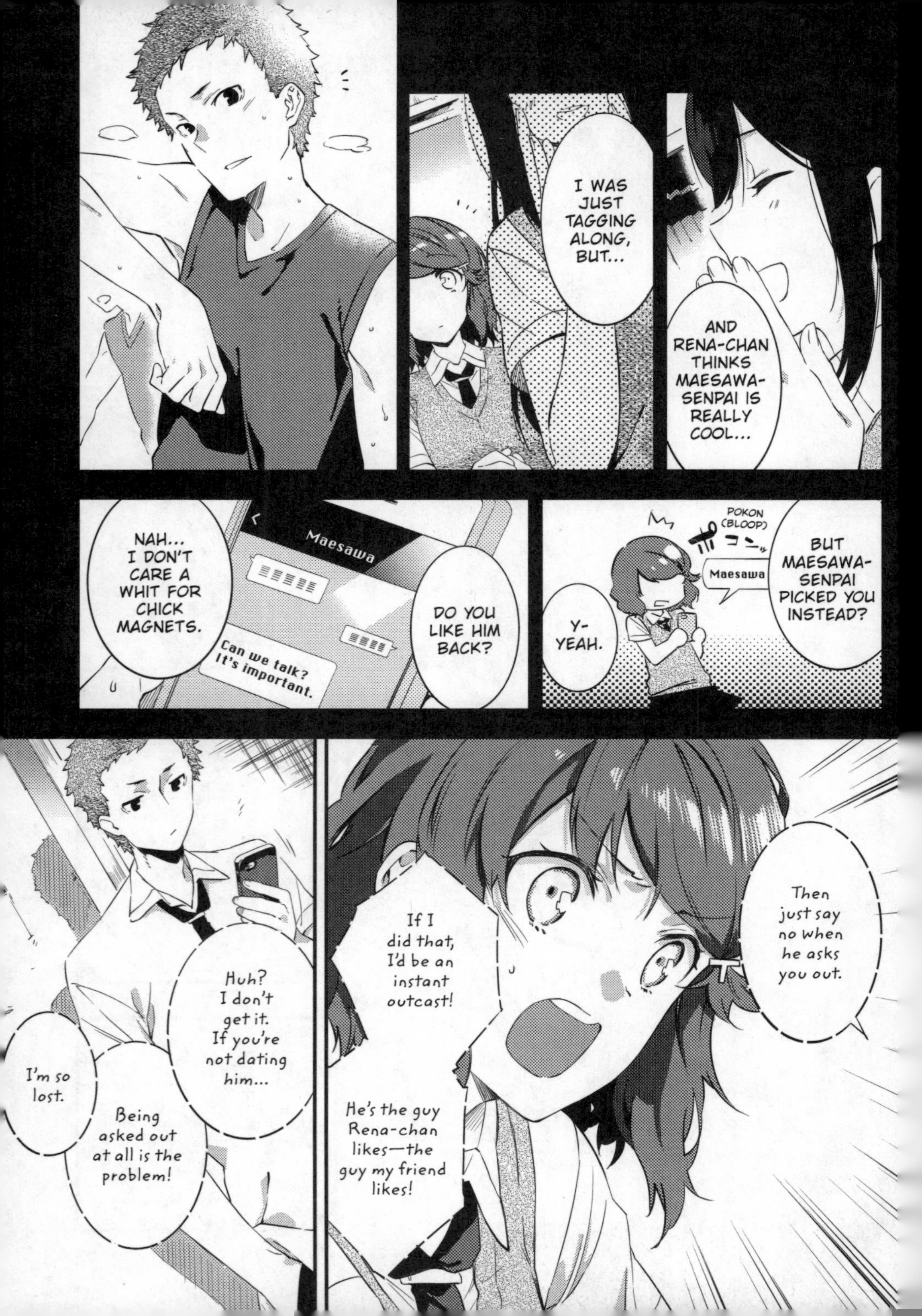
AND RENA-CHAN THINKS MAESAWA-SENPAI IS REALLY COOL...
I WAS JUST TAGGING ALONG, BUT...
BUT MAESAWA-SENPAI PICKED YOU INSTEAD?
POKON (BLOOP)
Maesawa
Y-YEAH.
DO YOU LIKE HIM BACK?
Maesawa
Can we talk? It's important.
NAH... I DON'T CARE A WHIT FOR CHICK MAGNETS.
Then just say no when he asks you out.
If I did that, I'd be an instant outcast!
He's the guy Rena-chan likes—the guy my friend likes!
Huh? I don't get it. If you're not dating him...
Being asked out at all is the problem!
I'm so lost.

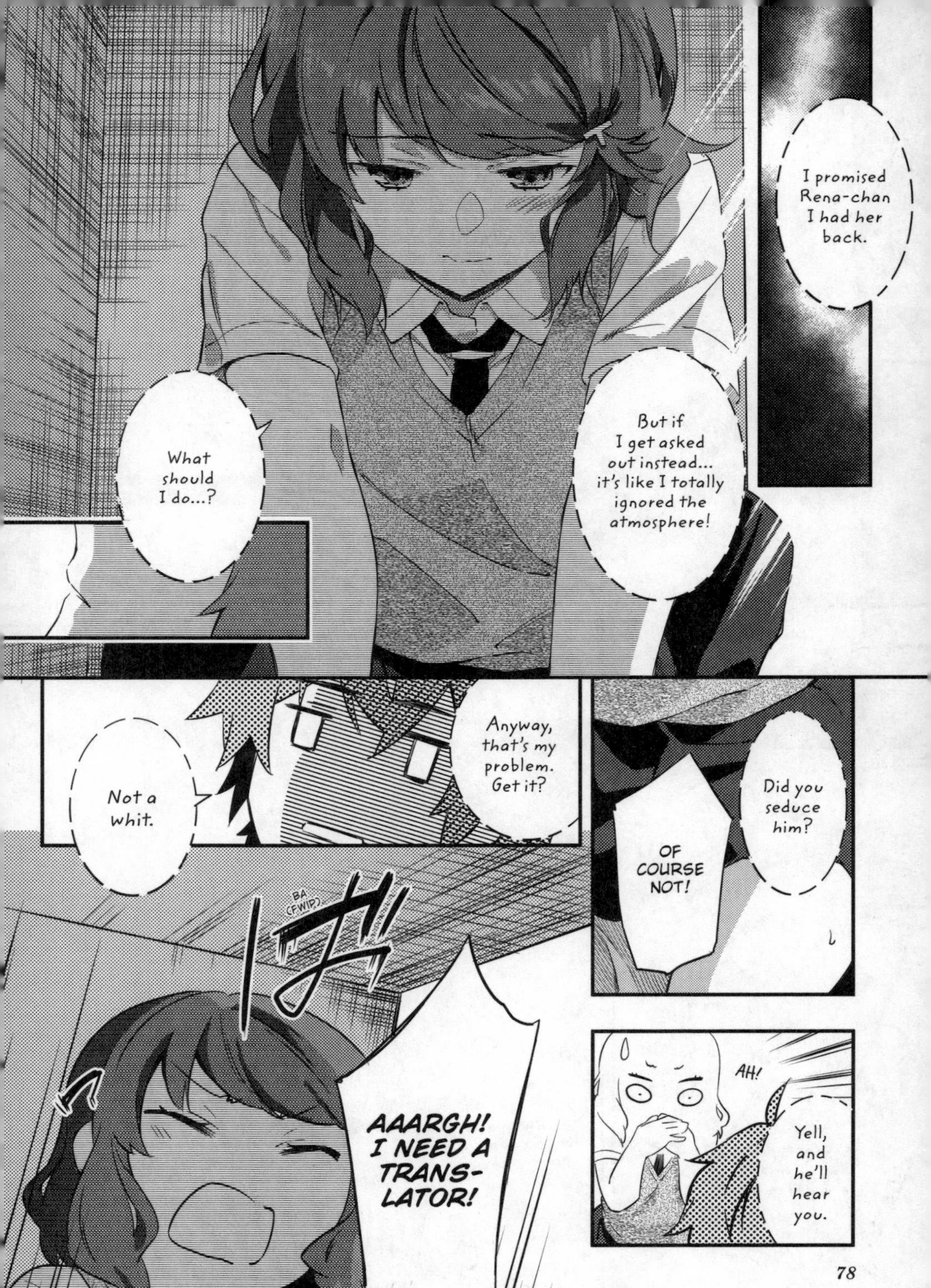
I promised Rena-chan I had her back.
But if I get asked out instead... it's like I totally ignored the atmosphere!
What should I do...?
Did you seduce him?
OF COURSE NOT!
Anyway, that's my problem. Get it?
Not a whit.
BA (FWIP)
AAARGH! I NEED A TRANSLATOR!
AH!
Yell, and he'll hear you.

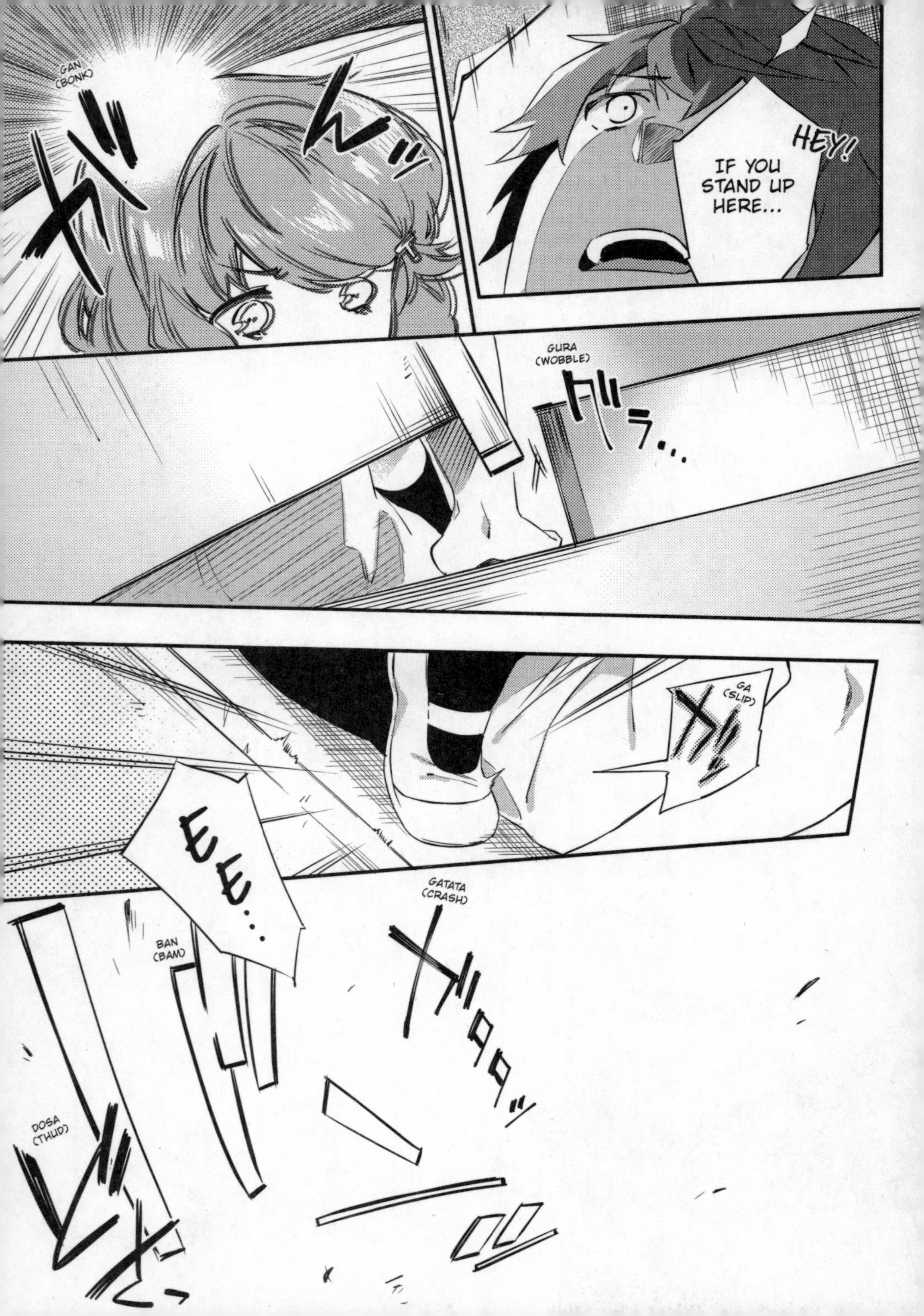
HEY!
IF YOU STAND UP HERE...
GAN (BONK)
GURA (WOBBLE)
GA (SLIP)
GATATA (CRASH)
EE...
BAN (BAM)
DOSA (THUD)

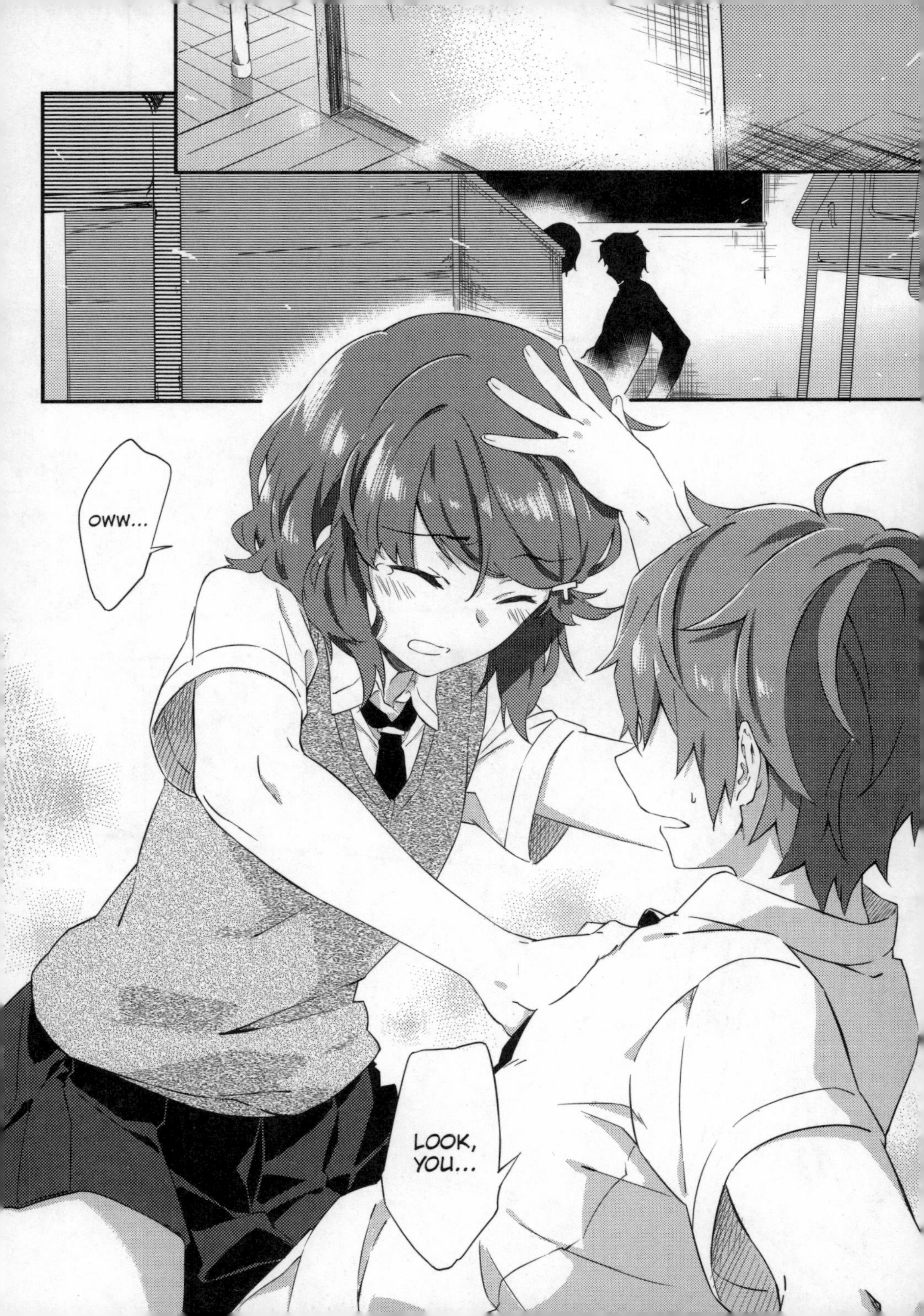
OWW...
LOOK, YOU...

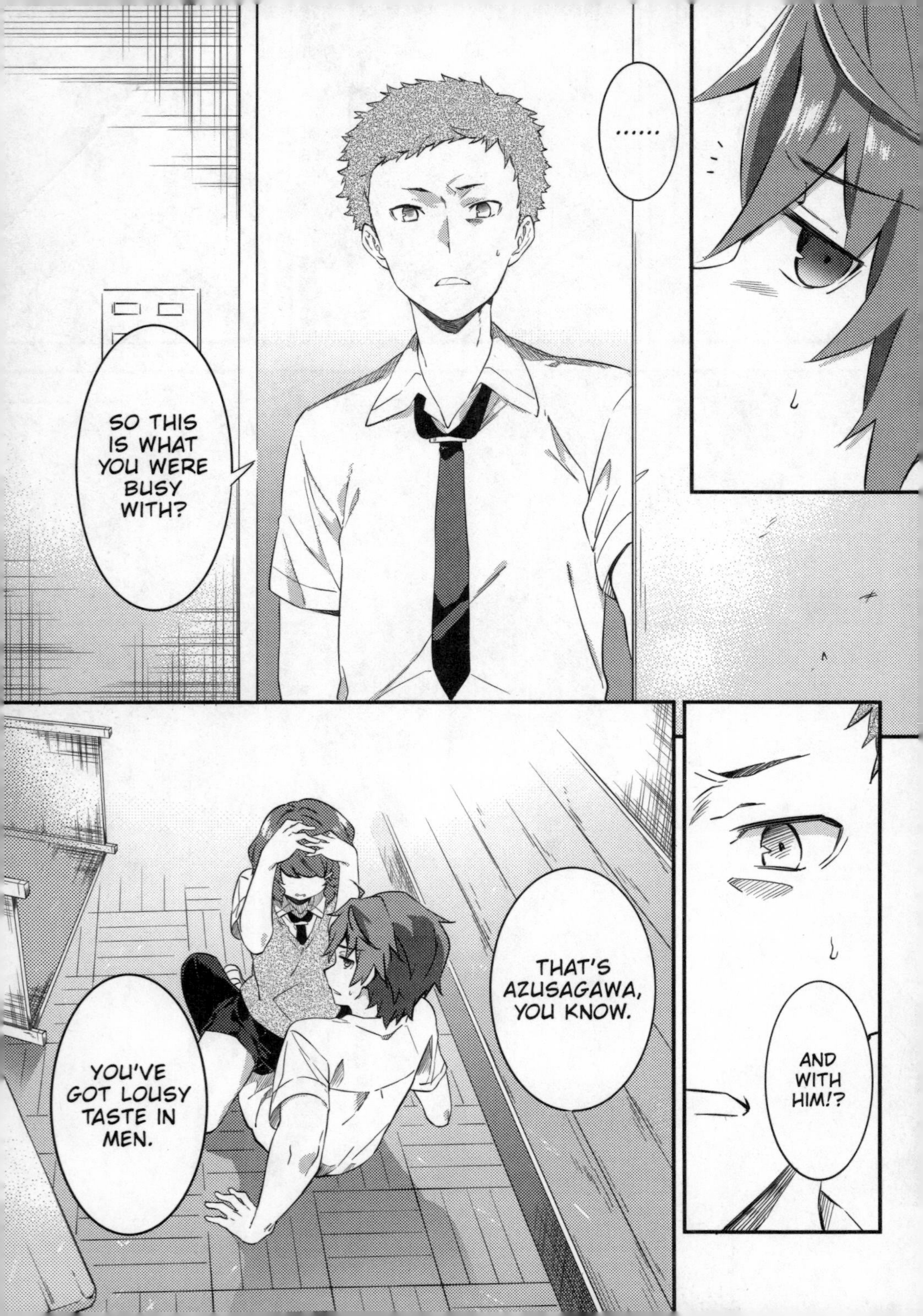
......
SO THIS IS WHAT YOU WERE BUSY WITH?
AND WITH HIM!?
THAT'S AZUSAGAWA, YOU KNOW.
YOU'VE GOT LOUSY TASTE IN MEN.

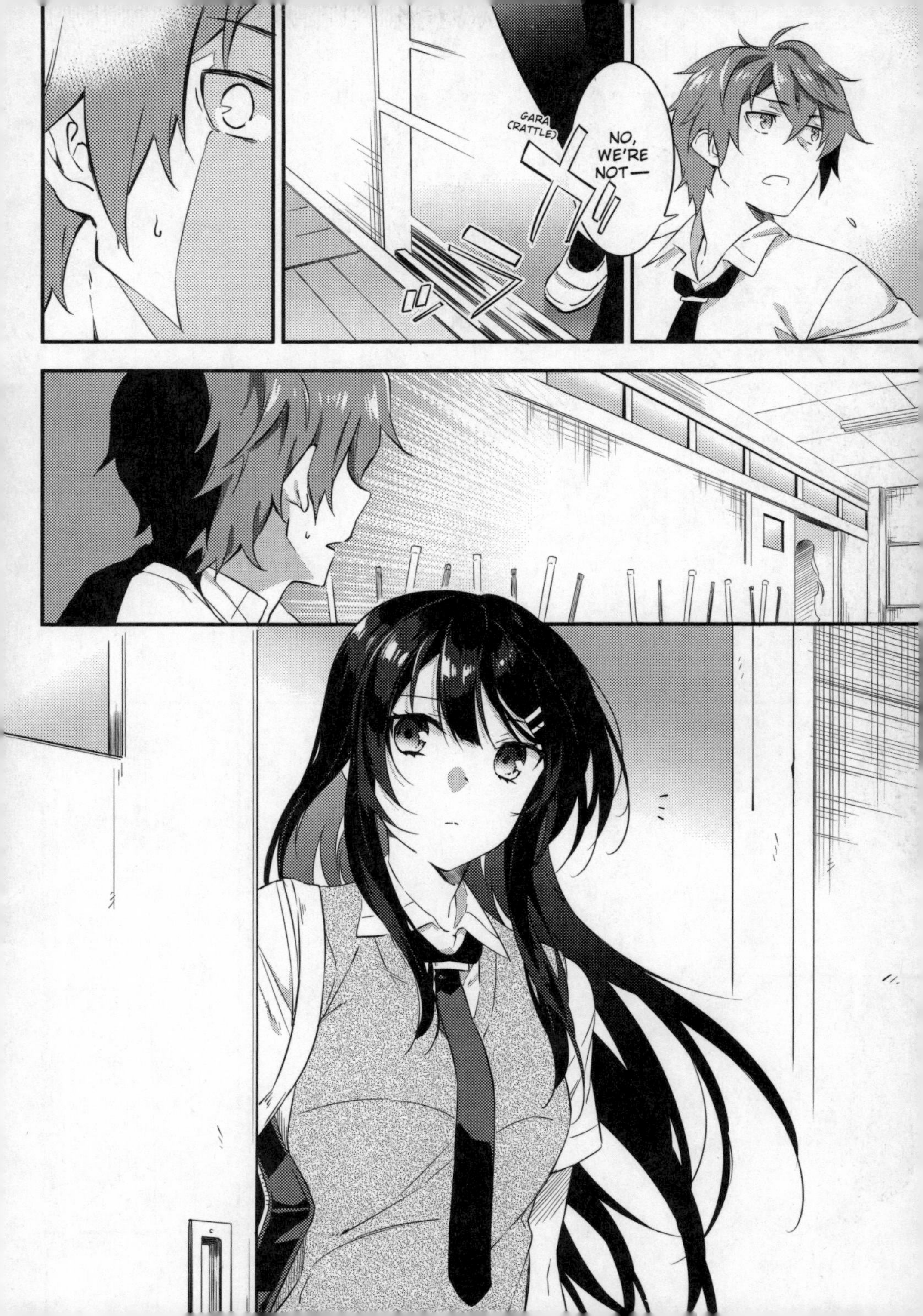
NO, WE'RE NOT—
GARA (RATTLE)

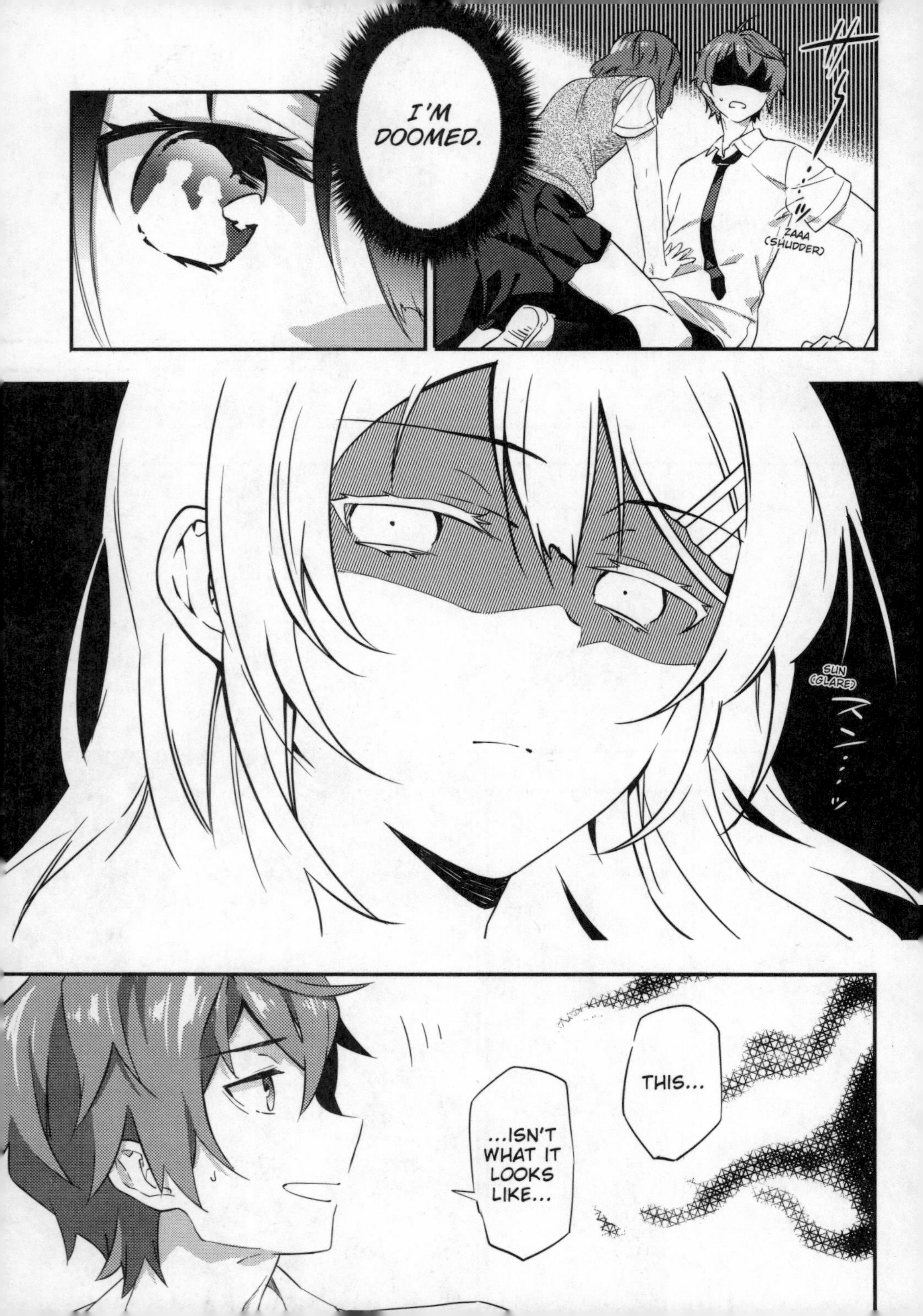
ZAAA (SHUDDER)
I'M DOOMED.
SUN (GLARE)
THIS...
...ISN'T WHAT IT LOOKS LIKE...

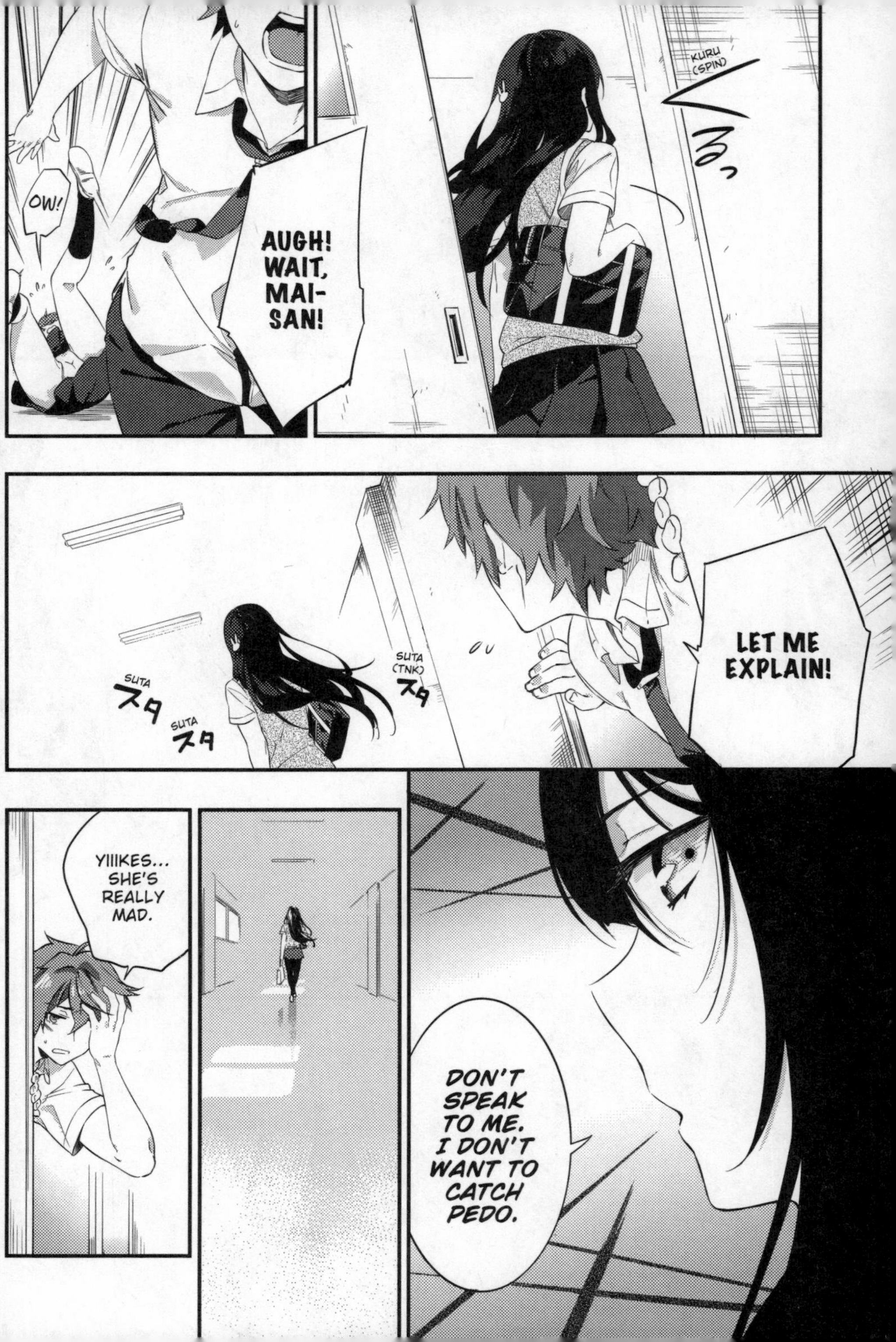
KURU (SPIN)
AUGH! WAIT, MAI-SAN!
OW!
LET ME EXPLAIN!
SUTA (TNK) スタ
SUTA スタ
SUTA スタ
DON'T SPEAK TO ME. I DON'T WANT TO CATCH PEDO.
YIIIKES... SHE'S REALLY MAD.

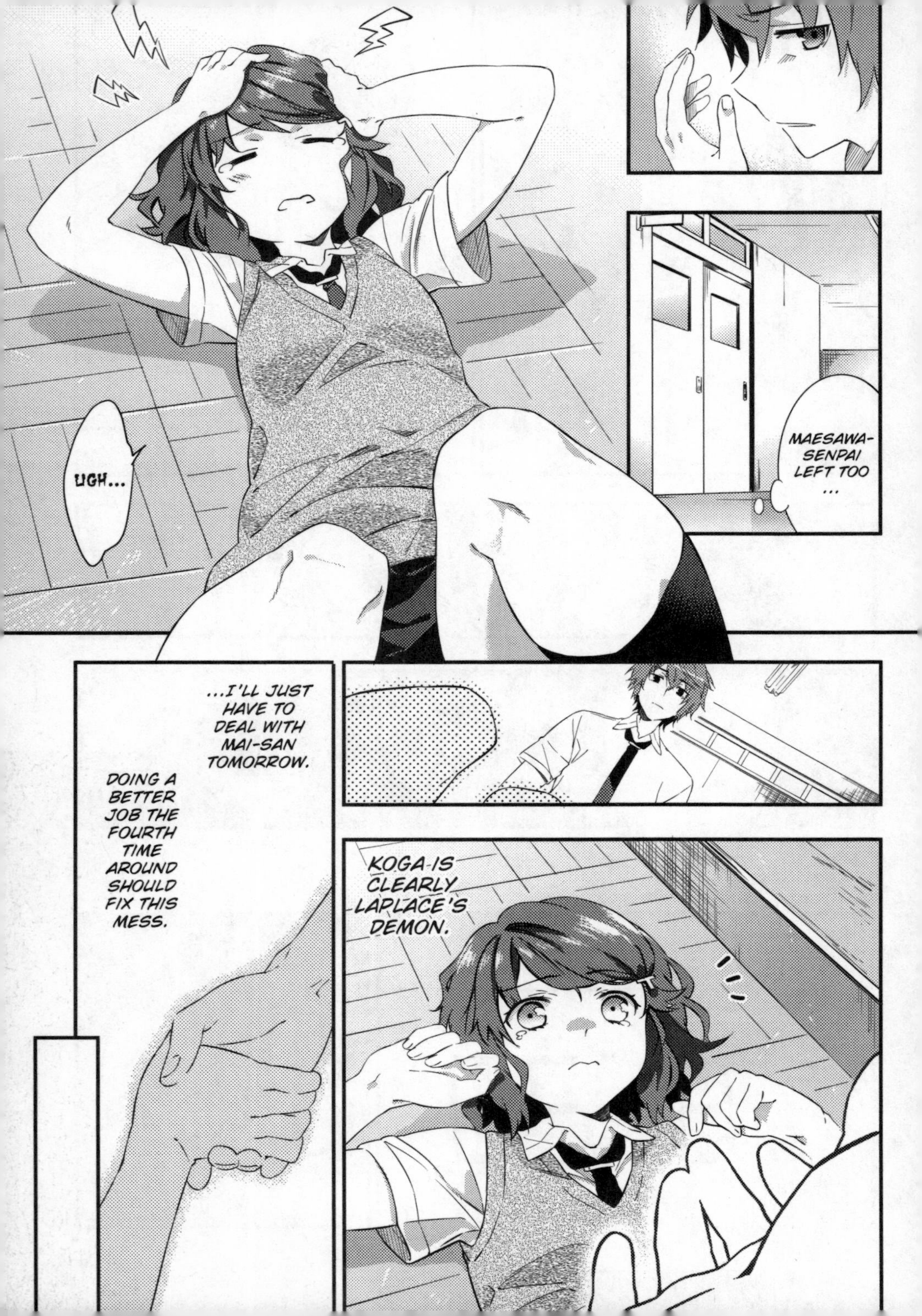
MAESAWA-SENPAI LEFT TOO ...
UGH...
KOGA IS CLEARLY LAPLACE'S DEMON.
...I'LL JUST HAVE TO DEAL WITH MAI-SAN TOMORROW.
DOING A BETTER JOB THE FOURTH TIME AROUND SHOULD FIX THIS MESS.

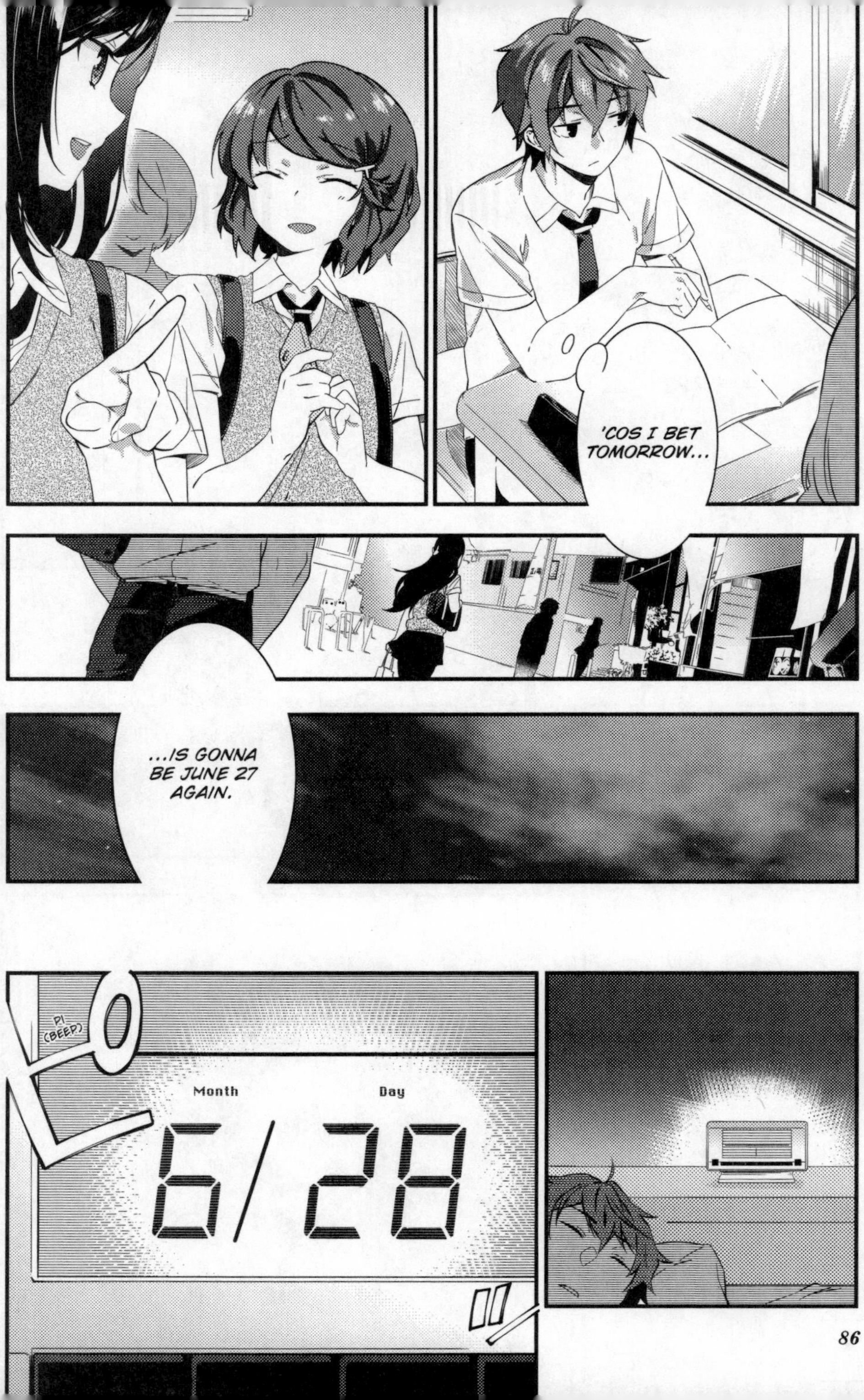
'COS I BET TOMORROW...
...IS GONNA BE JUNE 27 AGAIN.
PI (BEEP)
Month
Day
6/ 28

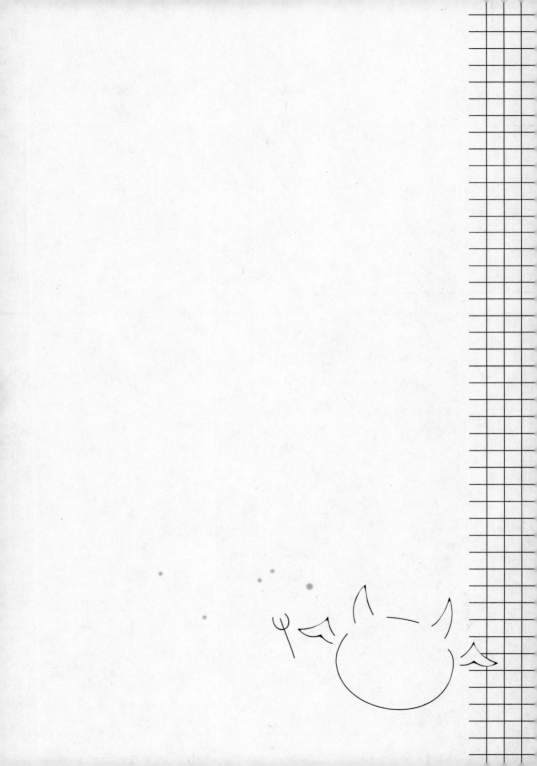

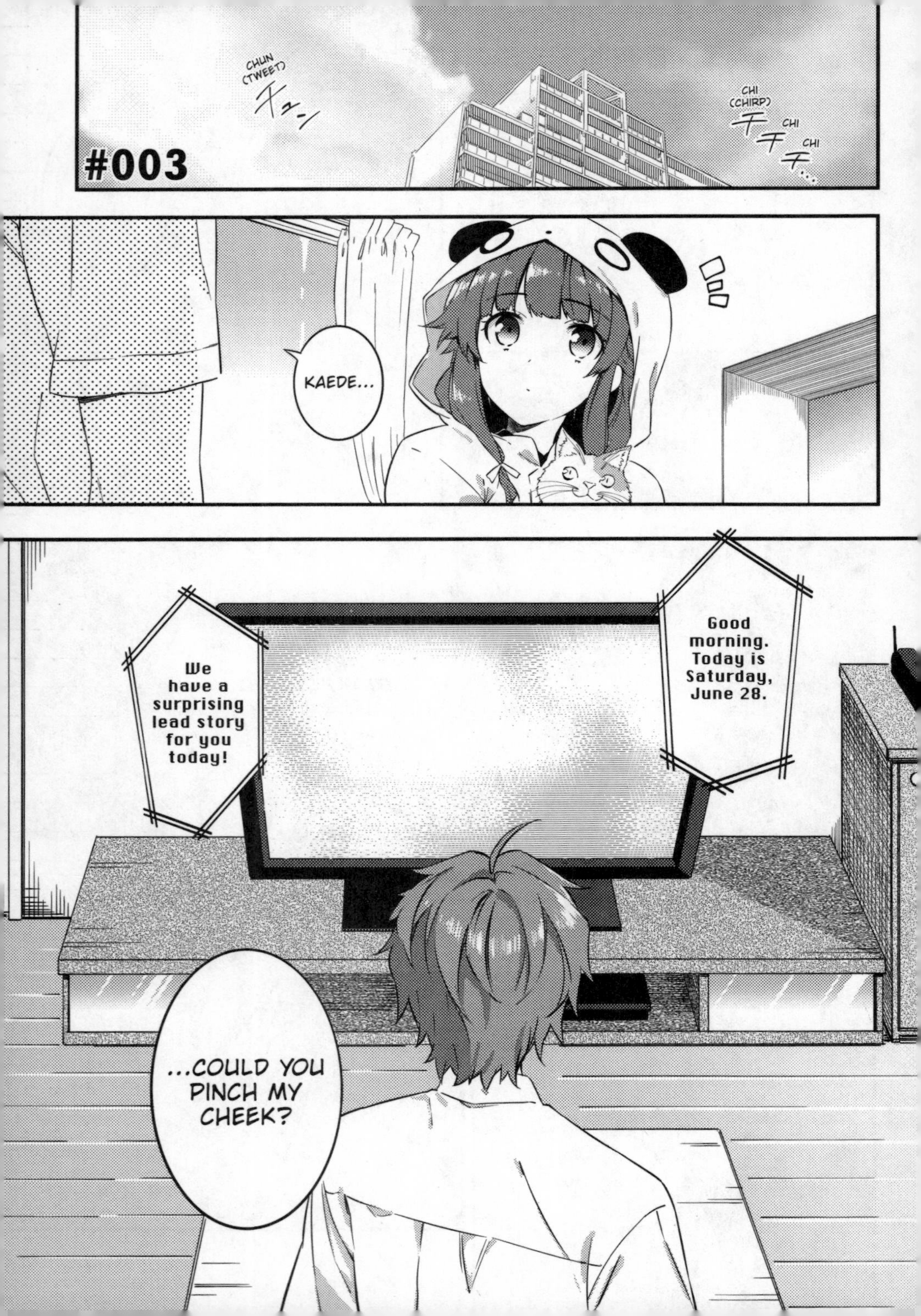
#003
CHI (CHIRP) CHI CHI
CHUN (TWEET)
KAEDE...
Good morning. Today is Saturday, June 28.
We have a surprising lead story for you today!
...COULD YOU PINCH MY CHEEK?

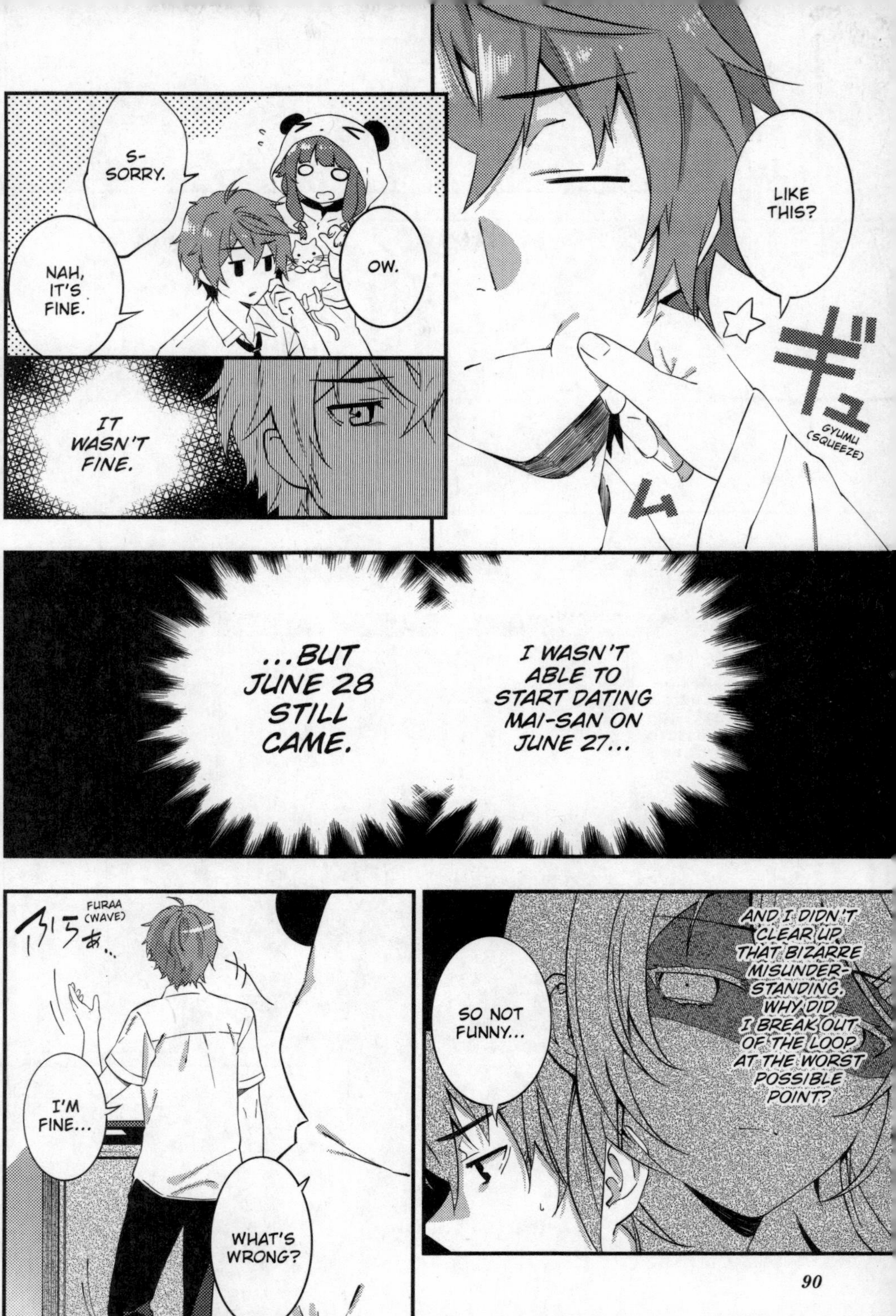
LIKE THIS?
ギュ
ム
GYUMU (SQUEEZE)
OW.
S-SORRY.
NAH, IT'S FINE.
IT WASN'T FINE.
I WASN'T ABLE TO START DATING MAI-SAN ON JUNE 27...
...BUT JUNE 28 STILL CAME.
AND I DIDN'T CLEAR UP THAT BIZARRE MISUNDER-STANDING. WHY DID I BREAK OUT OF THE LOOP AT THE WORST POSSIBLE POINT?
SO NOT FUNNY...
ふらぁ...
FURAA (WAVE)
WHAT'S WRONG?
I'M FINE...

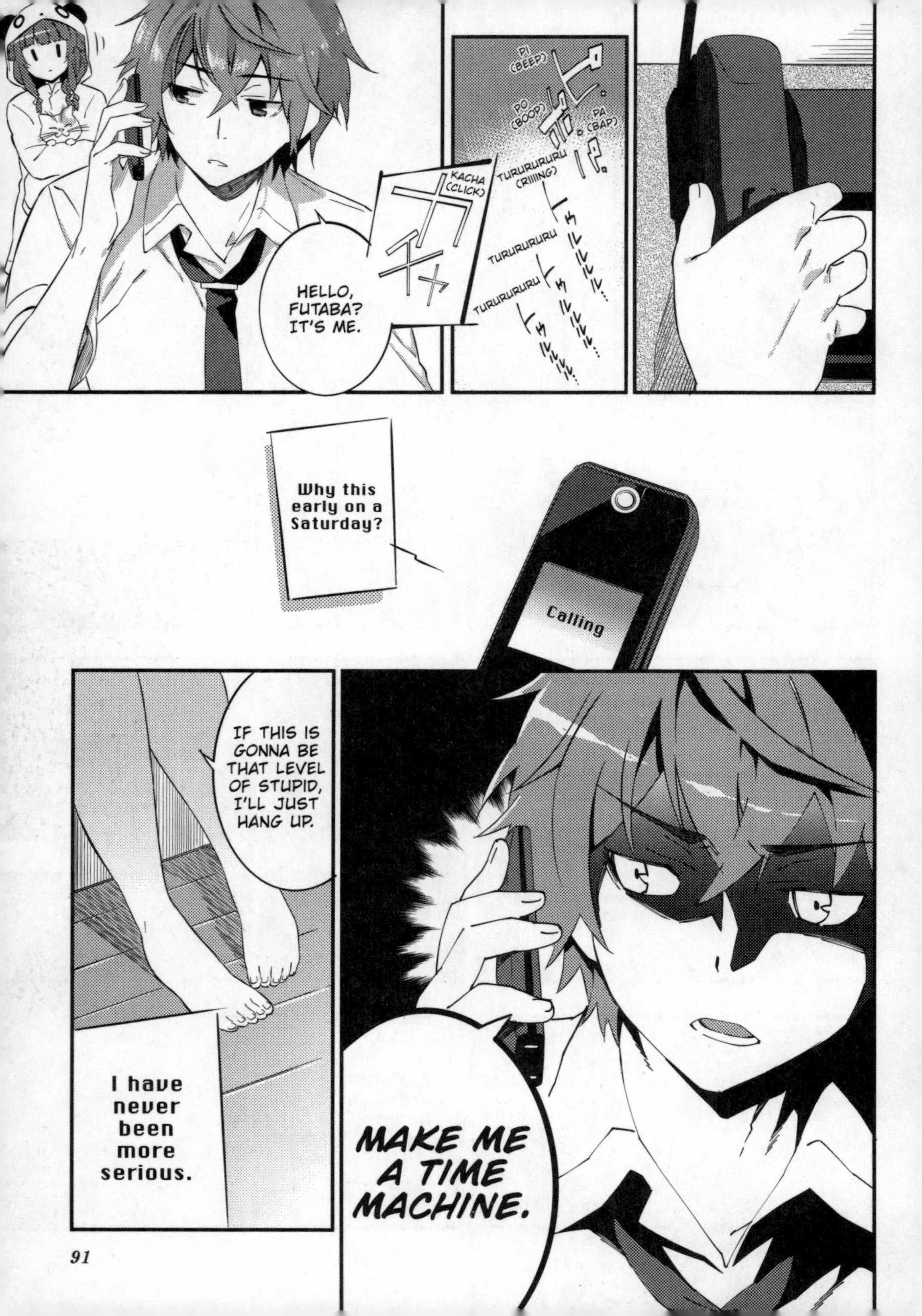
PI (BEEP)
PO (BOOP)
PA (BAP)
TURURURURU (RIIIING)
TURURURURU
TURURURURU
KACHA (CLICK)
HELLO, FUTABA? IT'S ME.
Calling
Why this early on a Saturday?
MAKE ME A TIME MACHINE.
IF THIS IS GONNA BE THAT LEVEL OF STUPID, I'LL JUST HANG UP.
I have never been more serious.

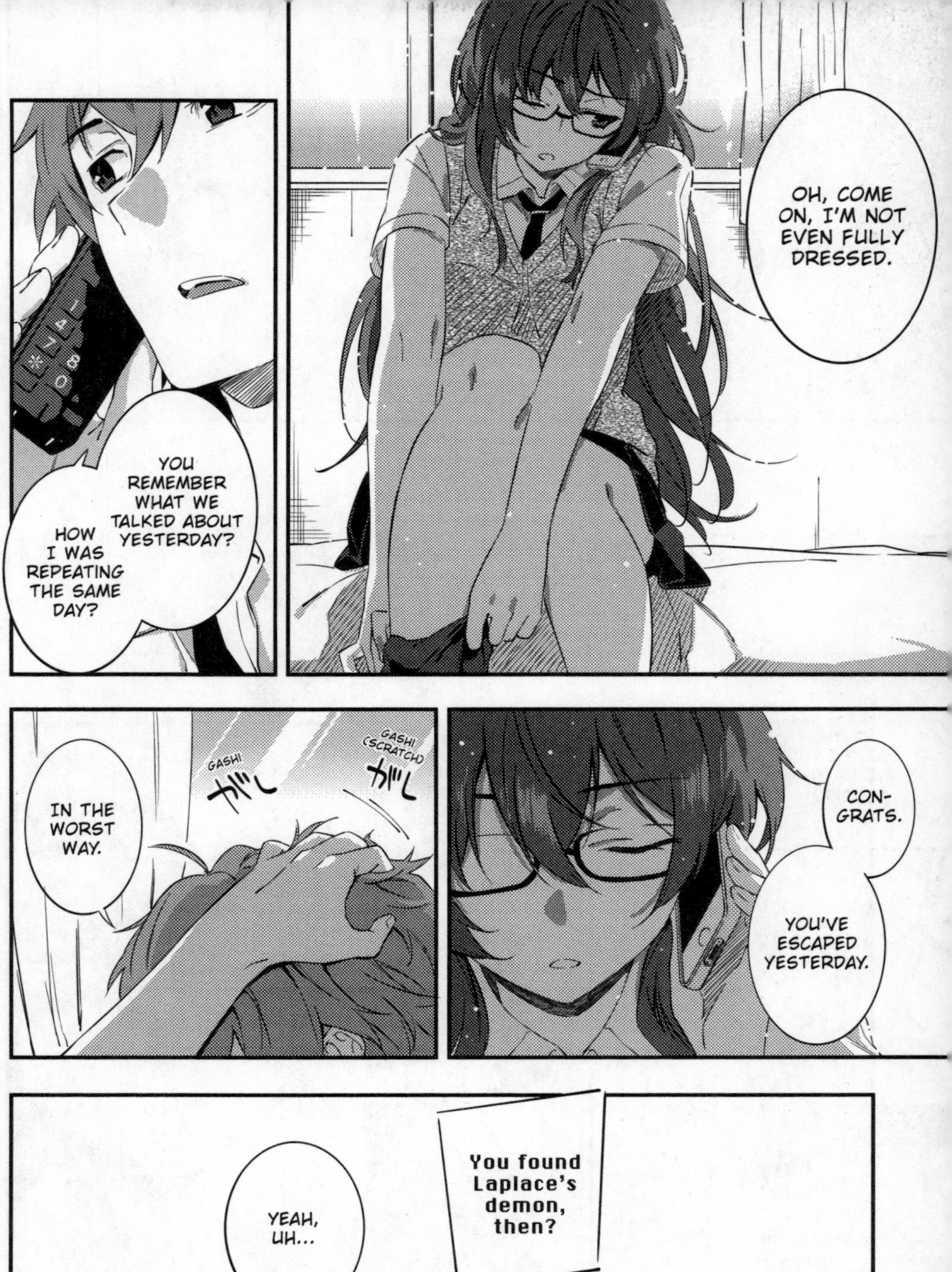
OH, COME ON, I'M NOT EVEN FULLY DRESSED.
YOU REMEMBER WHAT WE TALKED ABOUT YESTERDAY?
HOW I WAS REPEATING THE SAME DAY?
CON-GRATS.
YOU'VE ESCAPED YESTERDAY.
GASHI (SCRATCH)
がし
GASHI
がし
IN THE WORST WAY.
You found Laplace's demon, then?
YEAH, UH...

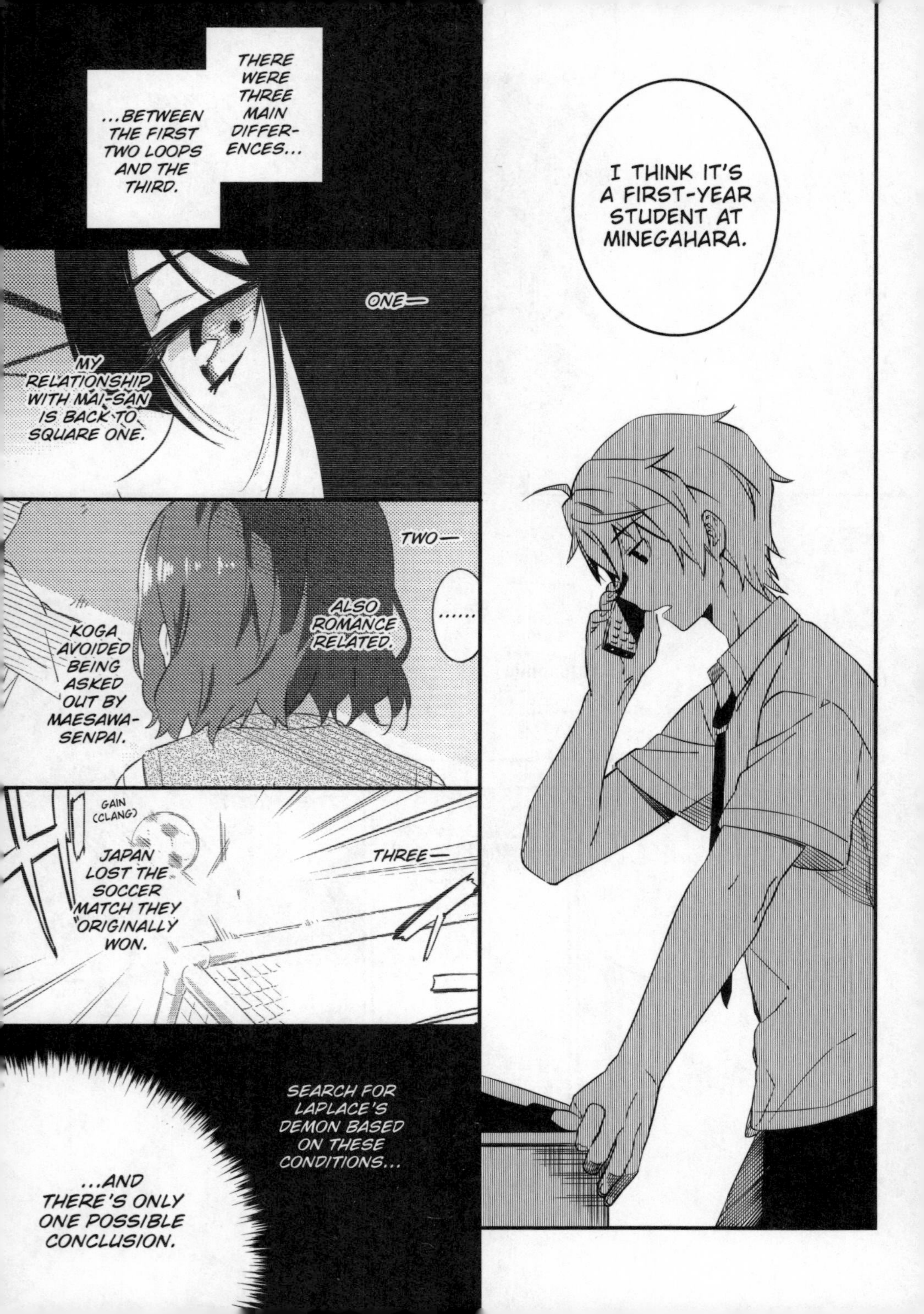
I THINK IT'S A FIRST-YEAR STUDENT AT MINEGAHARA.
THERE WERE THREE MAIN DIFFERENCES...
...BETWEEN THE FIRST TWO LOOPS AND THE THIRD.
ONE—
MY RELATIONSHIP WITH MAI-SAN IS BACK TO SQUARE ONE.
TWO—
......
ALSO ROMANCE RELATED.
KOGA AVOIDED BEING ASKED OUT BY MAESAWA-SENPAI.
THREE—
GAIN (CLANG)
JAPAN LOST THE SOCCER MATCH THEY ORIGINALLY WON.
SEARCH FOR LAPLACE'S DEMON BASED ON THESE CONDITIONS...
...AND THERE'S ONLY ONE POSSIBLE CONCLUSION.

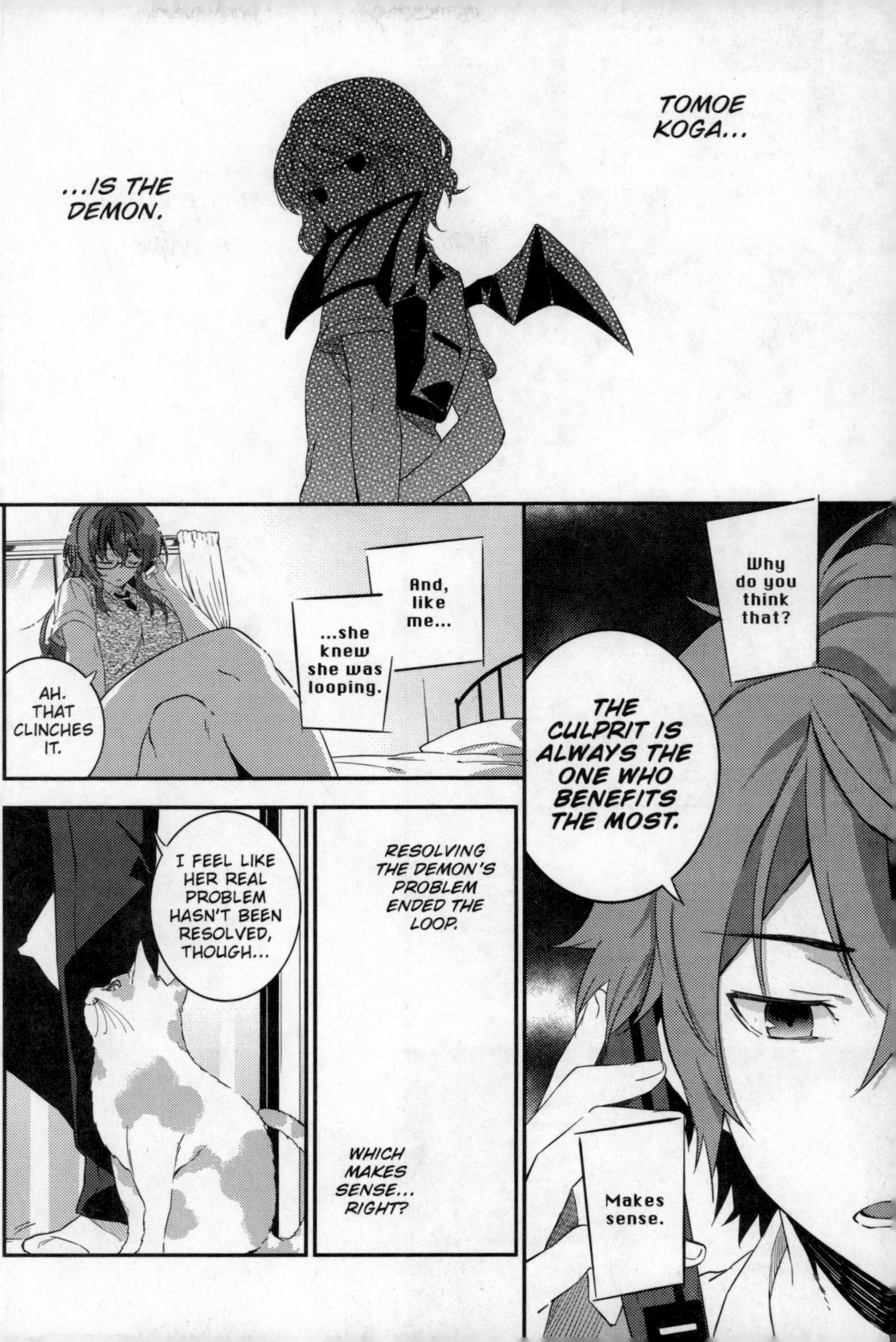
TOMOE KOGA...
...IS THE DEMON.
Why do you think that?
THE CULPRIT IS ALWAYS THE ONE WHO BENEFITS THE MOST.
Makes sense.
And, like me...
...she knew she was looping.
AH. THAT CLINCHES IT.
RESOLVING THE DEMON'S PROBLEM ENDED THE LOOP.
WHICH MAKES SENSE... RIGHT?
I FEEL LIKE HER REAL PROBLEM HASN'T BEEN RESOLVED, THOUGH...

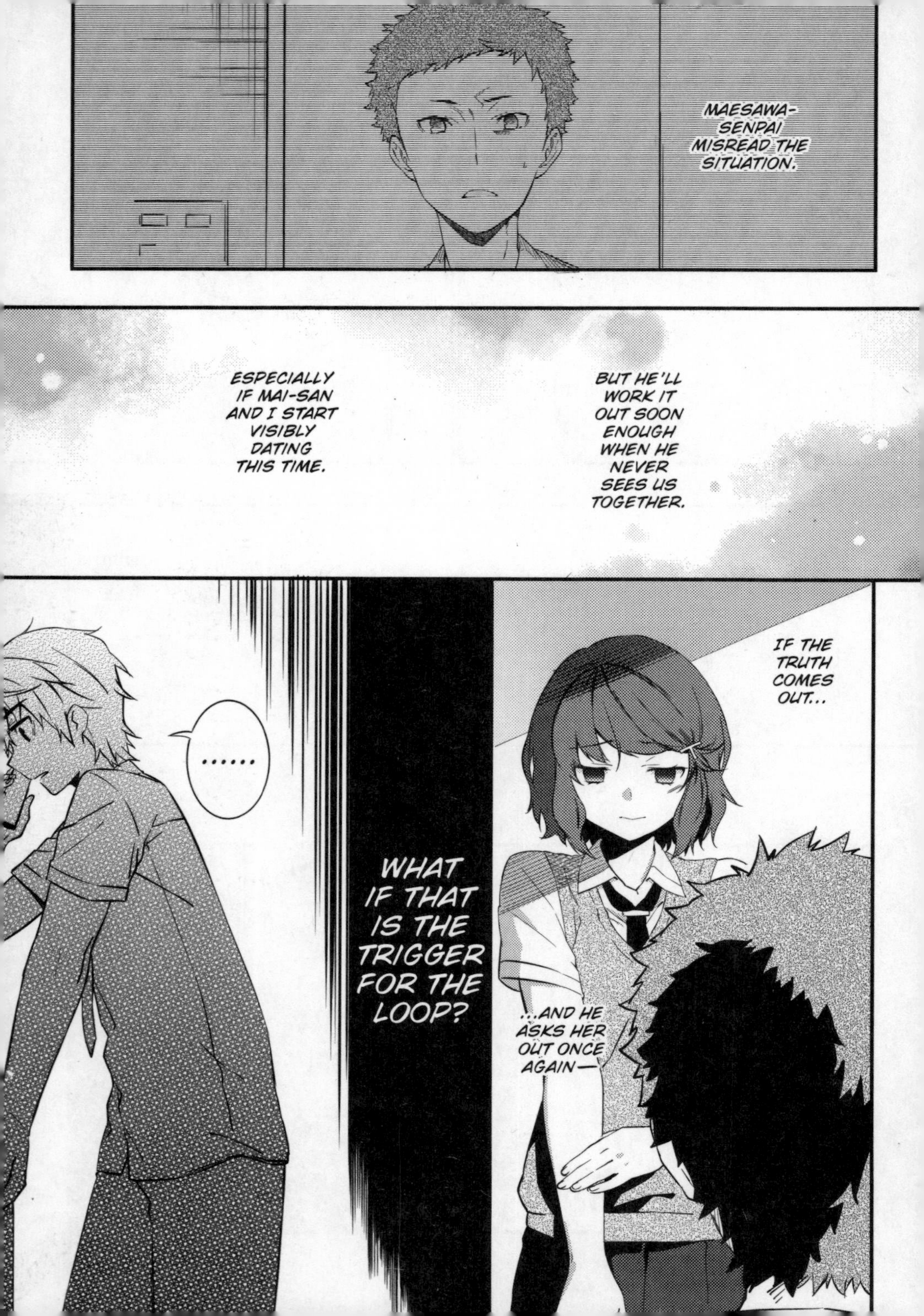
MAESAWA-SENPAI MISREAD THE SITUATION.
BUT HE'LL WORK IT OUT SOON ENOUGH WHEN HE NEVER SEES US TOGETHER.
ESPECIALLY IF MAI-SAN AND I START VISIBLY DATING THIS TIME.
IF THE TRUTH COMES OUT...
...AND HE ASKS HER OUT ONCE AGAIN—
WHAT IF THAT IS THE TRIGGER FOR THE LOOP?
......

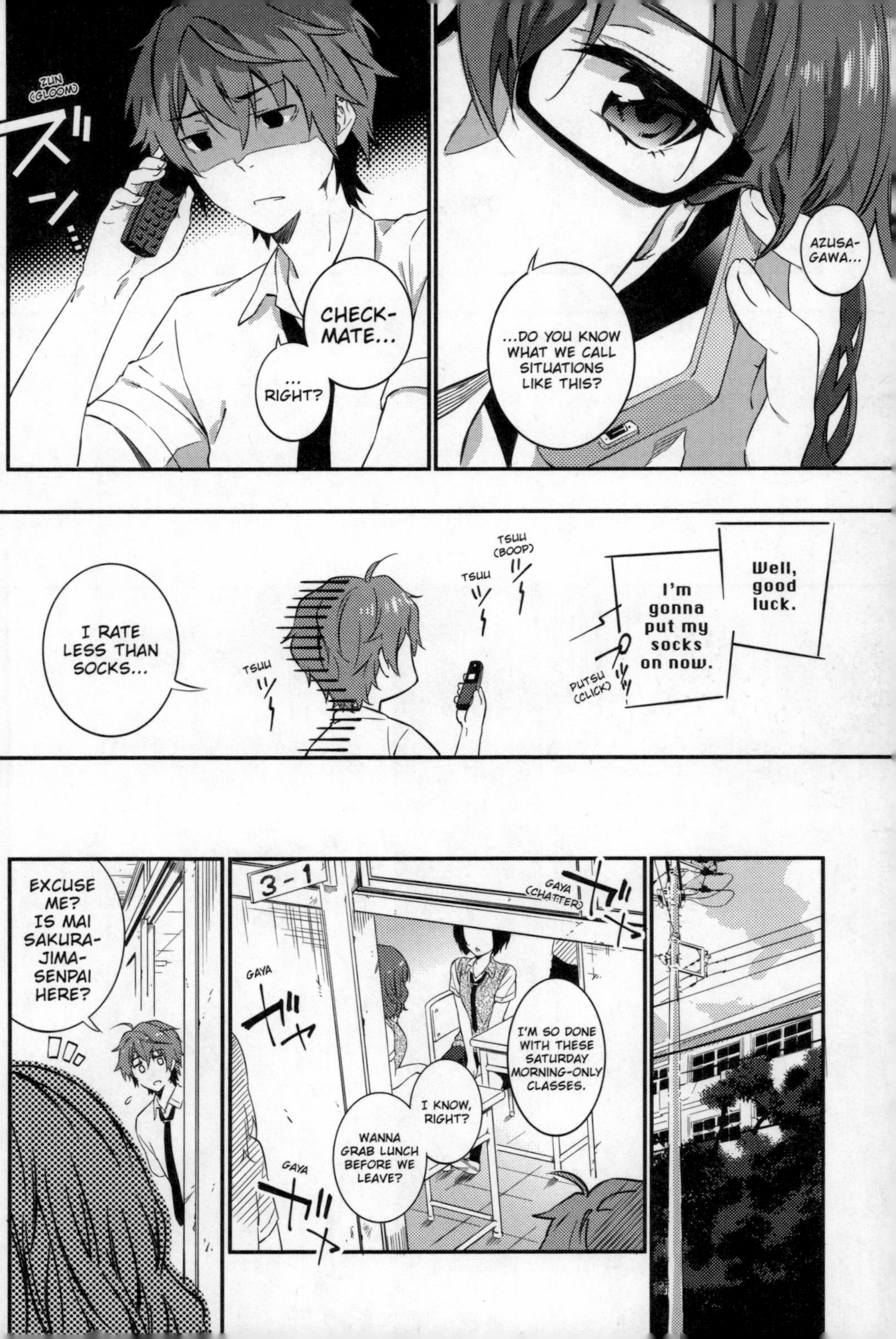
AZUSA-GAWA...
...DO YOU KNOW WHAT WE CALL SITUATIONS LIKE THIS?
ZUN (GLOOM)
CHECK-MATE...
...RIGHT?
Well, good luck.
I'm gonna put my socks on now.
PUTSU (CLICK)
TSUU (BOOP)
TSUU
TSUU
I RATE LESS THAN SOCKS...
3-1
GAYA (CHATTER)
I'M SO DONE WITH THESE SATURDAY MORNING-ONLY CLASSES.
I KNOW, RIGHT?
GAYA
WANNA GRAB LUNCH BEFORE WE LEAVE?
GAYA
EXCUSE ME? IS MAI SAKURA-JIMA-SENPAI HERE?

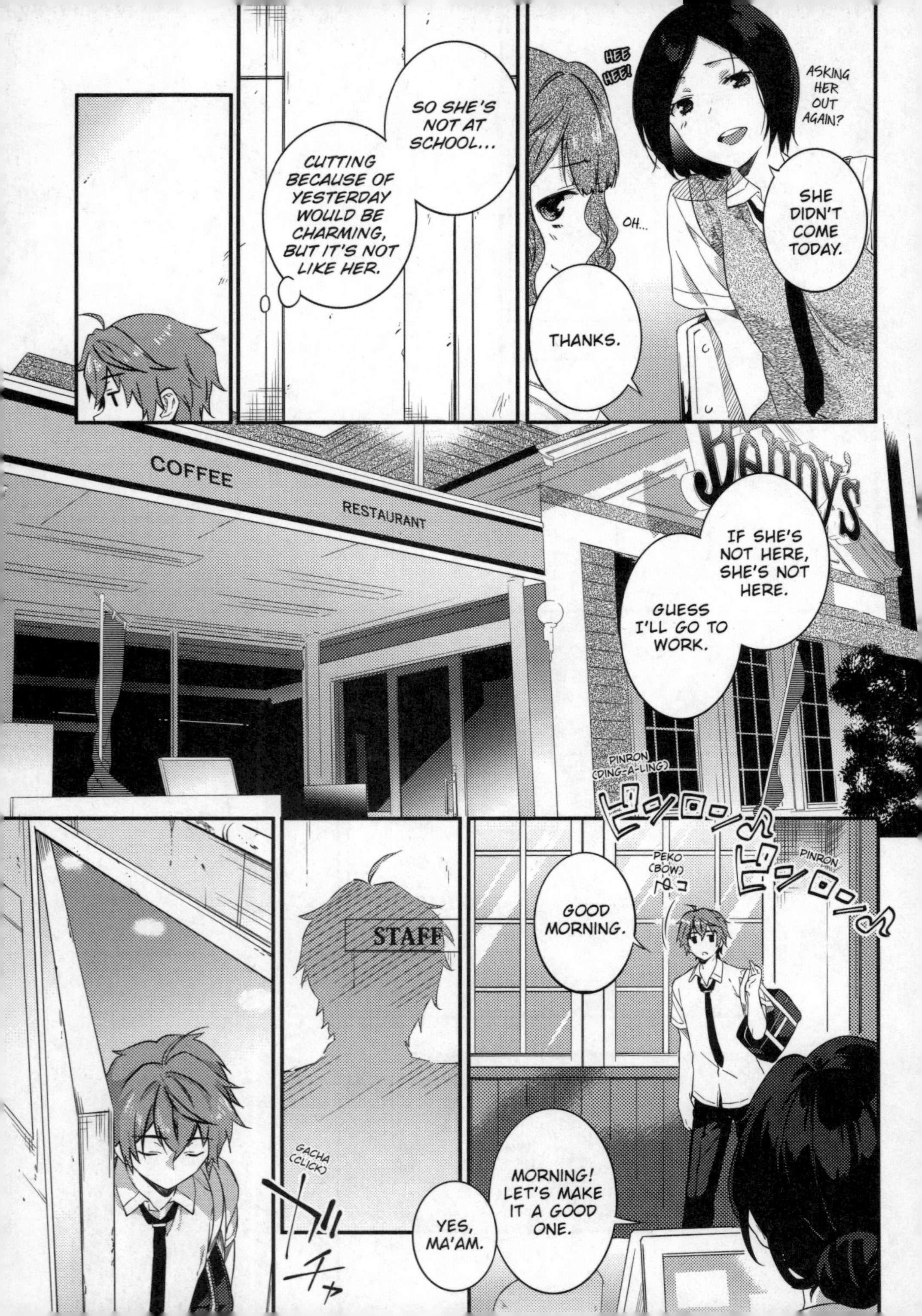
HEE HEE!
ASKING HER OUT AGAIN?
SHE DIDN'T COME TODAY.
OH...
THANKS.
SO SHE'S NOT AT SCHOOL...
CUTTING BECAUSE OF YESTERDAY WOULD BE CHARMING, BUT IT'S NOT LIKE HER.
COFFEE
RESTAURANT
IF SHE'S NOT HERE, SHE'S NOT HERE.
GUESS I'LL GO TO WORK.
PINRON (DING-A-LING)
PINRON
PEKO (BOW)
GOOD MORNING.
MORNING! LET'S MAKE IT A GOOD ONE.
YES, MA'AM.
STAFF
GACHA (CLICK)

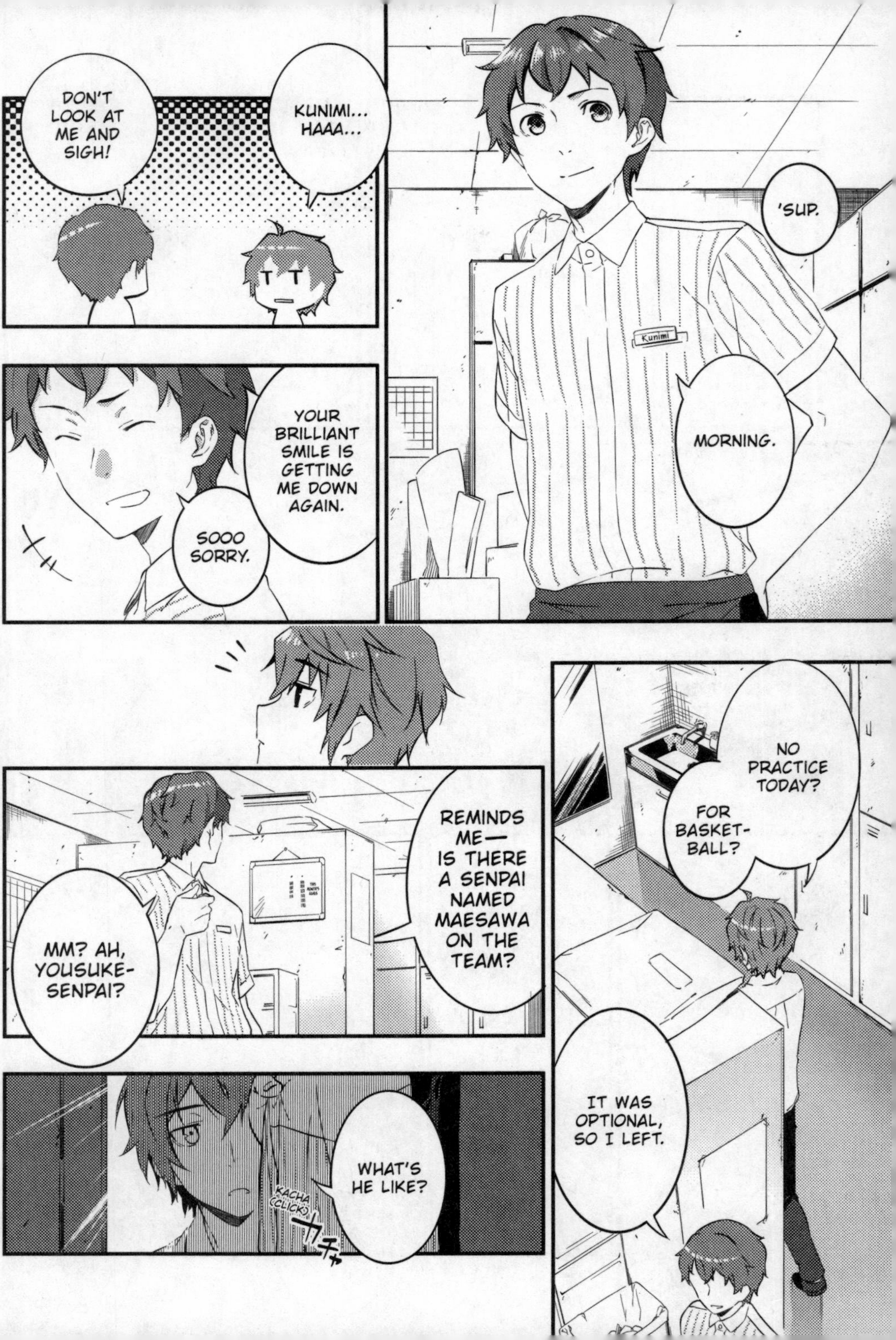
'SUP.
MORNING.
KUNIMI... HAAA...
DON'T LOOK AT ME AND SIGH!
YOUR BRILLIANT SMILE IS GETTING ME DOWN AGAIN.
SOOO SORRY.
NO PRACTICE TODAY?
FOR BASKET-BALL?
IT WAS OPTIONAL, SO I LEFT.
REMINDS ME— IS THERE A SENPAI NAMED MAESAWA ON THE TEAM?
MM? AH, YOUSUKE-SENPAI?
WHAT'S HE LIKE?
KACHA (CLICK)

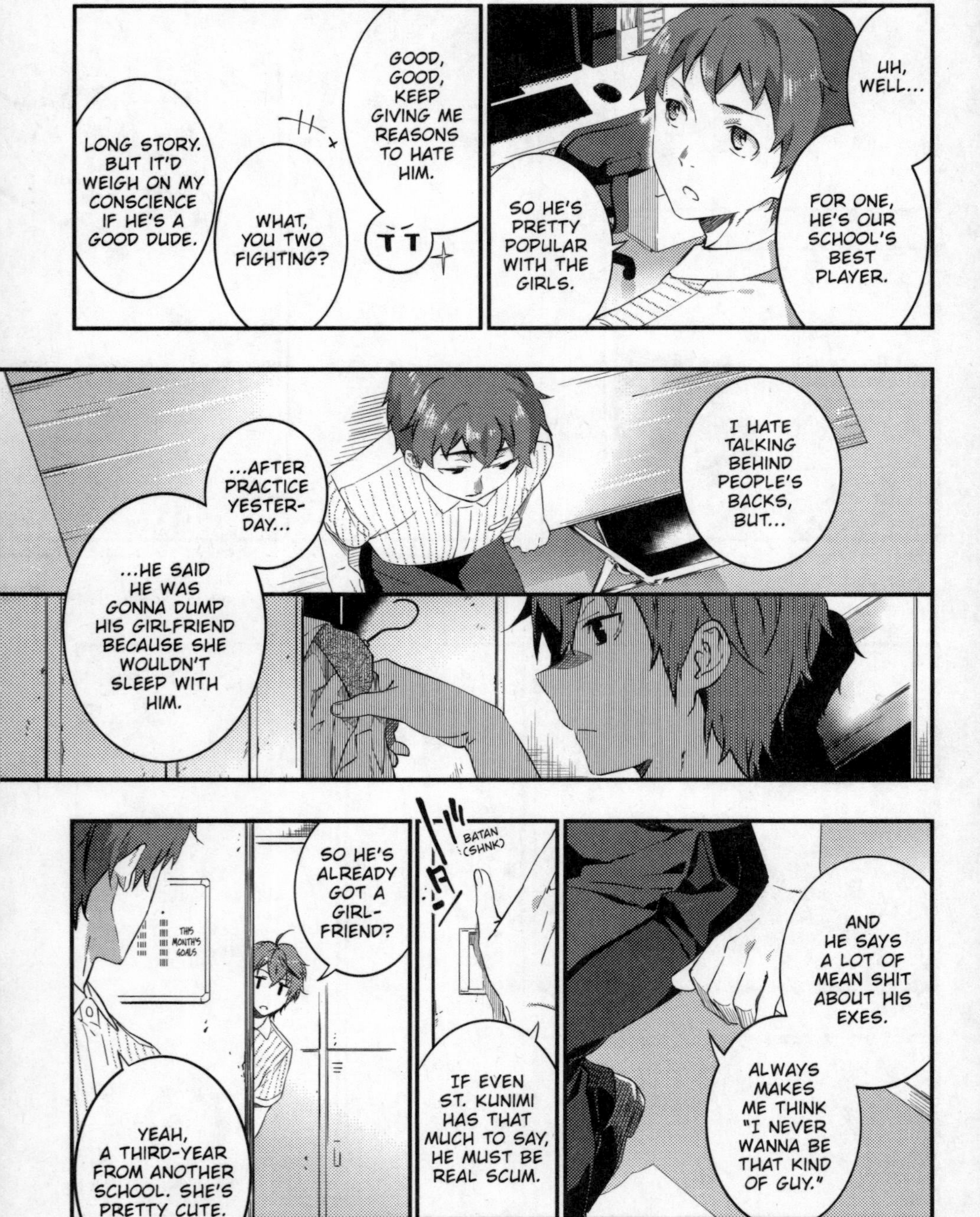
UH, WELL...
FOR ONE, HE'S OUR SCHOOL'S BEST PLAYER.
SO HE'S PRETTY POPULAR WITH THE GIRLS.
GOOD, GOOD, KEEP GIVING ME REASONS TO HATE HIM.
WHAT, YOU TWO FIGHTING?
LONG STORY. BUT IT'D WEIGH ON MY CONSCIENCE IF HE'S A GOOD DUDE.
I HATE TALKING BEHIND PEOPLE'S BACKS, BUT...
...AFTER PRACTICE YESTER-DAY...
...HE SAID HE WAS GONNA DUMP HIS GIRLFRIEND BECAUSE SHE WOULDN'T SLEEP WITH HIM.
AND HE SAYS A LOT OF MEAN SHIT ABOUT HIS EXES.
ALWAYS MAKES ME THINK "I NEVER WANNA BE THAT KIND OF GUY."
BATAN (SHNK)
IF EVEN ST. KUNIMI HAS THAT MUCH TO SAY, HE MUST BE REAL SCUM.
SO HE'S ALREADY GOT A GIRL-FRIEND?
THIS MONTH'S GOALS
YEAH, A THIRD-YEAR FROM ANOTHER SCHOOL. SHE'S PRETTY CUTE.

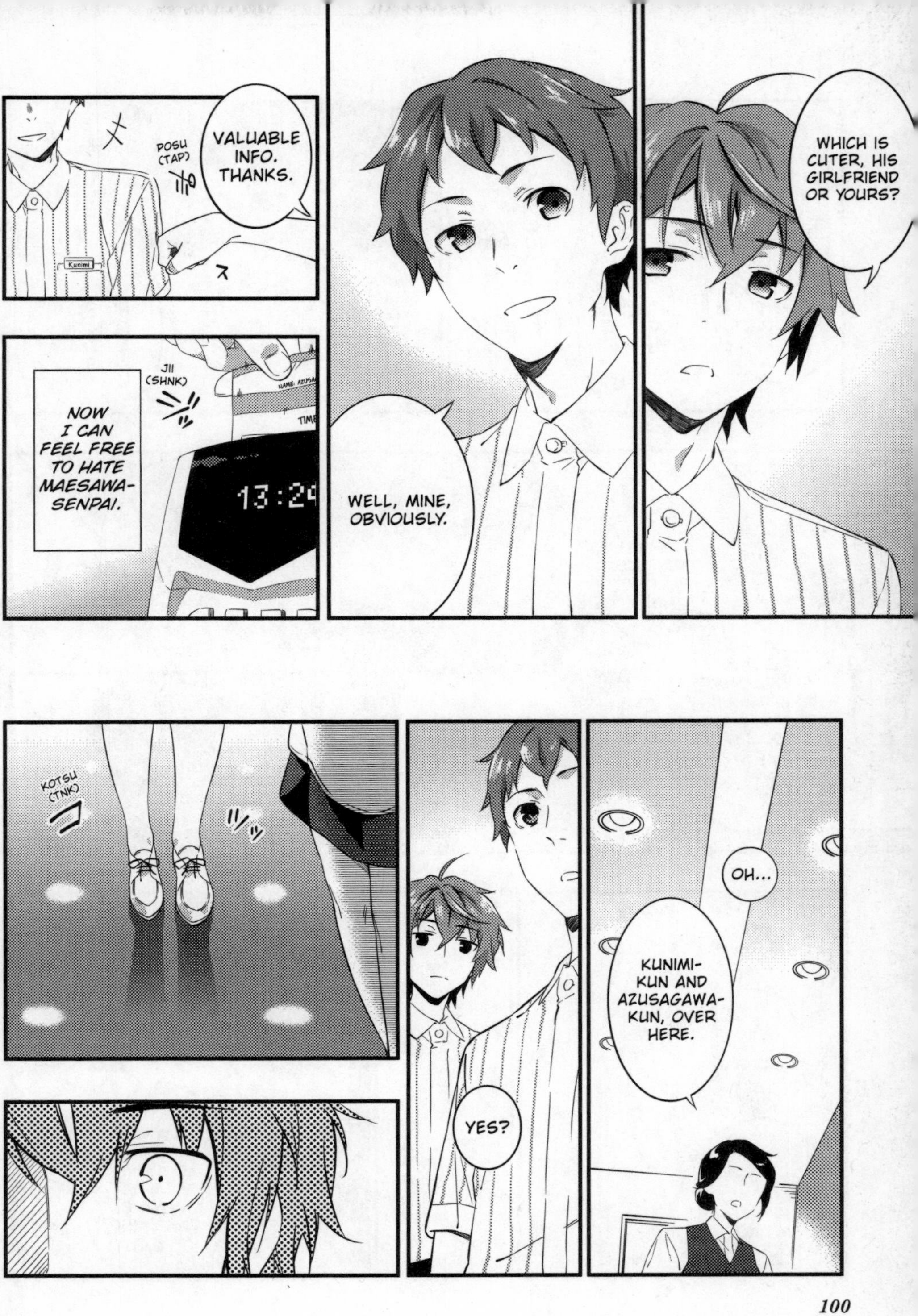
WHICH IS CUTER, HIS GIRLFRIEND OR YOURS?
WELL, MINE, OBVIOUSLY.
VALUABLE INFO. THANKS.
POSU (TAP)
Kunimi
JII (SHNK)
NOW I CAN FEEL FREE TO HATE MAESAWA-SENPAI.
13:24
OH...
KUNIMI-KUN AND AZUSAGAWA-KUN, OVER HERE.
YES?
KOTSU (TNK)

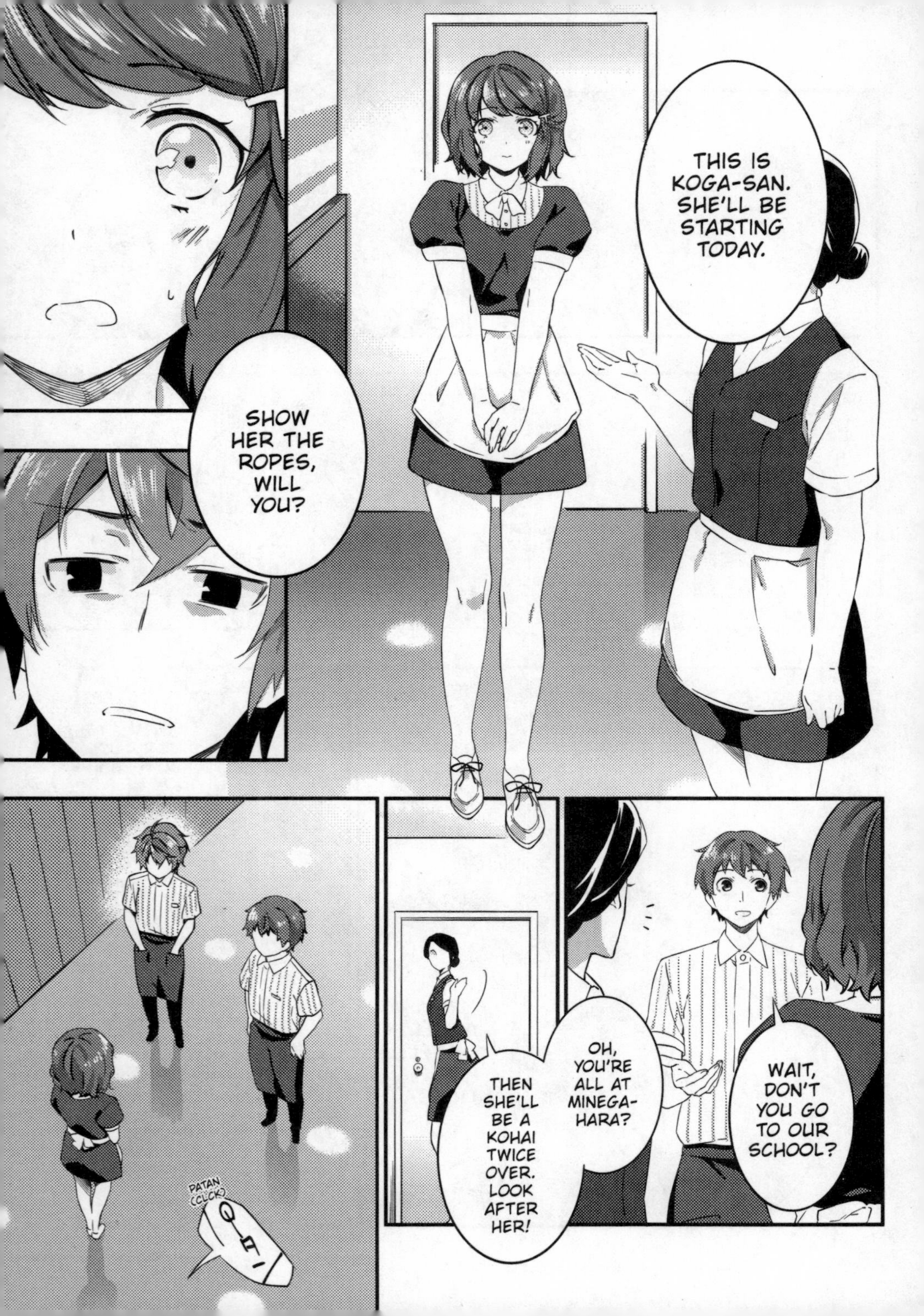
THIS IS KOGA-SAN. SHE'LL BE STARTING TODAY.
SHOW HER THE ROPES, WILL YOU?
WAIT, DON'T YOU GO TO OUR SCHOOL?
OH, YOU'RE ALL AT MINEGA-HARA?
THEN SHE'LL BE A KOHAI TWICE OVER. LOOK AFTER HER!
PATAN (CLICK)

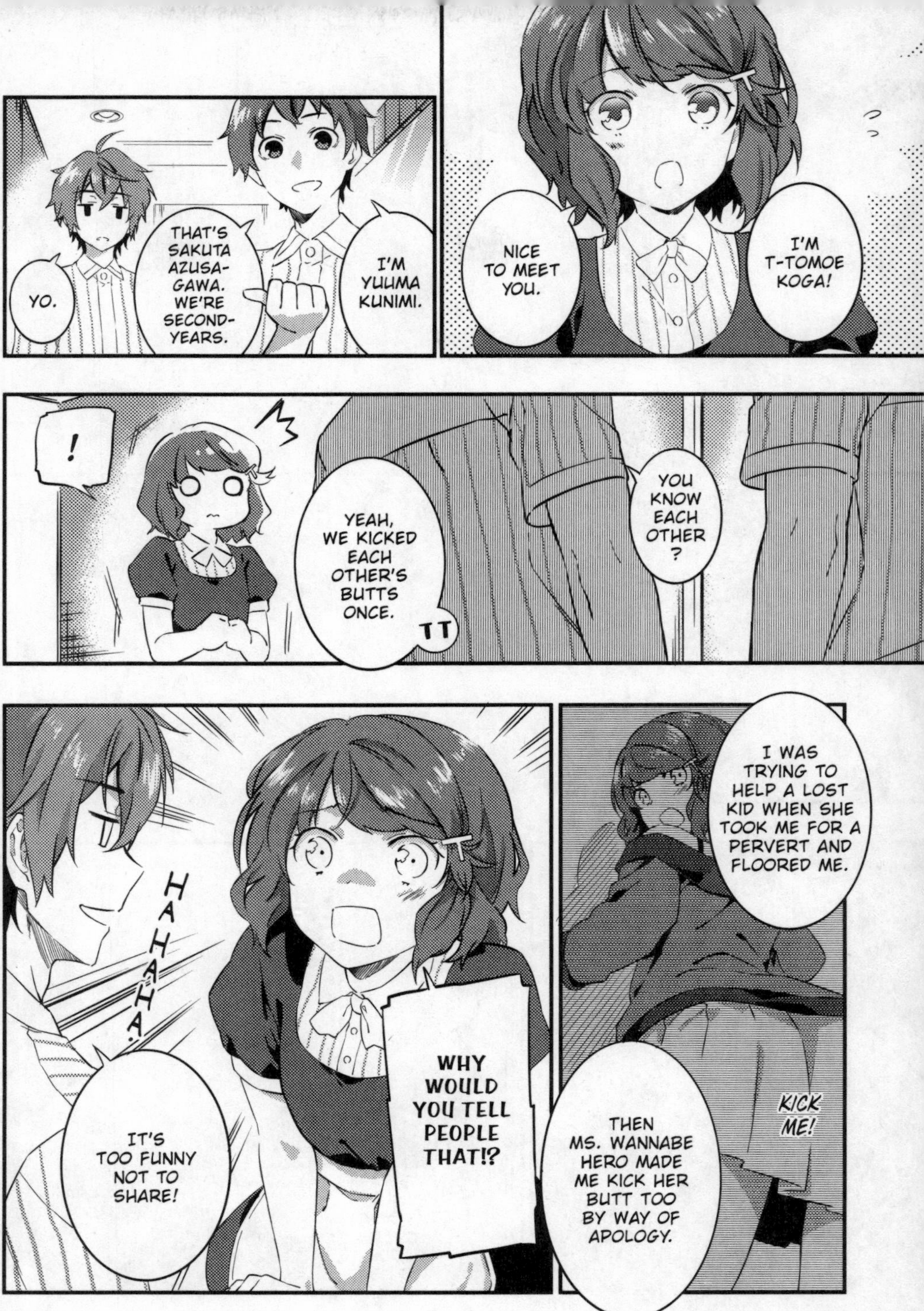
I'M T-TOMOE KOGA!
NICE TO MEET YOU.
I'M YUUMA KUNIMI.
THAT'S SAKUTA AZUSA-GAWA. WE'RE SECOND-YEARS.
YO.
YOU KNOW EACH OTHER?
YEAH, WE KICKED EACH OTHER'S BUTTS ONCE.
TT
!
I WAS TRYING TO HELP A LOST KID WHEN SHE TOOK ME FOR A PERVERT AND FLOORED ME.
KICK ME!
THEN MS. WANNABE HERO MADE ME KICK HER BUTT TOO BY WAY OF APOLOGY.
WHY WOULD YOU TELL PEOPLE THAT!?
HAHAHA!
IT'S TOO FUNNY NOT TO SHARE!

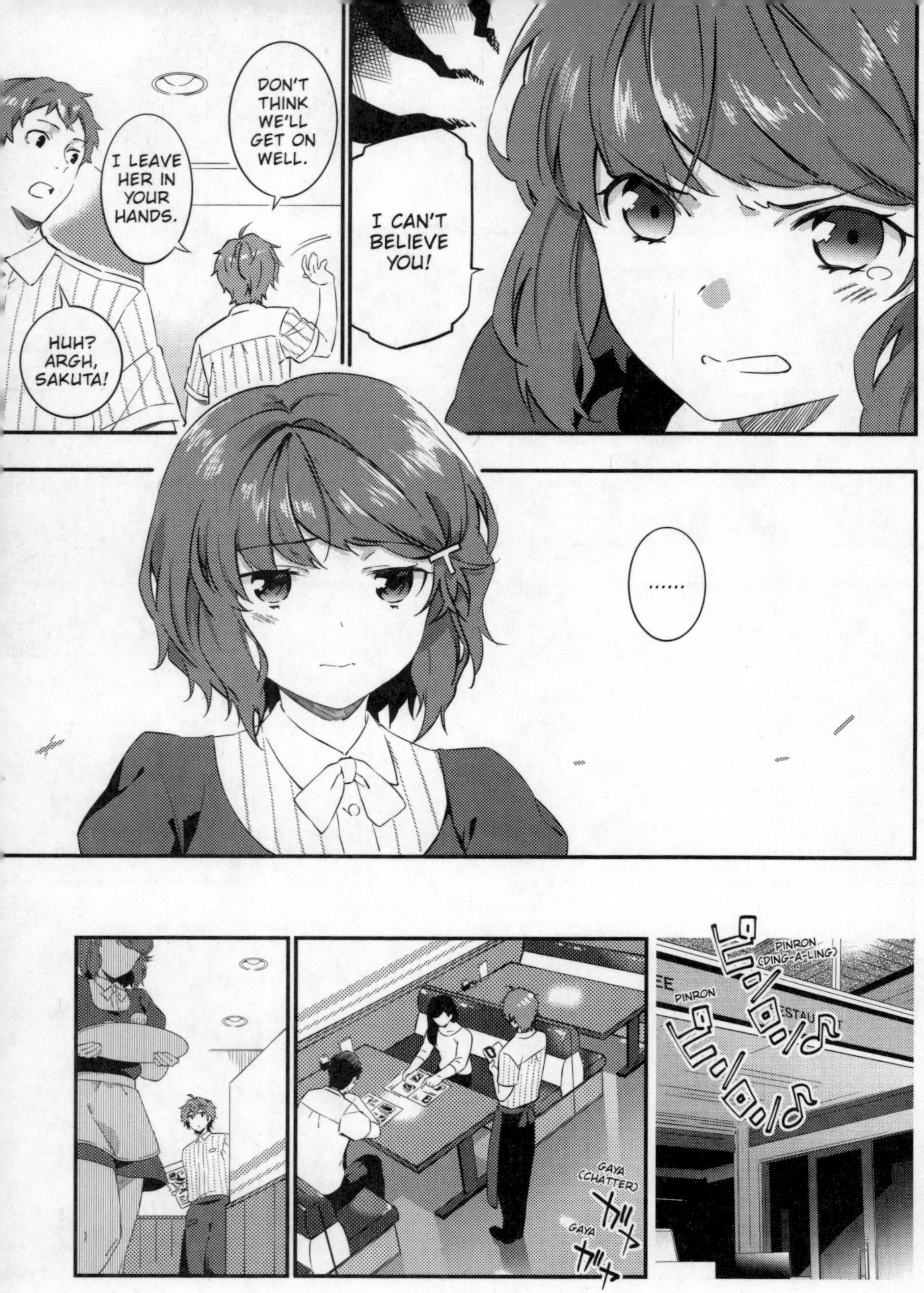
I CAN'T BELIEVE YOU!
DON'T THINK WE'LL GET ON WELL.
I LEAVE HER IN YOUR HANDS.
HUH? ARGH, SAKUTA!
......
PINRON (DING-A-LING)
PINRON
GAYA (CHATTER)
GAYA

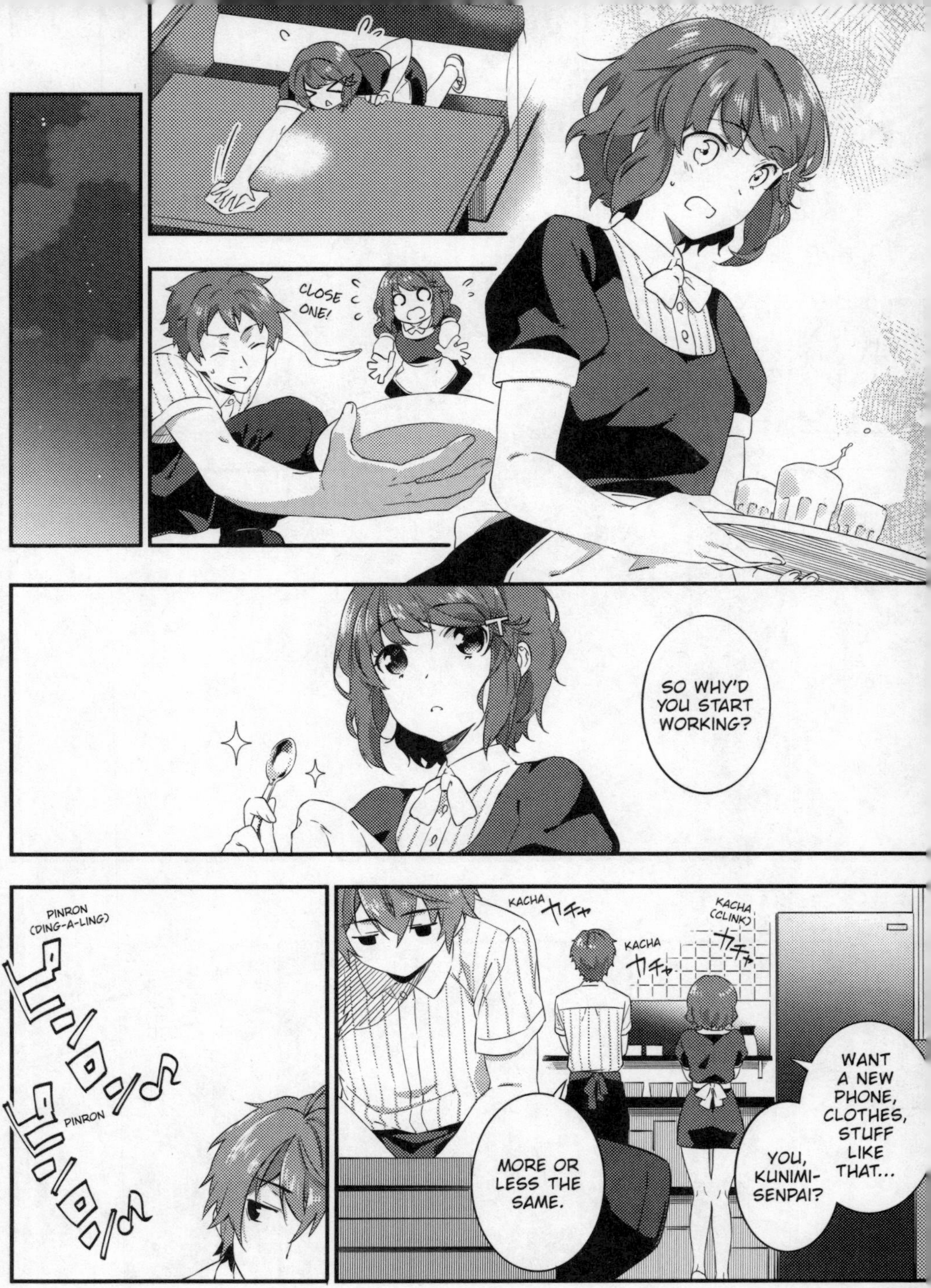
CLOSE ONE!
SO WHY'D YOU START WORKING?
KACHA
カチャ
KACHA (CLINK)
カチャ
KACHA
カチャ
WANT A NEW PHONE, CLOTHES, STUFF LIKE THAT...
YOU, KUNIMI-SENPAI?
MORE OR LESS THE SAME.
PINRON (DING-A-LING)
PINRON

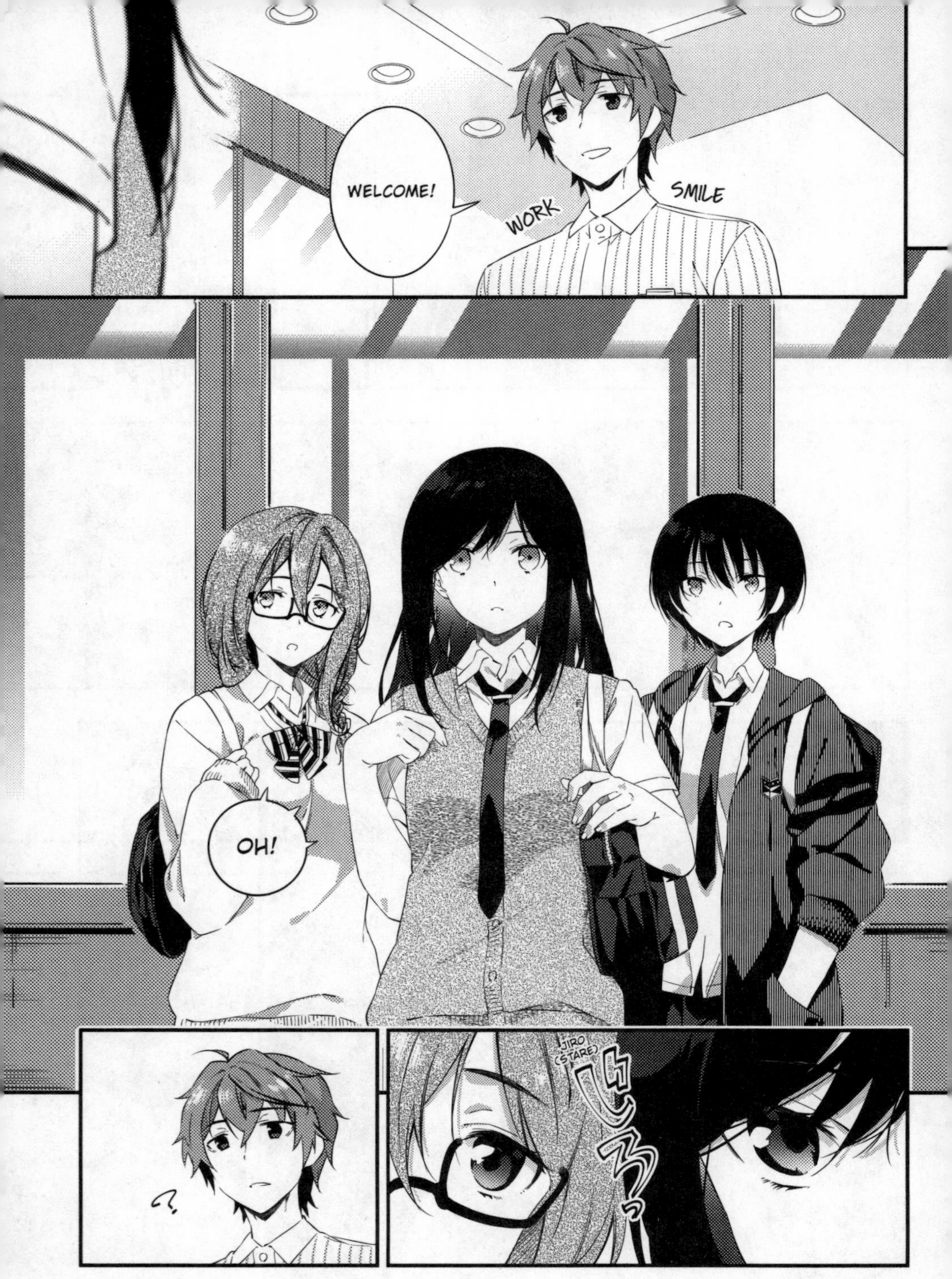
WELCOME!
WORK SMILE
OH!
JIRO (STARE)
?

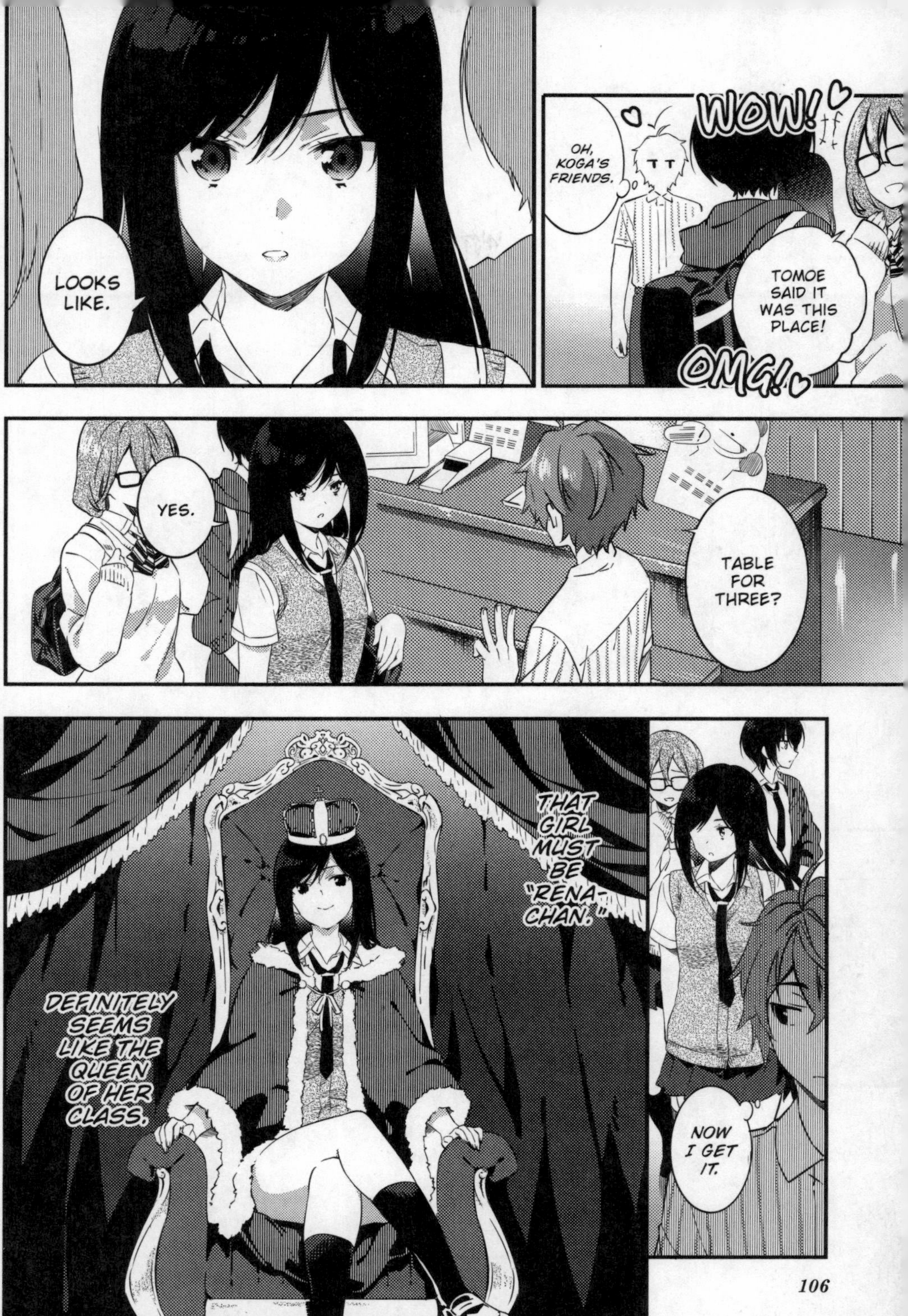
WOW!
OH, KOGA'S FRIENDS.
TOMOE SAID IT WAS THIS PLACE!
OMG!
LOOKS LIKE.
TABLE FOR THREE?
YES.
NOW I GET IT.
THAT GIRL MUST BE "RENA-CHAN."
DEFINITELY SEEMS LIKE THE QUEEN OF HER CLASS.

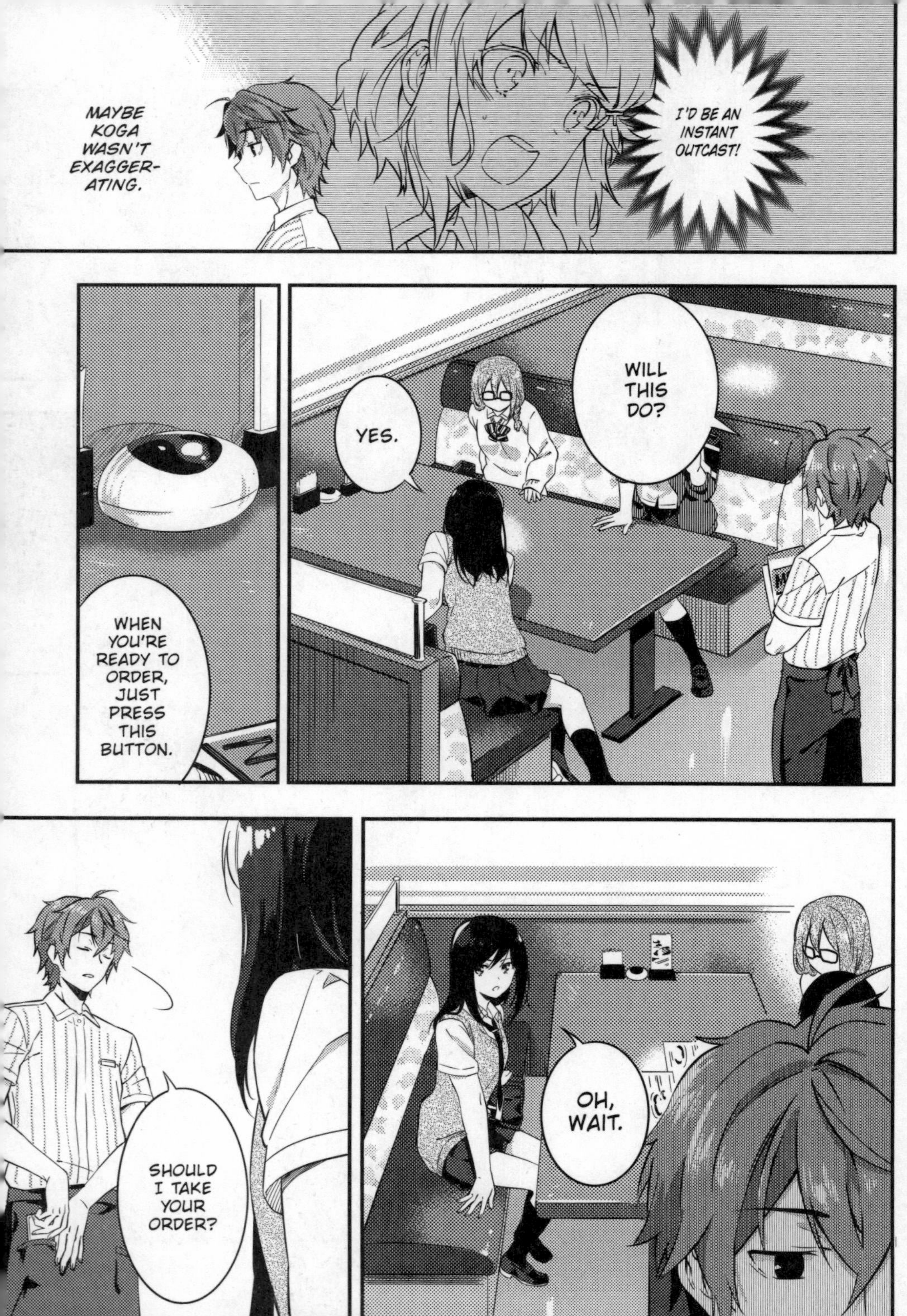
I'D BE AN INSTANT OUTCAST!
MAYBE KOGA WASN'T EXAGGER-ATING.
WILL THIS DO?
YES.
WHEN YOU'RE READY TO ORDER, JUST PRESS THIS BUTTON.
OH, WAIT.
SHOULD I TAKE YOUR ORDER?

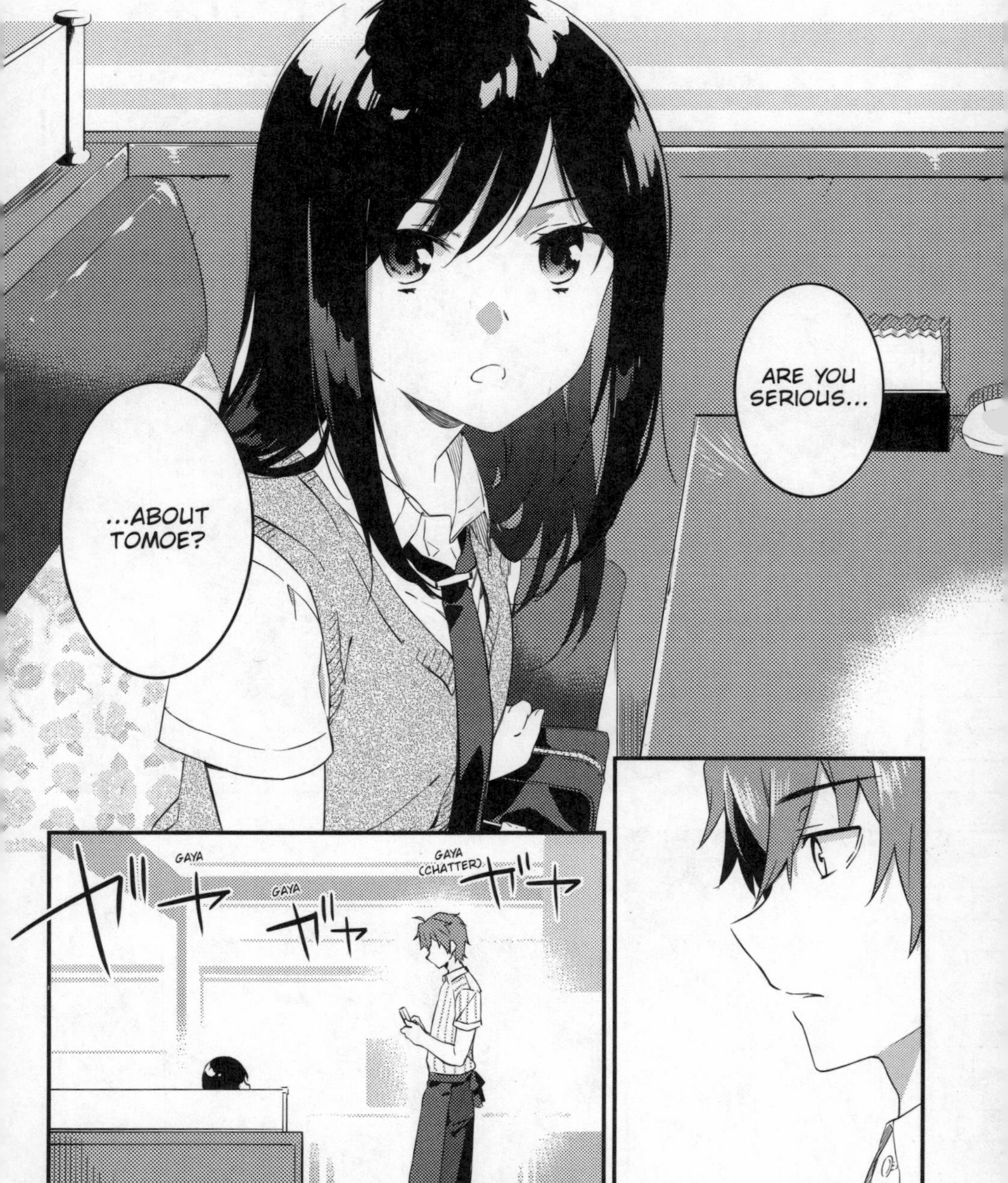
ARE YOU SERIOUS...
...ABOUT TOMOE?
GAYA (CHATTER)
ガヤ
GAYA
ガヤ
GAYA
ガヤ

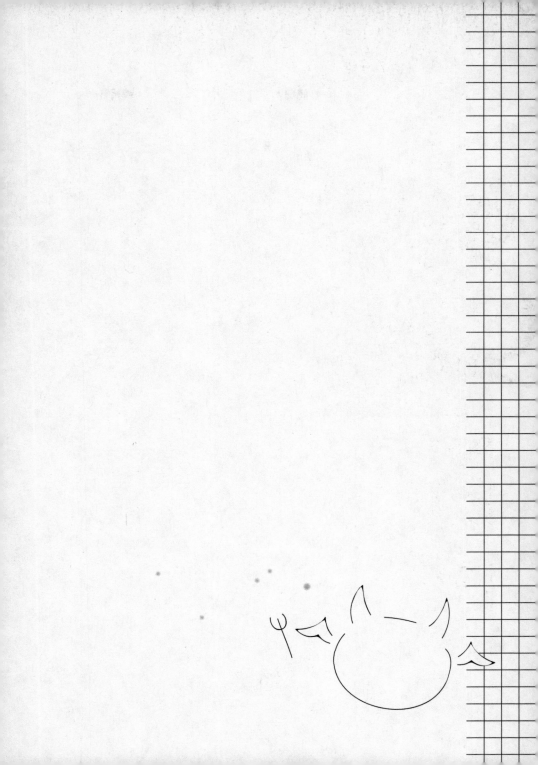

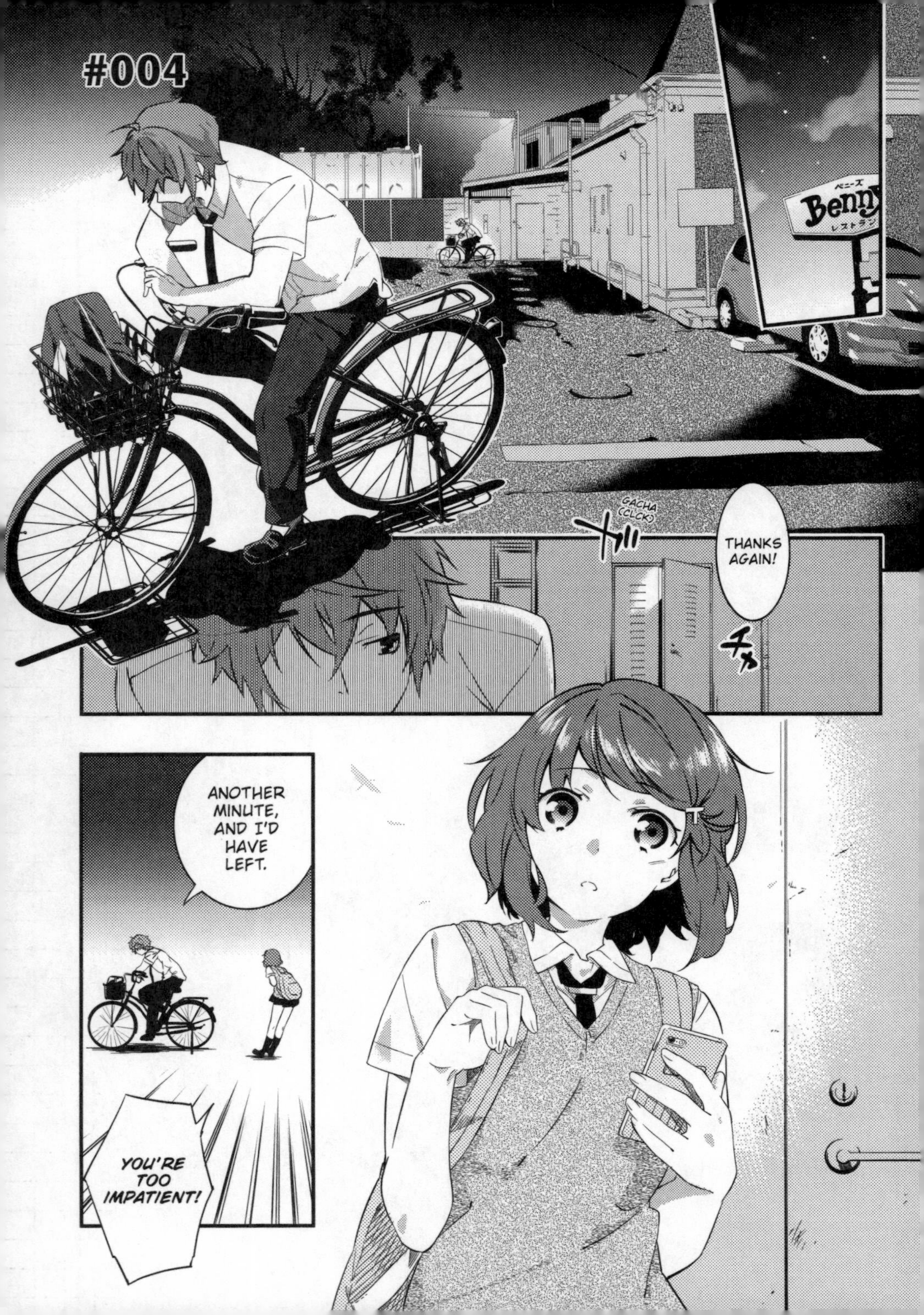
#004
ベニーズ
Benny
レストラン
GACHA (CLCK)
THANKS AGAIN!
ANOTHER MINUTE, AND I'D HAVE LEFT.
YOU'RE TOO IMPATIENT!

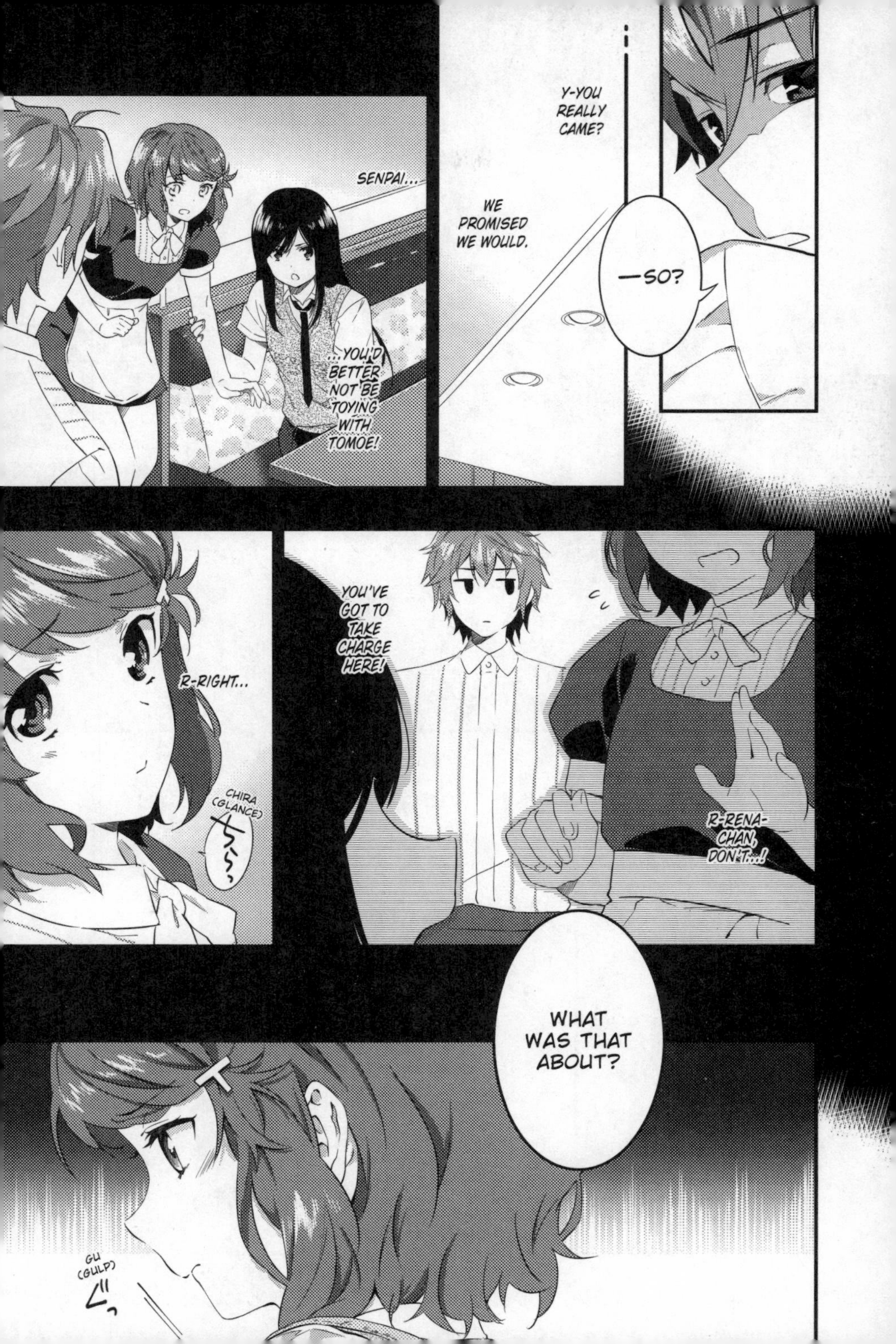
—SO?
Y-YOU REALLY CAME?
WE PROMISED WE WOULD.
SENPAI...
...YOU'D BETTER NOT BE TOYING WITH TOMOE!
YOU'VE GOT TO TAKE CHARGE HERE!
R-RENA-CHAN, DON'T...!
R-RIGHT...
CHIRA (GLANCE)
ちらっ
WHAT WAS THAT ABOUT?
GU (GULP)
ぐっ

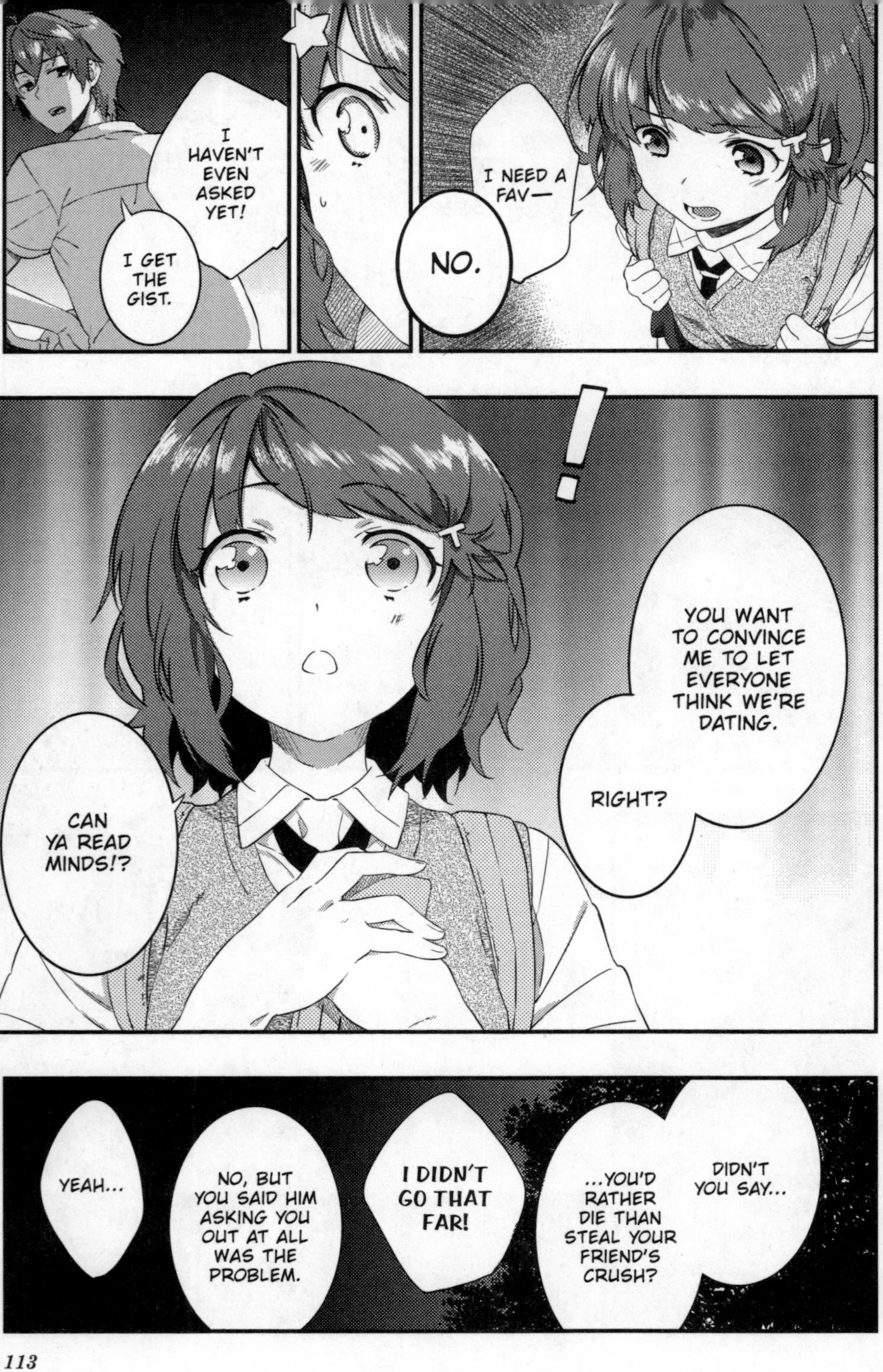
I NEED A FAV—
NO.
I HAVEN'T EVEN ASKED YET!
I GET THE GIST.
!
YOU WANT TO CONVINCE ME TO LET EVERYONE THINK WE'RE DATING.
RIGHT?
CAN YA READ MINDS!?
DIDN'T YOU SAY...
...YOU'D RATHER DIE THAN STEAL YOUR FRIEND'S CRUSH?
I DIDN'T GO THAT FAR!
NO, BUT YOU SAID HIM ASKING YOU OUT AT ALL WAS THE PROBLEM.
YEAH...

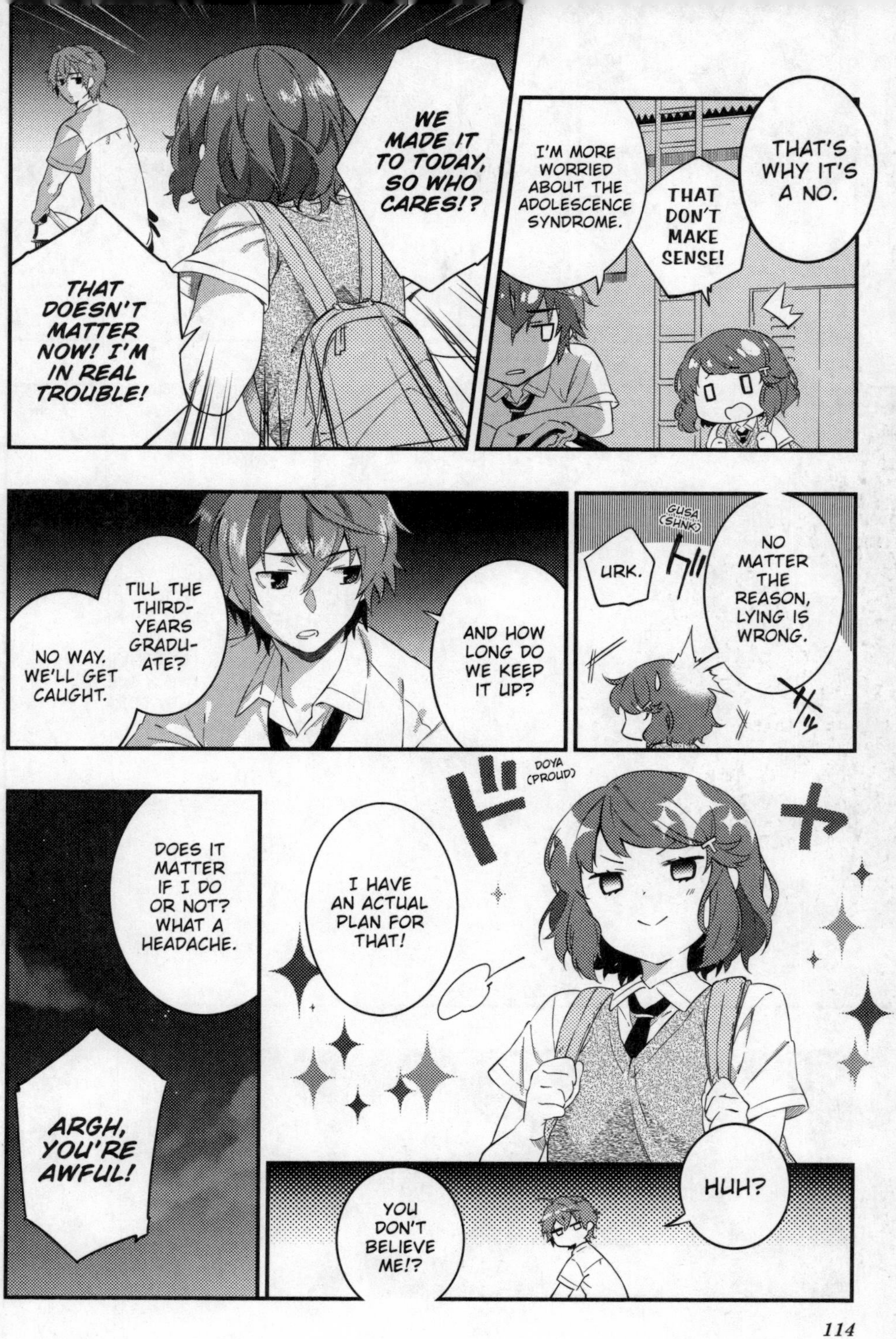
THAT'S WHY IT'S A NO.
THAT DON'T MAKE SENSE!
I'M MORE WORRIED ABOUT THE ADOLESCENCE SYNDROME.
WE MADE IT TO TODAY, SO WHO CARES!?
THAT DOESN'T MATTER NOW! I'M IN REAL TROUBLE!
GUSA (SHNK)
NO MATTER THE REASON, LYING IS WRONG.
URK.
AND HOW LONG DO WE KEEP IT UP?
TILL THE THIRD-YEARS GRADUATE?
NO WAY. WE'LL GET CAUGHT.
DOYA (PROUD)
I HAVE AN ACTUAL PLAN FOR THAT!
HUH?
YOU DON'T BELIEVE ME!?
DOES IT MATTER IF I DO OR NOT? WHAT A HEADACHE.
ARGH, YOU'RE AWFUL!

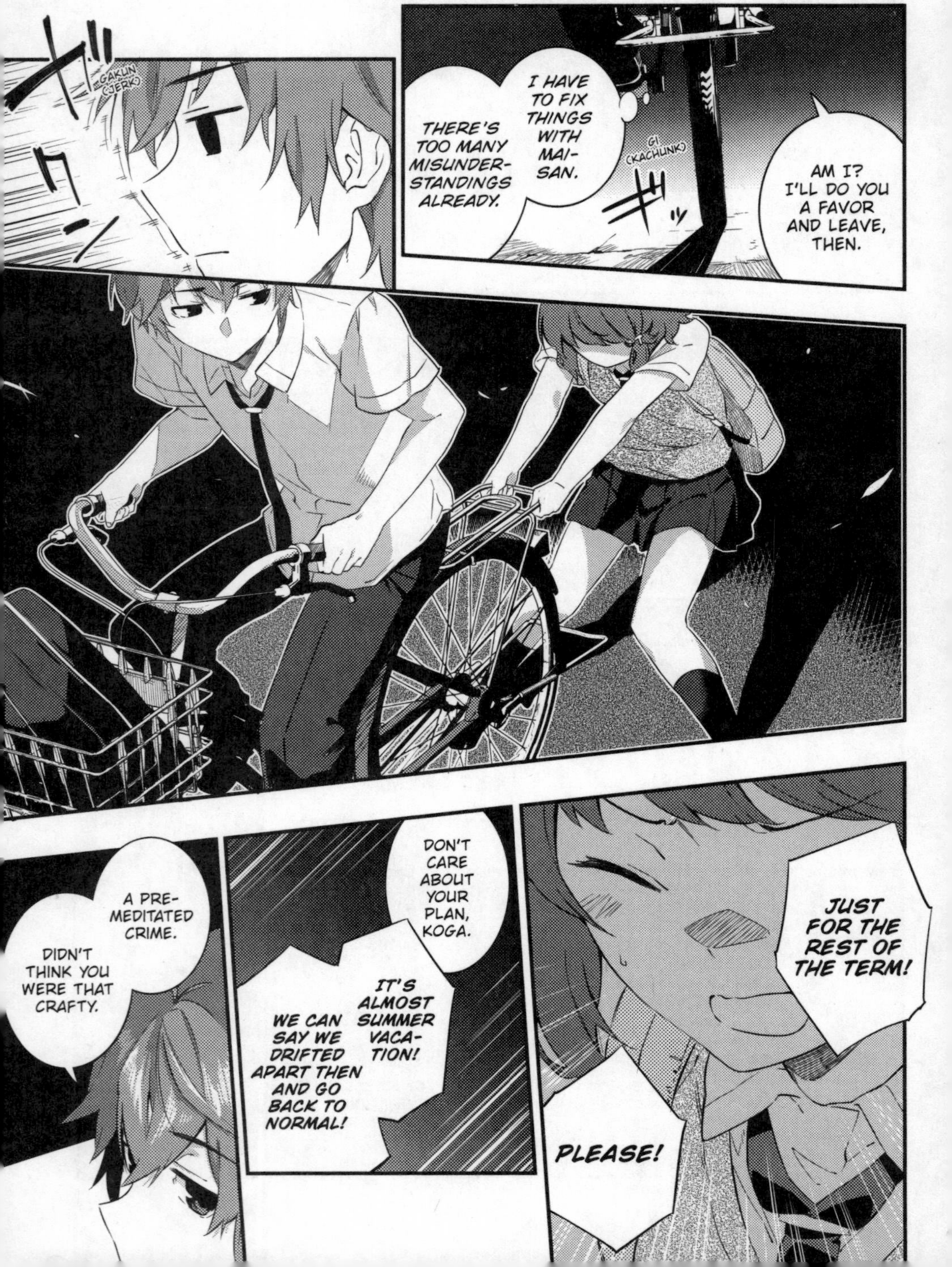
AM I? I'LL DO YOU A FAVOR AND LEAVE, THEN.
GI (KACHUNK)
I HAVE TO FIX THINGS WITH MAI-SAN.
THERE'S TOO MANY MISUNDERSTANDINGS ALREADY.
GAKUN (JERK)
JUST FOR THE REST OF THE TERM!
PLEASE!
DON'T CARE ABOUT YOUR PLAN, KOGA.
IT'S ALMOST SUMMER VACATION!
WE CAN SAY WE DRIFTED APART THEN AND GO BACK TO NORMAL!
A PRE-MEDITATED CRIME.
DIDN'T THINK YOU WERE THAT CRAFTY.

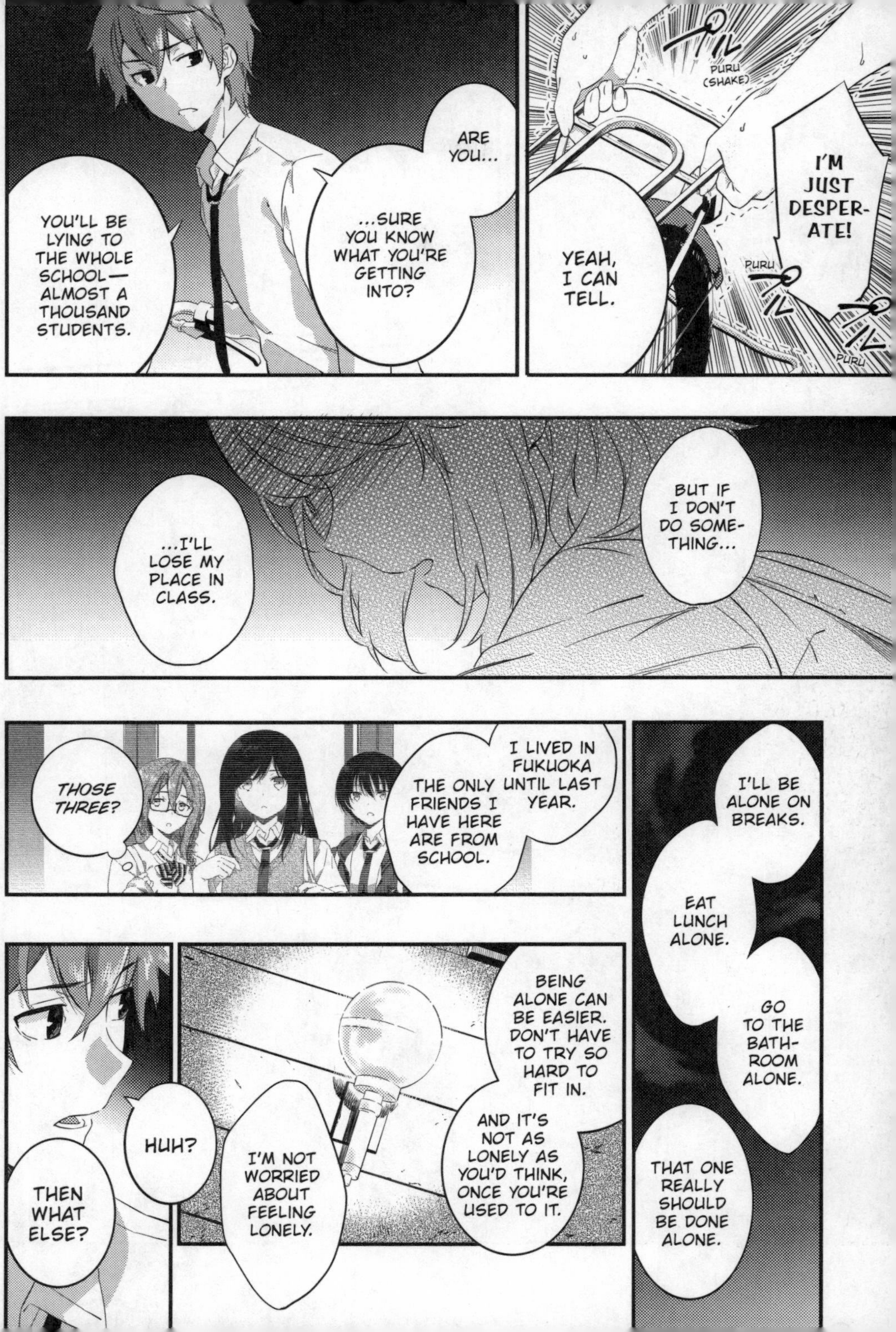
PURU (SHAKE)
I'M JUST DESPERATE!
YEAH, I CAN TELL.
PURU
PURU
ARE YOU...
...SURE YOU KNOW WHAT YOU'RE GETTING INTO?
YOU'LL BE LYING TO THE WHOLE SCHOOL—ALMOST A THOUSAND STUDENTS.
BUT IF I DON'T DO SOME-THING...
...I'LL LOSE MY PLACE IN CLASS.
I'LL BE ALONE ON BREAKS.
EAT LUNCH ALONE.
GO TO THE BATH-ROOM ALONE.
THAT ONE REALLY SHOULD BE DONE ALONE.
I LIVED IN FUKUOKA UNTIL LAST YEAR.
THE ONLY FRIENDS I HAVE HERE ARE FROM SCHOOL.
THOSE THREE?
BEING ALONE CAN BE EASIER. DON'T HAVE TO TRY SO HARD TO FIT IN.
AND IT'S NOT AS LONELY AS YOU'D THINK, ONCE YOU'RE USED TO IT.
I'M NOT WORRIED ABOUT FEELING LONELY.
HUH?
THEN WHAT ELSE?

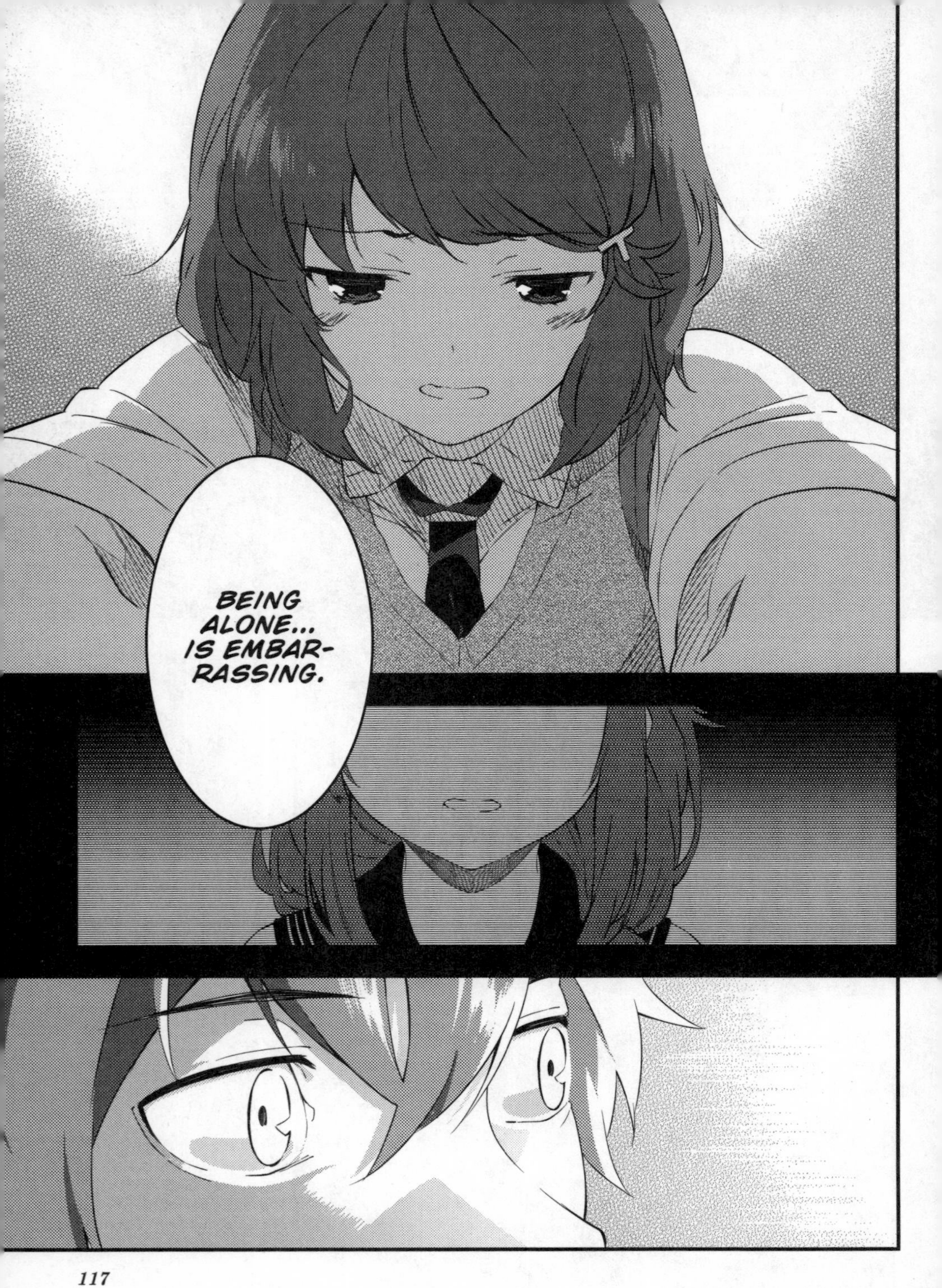
BEING ALONE... IS EMBAR-RASSING.

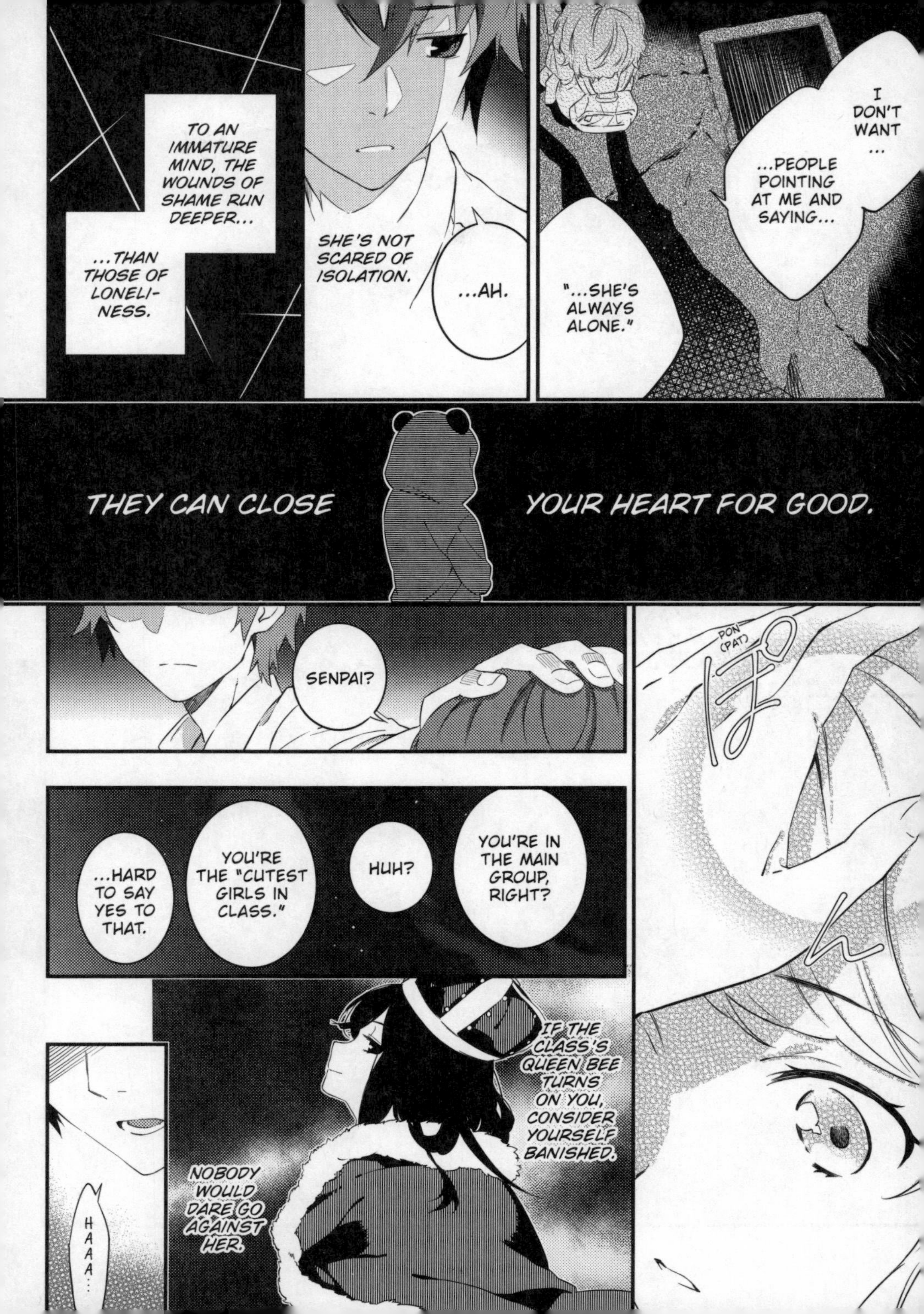
I DON'T WANT...
...PEOPLE POINTING AT ME AND SAYING...
"...SHE'S ALWAYS ALONE."
...AH.
SHE'S NOT SCARED OF ISOLATION.
TO AN IMMATURE MIND, THE WOUNDS OF SHAME RUN DEEPER...
...THAN THOSE OF LONELI-NESS.
THEY CAN CLOSE
YOUR HEART FOR GOOD.
PON (PAT)
ぽん
SENPAI?
YOU'RE IN THE MAIN GROUP, RIGHT?
HUH?
YOU'RE THE "CUTEST GIRLS IN CLASS."
...HARD TO SAY YES TO THAT.
IF THE CLASS'S QUEEN BEE TURNS ON YOU, CONSIDER YOURSELF BANISHED.
NOBODY WOULD DARE GO AGAINST HER.
HAAAA...

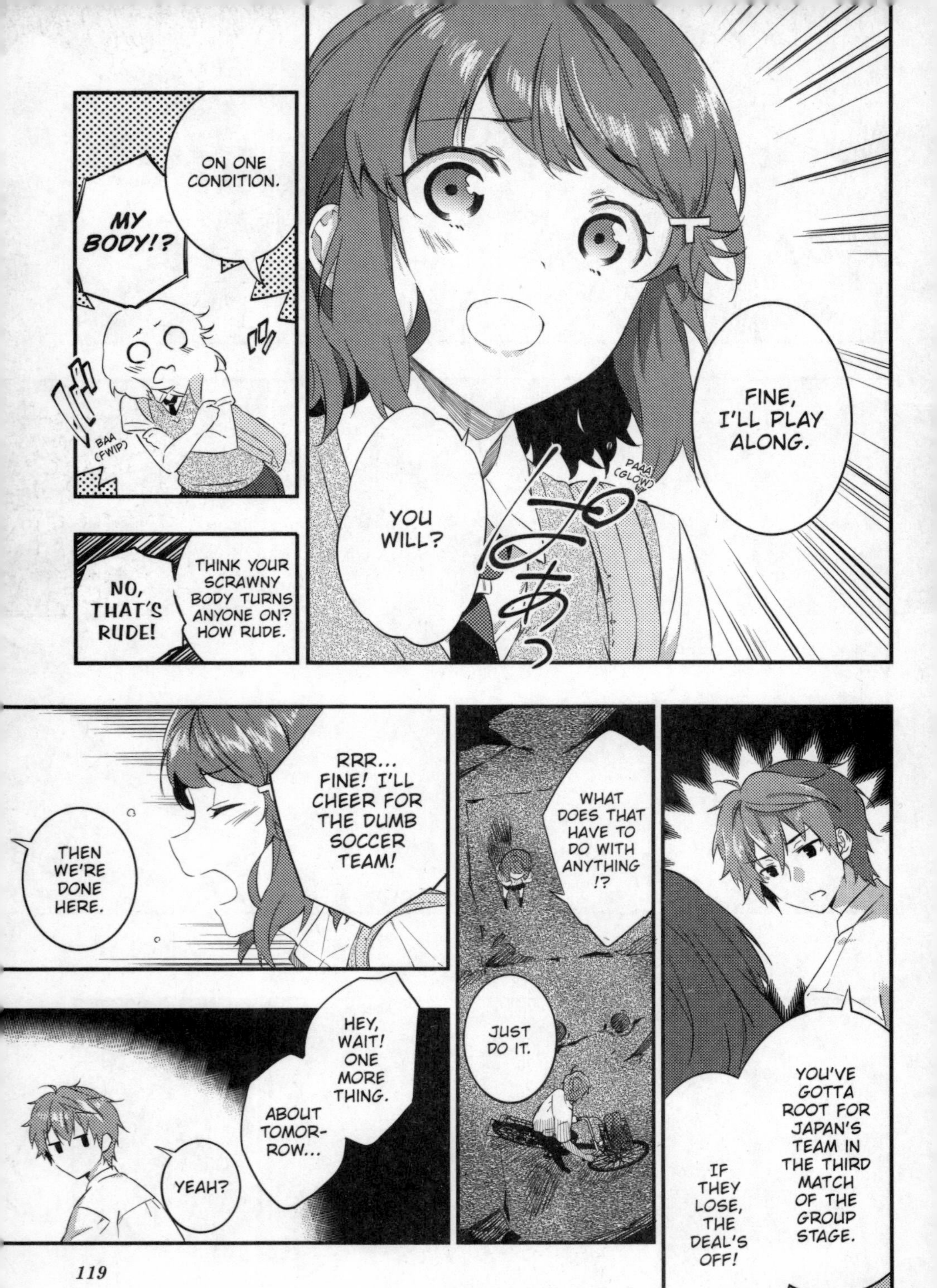
FINE, I'LL PLAY ALONG.
PAAA (GLOW)
YOU WILL?
ON ONE CONDITION.
MY BODY!?
BAA (FWIP)
THINK YOUR SCRAWNY BODY TURNS ANYONE ON? HOW RUDE.
NO, THAT'S RUDE!
YOU'VE GOTTA ROOT FOR JAPAN'S TEAM IN THE THIRD MATCH OF THE GROUP STAGE.
IF THEY LOSE, THE DEAL'S OFF!
WHAT DOES THAT HAVE TO DO WITH ANYTHING !?
JUST DO IT.
RRR... FINE! I'LL CHEER FOR THE DUMB SOCCER TEAM!
THEN WE'RE DONE HERE.
HEY, WAIT! ONE MORE THING.
ABOUT TOMOR-ROW...
YEAH?

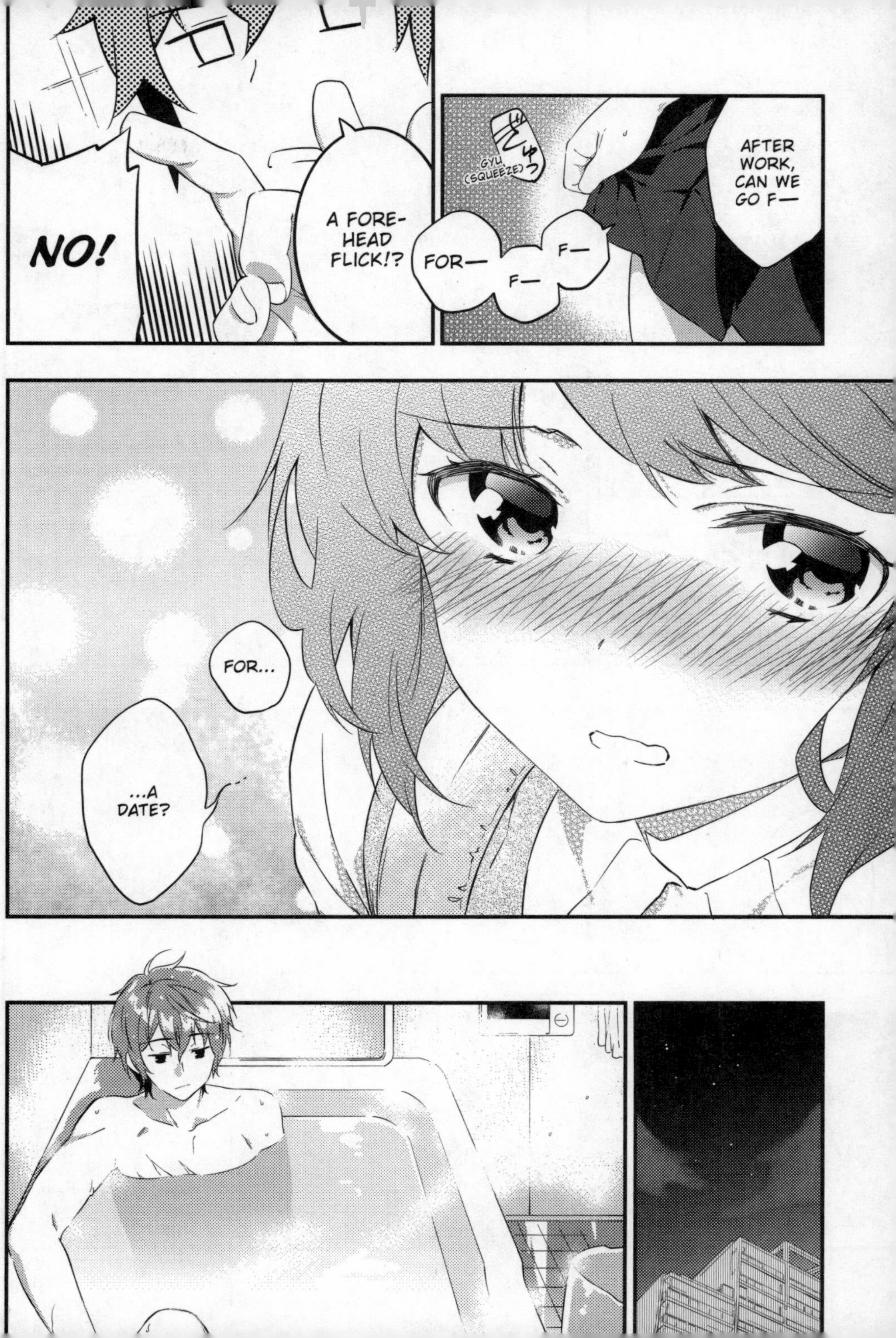
AFTER WORK, CAN WE GO F—
GYU (SQUEEZE)
FOR— F— F—
A FORE-HEAD FLICK!?
NO!
FOR...
...A DATE?

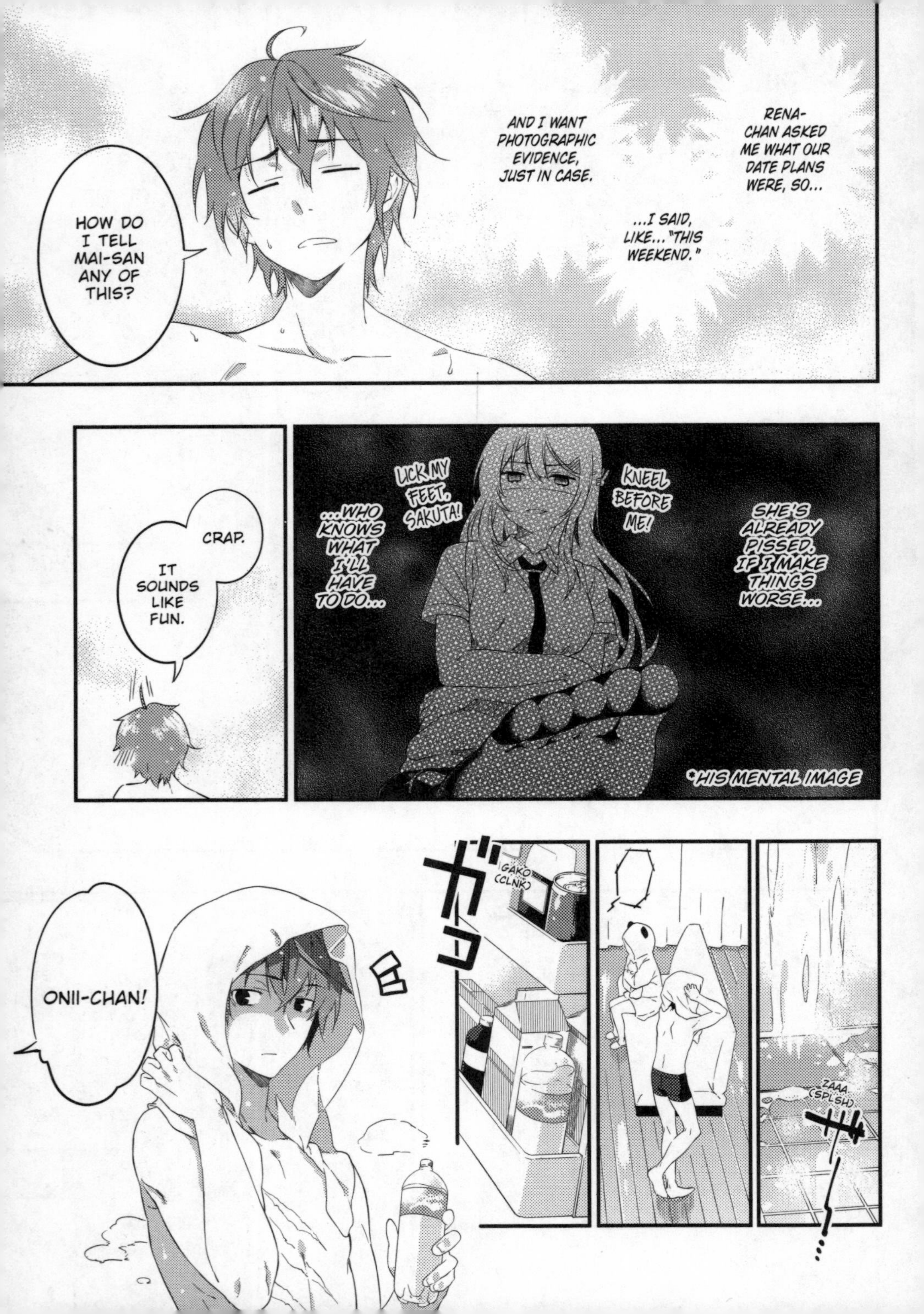
RENA-CHAN ASKED ME WHAT OUR DATE PLANS WERE, SO...
...I SAID, LIKE... "THIS WEEKEND."
AND I WANT PHOTOGRAPHIC EVIDENCE, JUST IN CASE.
HOW DO I TELL MAI-SAN ANY OF THIS?
SHE'S ALREADY PISSED. IF I MAKE THINGS WORSE...
KNEEL BEFORE ME!
LICK MY FEET, SAKUTA!
...WHO KNOWS WHAT I'LL HAVE TO DO...
*HIS MENTAL IMAGE
CRAP.
IT SOUNDS LIKE FUN.
ZAAA (SPLSH)
GAKO (CLNK)
ONII-CHAN!

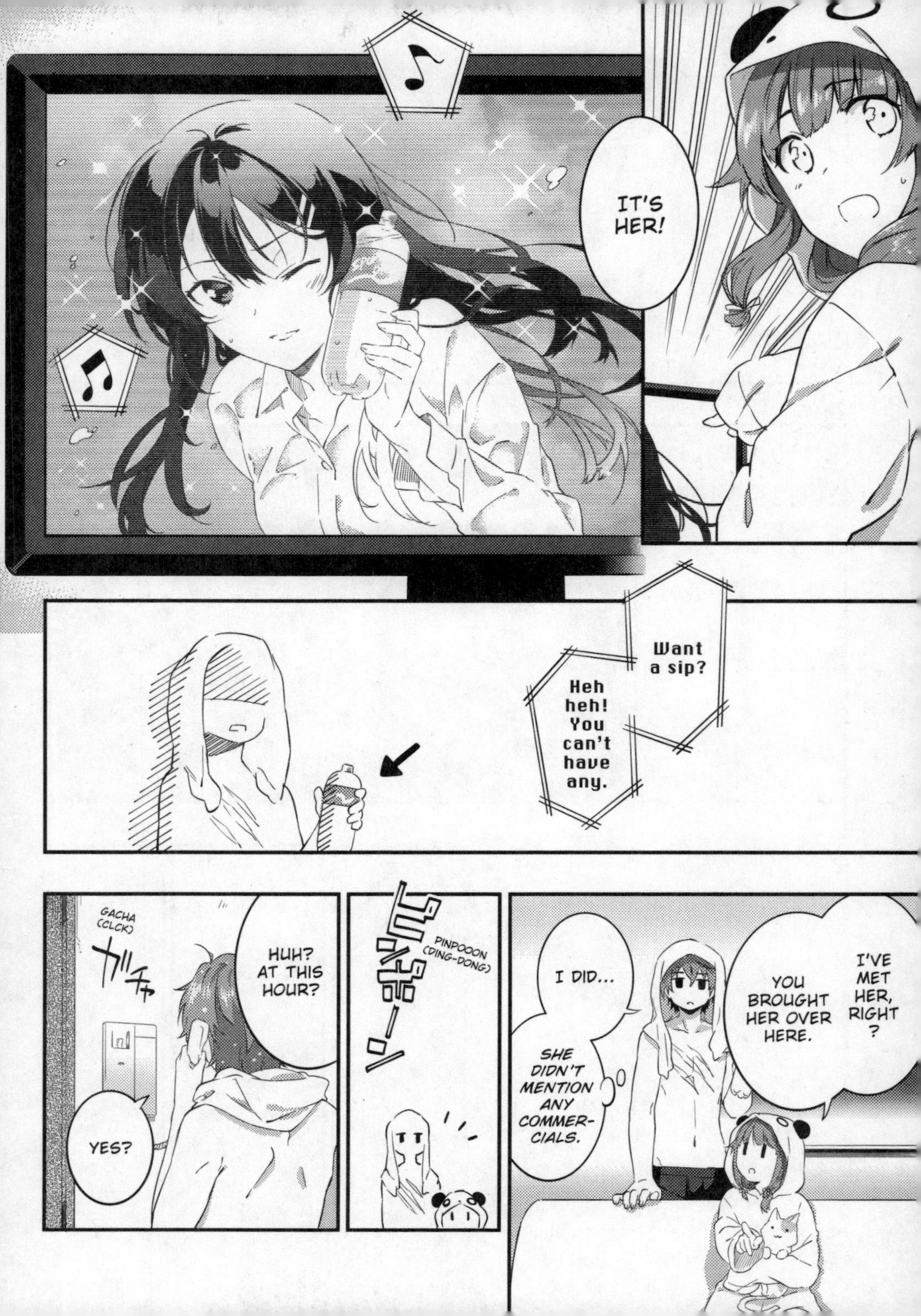
IT'S HER!
Want a sip?
Heh heh! You can't have any.
I'VE MET HER, RIGHT?
YOU BROUGHT HER OVER HERE.
I DID...
SHE DIDN'T MENTION ANY COMMERCIALS.
PINPOOON (DING-DONG)
GACHA (CLCK)
HUH? AT THIS HOUR?
YES?

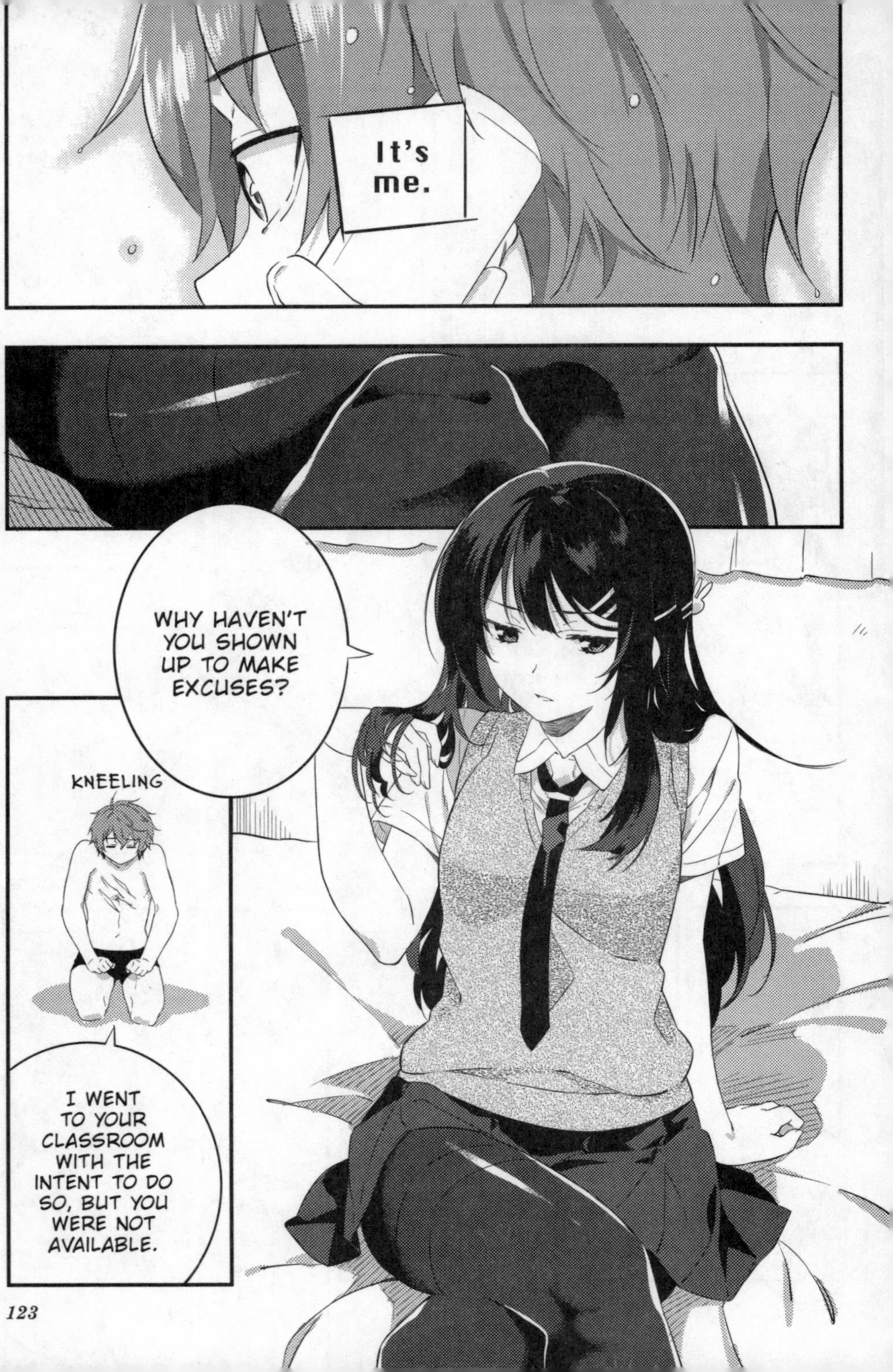
It's me.
WHY HAVEN'T YOU SHOWN UP TO MAKE EXCUSES?
KNEELING
I WENT TO YOUR CLASSROOM WITH THE INTENT TO DO SO, BUT YOU WERE NOT AVAILABLE.

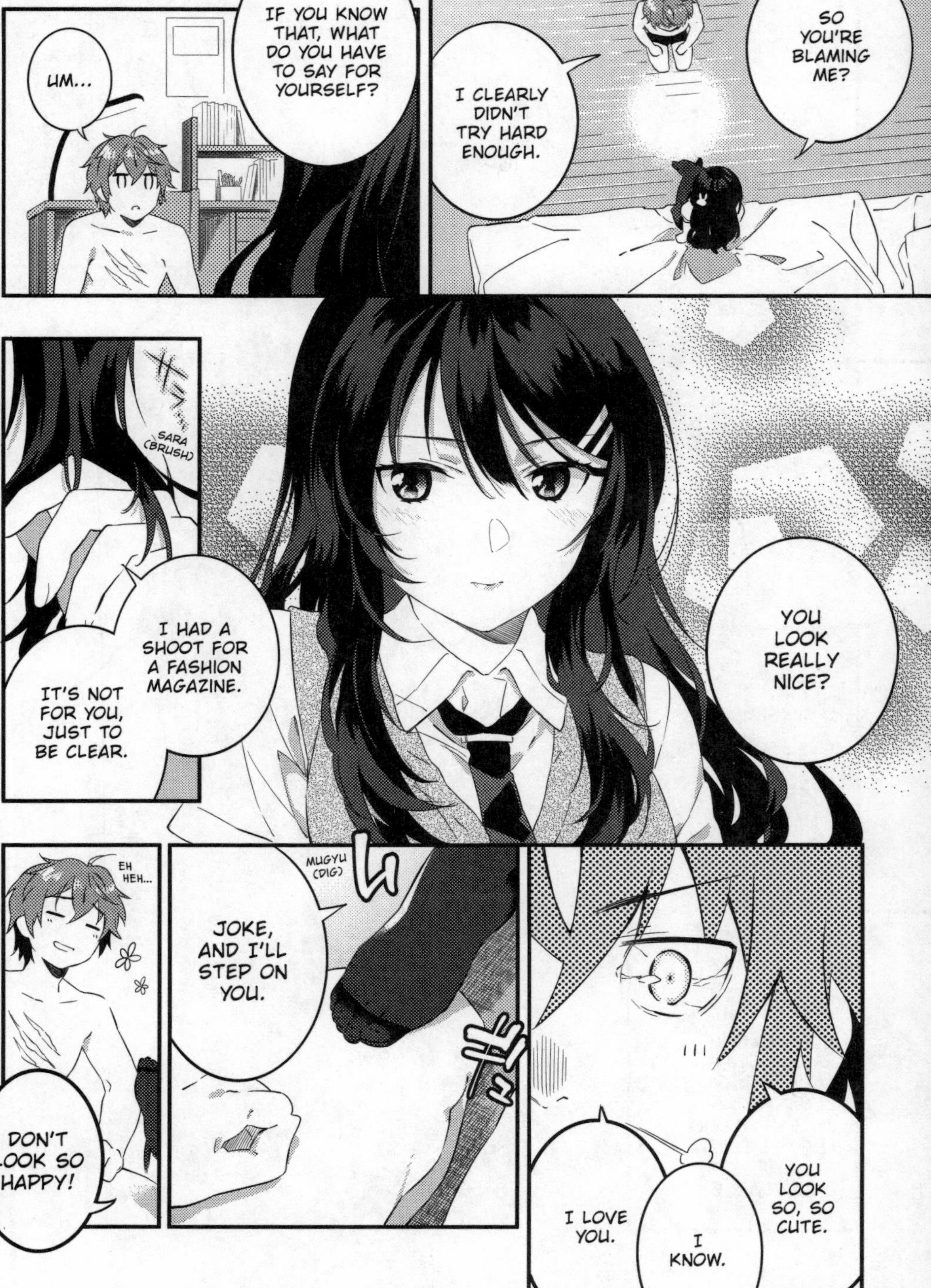
SO YOU'RE BLAMING ME?
I CLEARLY DIDN'T TRY HARD ENOUGH.
IF YOU KNOW THAT, WHAT DO YOU HAVE TO SAY FOR YOURSELF?
UM...
YOU LOOK REALLY NICE?
SARA (BRUSH)
I HAD A SHOOT FOR A FASHION MAGAZINE.
IT'S NOT FOR YOU, JUST TO BE CLEAR.
YOU LOOK SO, SO CUTE.
I LOVE YOU.
I KNOW.
MUGYU (DIG)
JOKE, AND I'LL STEP ON YOU.
EH HEH...
DON'T LOOK SO HAPPY!

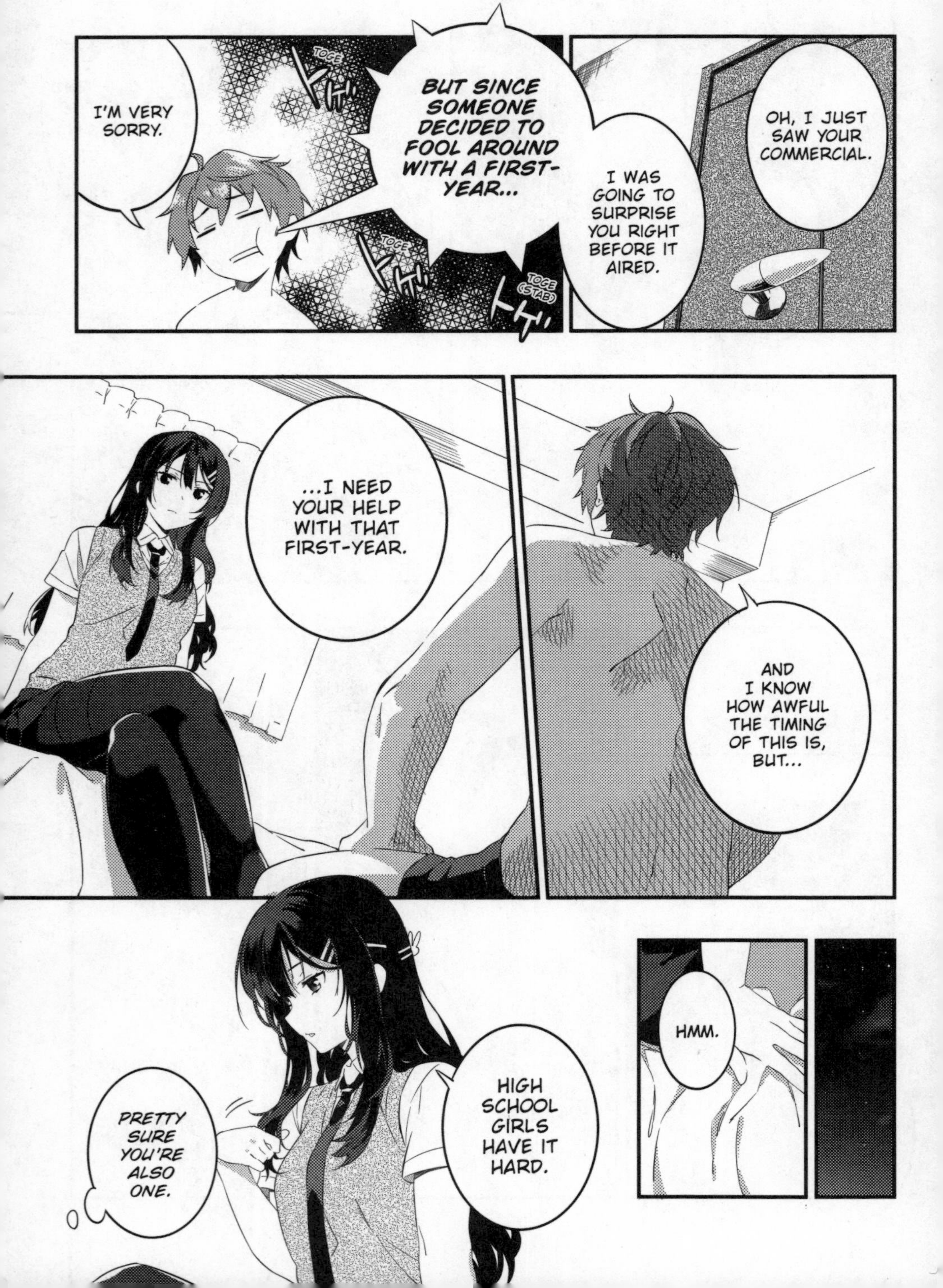
OH, I JUST SAW YOUR COMMERCIAL.
I WAS GOING TO SURPRISE YOU RIGHT BEFORE IT AIRED.
BUT SINCE SOMEONE DECIDED TO FOOL AROUND WITH A FIRST-YEAR...
TOGE
TOGE
TOGE (STAB)
I'M VERY SORRY.
AND I KNOW HOW AWFUL THE TIMING OF THIS IS, BUT...
...I NEED YOUR HELP WITH THAT FIRST-YEAR.
HMM.
HIGH SCHOOL GIRLS HAVE IT HARD.
PRETTY SURE YOU'RE ALSO ONE.

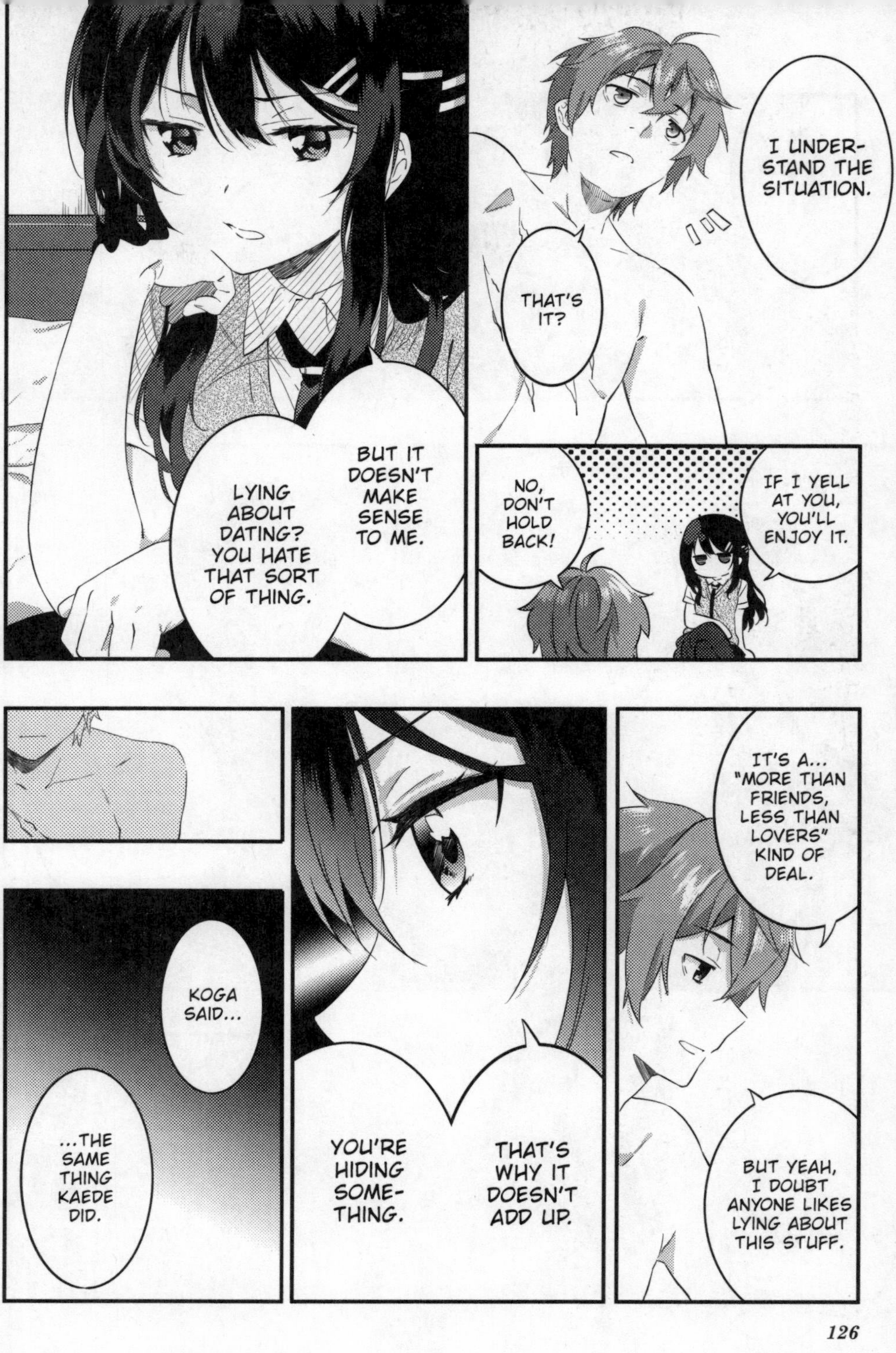
I UNDER-STAND THE SITUATION.
THAT'S IT?
IF I YELL AT YOU, YOU'LL ENJOY IT.
NO, DON'T HOLD BACK!
BUT IT DOESN'T MAKE SENSE TO ME.
LYING ABOUT DATING? YOU HATE THAT SORT OF THING.
IT'S A... "MORE THAN FRIENDS, LESS THAN LOVERS" KIND OF DEAL.
BUT YEAH, I DOUBT ANYONE LIKES LYING ABOUT THIS STUFF.
THAT'S WHY IT DOESN'T ADD UP.
YOU'RE HIDING SOME-THING.
KOGA SAID...
...THE SAME THING KAEDE DID.

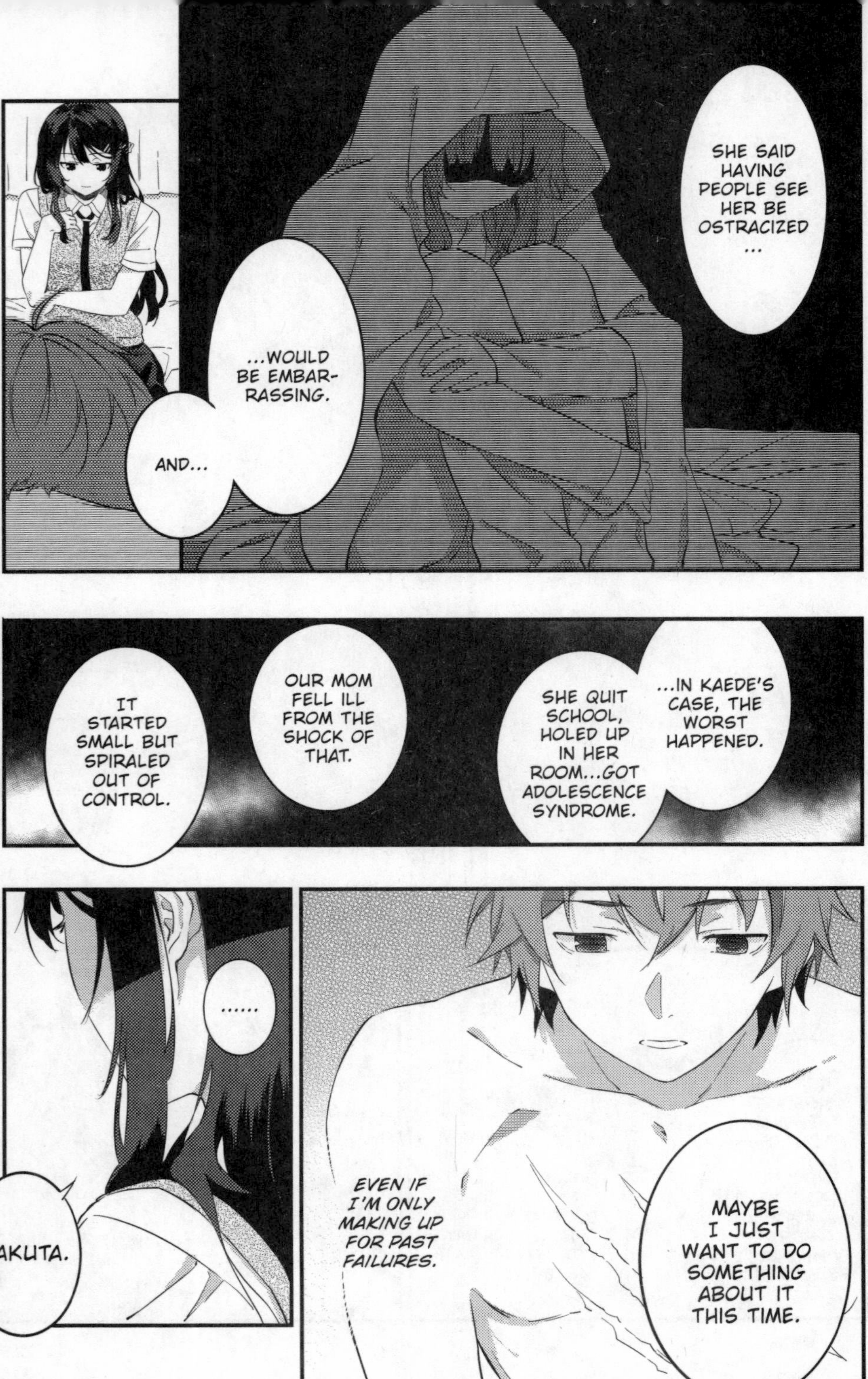
SHE SAID HAVING PEOPLE SEE HER BE OSTRACIZED ...
...WOULD BE EMBARRASSING.
AND...
...IN KAEDE'S CASE, THE WORST HAPPENED.
SHE QUIT SCHOOL, HOLED UP IN HER ROOM...GOT ADOLESCENCE SYNDROME.
OUR MOM FELL ILL FROM THE SHOCK OF THAT.
IT STARTED SMALL BUT SPIRALED OUT OF CONTROL.
MAYBE I JUST WANT TO DO SOMETHING ABOUT IT THIS TIME.
EVEN IF I'M ONLY MAKING UP FOR PAST FAILURES.
......
SAKUTA.

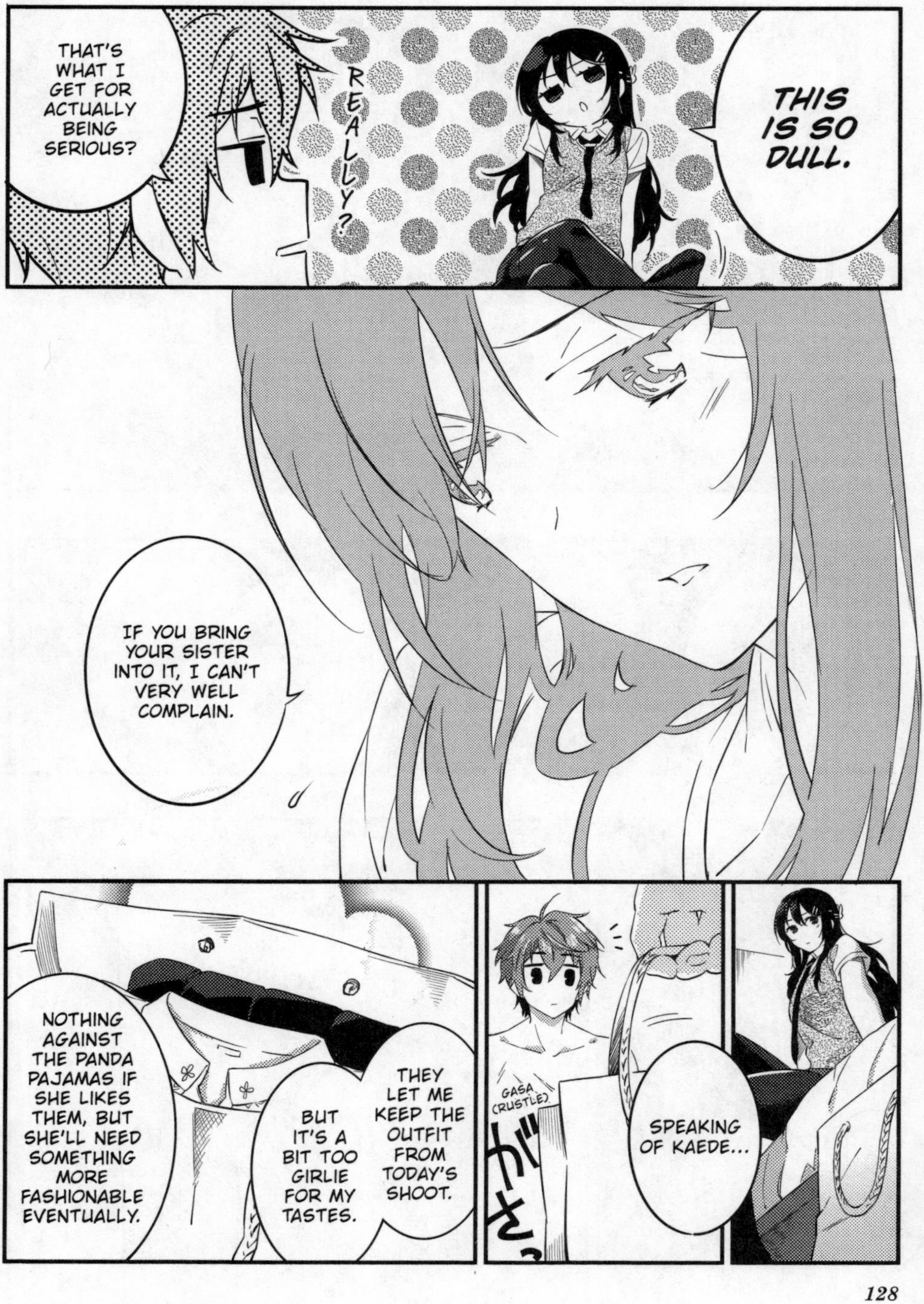
THIS IS SO DULL.
REALLY?
THAT'S WHAT I GET FOR ACTUALLY BEING SERIOUS?
IF YOU BRING YOUR SISTER INTO IT, I CAN'T VERY WELL COMPLAIN.
SPEAKING OF KAEDE...
GASA (RUSTLE)
がさっ
THEY LET ME KEEP THE OUTFIT FROM TODAY'S SHOOT.
BUT IT'S A BIT TOO GIRLIE FOR MY TASTES.
NOTHING AGAINST THE PANDA PAJAMAS IF SHE LIKES THEM, BUT SHE'LL NEED SOMETHING MORE FASHIONABLE EVENTUALLY.

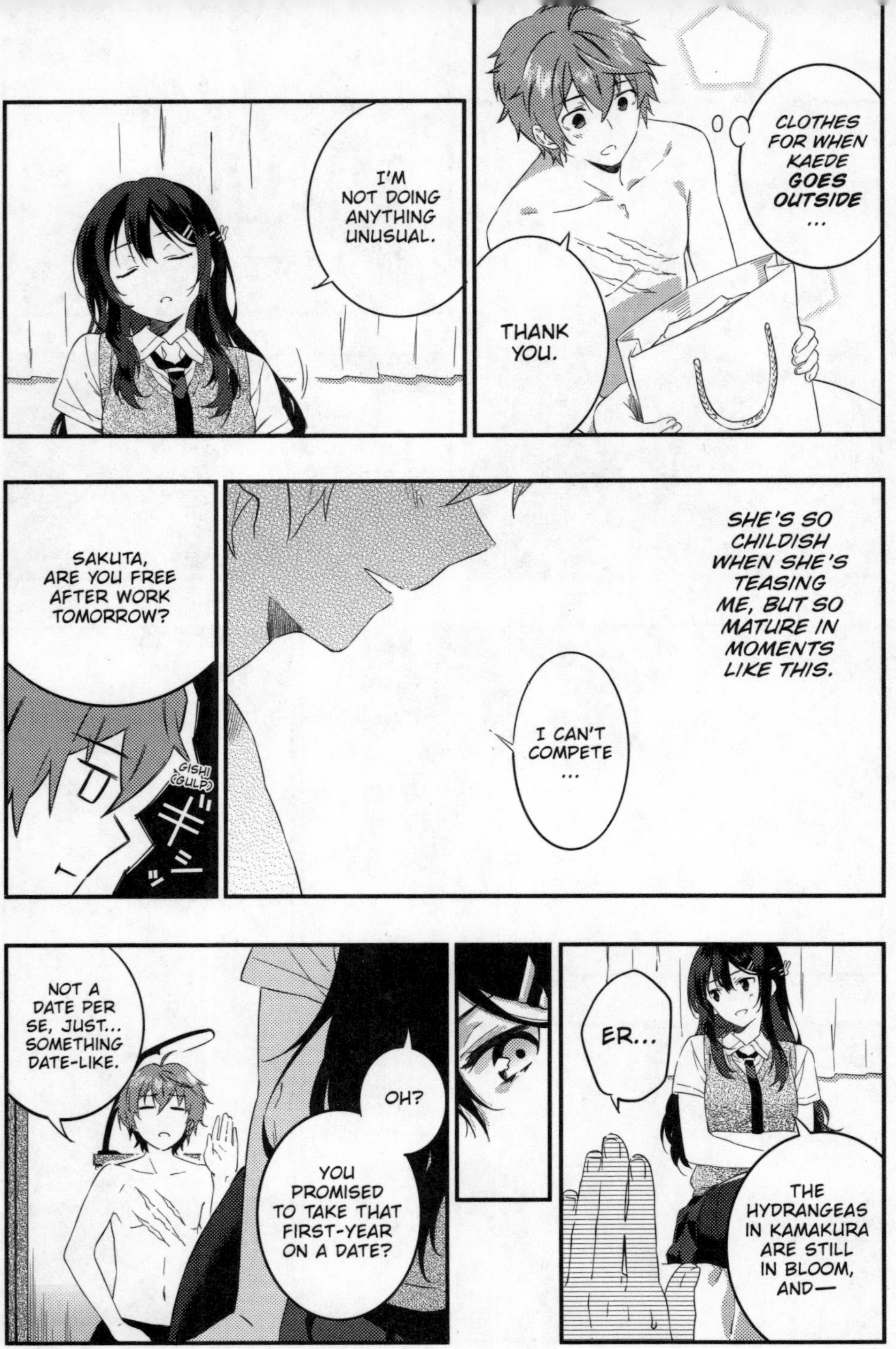
CLOTHES FOR WHEN KAEDE GOES OUTSIDE...
THANK YOU.
I'M NOT DOING ANYTHING UNUSUAL.
SHE'S SO CHILDISH WHEN SHE'S TEASING ME, BUT SO MATURE IN MOMENTS LIKE THIS.
I CAN'T COMPETE...
SAKUTA, ARE YOU FREE AFTER WORK TOMORROW?
GISHI (GULP)
ER...
THE HYDRANGEAS IN KAMAKURA ARE STILL IN BLOOM, AND—
OH?
YOU PROMISED TO TAKE THAT FIRST-YEAR ON A DATE?
NOT A DATE PER SE, JUST... SOMETHING DATE-LIKE.

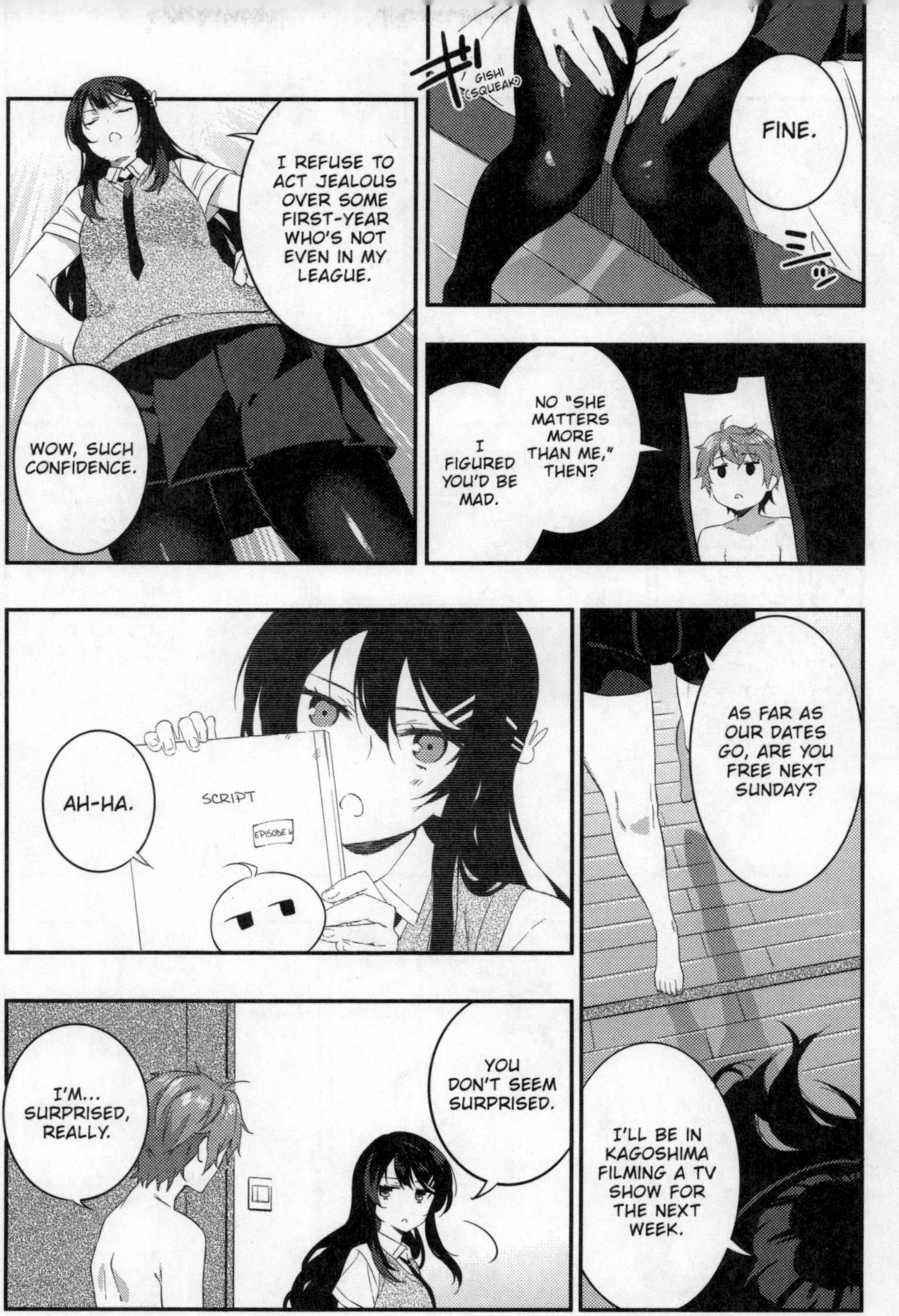
GISHI (SQUEAK)
FINE.
NO "SHE MATTERS MORE THAN ME," THEN?
I FIGURED YOU'D BE MAD.
I REFUSE TO ACT JEALOUS OVER SOME FIRST-YEAR WHO'S NOT EVEN IN MY LEAGUE.
WOW, SUCH CONFIDENCE.
AS FAR AS OUR DATES GO, ARE YOU FREE NEXT SUNDAY?
I'LL BE IN KAGOSHIMA FILMING A TV SHOW FOR THE NEXT WEEK.
AH-HA.
SCRIPT
EPISODE 4
YOU DON'T SEEM SURPRISED.
I'M... SURPRISED, REALLY.

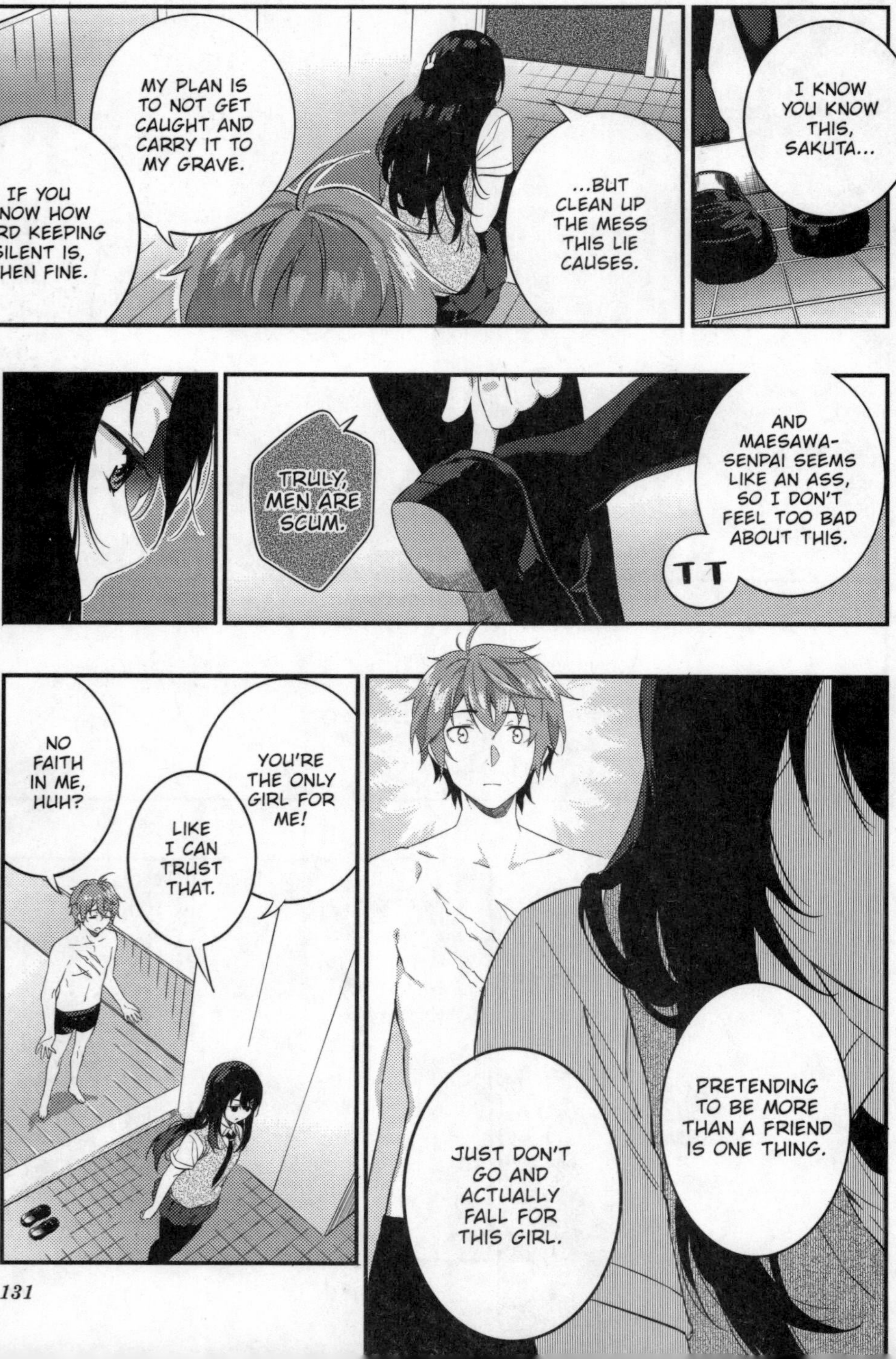
I KNOW YOU KNOW THIS, SAKUTA...
...BUT CLEAN UP THE MESS THIS LIE CAUSES.
MY PLAN IS TO NOT GET CAUGHT AND CARRY IT TO MY GRAVE.
IF YOU KNOW HOW HARD KEEPING SILENT IS, THEN FINE.
AND MAESAWA-SENPAI SEEMS LIKE AN ASS, SO I DON'T FEEL TOO BAD ABOUT THIS.
TT
TRULY, MEN ARE SCUM.
PRETENDING TO BE MORE THAN A FRIEND IS ONE THING.
JUST DON'T GO AND ACTUALLY FALL FOR THIS GIRL.
YOU'RE THE ONLY GIRL FOR ME!
LIKE I CAN TRUST THAT.
NO FAITH IN ME, HUH?

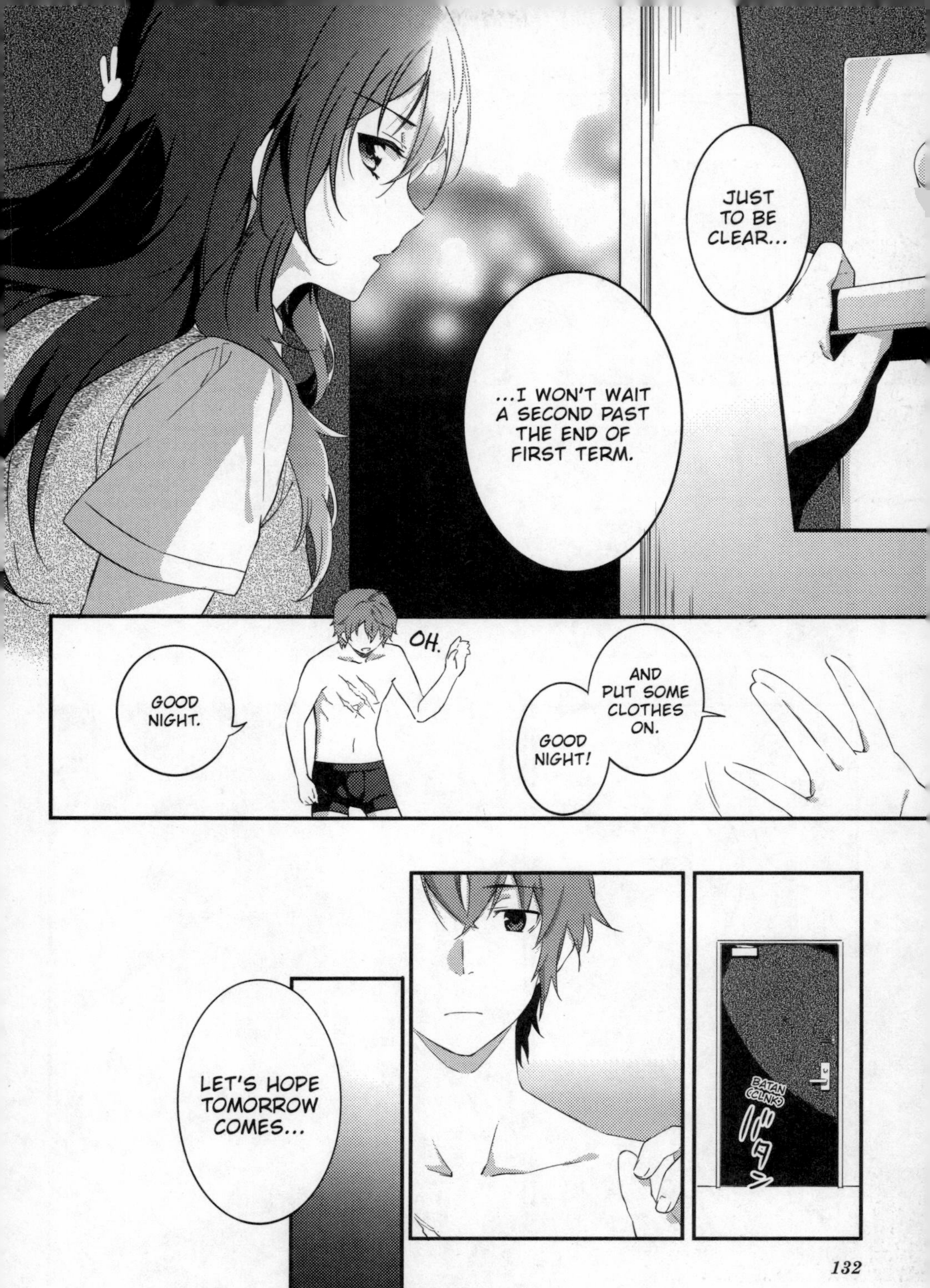
JUST TO BE CLEAR...
...I WON'T WAIT A SECOND PAST THE END OF FIRST TERM.
AND PUT SOME CLOTHES ON.
GOOD NIGHT!
OH.
GOOD NIGHT.
BATAN (CLNK)
バタン
LET'S HOPE TOMORROW COMES...

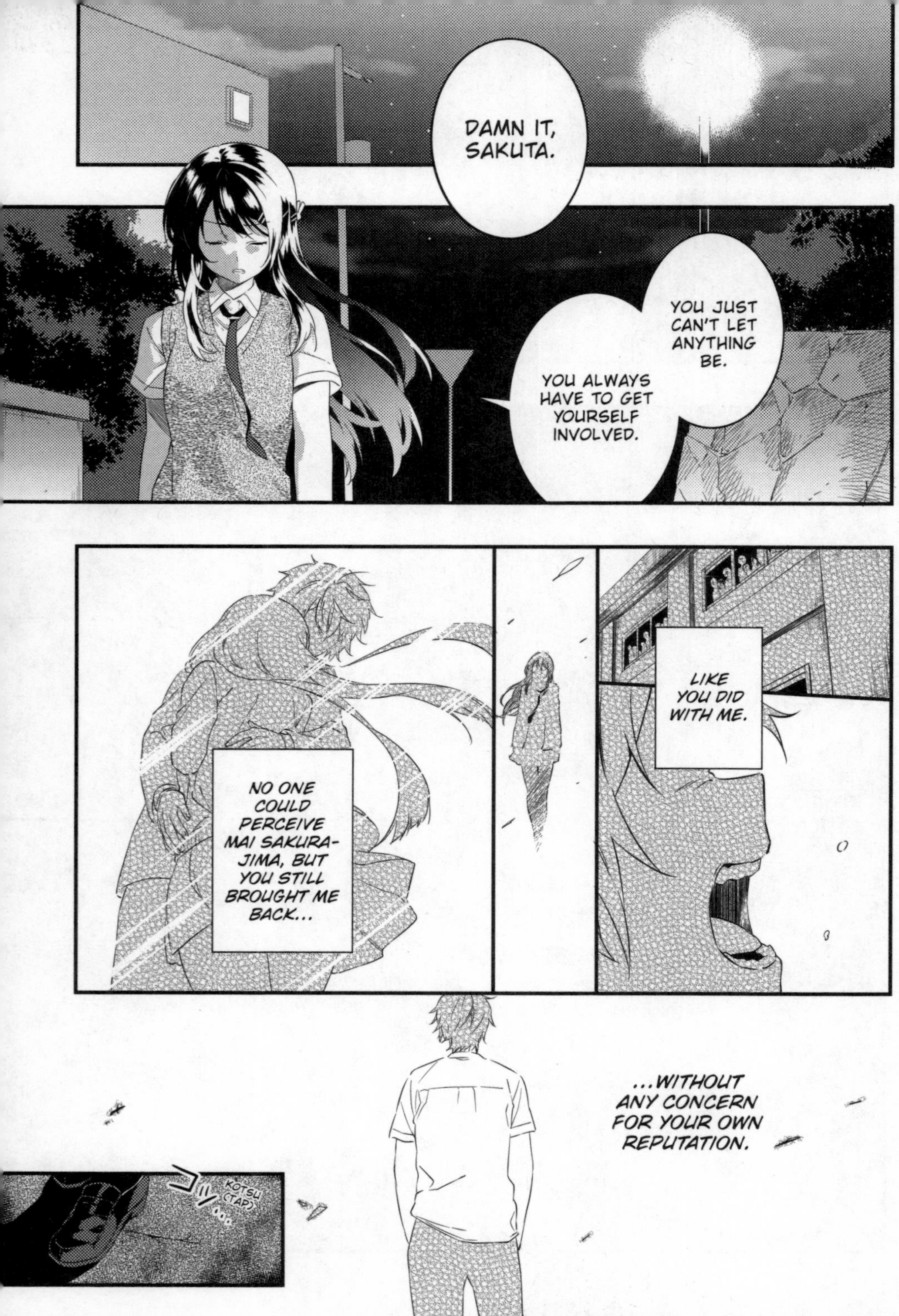
DAMN IT, SAKUTA.
YOU JUST CAN'T LET ANYTHING BE.
YOU ALWAYS HAVE TO GET YOURSELF INVOLVED.
LIKE YOU DID WITH ME.
NO ONE COULD PERCEIVE MAI SAKURA-JIMA, BUT YOU STILL BROUGHT ME BACK...
...WITHOUT ANY CONCERN FOR YOUR OWN REPUTATION.
KOTSU (TAP)

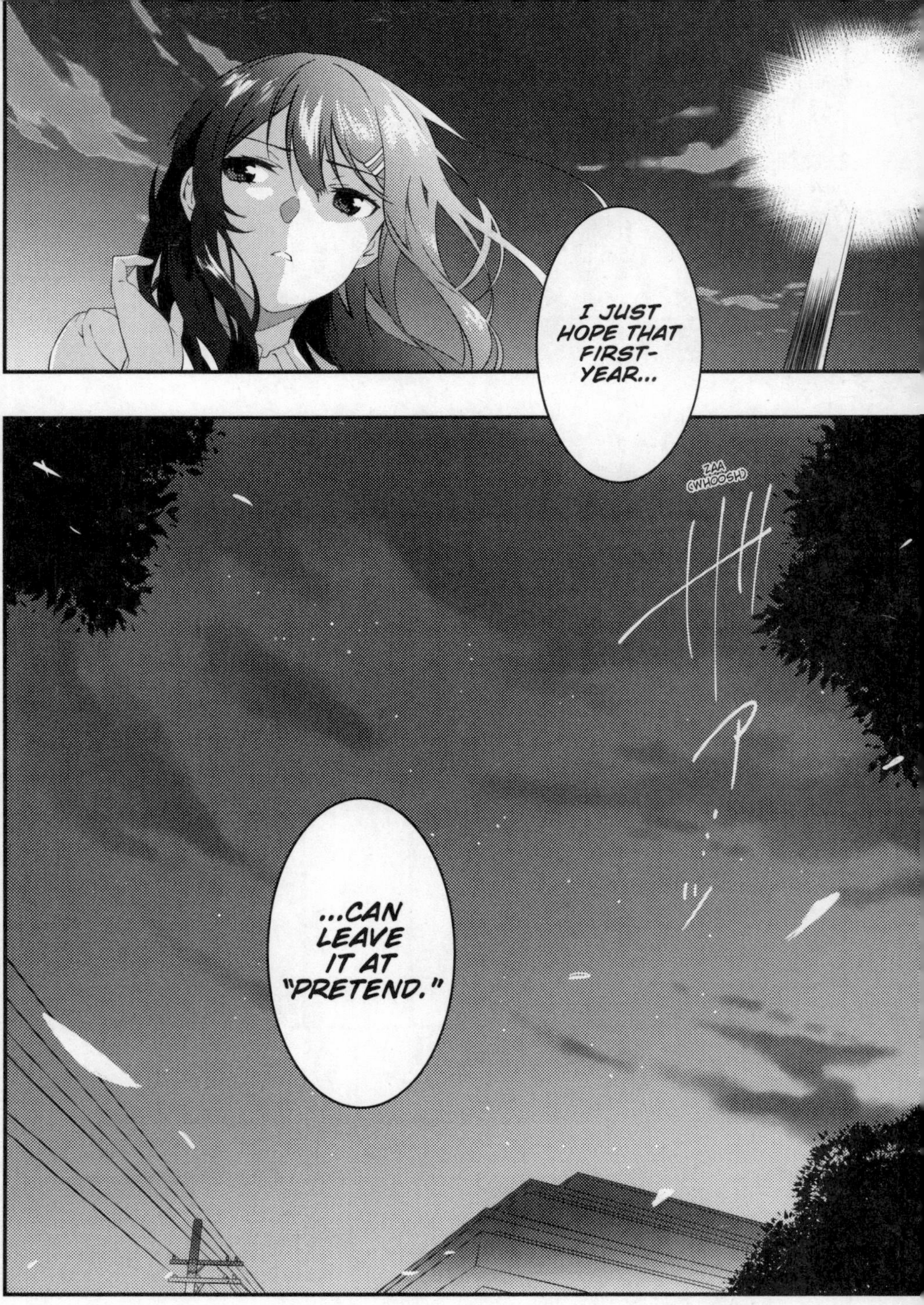
I JUST HOPE THAT FIRST-YEAR...
ZAA (WHOOSH)
...CAN LEAVE IT AT "PRETEND."

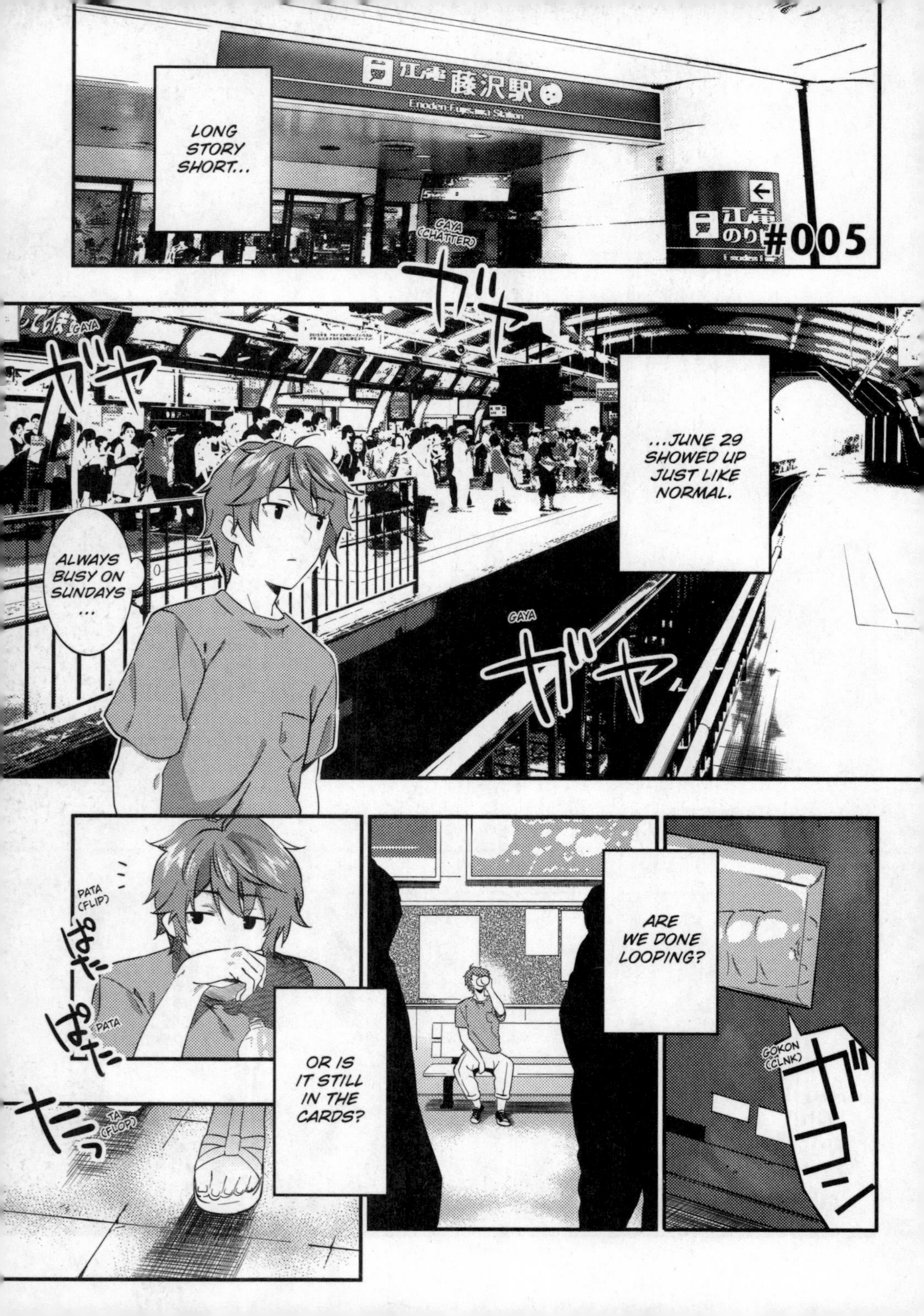
#005
LONG STORY SHORT...
GAYA (CHATTER)
...JUNE 29 SHOWED UP JUST LIKE NORMAL.
GAYA
ALWAYS BUSY ON SUNDAYS...
GAYA
GOKON (CLNK)
ARE WE DONE LOOPING?
OR IS IT STILL IN THE CARDS?
PATA (FLIP)
PATA
TA (FLOP)

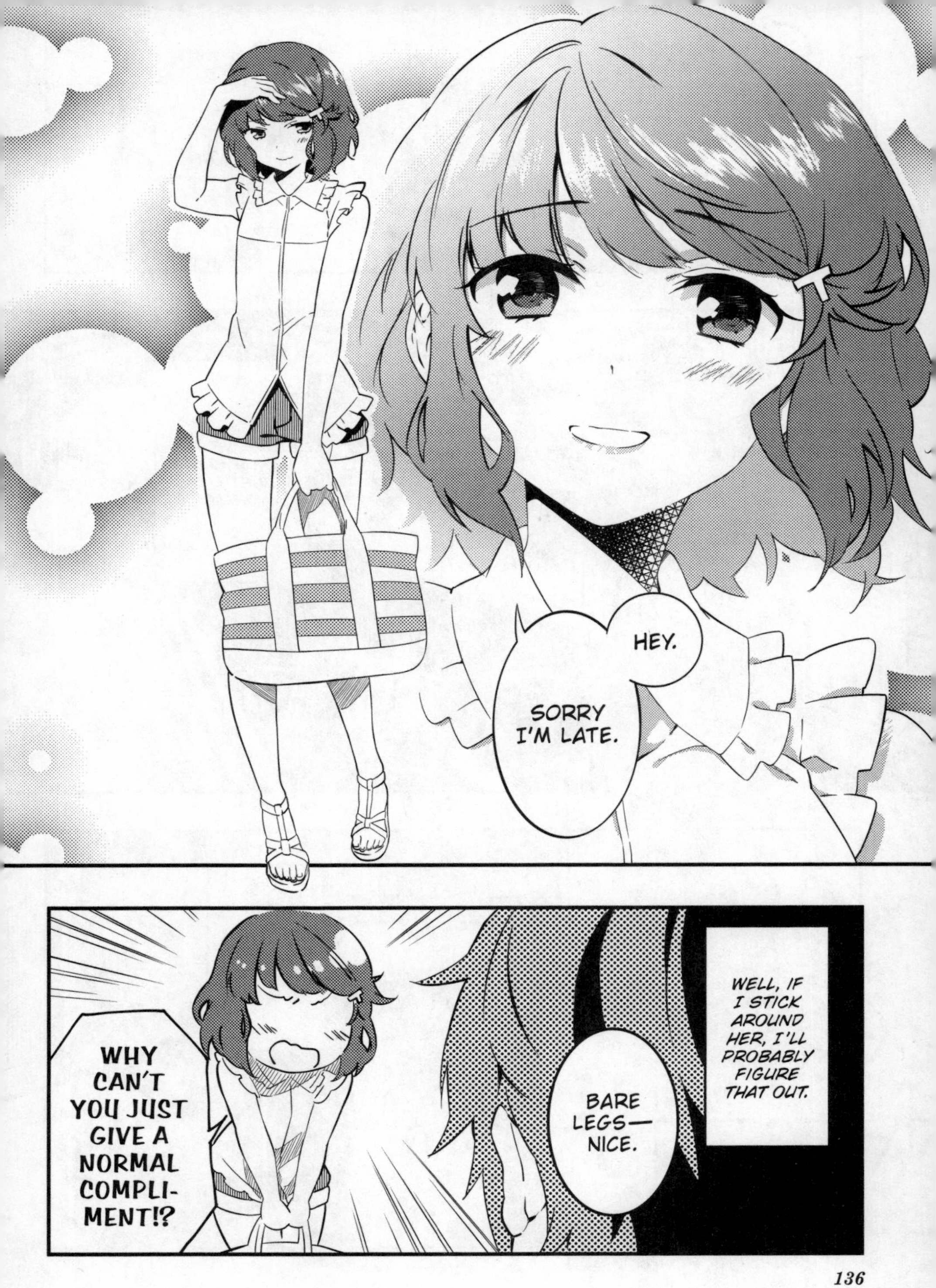
HEY.
SORRY I'M LATE.
WELL, IF I STICK AROUND HER, I'LL PROBABLY FIGURE THAT OUT.
BARE LEGS—NICE.
WHY CAN'T YOU JUST GIVE A NORMAL COMPLIMENT!?

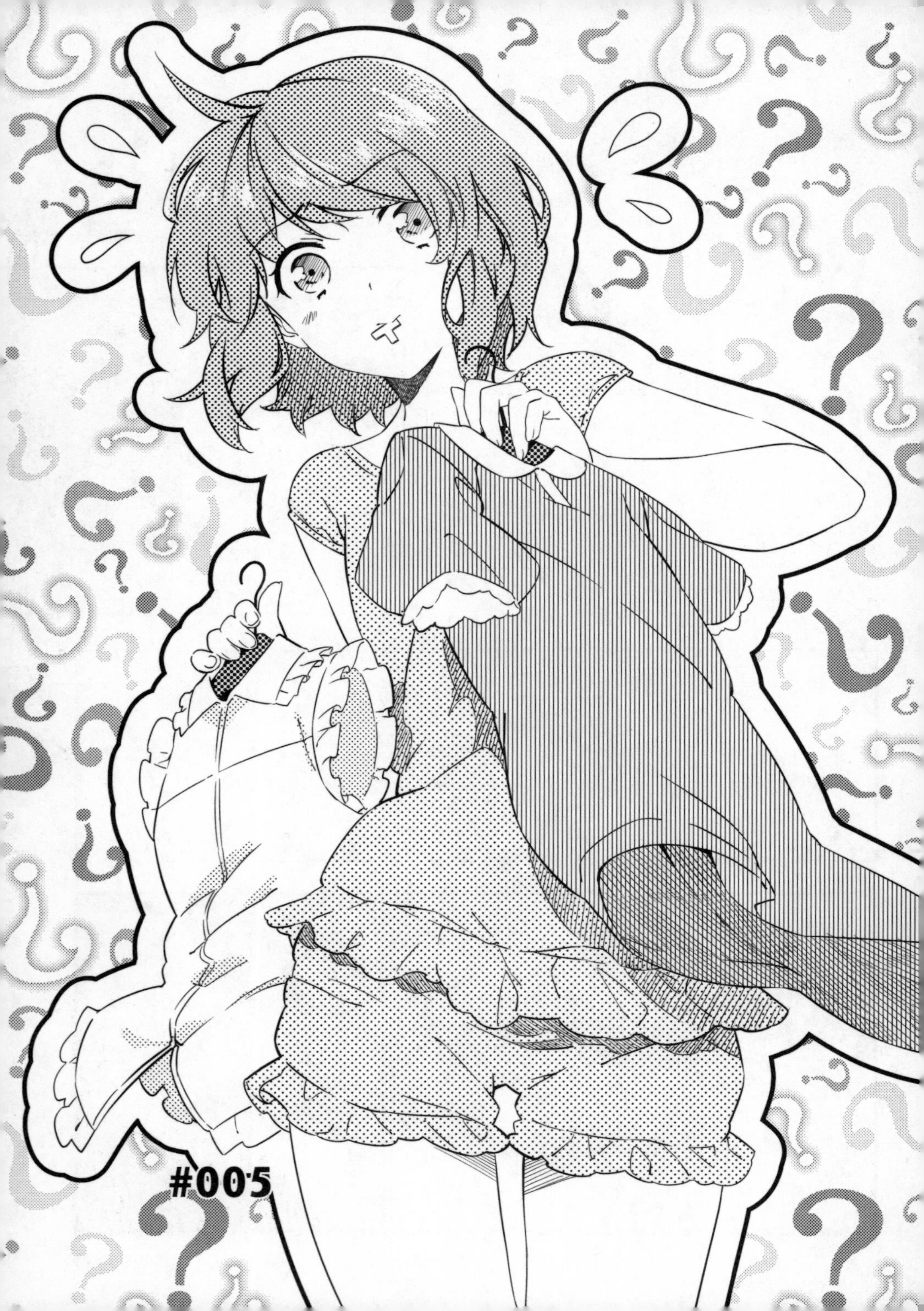
#005

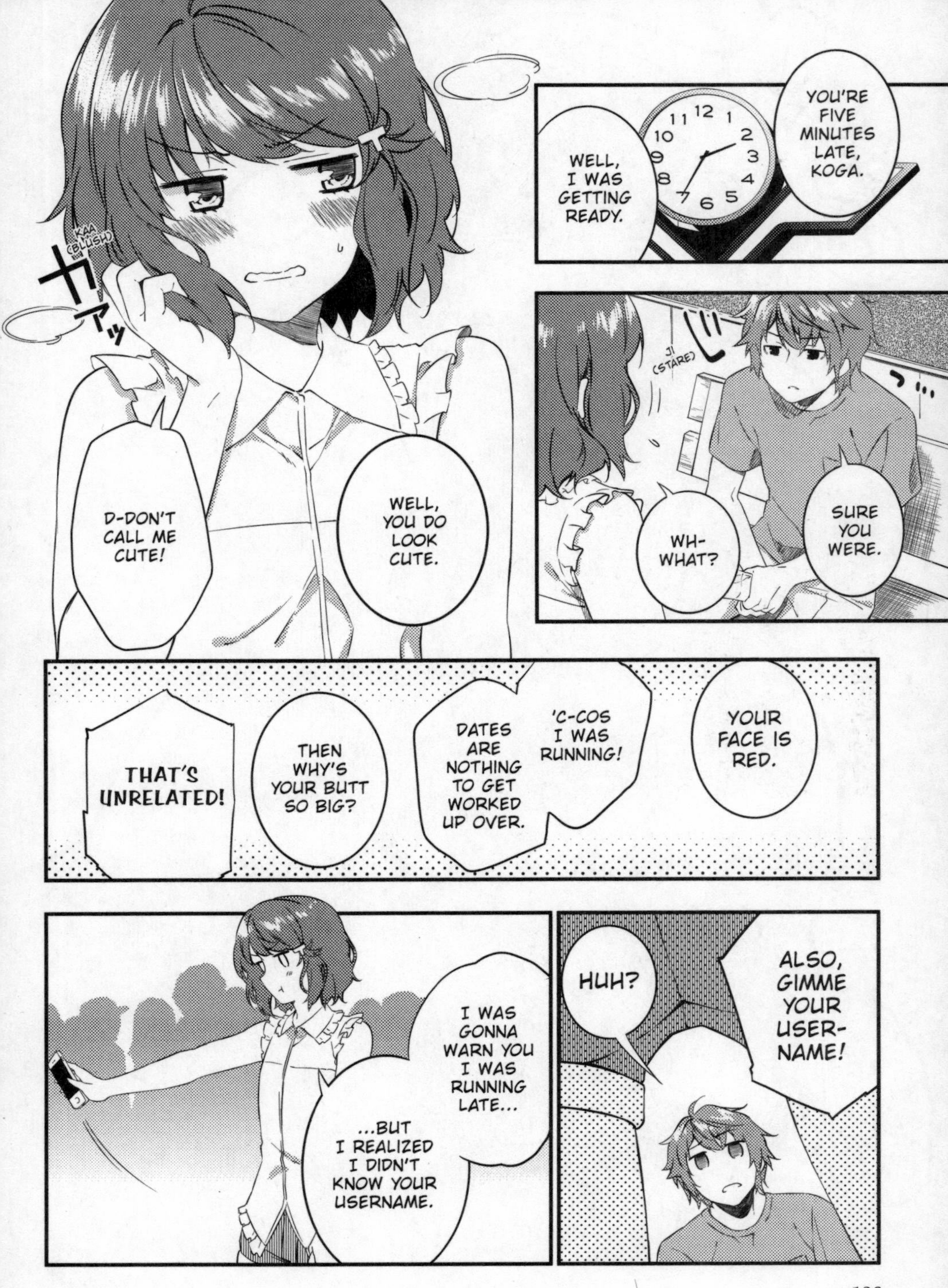
YOU'RE FIVE MINUTES LATE, KOGA.
WELL, I WAS GETTING READY.
JI (STARE)
SURE YOU WERE.
WH-WHAT?
KAA (BLUSH)
WELL, YOU DO LOOK CUTE.
D-DON'T CALL ME CUTE!
YOUR FACE IS RED.
'C-COS I WAS RUNNING!
DATES ARE NOTHING TO GET WORKED UP OVER.
THEN WHY'S YOUR BUTT SO BIG?
THAT'S UNRELATED!
ALSO, GIMME YOUR USER-NAME!
HUH?
I WAS GONNA WARN YOU I WAS RUNNING LATE...
...BUT I REALIZED I DIDN'T KNOW YOUR USERNAME.

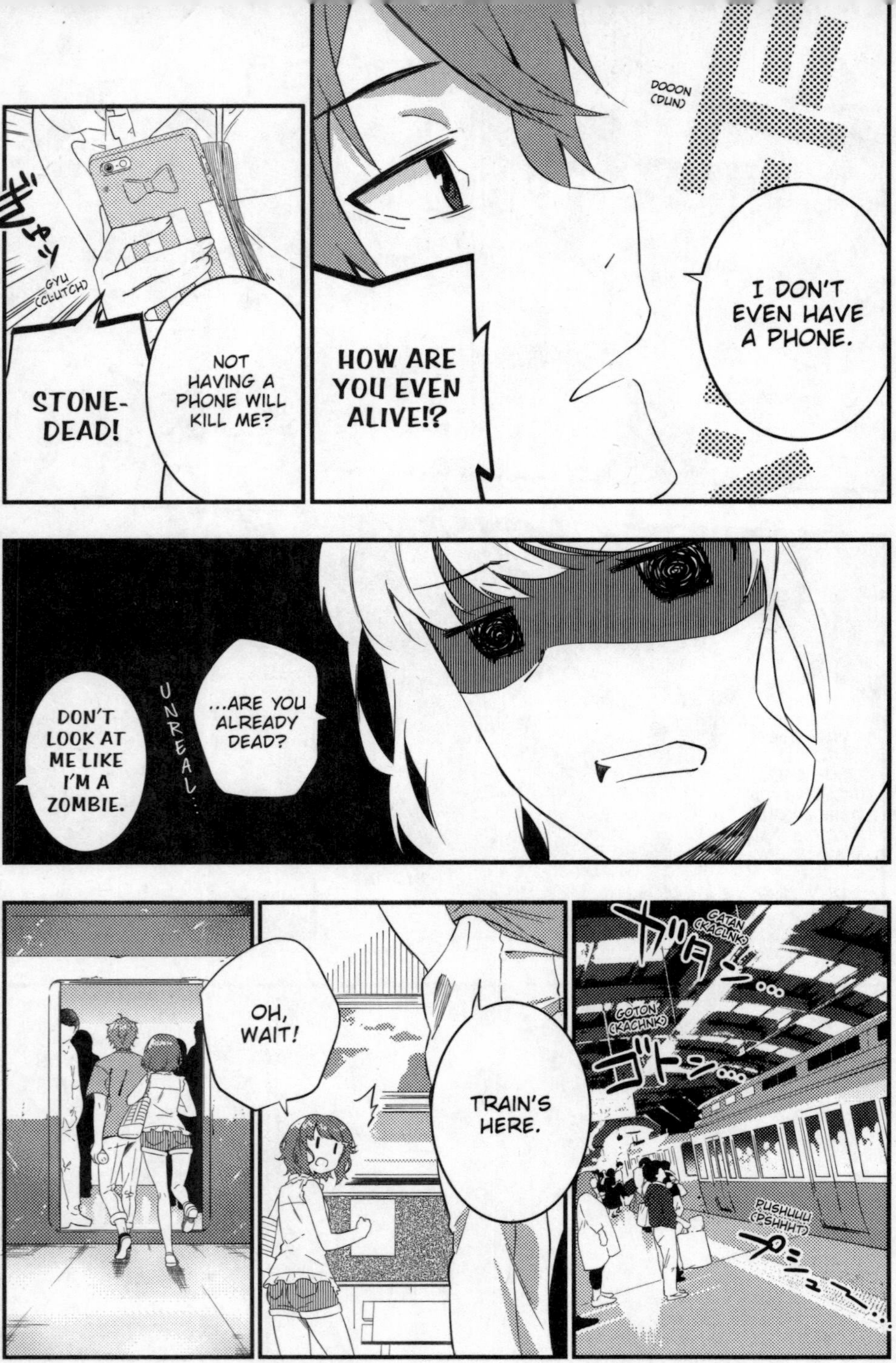
DOOON (DUN)
I DON'T EVEN HAVE A PHONE.
HOW ARE YOU EVEN ALIVE!?
NOT HAVING A PHONE WILL KILL ME?
GYU (CLUTCH)
STONE-DEAD!
...ARE YOU ALREADY DEAD?
UNREAL...
DON'T LOOK AT ME LIKE I'M A ZOMBIE.
GATAN (KACLNK)
GOTON (KACHNK)
PUSHUUU (PSHHHT)
TRAIN'S HERE.
OH, WAIT!

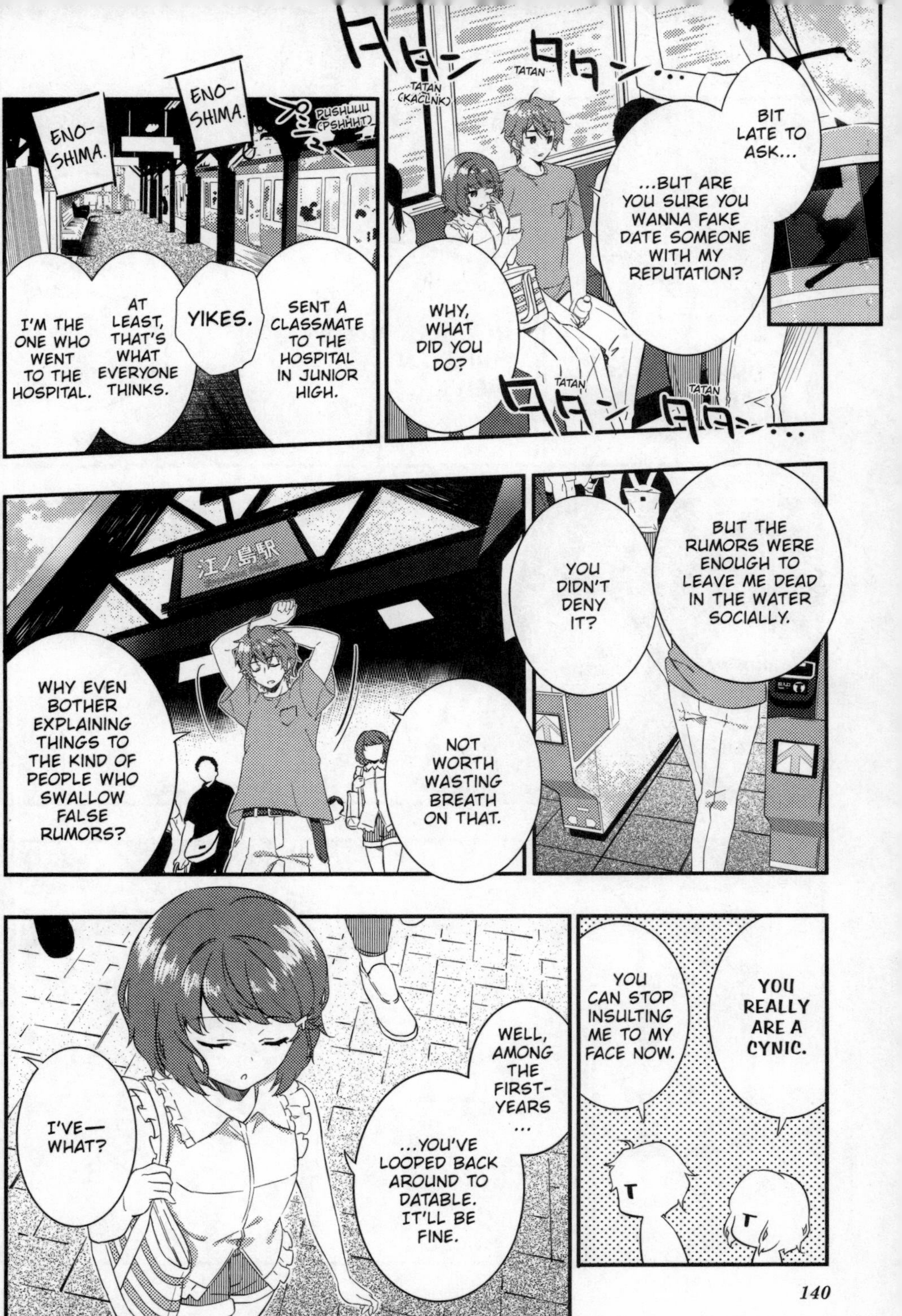
TATAN (KACLNK)
TATAN
BIT LATE TO ASK...
...BUT ARE YOU SURE YOU WANNA FAKE DATE SOMEONE WITH MY REPUTATION?
WHY, WHAT DID YOU DO?
TATAN
TATAN
ENO-SHIMA.
ENO-SHIMA.
PUSHUUU (PSHHHT)
SENT A CLASSMATE TO THE HOSPITAL IN JUNIOR HIGH.
YIKES.
AT LEAST, THAT'S WHAT EVERYONE THINKS.
I'M THE ONE WHO WENT TO THE HOSPITAL.
BUT THE RUMORS WERE ENOUGH TO LEAVE ME DEAD IN THE WATER SOCIALLY.
YOU DIDN'T DENY IT?
江ノ島駅
NOT WORTH WASTING BREATH ON THAT.
WHY EVEN BOTHER EXPLAINING THINGS TO THE KIND OF PEOPLE WHO SWALLOW FALSE RUMORS?
YOU REALLY ARE A CYNIC.
YOU CAN STOP INSULTING ME TO MY FACE NOW.
WELL, AMONG THE FIRST-YEARS...
...YOU'VE LOOPED BACK AROUND TO DATABLE. IT'LL BE FINE.
I'VE— WHAT?

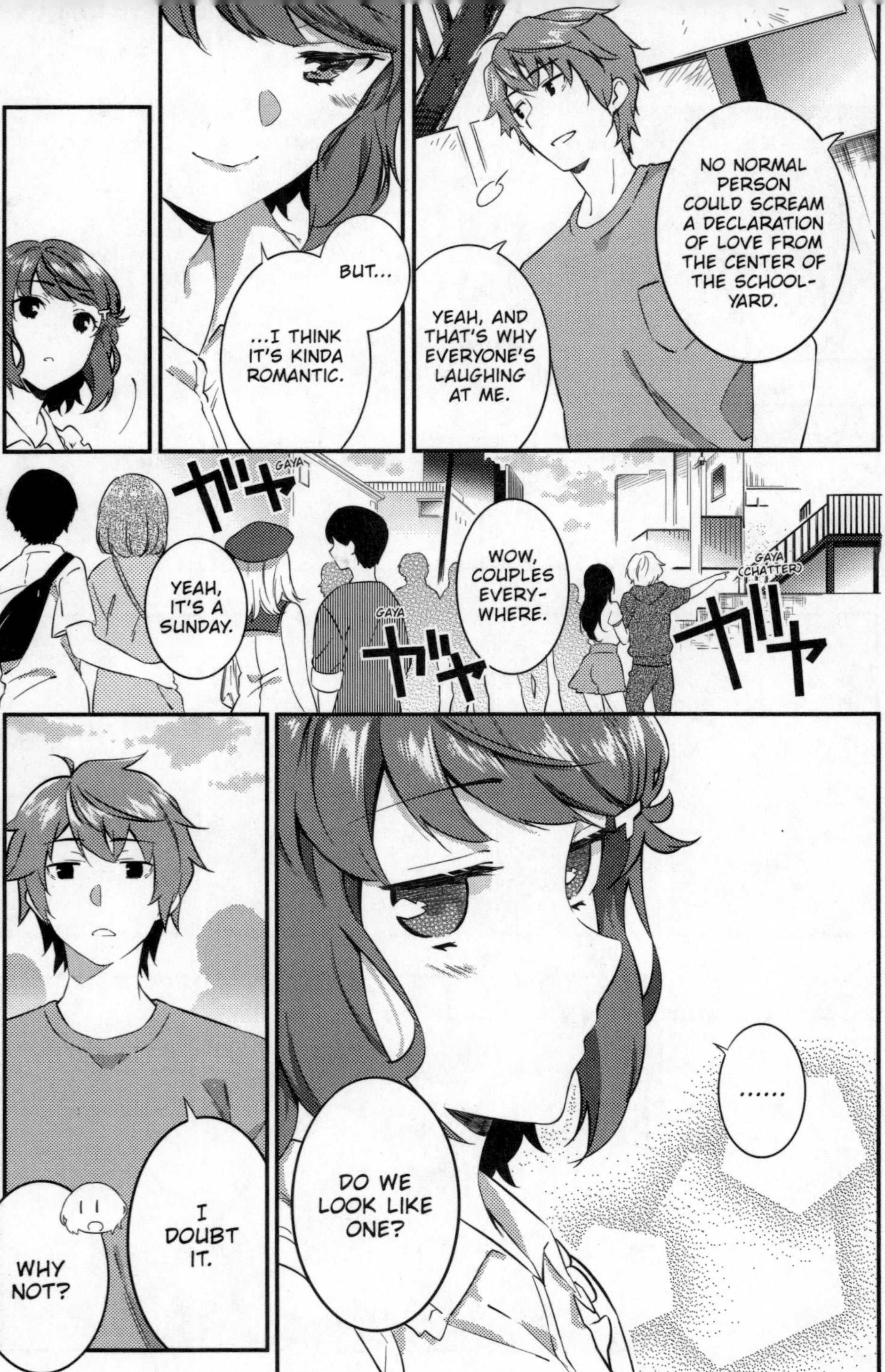
NO NORMAL PERSON COULD SCREAM A DECLARATION OF LOVE FROM THE CENTER OF THE SCHOOL-YARD.
YEAH, AND THAT'S WHY EVERYONE'S LAUGHING AT ME.
BUT...
...I THINK IT'S KINDA ROMANTIC.
GAYA (CHATTER)
WOW, COUPLES EVERY-WHERE.
GAYA
YEAH, IT'S A SUNDAY.
GAYA
......
DO WE LOOK LIKE ONE?
I DOUBT IT.
WHY NOT?

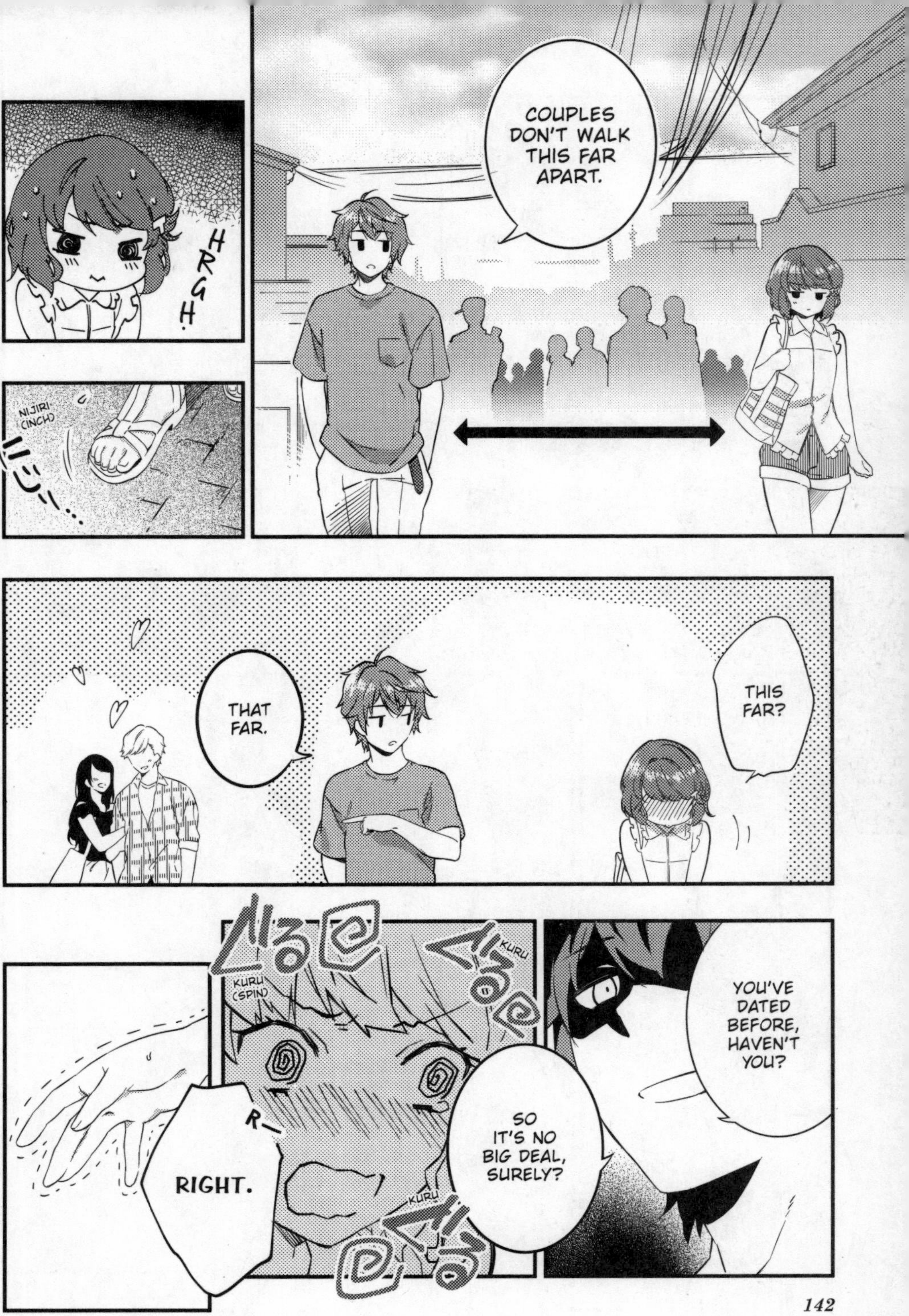
COUPLES DON'T WALK THIS FAR APART.
HRGH.
NIJIRI (INCH)
ニジリ…
THIS FAR?
THAT FAR.
YOU'VE DATED BEFORE, HAVEN'T YOU?
SO IT'S NO BIG DEAL, SURELY?
KURU
KURU (SPIN)
KURU
R—
RIGHT.

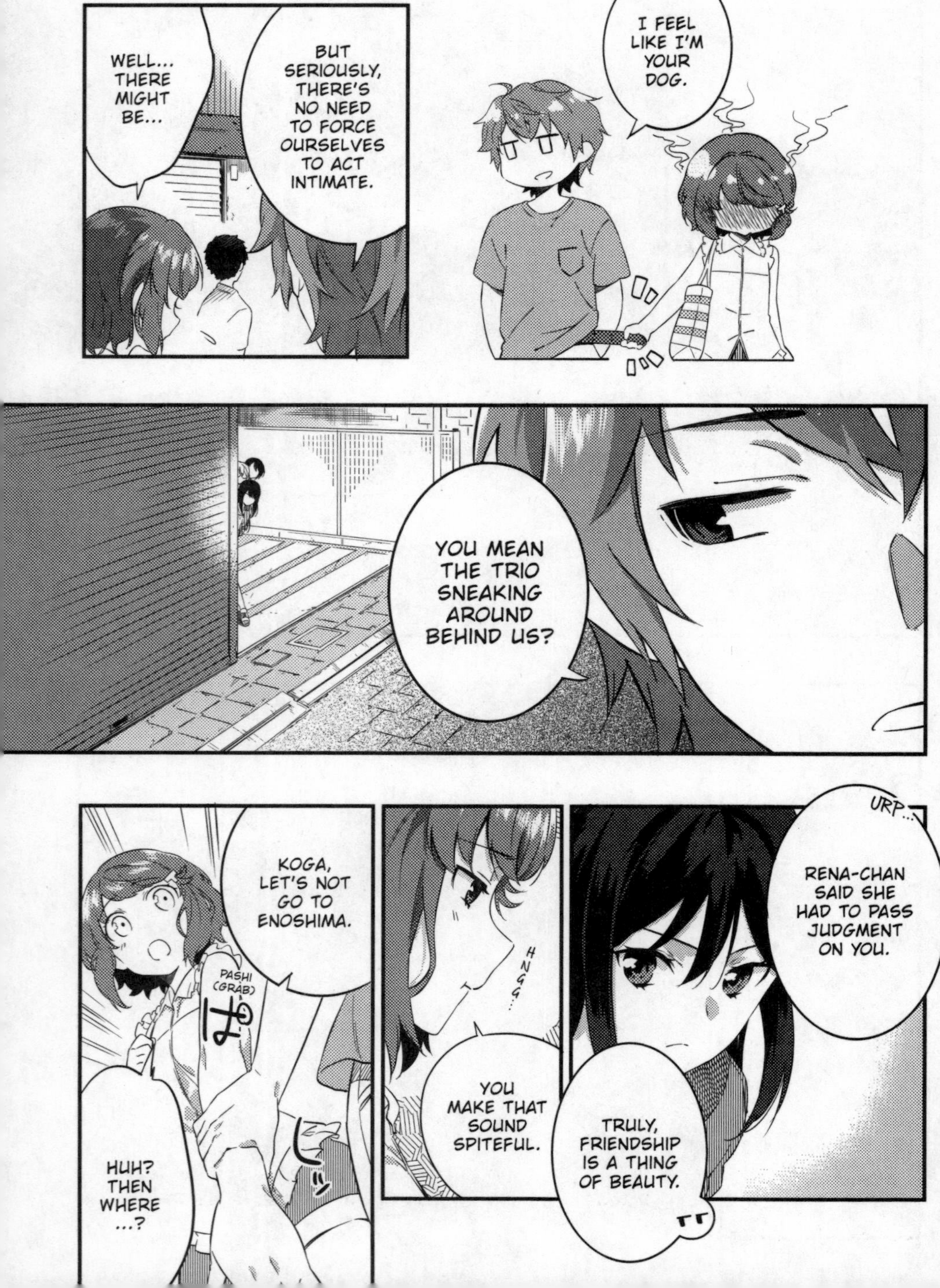
I FEEL LIKE I'M YOUR DOG.
BUT SERIOUSLY, THERE'S NO NEED TO FORCE OURSELVES TO ACT INTIMATE.
WELL... THERE MIGHT BE...
YOU MEAN THE TRIO SNEAKING AROUND BEHIND US?
URP...
RENA-CHAN SAID SHE HAD TO PASS JUDGMENT ON YOU.
TRULY, FRIENDSHIP IS A THING OF BEAUTY.
HNGG...
YOU MAKE THAT SOUND SPITEFUL.
KOGA, LET'S NOT GO TO ENOSHIMA.
PASHI (GRAB)
HUH? THEN WHERE ...?

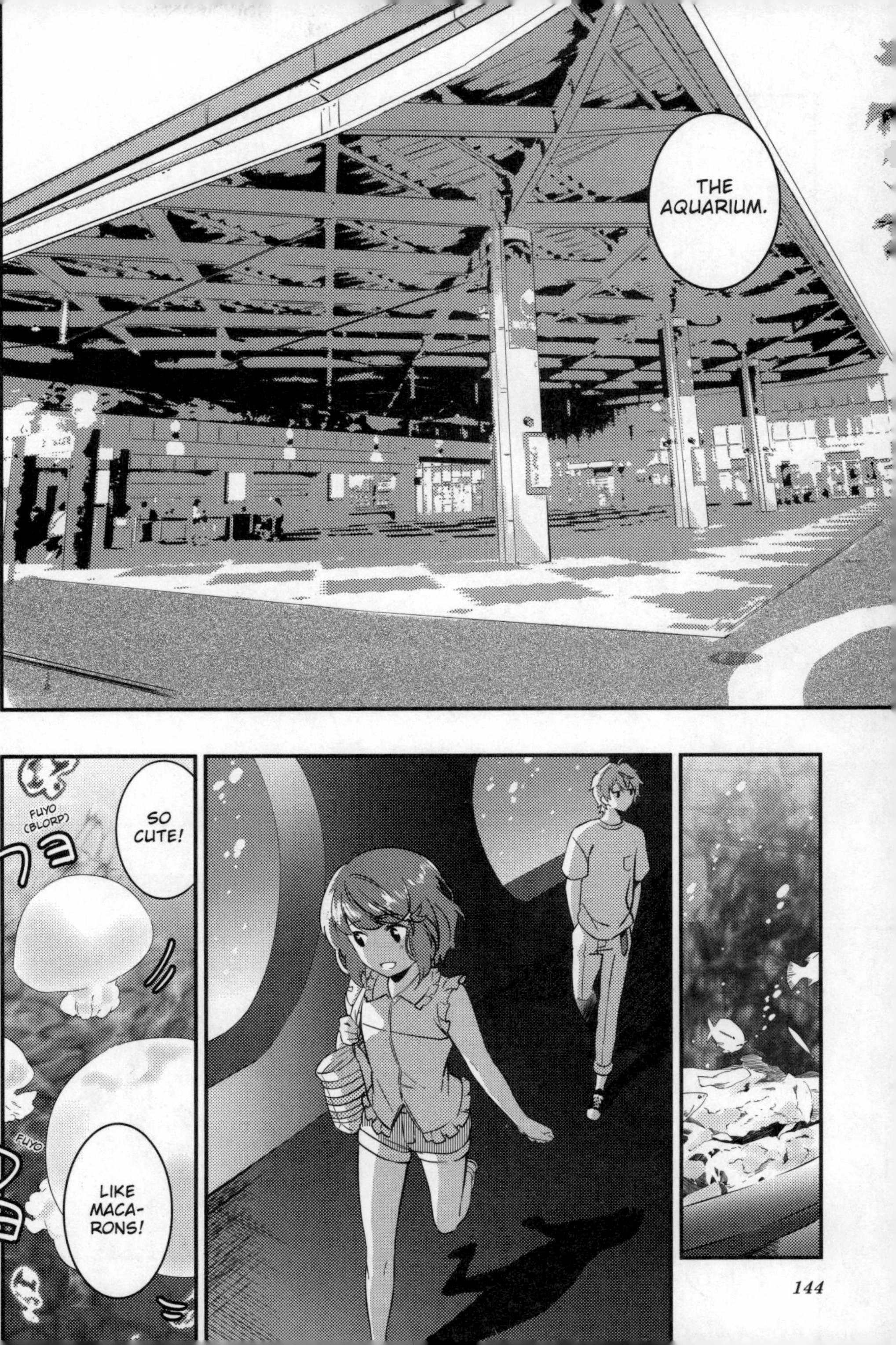
THE AQUARIUM.
FUYO (BLORP)
SO CUTE!
FUYO
LIKE MACA-RONS!

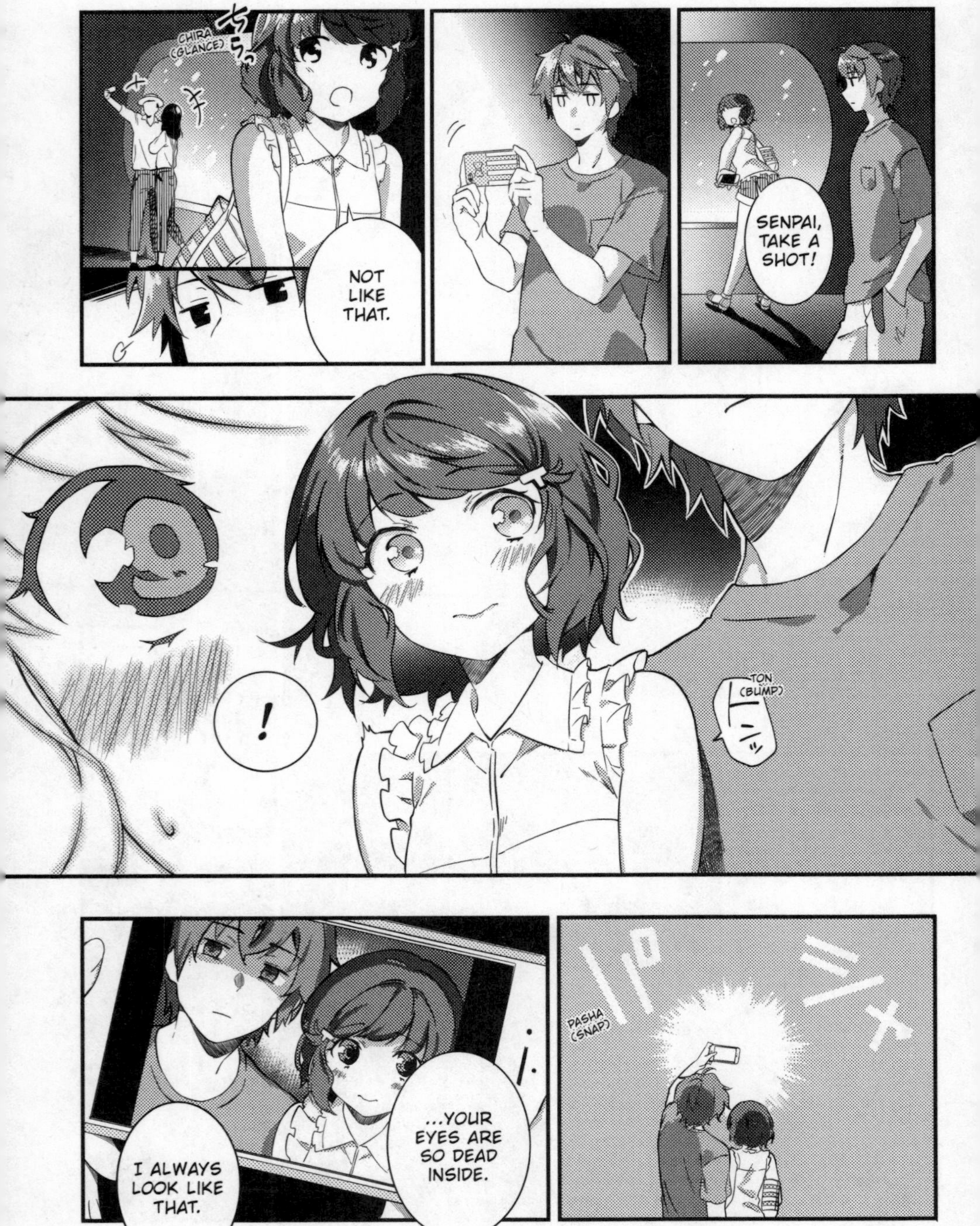
SENPAI, TAKE A SHOT!
CHIRA (GLANCE)
NOT LIKE THAT.
TON (BUMP)
!
PASHA (SNAP)
...YOUR EYES ARE SO DEAD INSIDE.
I ALWAYS LOOK LIKE THAT.

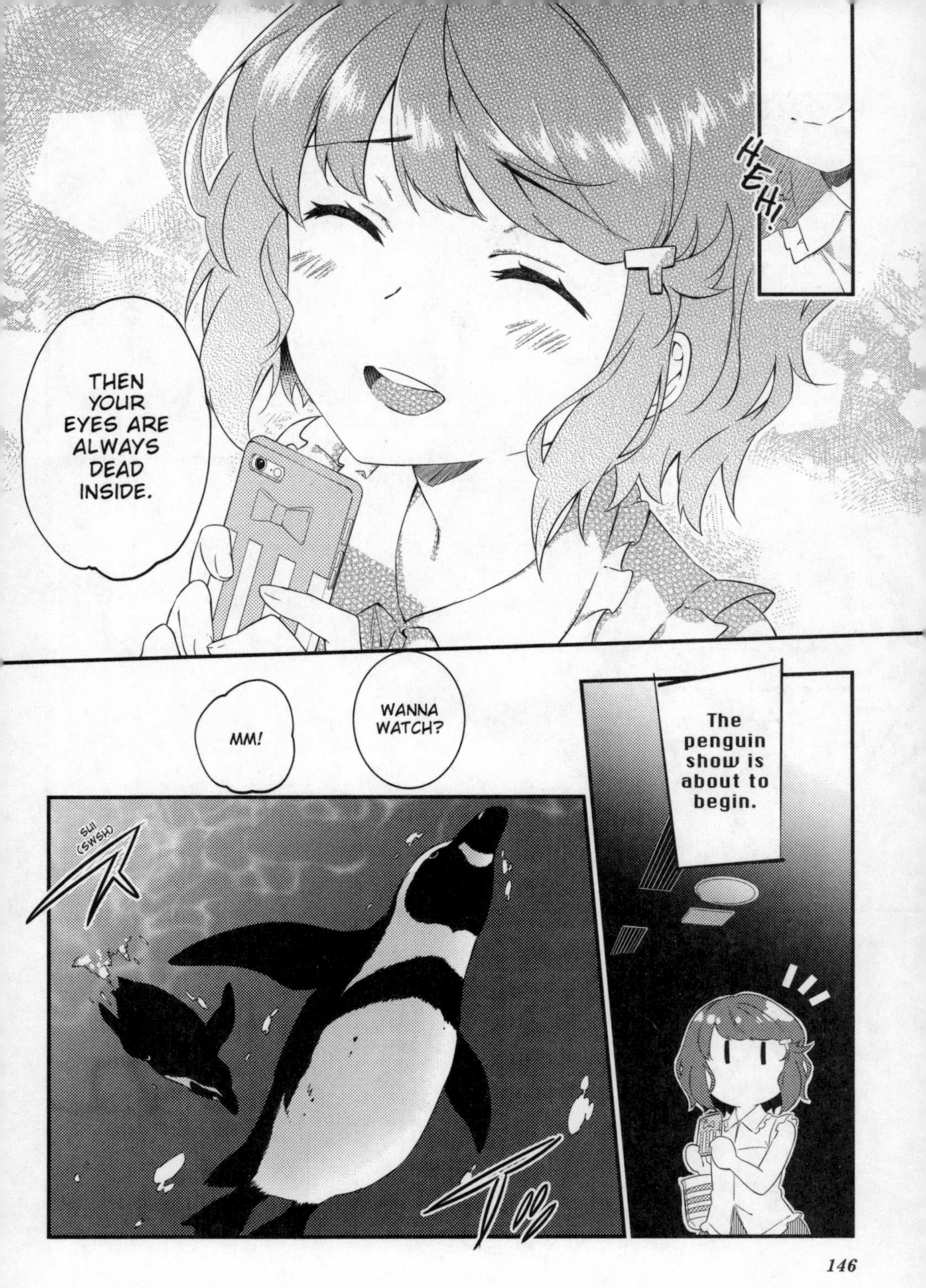
HEH!
THEN YOUR EYES ARE ALWAYS DEAD INSIDE.
The penguin show is about to begin.
WANNA WATCH?
MM!
SUI (SWSH)

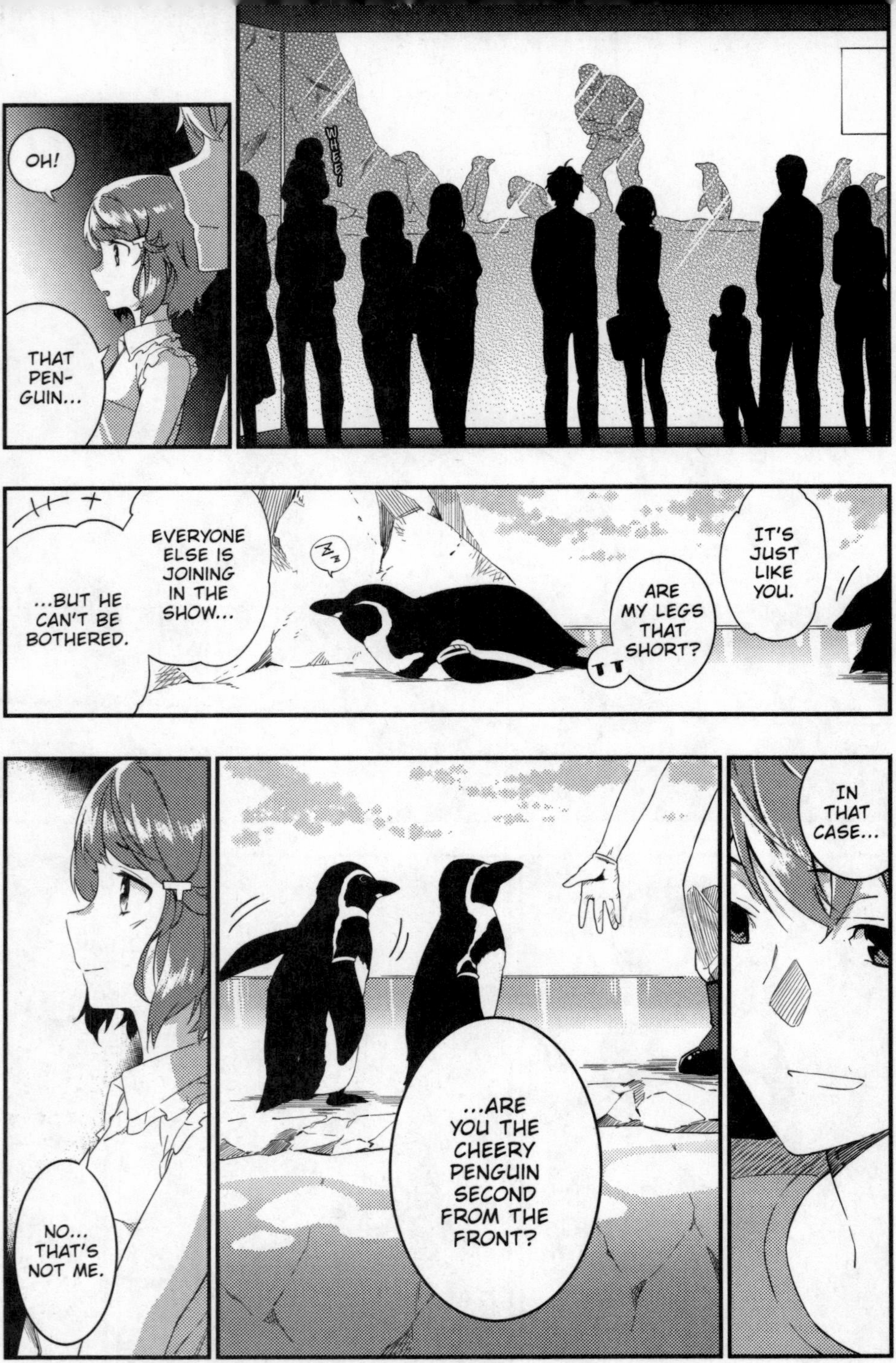
WHEE!
OH!
THAT PEN-GUIN...
IT'S JUST LIKE YOU.
ARE MY LEGS THAT SHORT?
EVERYONE ELSE IS JOINING IN THE SHOW...
...BUT HE CAN'T BE BOTHERED.
IN THAT CASE...
...ARE YOU THE CHEERY PENGUIN SECOND FROM THE FRONT?
NO... THAT'S NOT ME.

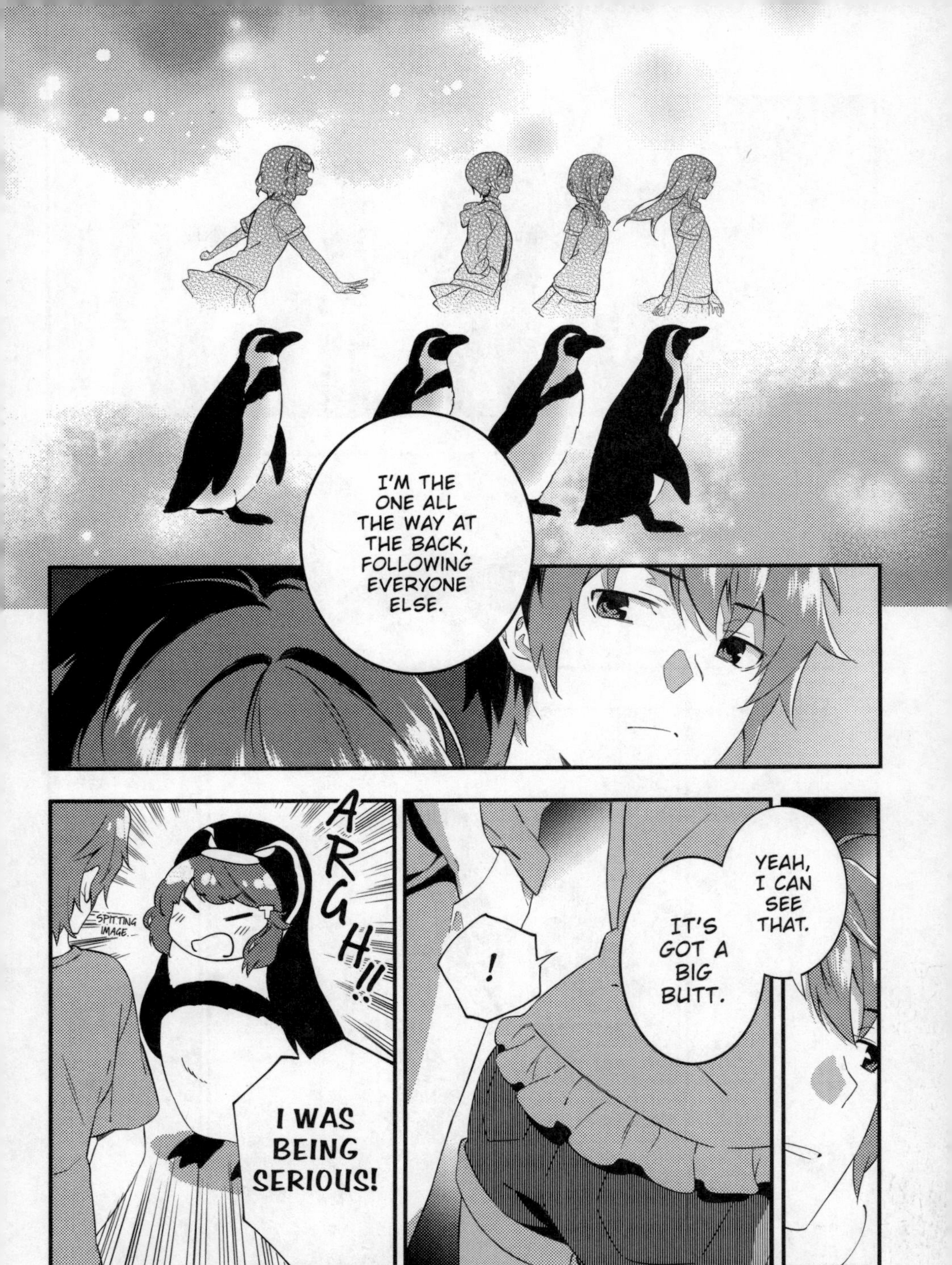
I'M THE ONE ALL THE WAY AT THE BACK, FOLLOWING EVERYONE ELSE.
YEAH, I CAN SEE THAT.
IT'S GOT A BIG BUTT.
!
ARGH!!
SPITTING IMAGE.
I WAS BEING SERIOUS!

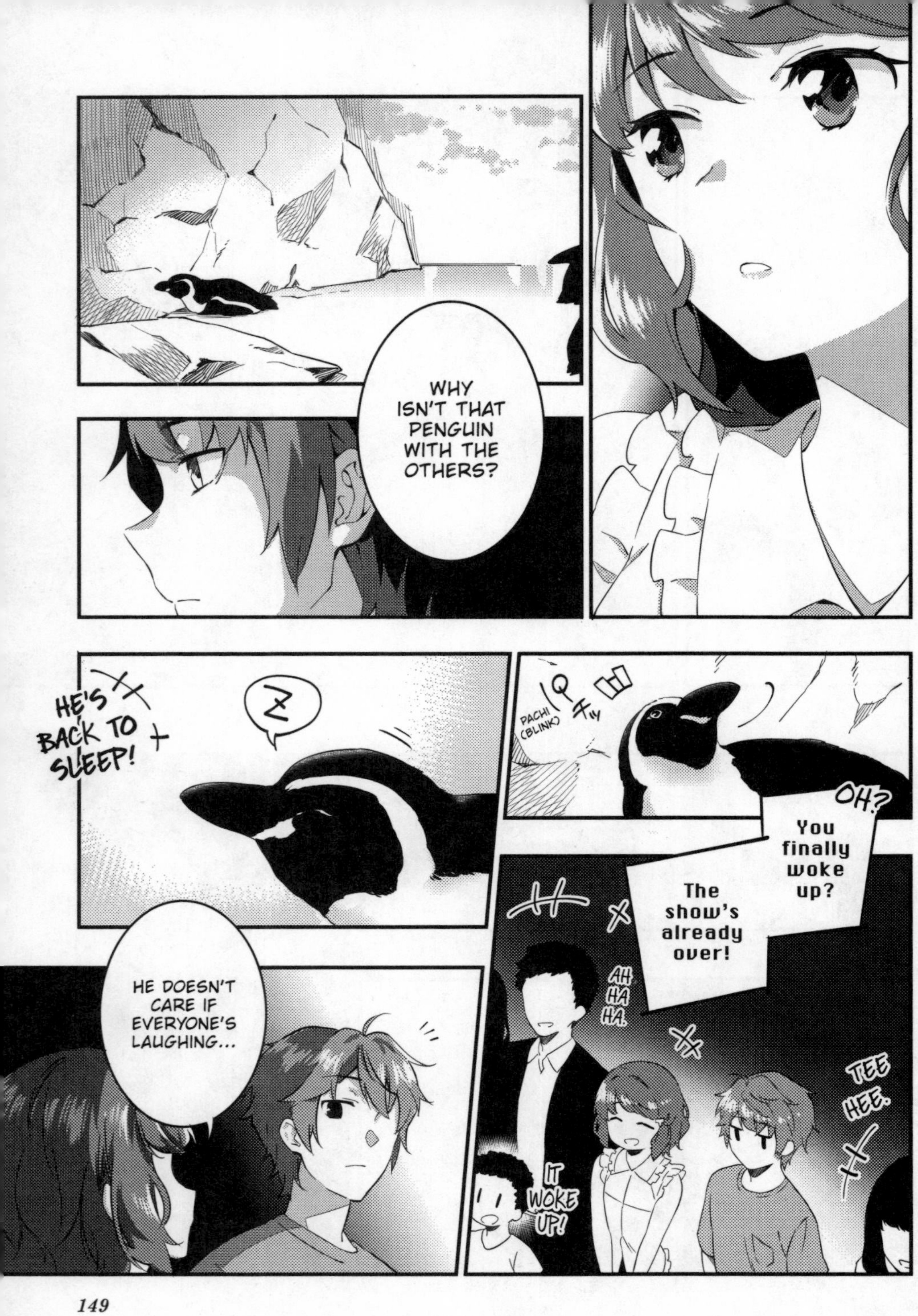
WHY ISN'T THAT PENGUIN WITH THE OTHERS?
PACHI (BLINK)
OH?
You finally woke up?
The show's already over!
Z
HE'S BACK TO SLEEP!
AH HA HA.
TEE HEE.
IT WOKE UP!
HE DOESN'T CARE IF EVERYONE'S LAUGHING...

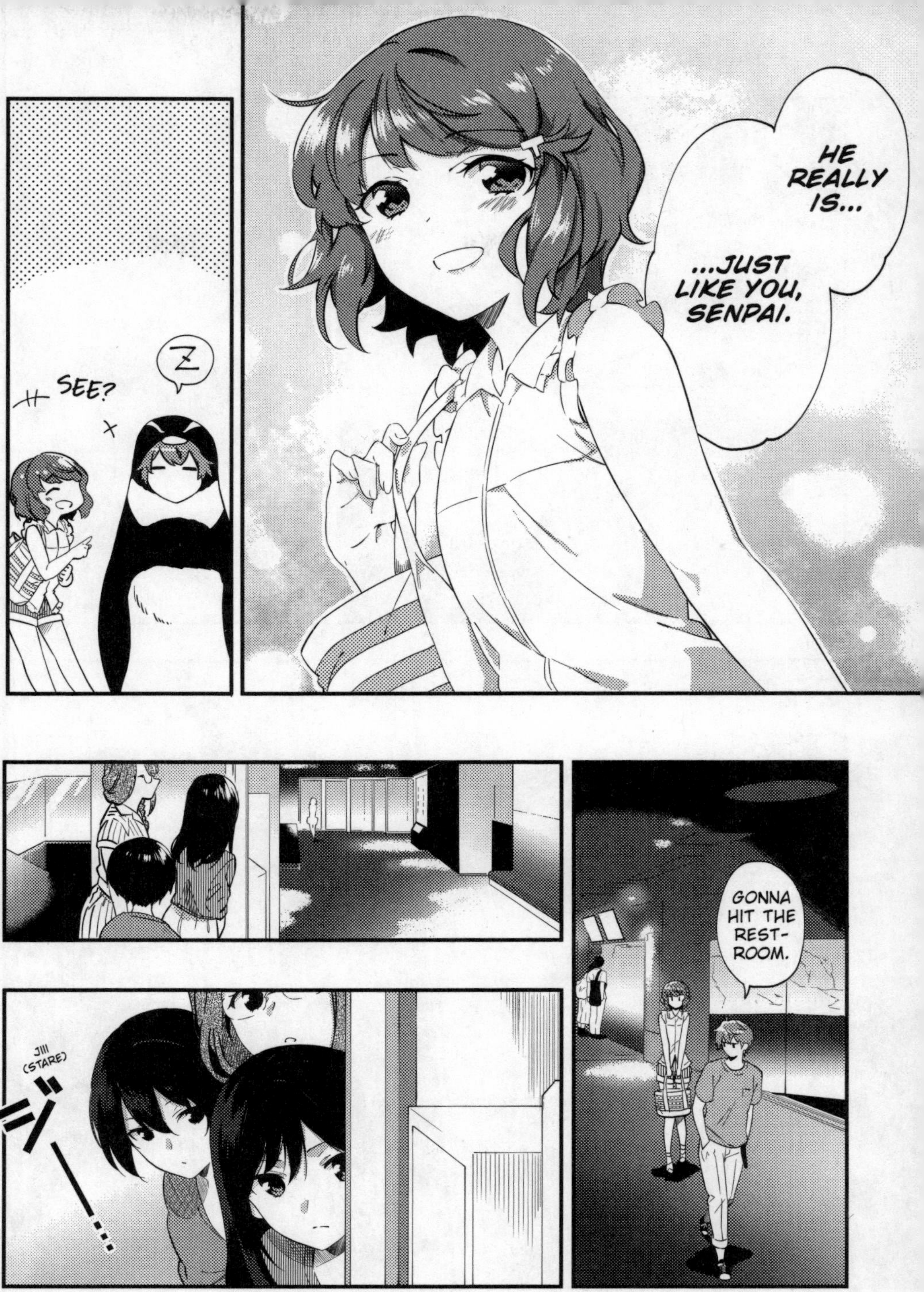
HE REALLY IS...
...JUST LIKE YOU, SENPAI.
Z
SEE?
GONNA HIT THE REST-ROOM.
JIII (STARE)
ジー…

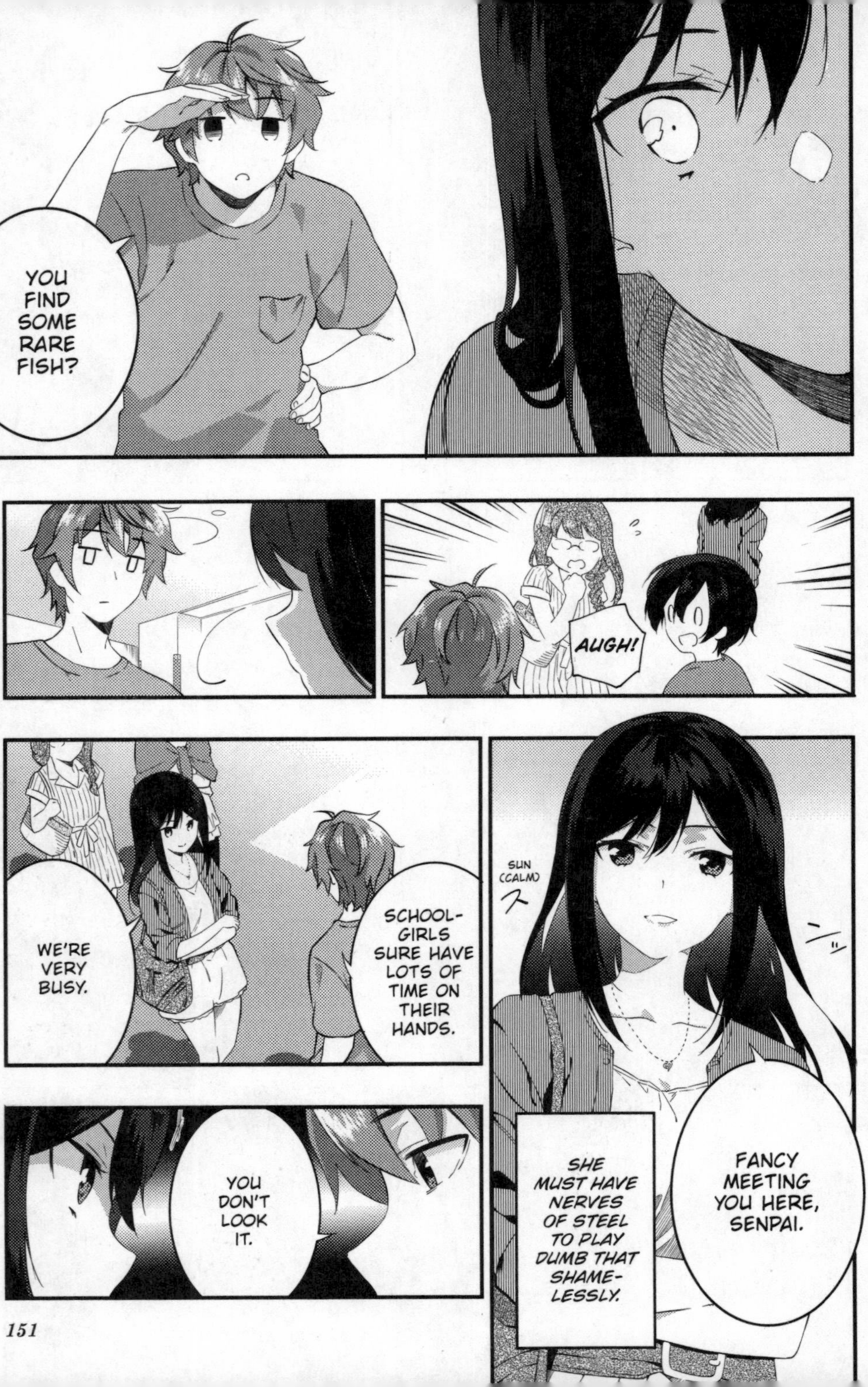
YOU FIND SOME RARE FISH?
AUGH!
SUN (CALM)
FANCY MEETING YOU HERE, SENPAI.
SHE MUST HAVE NERVES OF STEEL TO PLAY DUMB THAT SHAME-LESSLY.
SCHOOL-GIRLS SURE HAVE LOTS OF TIME ON THEIR HANDS.
WE'RE VERY BUSY.
YOU DON'T LOOK IT.

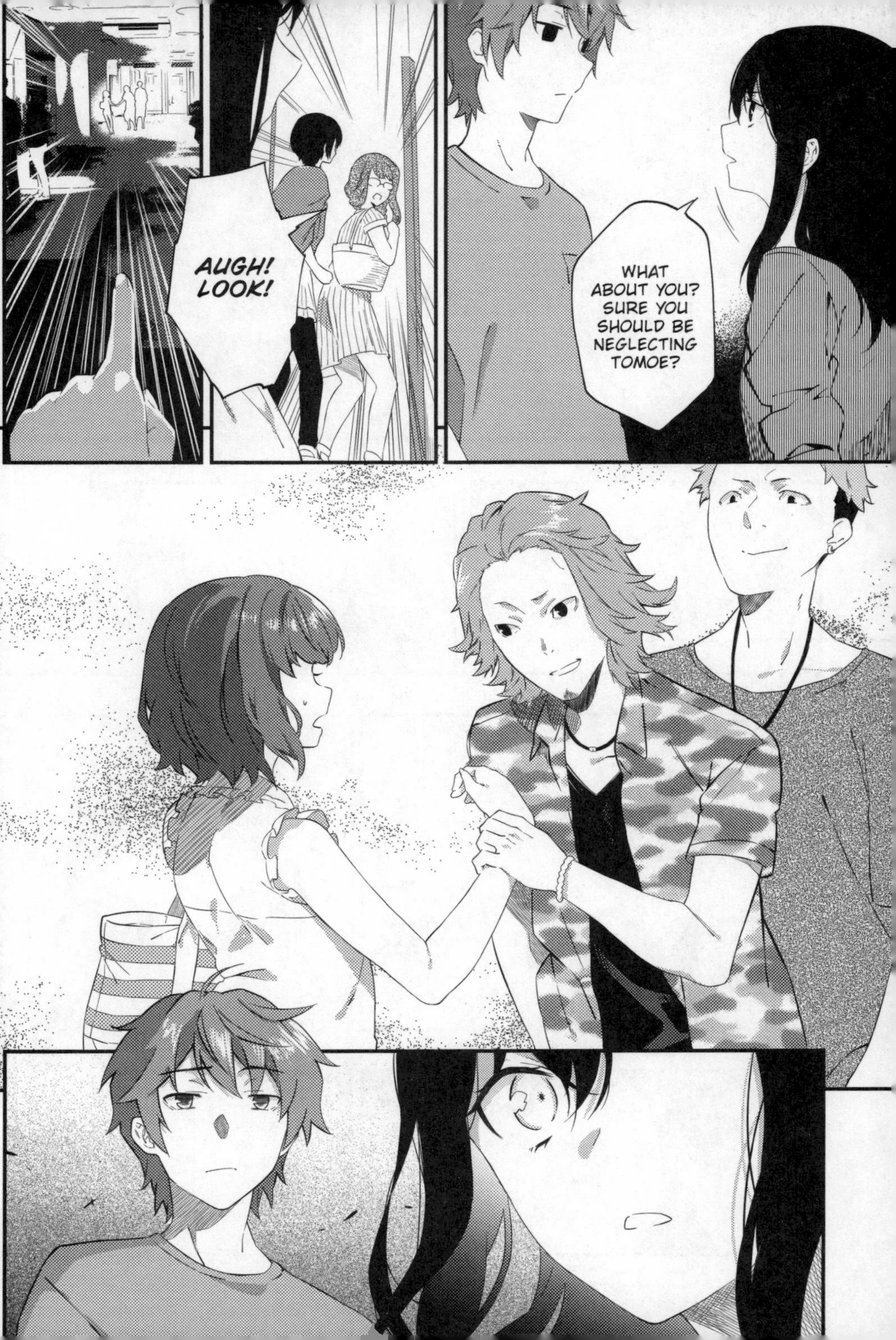
WHAT ABOUT YOU? SURE YOU SHOULD BE NEGLECTING TOMOE?
AUGH! LOOK!

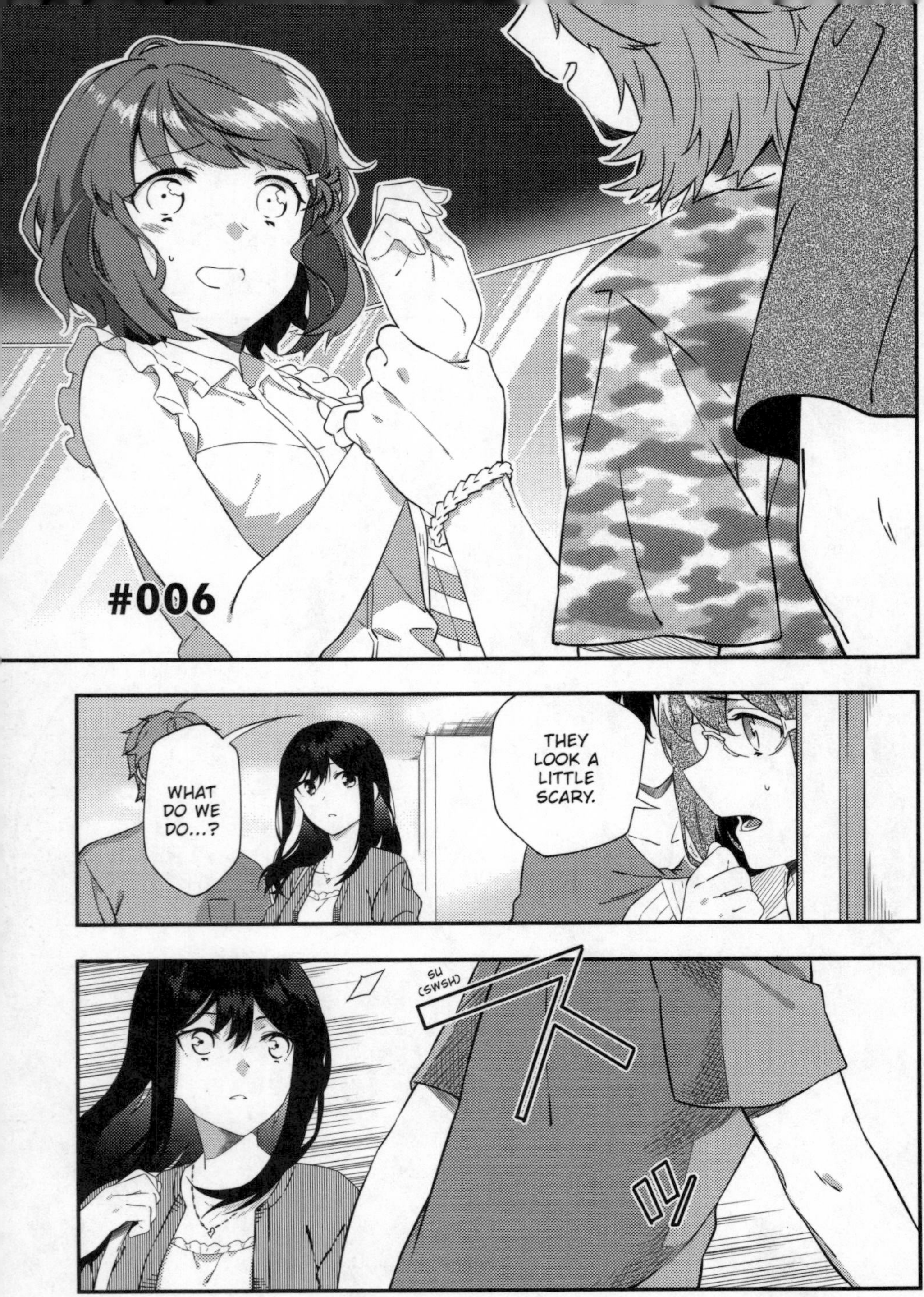
#006
THEY LOOK A LITTLE SCARY.
WHAT DO WE DO...?
SU (SWSH)

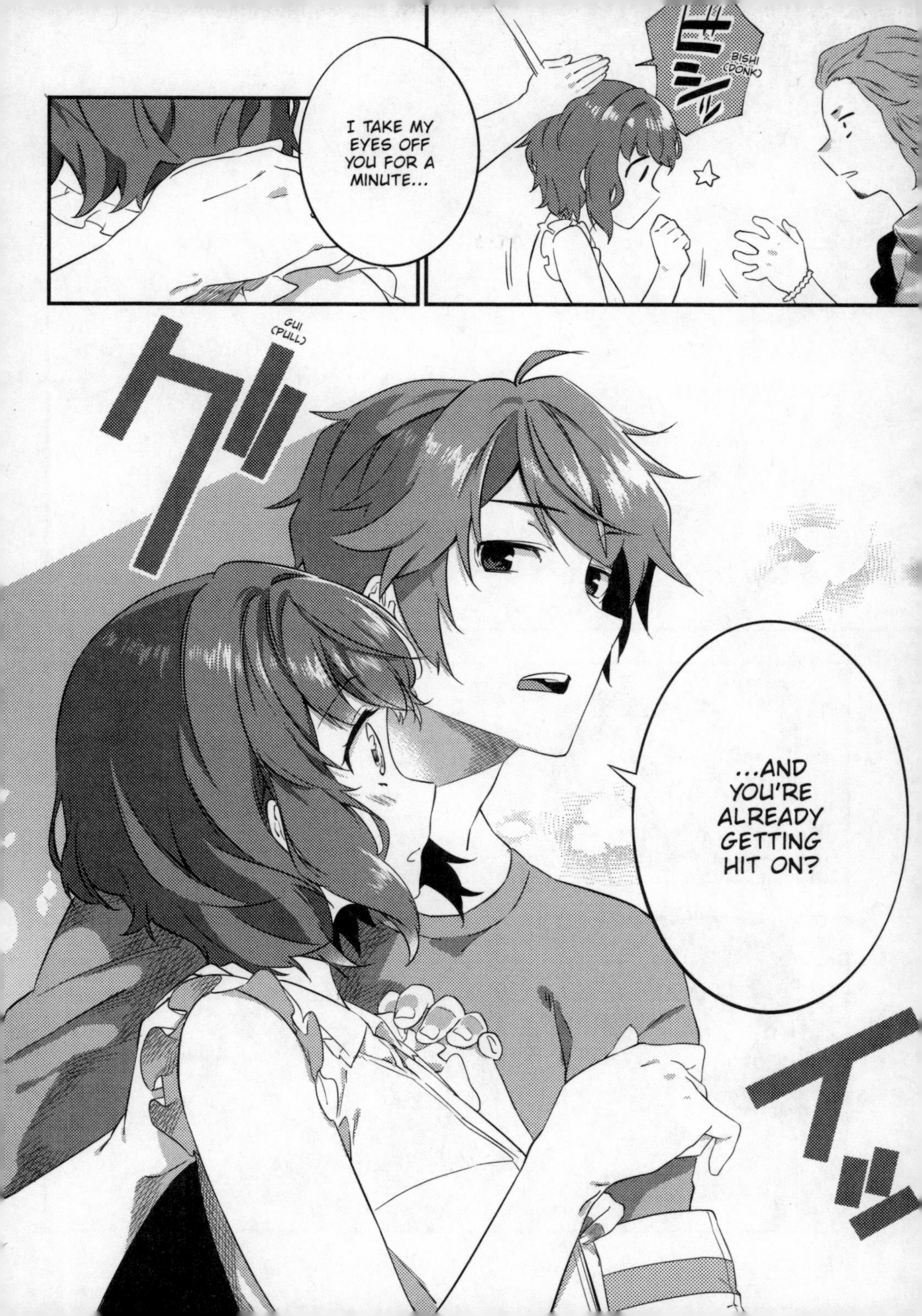
BISHI (DONK)
I TAKE MY EYES OFF YOU FOR A MINUTE...
GUI (PULL)
...AND YOU'RE ALREADY GETTING HIT ON?

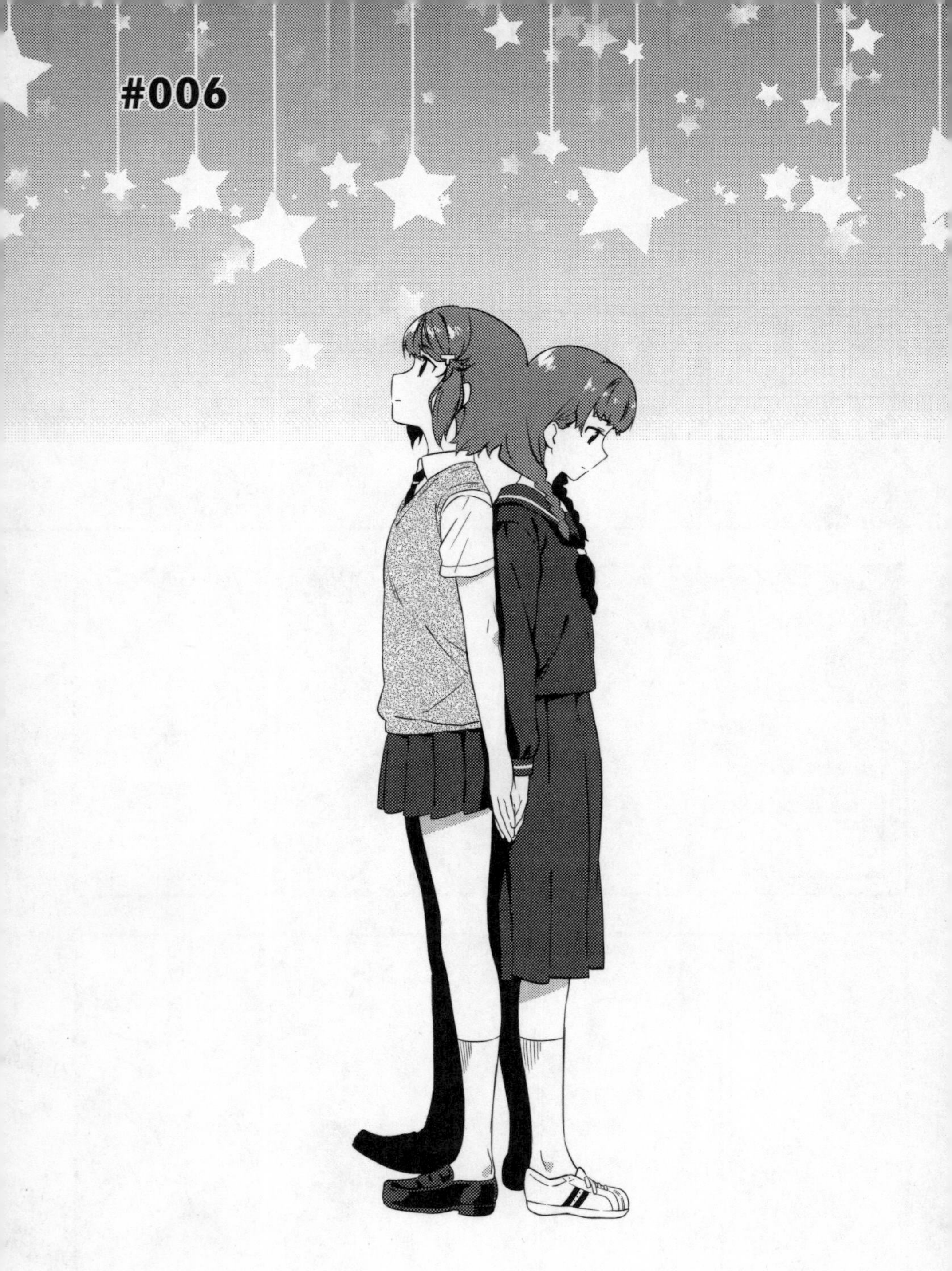
#006

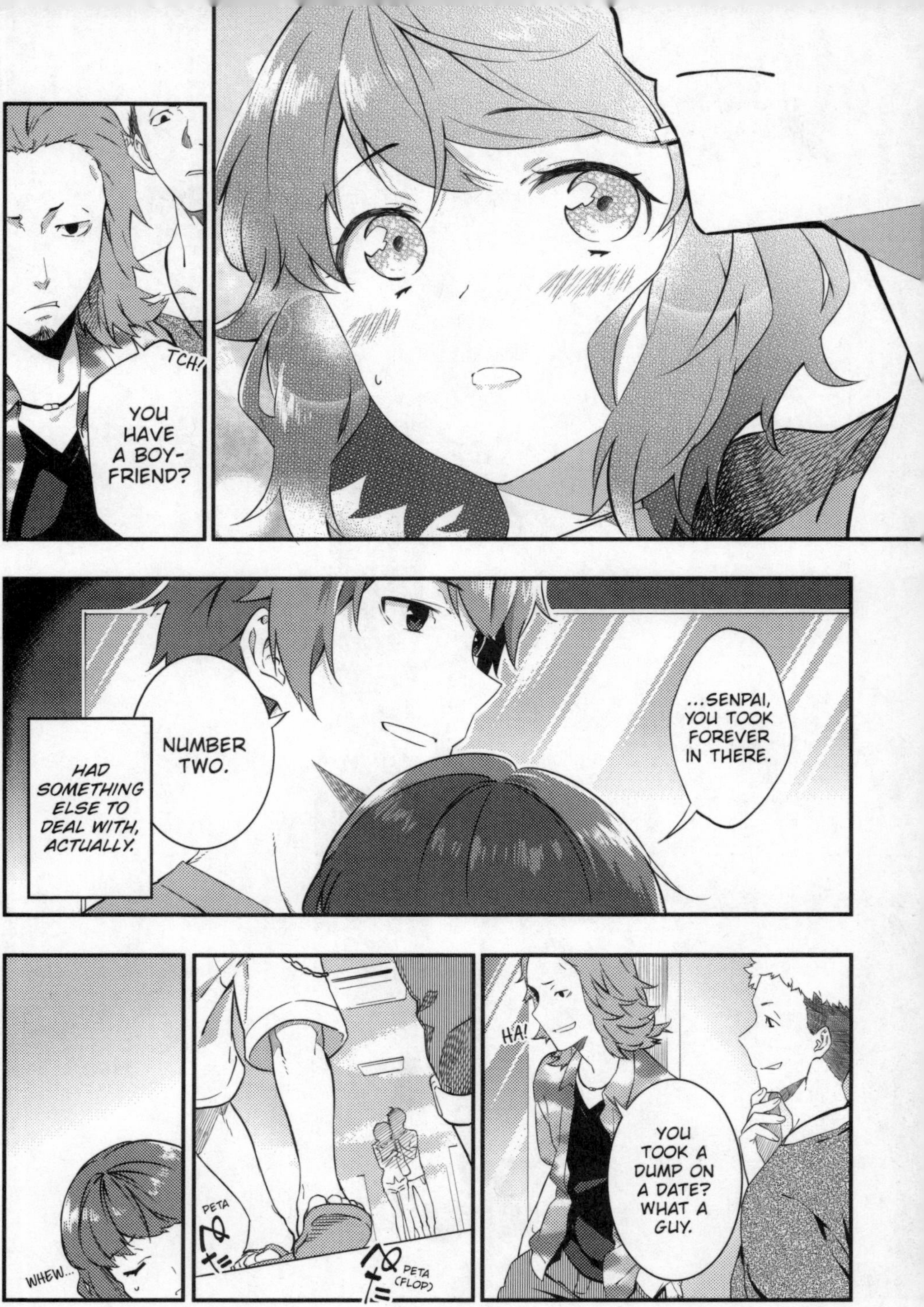
—
TCH!
YOU HAVE A BOY-FRIEND?
...SENPAI, YOU TOOK FOREVER IN THERE.
NUMBER TWO.
HAD SOMETHING ELSE TO DEAL WITH, ACTUALLY.
HA!
YOU TOOK A DUMP ON A DATE? WHAT A GUY.
PETA
PETA (FLOP)
WHEW...

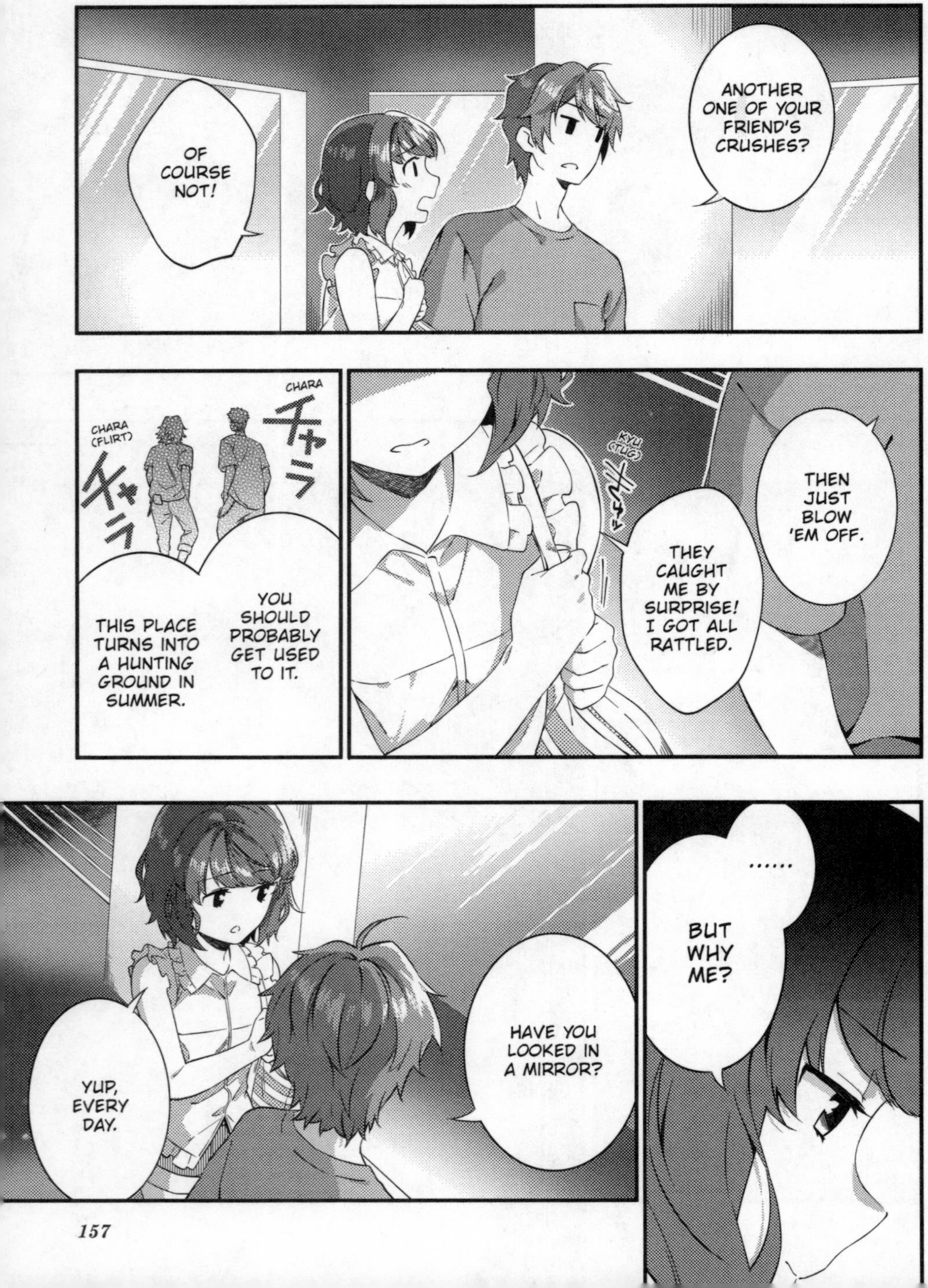
ANOTHER ONE OF YOUR FRIEND'S CRUSHES?
OF COURSE NOT!
THEN JUST BLOW 'EM OFF.
KYU (TUG)
THEY CAUGHT ME BY SURPRISE! I GOT ALL RATTLED.
CHARA
チャラ
CHARA (FLIRT)
チャラ
YOU SHOULD PROBABLY GET USED TO IT.
THIS PLACE TURNS INTO A HUNTING GROUND IN SUMMER.
......
BUT WHY ME?
HAVE YOU LOOKED IN A MIRROR?
YUP, EVERY DAY.

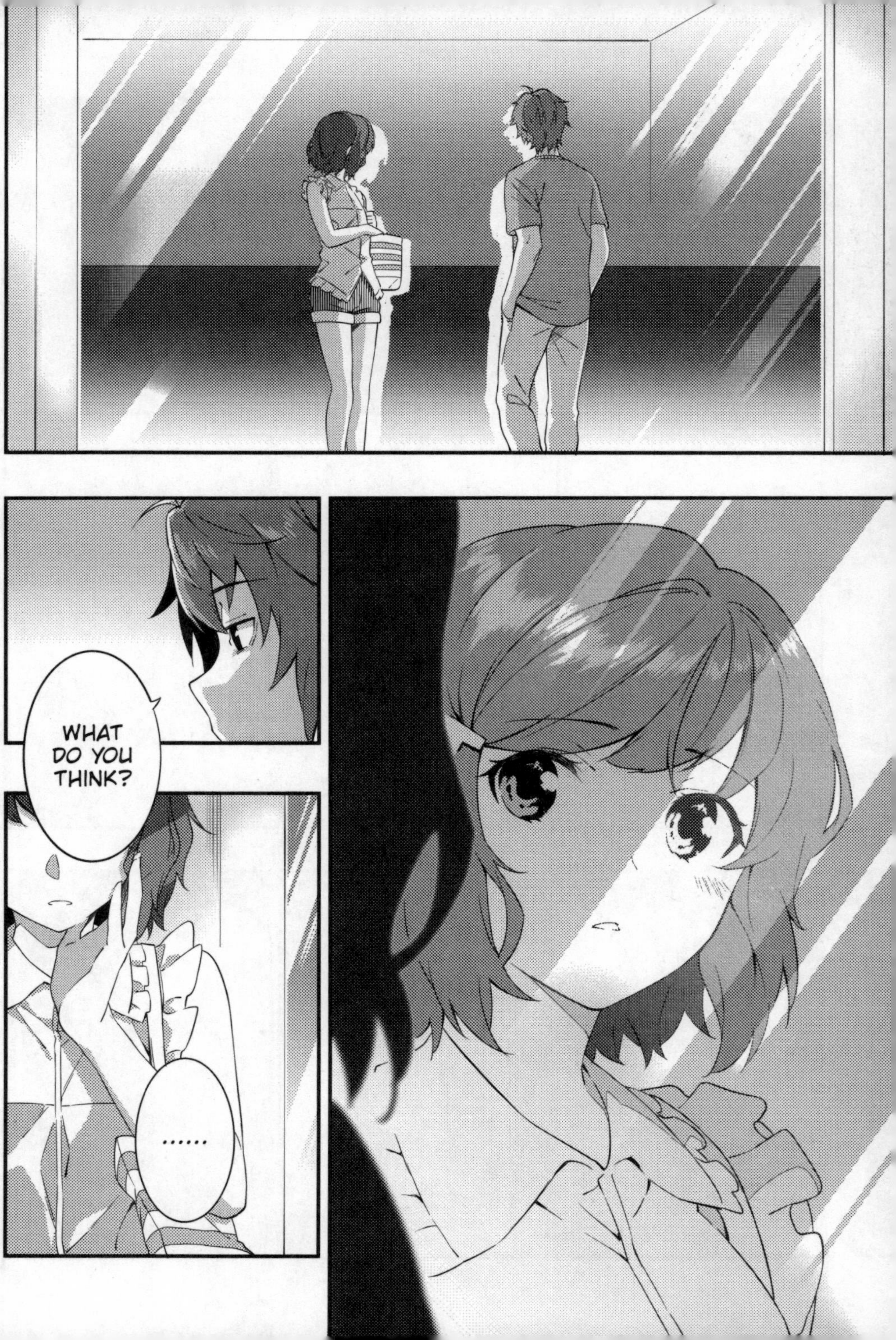
WHAT DO YOU THINK?
......

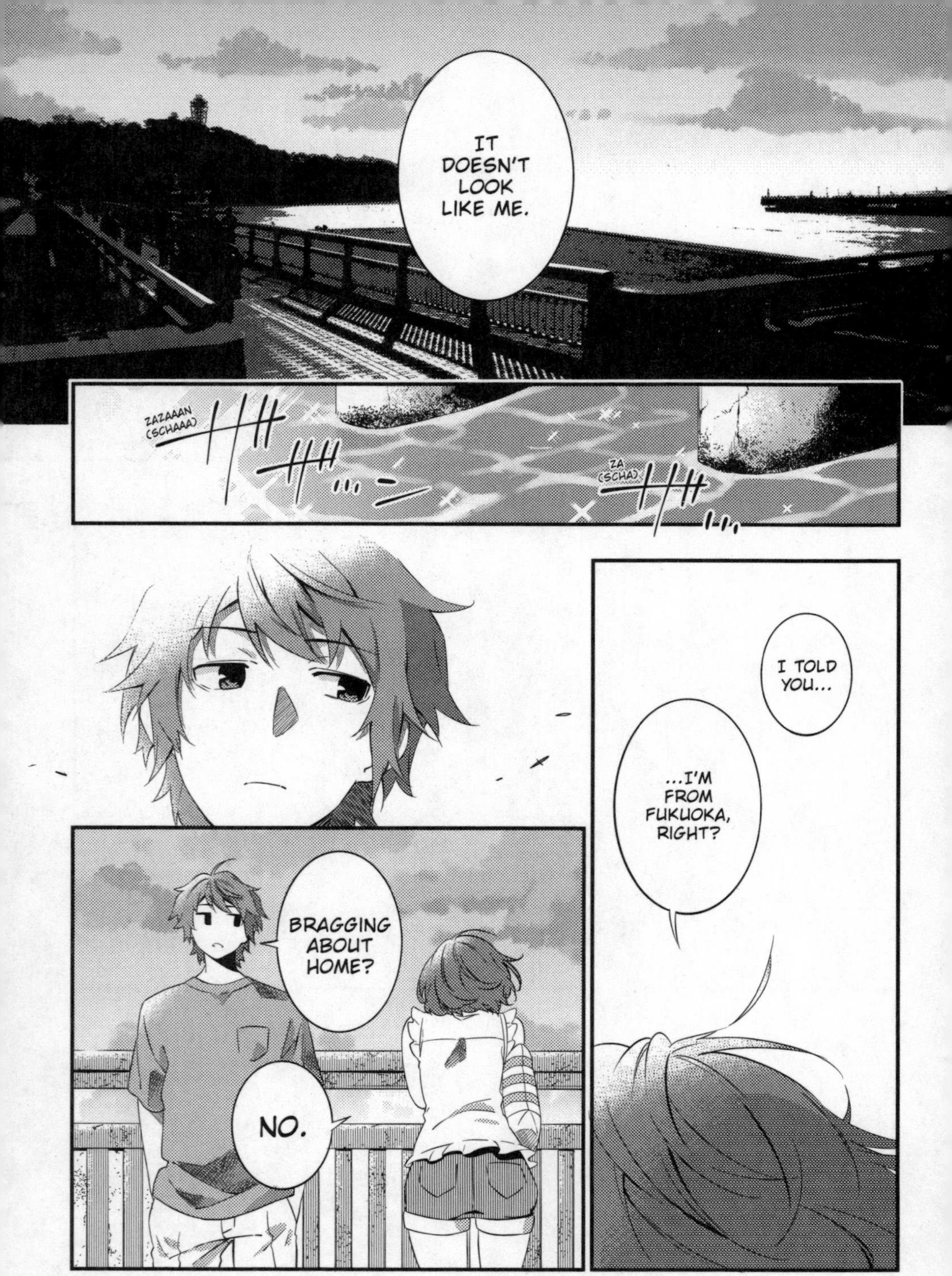
IT DOESN'T LOOK LIKE ME.
ZA (SCHA)
ZAZAAAN (SCHAAA)
I TOLD YOU...
...I'M FROM FUKUOKA, RIGHT?
BRAGGING ABOUT HOME?
NO.

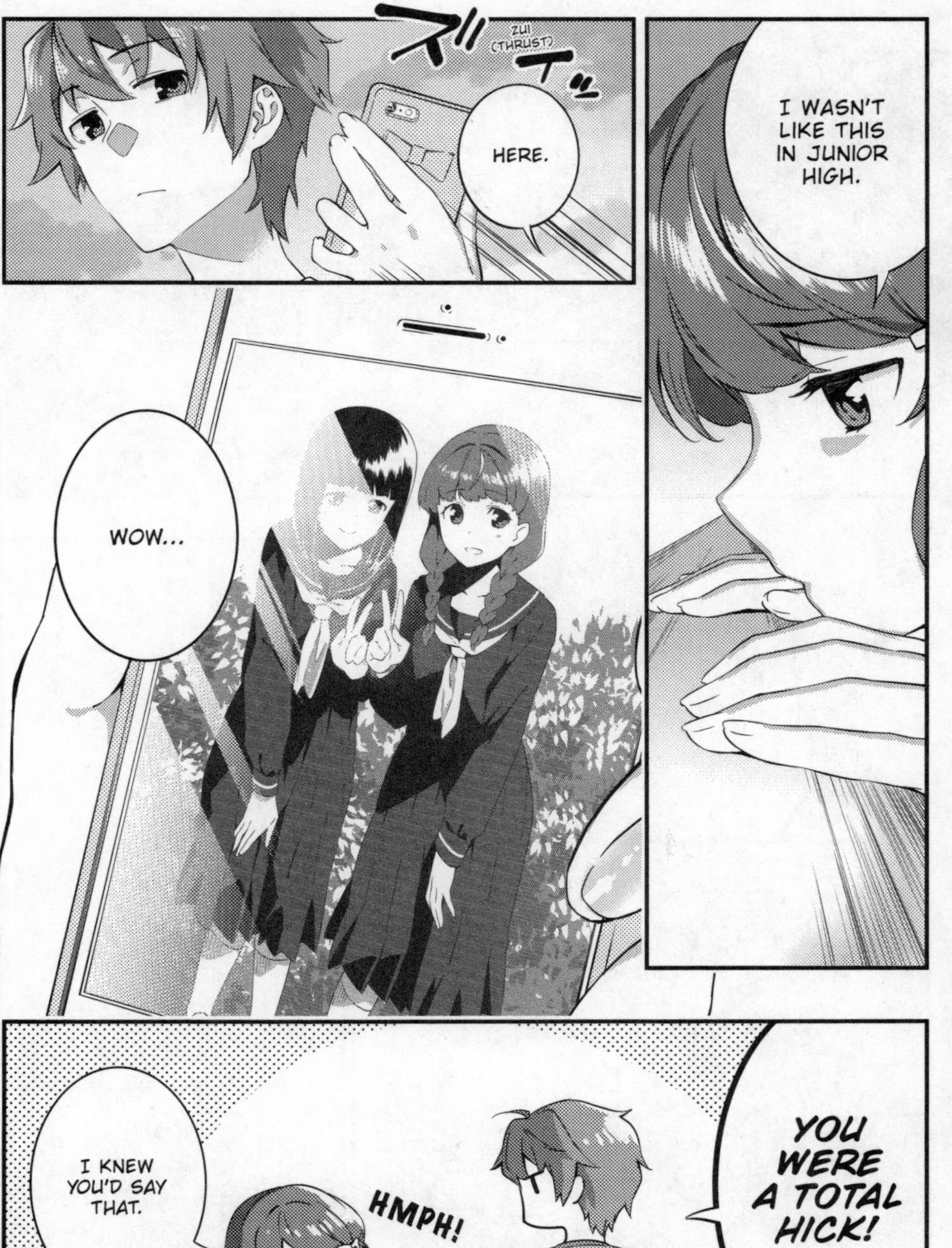
I WASN'T LIKE THIS IN JUNIOR HIGH.
ZUI (THRUST)
HERE.
WOW...
YOU WERE A TOTAL HICK!
HMPH!
I KNEW YOU'D SAY THAT.

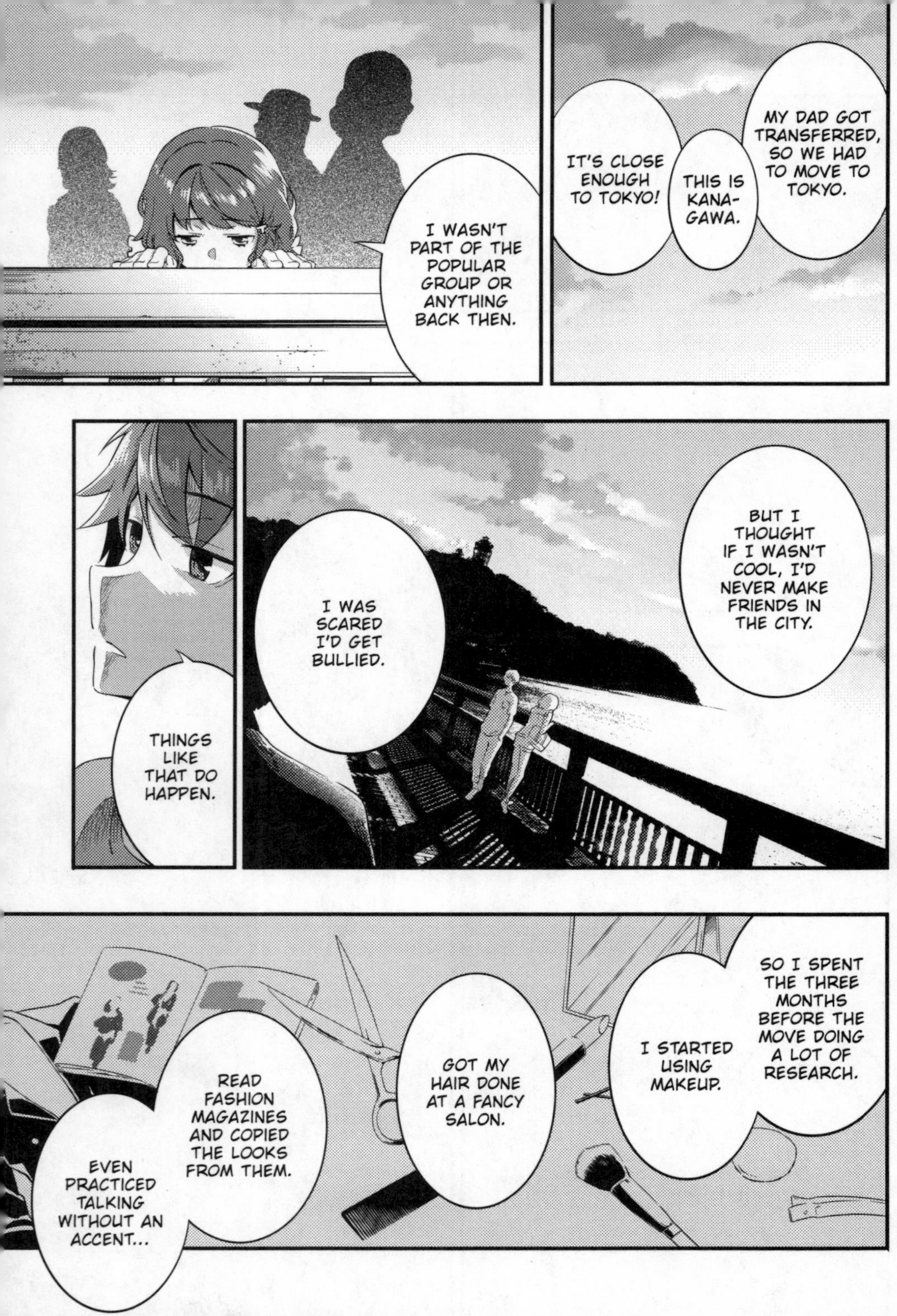
MY DAD GOT TRANSFERRED, SO WE HAD TO MOVE TO TOKYO.
THIS IS KANA-GAWA.
IT'S CLOSE ENOUGH TO TOKYO!
I WASN'T PART OF THE POPULAR GROUP OR ANYTHING BACK THEN.
BUT I THOUGHT IF I WASN'T COOL, I'D NEVER MAKE FRIENDS IN THE CITY.
I WAS SCARED I'D GET BULLIED.
THINGS LIKE THAT DO HAPPEN.
SO I SPENT THE THREE MONTHS BEFORE THE MOVE DOING A LOT OF RESEARCH.
I STARTED USING MAKEUP.
GOT MY HAIR DONE AT A FANCY SALON.
READ FASHION MAGAZINES AND COPIED THE LOOKS FROM THEM.
EVEN PRACTICED TALKING WITHOUT AN ACCENT...

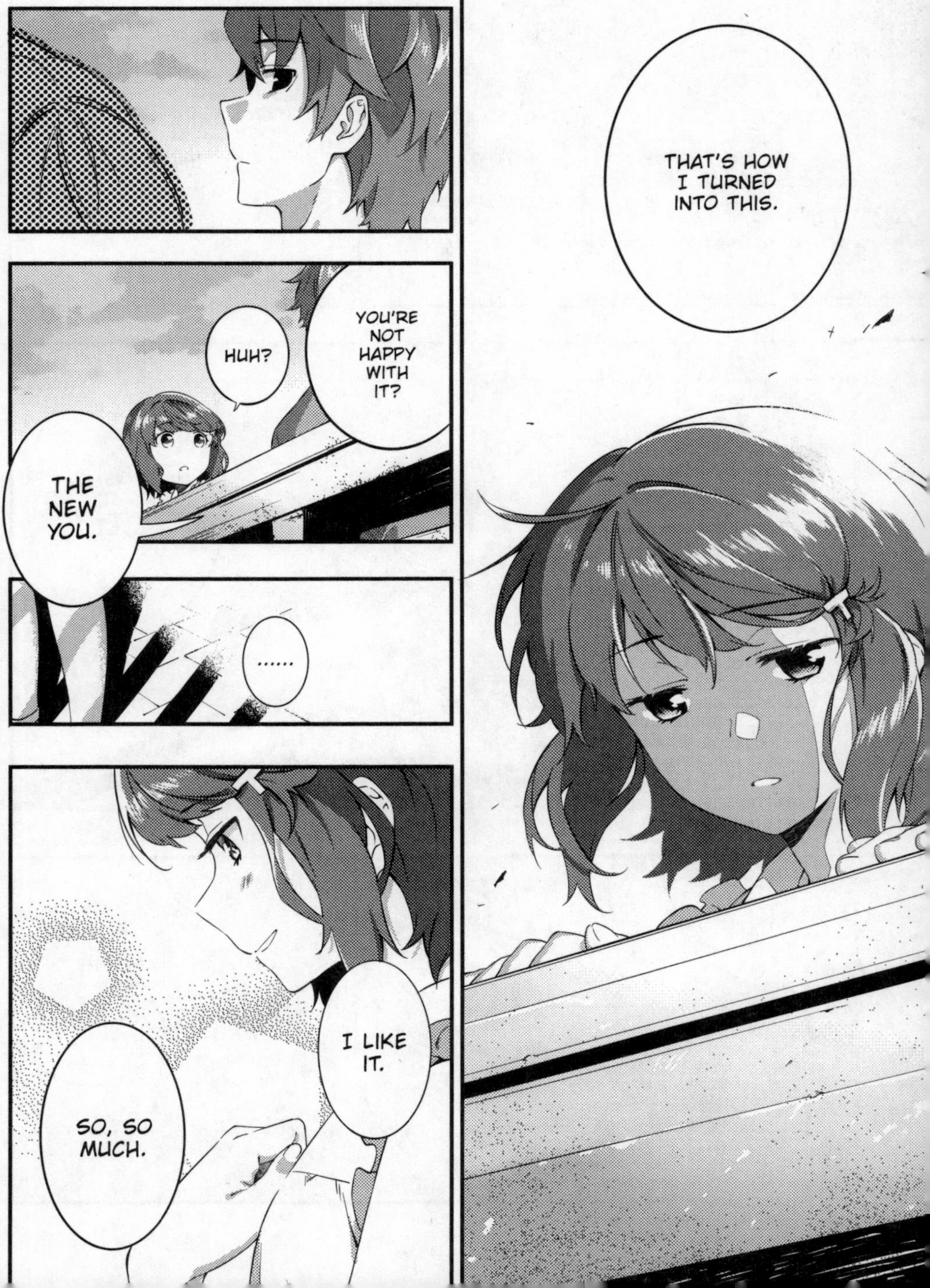
THAT'S HOW I TURNED INTO THIS.
YOU'RE NOT HAPPY WITH IT?
HUH?
THE NEW YOU.
......
I LIKE IT.
SO, SO MUCH.

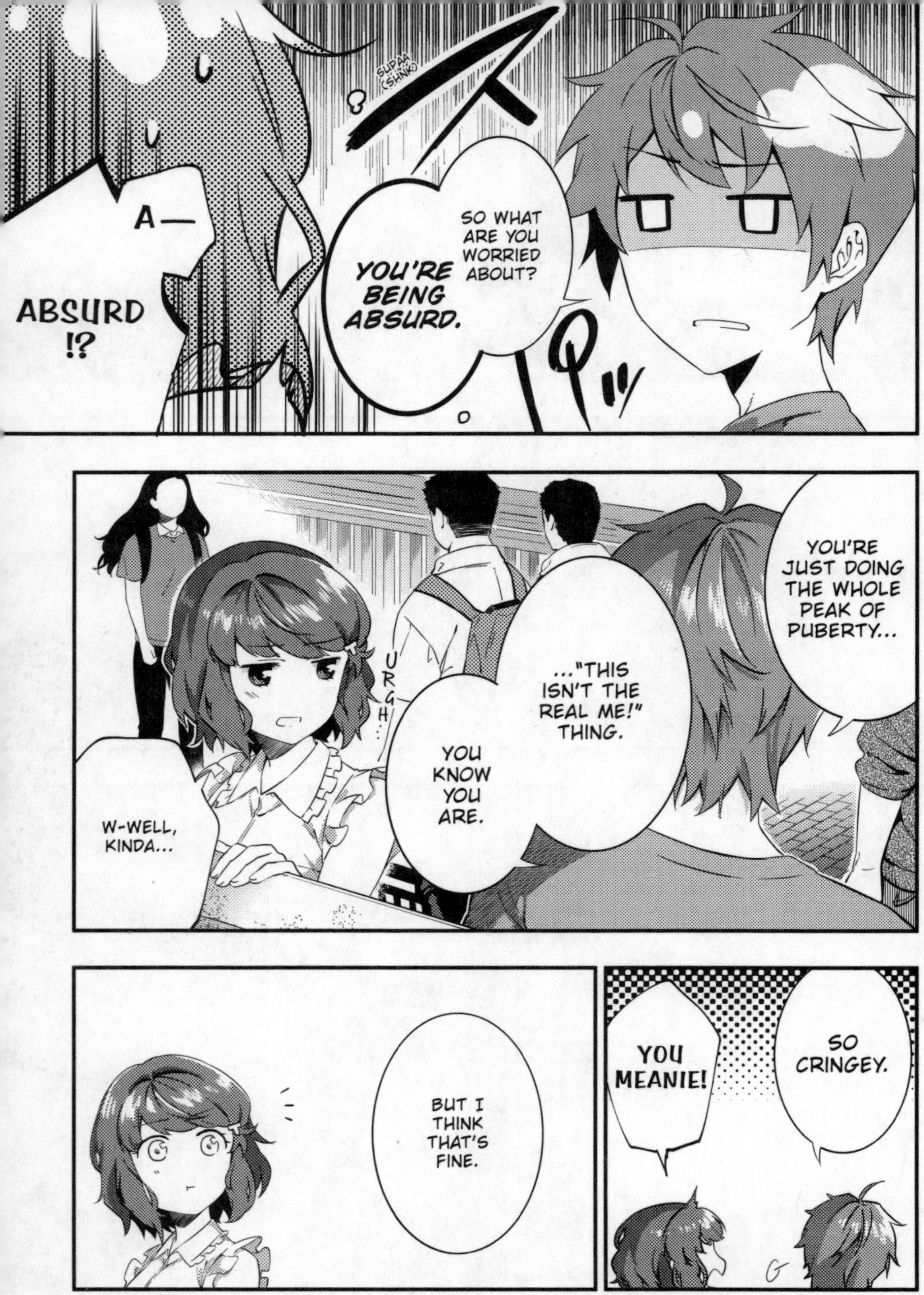
SUPAA (SHNK)
SO WHAT ARE YOU WORRIED ABOUT?
YOU'RE BEING ABSURD.
A—
ABSURD !?
YOU'RE JUST DOING THE WHOLE PEAK OF PUBERTY...
..."THIS ISN'T THE REAL ME!" THING.
YOU KNOW YOU ARE.
URGH...
W-WELL, KINDA...
SO CRINGEY.
YOU MEANIE!
BUT I THINK THAT'S FINE.

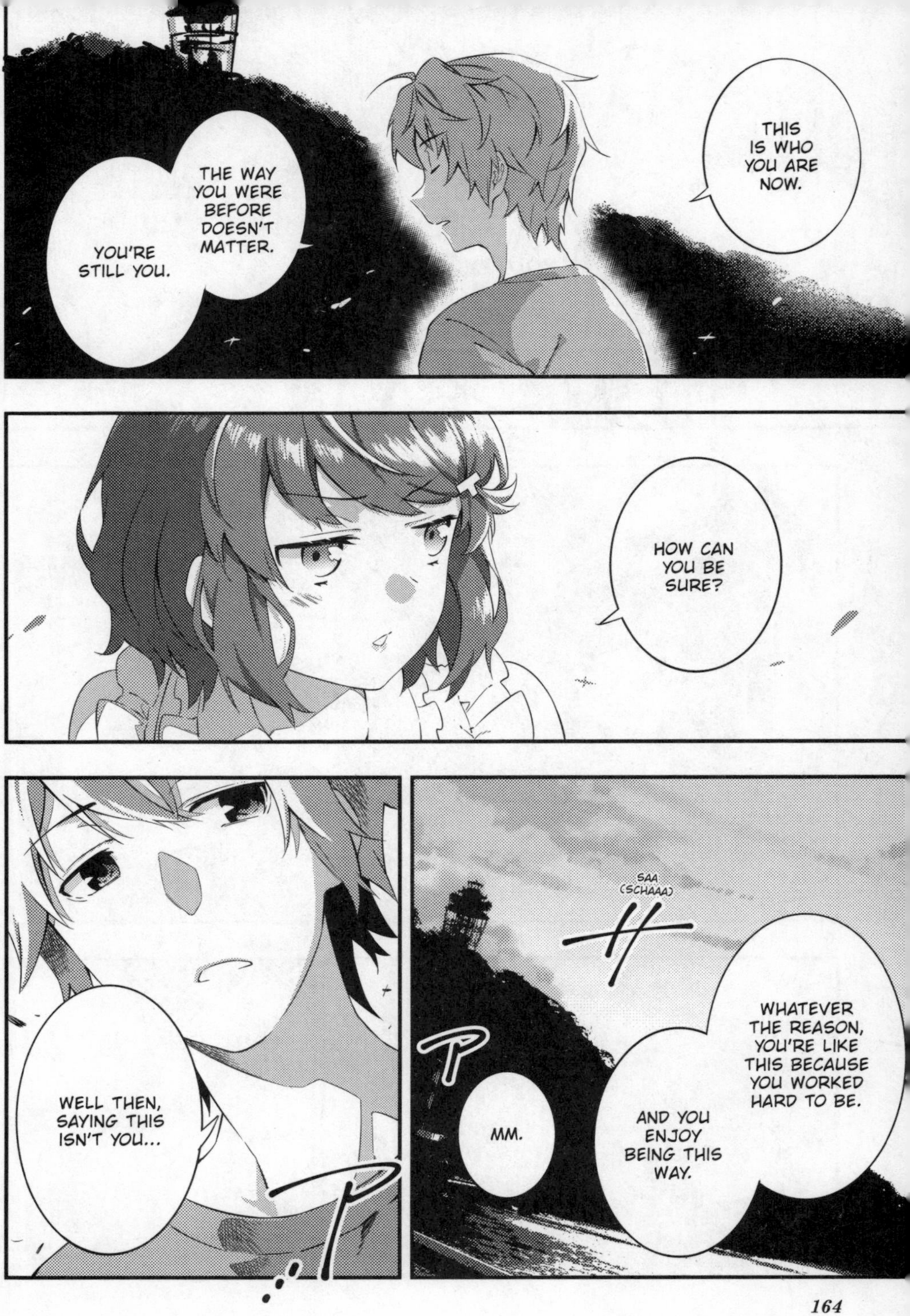
THIS IS WHO YOU ARE NOW.
THE WAY YOU WERE BEFORE DOESN'T MATTER.
YOU'RE STILL YOU.
HOW CAN YOU BE SURE?
SAA (SCHAAA)
WHATEVER THE REASON, YOU'RE LIKE THIS BECAUSE YOU WORKED HARD TO BE.
AND YOU ENJOY BEING THIS WAY.
MM.
WELL THEN, SAYING THIS ISN'T YOU...

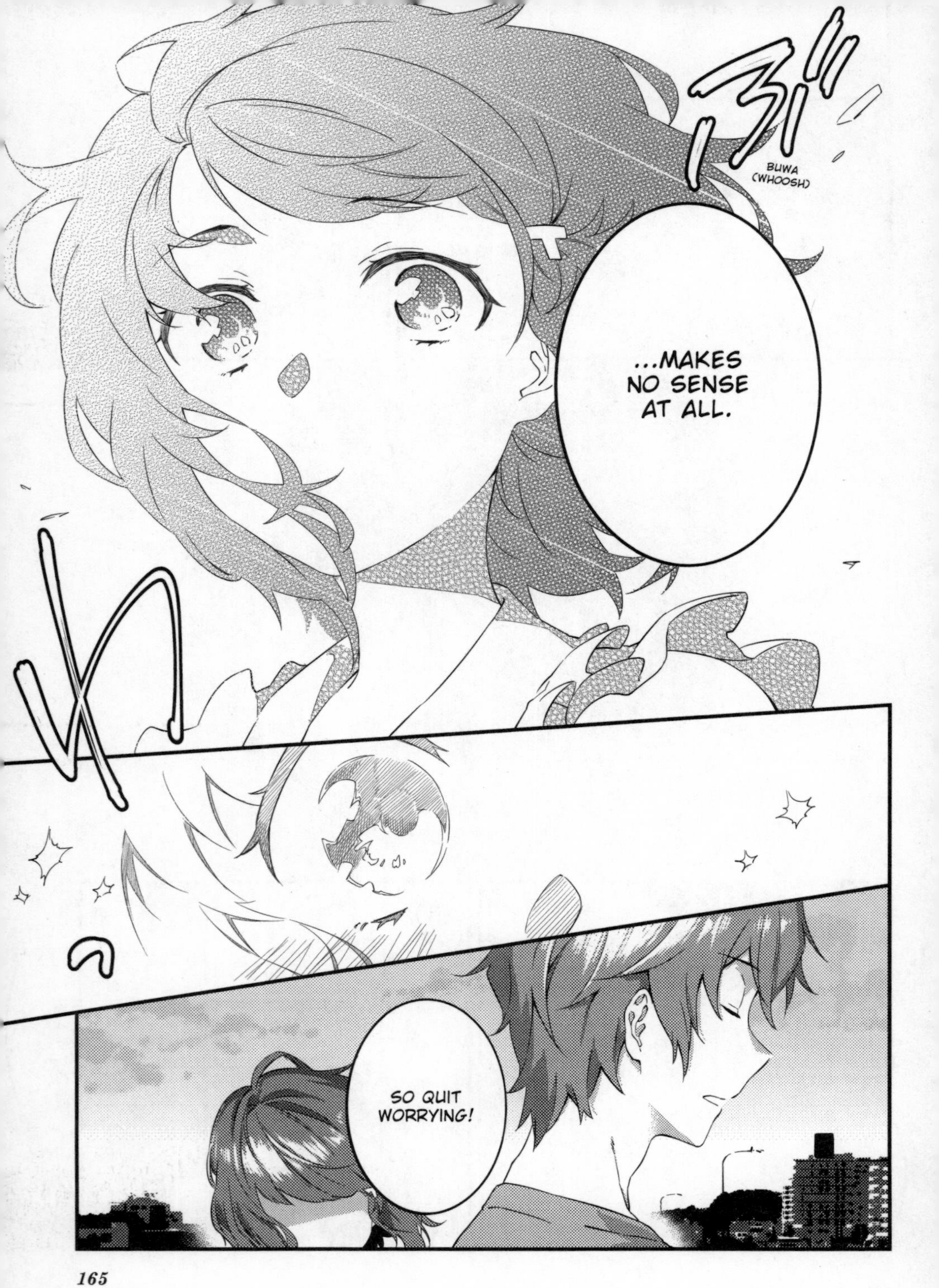
BUWA
(WHOOSH)
...MAKES NO SENSE AT ALL.
SO QUIT WORRYING!

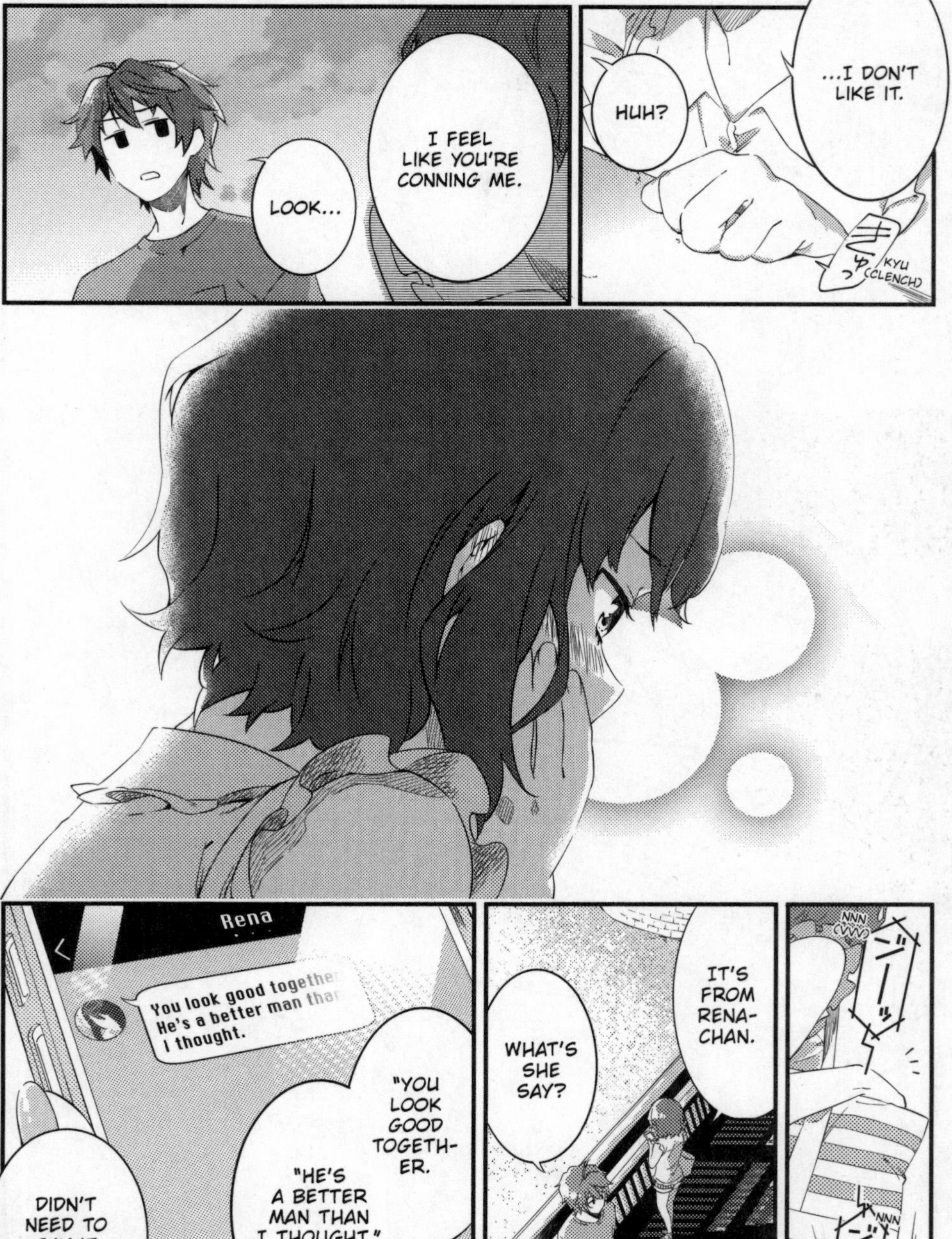
...I DON'T LIKE IT.
HUH?
きゅっ
KYU (CLENCH)
I FEEL LIKE YOU'RE CONNING ME.
LOOK...
NNN (VVV)
ジーッ
NNN
ジーッ
IT'S FROM RENA-CHAN.
WHAT'S SHE SAY?
Rena
You look good togethe
He's a better man tha
I thought.
"YOU LOOK GOOD TOGETH-ER.
"HE'S A BETTER MAN THAN I THOUGHT."
DIDN'T NEED TO SAY IT LIKE THAT.

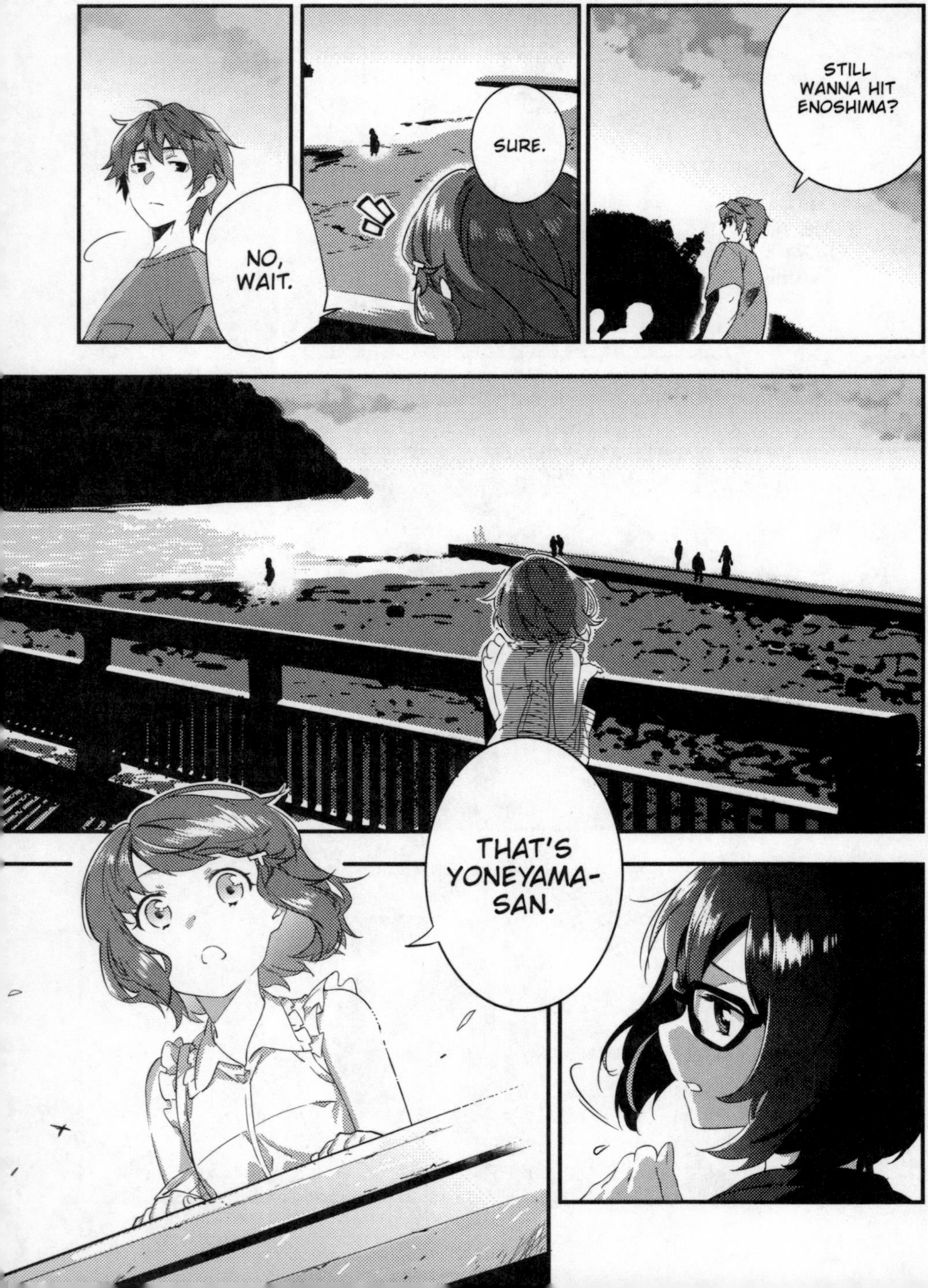
STILL WANNA HIT ENOSHIMA?
SURE.
NO, WAIT.
THAT'S YONEYAMA-SAN.

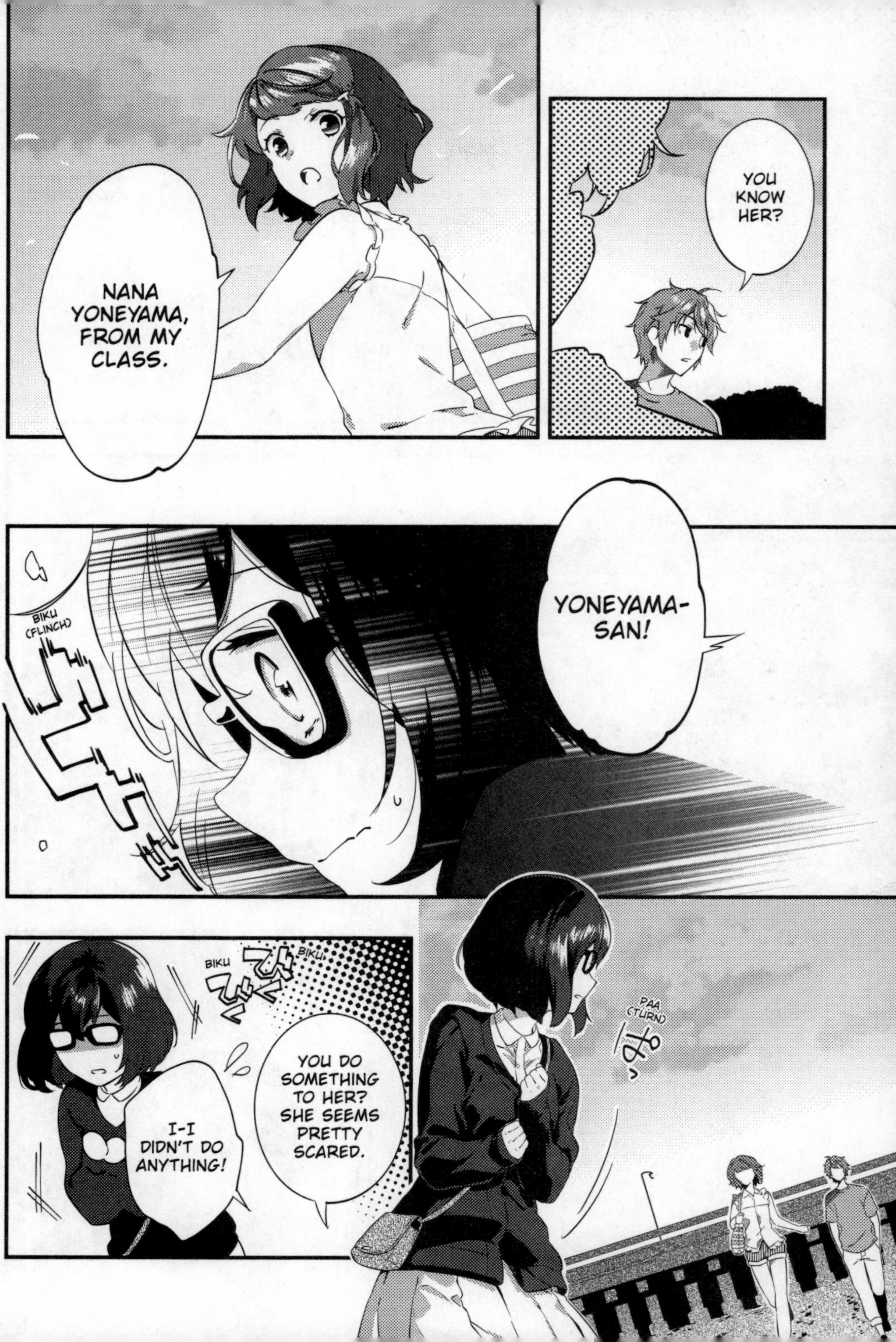
YOU KNOW HER?
NANA YONEYAMA, FROM MY CLASS.
YONEYAMA-SAN!
BIKU (FLINCH)
PAA (TURN)
BIKU BIKU
YOU DO SOMETHING TO HER? SHE SEEMS PRETTY SCARED.
I-I DIDN'T DO ANYTHING!

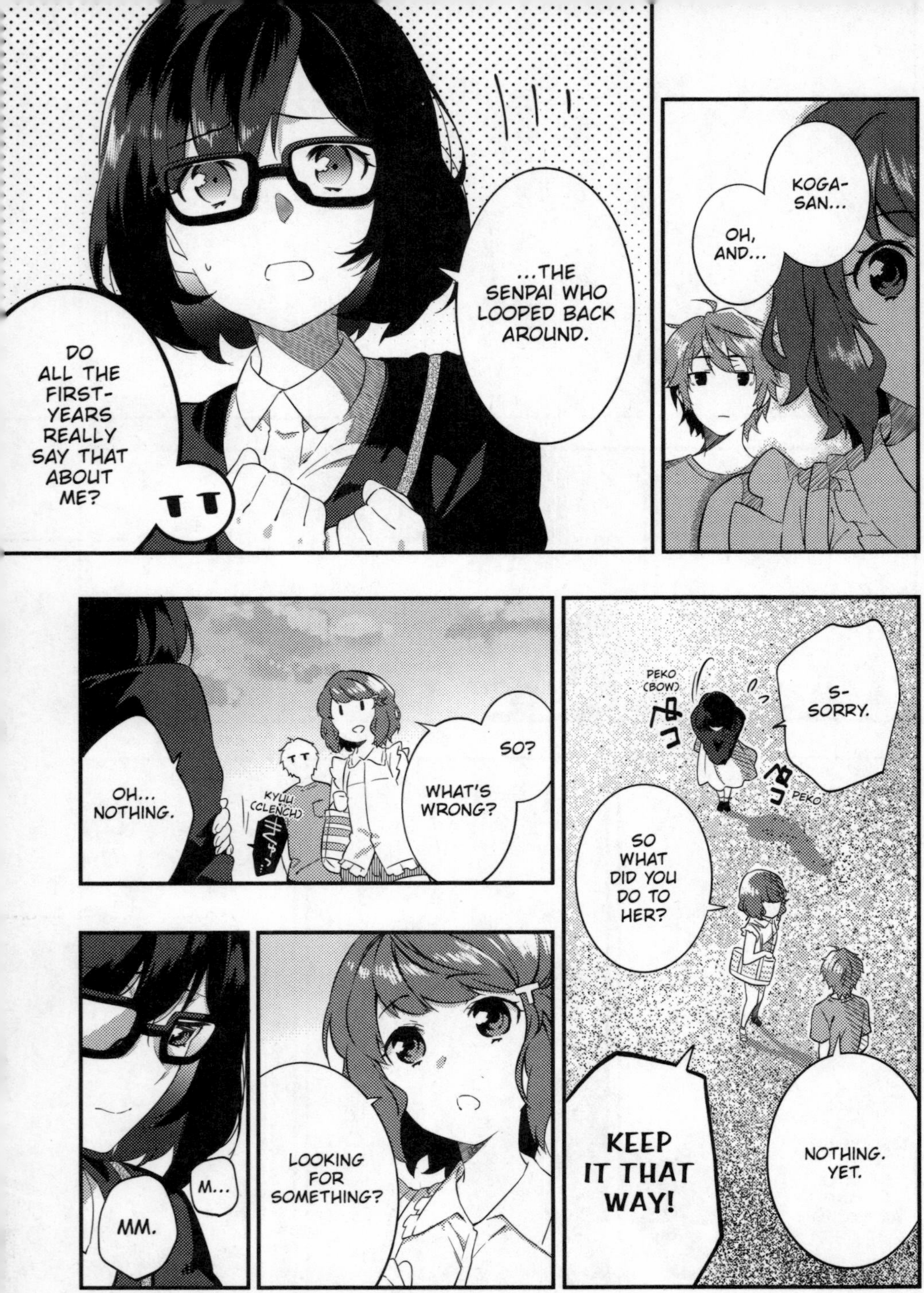
KOGA-SAN...
OH, AND...
...THE SENPAI WHO LOOPED BACK AROUND.
DO ALL THE FIRST-YEARS REALLY SAY THAT ABOUT ME?
S-SORRY.
PEKO (BOW)
PEKO
SO WHAT DID YOU DO TO HER?
NOTHING. YET.
KEEP IT THAT WAY!
SO?
WHAT'S WRONG?
KYUU (CLENCH)
OH... NOTHING.
LOOKING FOR SOMETHING?
M...
MM.

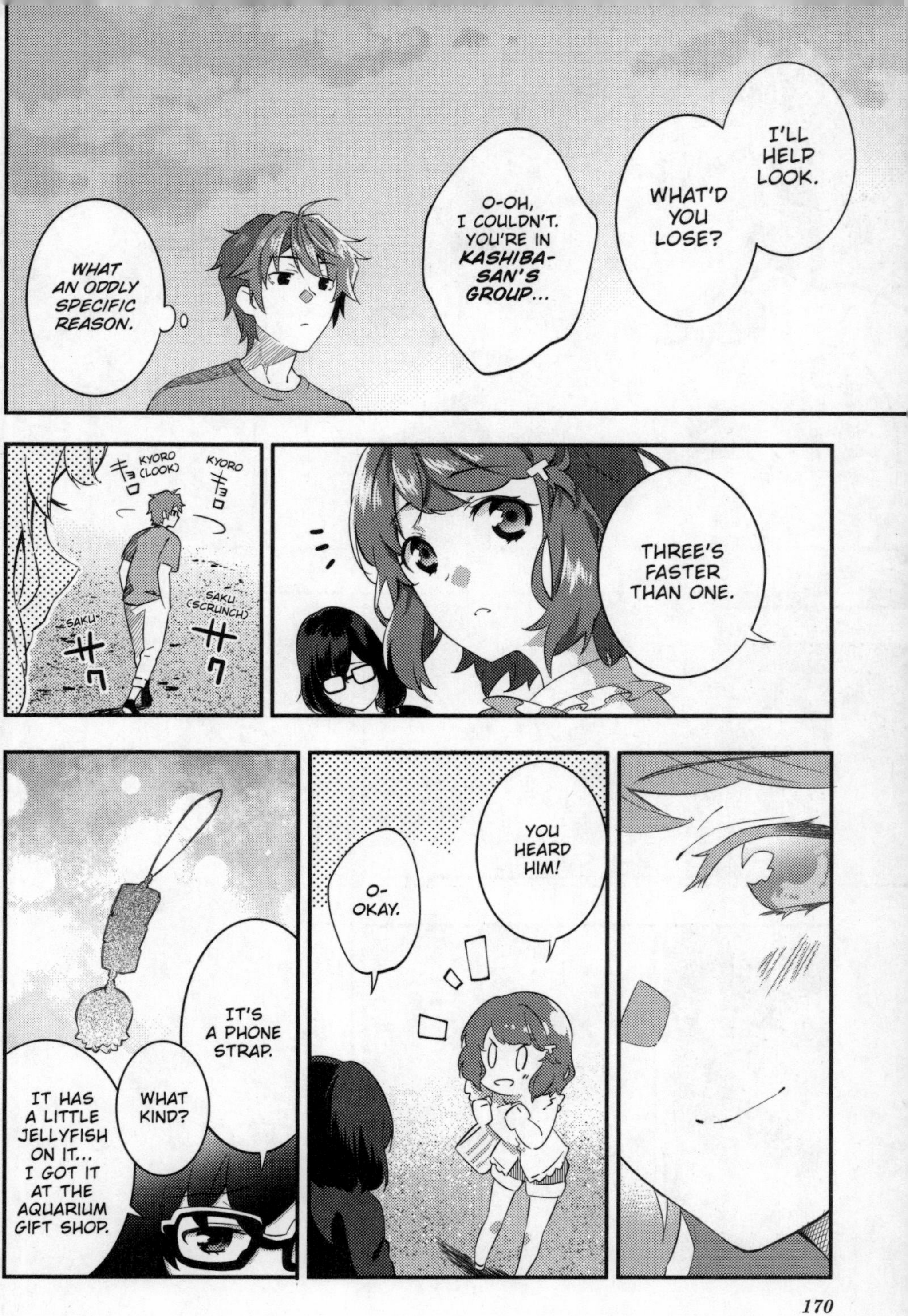
I'LL HELP LOOK.
WHAT'D YOU LOSE?
O-OH, I COULDN'T. YOU'RE IN ***KASHIBA-SAN'S*** GROUP...
WHAT AN ODDLY SPECIFIC REASON.
THREE'S FASTER THAN ONE.
KYORO
KYORO (LOOK)
SAKU (SCRUNCH)
SAKU
YOU HEARD HIM!
O-OKAY.
IT'S A PHONE STRAP.
WHAT KIND?
IT HAS A LITTLE JELLYFISH ON IT... I GOT IT AT THE AQUARIUM GIFT SHOP.

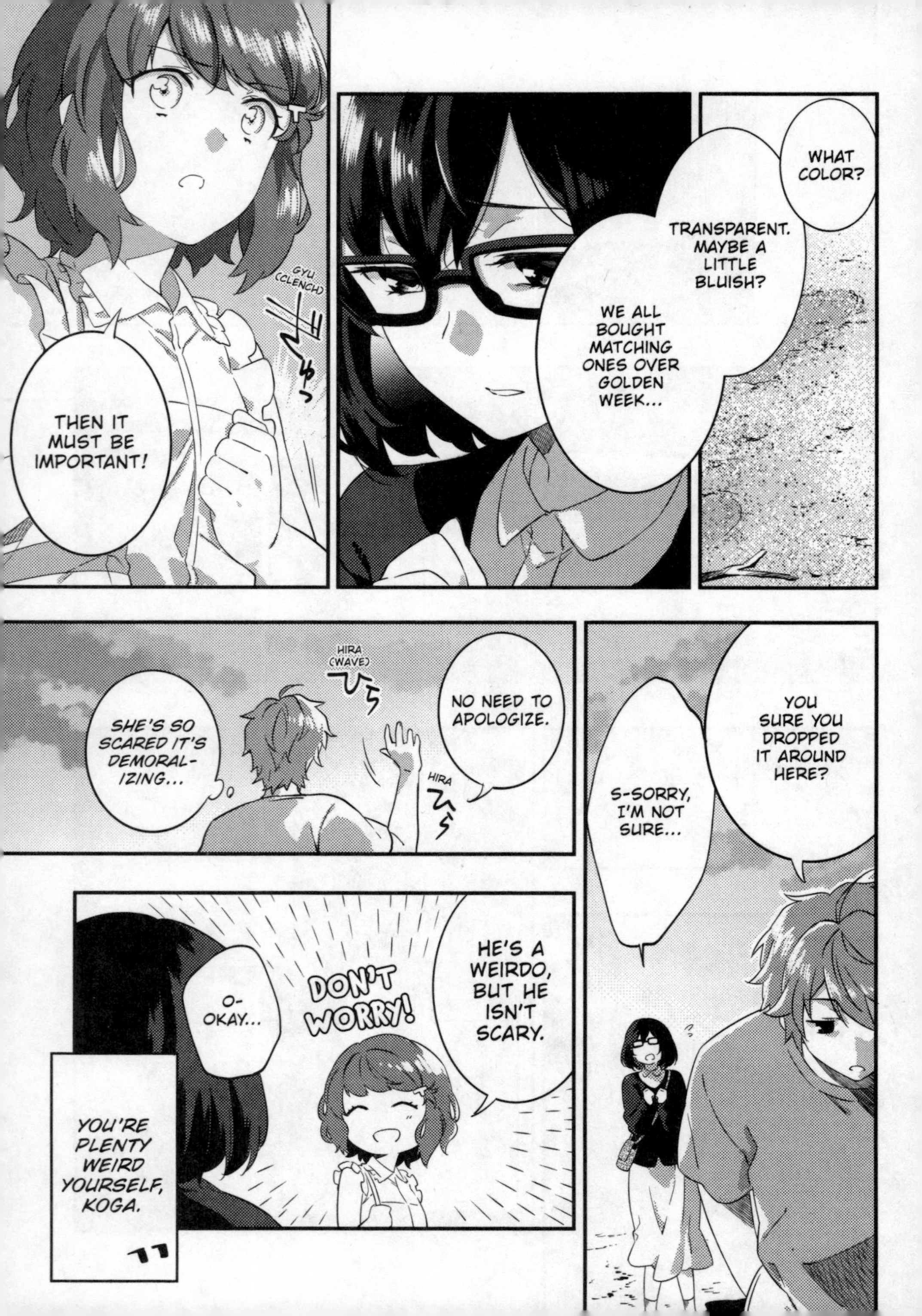
WHAT COLOR?
TRANSPARENT. MAYBE A LITTLE BLUISH?
WE ALL BOUGHT MATCHING ONES OVER GOLDEN WEEK...
GYU (CLENCH)
THEN IT MUST BE IMPORTANT!
YOU SURE YOU DROPPED IT AROUND HERE?
S-SORRY, I'M NOT SURE...
NO NEED TO APOLOGIZE.
HIRA (WAVE)
HIRA
SHE'S SO SCARED IT'S DEMORALIZING...
HE'S A WEIRDO, BUT HE ISN'T SCARY.
DON'T WORRY!
O-OKAY...
YOU'RE PLENTY WEIRD YOURSELF, KOGA.

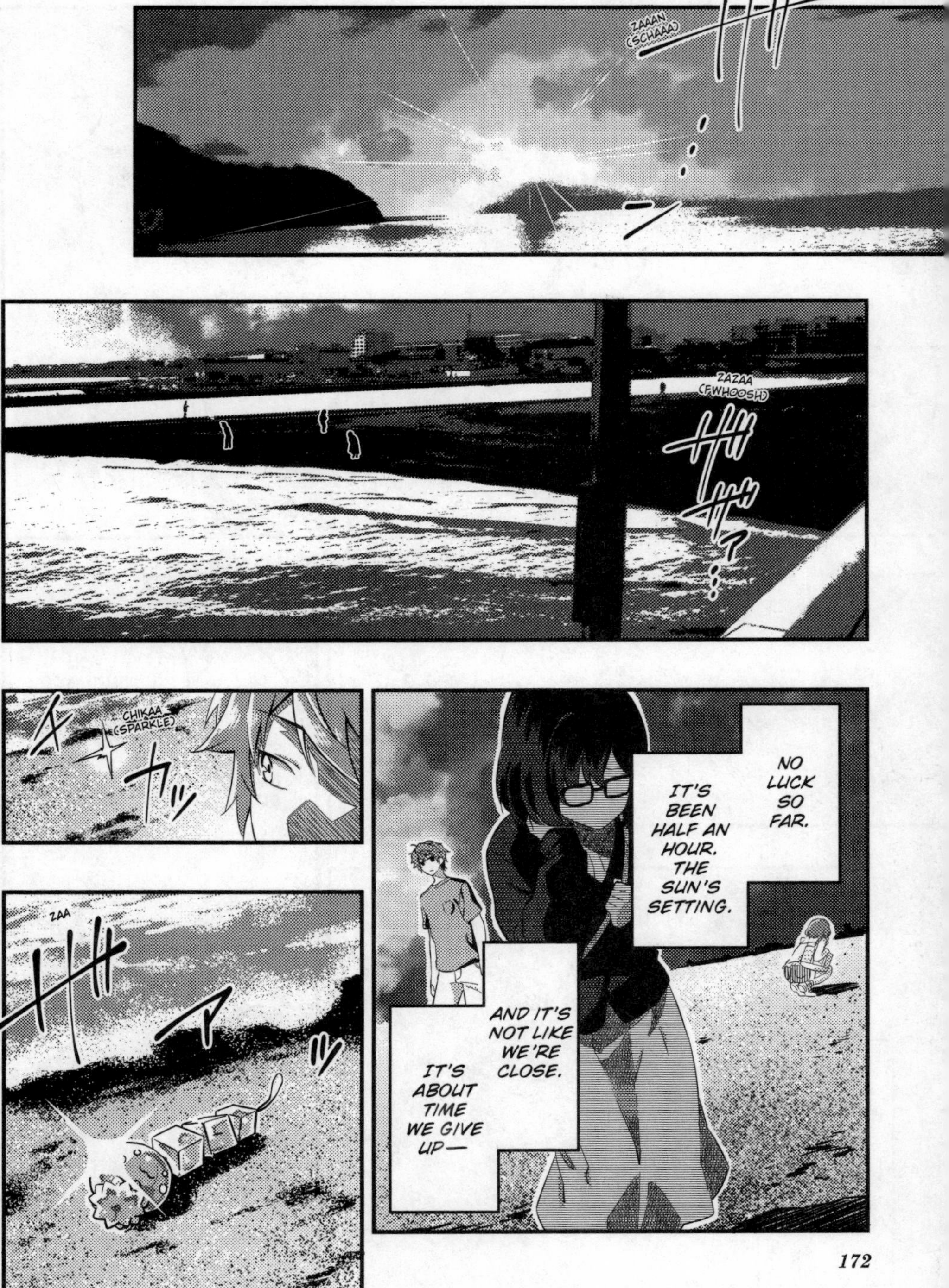
ZAAAN (SCHAAA)
ZAZAA (FWHOOSH)
NO LUCK SO FAR.
IT'S BEEN HALF AN HOUR. THE SUN'S SETTING.
AND IT'S NOT LIKE WE'RE CLOSE.
IT'S ABOUT TIME WE GIVE UP—
CHIKAA (SPARKLE)
ZAA

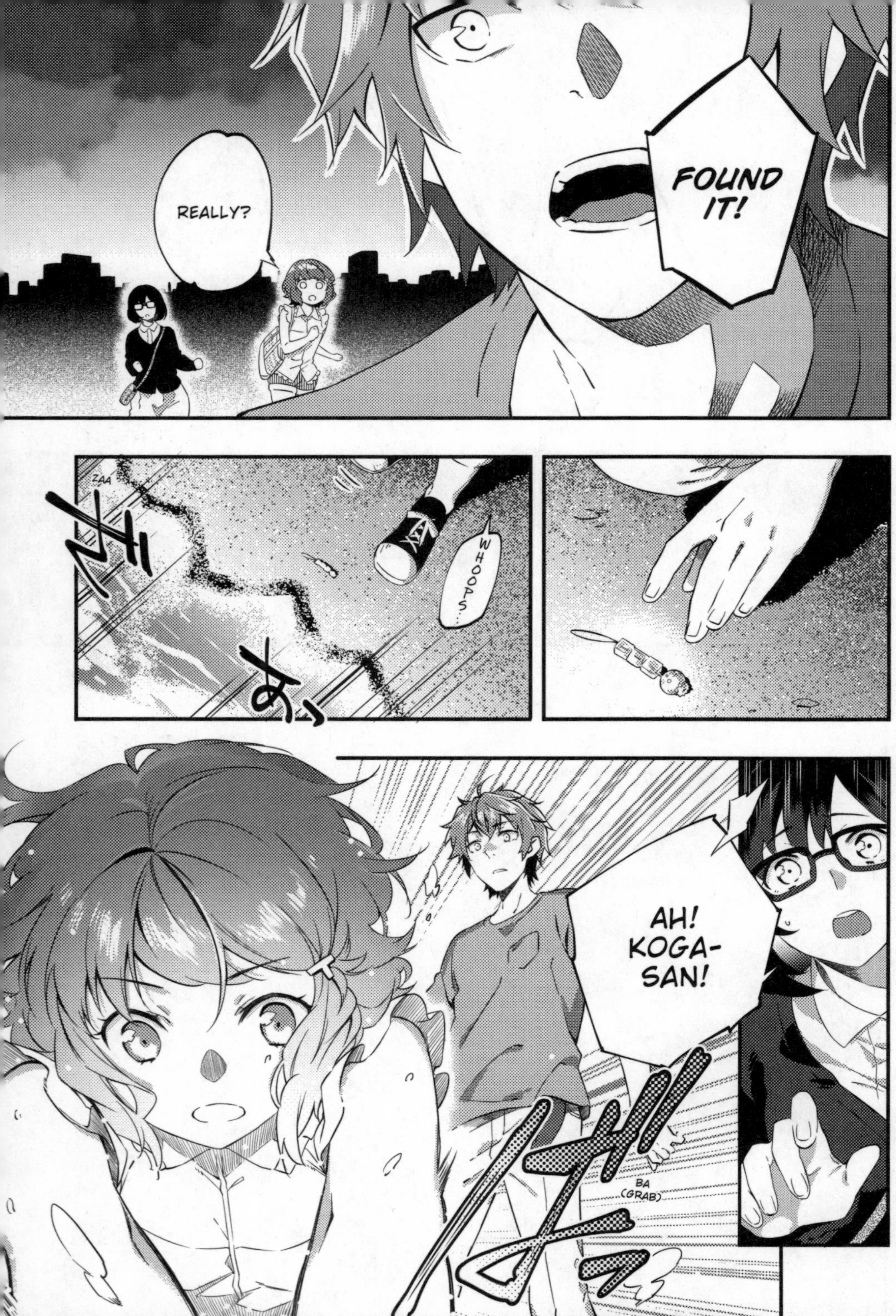
FOUND IT!
REALLY?
ZAA
WHOOPS...
あっ
AH! KOGA-SAN!
BA (GRAB)

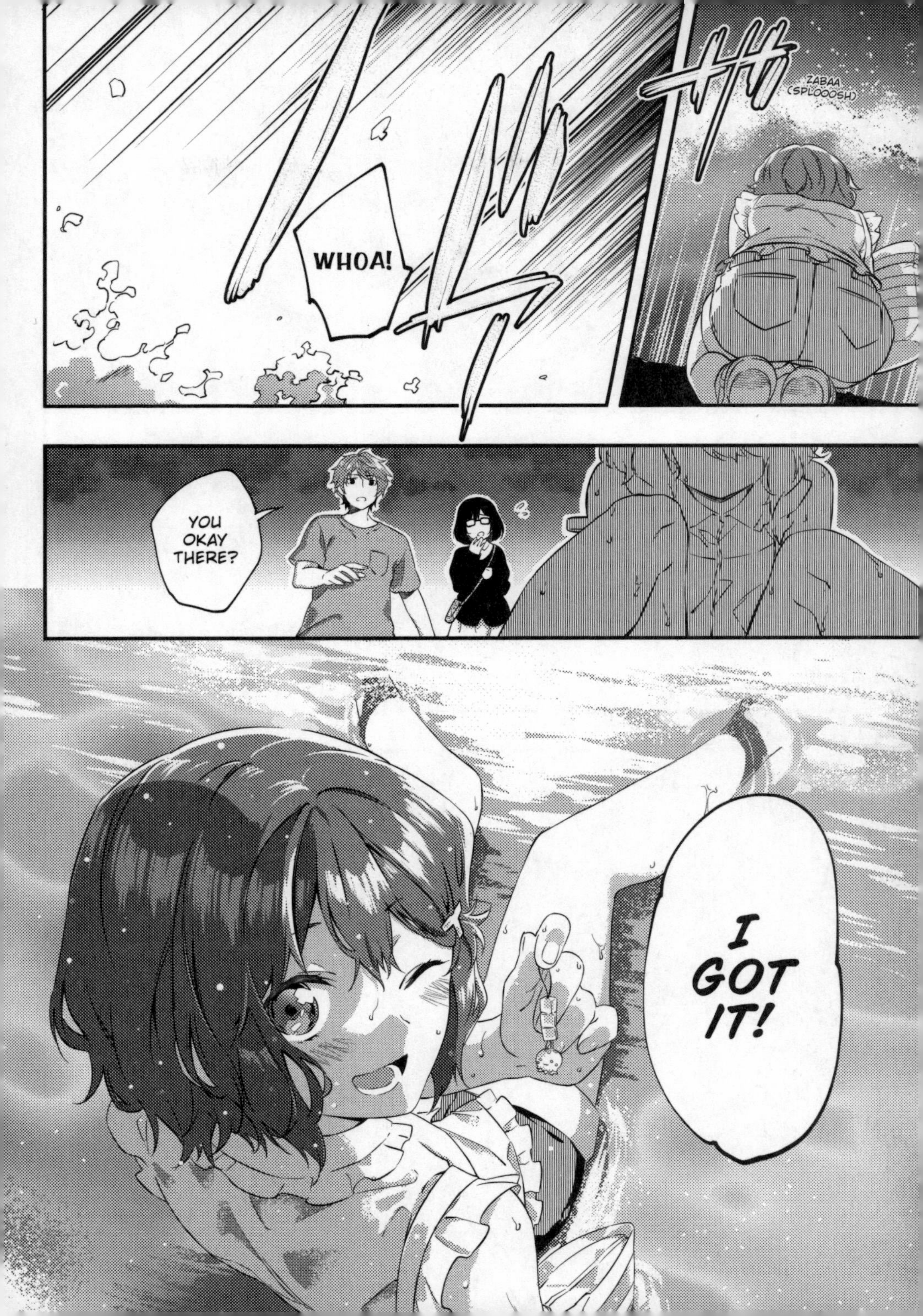
ZABAA (SPLOOOSH)
WHOA!
YOU OKAY THERE?
I GOT IT!

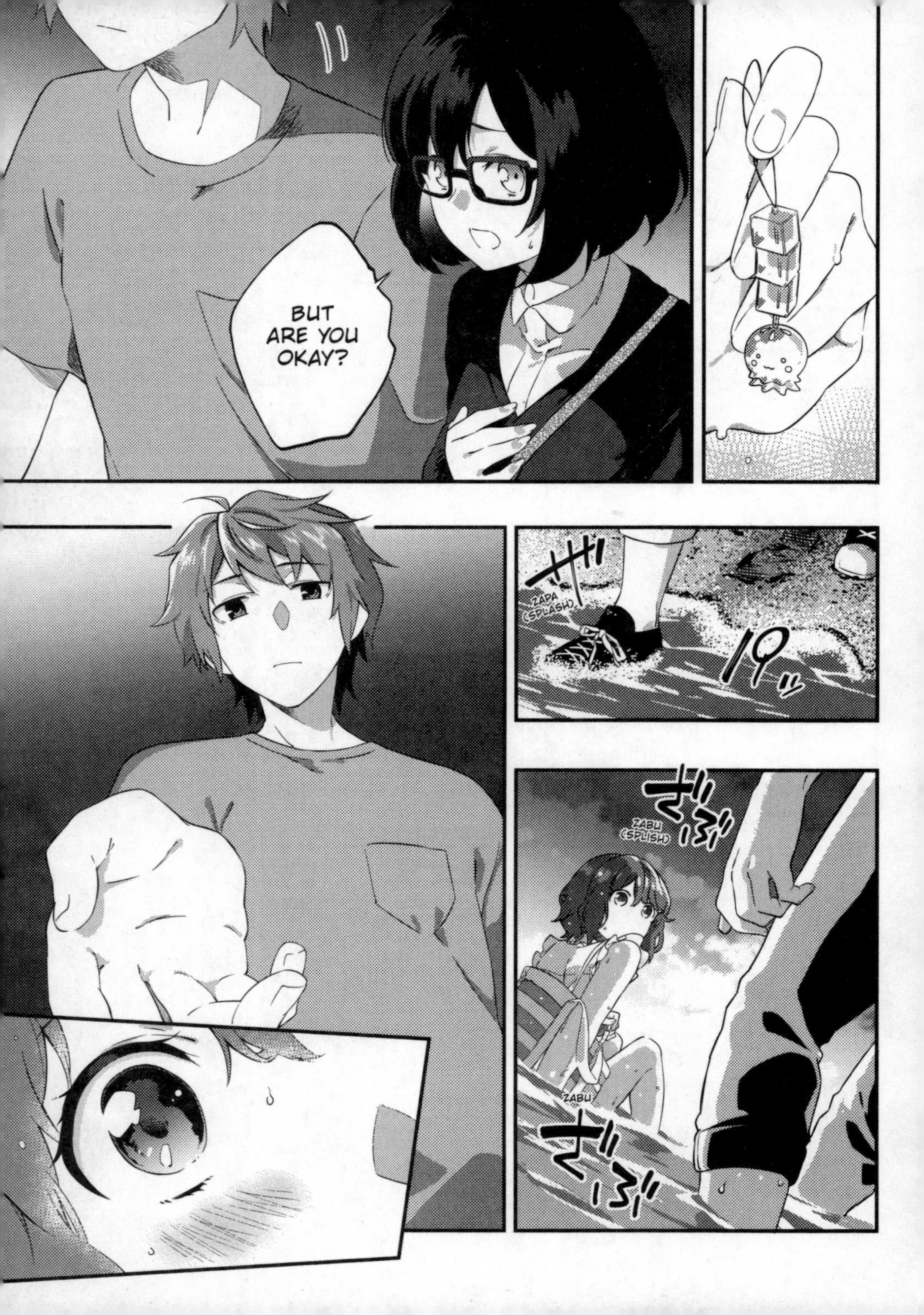
BUT ARE YOU OKAY?
ZAPA (SPLASH)
ZABU (SPLASH)
ZABU

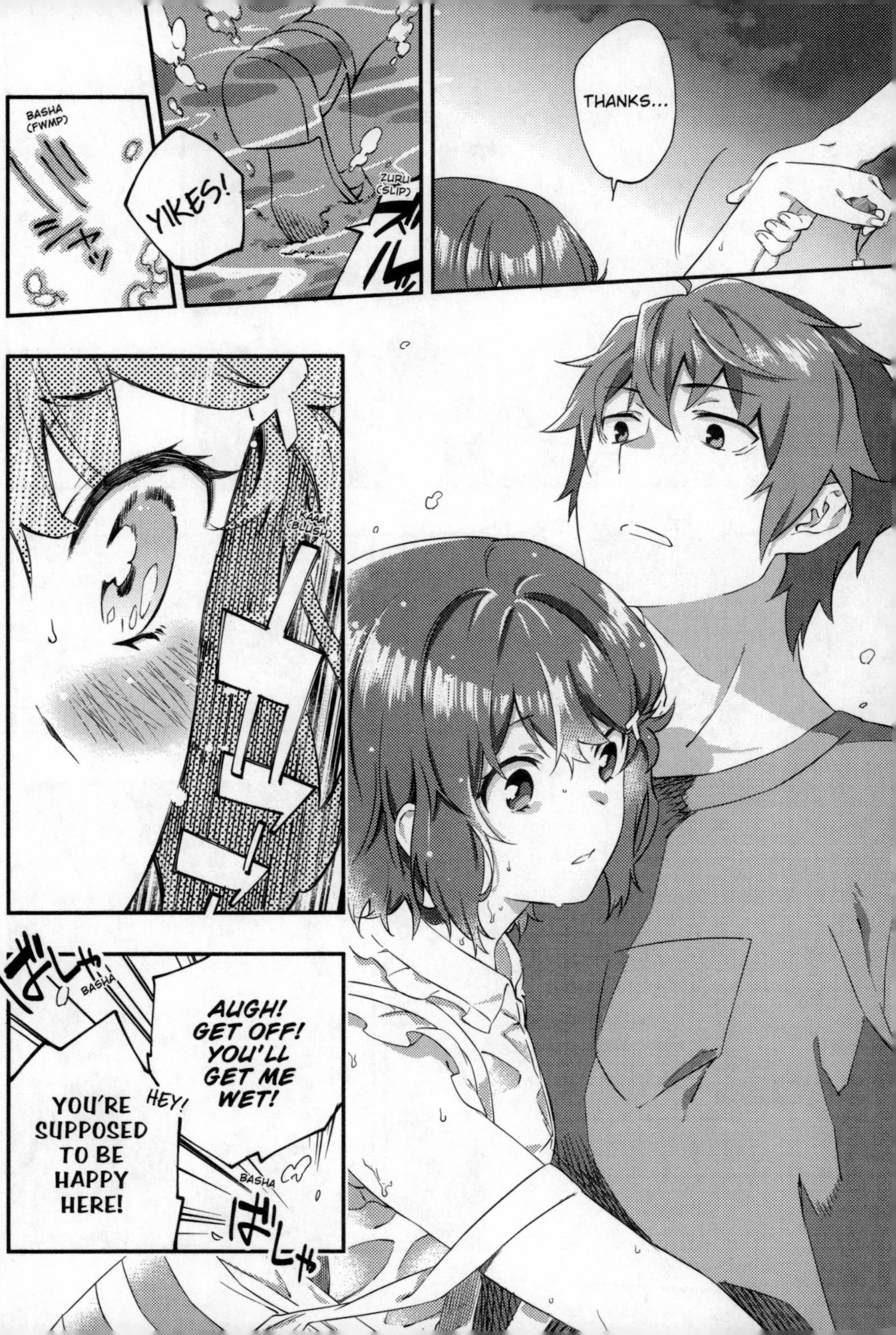
THANKS...
ZURU (SLIP)
YIKES!
BASHA (FWMP)
KAAA! (BLUSH)
ばしゃ
BASHA
AUGH! GET OFF! YOU'LL GET ME WET!
HEY!
YOU'RE SUPPOSED TO BE HAPPY HERE!
BASHA
ばしゃ

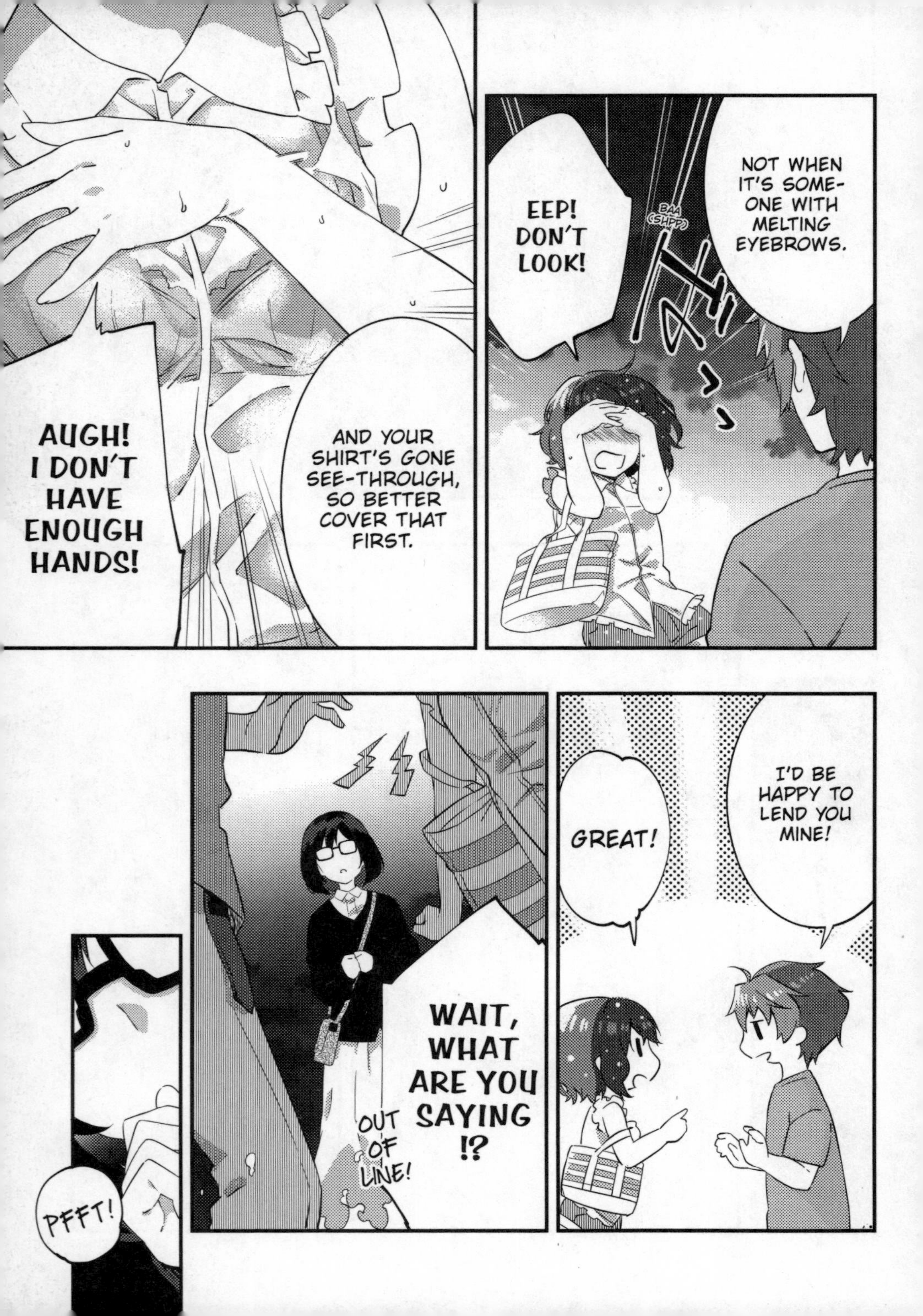
NOT WHEN IT'S SOME-ONE WITH MELTING EYEBROWS.
BAA (SHPP)
EEP! DON'T LOOK!
AND YOUR SHIRT'S GONE SEE-THROUGH, SO BETTER COVER THAT FIRST.
AUGH! I DON'T HAVE ENOUGH HANDS!
I'D BE HAPPY TO LEND YOU MINE!
GREAT!
WAIT, WHAT ARE YOU SAYING !?
OUT OF LINE!
PFFT!

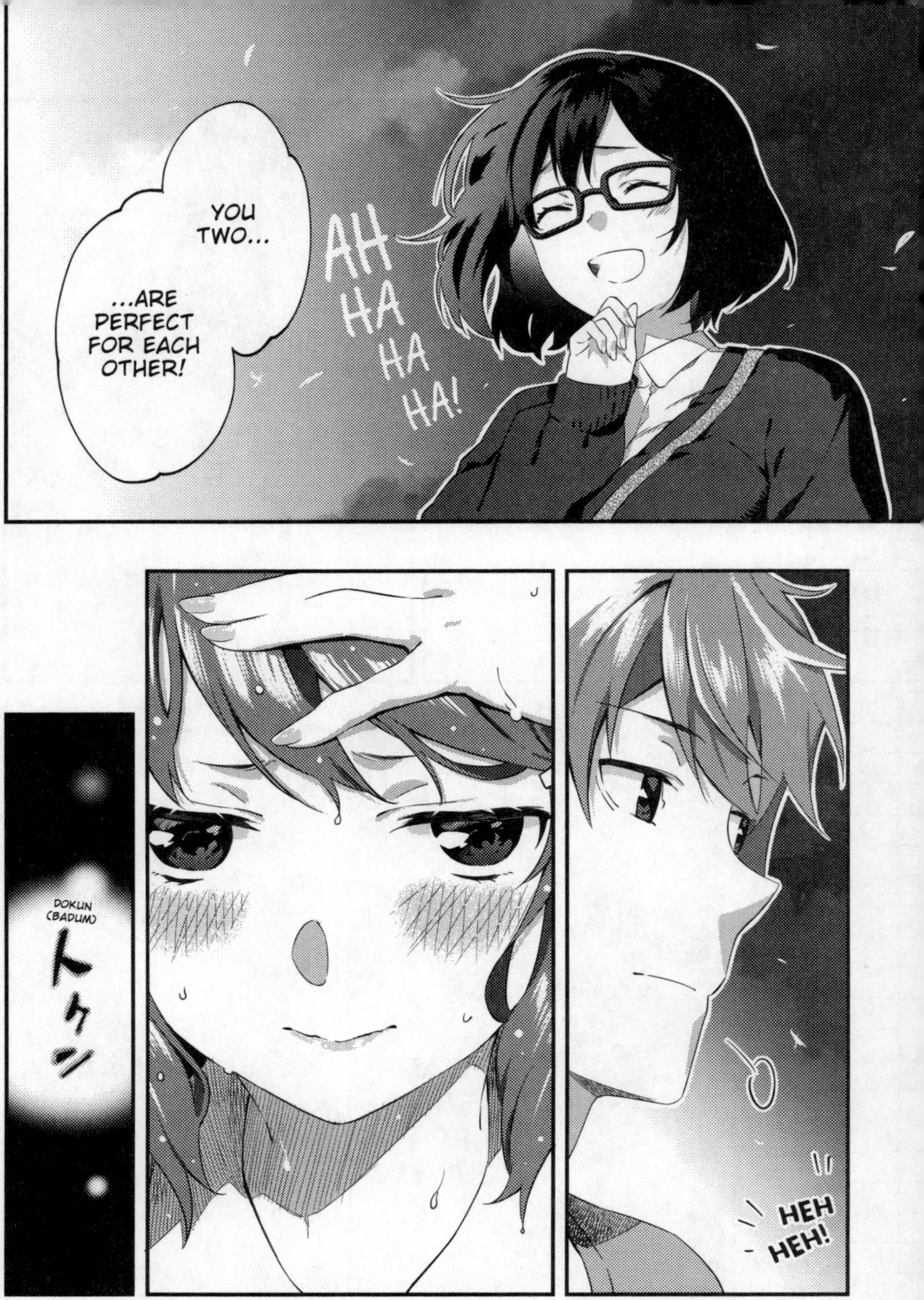
YOU TWO...
...ARE PERFECT FOR EACH OTHER!
AH HA HA HA!
HEH HEH!
DOKUN (BADUM)
トクン

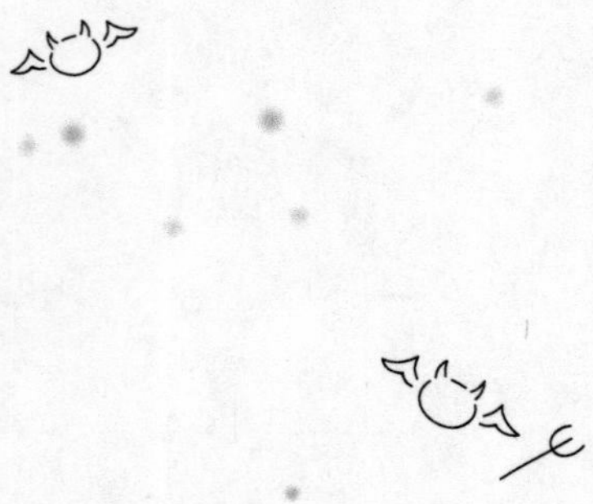

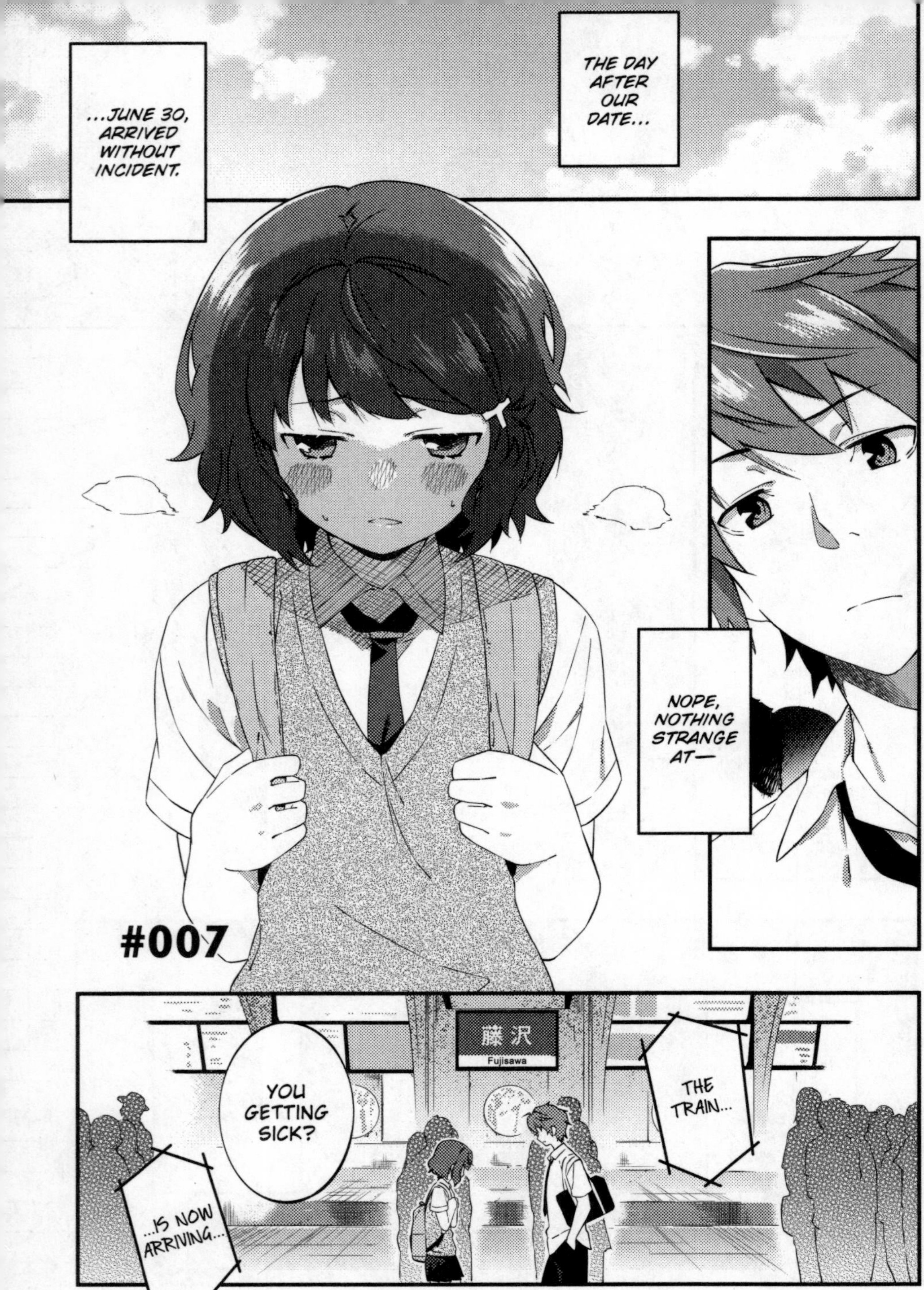
THE DAY AFTER OUR DATE...
...JUNE 30, ARRIVED WITHOUT INCIDENT.
NOPE, NOTHING STRANGE AT—
#007
THE TRAIN...
藤沢
Fujisawa
YOU GETTING SICK?
...IS NOW ARRIVING...

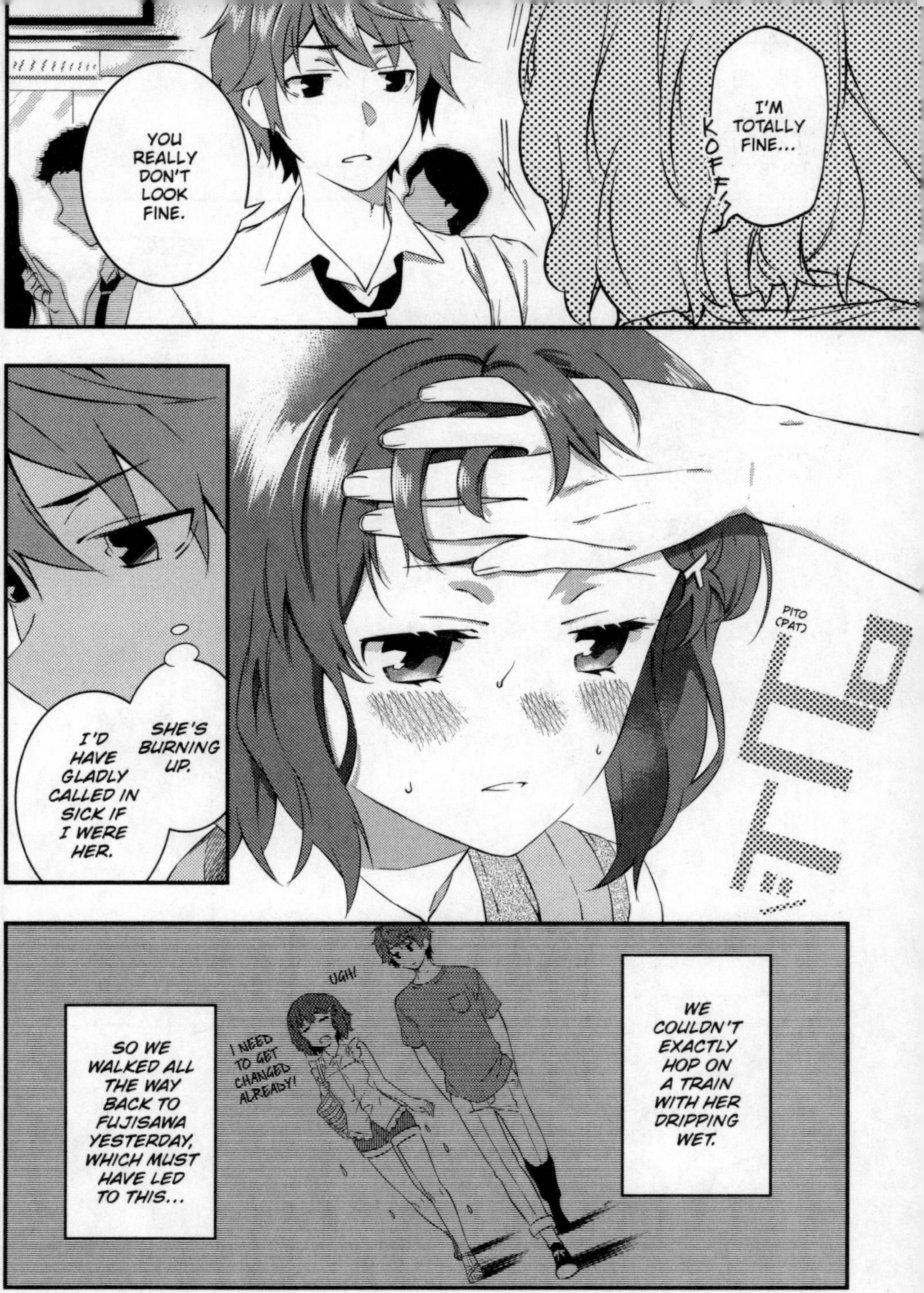
I'M TOTALLY FINE...
KOFF
YOU REALLY DON'T LOOK FINE.
PITO (PAT)
SHE'S BURNING UP.
I'D HAVE GLADLY CALLED IN SICK IF I WERE HER.
WE COULDN'T EXACTLY HOP ON A TRAIN WITH HER DRIPPING WET.
UGH!
I NEED TO GET CHANGED ALREADY!
SO WE WALKED ALL THE WAY BACK TO FUJISAWA YESTERDAY, WHICH MUST HAVE LED TO THIS...

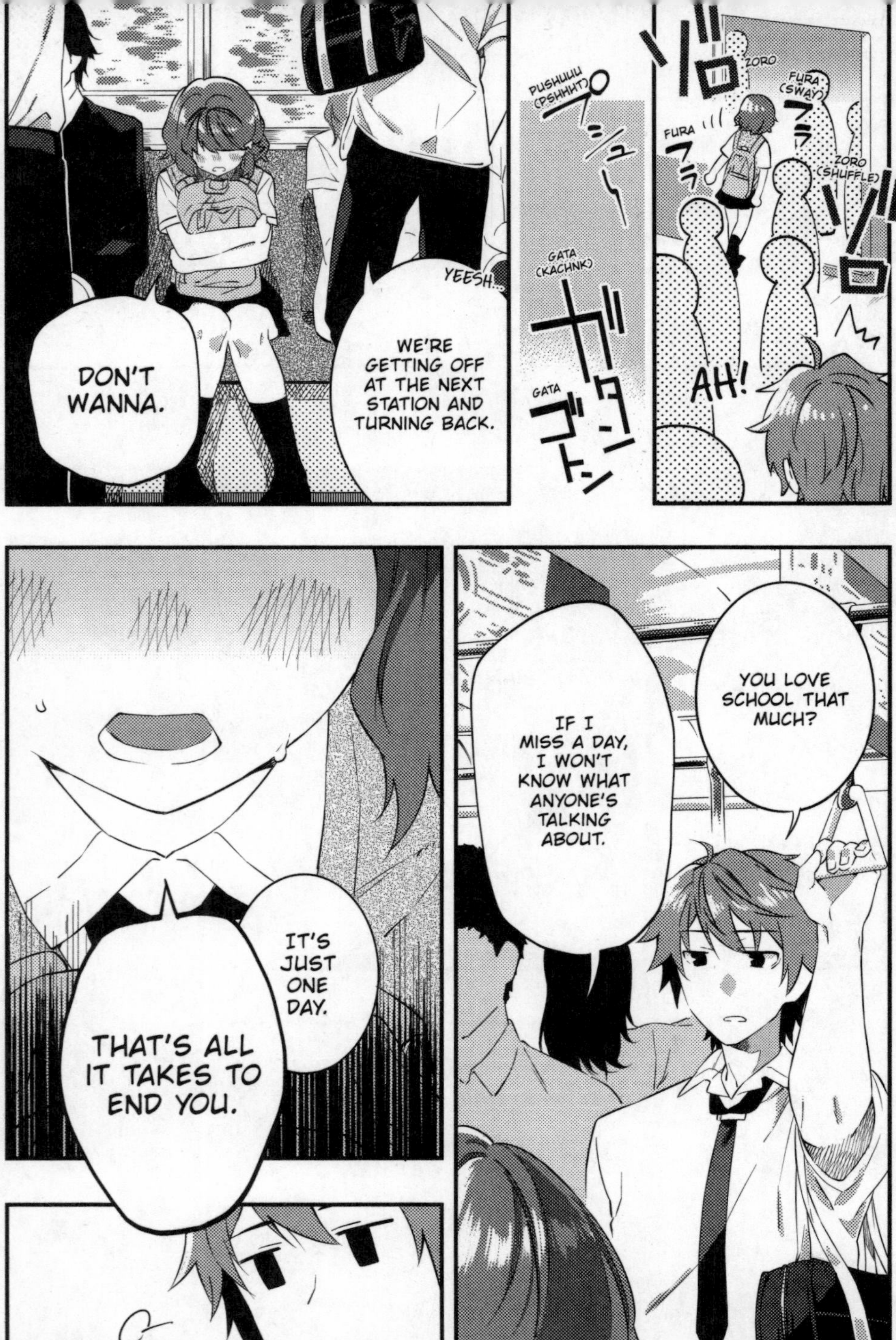
ZORO
FURA (SWAY)
ZORO (SHUFFLE)
FURA
AH!
PUSHUUU (PSHHHT)
GATA (KACHNK)
GATA
YEESH...
WE'RE GETTING OFF AT THE NEXT STATION AND TURNING BACK.
DON'T WANNA.
YOU LOVE SCHOOL THAT MUCH?
IF I MISS A DAY, I WON'T KNOW WHAT ANYONE'S TALKING ABOUT.
IT'S JUST ONE DAY.
THAT'S ALL IT TAKES TO END YOU.

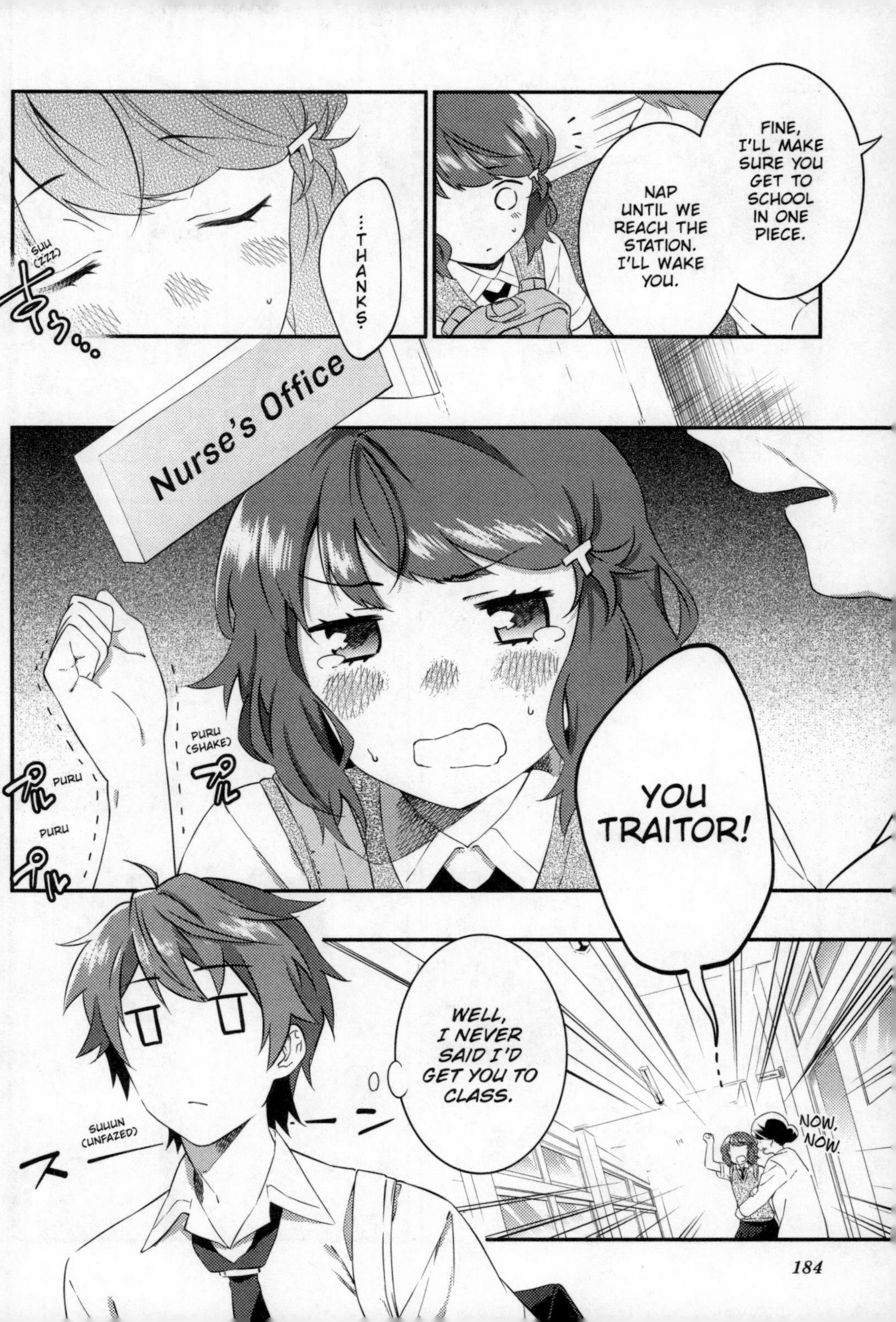
FINE, I'LL MAKE SURE YOU GET TO SCHOOL IN ONE PIECE.
NAP UNTIL WE REACH THE STATION. I'LL WAKE YOU.
...THANKS.
SUU (ZZZ)
Nurse's Office
YOU TRAITOR!
PURU (SHAKE)
PURU
PURU
NOW, NOW.
WELL, I NEVER SAID I'D GET YOU TO CLASS.
SUUUN (UNFAZED)

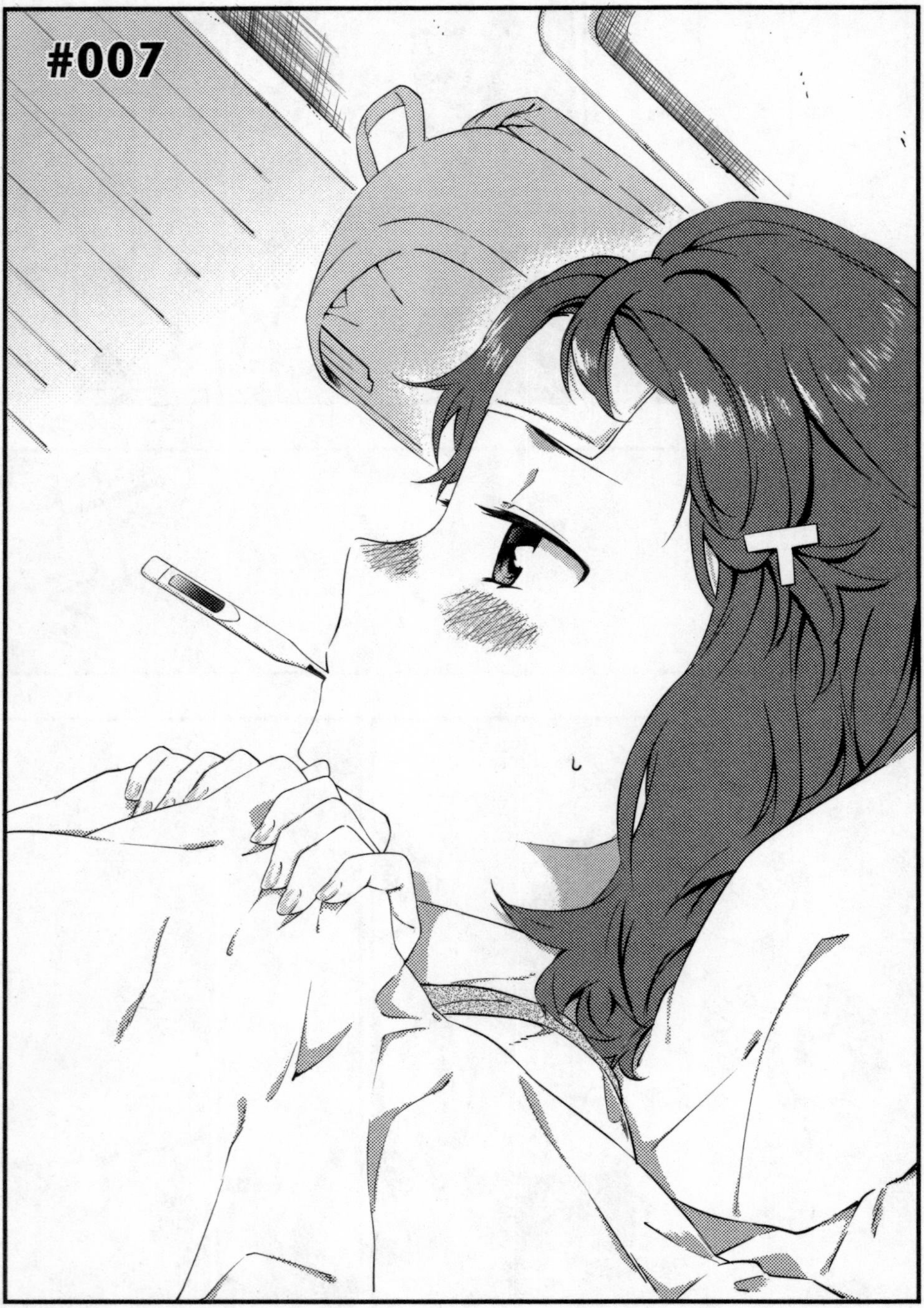
#007

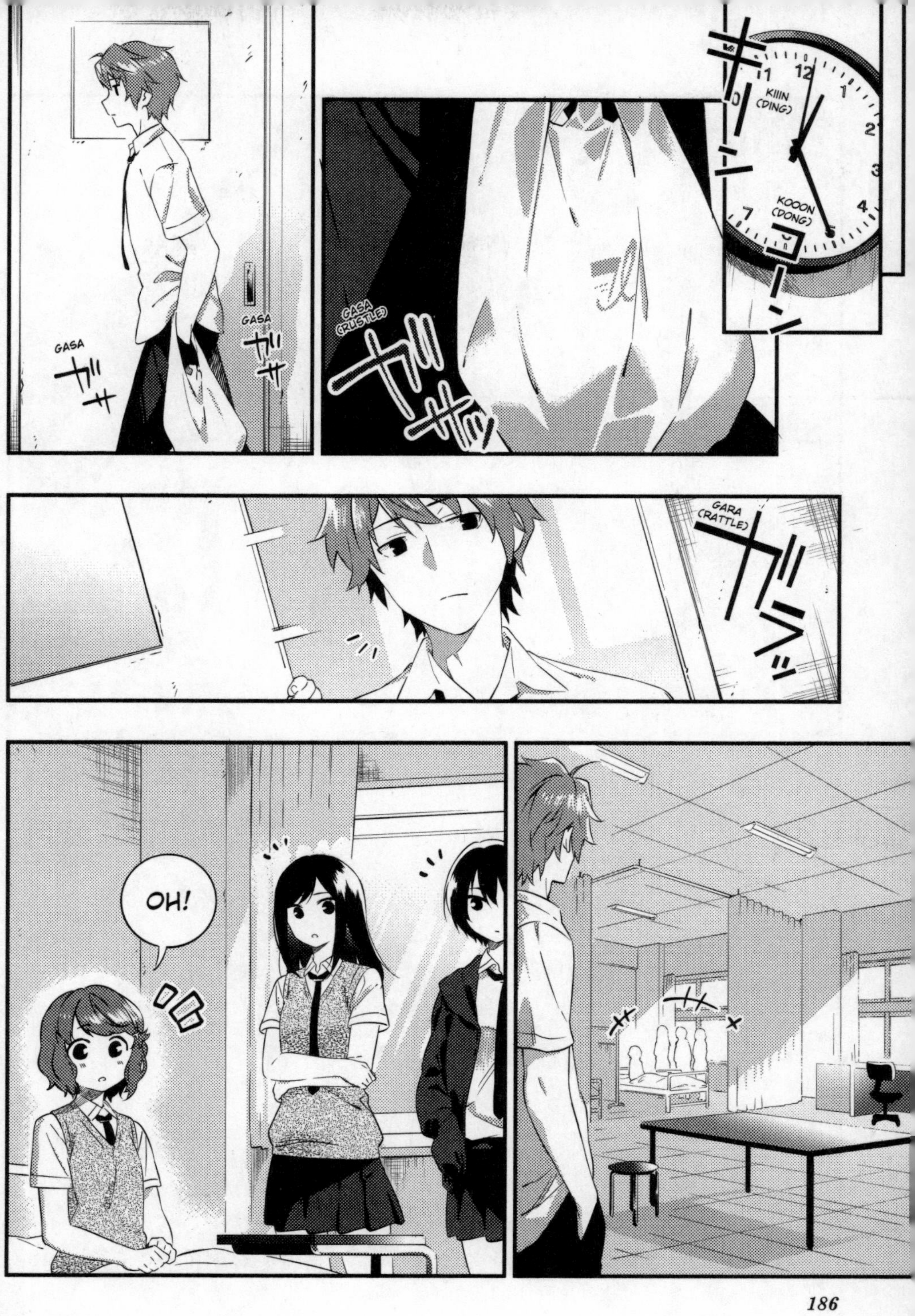
KIIIN
(DING)
KOOON
(DONG)
GASA
(RUSTLE)
GASA
GASA
GARA
(RATTLE)
OH!

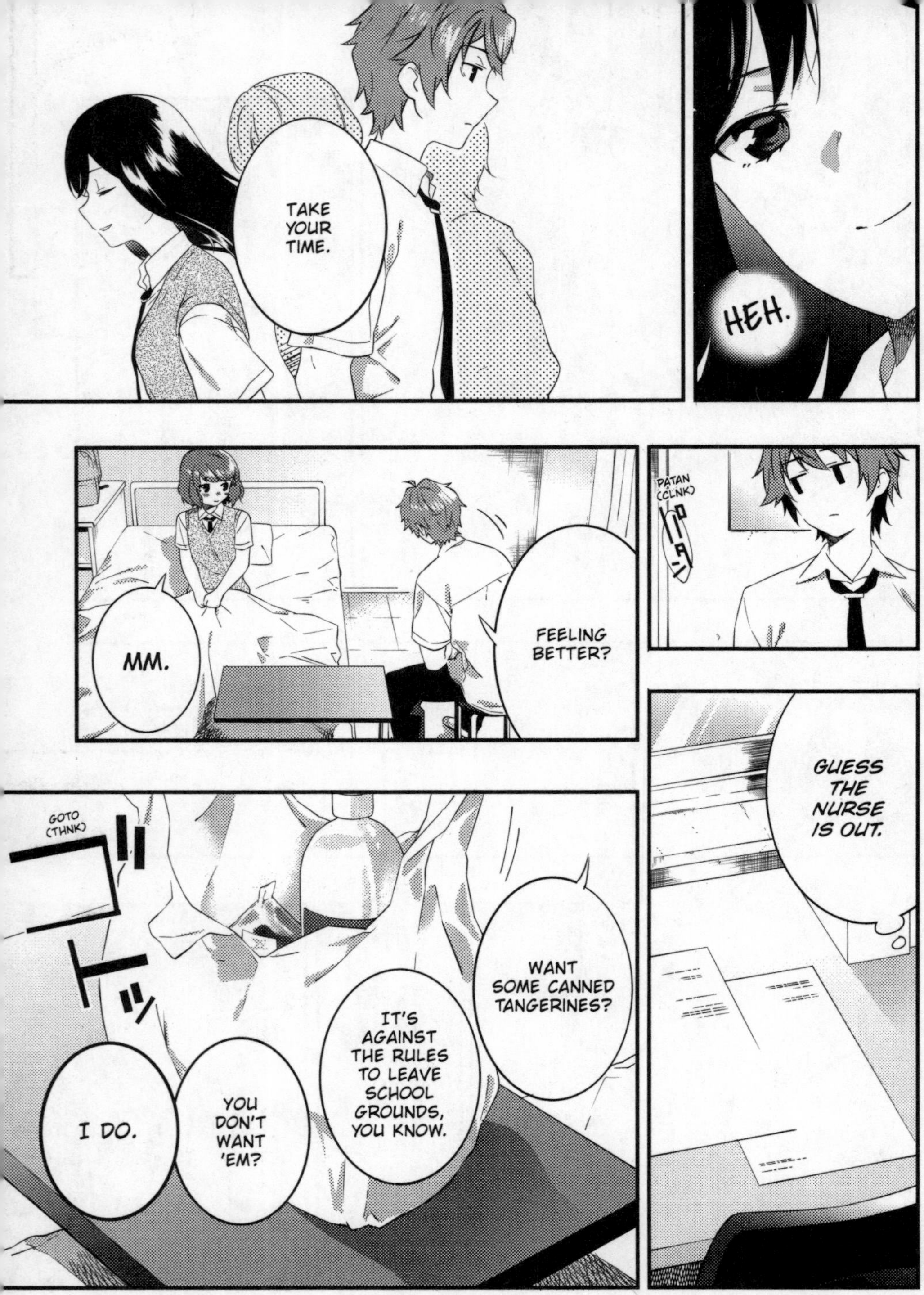
HEH.
TAKE YOUR TIME.
PATAN (CLNK)
FEELING BETTER?
MM.
GUESS THE NURSE IS OUT.
GOTO (THNK)
WANT SOME CANNED TANGERINES?
IT'S AGAINST THE RULES TO LEAVE SCHOOL GROUNDS, YOU KNOW.
YOU DON'T WANT 'EM?
I DO.

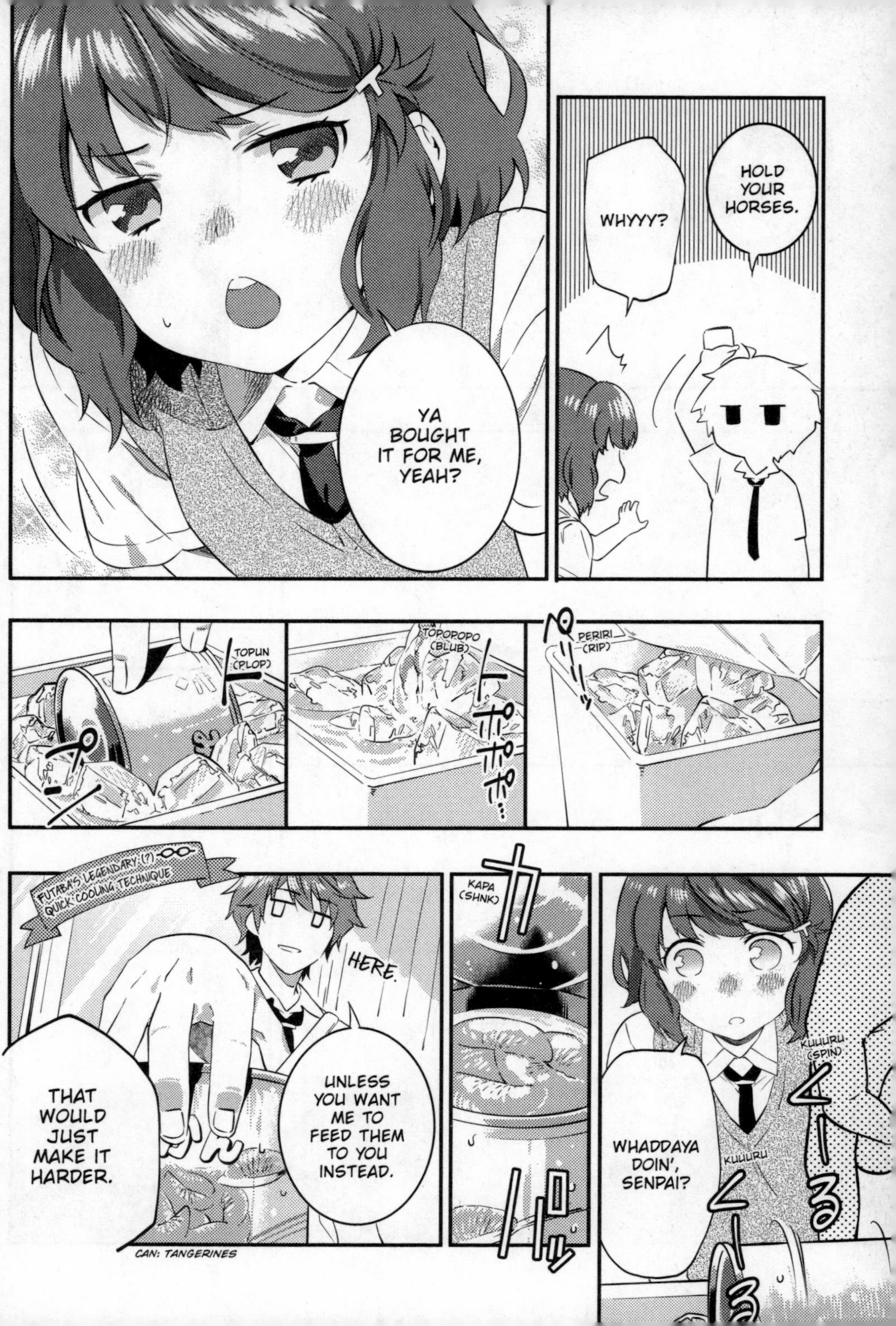
HOLD YOUR HORSES.
WHYYY?
YA BOUGHT IT FOR ME, YEAH?
PERIRI (RIP)
TOPOPOPO (BLUB)
TOPUN (PLOP)
KUUURU (SPIN)
KUUURU
WHADDAYA DOIN', SENPAI?
KAPA (SHNK)
FUTABA'S LEGENDARY (?) QUICK COOLING TECHNIQUE
HERE.
UNLESS YOU WANT ME TO FEED THEM TO YOU INSTEAD.
THAT WOULD JUST MAKE IT HARDER.
CAN: TANGERINES

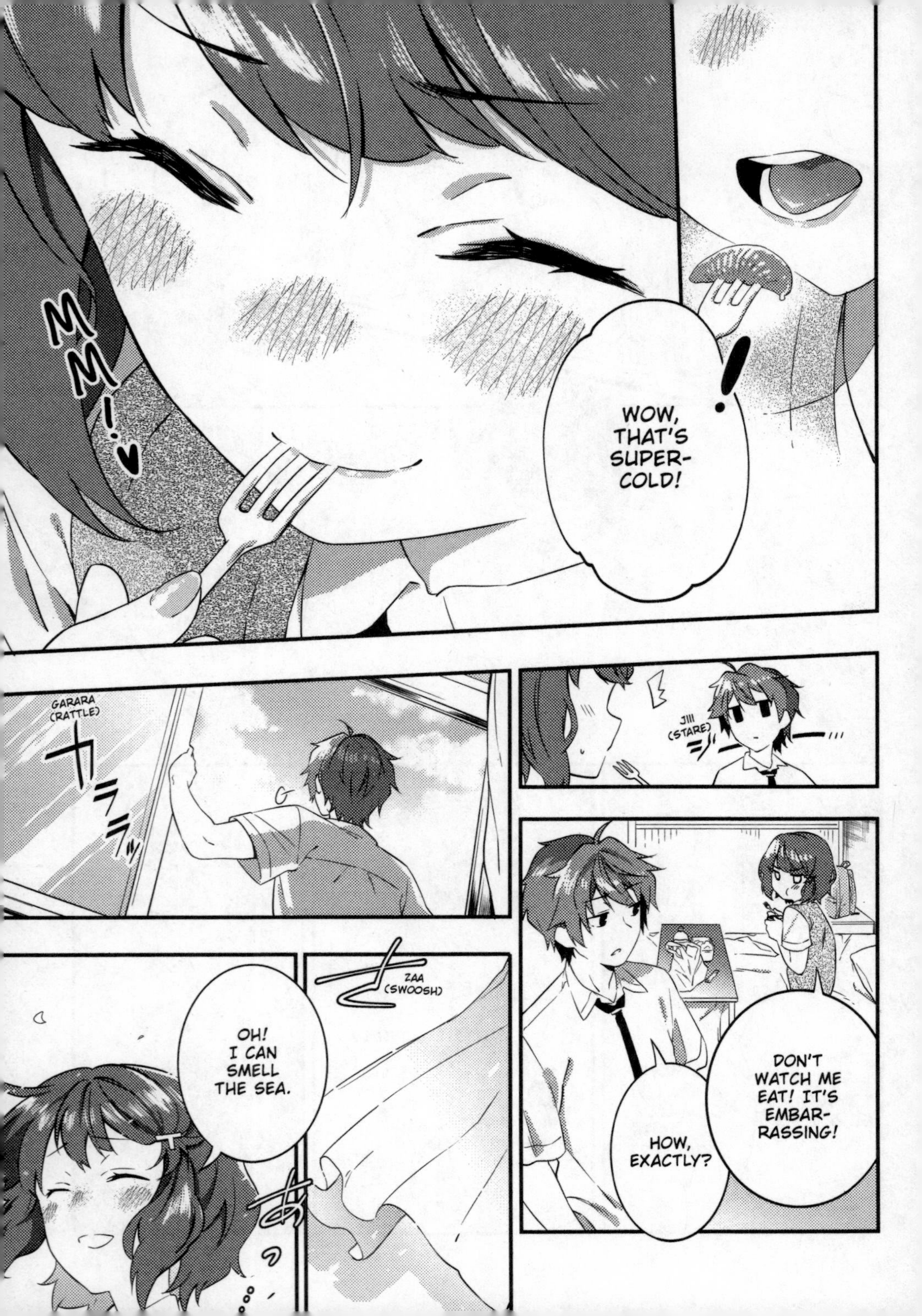
!
WOW, THAT'S SUPER-COLD!
MMM!♥
JIII (STARE)
DON'T WATCH ME EAT! IT'S EMBARRASSING!
HOW, EXACTLY?
GARARA (RATTLE)
ZAA (SWOOSH)
OH! I CAN SMELL THE SEA.

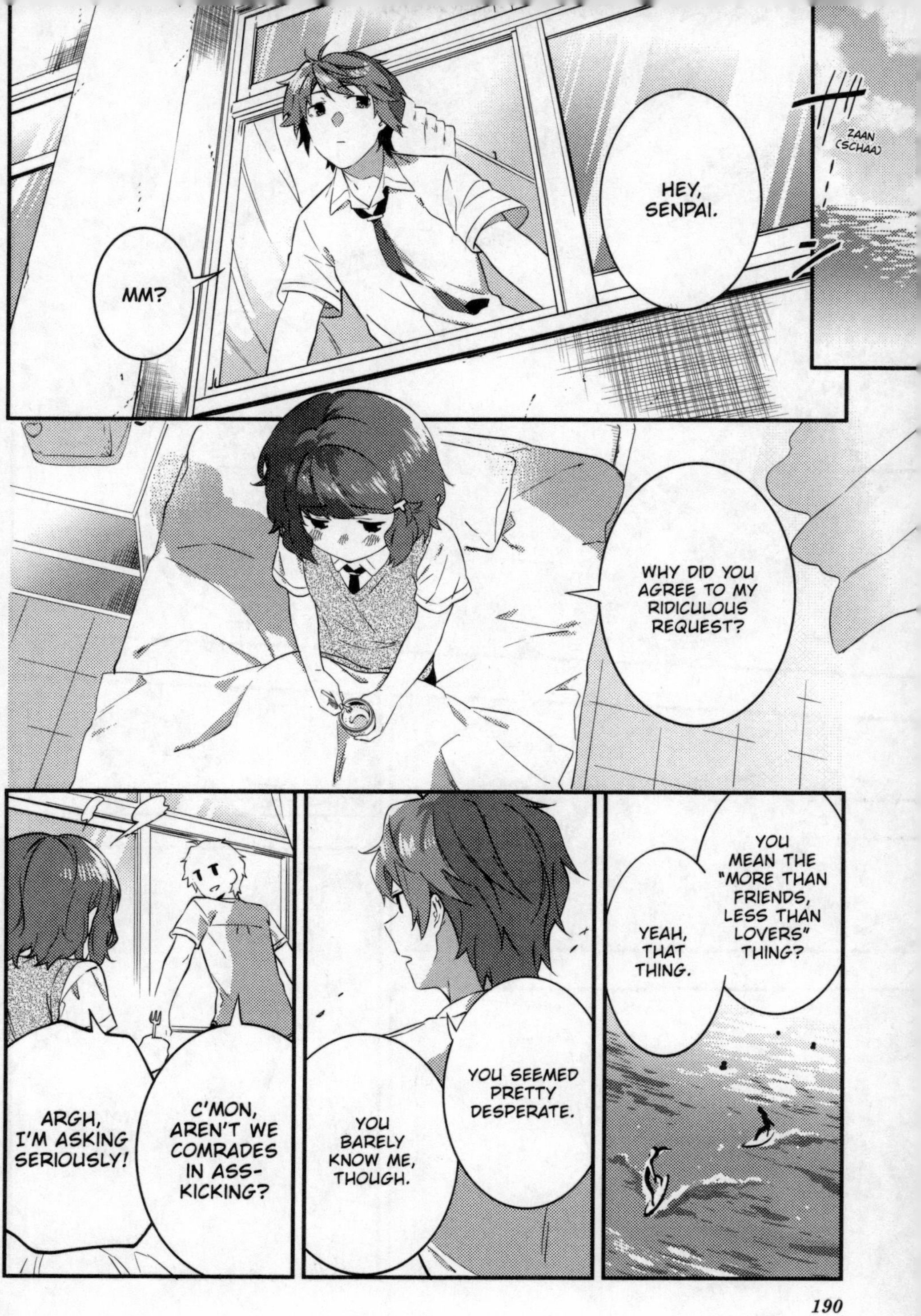
ZAAN (SCHAA)
HEY, SENPAI.
MM?
WHY DID YOU AGREE TO MY RIDICULOUS REQUEST?
YOU MEAN THE "MORE THAN FRIENDS, LESS THAN LOVERS" THING?
YEAH, THAT THING.
YOU SEEMED PRETTY DESPERATE.
YOU BARELY KNOW ME, THOUGH.
C'MON, AREN'T WE COMRADES IN ASS-KICKING?
ARGH, I'M ASKING SERIOUSLY!

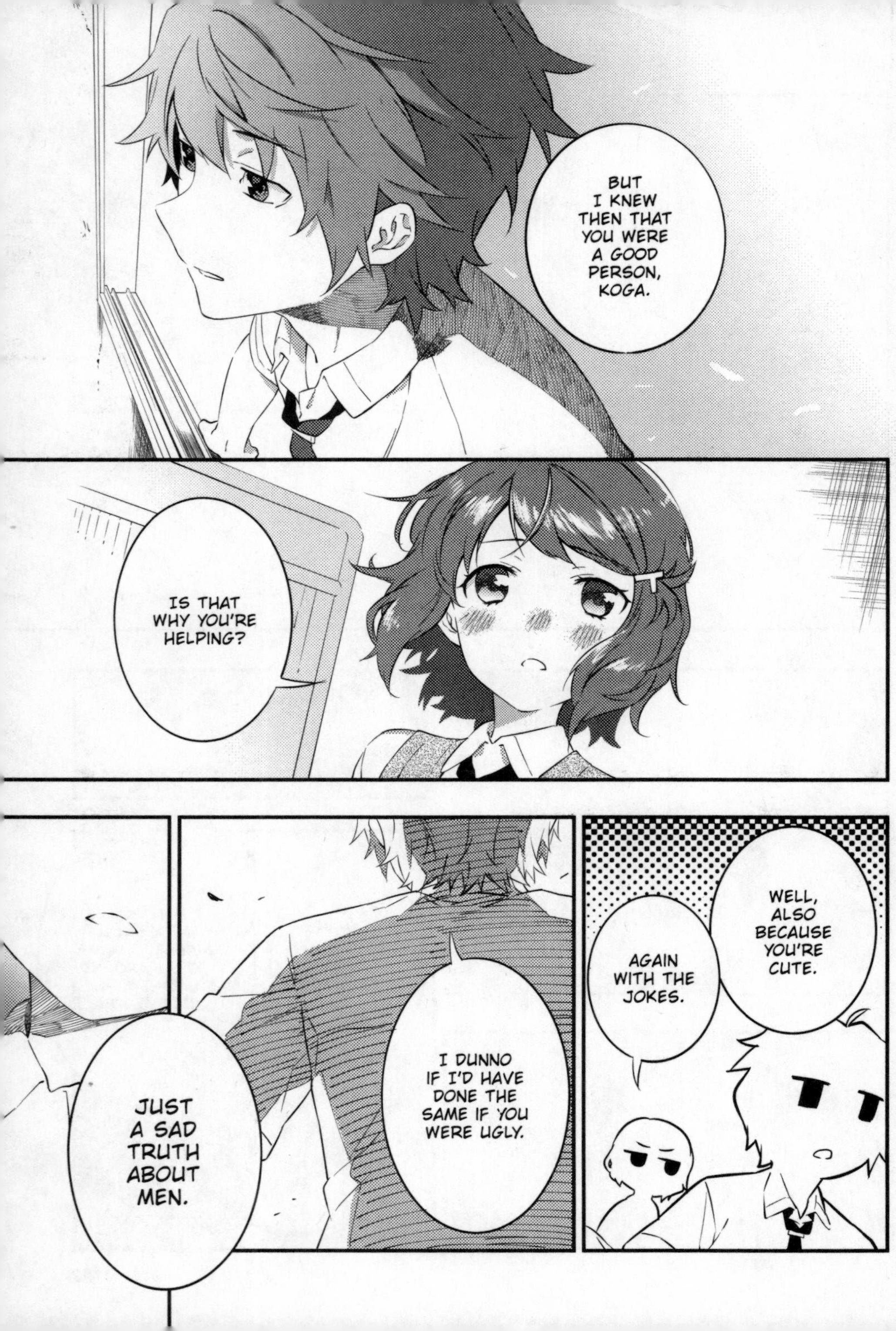
BUT I KNEW THEN THAT YOU WERE A GOOD PERSON, KOGA.
IS THAT WHY YOU'RE HELPING?
WELL, ALSO BECAUSE YOU'RE CUTE.
AGAIN WITH THE JOKES.
I DUNNO IF I'D HAVE DONE THE SAME IF YOU WERE UGLY.
JUST A SAD TRUTH ABOUT MEN.

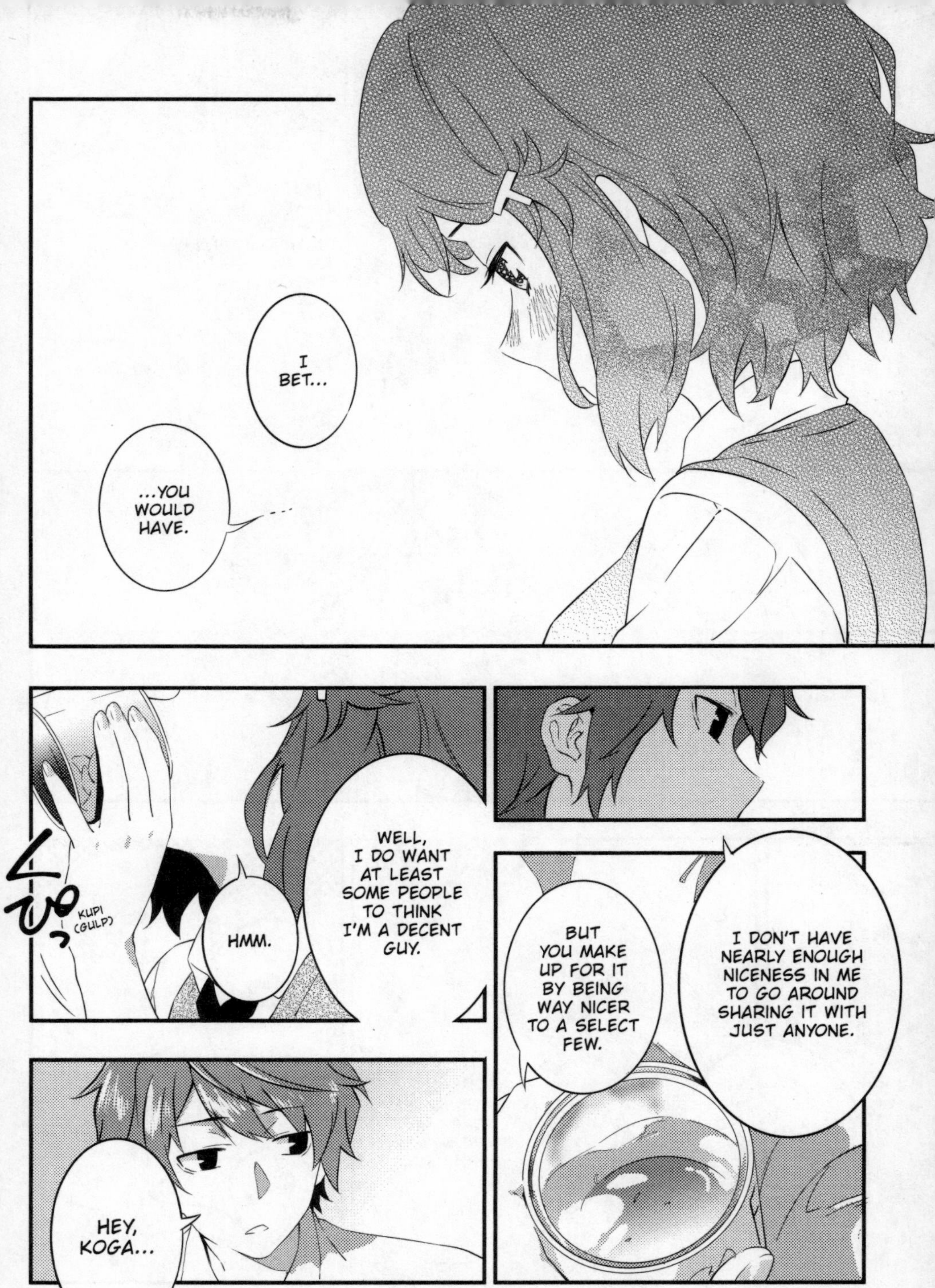
I BET...
...YOU WOULD HAVE.
WELL, I DO WANT AT LEAST SOME PEOPLE TO THINK I'M A DECENT GUY.
HMM.
KUPI (GULP)
I DON'T HAVE NEARLY ENOUGH NICENESS IN ME TO GO AROUND SHARING IT WITH JUST ANYONE.
BUT YOU MAKE UP FOR IT BY BEING WAY NICER TO A SELECT FEW.
HEY, KOGA...

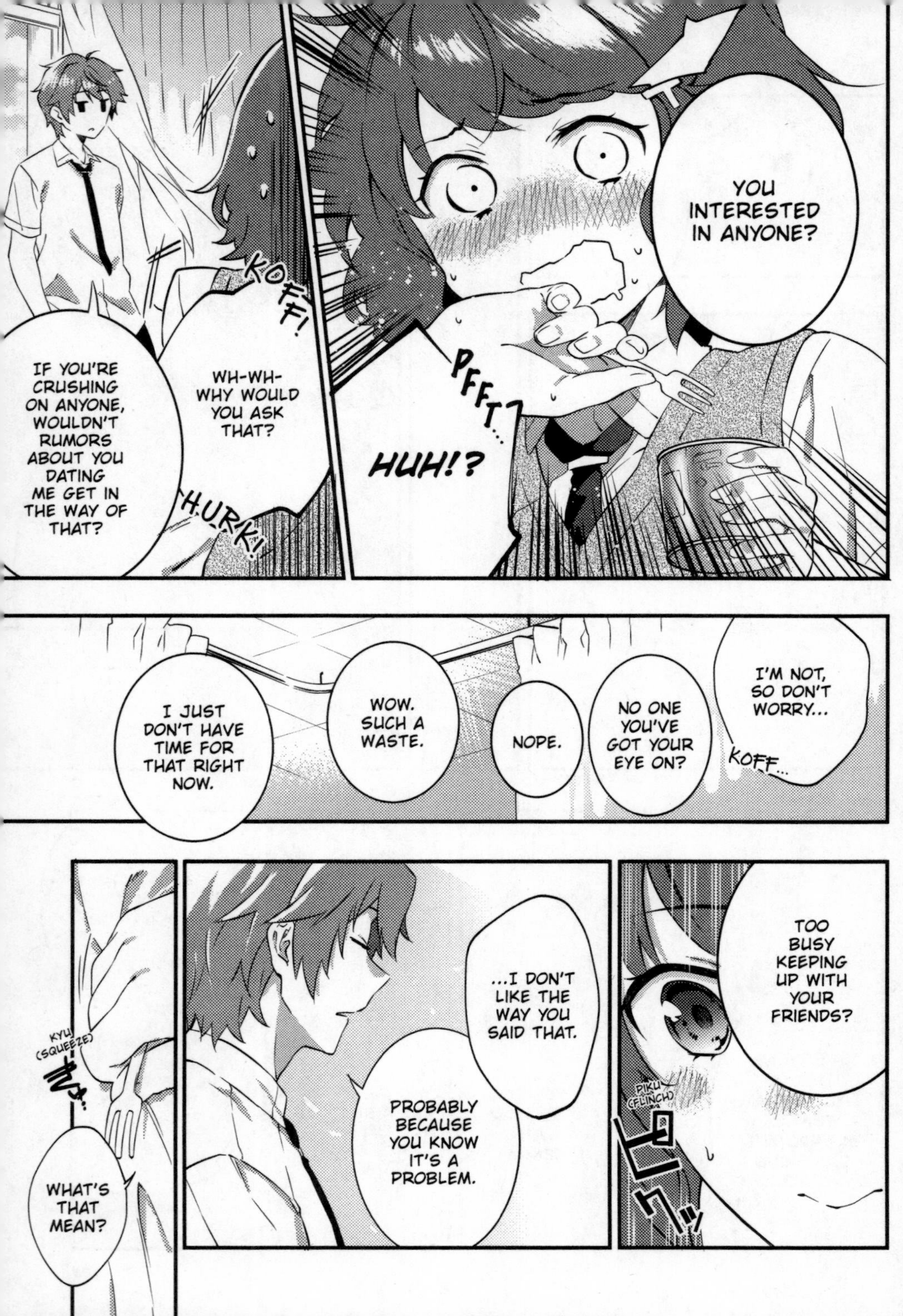
YOU INTERESTED IN ANYONE?
PFFT...
HUH!?
KOFF!
WH-WH-WHY WOULD YOU ASK THAT?
HURK!
IF YOU'RE CRUSHING ON ANYONE, WOULDN'T RUMORS ABOUT YOU DATING ME GET IN THE WAY OF THAT?
I'M NOT, SO DON'T WORRY...
KOFF...
NO ONE YOU'VE GOT YOUR EYE ON?
NOPE.
WOW. SUCH A WASTE.
I JUST DON'T HAVE TIME FOR THAT RIGHT NOW.
TOO BUSY KEEPING UP WITH YOUR FRIENDS?
PIKU (FLINCH)
...I DON'T LIKE THE WAY YOU SAID THAT.
PROBABLY BECAUSE YOU KNOW IT'S A PROBLEM.
KYU (SQUEEZE)
WHAT'S THAT MEAN?

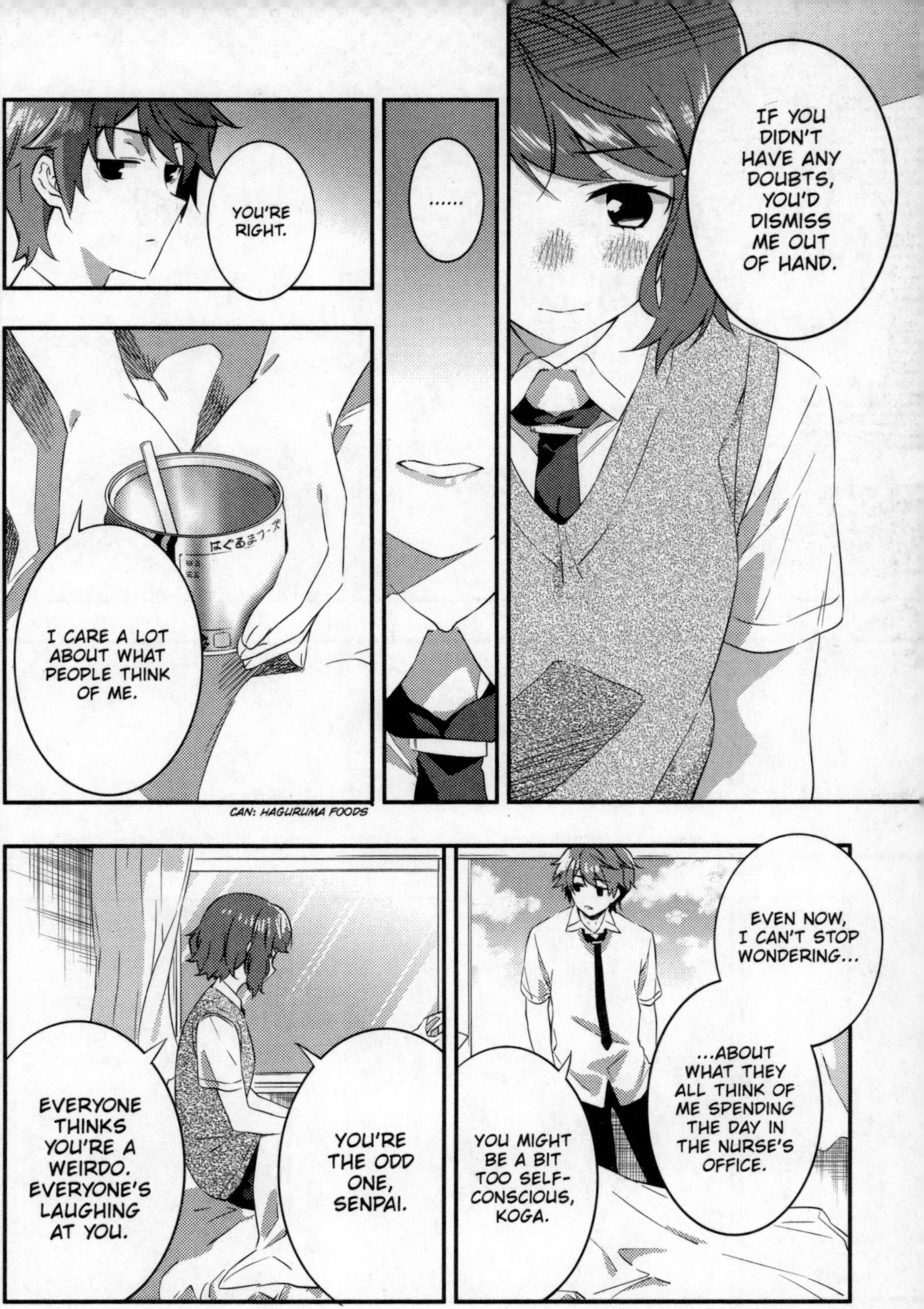
IF YOU DIDN'T HAVE ANY DOUBTS, YOU'D DISMISS ME OUT OF HAND.
......
YOU'RE RIGHT.
I CARE A LOT ABOUT WHAT PEOPLE THINK OF ME.
はぐるまフーズ
CAN: HAGURUMA FOODS
EVEN NOW, I CAN'T STOP WONDERING...
...ABOUT WHAT THEY ALL THINK OF ME SPENDING THE DAY IN THE NURSE'S OFFICE.
YOU MIGHT BE A BIT TOO SELF-CONSCIOUS, KOGA.
YOU'RE THE ODD ONE, SENPAI.
EVERYONE THINKS YOU'RE A WEIRDO. EVERYONE'S LAUGHING AT YOU.

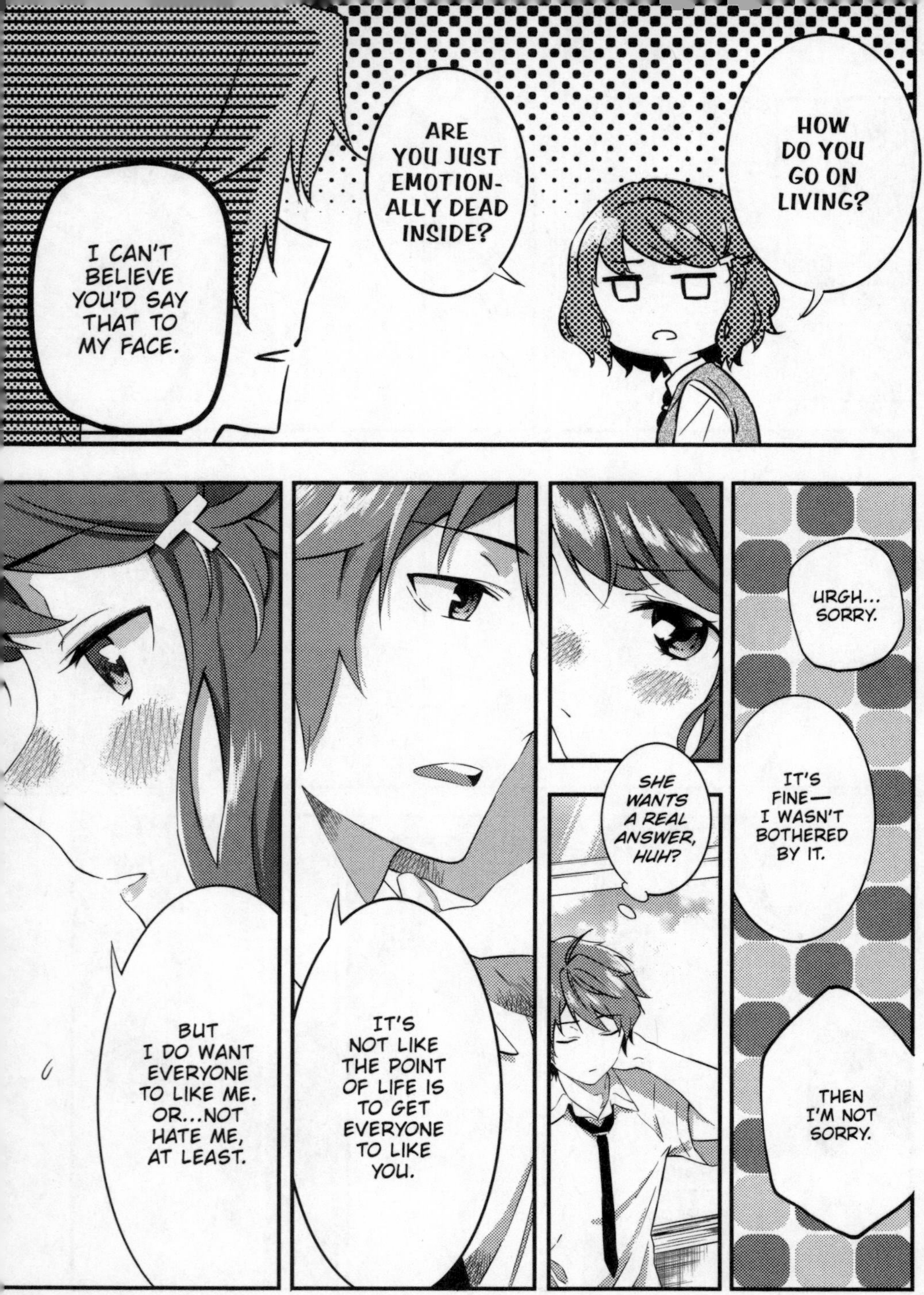
HOW DO YOU GO ON LIVING?
ARE YOU JUST EMOTION-ALLY DEAD INSIDE?
I CAN'T BELIEVE YOU'D SAY THAT TO MY FACE.
URGH... SORRY.
IT'S FINE— I WASN'T BOTHERED BY IT.
THEN I'M NOT SORRY.
SHE WANTS A REAL ANSWER, HUH?
IT'S NOT LIKE THE POINT OF LIFE IS TO GET EVERYONE TO LIKE YOU.
BUT I DO WANT EVERYONE TO LIKE ME. OR...NOT HATE ME, AT LEAST.

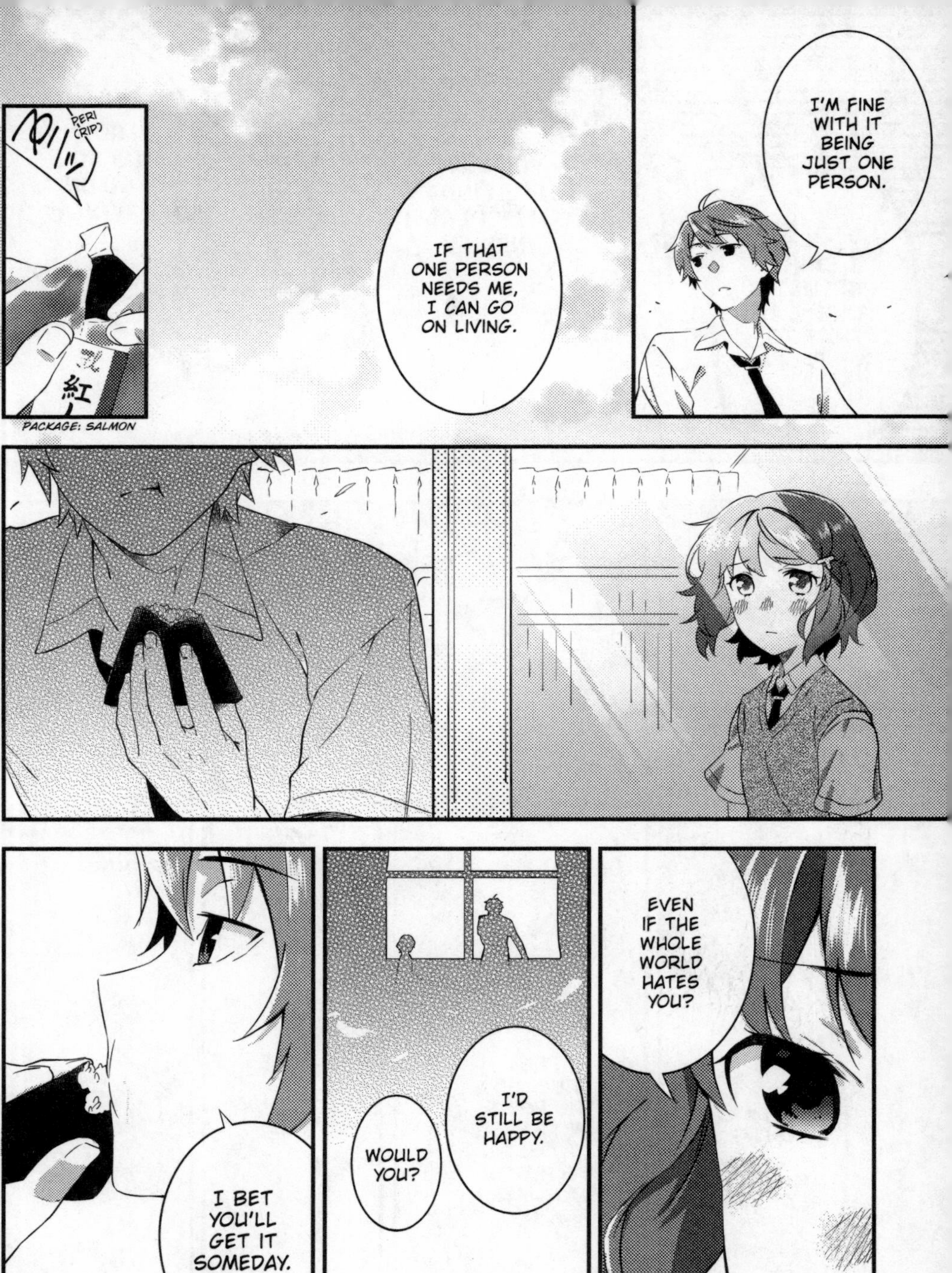
I'M FINE WITH IT BEING JUST ONE PERSON.
IF THAT ONE PERSON NEEDS ME, I CAN GO ON LIVING.
PERI (RIP)
PACKAGE: SALMON
EVEN IF THE WHOLE WORLD HATES YOU?
I'D STILL BE HAPPY.
WOULD YOU?
I BET YOU'LL GET IT SOMEDAY.

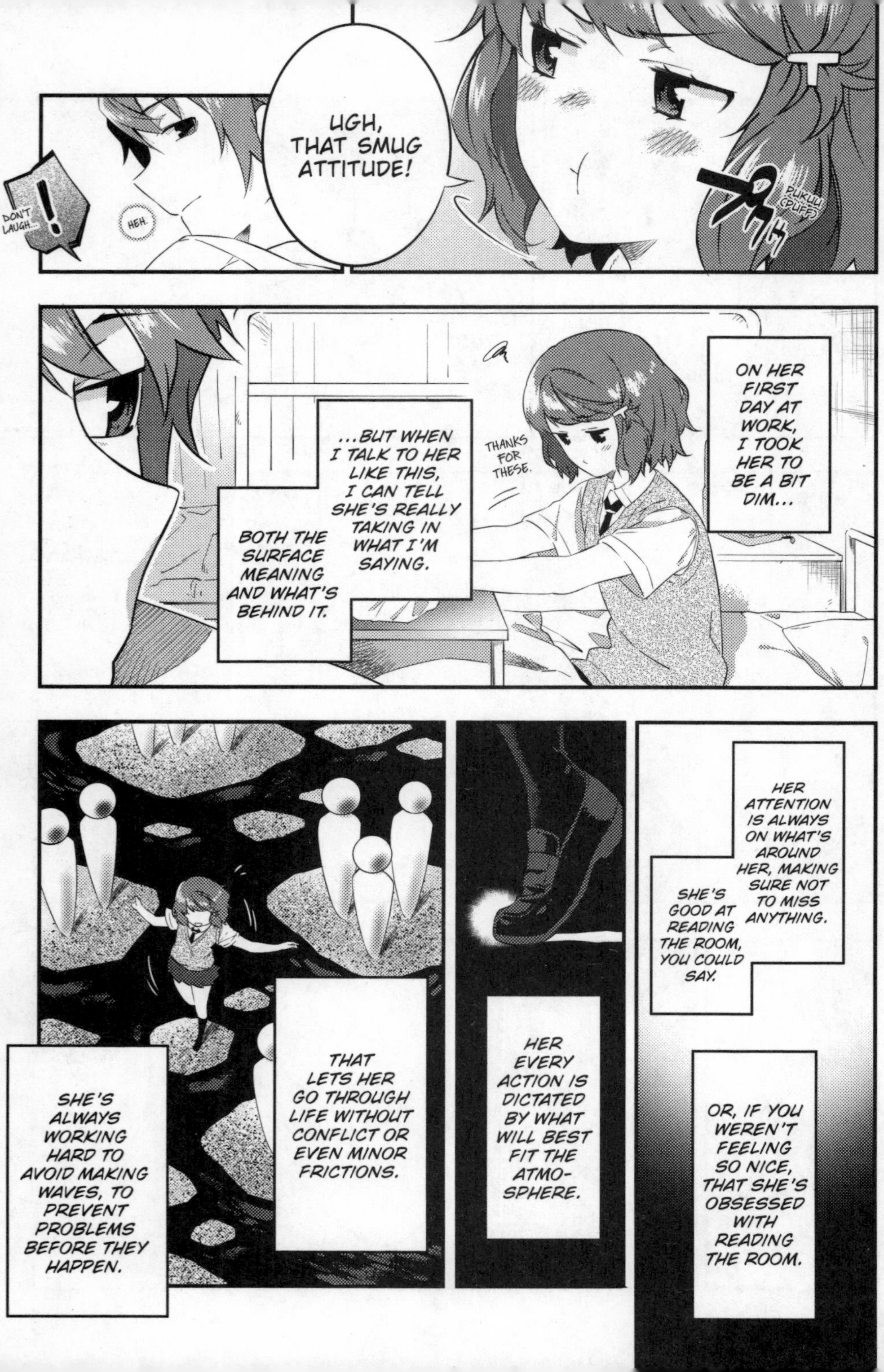
UGH, THAT SMUG ATTITUDE!
PUKUU (PUFF)
HEH.
DON'T LAUGH...
ON HER FIRST DAY AT WORK, I TOOK HER TO BE A BIT DIM...
THANKS FOR THESE.
...BUT WHEN I TALK TO HER LIKE THIS, I CAN TELL SHE'S REALLY TAKING IN WHAT I'M SAYING.
BOTH THE SURFACE MEANING AND WHAT'S BEHIND IT.
HER ATTENTION IS ALWAYS ON WHAT'S AROUND HER, MAKING SURE NOT TO MISS ANYTHING.
SHE'S GOOD AT READING THE ROOM, YOU COULD SAY.
OR, IF YOU WEREN'T FEELING SO NICE, THAT SHE'S OBSESSED WITH READING THE ROOM.
HER EVERY ACTION IS DICTATED BY WHAT WILL BEST FIT THE ATMO-SPHERE.
THAT LETS HER GO THROUGH LIFE WITHOUT CONFLICT OR EVEN MINOR FRICTIONS.
SHE'S ALWAYS WORKING HARD TO AVOID MAKING WAVES, TO PREVENT PROBLEMS BEFORE THEY HAPPEN.

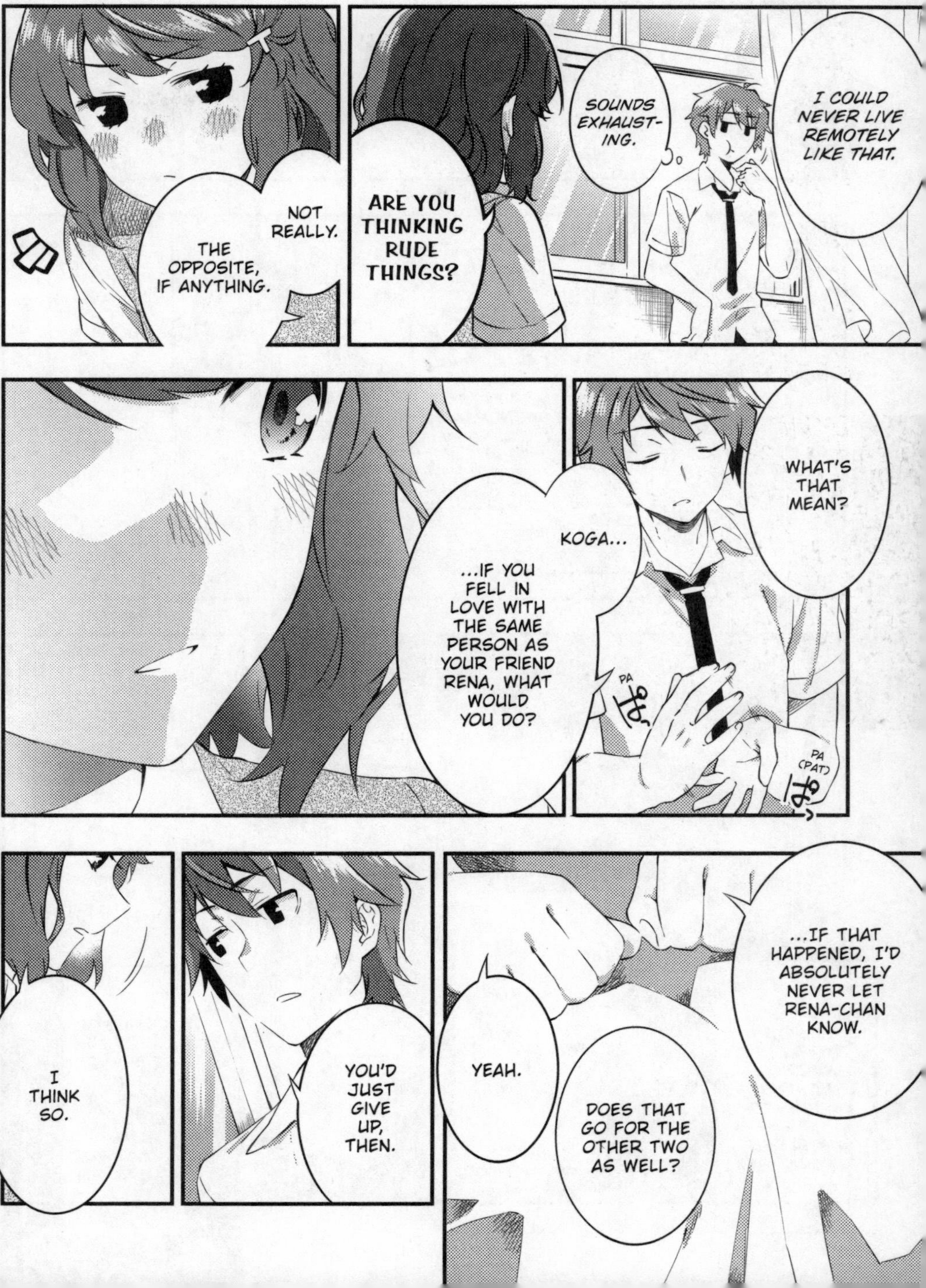
I COULD NEVER LIVE REMOTELY LIKE THAT.
SOUNDS EXHAUST-ING.
ARE YOU THINKING RUDE THINGS?
NOT REALLY.
THE OPPOSITE, IF ANYTHING.
WHAT'S THAT MEAN?
KOGA...
...IF YOU FELL IN LOVE WITH THE SAME PERSON AS YOUR FRIEND RENA, WHAT WOULD YOU DO?
PA
PA (PAT)
...IF THAT HAPPENED, I'D ABSOLUTELY NEVER LET RENA-CHAN KNOW.
YEAH.
DOES THAT GO FOR THE OTHER TWO AS WELL?
YOU'D JUST GIVE UP, THEN.
I THINK SO.

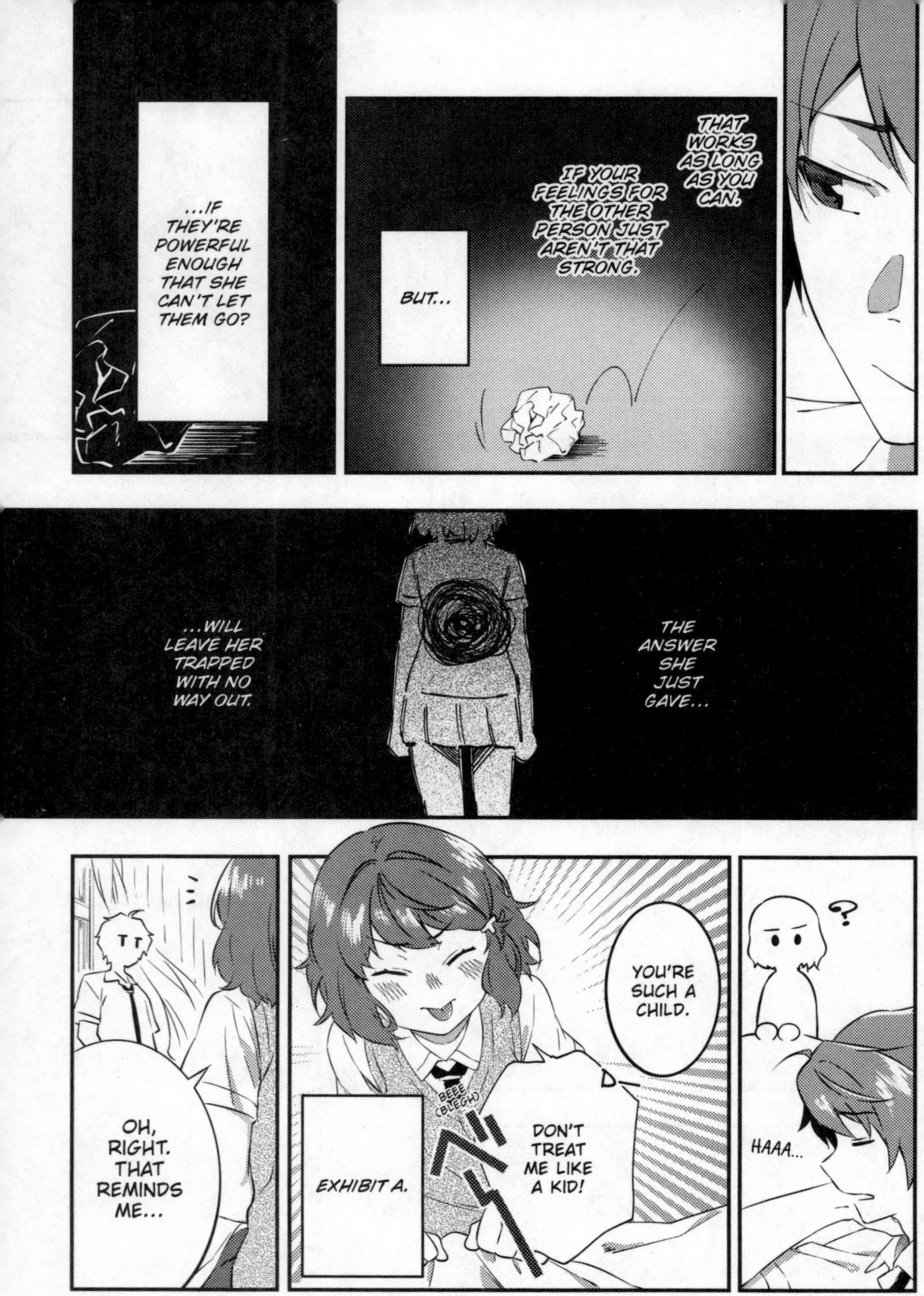
THAT WORKS AS LONG AS YOU CAN.
IF YOUR FEELINGS FOR THE OTHER PERSON JUST AREN'T THAT STRONG.
BUT...
...IF THEY'RE POWERFUL ENOUGH THAT SHE CAN'T LET THEM GO?
THE ANSWER SHE JUST GAVE...
...WILL LEAVE HER TRAPPED WITH NO WAY OUT.
?
HAAA...
YOU'RE SUCH A CHILD.
DON'T TREAT ME LIKE A KID!
BEEE (BLEGH)
EXHIBIT A.
OH, RIGHT. THAT REMINDS ME...

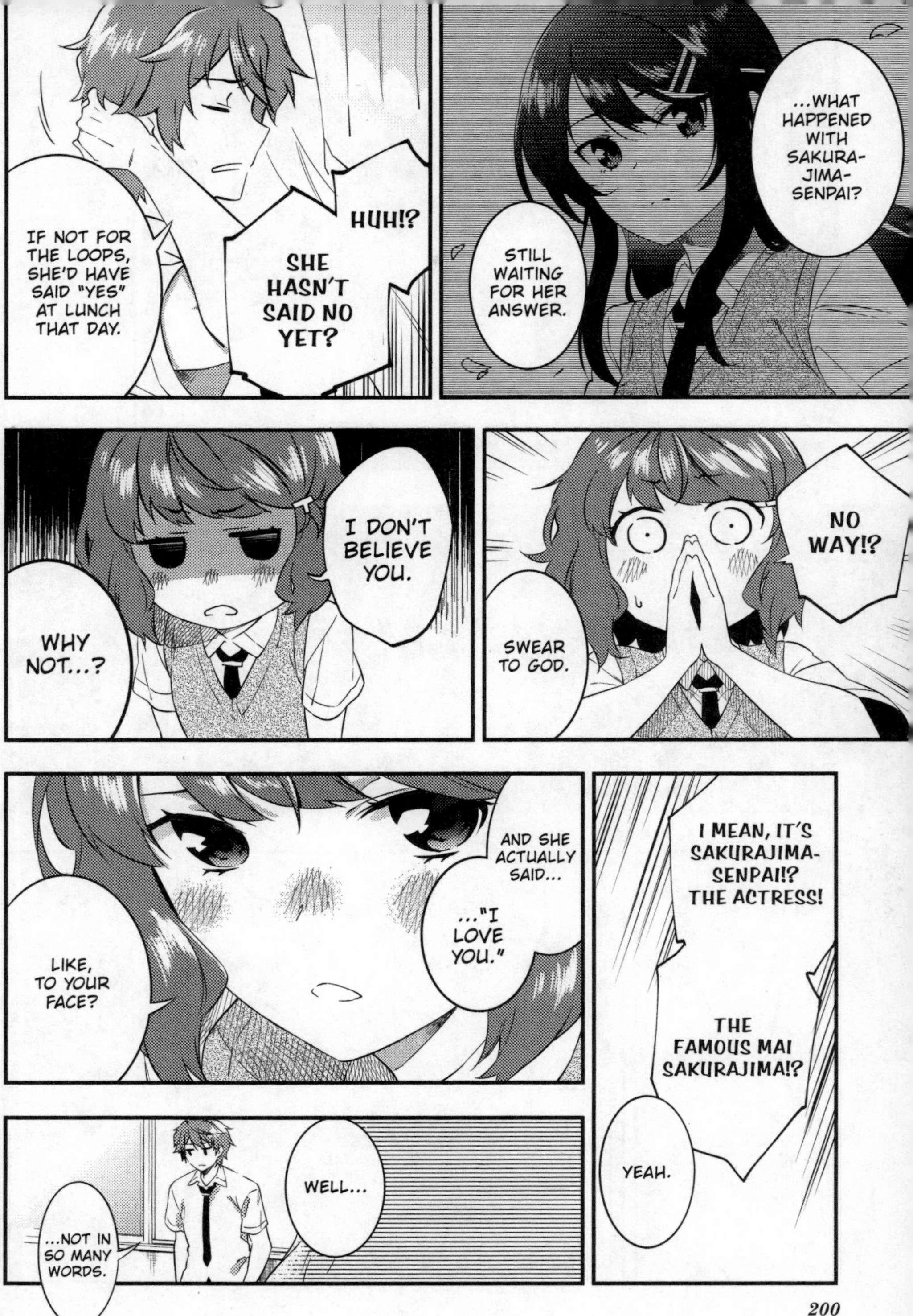
...WHAT HAPPENED WITH SAKURAJIMA-SENPAI?
STILL WAITING FOR HER ANSWER.
HUH!?
SHE HASN'T SAID NO YET?
IF NOT FOR THE LOOPS, SHE'D HAVE SAID "YES" AT LUNCH THAT DAY.
NO WAY!?
SWEAR TO GOD.
I DON'T BELIEVE YOU.
WHY NOT...?
I MEAN, IT'S SAKURAJIMA-SENPAI!? THE ACTRESS!
THE FAMOUS MAI SAKURAJIMA!?
YEAH.
AND SHE ACTUALLY SAID...
..."I LOVE YOU."
LIKE, TO YOUR FACE?
WELL...
...NOT IN SO MANY WORDS.

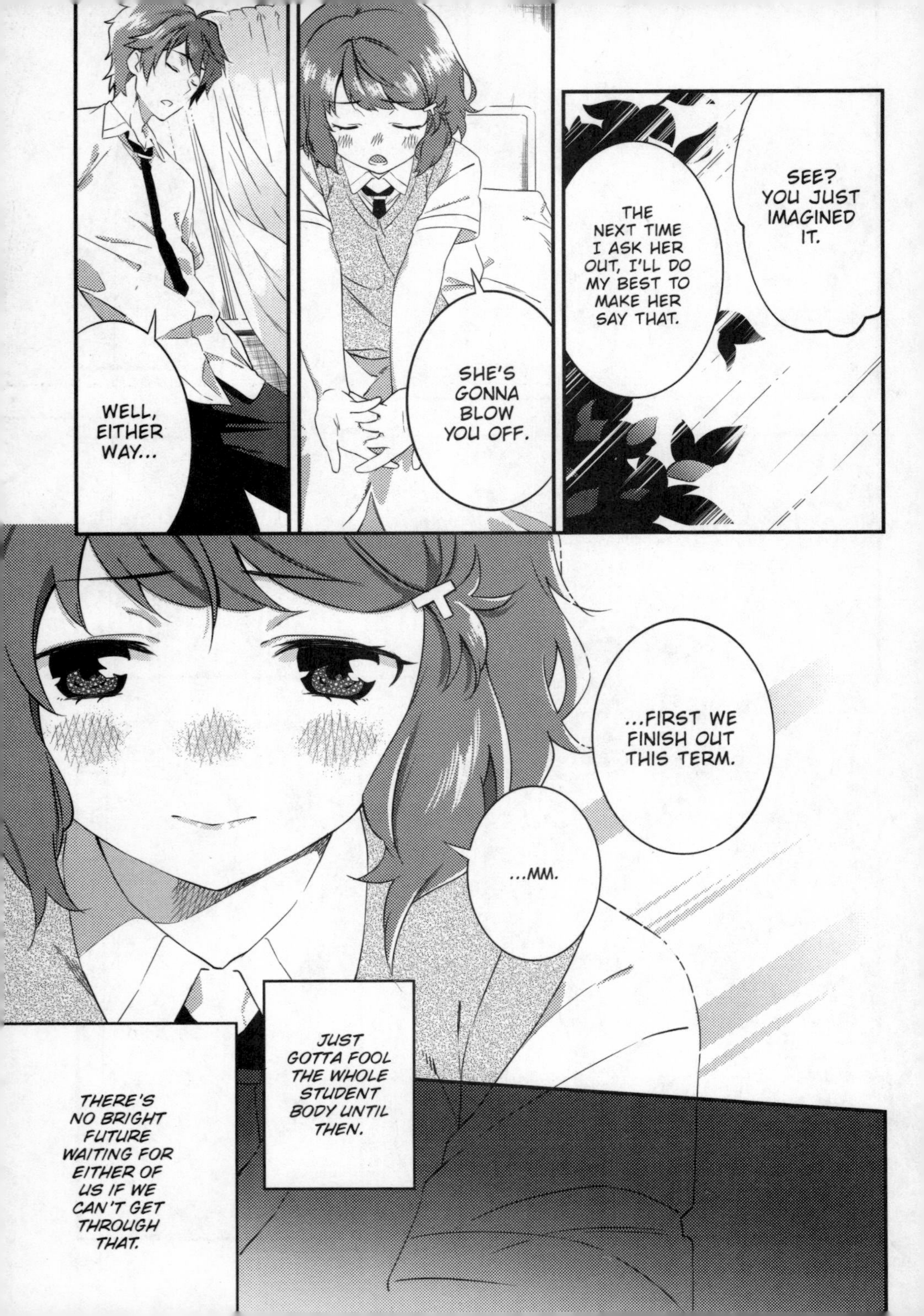
SEE? YOU JUST IMAGINED IT.
THE NEXT TIME I ASK HER OUT, I'LL DO MY BEST TO MAKE HER SAY THAT.
SHE'S GONNA BLOW YOU OFF.
WELL, EITHER WAY...
...FIRST WE FINISH OUT THIS TERM.
...MM.
JUST GOTTA FOOL THE WHOLE STUDENT BODY UNTIL THEN.
THERE'S NO BRIGHT FUTURE WAITING FOR EITHER OF US IF WE CAN'T GET THROUGH THAT.

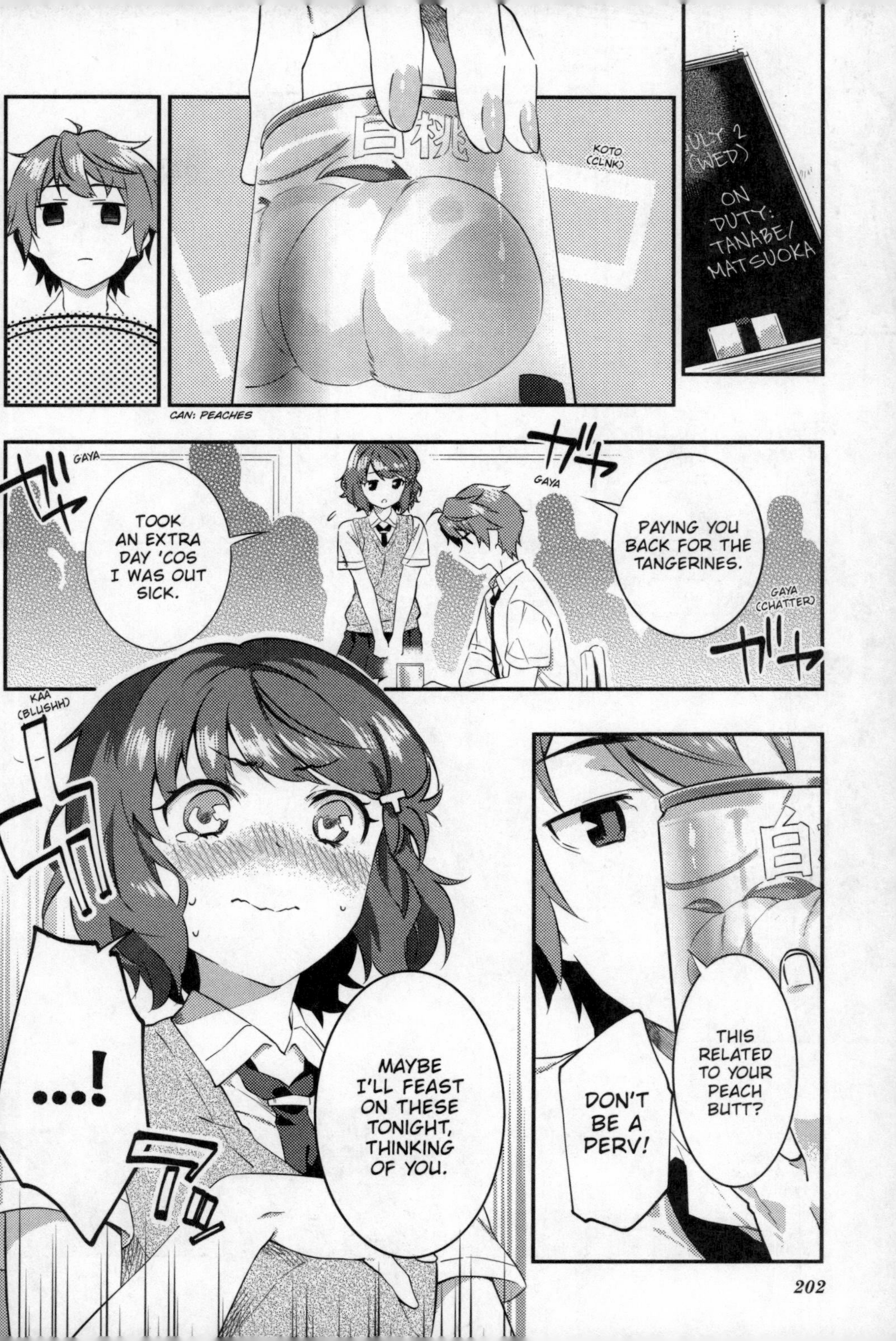

JULY 2 (WED)
ON DUTY: TANABE/ MATSUOKA
KOTO (CLNK)
CAN: PEACHES
GAYA
PAYING YOU BACK FOR THE TANGERINES.
GAYA (CHATTER)
GAYA
TOOK AN EXTRA DAY 'COS I WAS OUT SICK.
THIS RELATED TO YOUR PEACH BUTT?
DON'T BE A PERV!
MAYBE I'LL FEAST ON THESE TONIGHT, THINKING OF YOU.
KAA (BLUSHH)
...!

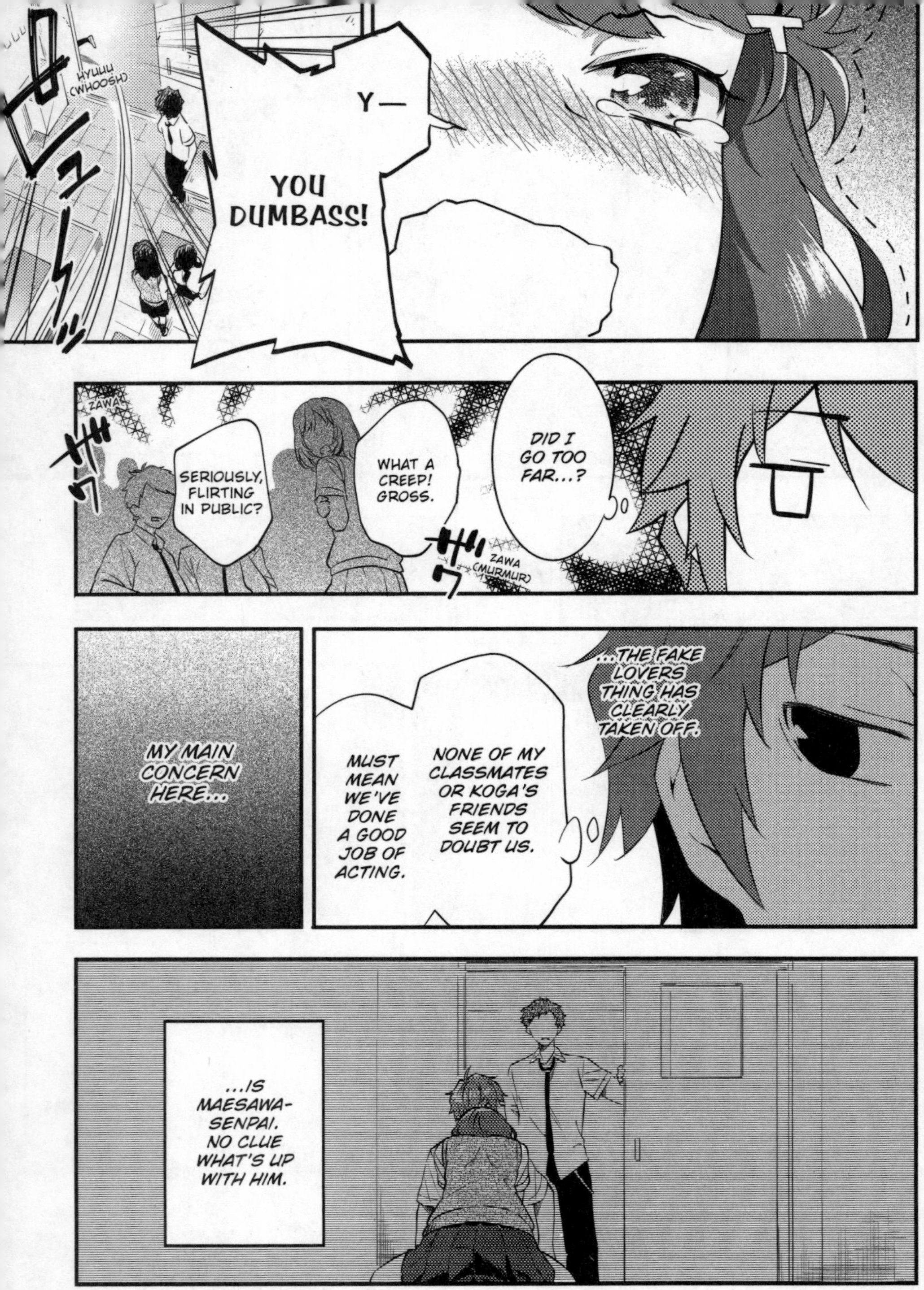
Y—
YOU DUMBASS!
HYUUU (WHOOSH)
DID I GO TOO FAR...?
ZAWA (MURMUR)
WHAT A CREEP! GROSS.
SERIOUSLY, FLIRTING IN PUBLIC?
ZAWA
...THE FAKE LOVERS THING HAS CLEARLY TAKEN OFF.
NONE OF MY CLASSMATES OR KOGA'S FRIENDS SEEM TO DOUBT US.
MUST MEAN WE'VE DONE A GOOD JOB OF ACTING.
MY MAIN CONCERN HERE...
...IS MAESAWA-SENPAI. NO CLUE WHAT'S UP WITH HIM.

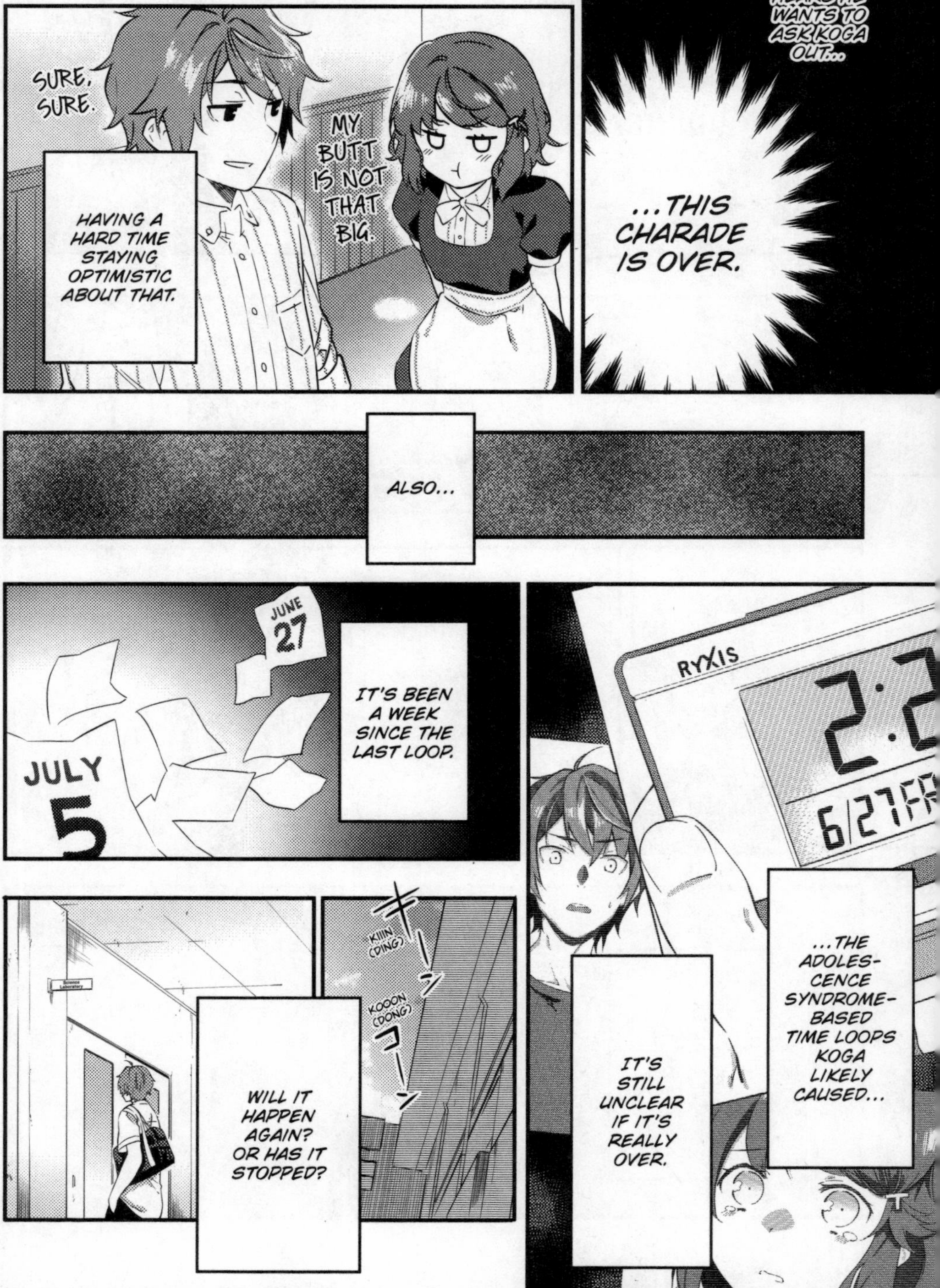

IF RENA HEARS HE WANTS TO ASK KOGA OUT...
...THIS CHARADE IS OVER.
MY BUTT IS NOT THAT BIG.
SURE, SURE.
HAVING A HARD TIME STAYING OPTIMISTIC ABOUT THAT.
ALSO...
RYXIS
2:2
6/27FR
...THE ADOLES-CENCE SYNDROME-BASED TIME LOOPS KOGA LIKELY CAUSED...
IT'S STILL UNCLEAR IF IT'S REALLY OVER.
JUNE 27
IT'S BEEN A WEEK SINCE THE LAST LOOP.
JULY 5
KIIN (DING)
KOOON (DONG)
Science Laboratory
WILL IT HAPPEN AGAIN? OR HAS IT STOPPED?

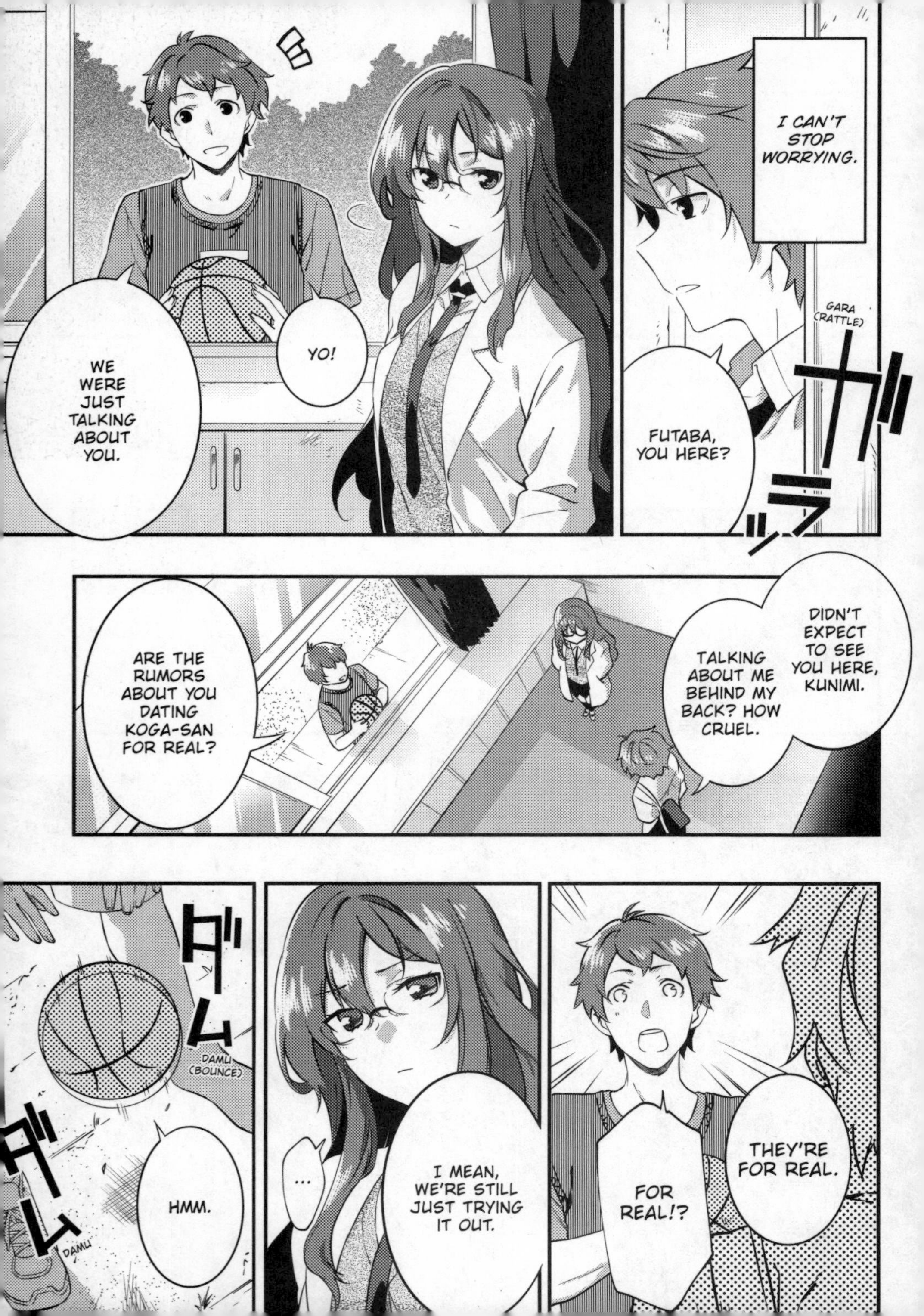

I CAN'T STOP WORRYING.
GARA (RATTLE)
FUTABA, YOU HERE?
YO!
WE WERE JUST TALKING ABOUT YOU.
DIDN'T EXPECT TO SEE YOU HERE, KUNIMI.
TALKING ABOUT ME BEHIND MY BACK? HOW CRUEL.
ARE THE RUMORS ABOUT YOU DATING KOGA-SAN FOR REAL?
THEY'RE FOR REAL.
FOR REAL!?
I MEAN, WE'RE STILL JUST TRYING IT OUT.
...
DAMU (BOUNCE)
HMM.
DAMU

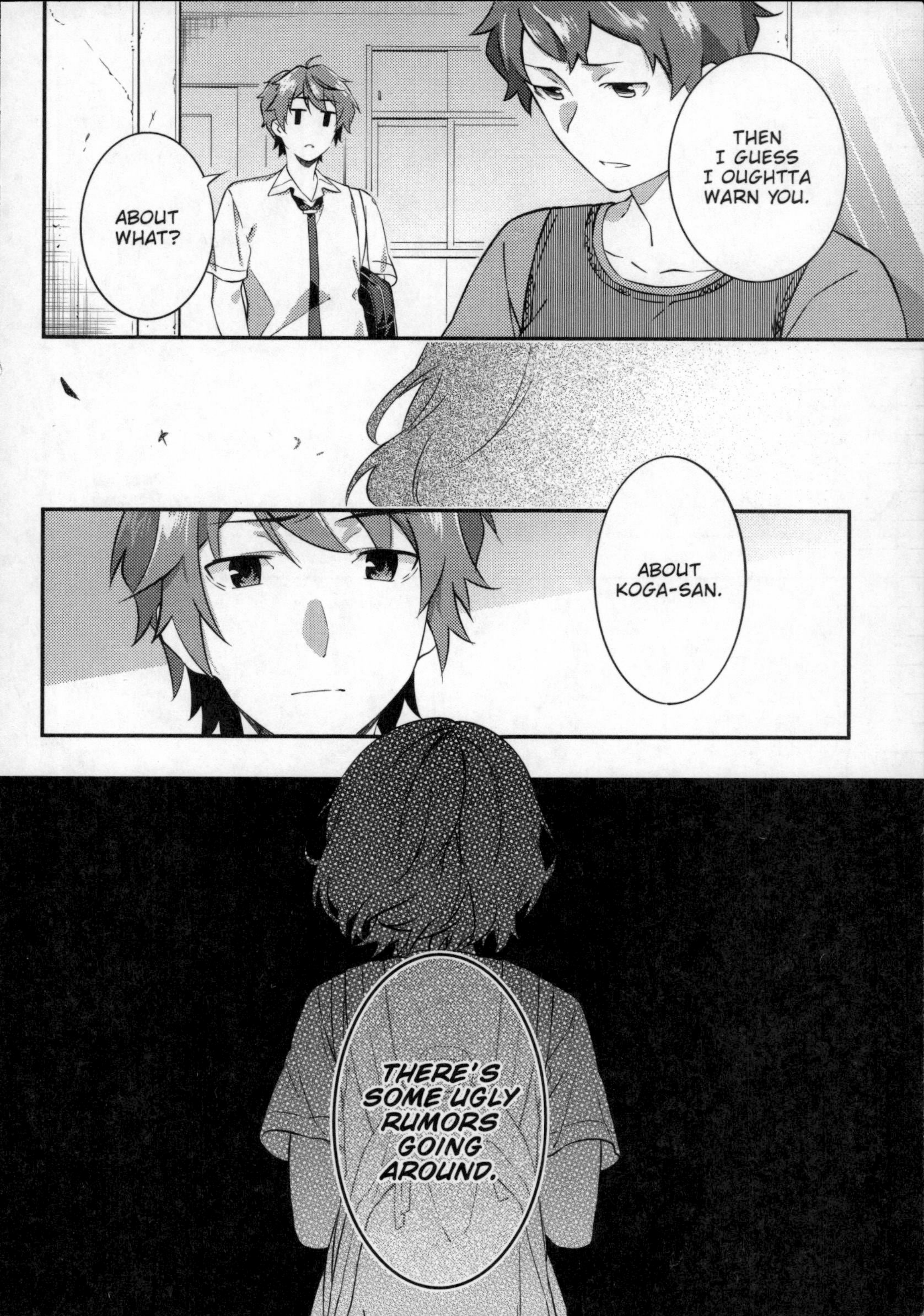
THEN I GUESS I OUGHTTA WARN YOU.
ABOUT WHAT?
ABOUT KOGA-SAN.
THERE'S SOME UGLY RUMORS GOING AROUND.

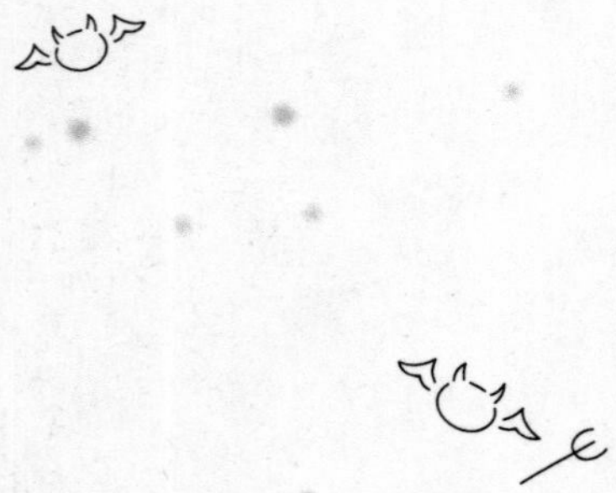

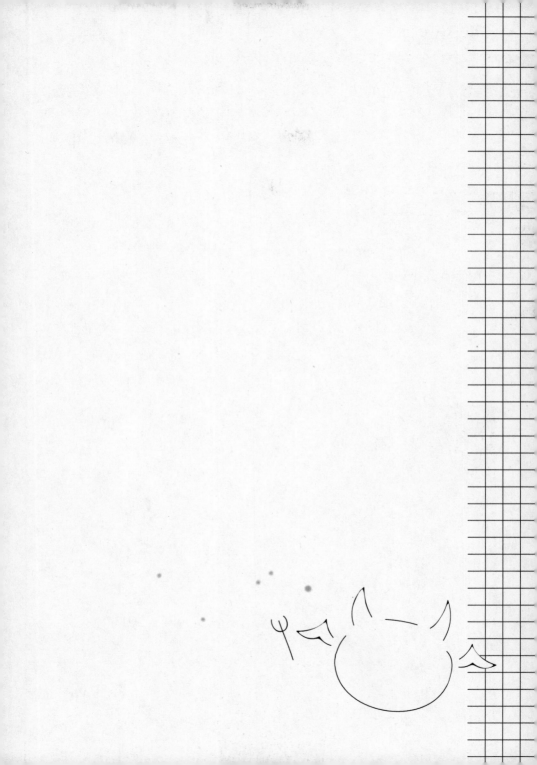

# #008

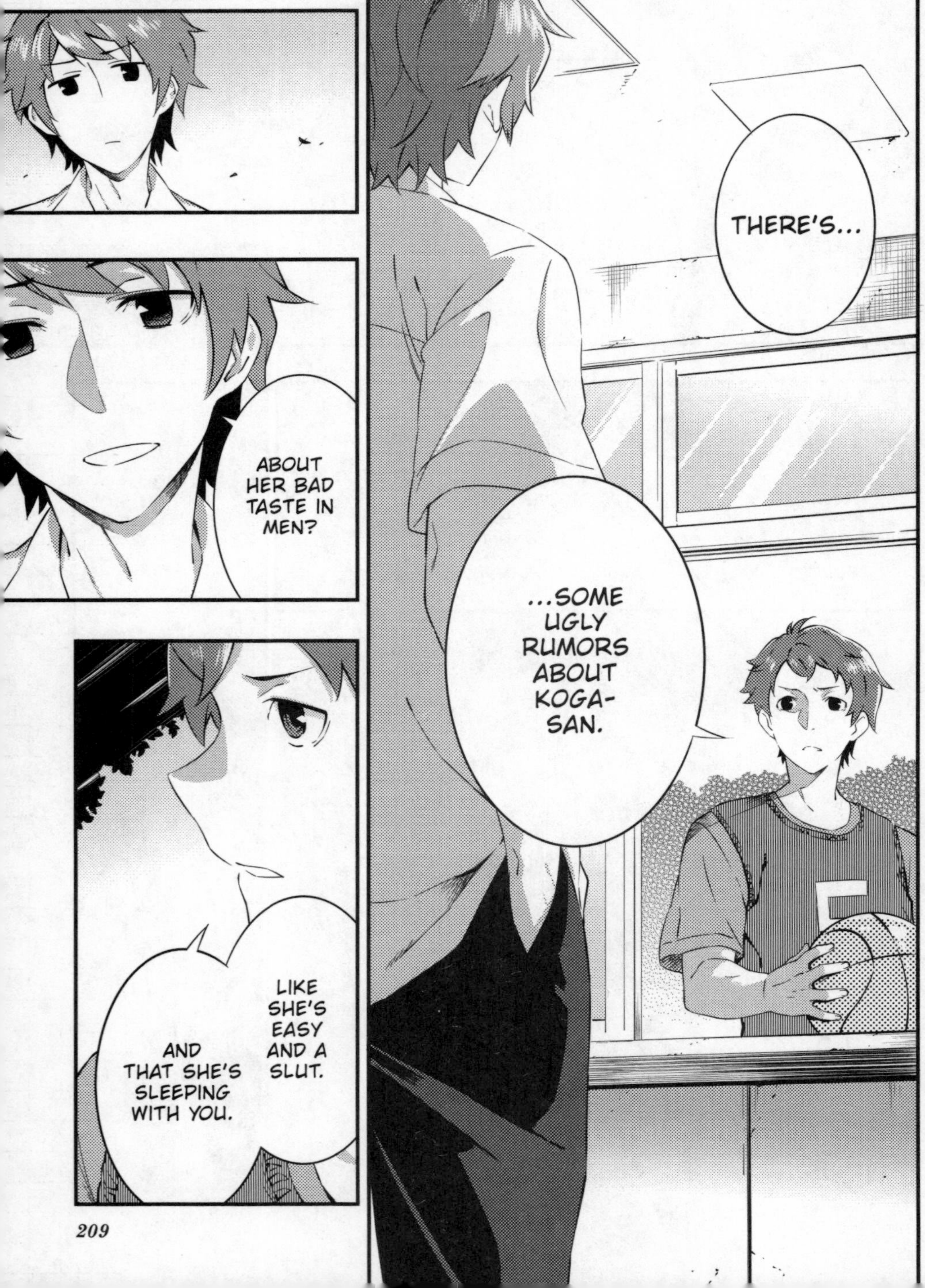
THERE'S...
...SOME UGLY RUMORS ABOUT KOGA-SAN.
ABOUT HER BAD TASTE IN MEN?
LIKE SHE'S EASY AND A SLUT.
AND THAT SHE'S SLEEPING WITH YOU.

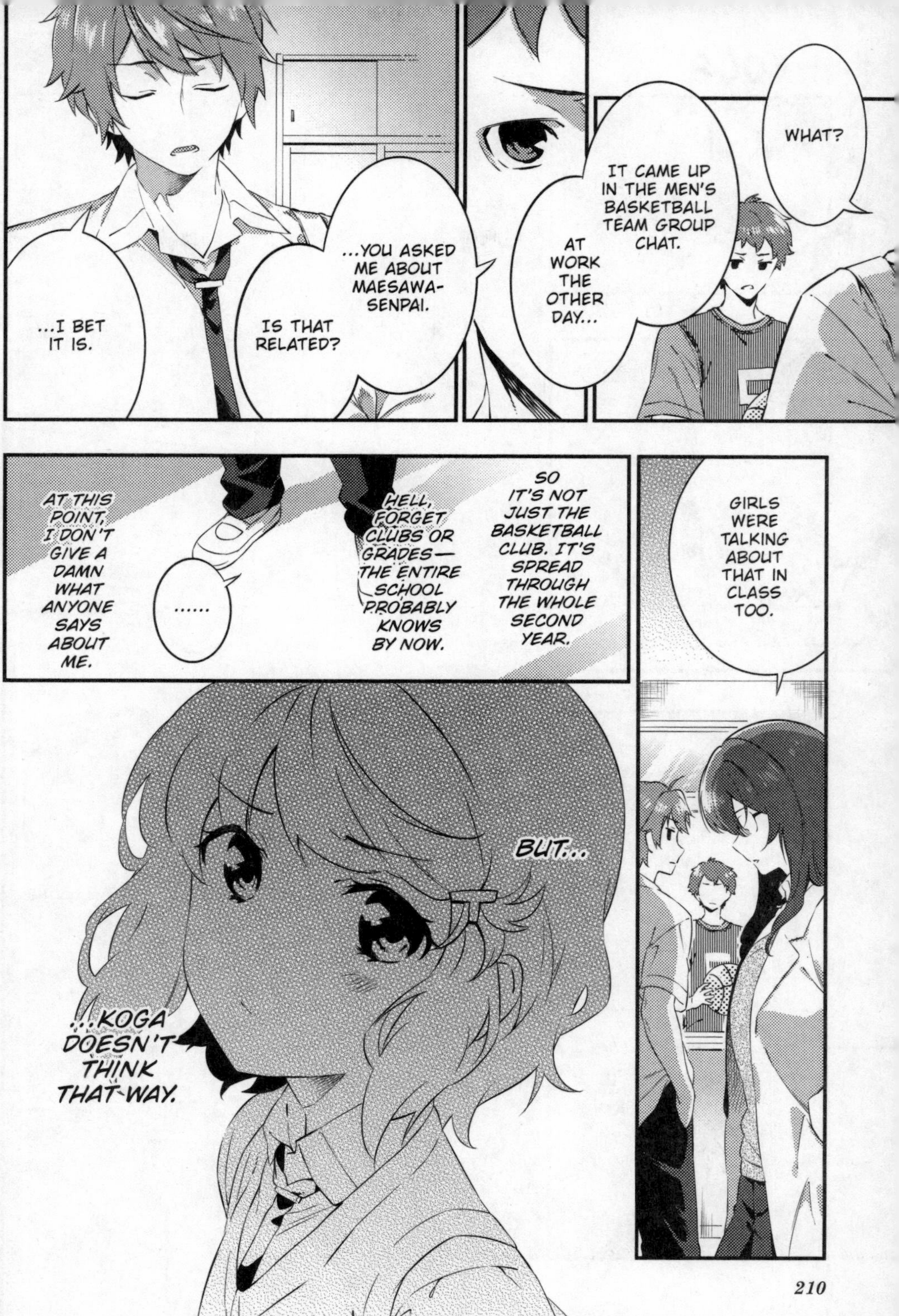
WHAT?
IT CAME UP IN THE MEN'S BASKETBALL TEAM GROUP CHAT.
AT WORK THE OTHER DAY...
...YOU ASKED ME ABOUT MAESAWA-SENPAI.
IS THAT RELATED?
...I BET IT IS.
GIRLS WERE TALKING ABOUT THAT IN CLASS TOO.
SO IT'S NOT JUST THE BASKETBALL CLUB. IT'S SPREAD THROUGH THE WHOLE SECOND YEAR.
HELL, FORGET CLUBS OR GRADES—THE ENTIRE SCHOOL PROBABLY KNOWS BY NOW.
......
AT THIS POINT, I DON'T GIVE A DAMN WHAT ANYONE SAYS ABOUT ME.
BUT...
...KOGA DOESN'T THINK THAT WAY.

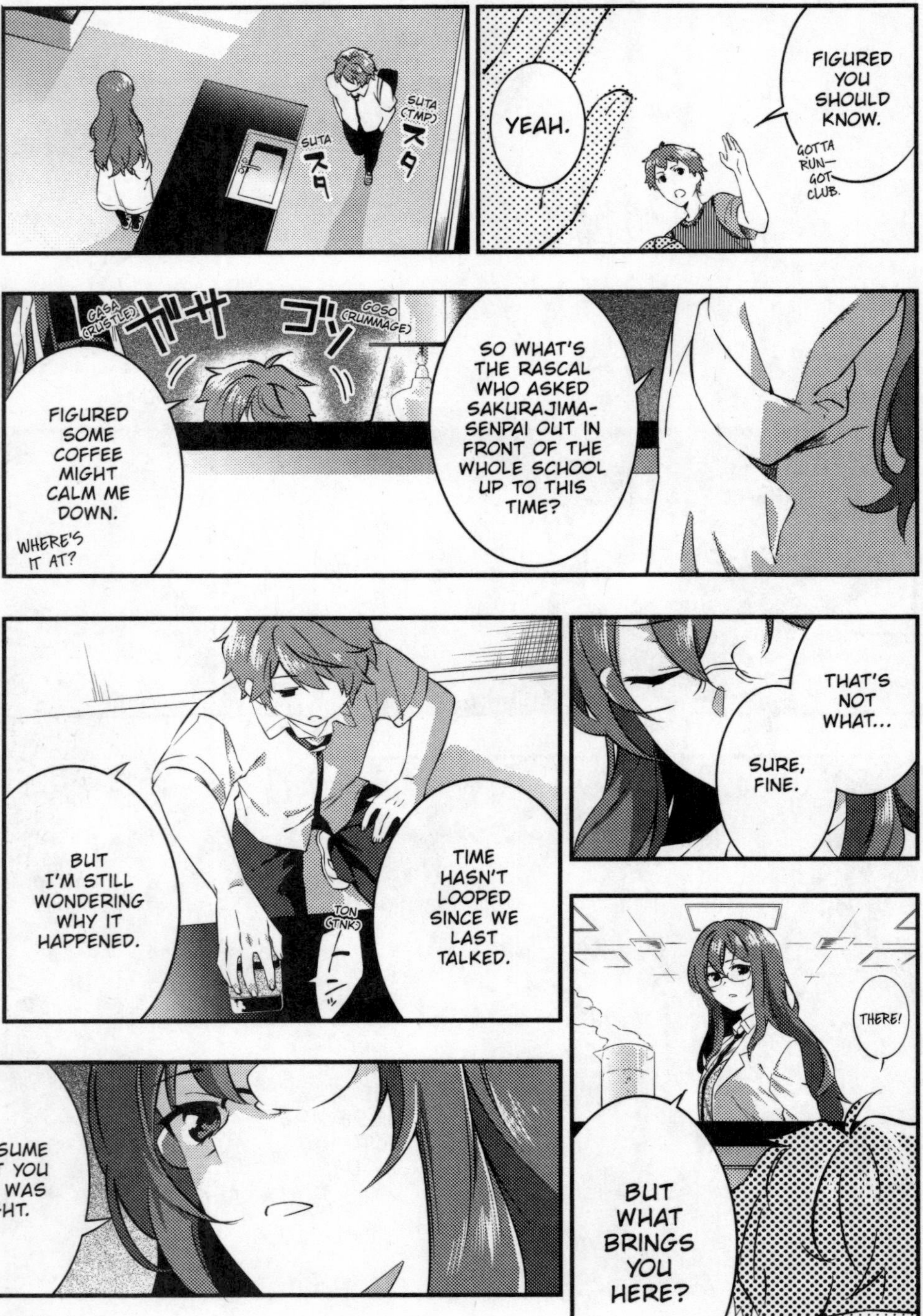

FIGURED YOU SHOULD KNOW.
GOTTA RUN—GOT CLUB.
YEAH.
SUTA (TMP) スタ
SUTA スタ
SO WHAT'S THE RASCAL WHO ASKED SAKURAJIMA-SENPAI OUT IN FRONT OF THE WHOLE SCHOOL UP TO THIS TIME?
GOSO (RUMMAGE) ゴソ
GASA (RUSTLE) ガサ
FIGURED SOME COFFEE MIGHT CALM ME DOWN.
WHERE'S IT AT?
THAT'S NOT WHAT...
SURE, FINE.
TIME HASN'T LOOPED SINCE WE LAST TALKED.
TON (TNK)
BUT I'M STILL WONDERING WHY IT HAPPENED.
THERE!
BUT WHAT BRINGS YOU HERE?
I ASSUME WHAT YOU SAID WAS RIGHT.

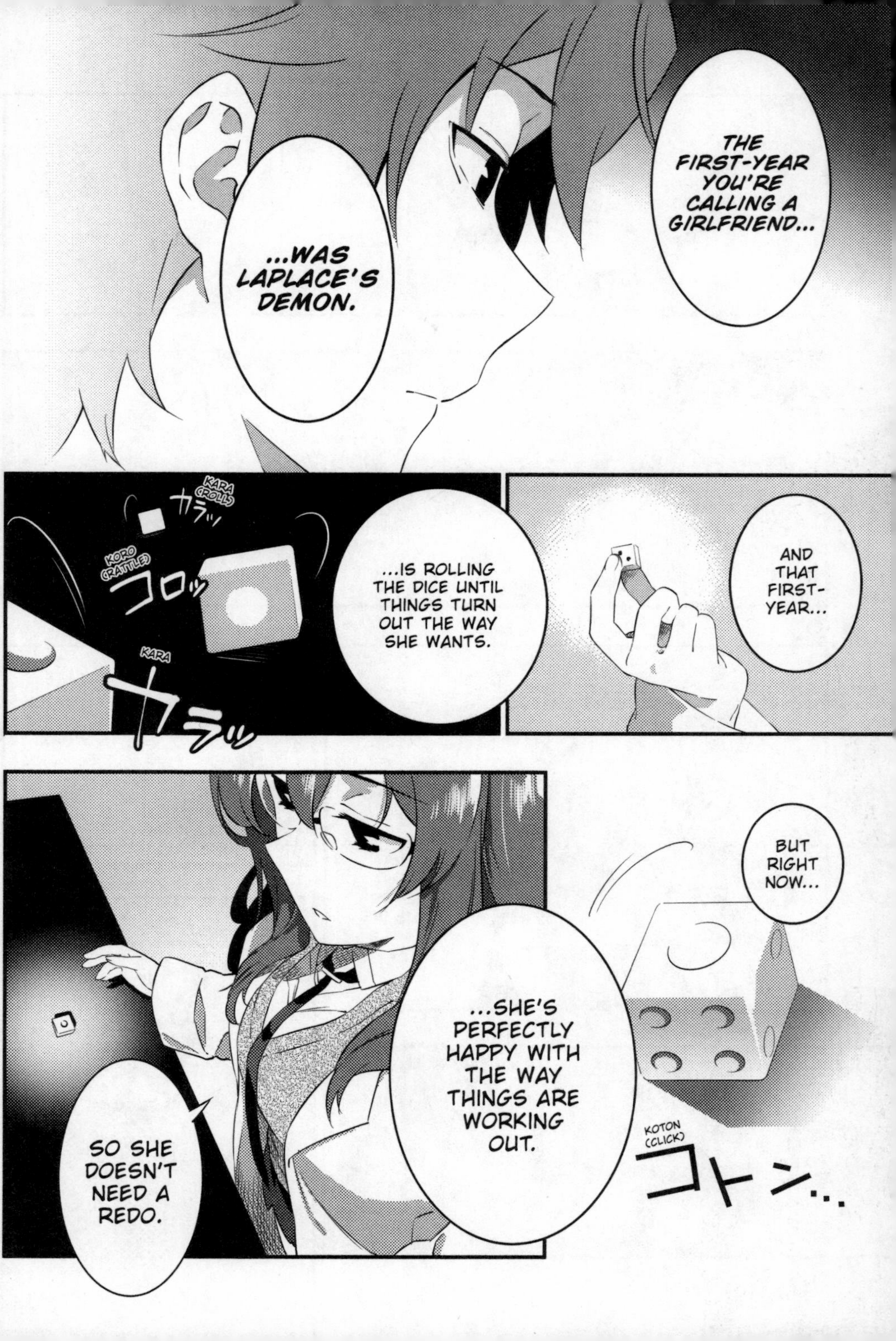
THE FIRST-YEAR YOU'RE CALLING A GIRLFRIEND...
...WAS LAPLACE'S DEMON.
AND THAT FIRST-YEAR...
...IS ROLLING THE DICE UNTIL THINGS TURN OUT THE WAY SHE WANTS.
KARA (ROLL)
カラッ
KORO (RATTLE)
コロッ
KARA
カラッ
BUT RIGHT NOW...
...SHE'S PERFECTLY HAPPY WITH THE WAY THINGS ARE WORKING OUT.
KOTON (CLICK)
コトン…
SO SHE DOESN'T NEED A REDO.

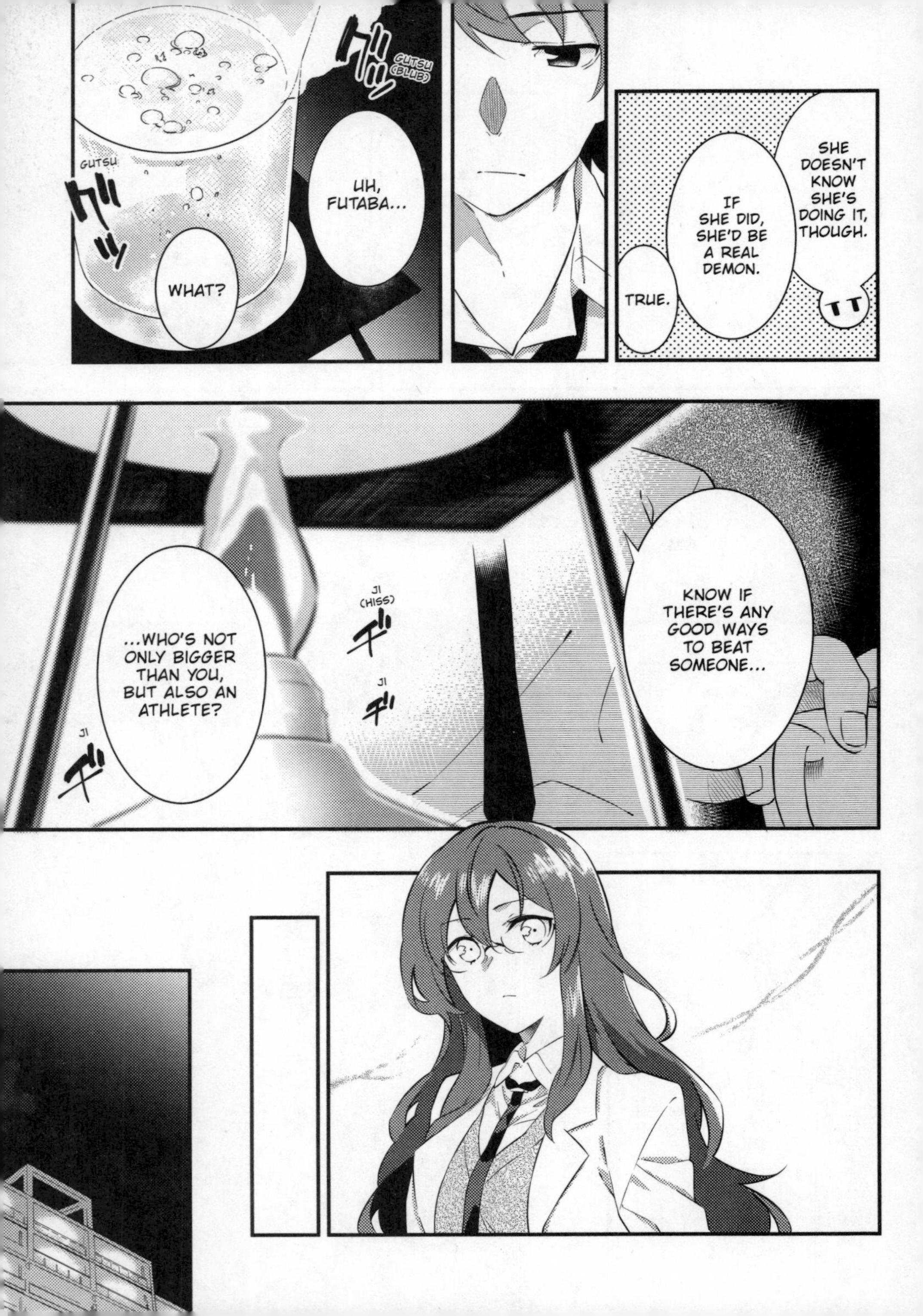
SHE DOESN'T KNOW SHE'S DOING IT, THOUGH.
IF SHE DID, SHE'D BE A REAL DEMON.
TRUE.
GUTSU (BLUB)
UH, FUTABA...
GUTSU
WHAT?
KNOW IF THERE'S ANY GOOD WAYS TO BEAT SOMEONE...
JI (HISS)
JI
...WHO'S NOT ONLY BIGGER THAN YOU, BUT ALSO AN ATHLETE?
JI

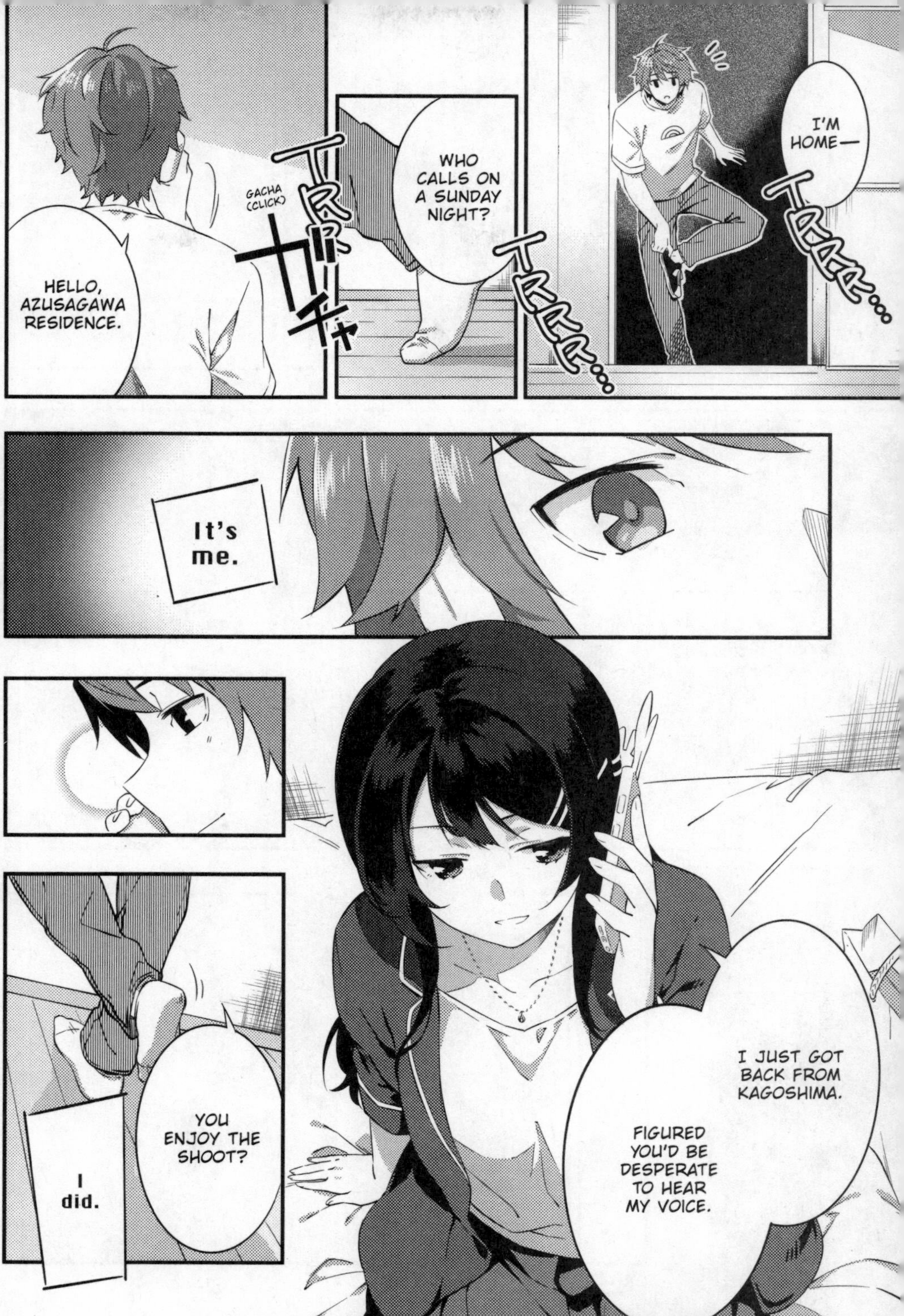
I'M HOME—
TRRR...
WHO CALLS ON A SUNDAY NIGHT?
TRRR...
TRR
GACHA (CLICK)
ガチャ
HELLO, AZUSAGAWA RESIDENCE.
It's me.
I JUST GOT BACK FROM KAGOSHIMA.
FIGURED YOU'D BE DESPERATE TO HEAR MY VOICE.
YOU ENJOY THE SHOOT?
I did.

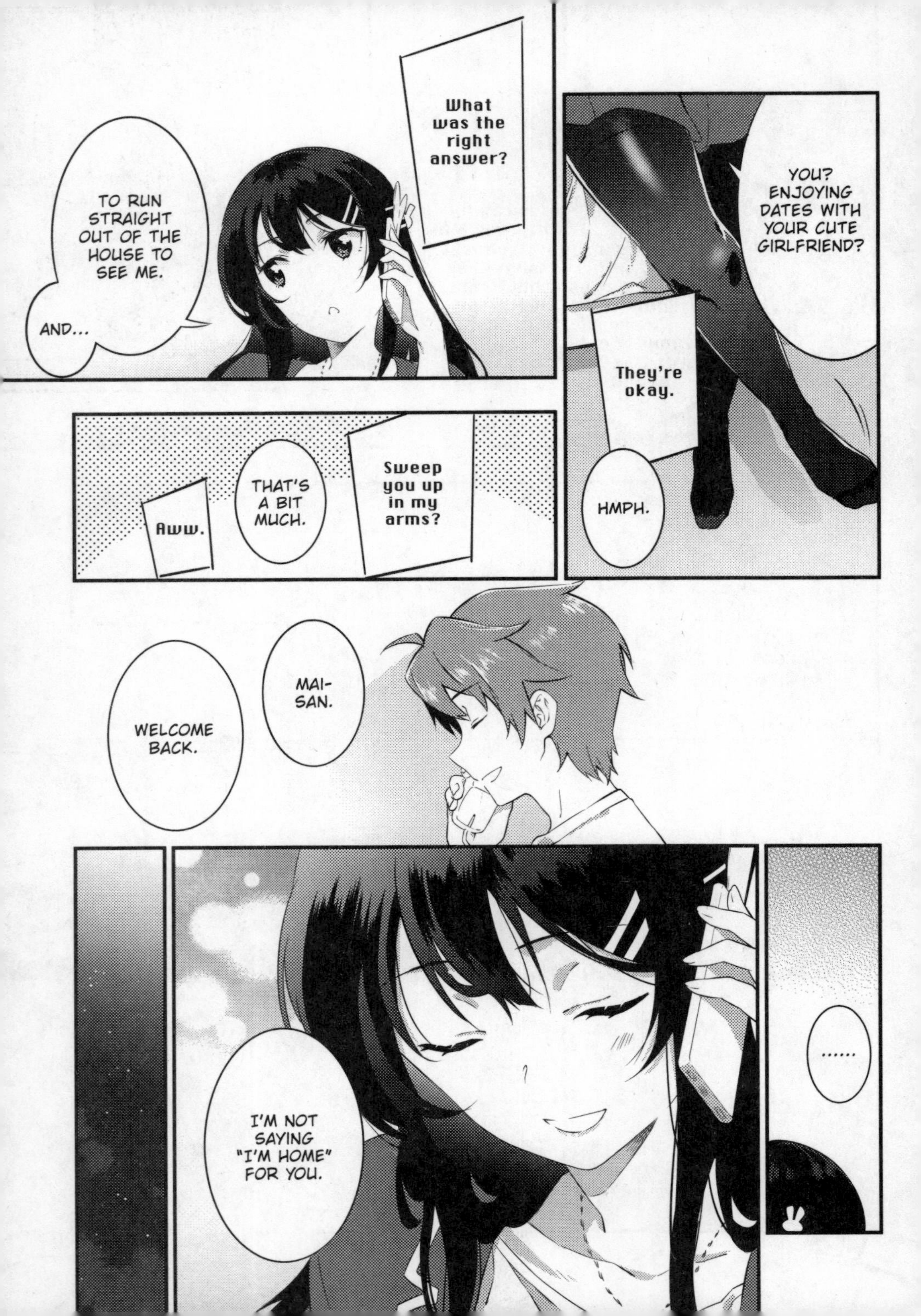
YOU? ENJOYING DATES WITH YOUR CUTE GIRLFRIEND?
They're okay.
HMPH.
What was the right answer?
TO RUN STRAIGHT OUT OF THE HOUSE TO SEE ME.
AND...
Sweep you up in my arms?
THAT'S A BIT MUCH.
Aww.
MAI-SAN.
WELCOME BACK.
......
I'M NOT SAYING "I'M HOME" FOR YOU.

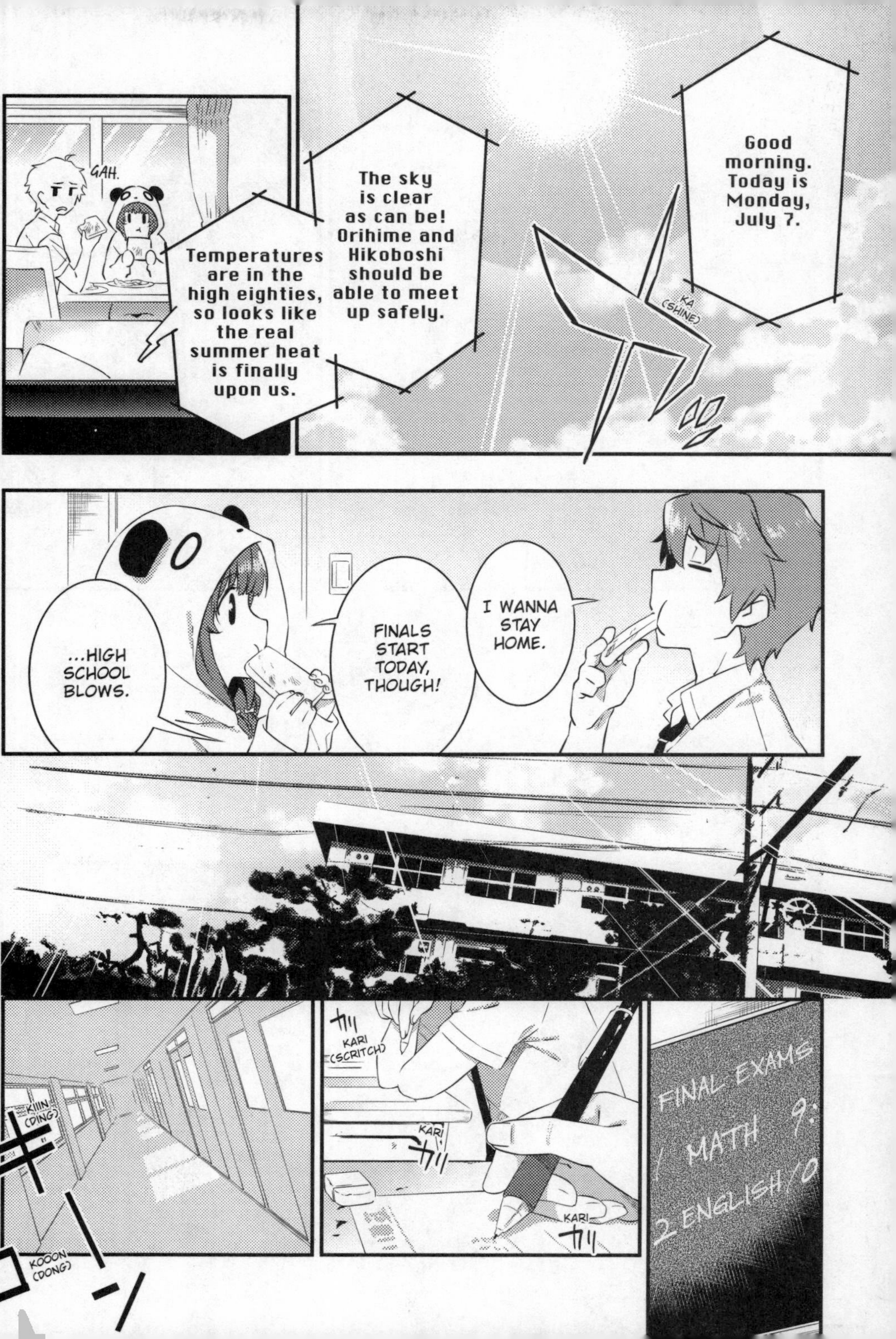
Good morning. Today is Monday, July 7.
KA (SHINE)
The sky is clear as can be! Orihime and Hikoboshi should be able to meet up safely.
Temperatures are in the high eighties, so looks like the real summer heat is finally upon us.
GAH.
I WANNA STAY HOME.
FINALS START TODAY, THOUGH!
...HIGH SCHOOL BLOWS.
FINAL EXAMS
1 MATH 9:
2 ENGLISH 10
カリ
KARI (SCRITCH)
KARI
カリ
KARI
カリ
KIIN (DING)
KOOON (DONG)

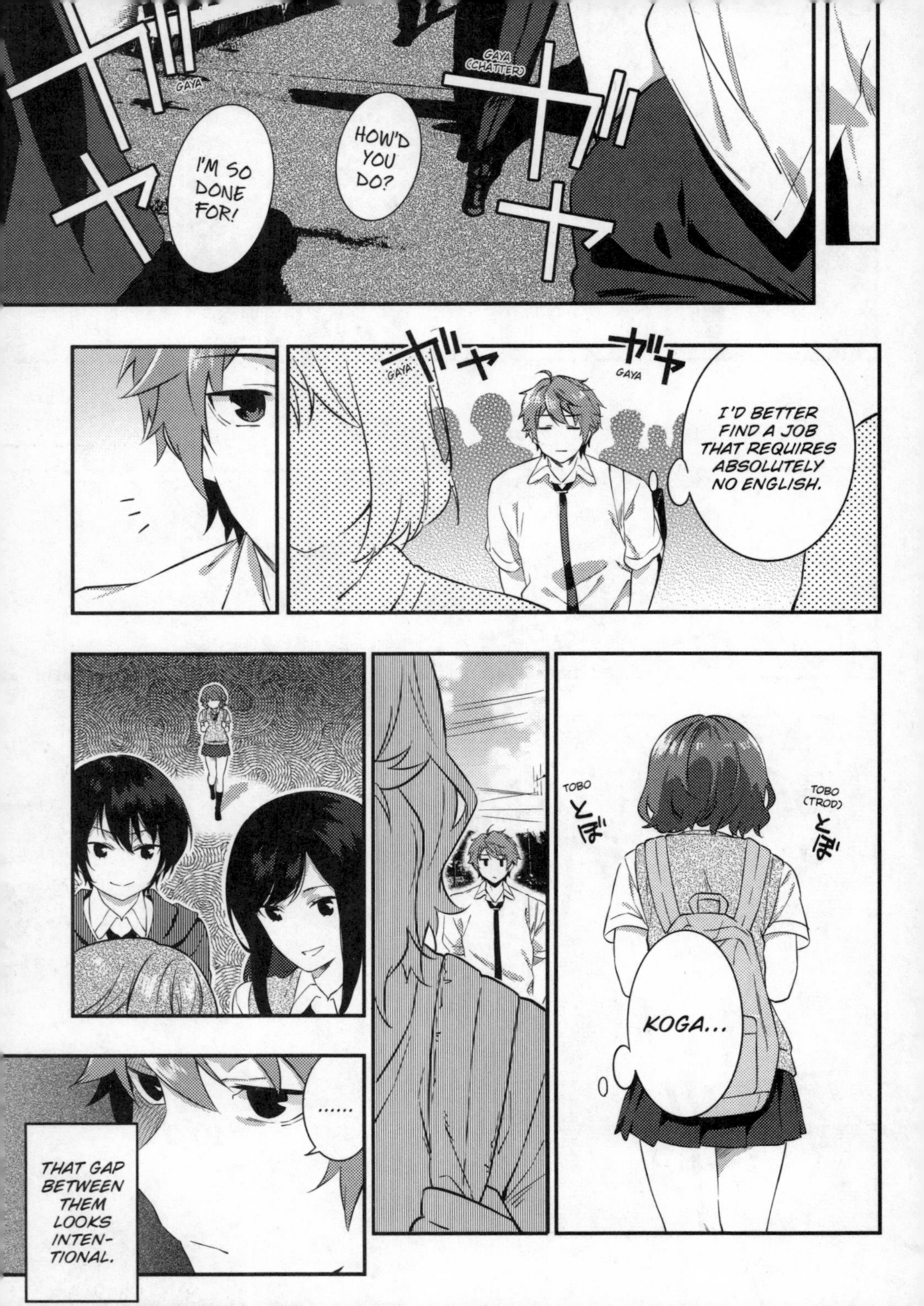

GAYA (CHATTER)
HOW'D YOU DO?
GAYA
I'M SO DONE FOR!
GAYA
GAYA
I'D BETTER FIND A JOB THAT REQUIRES ABSOLUTELY NO ENGLISH.
TOBO (TROD)
とぼ
TOBO
とぼ
KOGA...
......
THAT GAP BETWEEN THEM LOOKS INTENTIONAL.

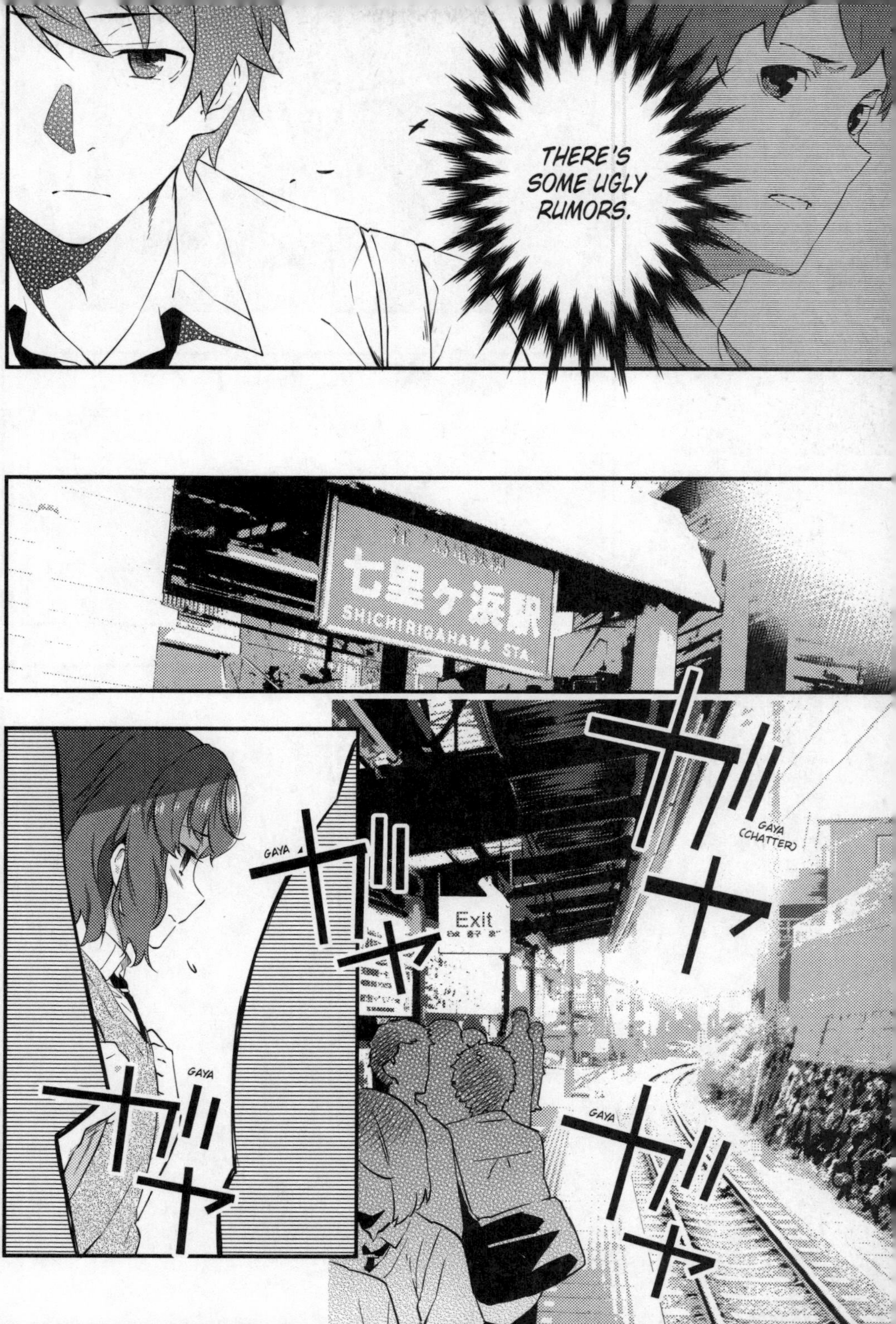
THERE'S SOME UGLY RUMORS.
七里ヶ浜駅
SHICHIRIGAHAMA STA.
GAYA (CHATTER)
GAYA
Exit
GAYA
GAYA

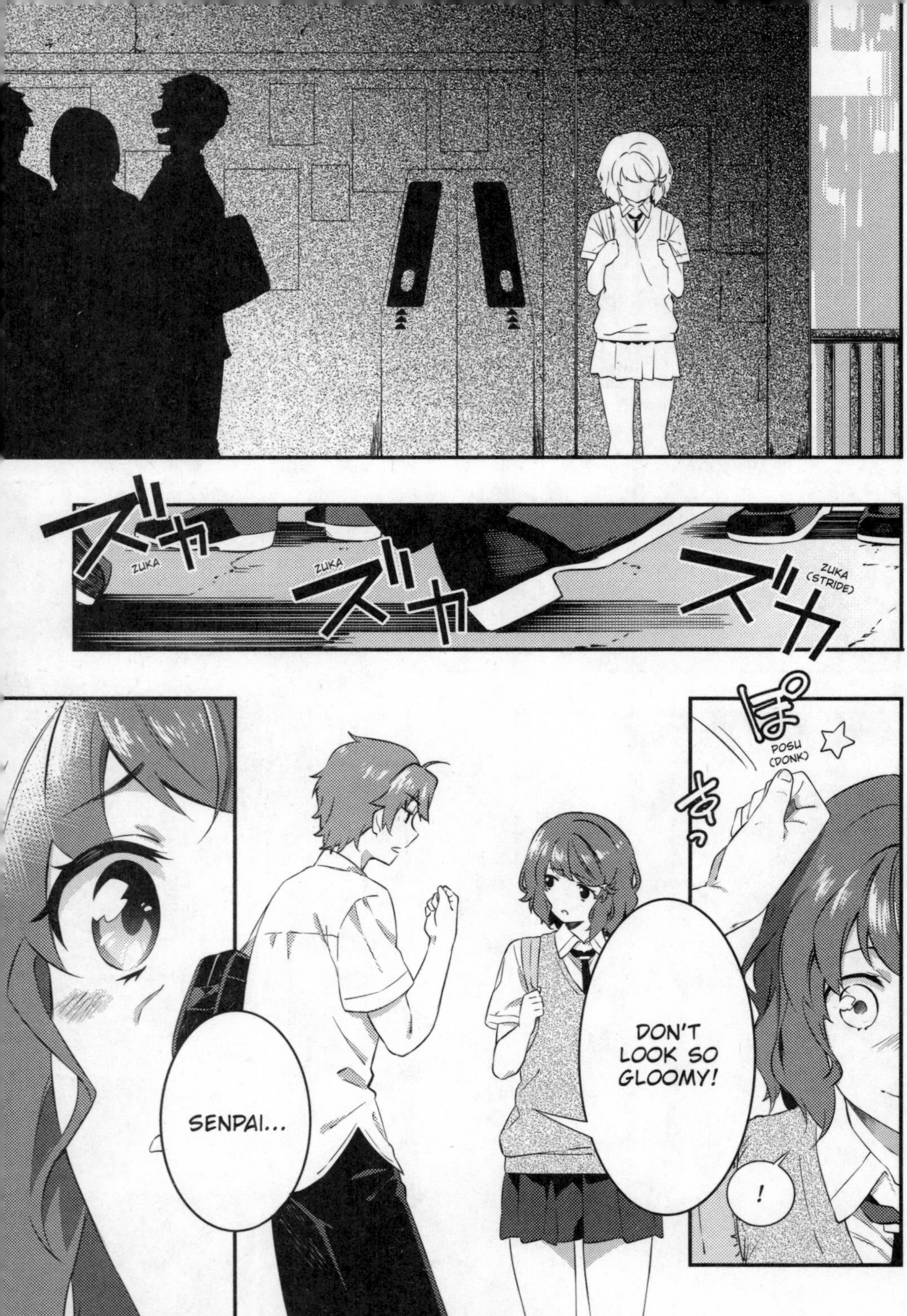
ZUKA (STRIDE)
ZUKA
ZUKA
POSU (DONK)
DON'T LOOK SO GLOOMY!
!
SENPAI...

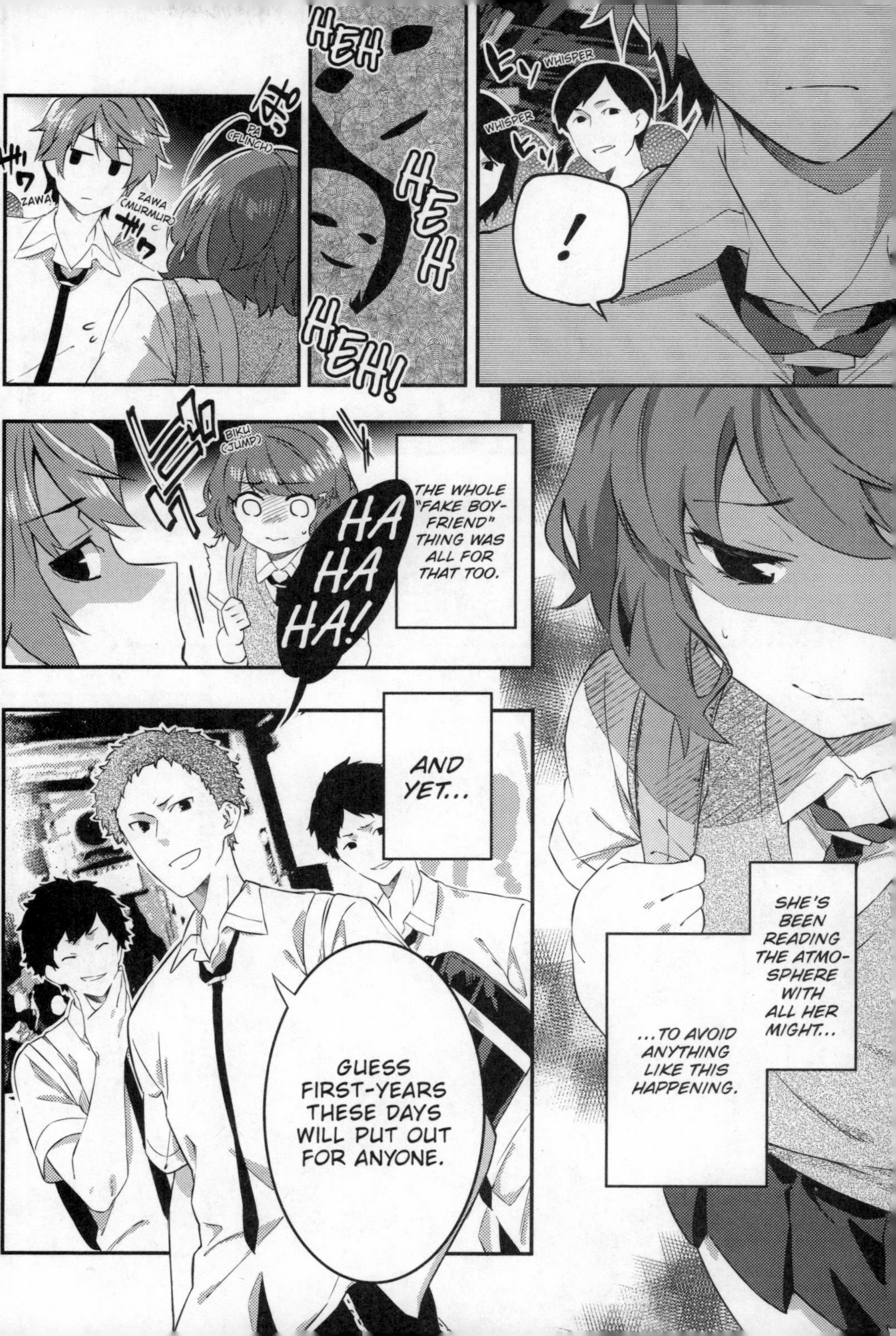

WHISPER
WHISPER
!
HEH HEH HEH HEH!
PA (FLINCH)
ZAWA (MURMUR)
ZAWA
SHE'S BEEN READING THE ATMOSPHERE WITH ALL HER MIGHT...
...TO AVOID ANYTHING LIKE THIS HAPPENING.
THE WHOLE "FAKE BOY-FRIEND" THING WAS ALL FOR THAT TOO.
BIKU (JUMP)
HA HA HA HA!
AND YET...
GUESS FIRST-YEARS THESE DAYS WILL PUT OUT FOR ANYONE.

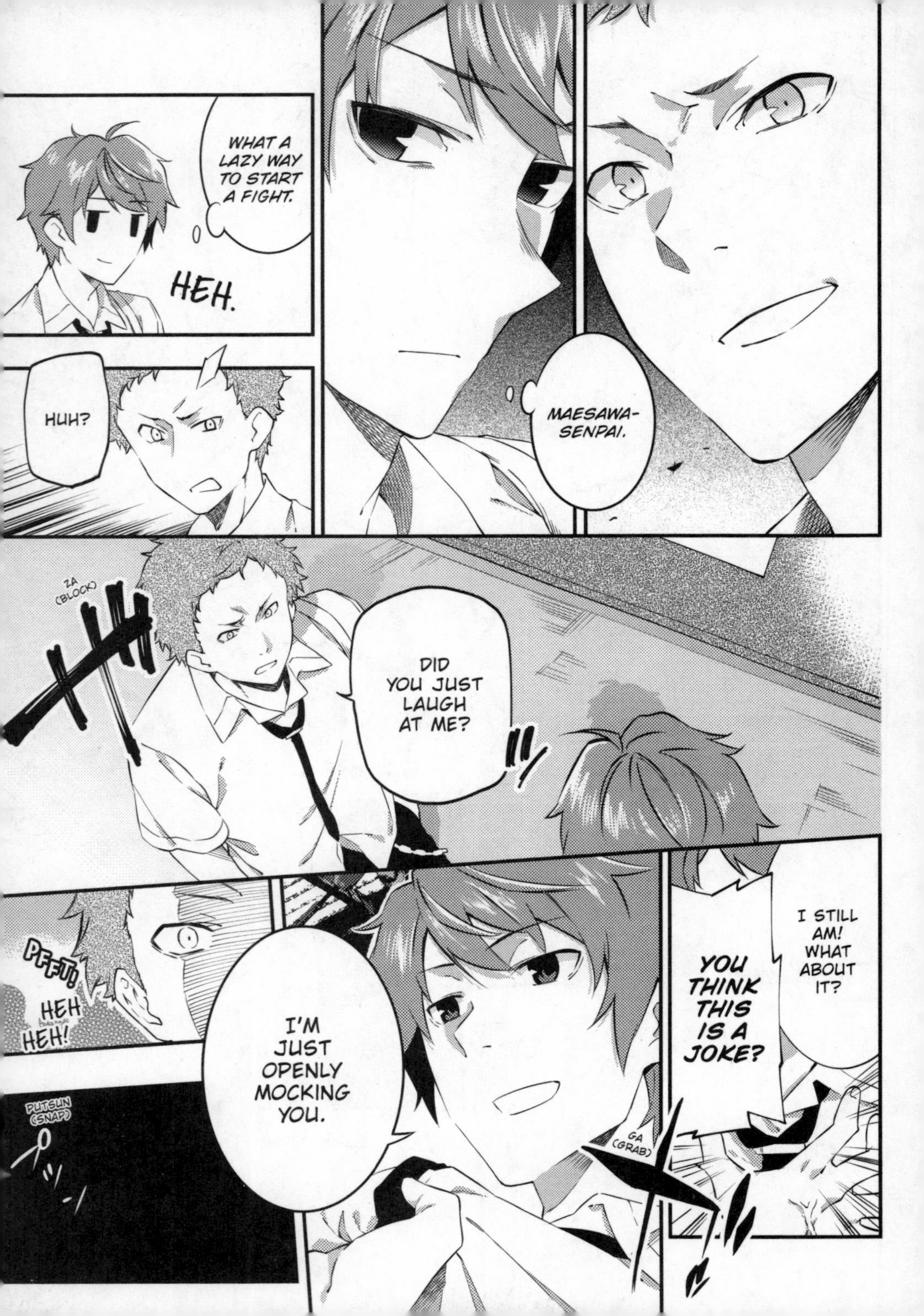
MAESAWA-SENPAI.
WHAT A LAZY WAY TO START A FIGHT.
HEH.
HUH?
ZA (BLOCK)
DID YOU JUST LAUGH AT ME?
I STILL AM! WHAT ABOUT IT?
YOU THINK THIS IS A JOKE?
GA (GRAB)
I'M JUST OPENLY MOCKING YOU.
PFFT! HEH HEH!
PUTSUN (SNAP)

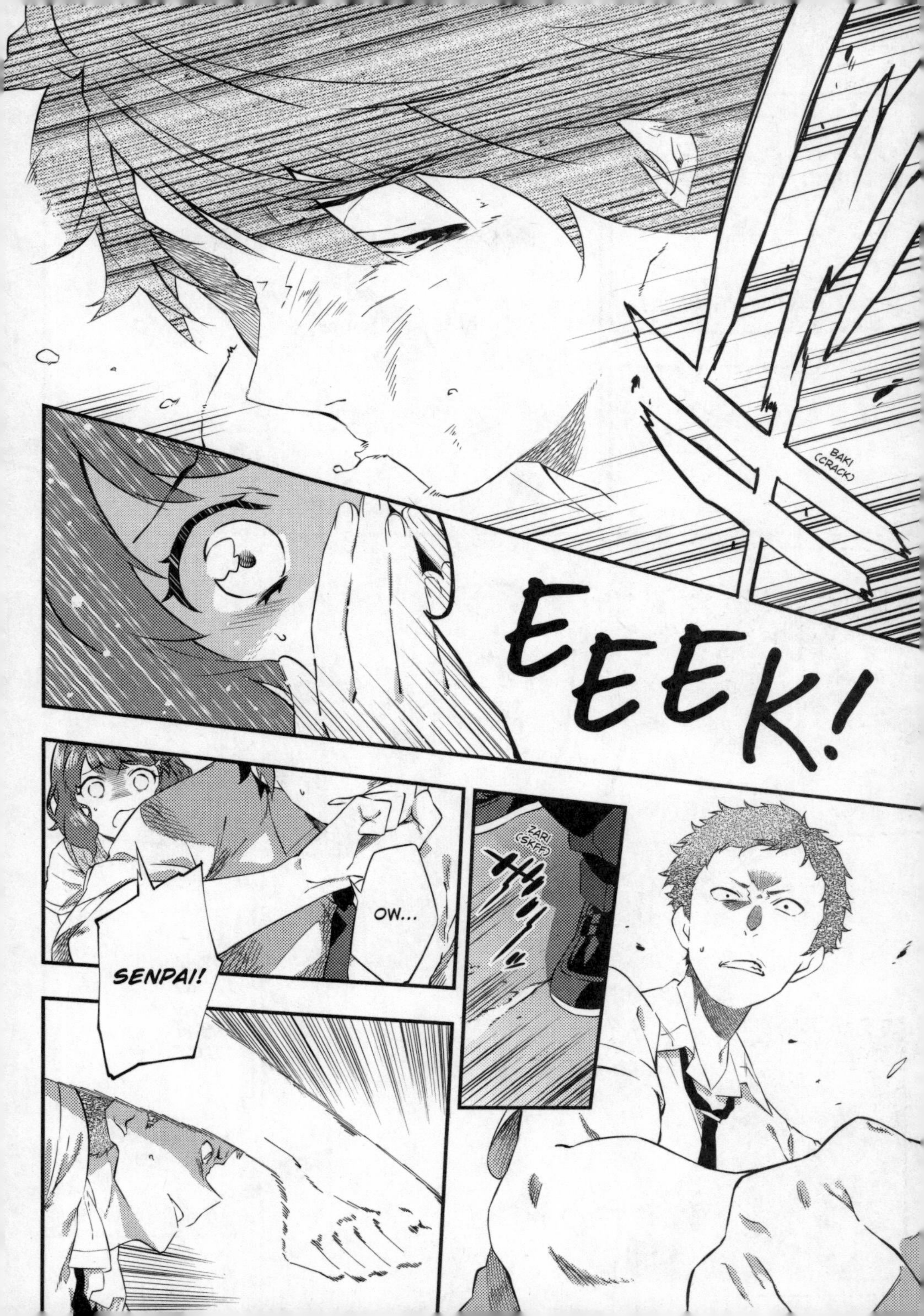
BAKI (CRACK)
EEEK!
OW...
SENPAI!
ZARI (SKFF)

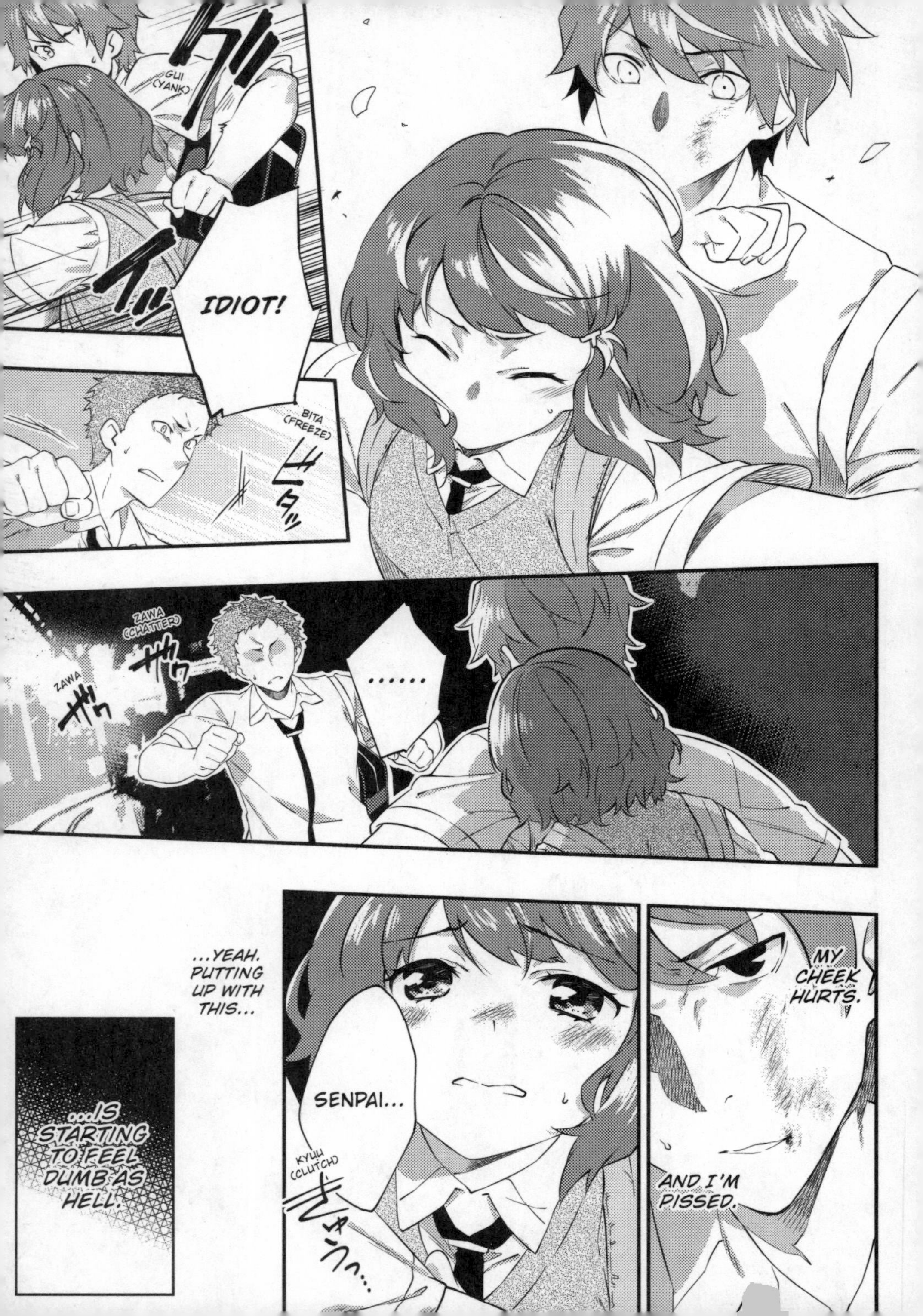
IDIOT!
GUI (YANK)
BITA (FREEZE)
......
ZAWA (CHATTER)
ZAWA
MY CHEEK HURTS.
AND I'M PISSED.
...YEAH. PUTTING UP WITH THIS...
SENPAI...
KYUU (CLUTCH)
...IS STARTING TO FEEL DUMB AS HELL.

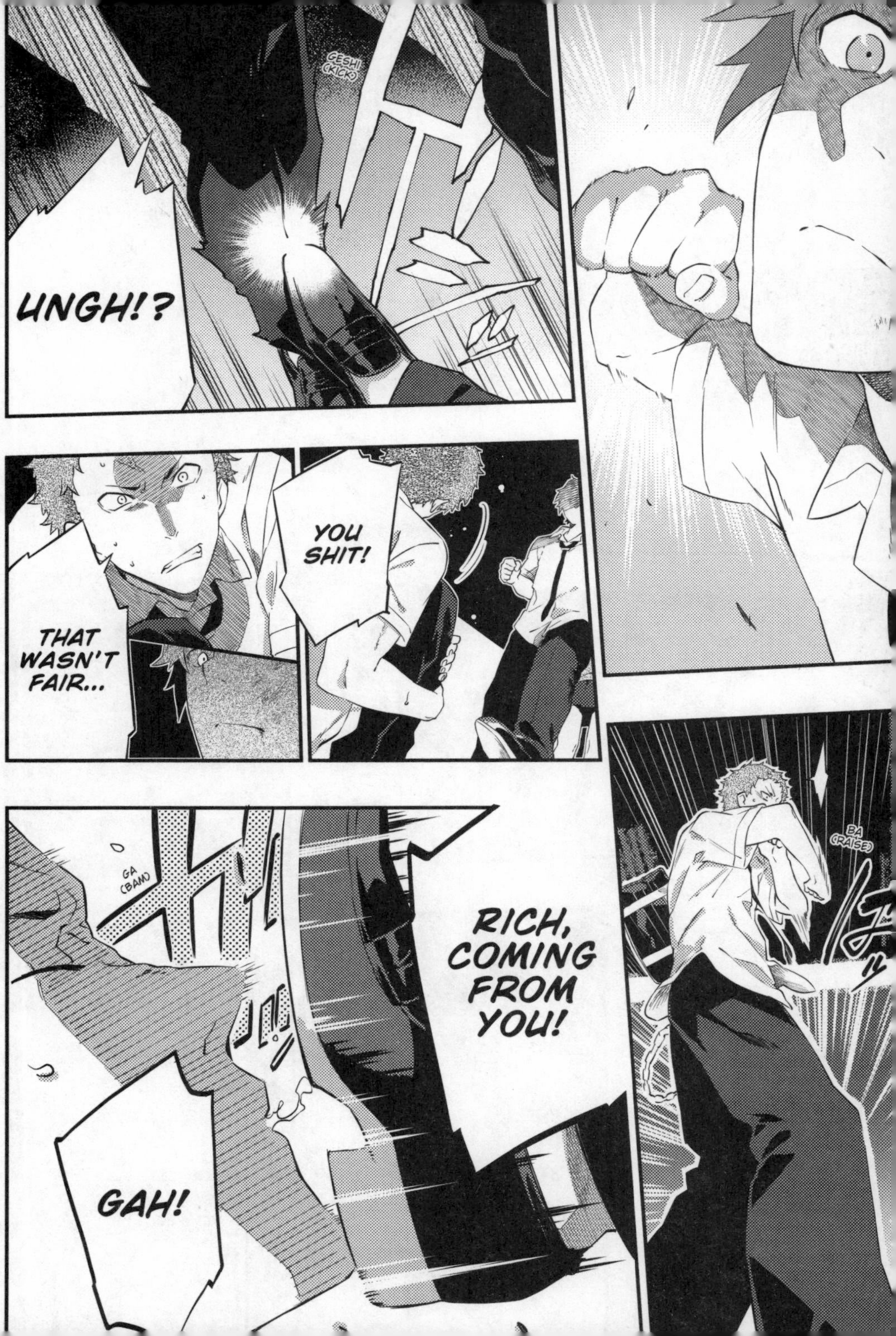
GESHI (KICK)
UNGH!?
YOU SHIT!
THAT WASN'T FAIR...
BA (RAISE)
RICH, COMING FROM YOU!
GA (BAM)
GAH!

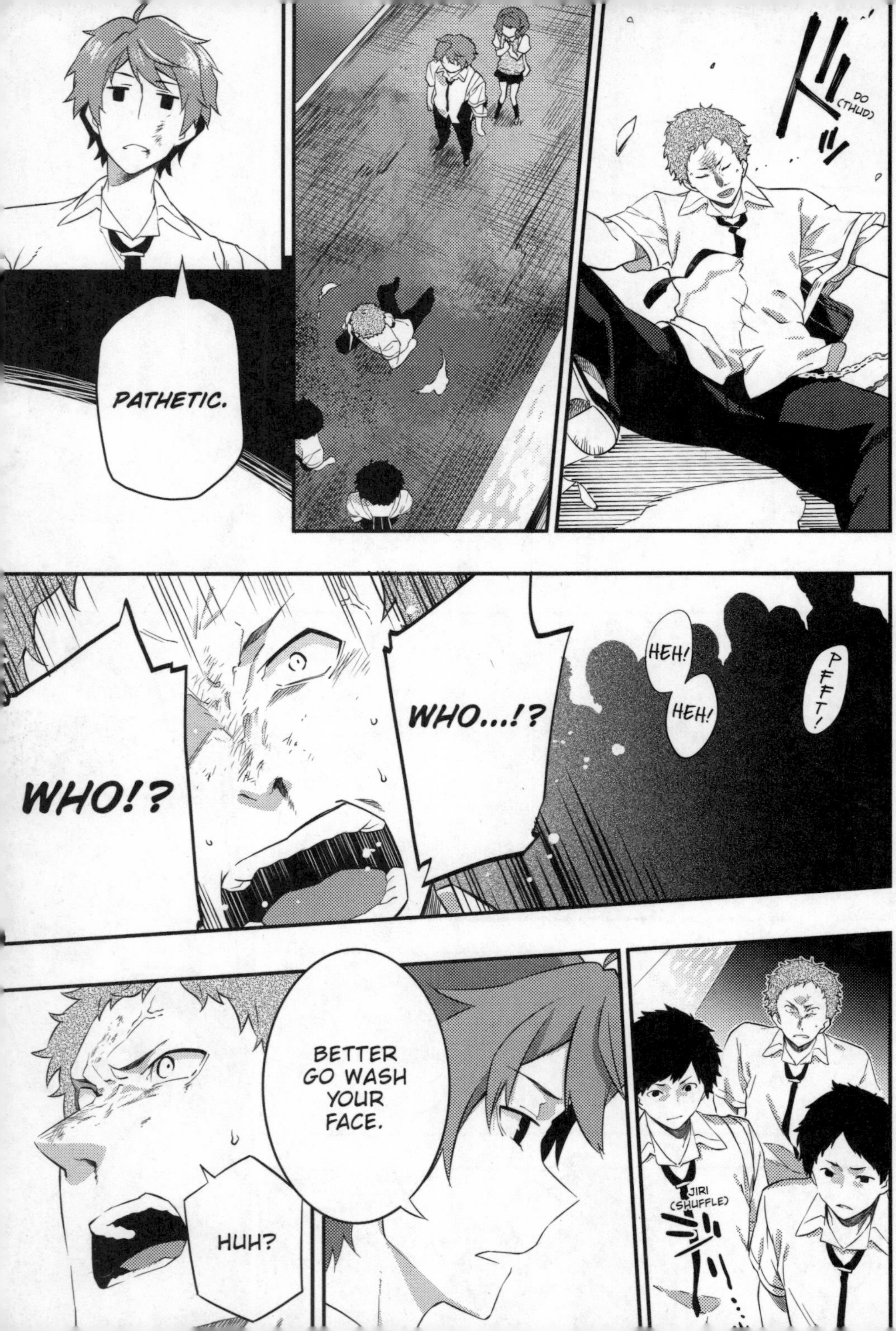
DO
(THUD)
PATHETIC.
HEH!
HEH!
PFFT!
WHO...!?
WHO!?
JIRI
(SHUFFLE)
BETTER GO WASH YOUR FACE.
HUH?

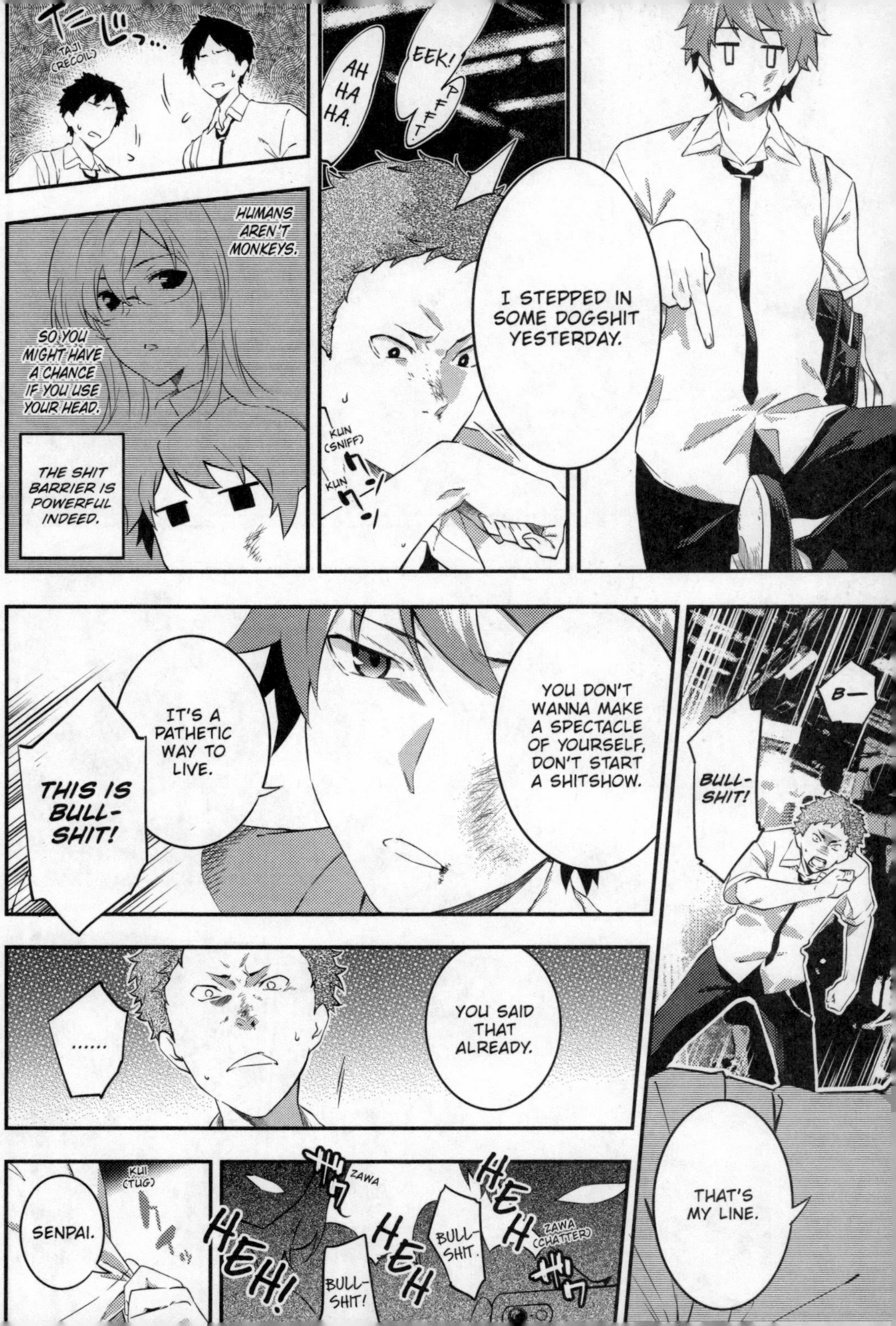
I STEPPED IN SOME DOGSHIT YESTERDAY.
EEK!
PFFT
AH HA HA.
KUN (SNIFF)
KUN
TAJI (RECOIL)
HUMANS AREN'T MONKEYS.
SO YOU MIGHT HAVE A CHANCE IF YOU USE YOUR HEAD.
THE SHIT BARRIER IS POWERFUL INDEED.
B—
BULL-SHIT!
THAT'S MY LINE.
YOU DON'T WANNA MAKE A SPECTACLE OF YOURSELF, DON'T START A SHITSHOW.
IT'S A PATHETIC WAY TO LIVE.
THIS IS BULL-SHIT!
YOU SAID THAT ALREADY.
......
ZAWA
HEH HEH
BULL-SHIT.
ZAWA (CHATTER)
HEH HEH
HEH!
BULL-SHIT!
KUI (TUG)
SENPAI.

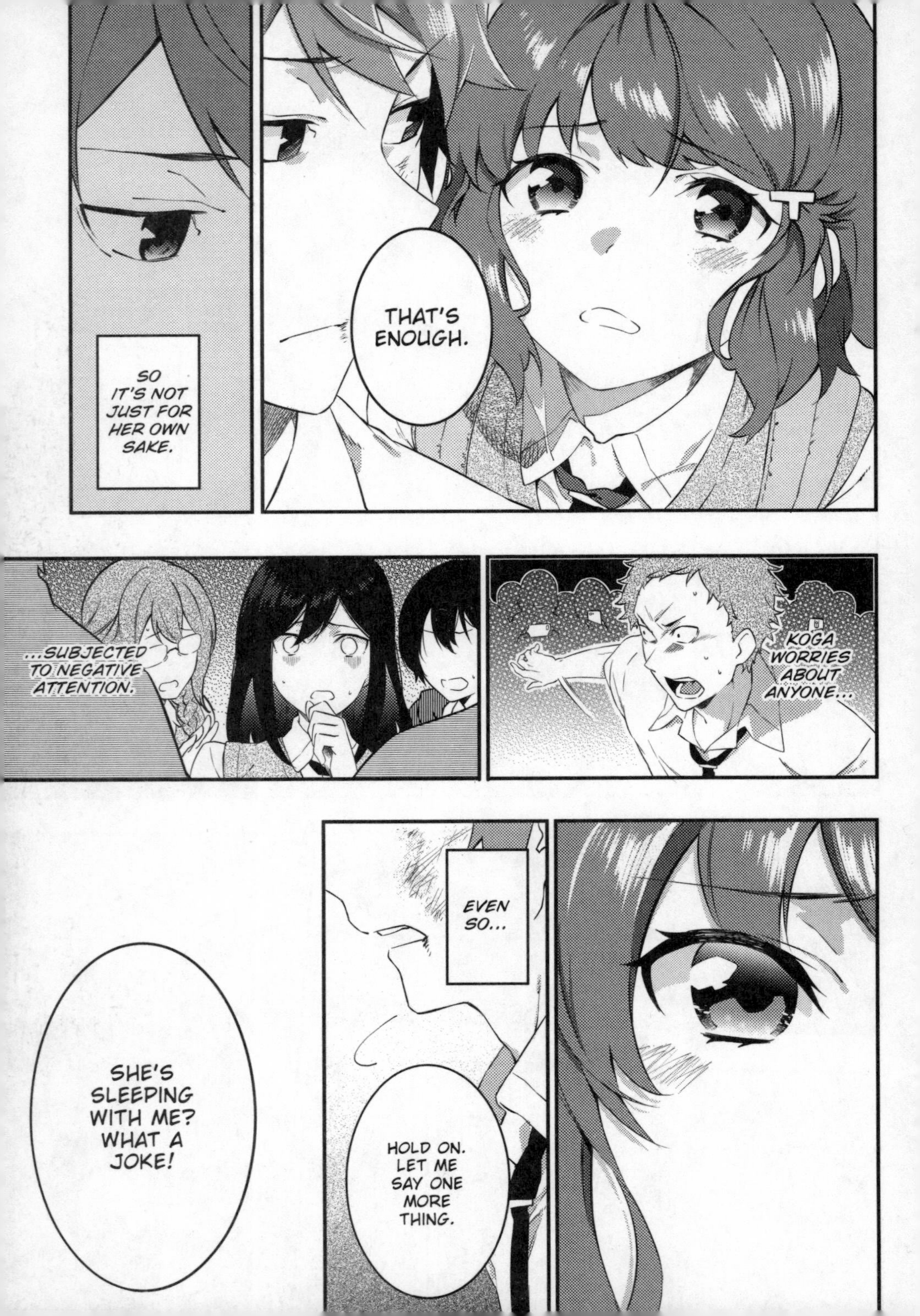
THAT'S ENOUGH.
SO IT'S NOT JUST FOR HER OWN SAKE.
KOGA WORRIES ABOUT ANYONE...
...SUBJECTED TO NEGATIVE ATTENTION.
EVEN SO...
HOLD ON. LET ME SAY ONE MORE THING.
SHE'S SLEEPING WITH ME? WHAT A JOKE!

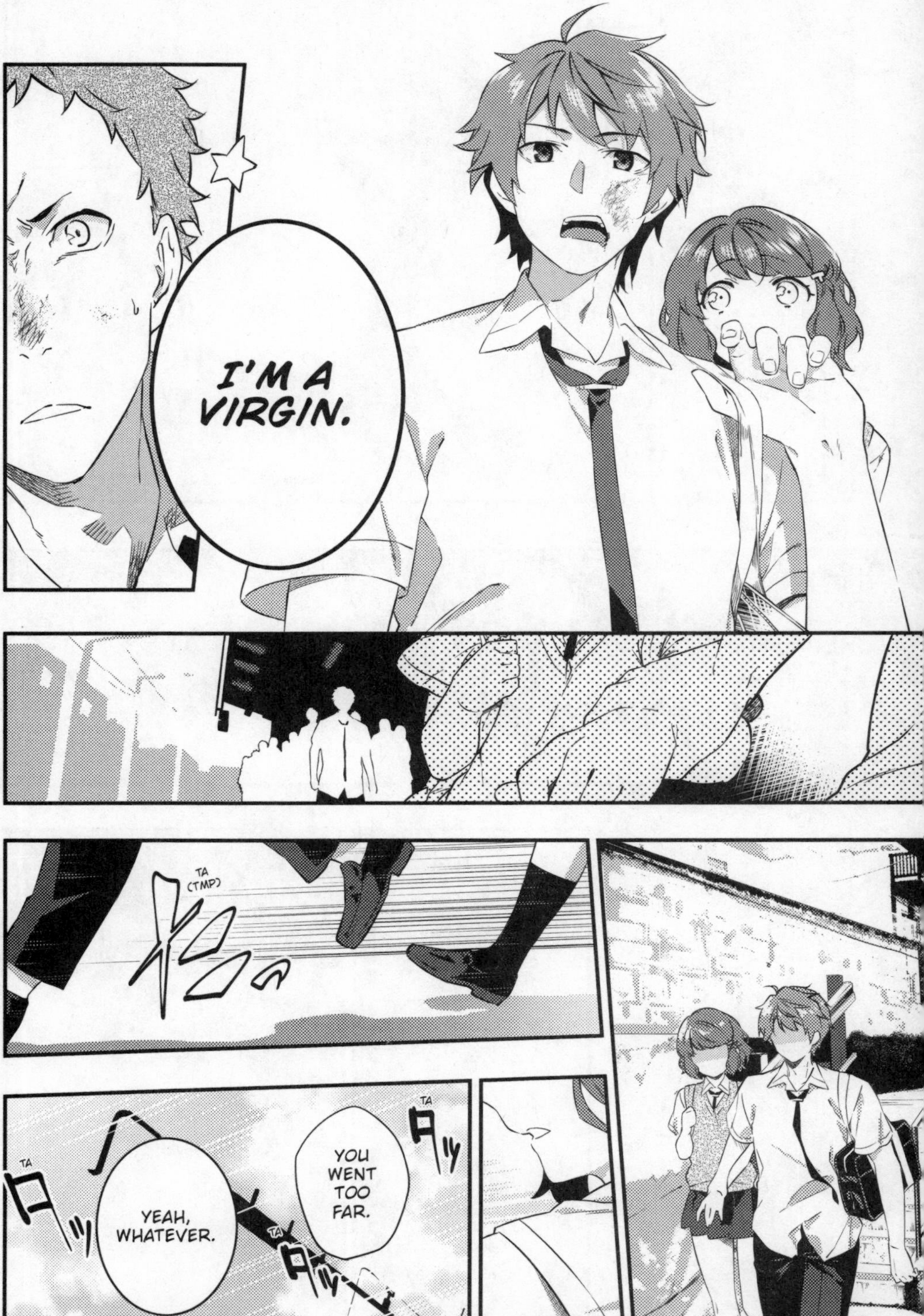
I'M A VIRGIN.
TA (TMP)
TA
YOU WENT TOO FAR.
TA
YEAH, WHATEVER.
TA

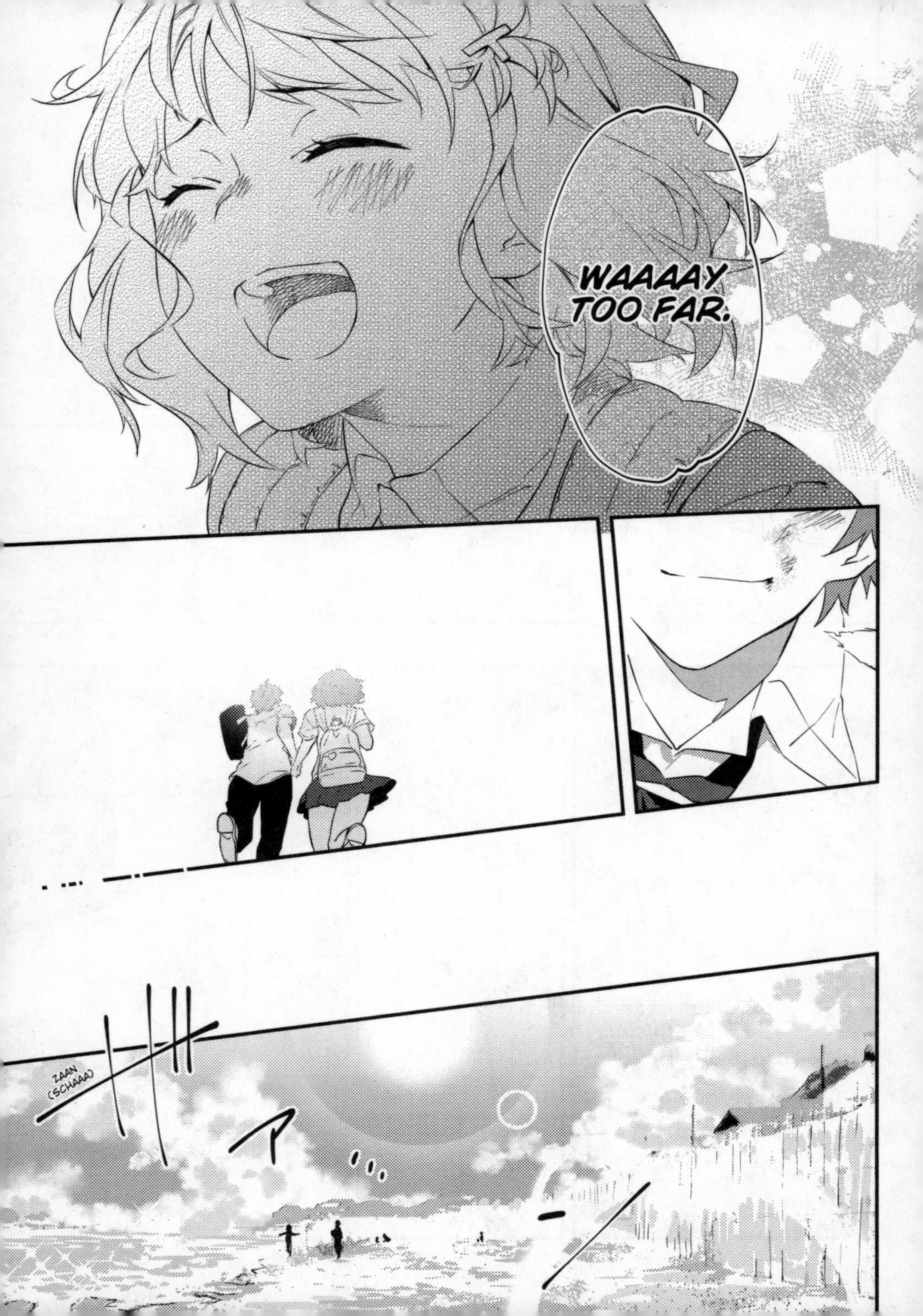
WAAAAY TOO FAR.
ZAAN (SCHAAA)

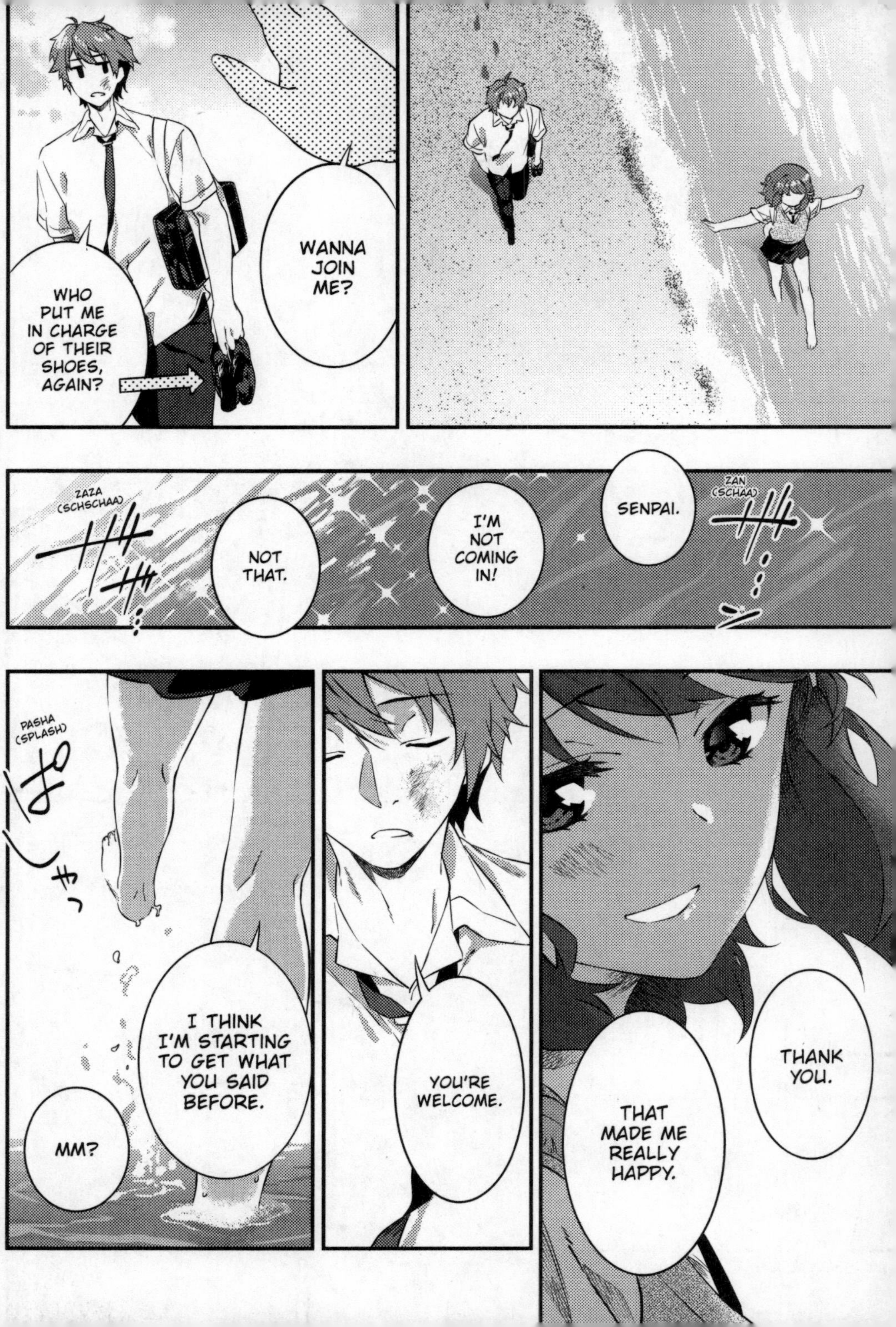
WANNA JOIN ME?
WHO PUT ME IN CHARGE OF THEIR SHOES, AGAIN?
ZAN (SCHAA)
SENPAI.
I'M NOT COMING IN!
NOT THAT.
ZAZA (SCHSCHAA)
THANK YOU.
THAT MADE ME REALLY HAPPY.
YOU'RE WELCOME.
PASHA (SPLASH)
I THINK I'M STARTING TO GET WHAT YOU SAID BEFORE.
MM?

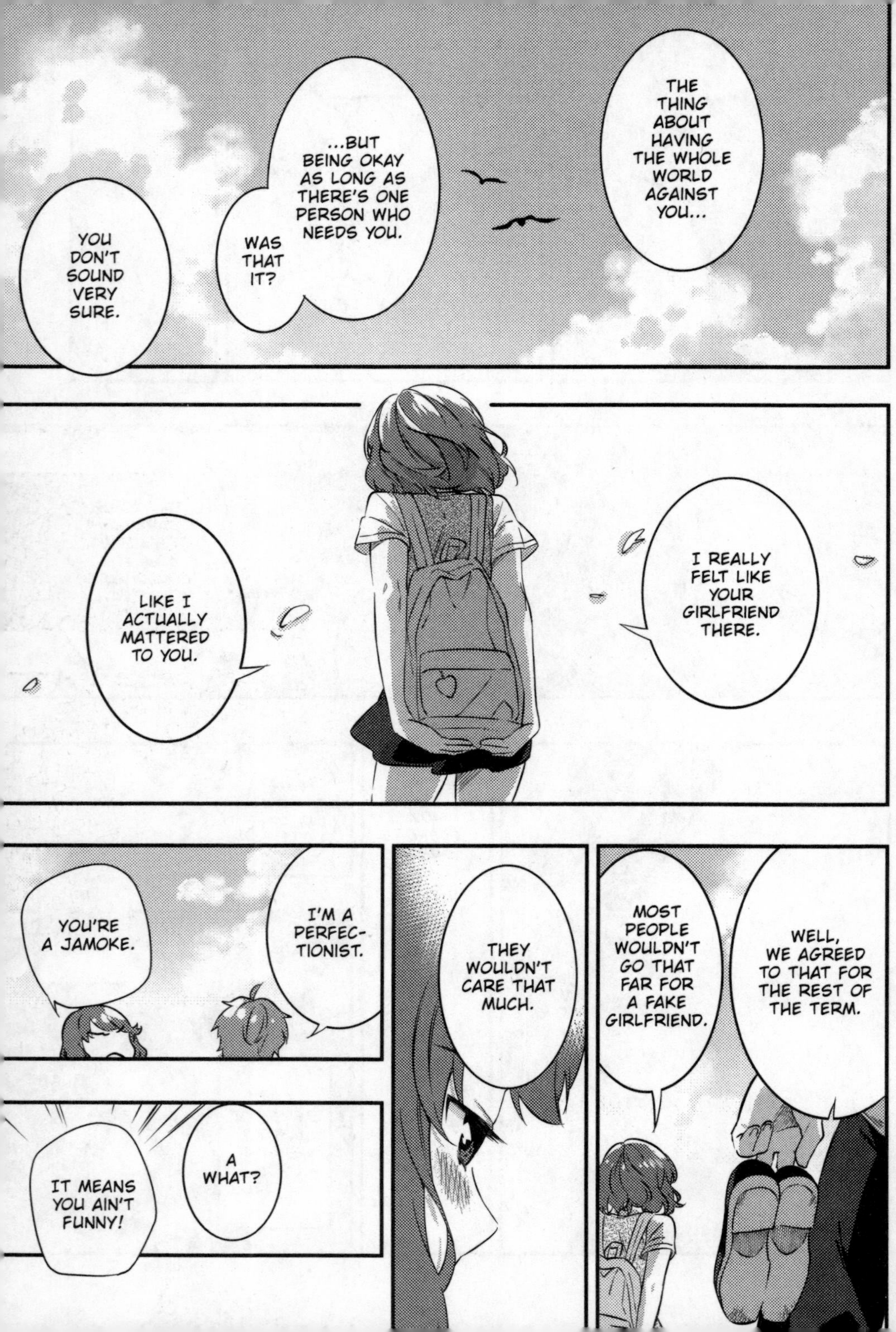
THE THING ABOUT HAVING THE WHOLE WORLD AGAINST YOU...
...BUT BEING OKAY AS LONG AS THERE'S ONE PERSON WHO NEEDS YOU.
WAS THAT IT?
YOU DON'T SOUND VERY SURE.
I REALLY FELT LIKE YOUR GIRLFRIEND THERE.
LIKE I ACTUALLY MATTERED TO YOU.
WELL, WE AGREED TO THAT FOR THE REST OF THE TERM.
MOST PEOPLE WOULDN'T GO THAT FAR FOR A FAKE GIRLFRIEND.
THEY WOULDN'T CARE THAT MUCH.
I'M A PERFECTIONIST.
YOU'RE A JAMOKE.
A WHAT?
IT MEANS YOU AIN'T FUNNY!

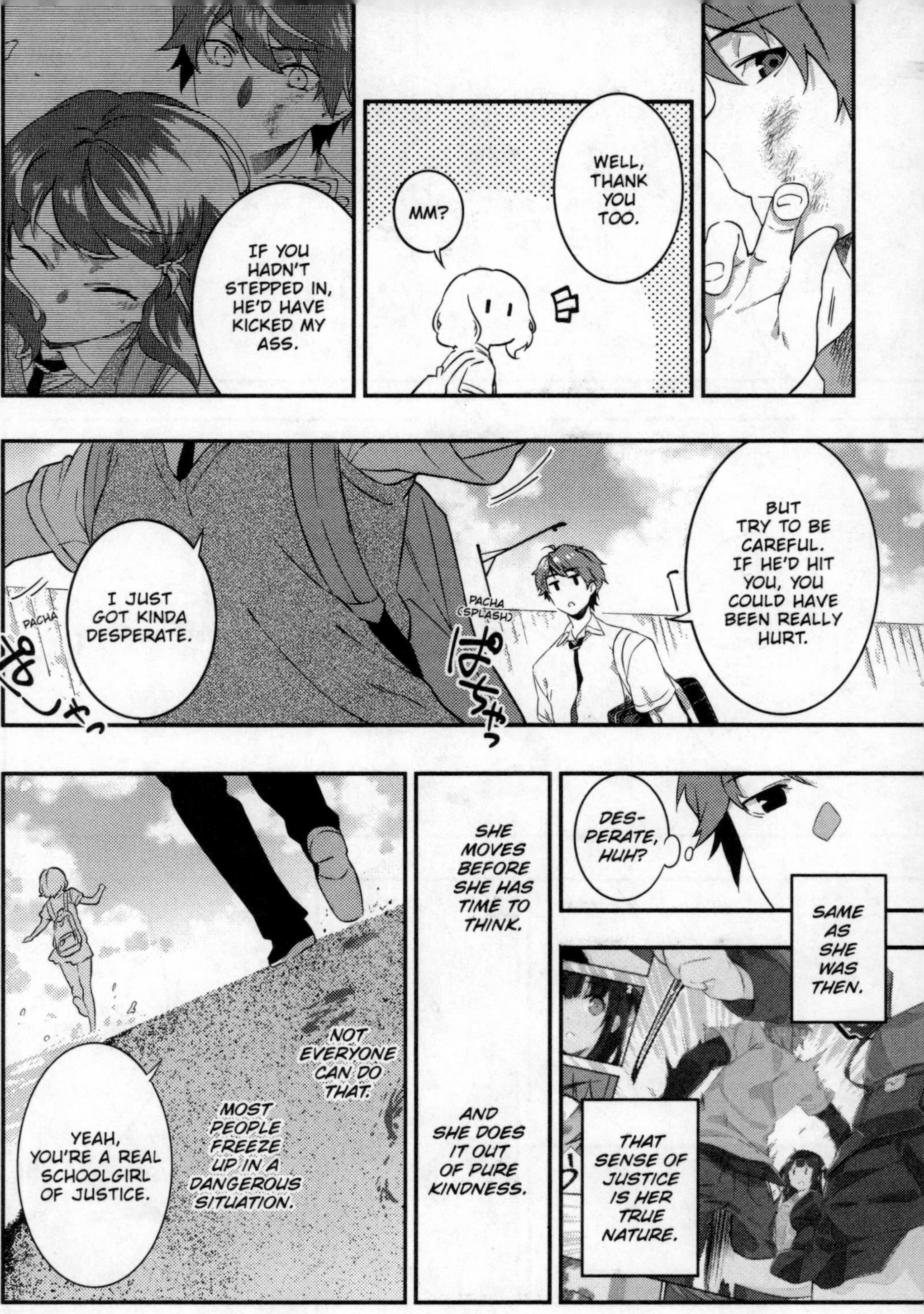
WELL, THANK YOU TOO.
MM?
IF YOU HADN'T STEPPED IN, HE'D HAVE KICKED MY ASS.
BUT TRY TO BE CAREFUL. IF HE'D HIT YOU, YOU COULD HAVE BEEN REALLY HURT.
PACHA (SPLASH)
I JUST GOT KINDA DESPERATE.
PACHA
DES-PERATE, HUH?
SAME AS SHE WAS THEN.
THAT SENSE OF JUSTICE IS HER TRUE NATURE.
SHE MOVES BEFORE SHE HAS TIME TO THINK.
AND SHE DOES IT OUT OF PURE KINDNESS.
NOT EVERYONE CAN DO THAT.
MOST PEOPLE FREEZE UP IN A DANGEROUS SITUATION.
YEAH, YOU'RE A REAL SCHOOLGIRL OF JUSTICE.

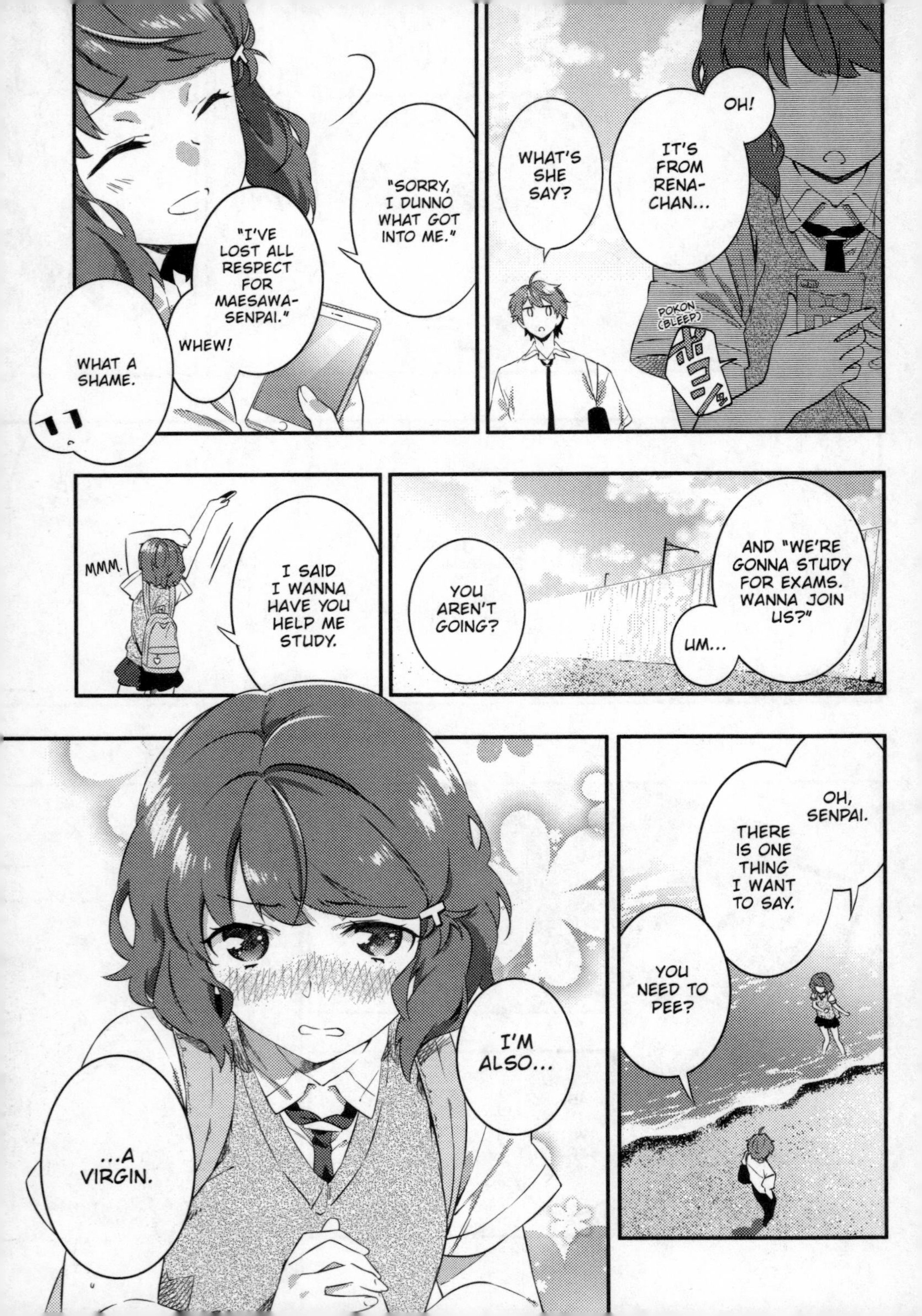
OH!
IT'S FROM RENA-CHAN...
WHAT'S SHE SAY?
POKON (BLEEP)
"SORRY, I DUNNO WHAT GOT INTO ME."
"I'VE LOST ALL RESPECT FOR MAESAWA-SENPAI."
WHEW!
WHAT A SHAME.
AND "WE'RE GONNA STUDY FOR EXAMS. WANNA JOIN US?"
UM...
YOU AREN'T GOING?
I SAID I WANNA HAVE YOU HELP ME STUDY.
MMM.
OH, SENPAI.
THERE IS ONE THING I WANT TO SAY.
YOU NEED TO PEE?
I'M ALSO...
...A VIRGIN.

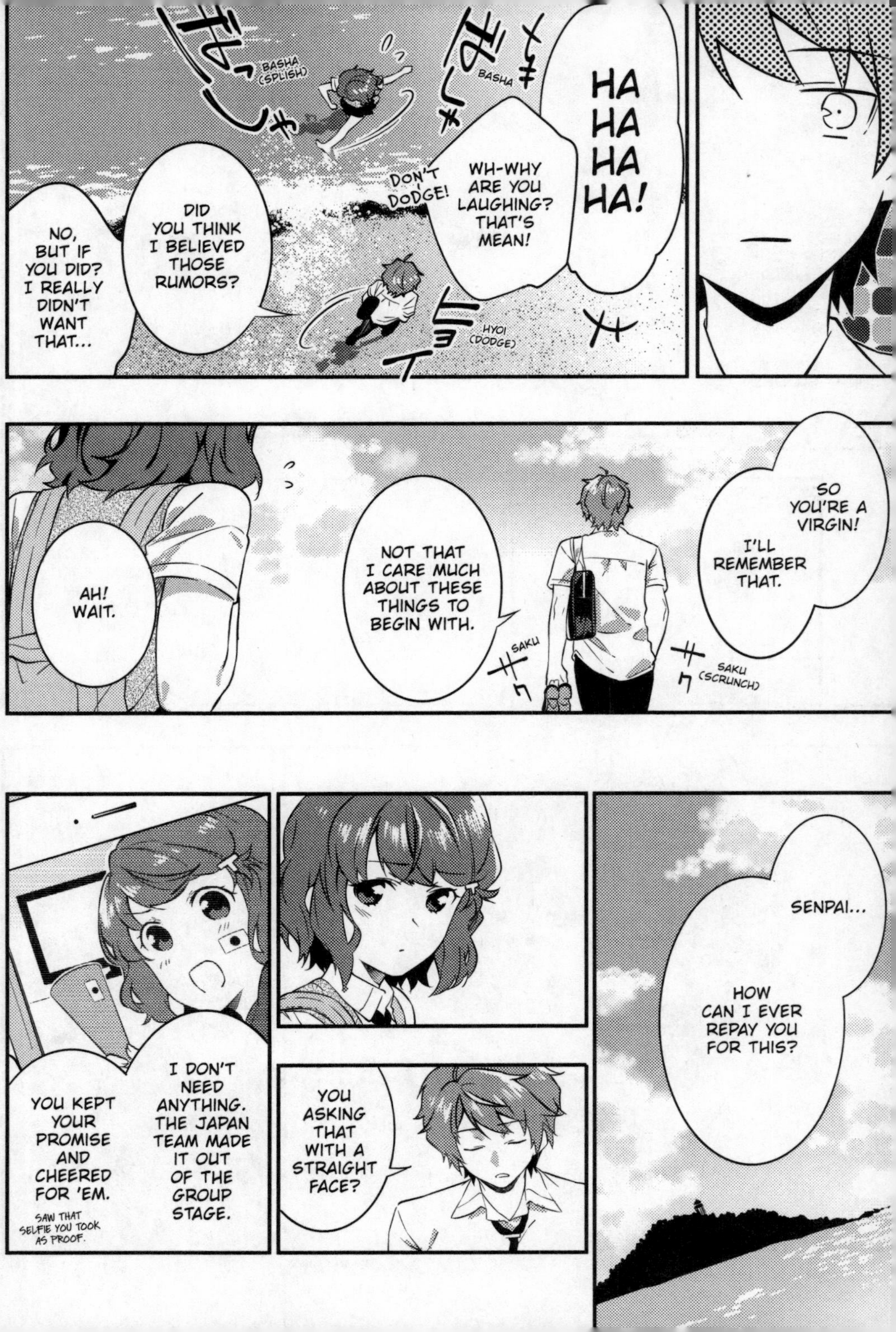
HA HA HA HA!
WH-WHY ARE YOU LAUGHING? THAT'S MEAN!
BASHA
DON'T DODGE!
BASHA (SPLISH)
DID YOU THINK I BELIEVED THOSE RUMORS?
HYOI (DODGE)
NO, BUT IF YOU DID? I REALLY DIDN'T WANT THAT...
SO YOU'RE A VIRGIN!
I'LL REMEMBER THAT.
SAKU (SCRUNCH)
SAKU
NOT THAT I CARE MUCH ABOUT THESE THINGS TO BEGIN WITH.
AH! WAIT.
SENPAI...
HOW CAN I EVER REPAY YOU FOR THIS?
YOU ASKING THAT WITH A STRAIGHT FACE?
I DON'T NEED ANYTHING. THE JAPAN TEAM MADE IT OUT OF THE GROUP STAGE.
YOU KEPT YOUR PROMISE AND CHEERED FOR 'EM.
SAW THAT SELFIE YOU TOOK AS PROOF.

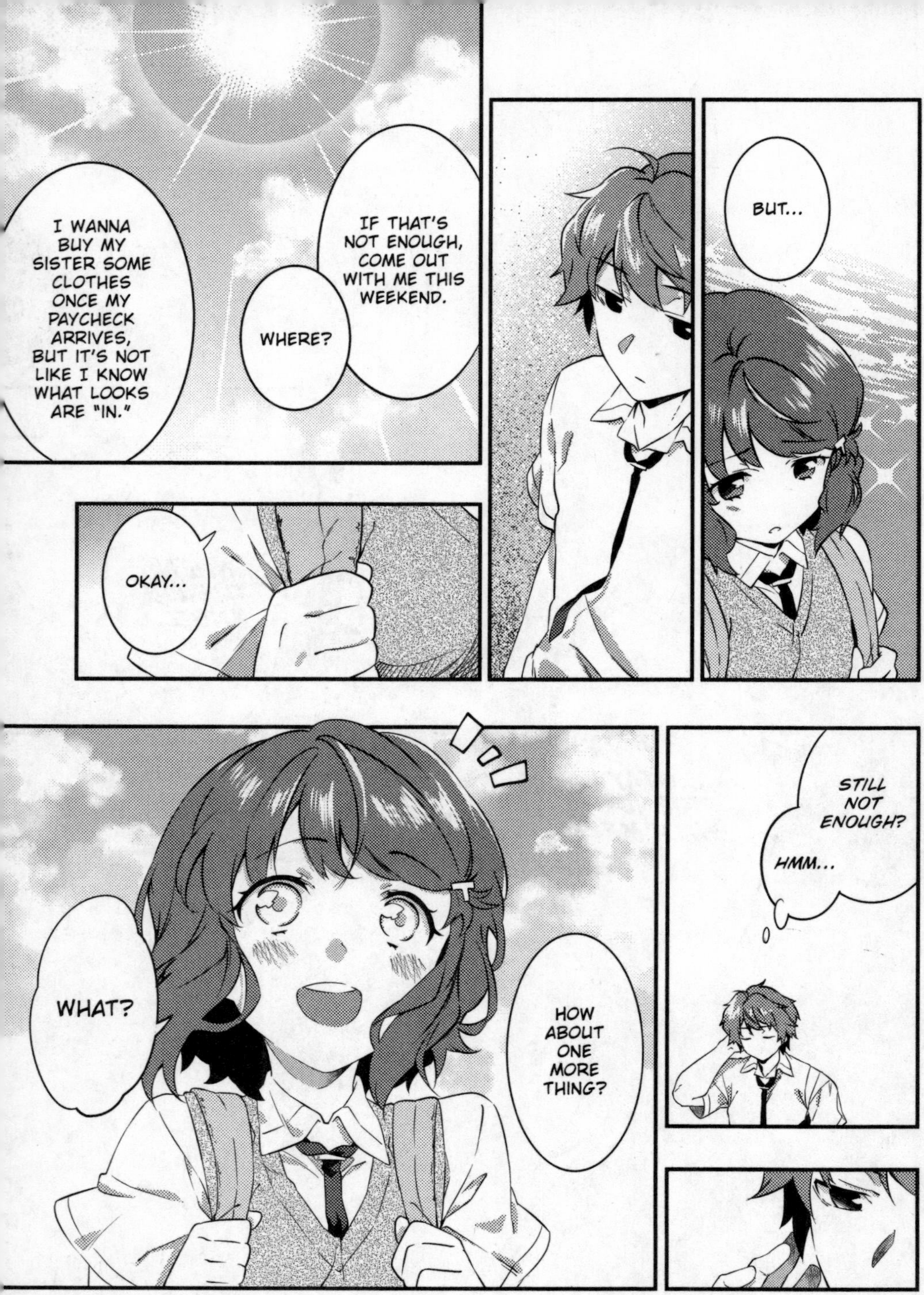
IF THAT'S NOT ENOUGH, COME OUT WITH ME THIS WEEKEND.
WHERE?
I WANNA BUY MY SISTER SOME CLOTHES ONCE MY PAYCHECK ARRIVES, BUT IT'S NOT LIKE I KNOW WHAT LOOKS ARE "IN."
OKAY...
BUT...
STILL NOT ENOUGH?
HMM...
HOW ABOUT ONE MORE THING?
WHAT?

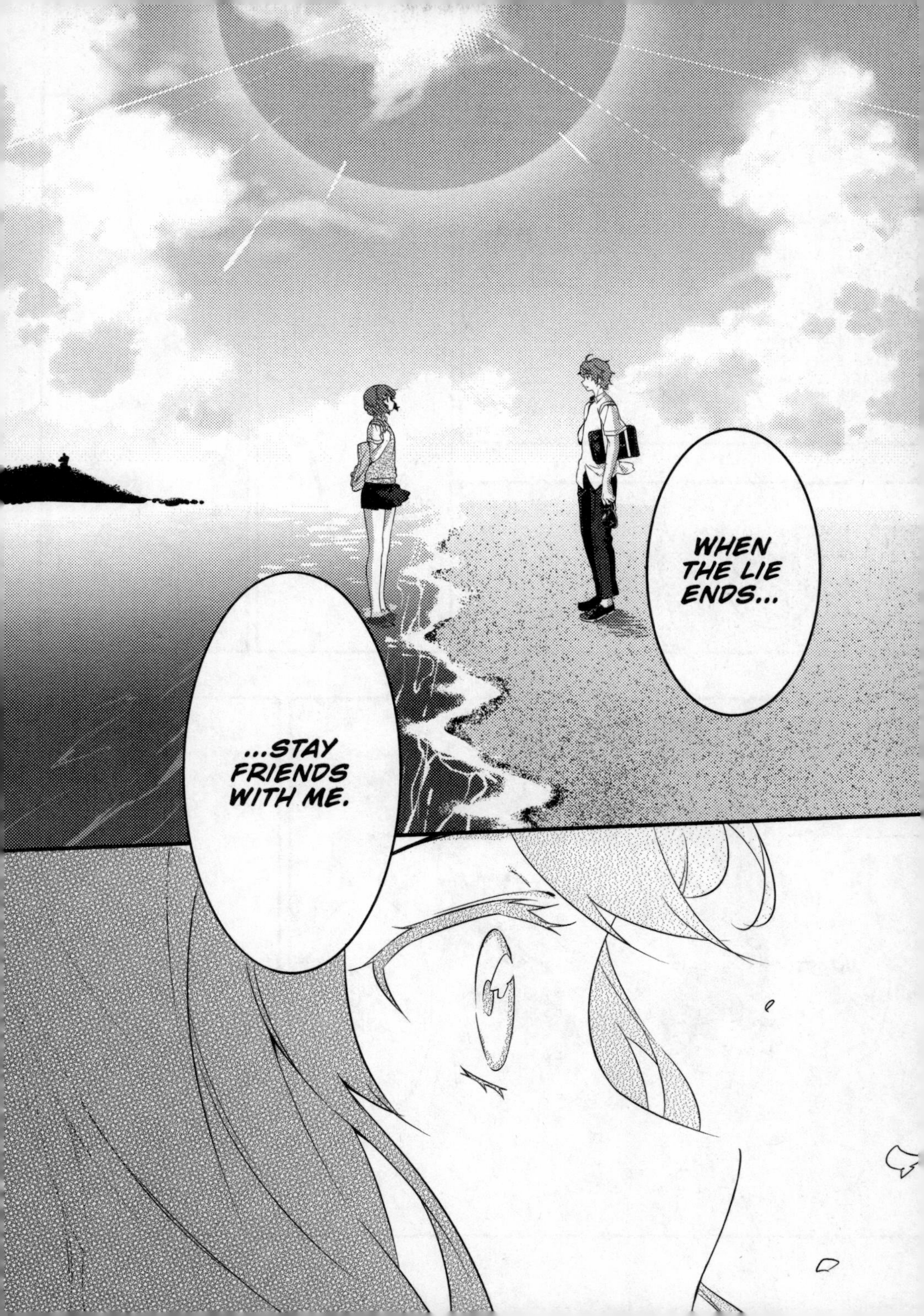
WHEN THE LIE ENDS...
...STAY FRIENDS WITH ME.

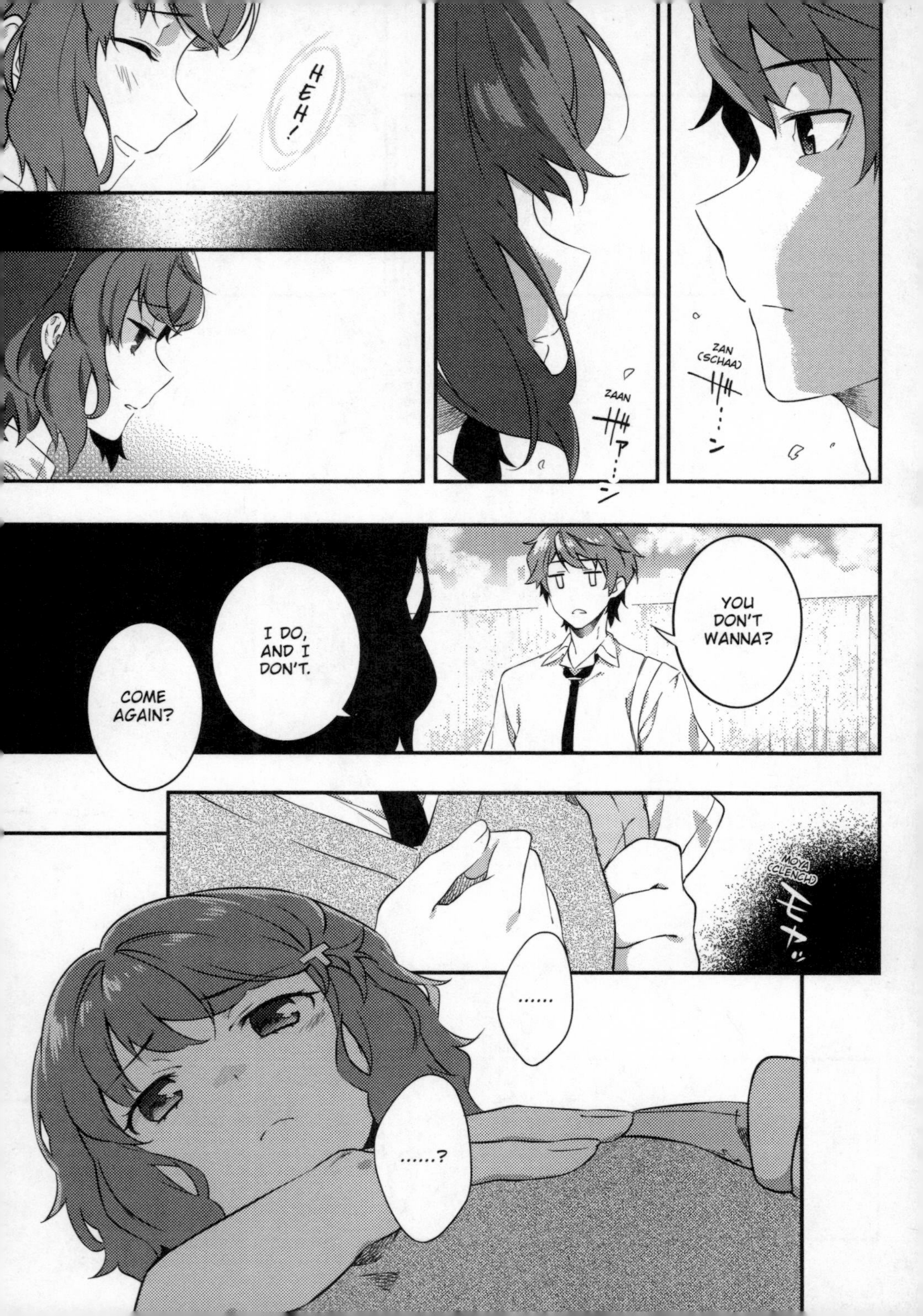
ZAN (SCHAA)
ZAAN
HEH!
YOU DON'T WANNA?
I DO, AND I DON'T.
COME AGAIN?
MOYA (CLENCH)
......
......?

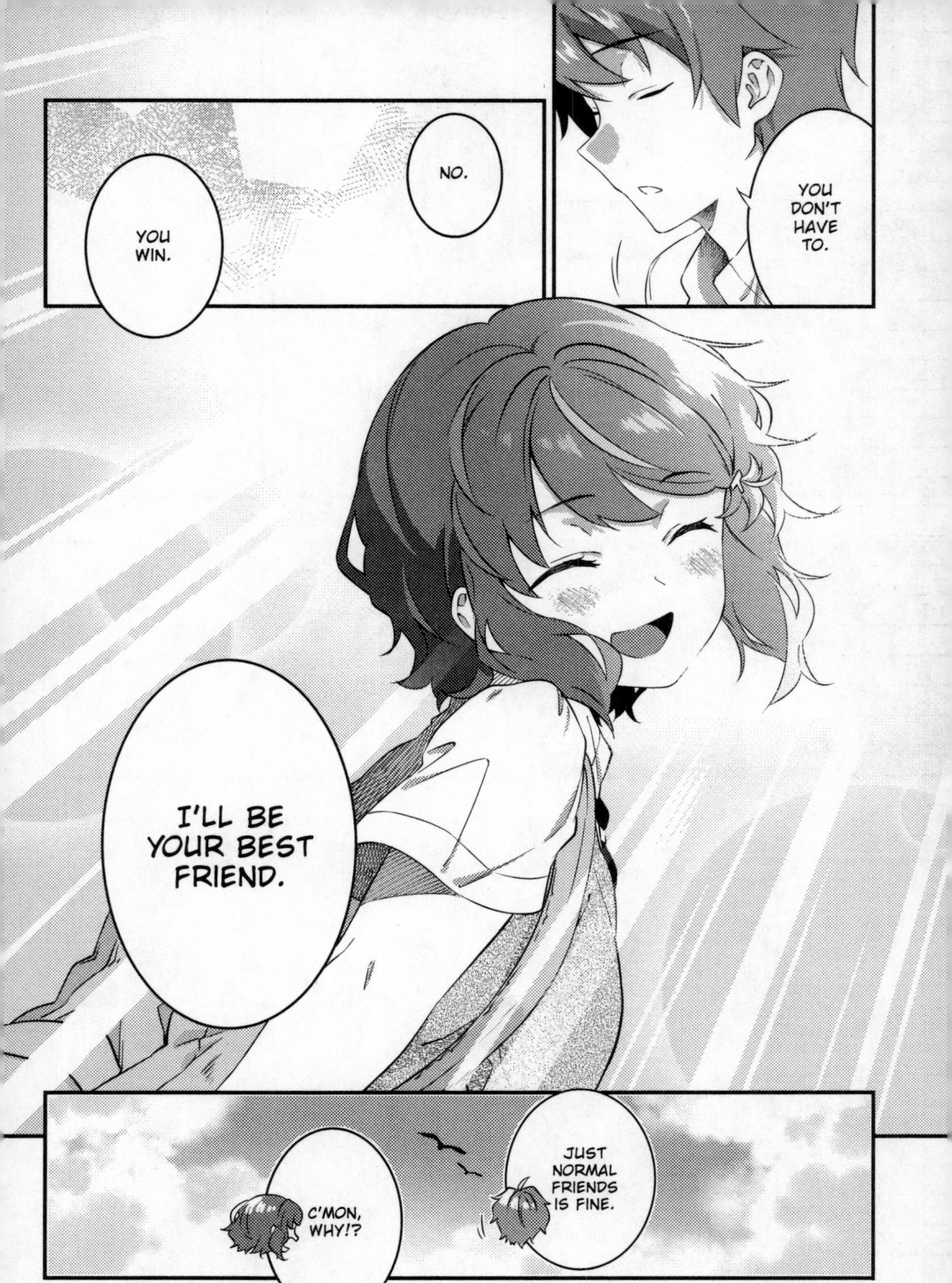

YOU DON'T HAVE TO.
NO.
YOU WIN.
I'LL BE YOUR BEST FRIEND.
JUST NORMAL FRIENDS IS FINE.
C'MON, WHY!?

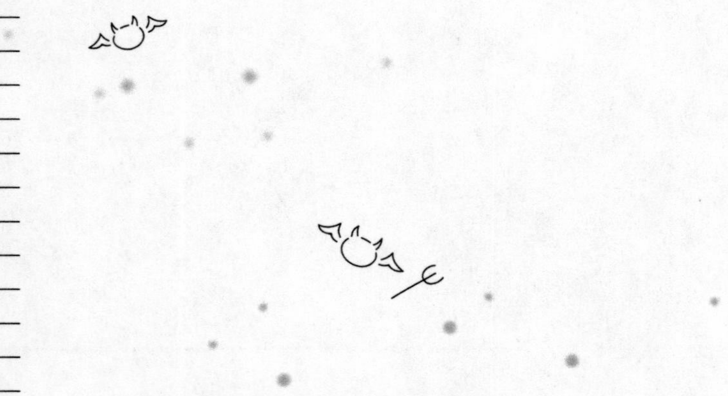

# #009

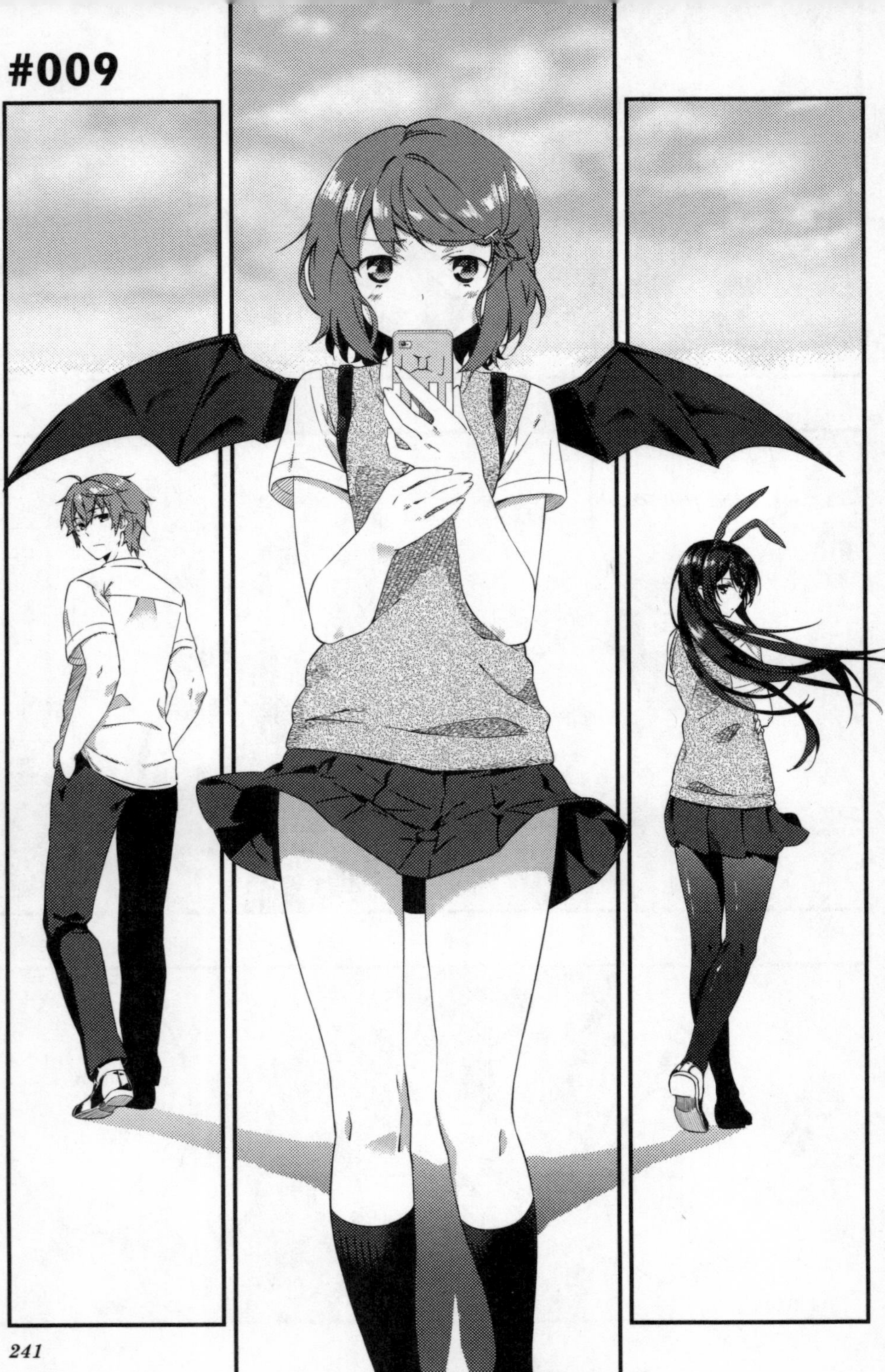

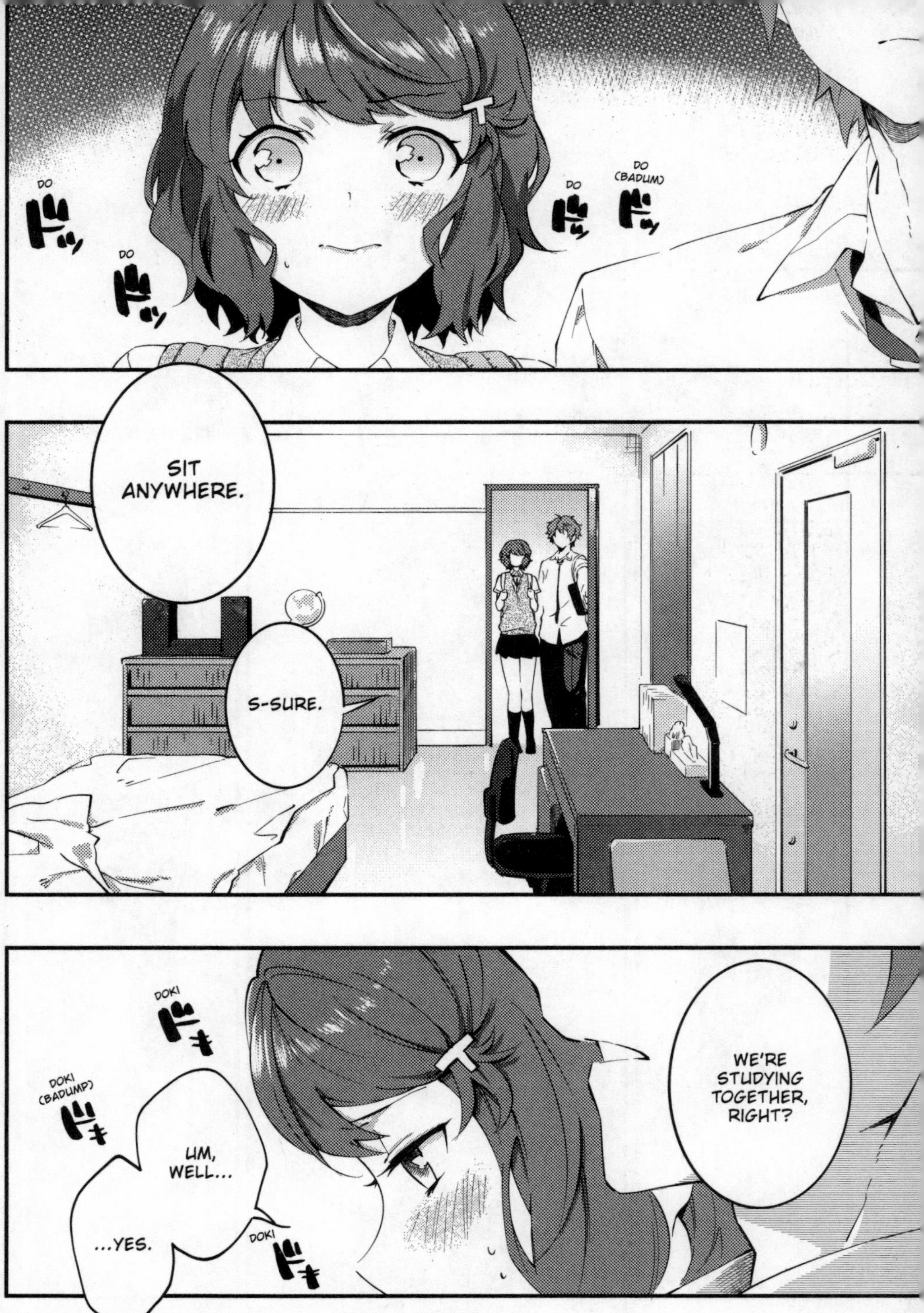

DO (BADUM)
DO
DO
DO
SIT ANYWHERE.
S-SURE.
WE'RE STUDYING TOGETHER, RIGHT?
DOKI
UM, WELL...
DOKI (BADUMP)
...YES.
DOKI

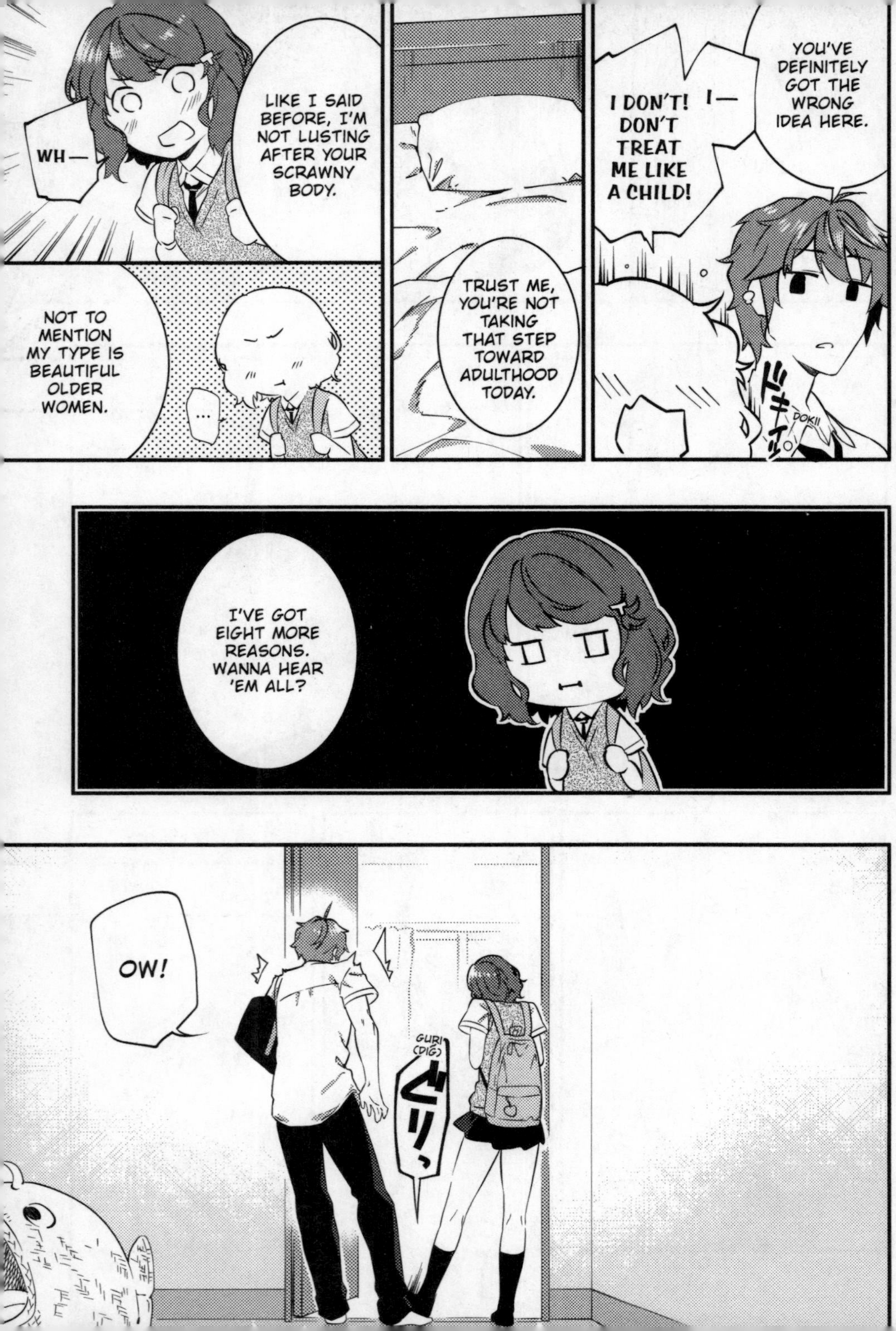
YOU'VE DEFINITELY GOT THE WRONG IDEA HERE.
I—
I DON'T! DON'T TREAT ME LIKE A CHILD!
ドキッ
DOKI!
TRUST ME, YOU'RE NOT TAKING THAT STEP TOWARD ADULTHOOD TODAY.
LIKE I SAID BEFORE, I'M NOT LUSTING AFTER YOUR SCRAWNY BODY.
WH—
NOT TO MENTION MY TYPE IS BEAUTIFUL OLDER WOMEN.
...
I'VE GOT EIGHT MORE REASONS. WANNA HEAR 'EM ALL?
GURI (DIG)
ぐりっ
OW!

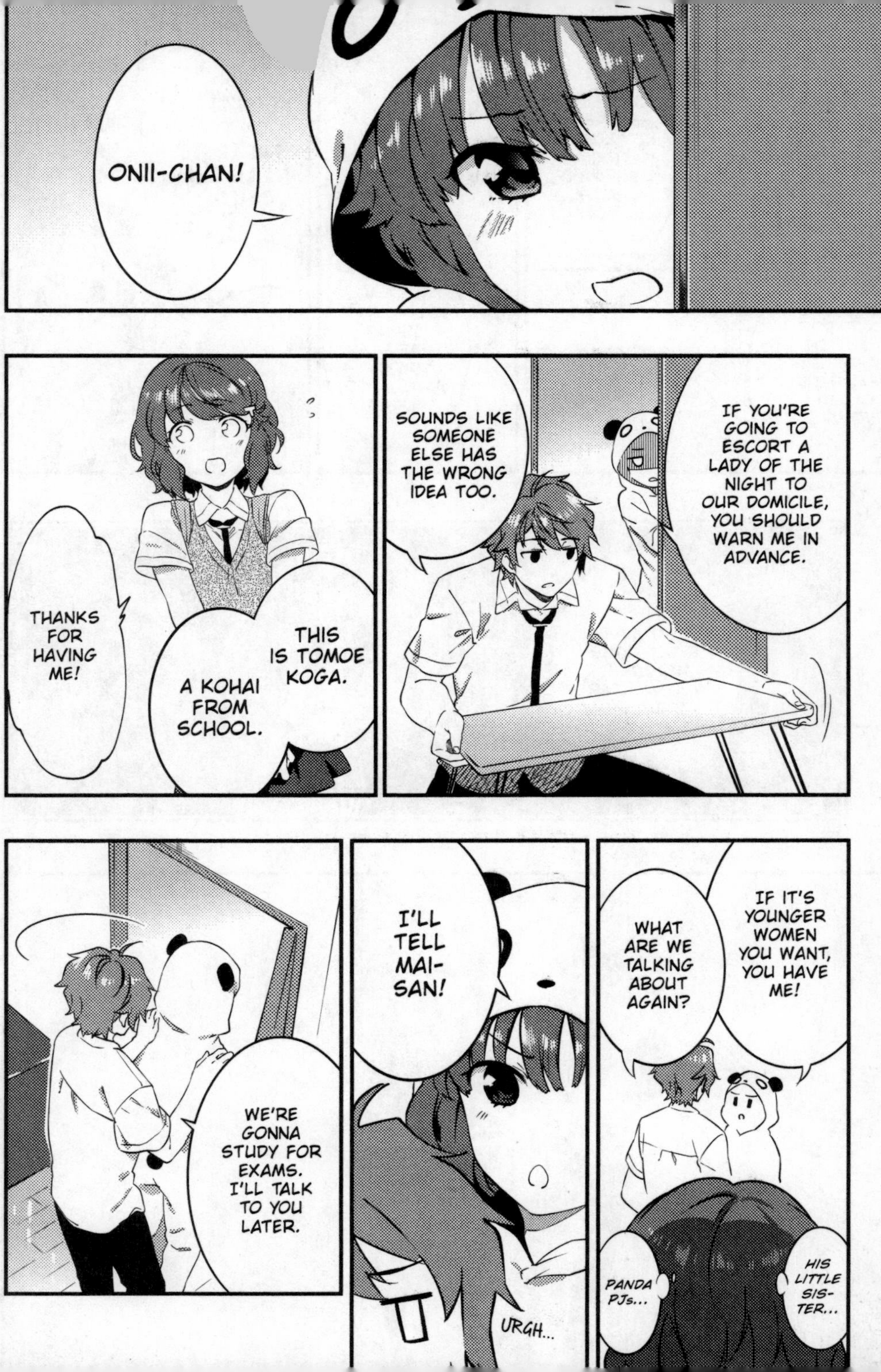
ONII-CHAN!
IF YOU'RE GOING TO ESCORT A LADY OF THE NIGHT TO OUR DOMICILE, YOU SHOULD WARN ME IN ADVANCE.
SOUNDS LIKE SOMEONE ELSE HAS THE WRONG IDEA TOO.
THIS IS TOMOE KOGA.
A KOHAI FROM SCHOOL.
THANKS FOR HAVING ME!
IF IT'S YOUNGER WOMEN YOU WANT, YOU HAVE ME!
WHAT ARE WE TALKING ABOUT AGAIN?
HIS LITTLE SIS-TER...
PANDA PJs...
I'LL TELL MAI-SAN!
URGH...
WE'RE GONNA STUDY FOR EXAMS. I'LL TALK TO YOU LATER.

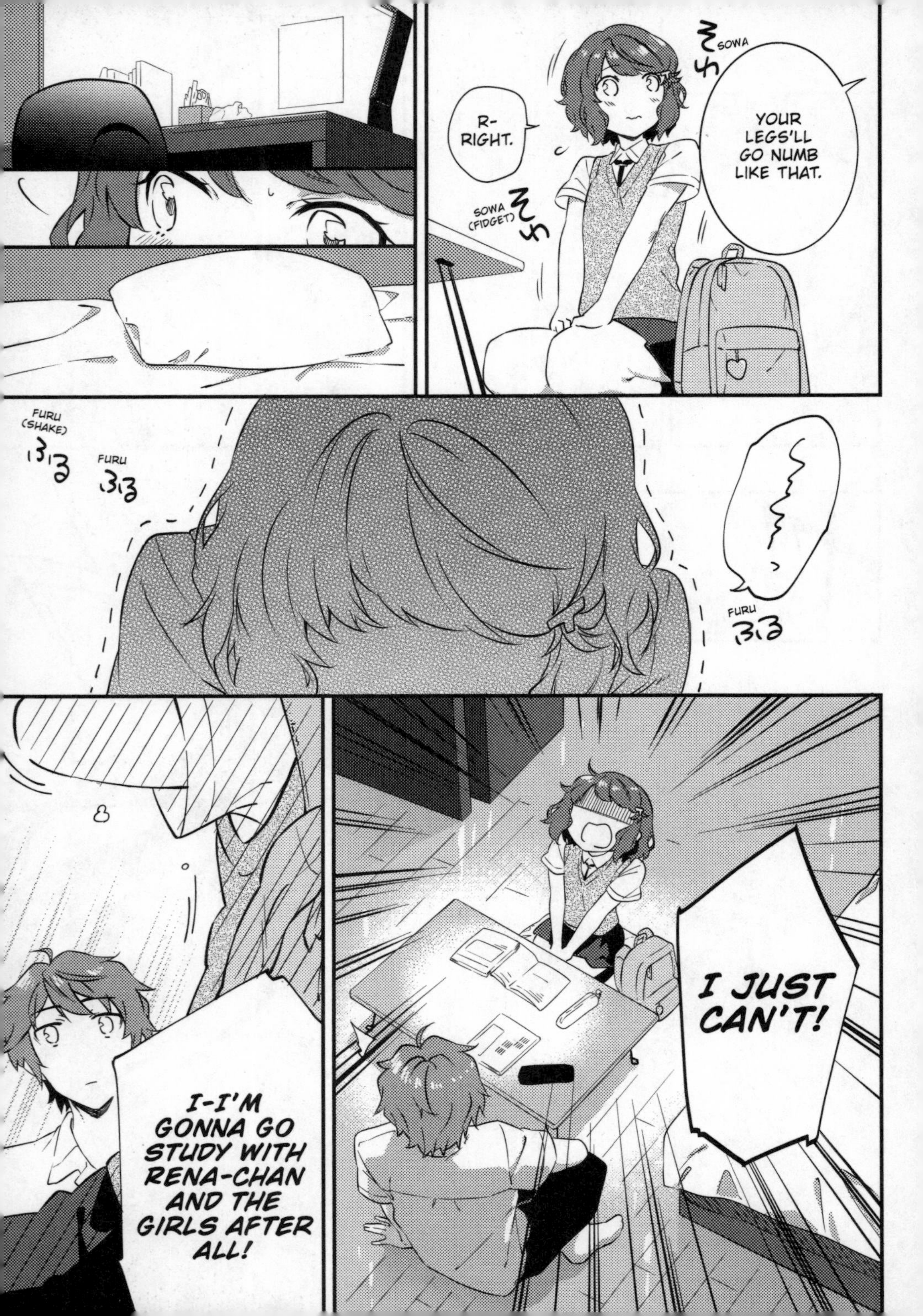
SOWA そわ
YOUR LEGS'LL GO NUMB LIKE THAT.
R-RIGHT.
SOWA (FIDGET) そわ
FURU ふる
FURU ふる
FURU (SHAKE) ふる
I JUST CAN'T!
I-I'M GONNA GO STUDY WITH RENA-CHAN AND THE GIRLS AFTER ALL!

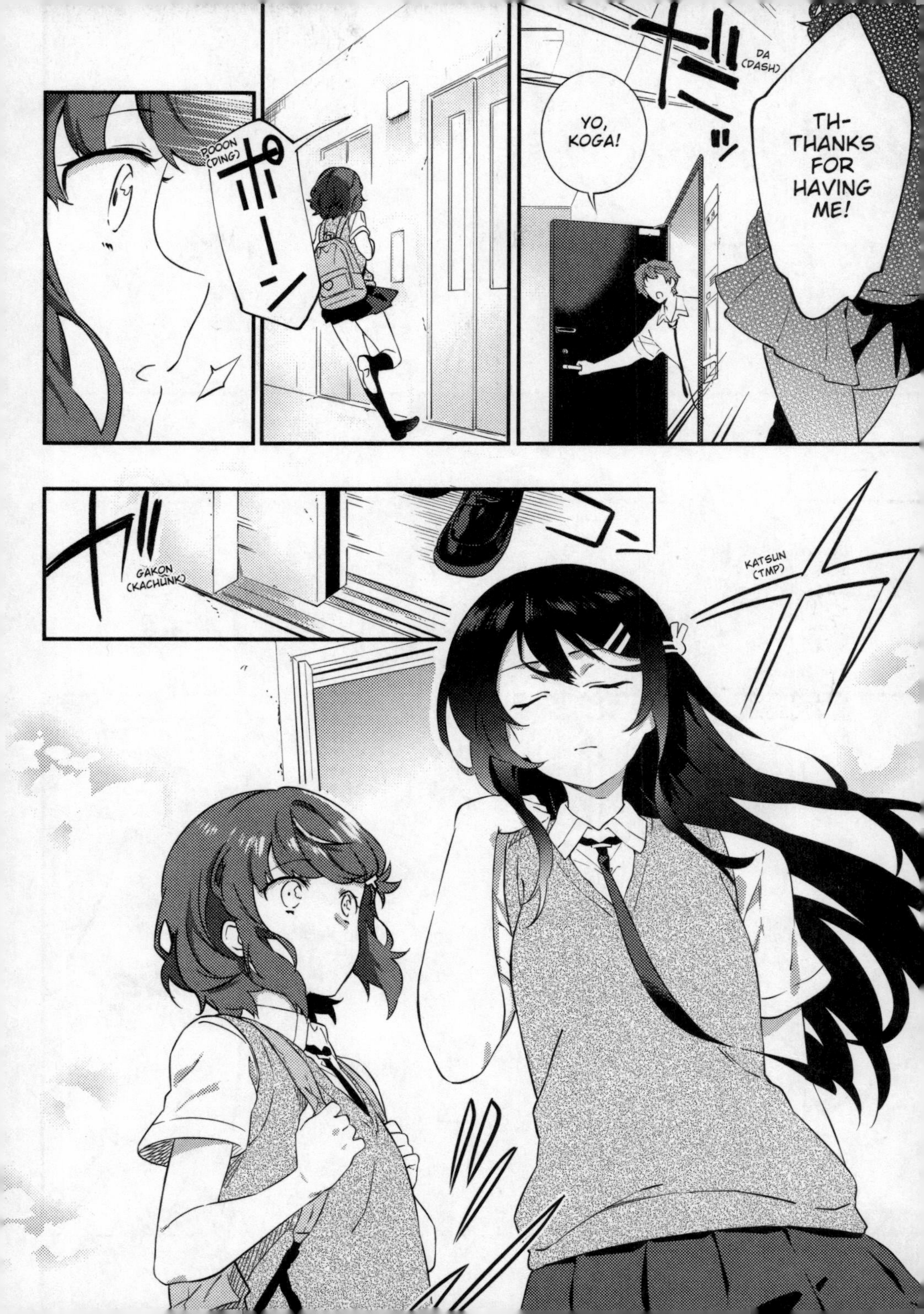
TH-THANKS FOR HAVING ME!
DA (DASH)
YO, KOGA!
POOON (DING)
GAKON (KACHUNK)
KATSUN (TMP)

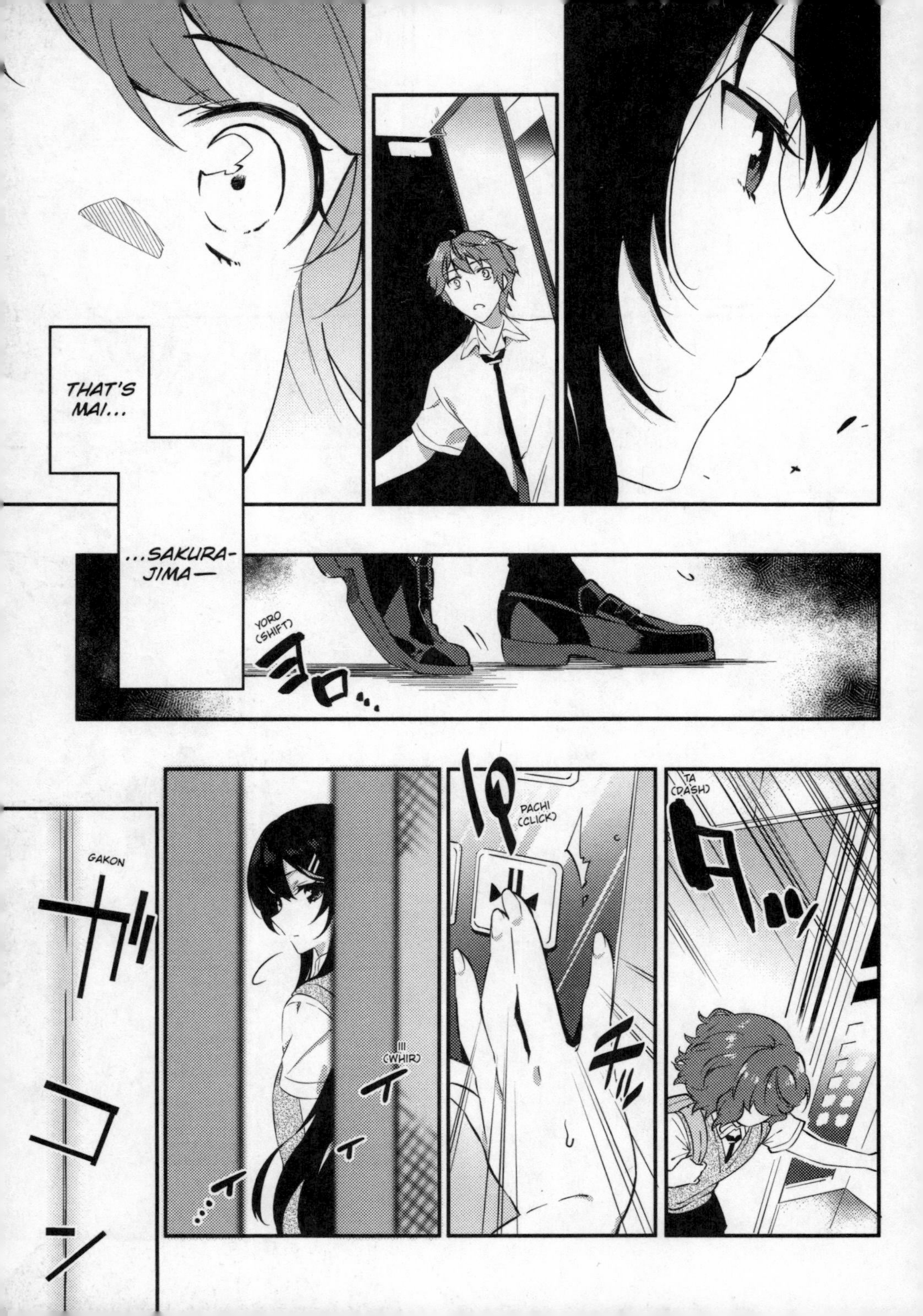
THAT'S MAI...
...SAKURA-JIMA—
YORO (SHIFT)
TA (DASH)
PACHI (CLICK)
III (WHIR)
GAKON

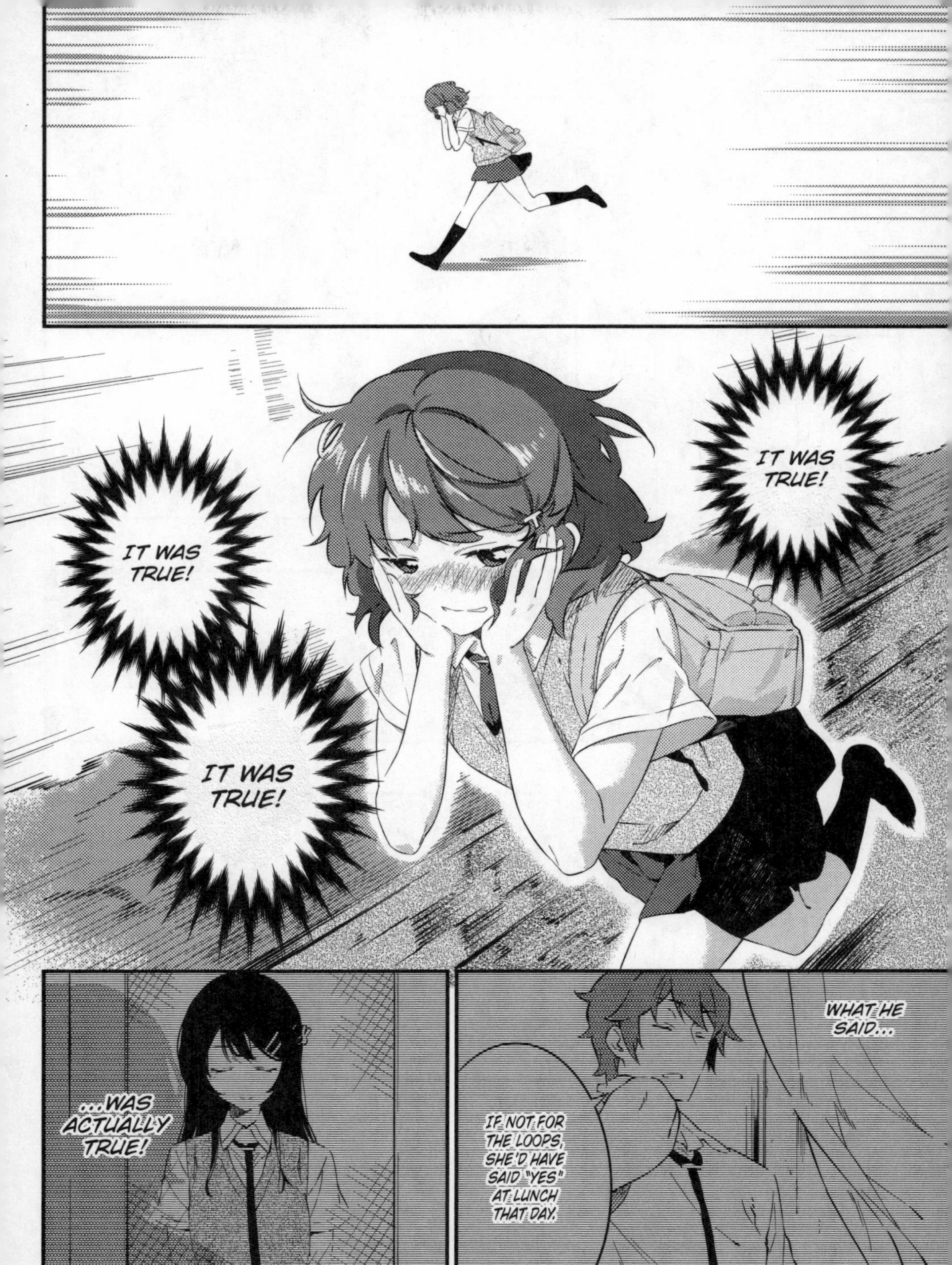
IT WAS TRUE!
IT WAS TRUE!
IT WAS TRUE!
WHAT HE SAID...
IF NOT FOR THE LOOPS, SHE'D HAVE SAID "YES" AT LUNCH THAT DAY.
...WAS ACTUALLY TRUE!

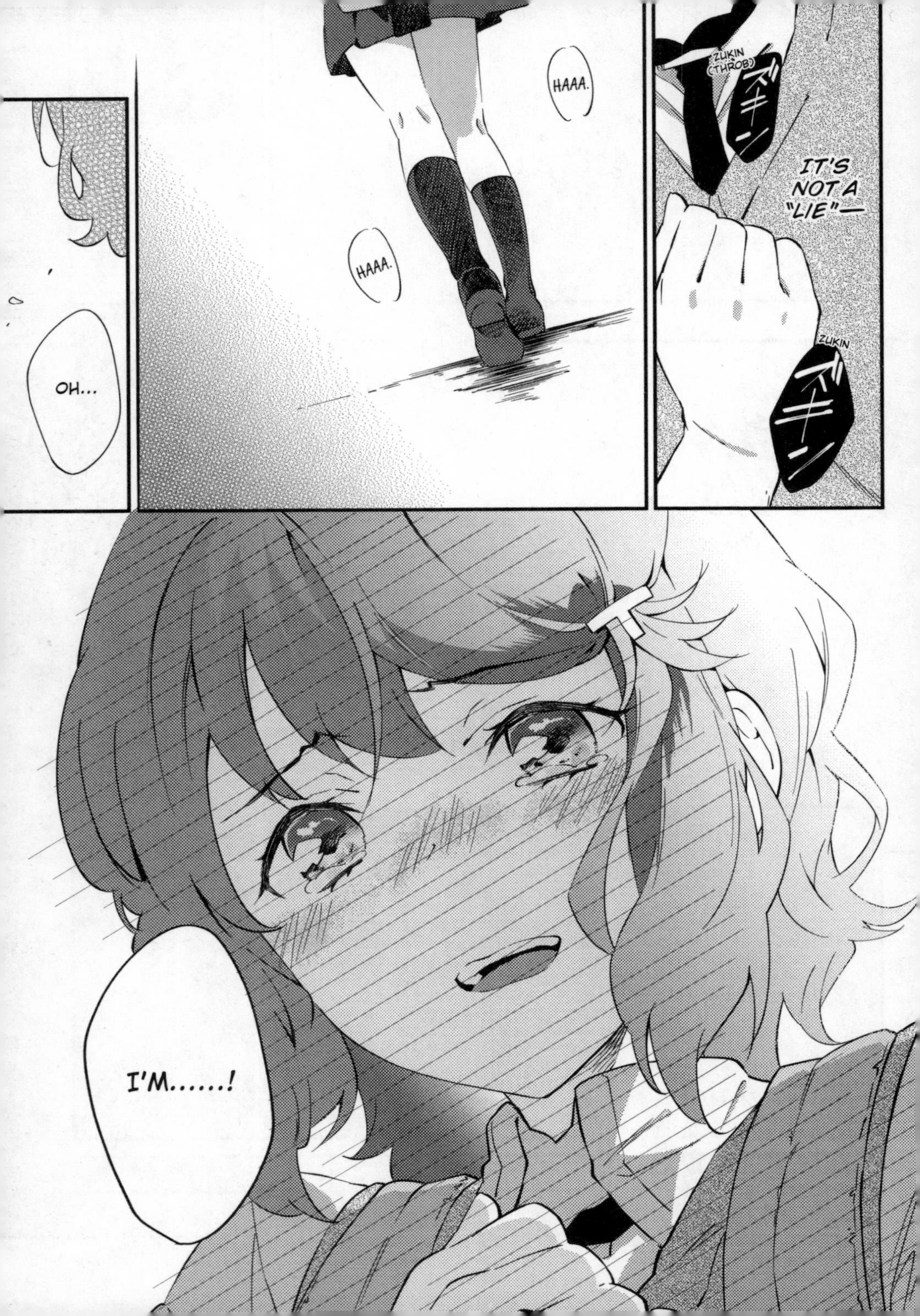
ZUKIN (THROB)
ズキン
IT'S NOT A "LIE"—
ZUKIN
ズキン
HAAA.
HAAA.
OH...
I'M......!

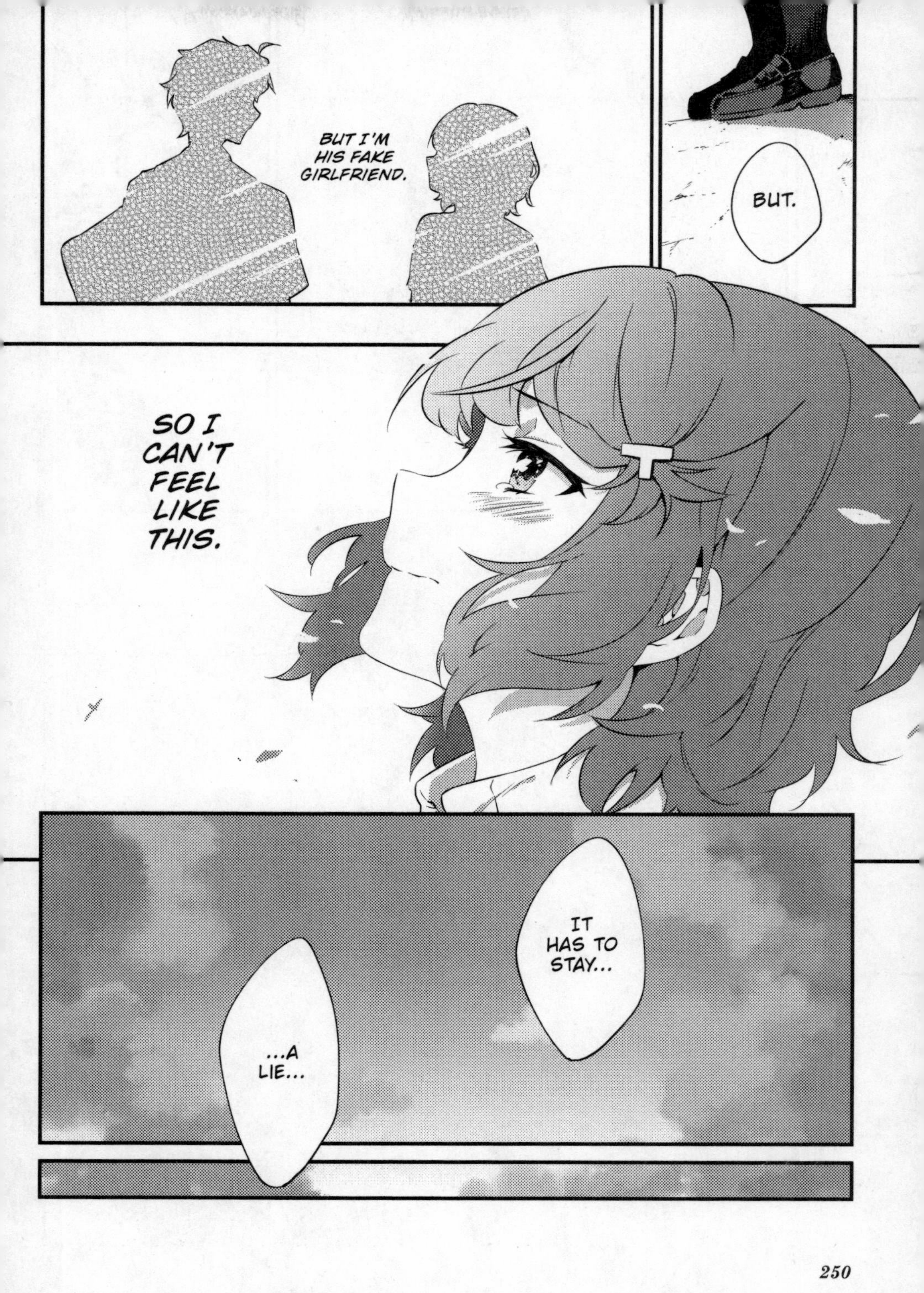
BUT.
BUT I'M HIS FAKE GIRLFRIEND.
SO I CAN'T FEEL LIKE THIS.
IT HAS TO STAY...
...A LIE...

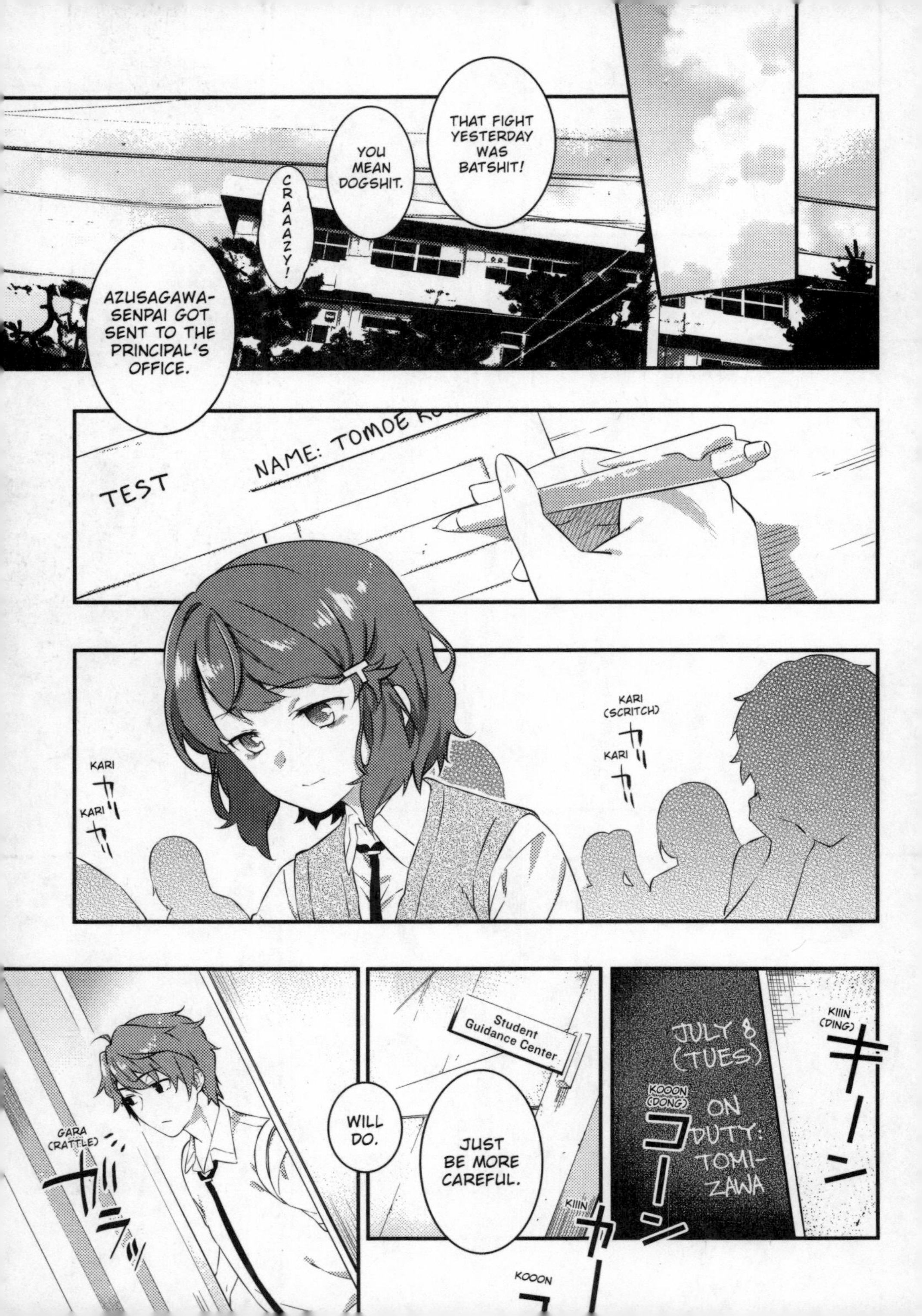
THAT FIGHT YESTERDAY WAS BATSHIT!
YOU MEAN DOGSHIT.
CRAAAZY!
AZUSAGAWA-SENPAI GOT SENT TO THE PRINCIPAL'S OFFICE.
NAME: TOMOE
TEST
KARI (SCRITCH)
KARI
KARI
KARI
KIIIN (DING)
JULY 8 (TUES)
ON DUTY: TOMI-ZAWA
KOOON (DONG)
KIIIN
KOOON
Student Guidance Center
JUST BE MORE CAREFUL.
WILL DO.
GARA (RATTLE)

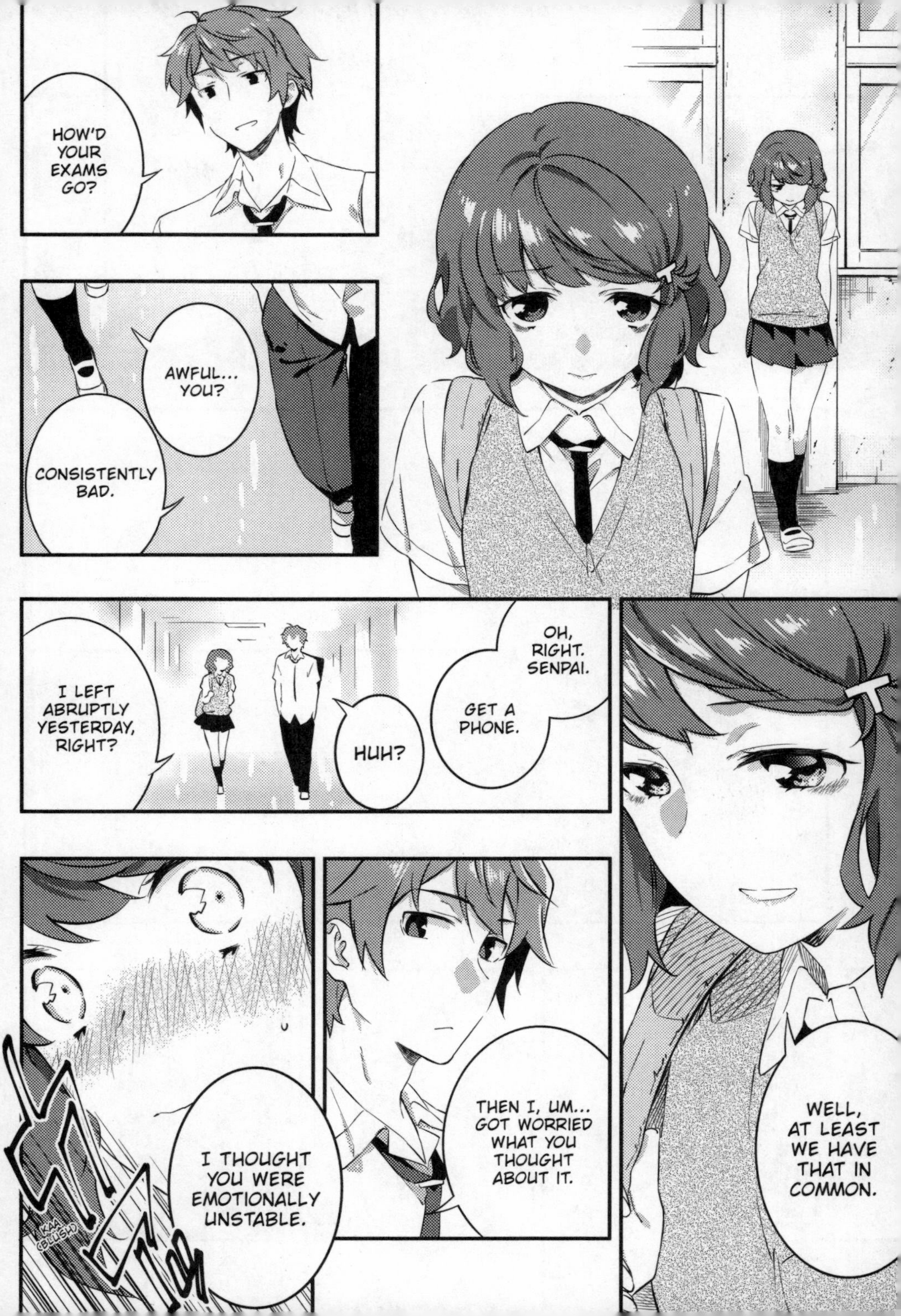
HOW'D YOUR EXAMS GO?
AWFUL... YOU?
CONSISTENTLY BAD.
WELL, AT LEAST WE HAVE THAT IN COMMON.
OH, RIGHT. SENPAI.
GET A PHONE.
HUH?
I LEFT ABRUPTLY YESTERDAY, RIGHT?
THEN I, UM... GOT WORRIED WHAT YOU THOUGHT ABOUT IT.
I THOUGHT YOU WERE EMOTIONALLY UNSTABLE.
KAA (BLUSH)

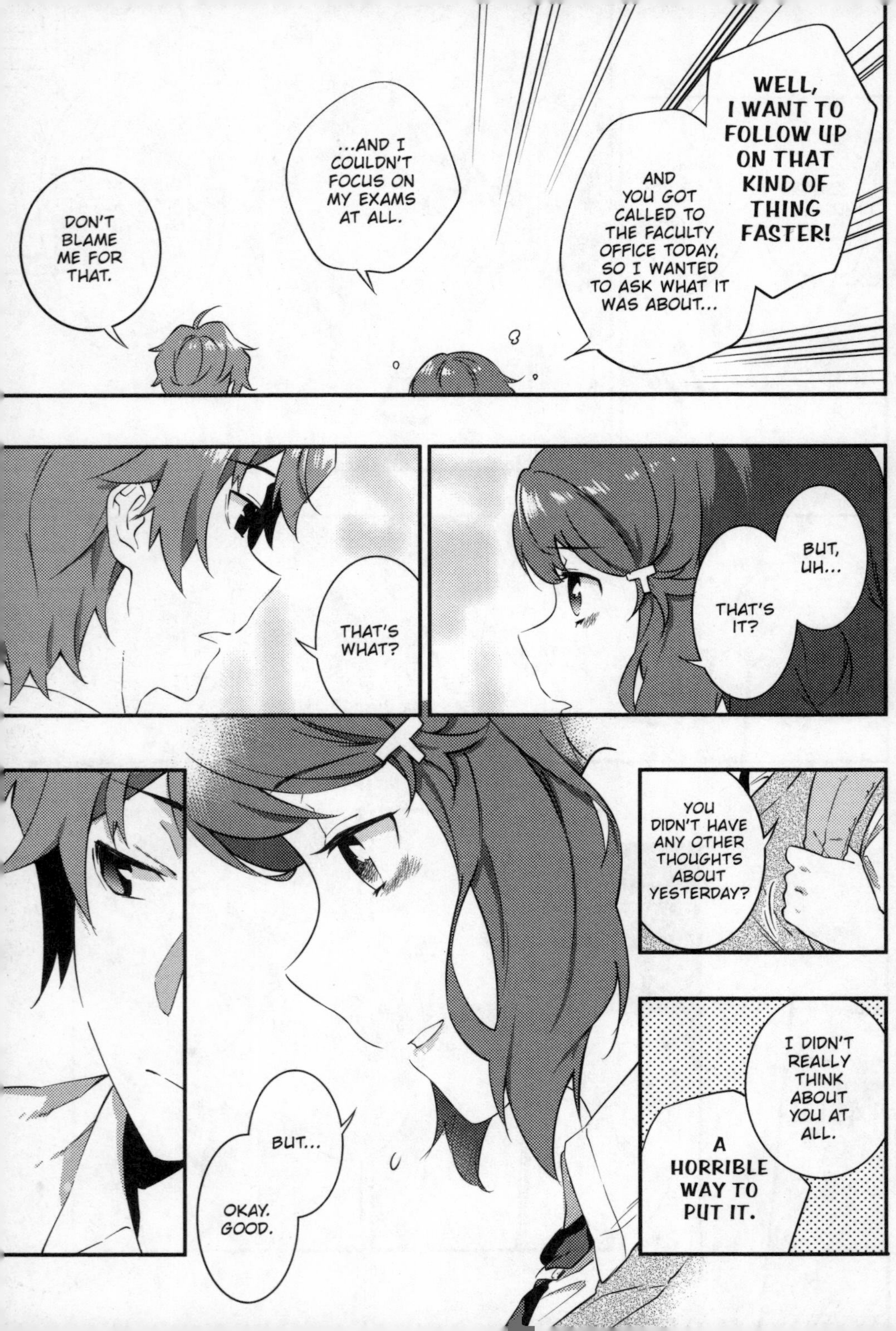
WELL, I WANT TO FOLLOW UP ON THAT KIND OF THING FASTER!
AND YOU GOT CALLED TO THE FACULTY OFFICE TODAY, SO I WANTED TO ASK WHAT IT WAS ABOUT...
...AND I COULDN'T FOCUS ON MY EXAMS AT ALL.
DON'T BLAME ME FOR THAT.
BUT, UH...
THAT'S IT?
THAT'S WHAT?
YOU DIDN'T HAVE ANY OTHER THOUGHTS ABOUT YESTERDAY?
I DIDN'T REALLY THINK ABOUT YOU AT ALL.
A HORRIBLE WAY TO PUT IT.
BUT...
OKAY. GOOD.

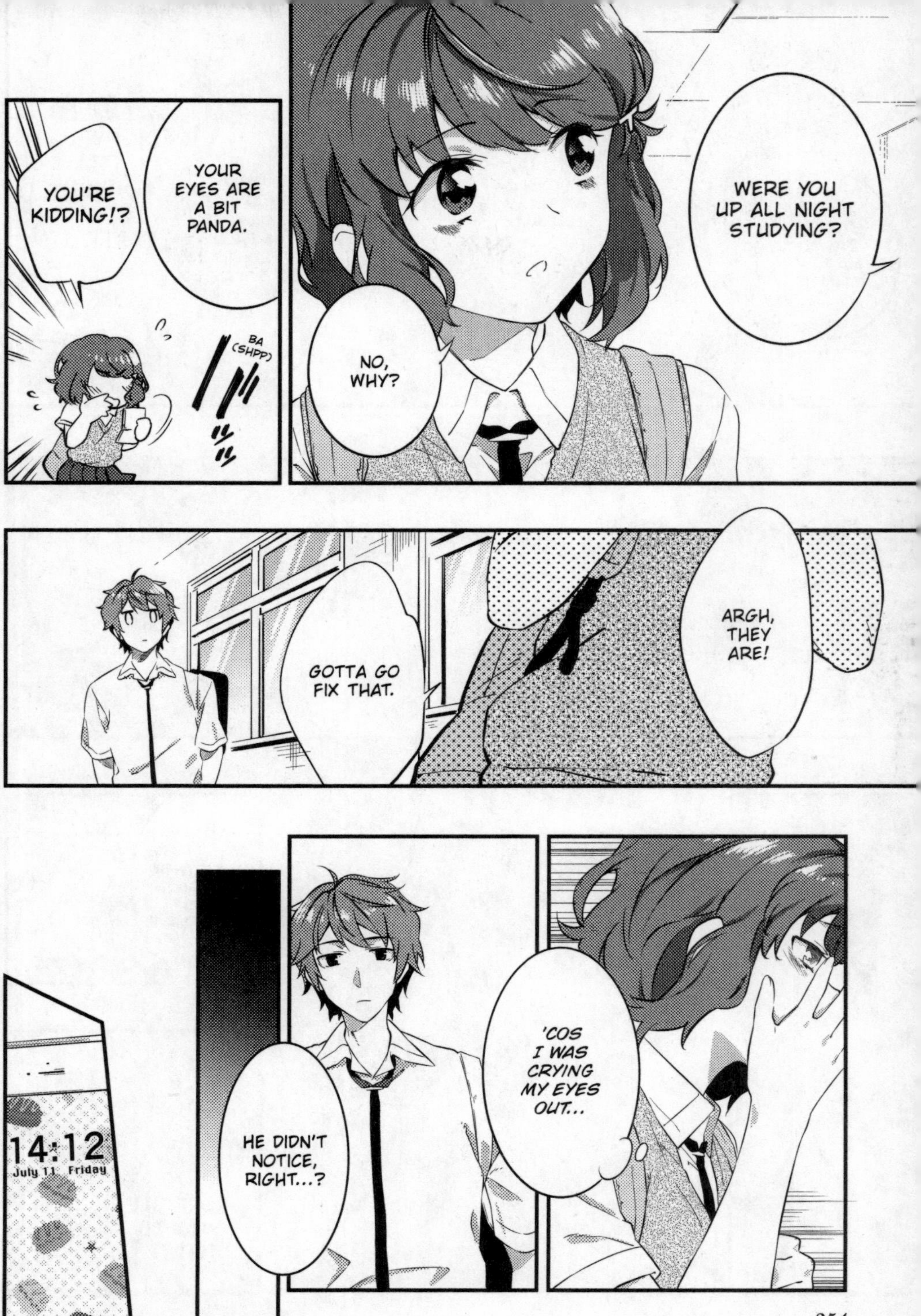
WERE YOU UP ALL NIGHT STUDYING?
NO, WHY?
YOUR EYES ARE A BIT PANDA.
YOU'RE KIDDING!?
BA (SHPP)
ARGH, THEY ARE!
GOTTA GO FIX THAT.
'COS I WAS CRYING MY EYES OUT...
HE DIDN'T NOTICE, RIGHT...?
14:12
July 11 Friday

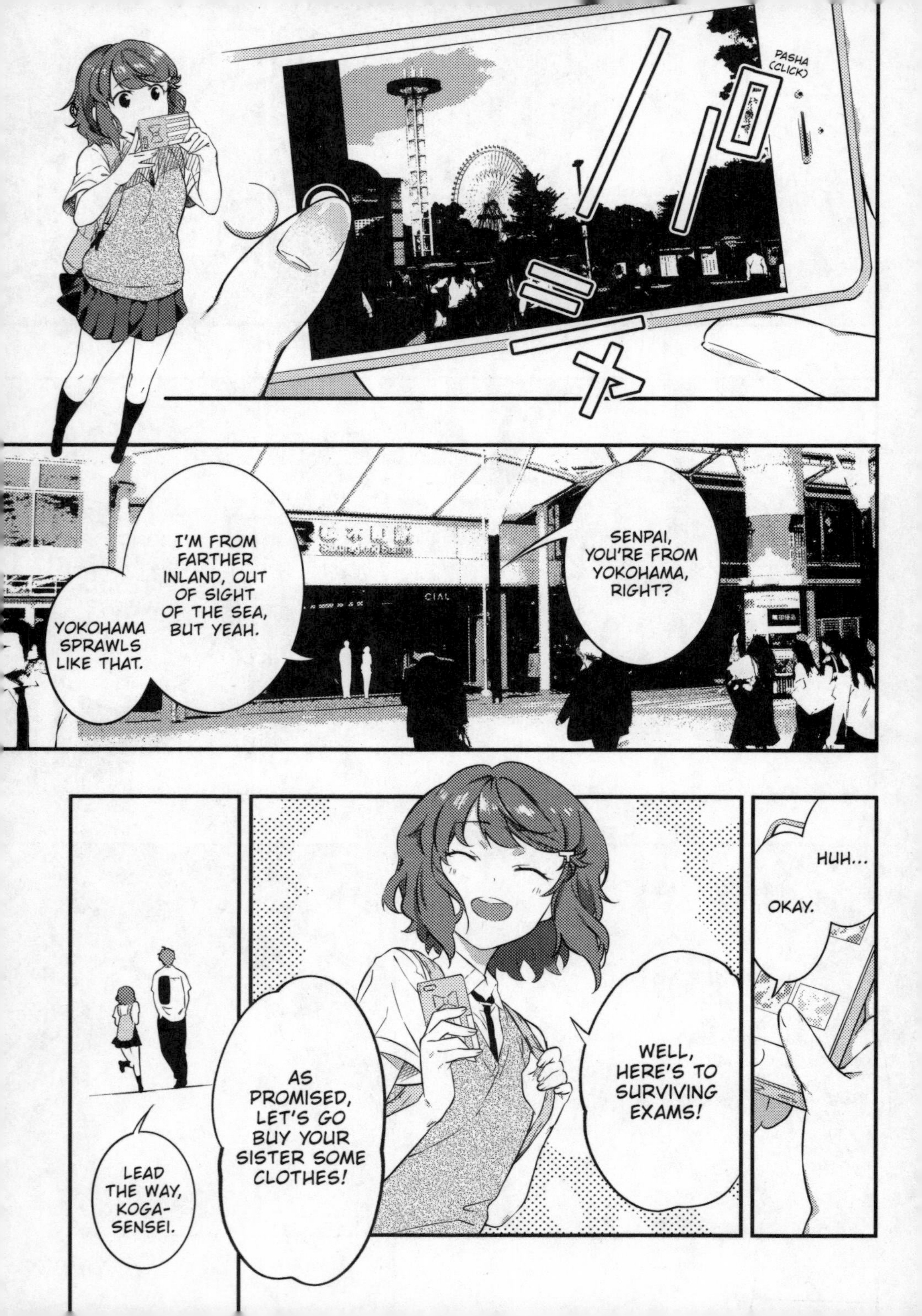
PASHA (CLICK)
SENPAI, YOU'RE FROM YOKOHAMA, RIGHT?
I'M FROM FARTHER INLAND, OUT OF SIGHT OF THE SEA, BUT YEAH.
YOKOHAMA SPRAWLS LIKE THAT.
HUH...
OKAY.
WELL, HERE'S TO SURVIVING EXAMS!
AS PROMISED, LET'S GO BUY YOUR SISTER SOME CLOTHES!
LEAD THE WAY, KOGA-SENSEI.

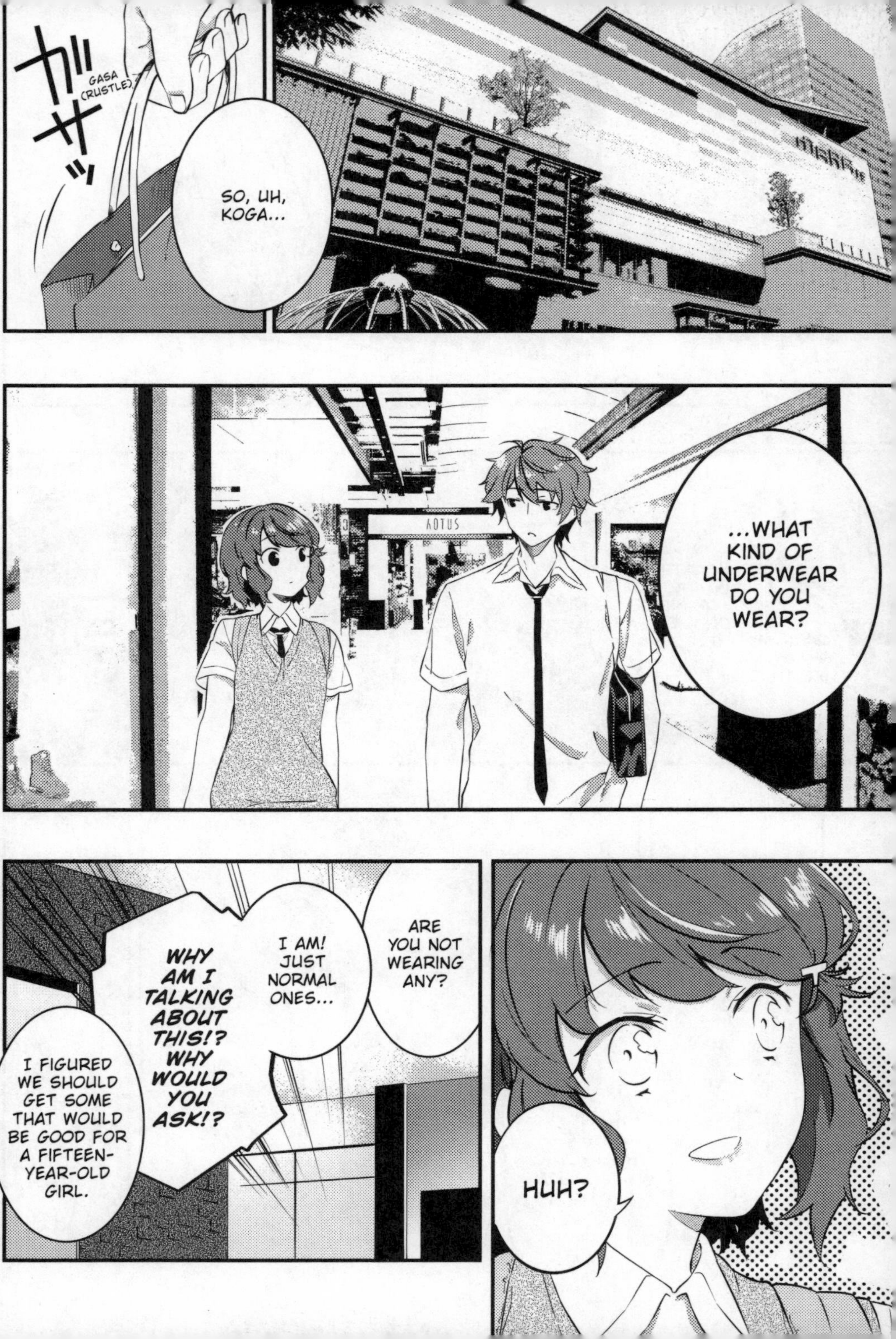
ガサッ
GASA (RUSTLE)
SO, UH, KOGA...
...WHAT KIND OF UNDERWEAR DO YOU WEAR?
HUH?
ARE YOU NOT WEARING ANY?
I AM! JUST NORMAL ONES...
WHY AM I TALKING ABOUT THIS!? WHY WOULD YOU ASK!?
I FIGURED WE SHOULD GET SOME THAT WOULD BE GOOD FOR A FIFTEEN-YEAR-OLD GIRL.

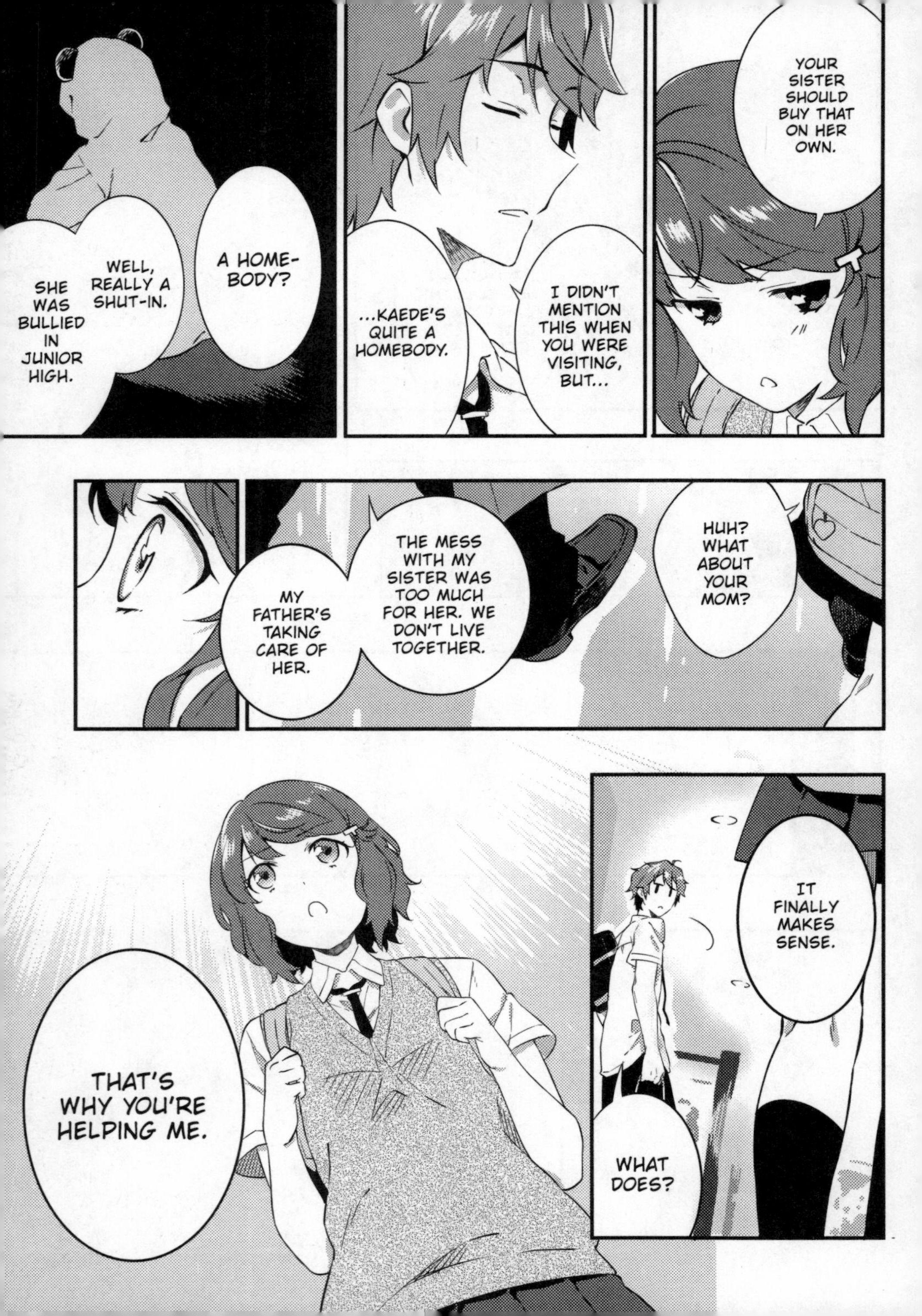
YOUR SISTER SHOULD BUY THAT ON HER OWN.
I DIDN'T MENTION THIS WHEN YOU WERE VISITING, BUT...
...KAEDE'S QUITE A HOMEBODY.
A HOME-BODY?
WELL, REALLY A SHUT-IN.
SHE WAS BULLIED IN JUNIOR HIGH.
HUH? WHAT ABOUT YOUR MOM?
THE MESS WITH MY SISTER WAS TOO MUCH FOR HER. WE DON'T LIVE TOGETHER.
MY FATHER'S TAKING CARE OF HER.
IT FINALLY MAKES SENSE.
WHAT DOES?
THAT'S WHY YOU'RE HELPING ME.

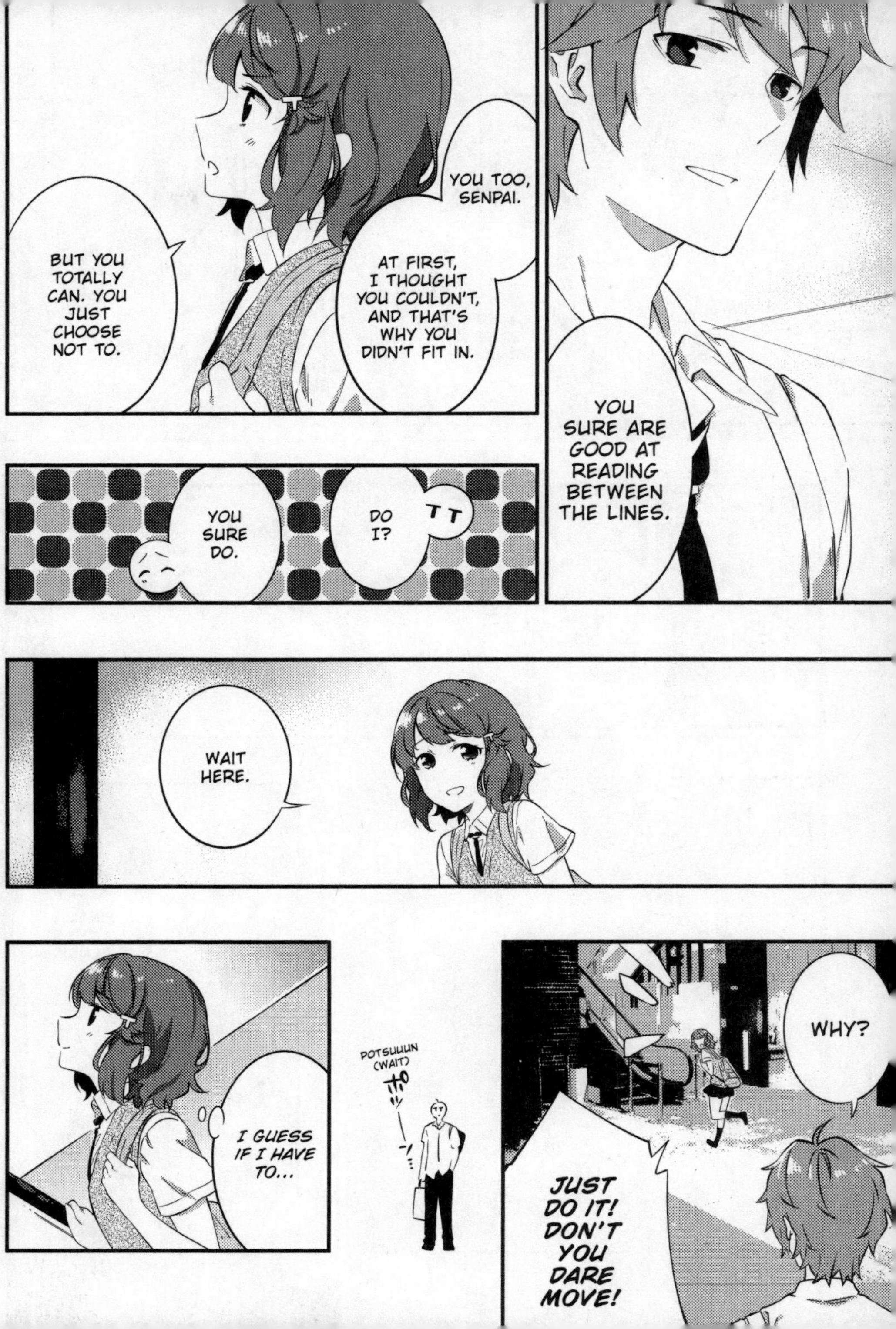
YOU SURE ARE GOOD AT READING BETWEEN THE LINES.
YOU TOO, SENPAI.
AT FIRST, I THOUGHT YOU COULDN'T, AND THAT'S WHY YOU DIDN'T FIT IN.
BUT YOU TOTALLY CAN. YOU JUST CHOOSE NOT TO.
DO I?
YOU SURE DO.
WAIT HERE.
WHY?
JUST DO IT! DON'T YOU DARE MOVE!
POTSUUUN (WAIT)
I GUESS IF I HAVE TO...

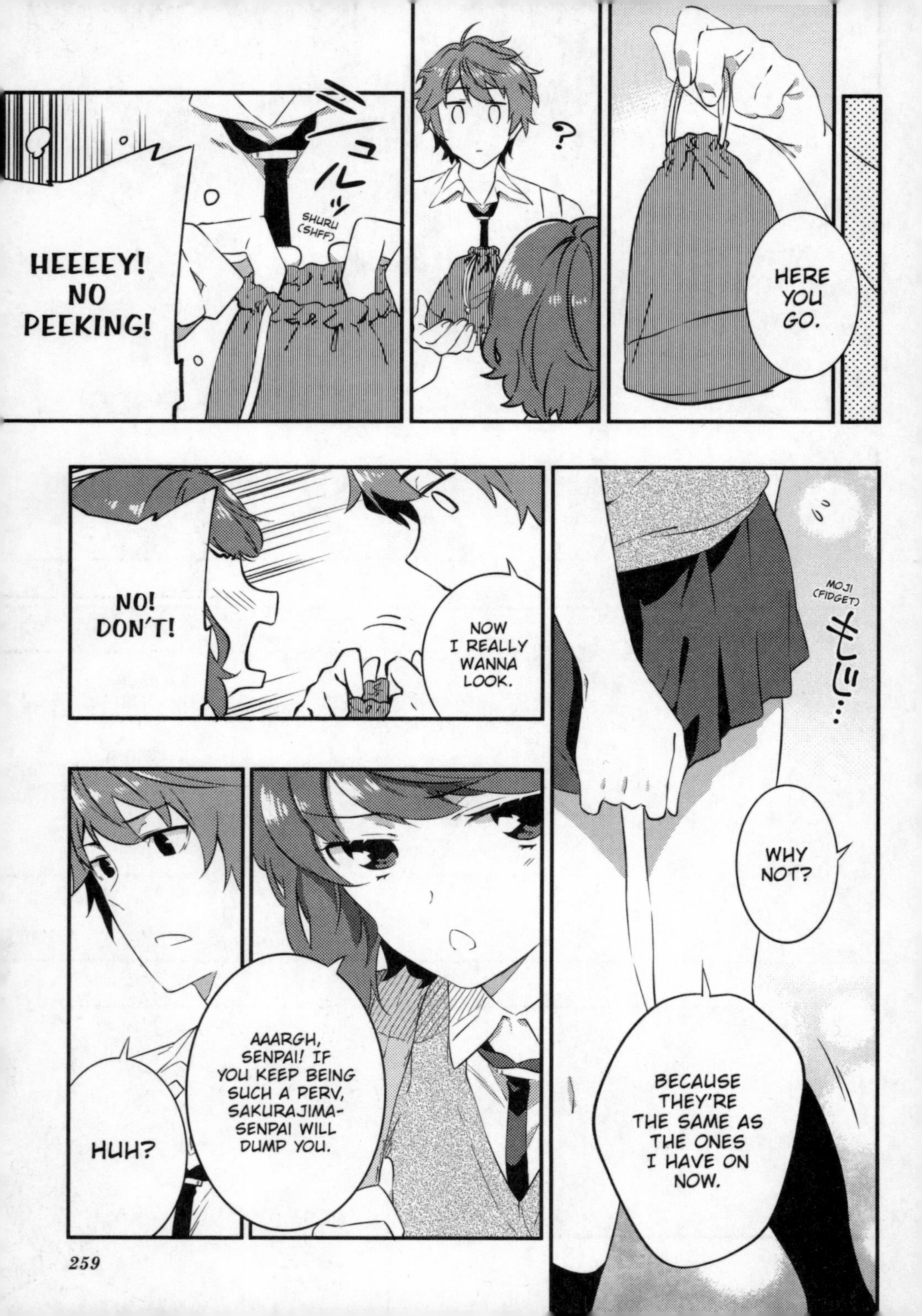
HERE YOU GO.
?
シュルッ
SHURU (SHFF)
HEEEEY! NO PEEKING!
NOW I REALLY WANNA LOOK.
NO! DON'T!
MOJI (FIDGET)
モジ…
WHY NOT?
BECAUSE THEY'RE THE SAME AS THE ONES I HAVE ON NOW.
AAARGH, SENPAI! IF YOU KEEP BEING SUCH A PERV, SAKURAJIMA-SENPAI WILL DUMP YOU.
HUH?

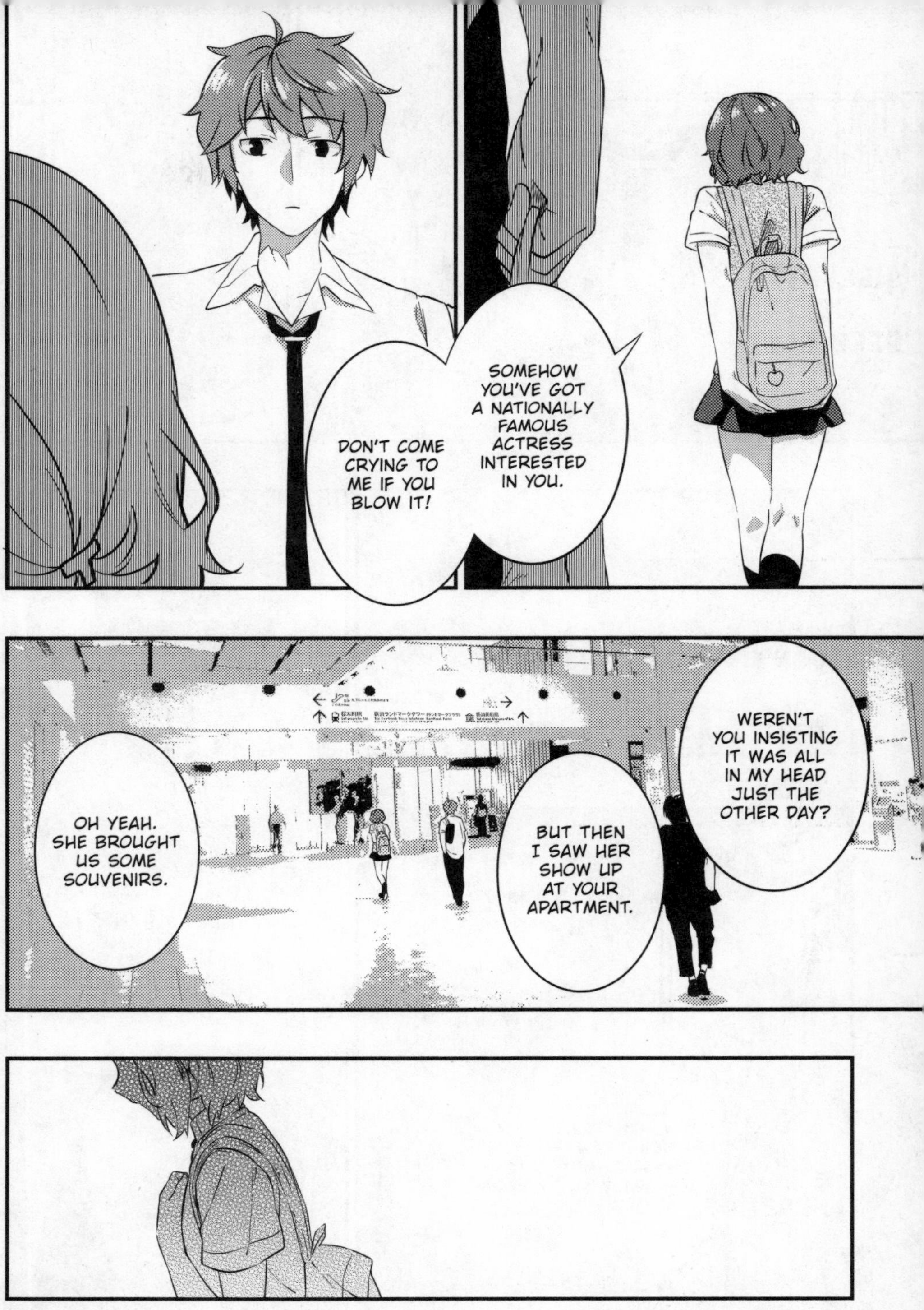
SOMEHOW YOU'VE GOT A NATIONALLY FAMOUS ACTRESS INTERESTED IN YOU.
DON'T COME CRYING TO ME IF YOU BLOW IT!
WEREN'T YOU INSISTING IT WAS ALL IN MY HEAD JUST THE OTHER DAY?
BUT THEN I SAW HER SHOW UP AT YOUR APARTMENT.
OH YEAH. SHE BROUGHT US SOME SOUVENIRS.

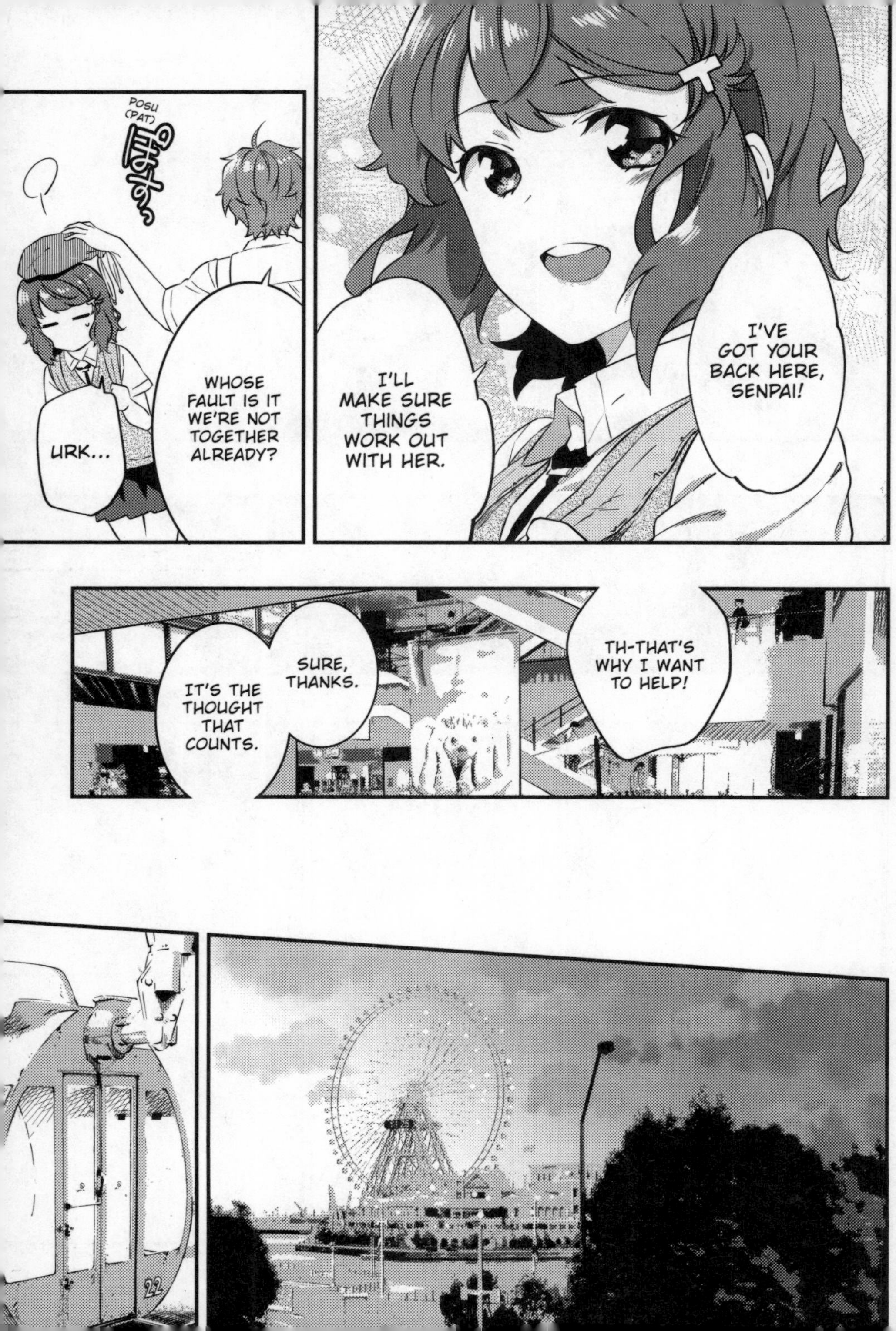
I'VE GOT YOUR BACK HERE, SENPAI!
I'LL MAKE SURE THINGS WORK OUT WITH HER.
POSU (PAT)
WHOSE FAULT IS IT WE'RE NOT TOGETHER ALREADY?
URK...
TH-THAT'S WHY I WANT TO HELP!
SURE, THANKS.
IT'S THE THOUGHT THAT COUNTS.

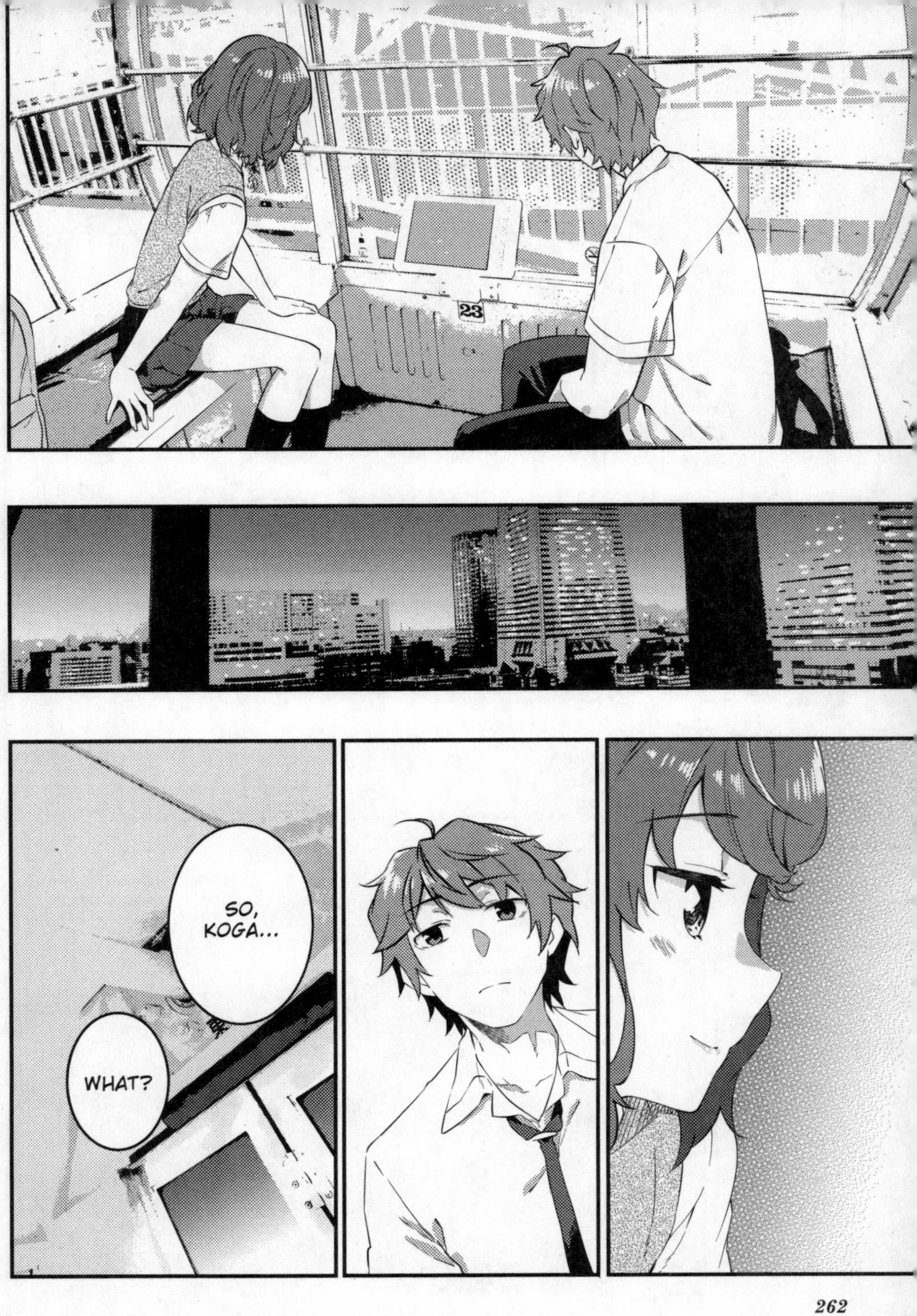
SO, KOGA...
WHAT?

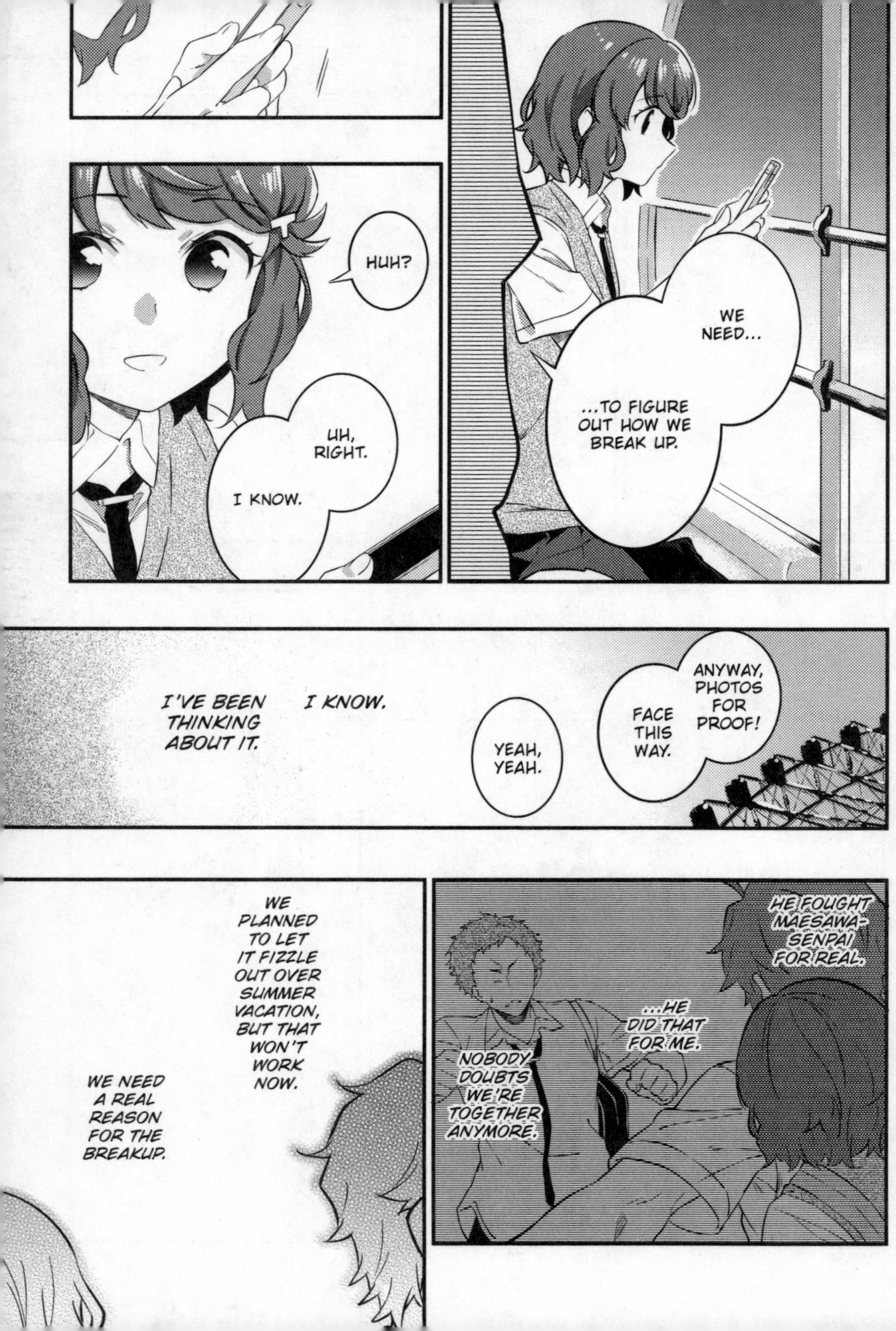
WE NEED...
...TO FIGURE OUT HOW WE BREAK UP.
HUH?
UH, RIGHT.
I KNOW.
ANYWAY, PHOTOS FOR PROOF!
FACE THIS WAY.
YEAH, YEAH.
I KNOW.
I'VE BEEN THINKING ABOUT IT.
HE FOUGHT MAESAWA-SENPAI FOR REAL.
...HE DID THAT FOR ME.
NOBODY DOUBTS WE'RE TOGETHER ANYMORE.
WE PLANNED TO LET IT FIZZLE OUT OVER SUMMER VACATION, BUT THAT WON'T WORK NOW.
WE NEED A REAL REASON FOR THE BREAKUP.

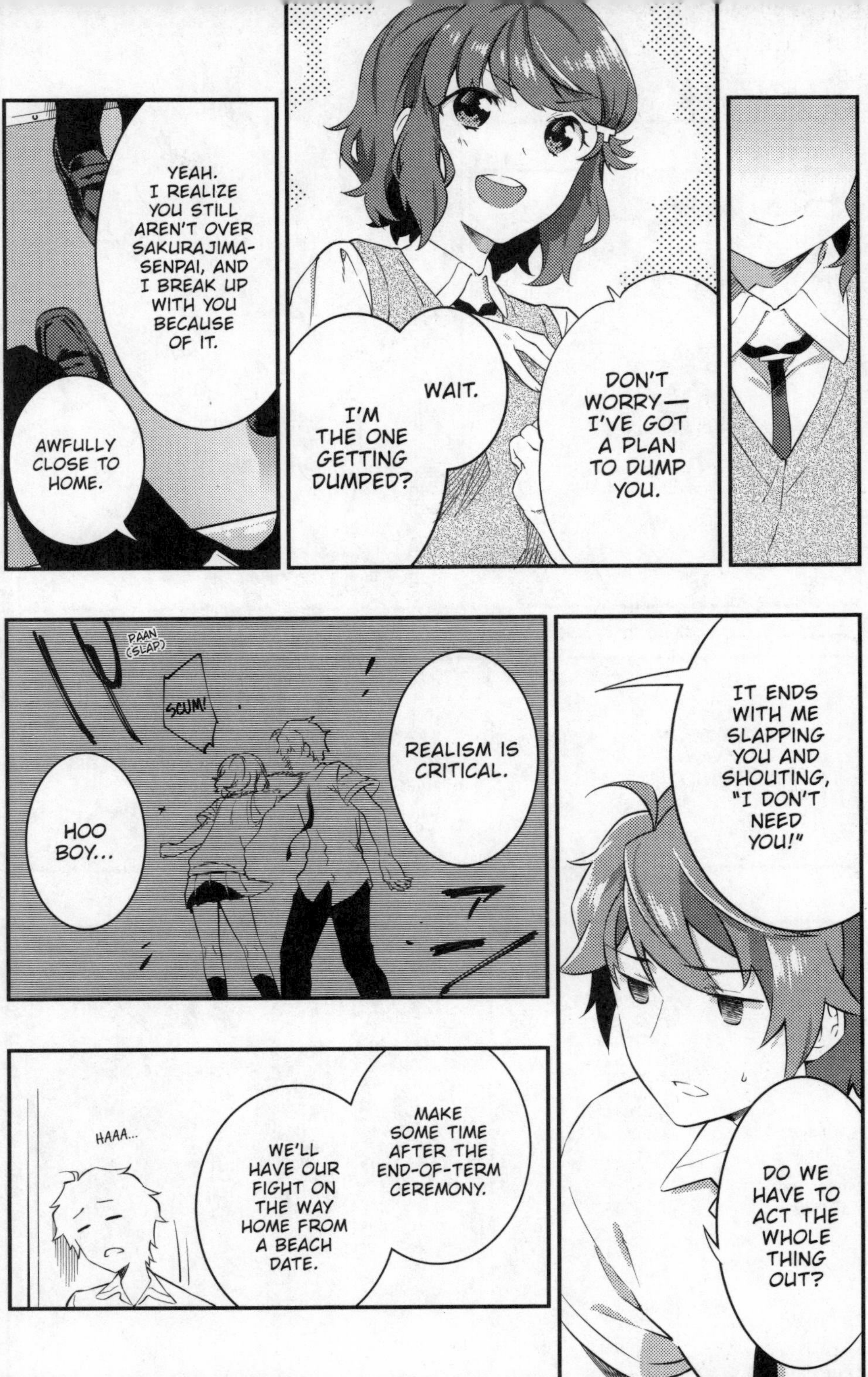
DON'T WORRY—I'VE GOT A PLAN TO DUMP YOU.
WAIT.
I'M THE ONE GETTING DUMPED?
YEAH. I REALIZE YOU STILL AREN'T OVER SAKURAJIMA-SENPAI, AND I BREAK UP WITH YOU BECAUSE OF IT.
AWFULLY CLOSE TO HOME.
IT ENDS WITH ME SLAPPING YOU AND SHOUTING, "I DON'T NEED YOU!"
DO WE HAVE TO ACT THE WHOLE THING OUT?
REALISM IS CRITICAL.
SCUM!
PAAN (SLAP)
HOO BOY...
MAKE SOME TIME AFTER THE END-OF-TERM CEREMONY.
WE'LL HAVE OUR FIGHT ON THE WAY HOME FROM A BEACH DATE.
HAAA...

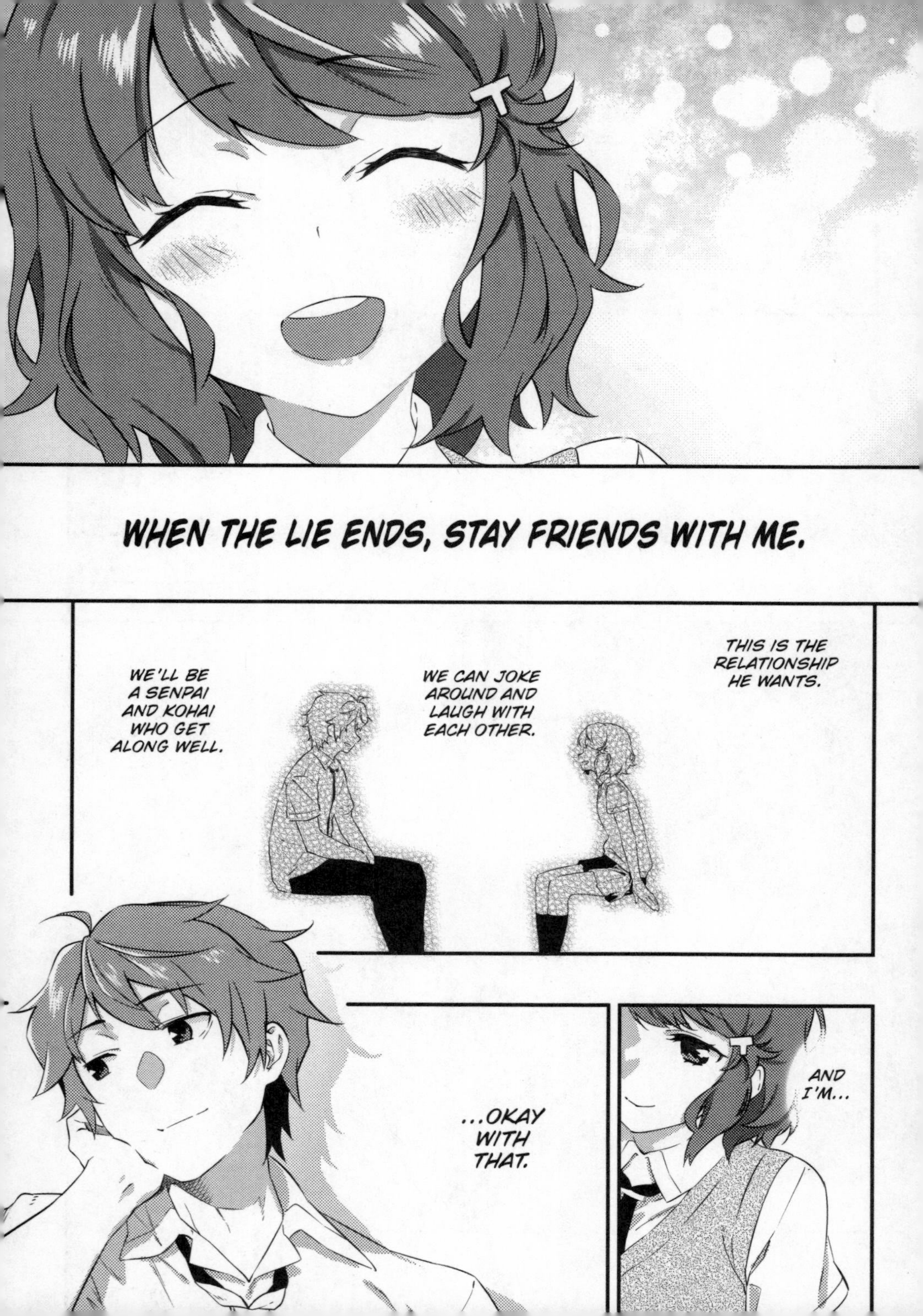
WHEN THE LIE ENDS, STAY FRIENDS WITH ME.
THIS IS THE RELATIONSHIP HE WANTS.
WE CAN JOKE AROUND AND LAUGH WITH EACH OTHER.
WE'LL BE A SENPAI AND KOHAI WHO GET ALONG WELL.
AND I'M...
...OKAY WITH THAT.

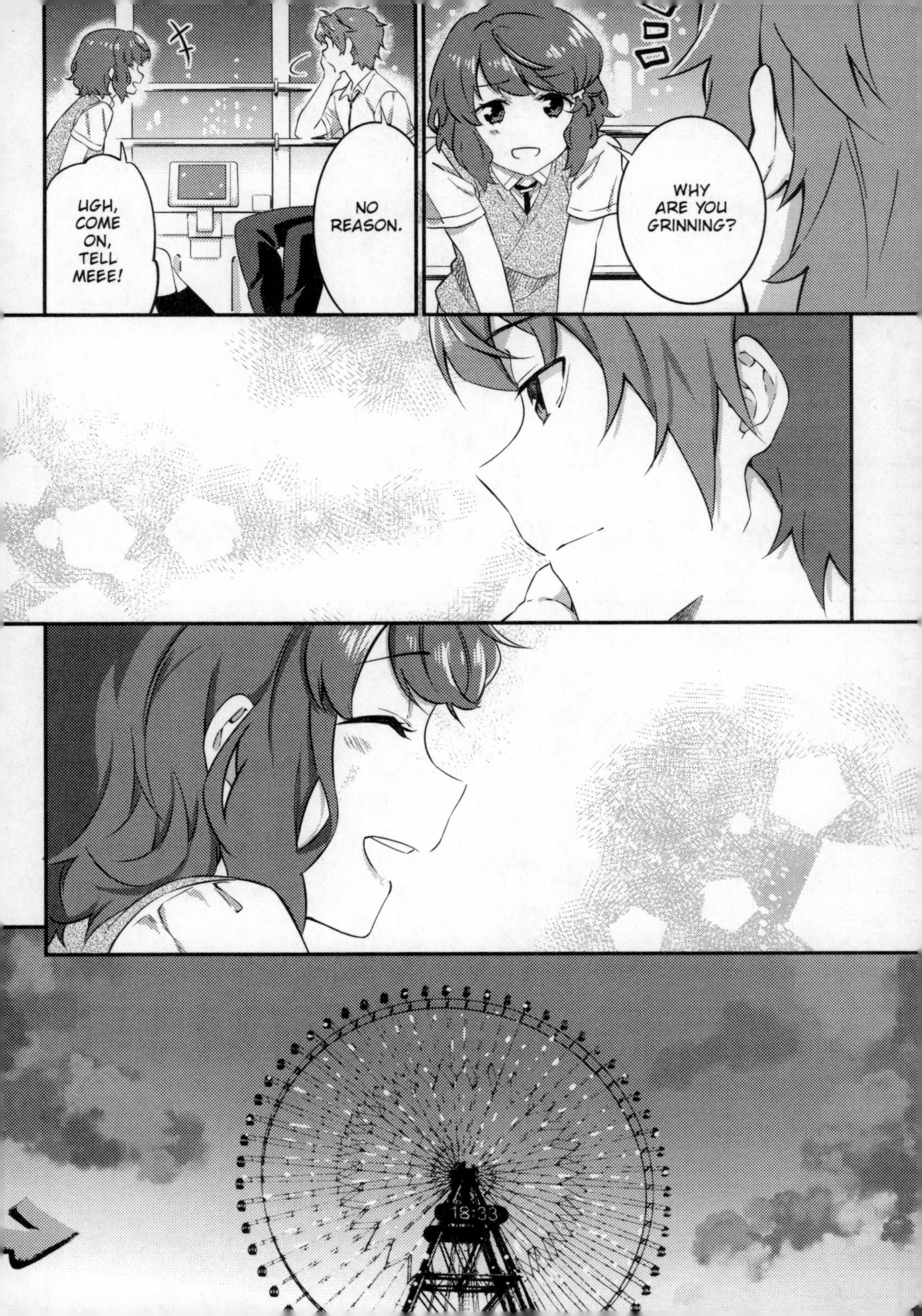
WHY ARE YOU GRINNING?
NO REASON.
UGH, COME ON, TELL MEEE!
18:33

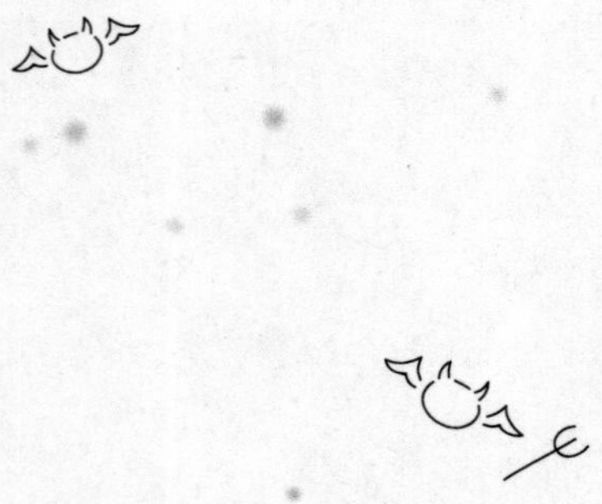

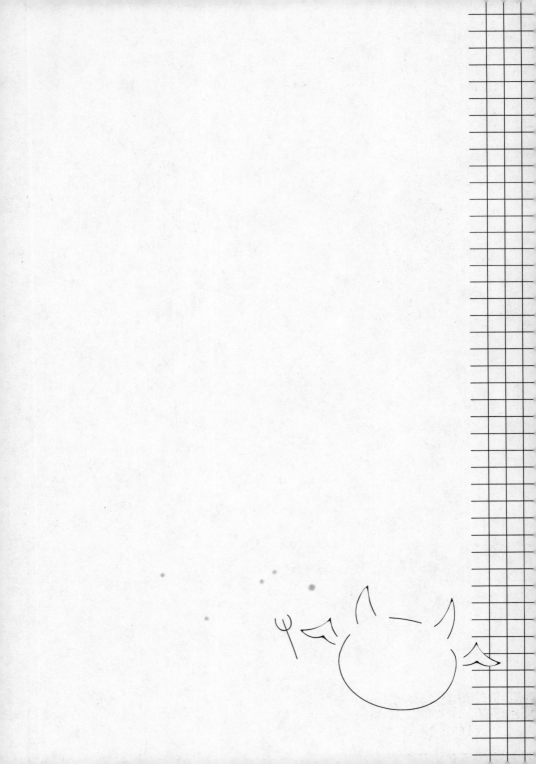

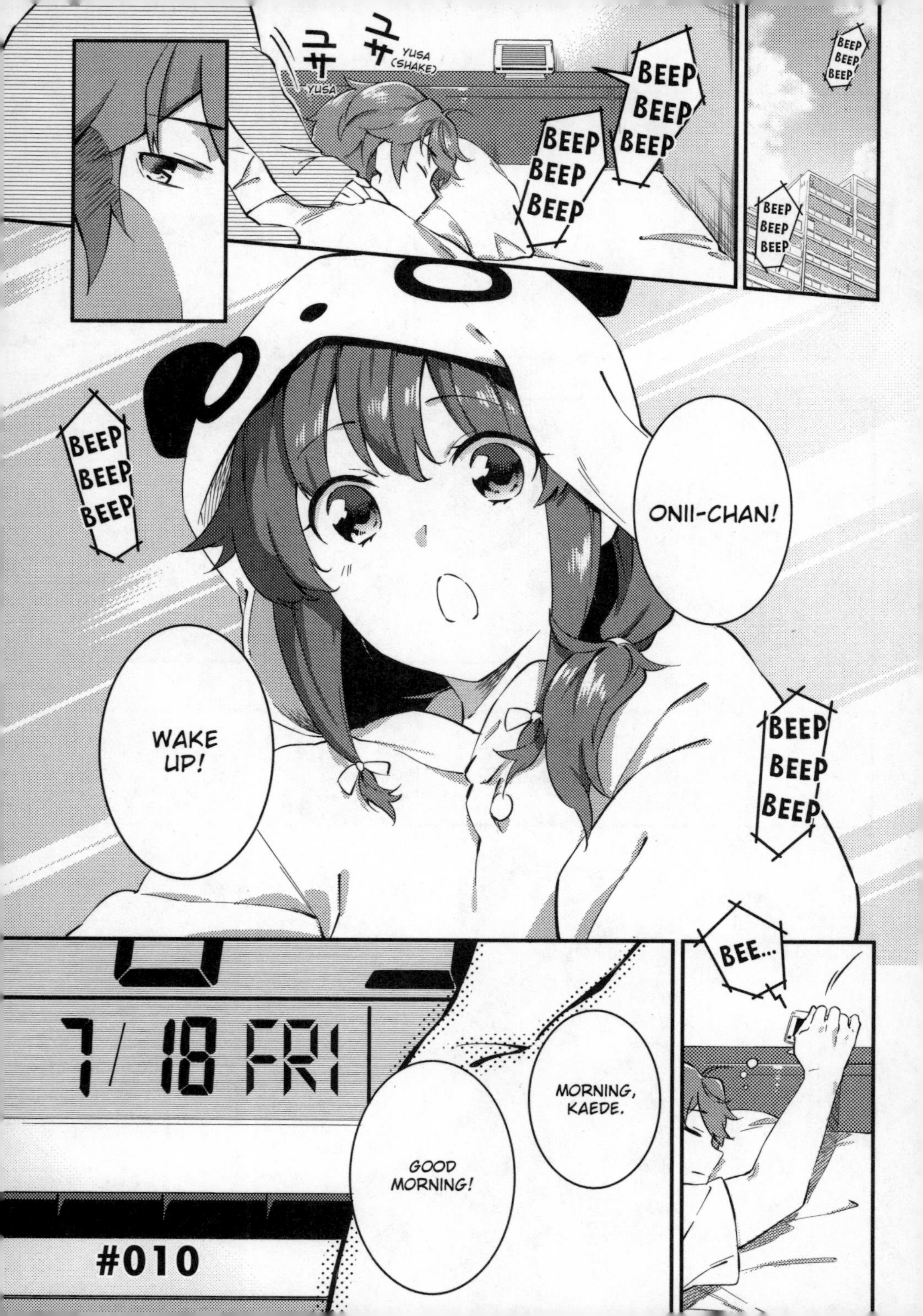

BEEP BEEP BEEP
BEEP BEEP BEEP
BEEP BEEP BEEP
ユサ YUSA (SHAKE)
BEEP BEEP BEEP
ユサ YUSA
ONII-CHAN!
BEEP BEEP BEEP
WAKE UP!
BEEP BEEP BEEP
BEE...
MORNING, KAEDE.
GOOD MORNING!
7/18 FRI
#010

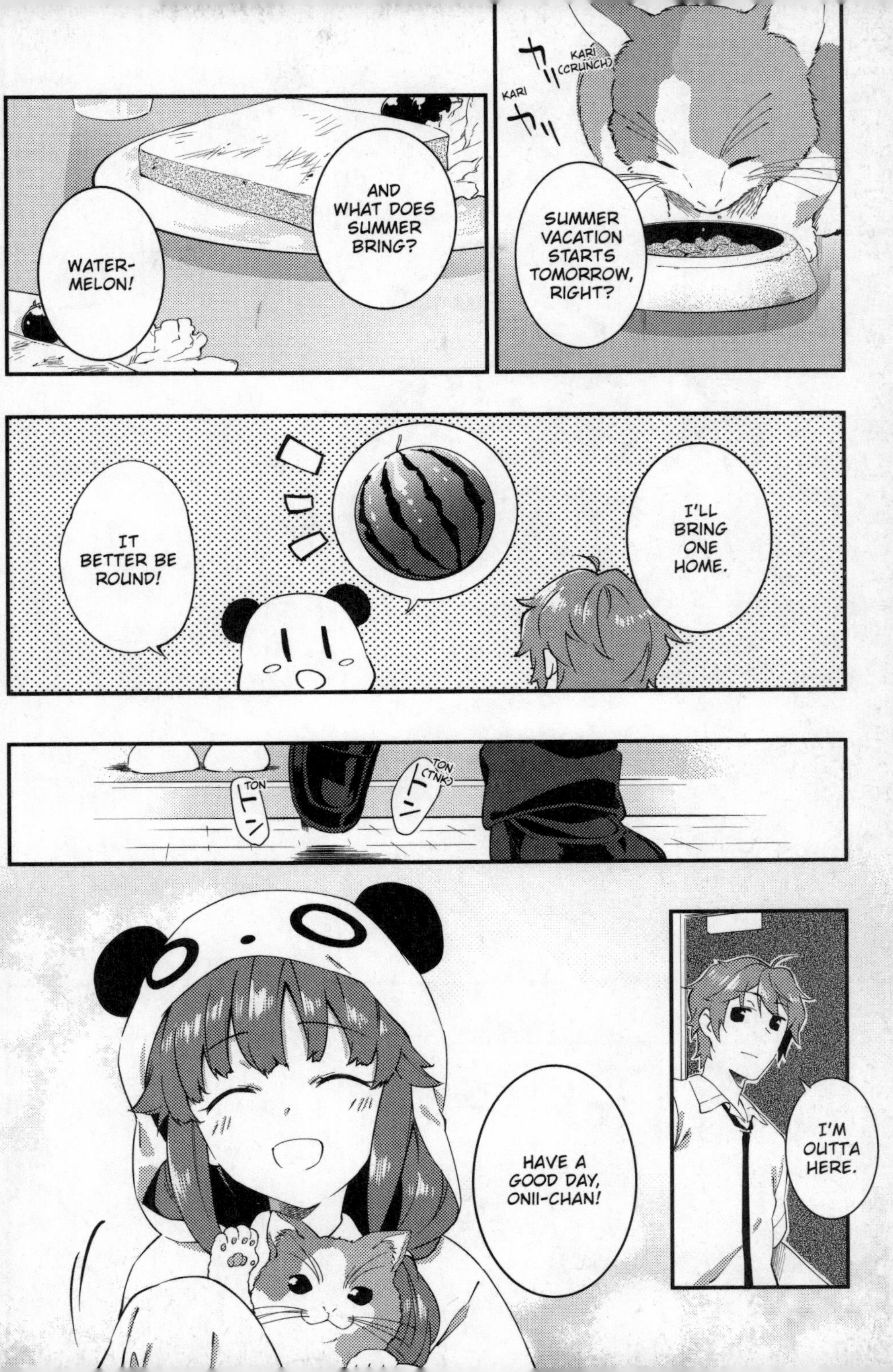
カリ
KARI (CRUNCH)
カリ
KARI
SUMMER VACATION STARTS TOMORROW, RIGHT?
AND WHAT DOES SUMMER BRING?
WATER-MELON!
I'LL BRING ONE HOME.
IT BETTER BE ROUND!
トン
TON (TNK)
トン
TON
I'M OUTTA HERE.
HAVE A GOOD DAY, ONII-CHAN!

# #010

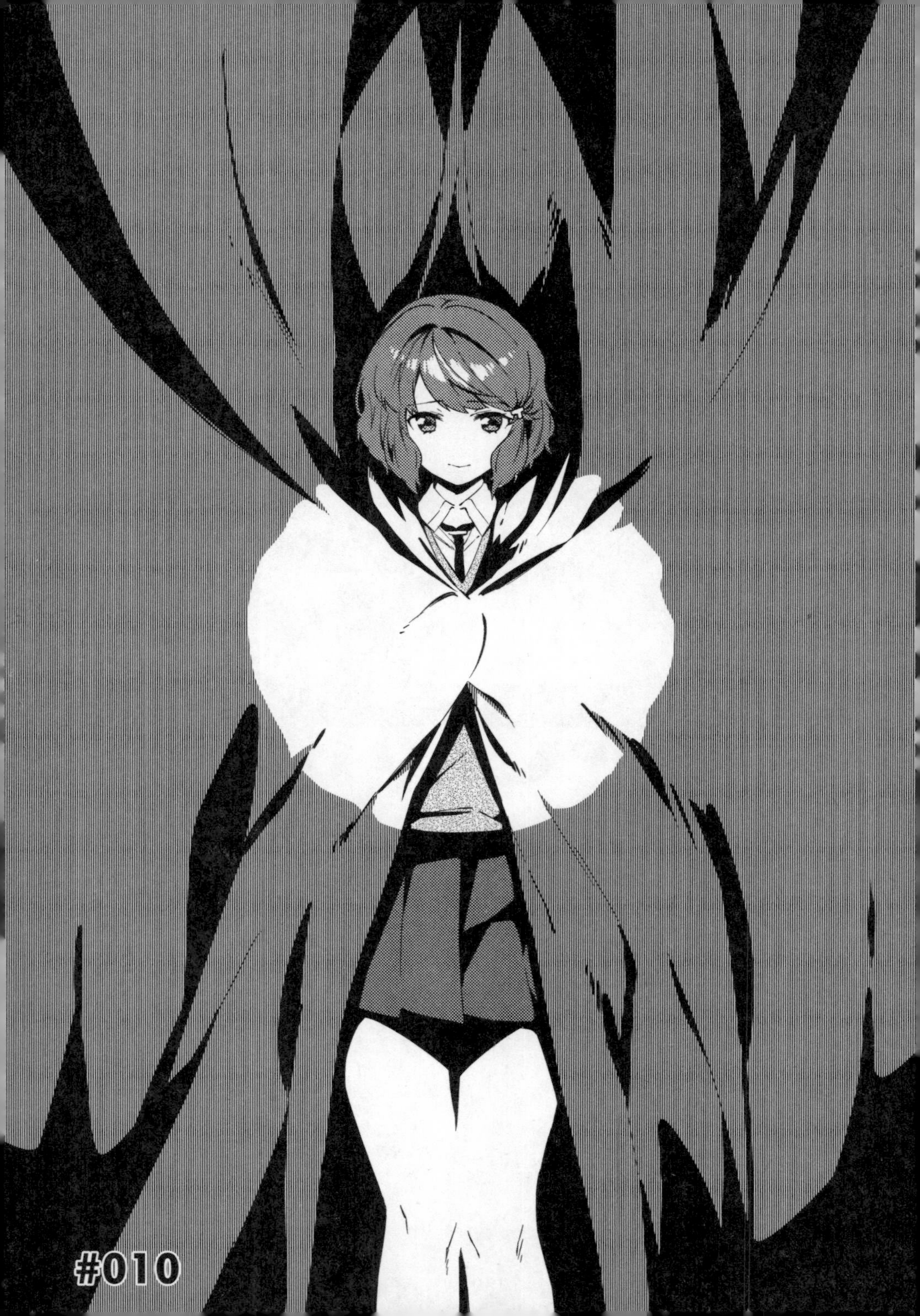

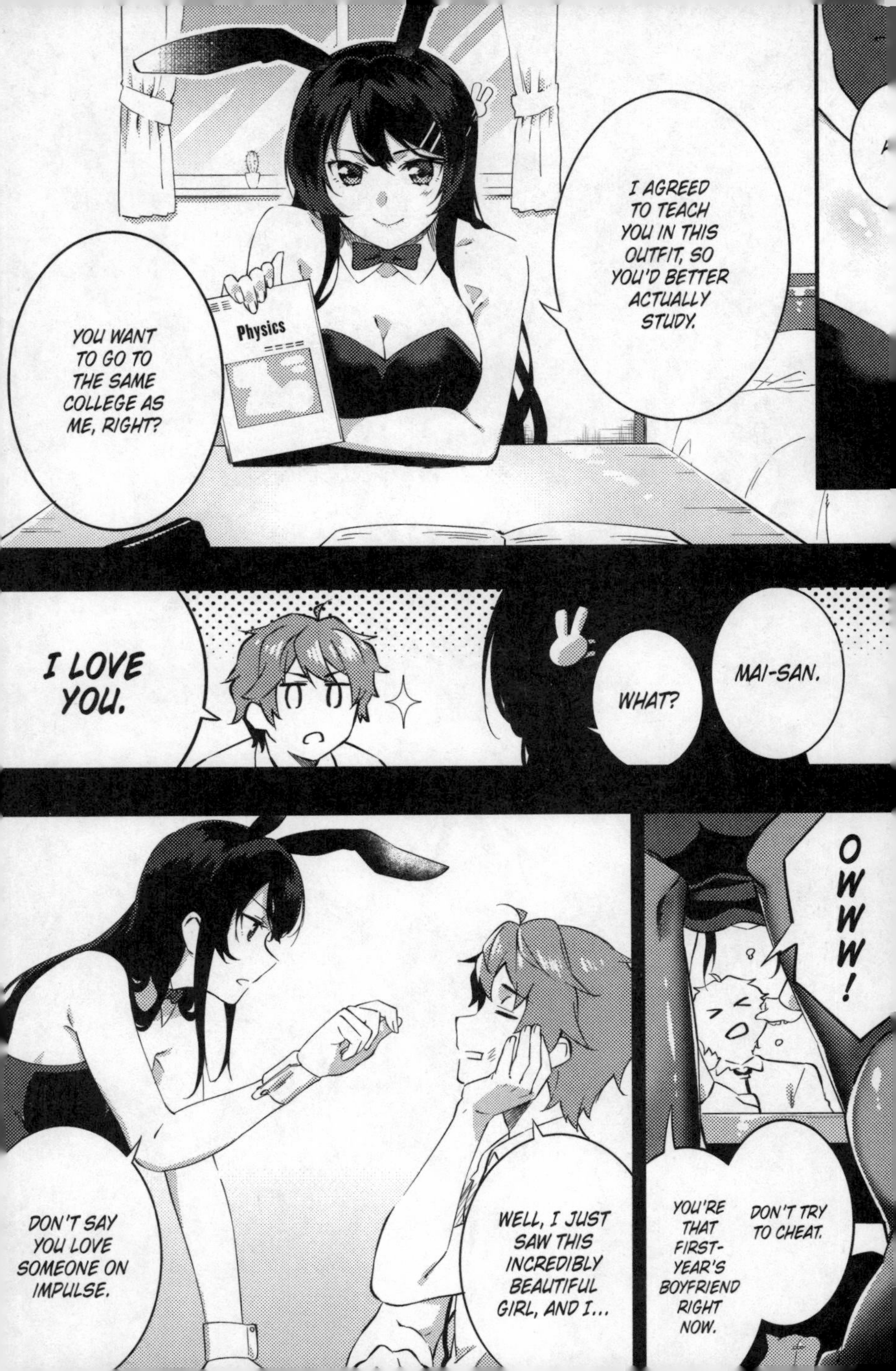
I AGREED TO TEACH YOU IN THIS OUTFIT, SO YOU'D BETTER ACTUALLY STUDY.
Physics
YOU WANT TO GO TO THE SAME COLLEGE AS ME, RIGHT?
MAI-SAN.
WHAT?
I LOVE YOU.
OWWW!
DON'T TRY TO CHEAT.
YOU'RE THAT FIRST-YEAR'S BOYFRIEND RIGHT NOW.
WELL, I JUST SAW THIS INCREDIBLY BEAUTIFUL GIRL, AND I...
DON'T SAY YOU LOVE SOMEONE ON IMPULSE.

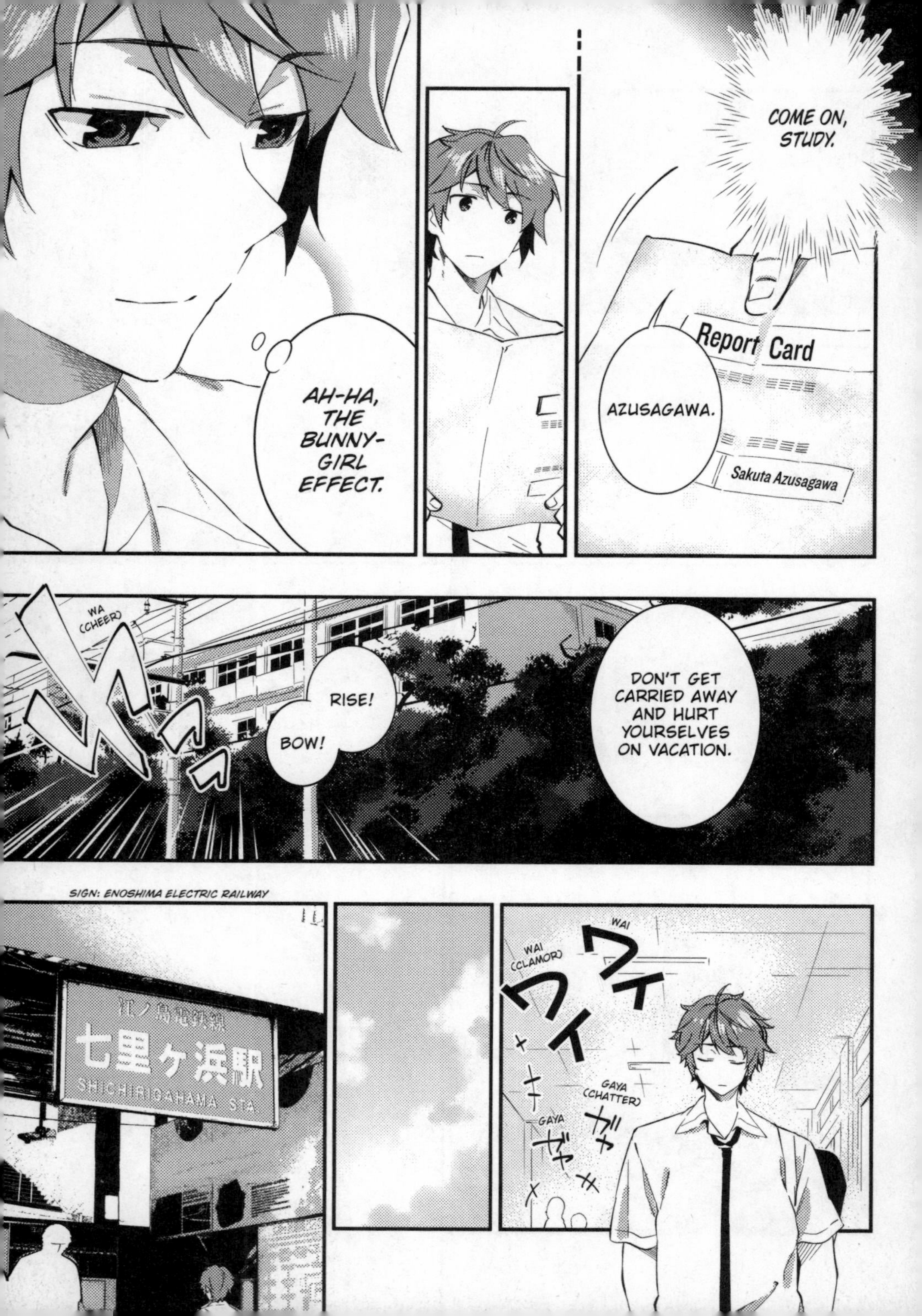
COME ON, STUDY.
Report Card
AZUSAGAWA.
Sakuta Azusagawa
AH-HA, THE BUNNY-GIRL EFFECT.
DON'T GET CARRIED AWAY AND HURT YOURSELVES ON VACATION.
RISE!
BOW!
WA (CHEER)
SIGN: ENOSHIMA ELECTRIC RAILWAY
WAI
WAI (CLAMOR)
ワイワイ
GAYA (CHATTER)
GAYA
ガヤガヤ
江ノ島電鉄線
七里ヶ浜駅
SHICHIRIGAHAMA STA

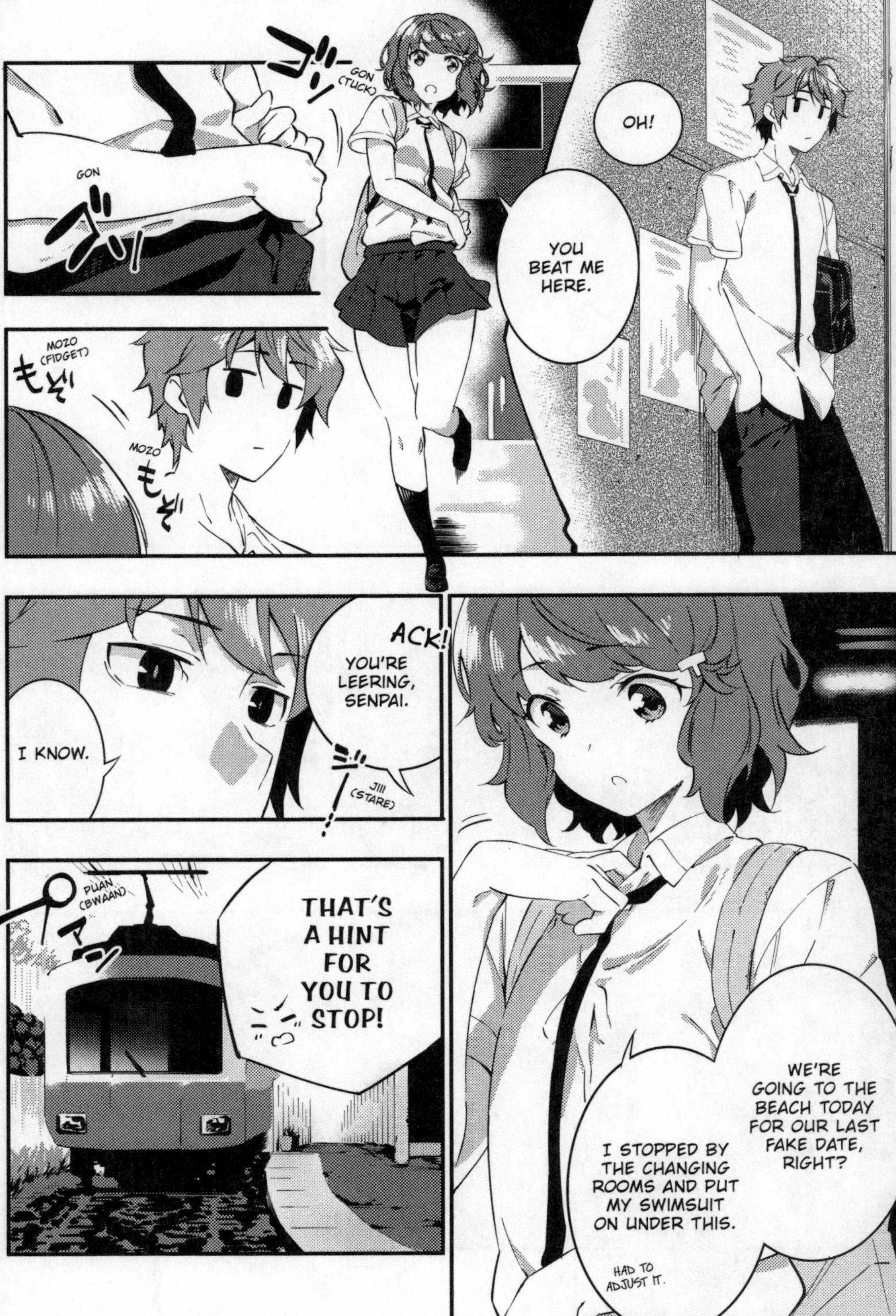
OH!
YOU BEAT ME HERE.
GON (TUCK)
GON
MOZO (FIDGET)
MOZO
WE'RE GOING TO THE BEACH TODAY FOR OUR LAST FAKE DATE, RIGHT?
I STOPPED BY THE CHANGING ROOMS AND PUT MY SWIMSUIT ON UNDER THIS.
HAD TO ADJUST IT.
ACK!
YOU'RE LEERING, SENPAI.
JIII (STARE)
I KNOW.
PUAN (BWAAN)
THAT'S A HINT FOR YOU TO STOP!

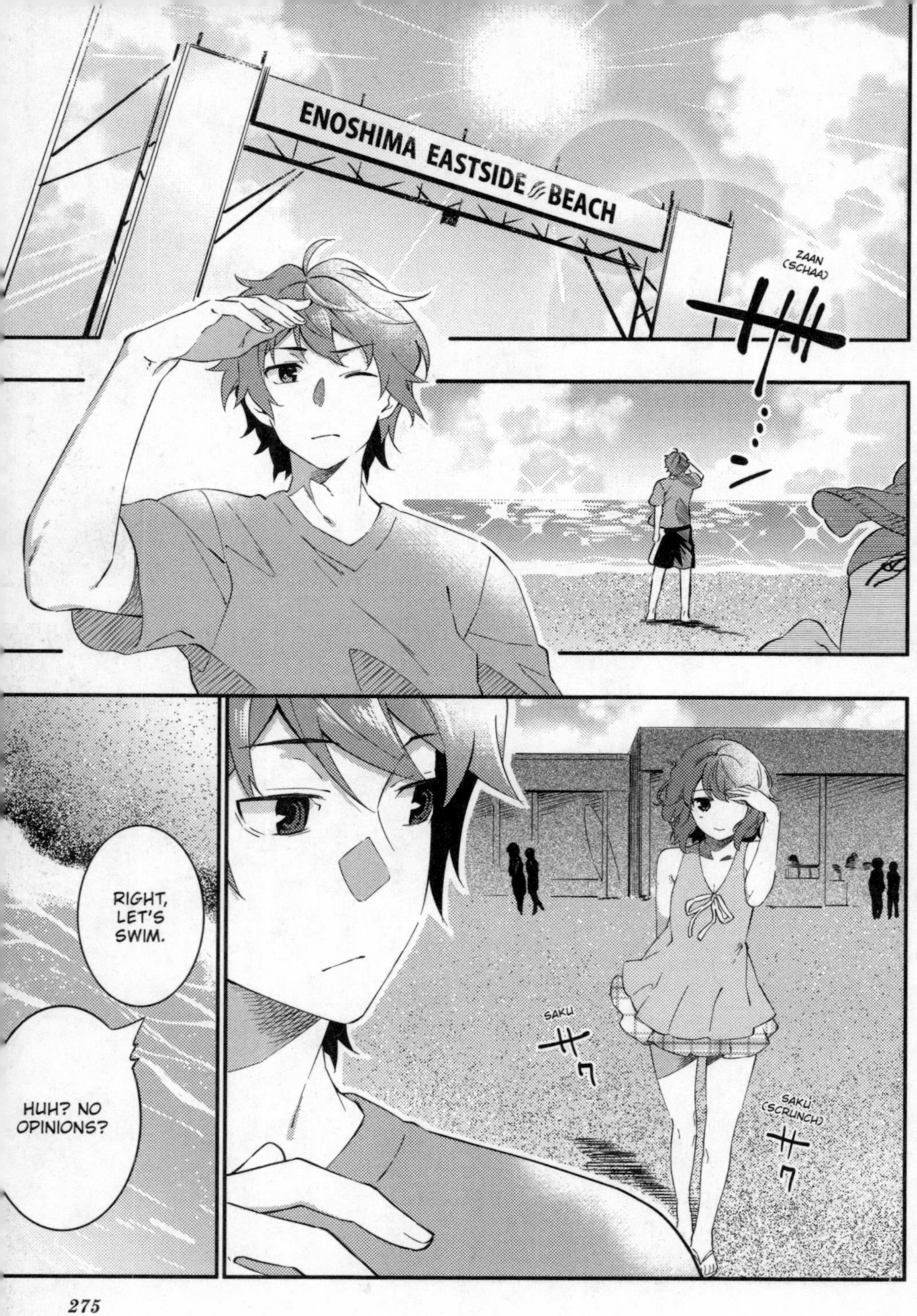
ENOSHIMA EASTSIDE BEACH
ZAAN (SCHAA)
SAKU
SAKU (SCRUNCH)
RIGHT, LET'S SWIM.
HUH? NO OPINIONS?

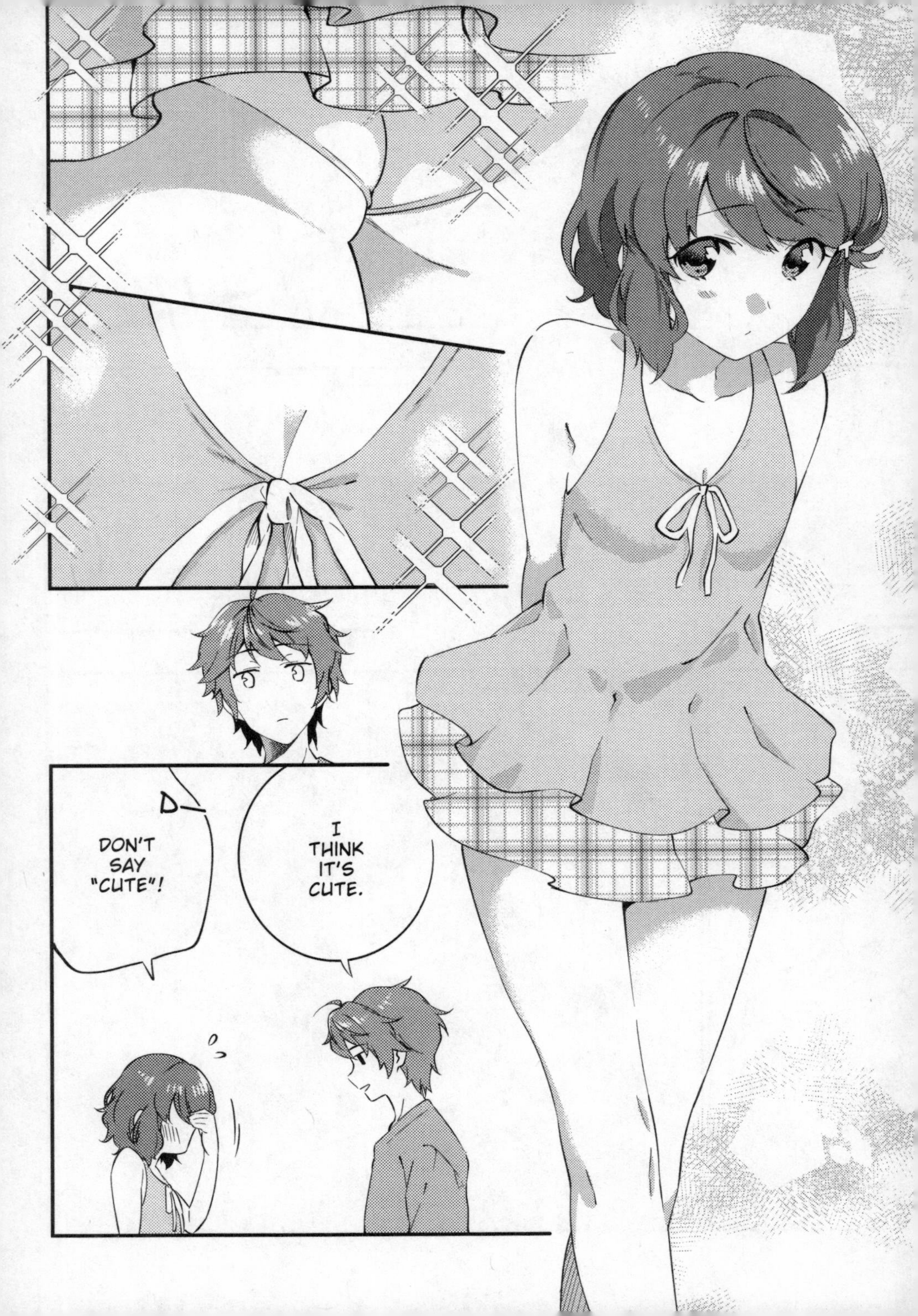
I THINK IT'S CUTE.
D—
DON'T SAY "CUTE"!

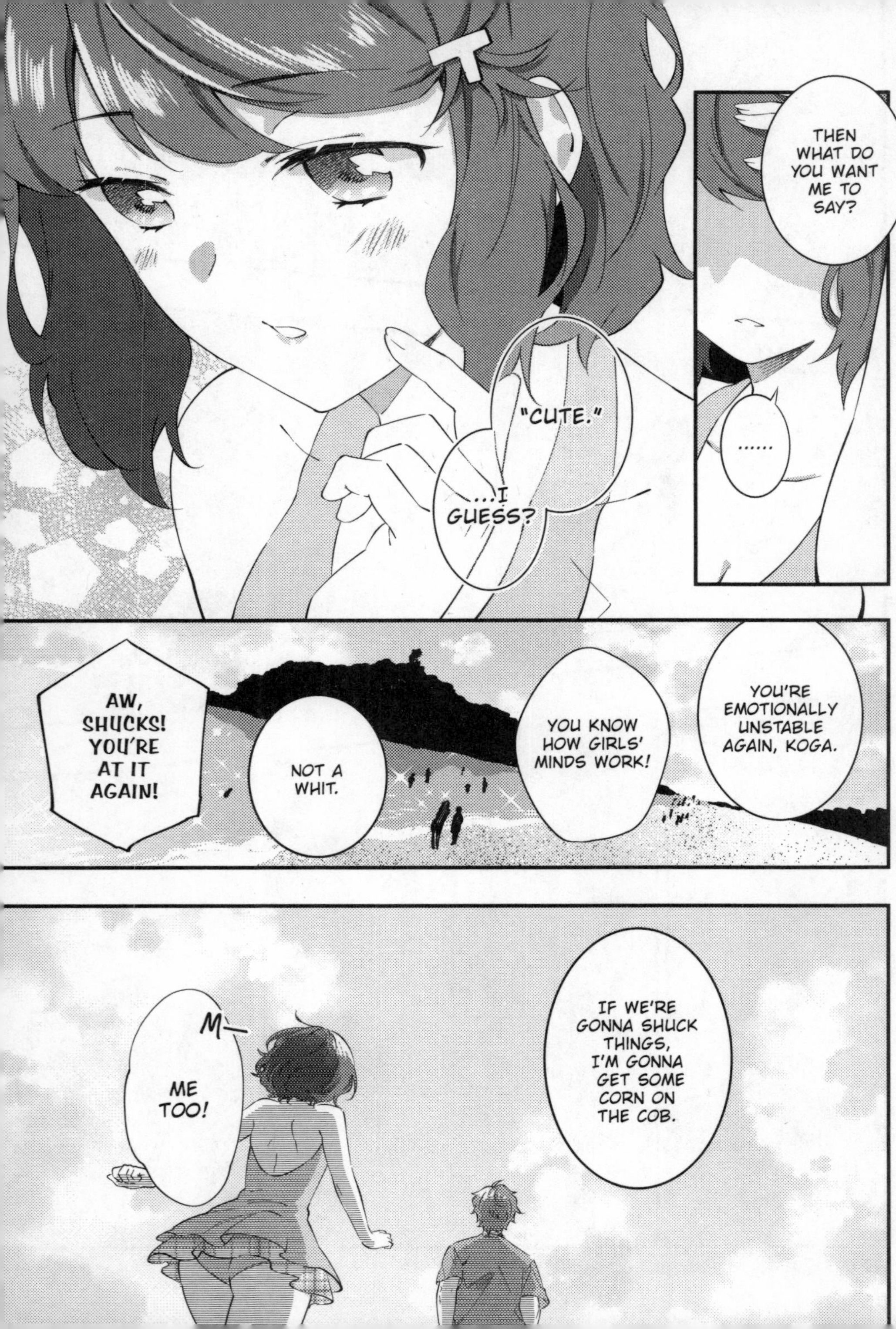
THEN WHAT DO YOU WANT ME TO SAY?
......
"CUTE."
...I GUESS?
YOU'RE EMOTIONALLY UNSTABLE AGAIN, KOGA.
YOU KNOW HOW GIRLS' MINDS WORK!
NOT A WHIT.
AW, SHUCKS! YOU'RE AT IT AGAIN!
IF WE'RE GONNA SHUCK THINGS, I'M GONNA GET SOME CORN ON THE COB.
M—
ME TOO!

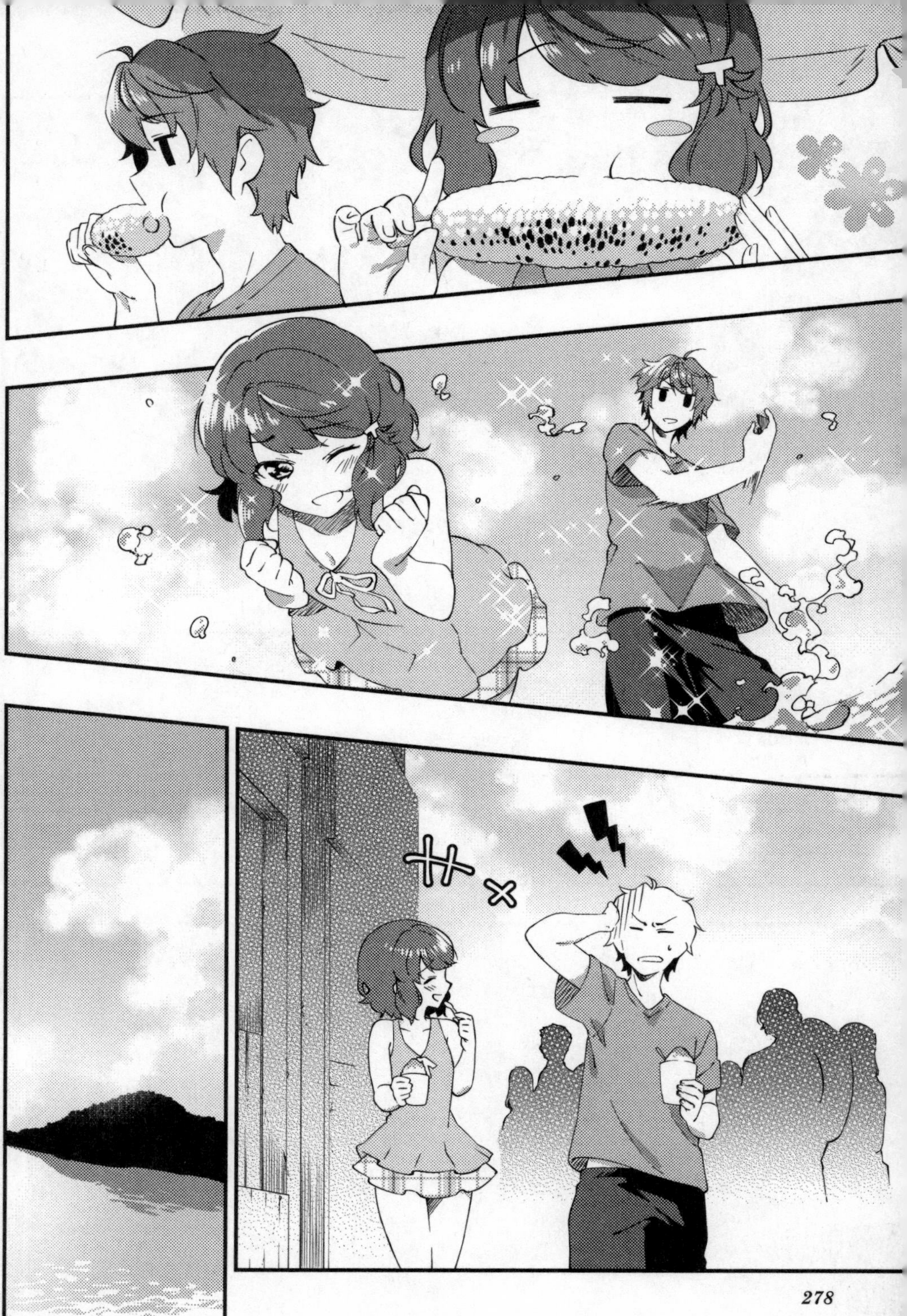

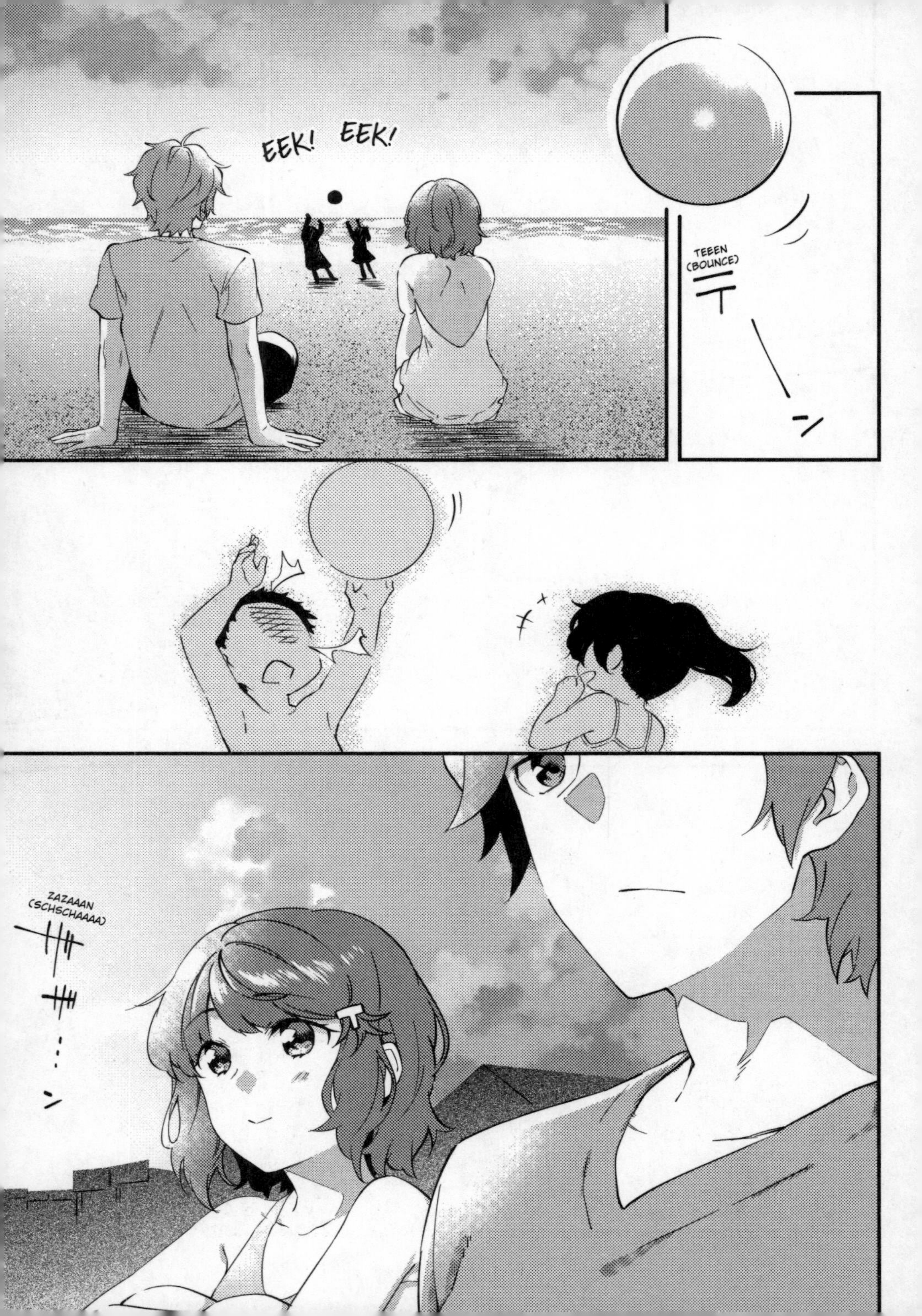
TEEEN
(BOUNCE)
EEK! EEK!
ZAZAAAN
(SCHSCHAAAA)

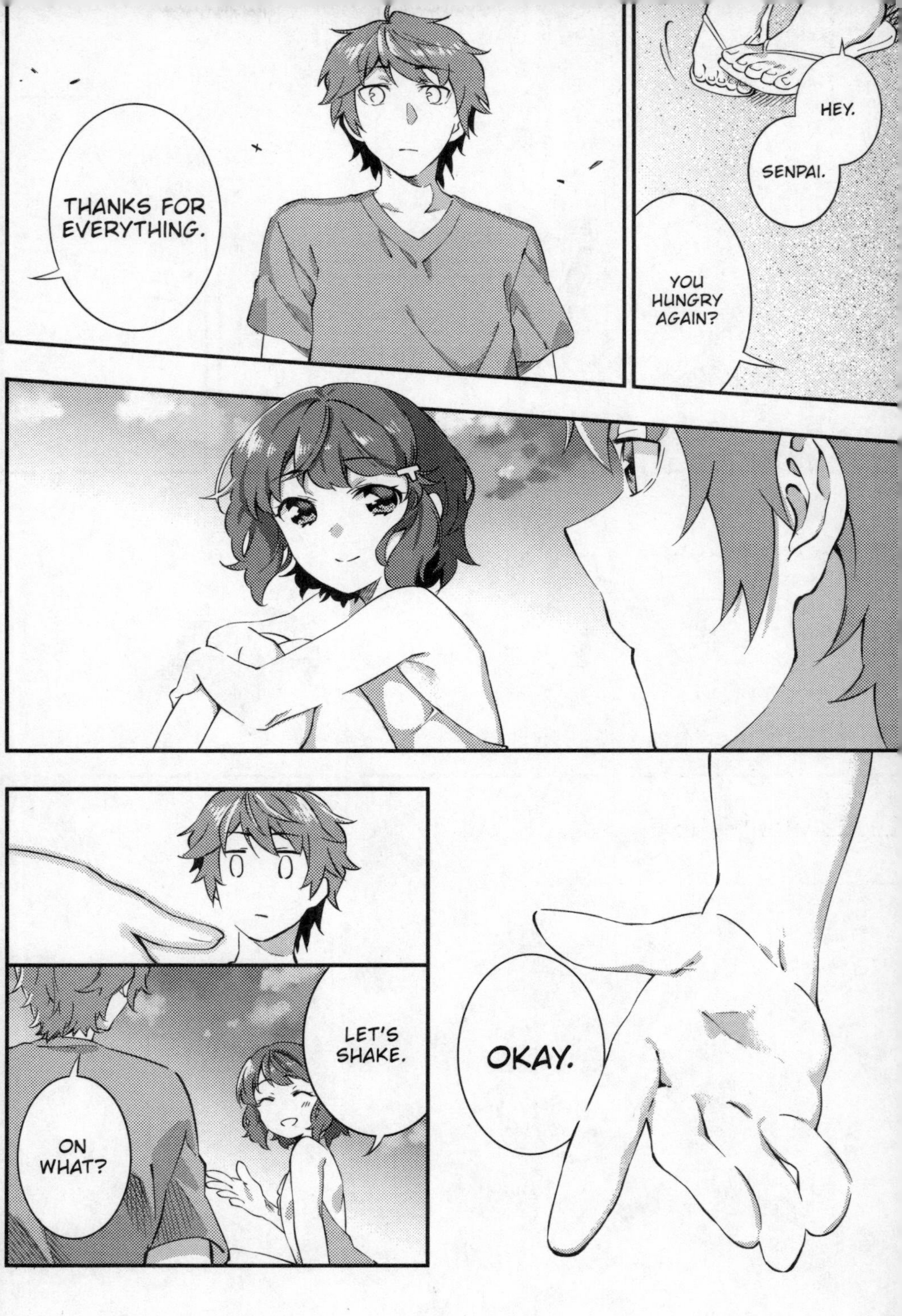
HEY.
SENPAI.
YOU HUNGRY AGAIN?
THANKS FOR EVERYTHING.
OKAY.
LET'S SHAKE.
ON WHAT?

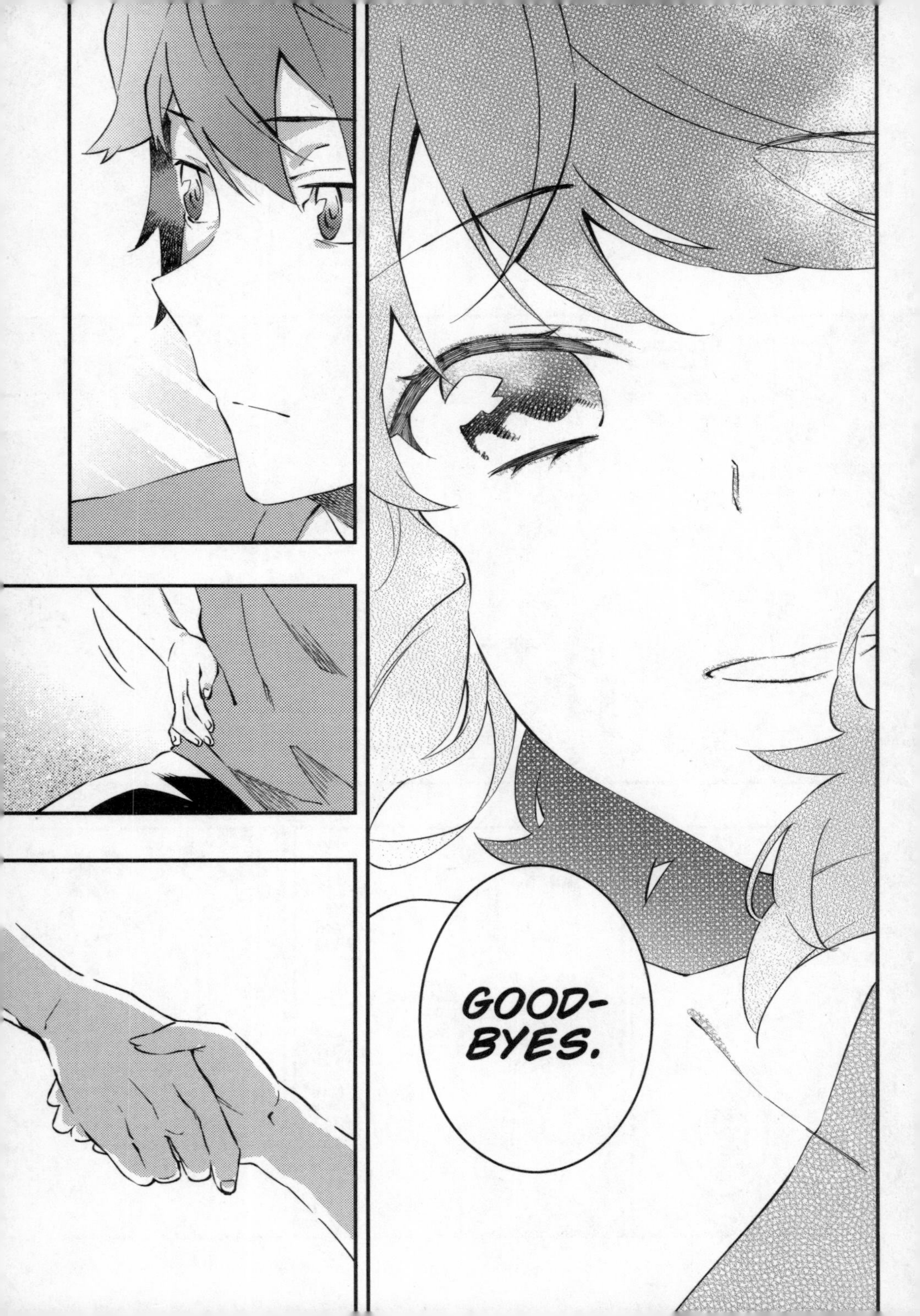
GOOD-BYES.

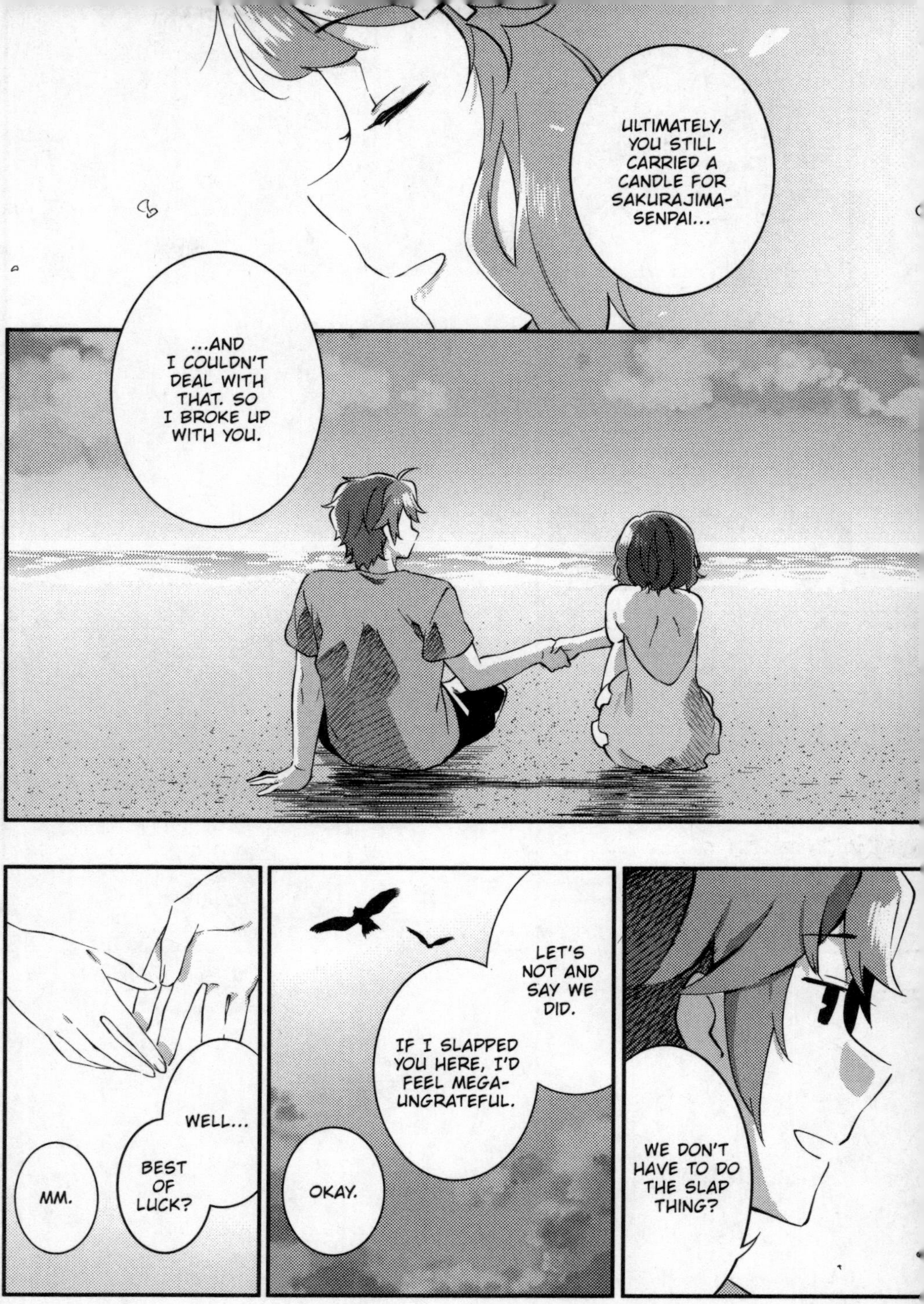
ULTIMATELY, YOU STILL CARRIED A CANDLE FOR SAKURAJIMA-SENPAI...
...AND I COULDN'T DEAL WITH THAT. SO I BROKE UP WITH YOU.
WE DON'T HAVE TO DO THE SLAP THING?
LET'S NOT AND SAY WE DID.
IF I SLAPPED YOU HERE, I'D FEEL MEGA-UNGRATEFUL.
OKAY.
WELL...
BEST OF LUCK?
MM.

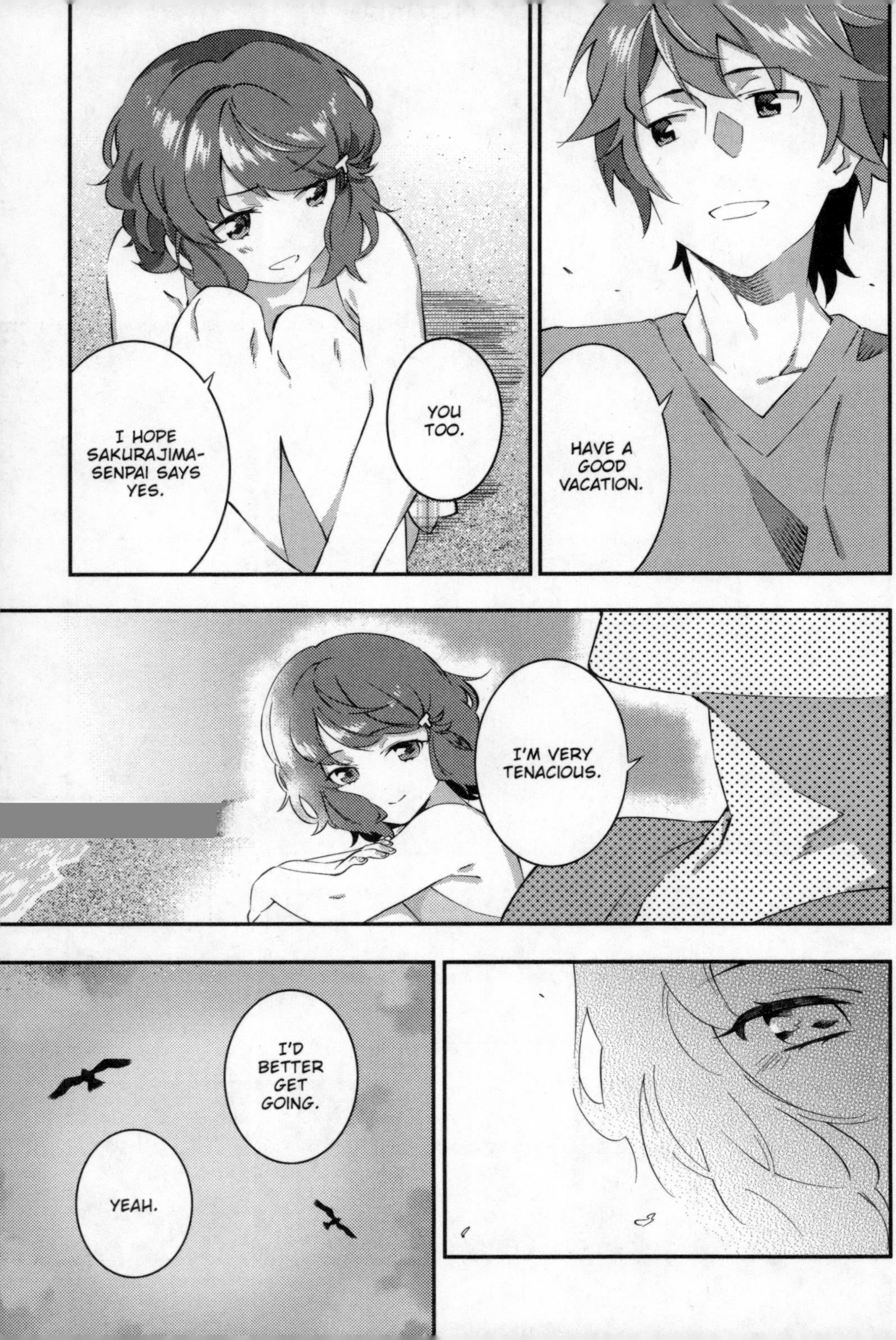
HAVE A GOOD VACATION.
YOU TOO.
I HOPE SAKURAJIMA-SENPAI SAYS YES.
I'M VERY TENACIOUS.
I'D BETTER GET GOING.
YEAH.

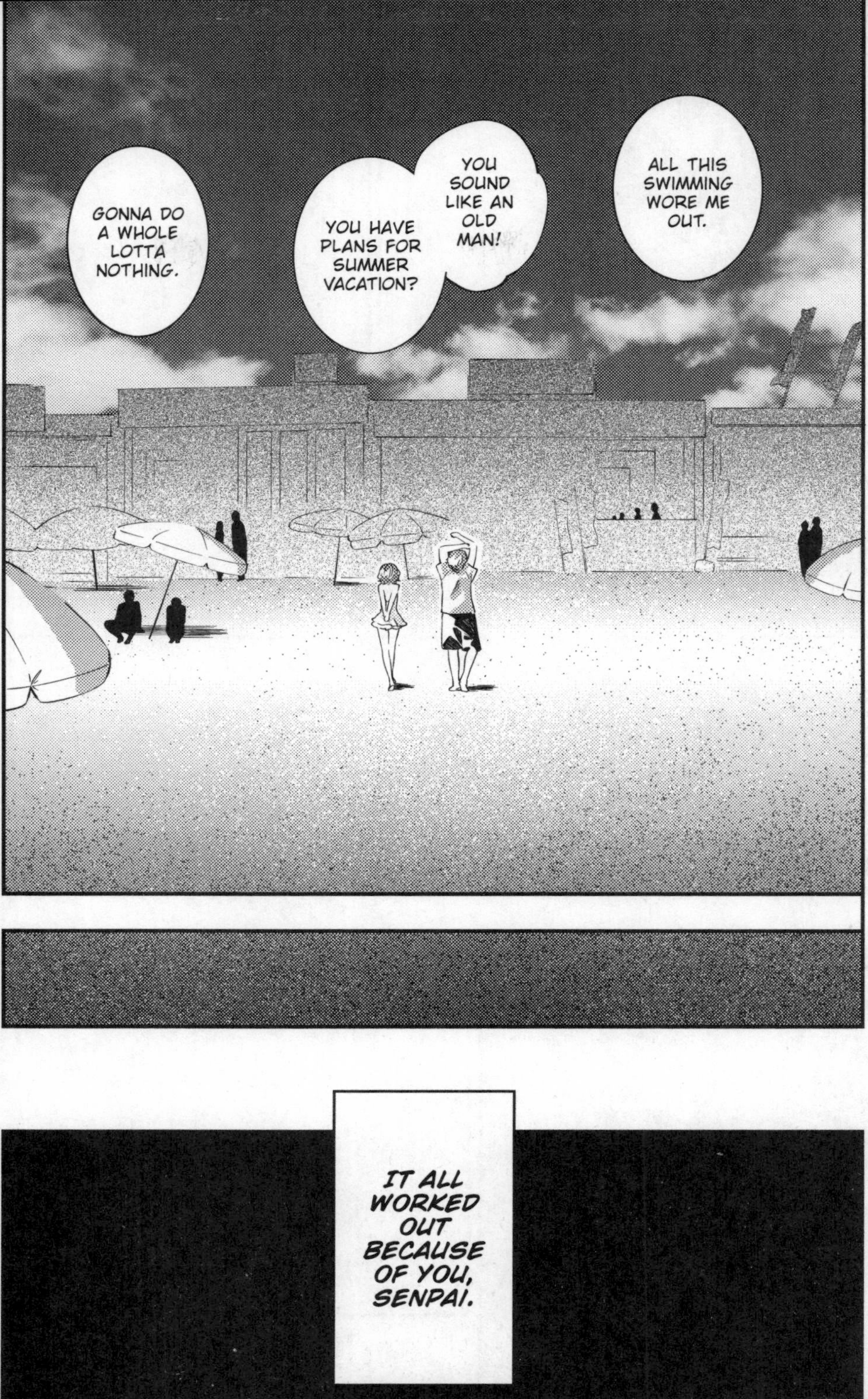
ALL THIS SWIMMING WORE ME OUT.
YOU SOUND LIKE AN OLD MAN!
YOU HAVE PLANS FOR SUMMER VACATION?
GONNA DO A WHOLE LOTTA NOTHING.
IT ALL WORKED OUT BECAUSE OF YOU, SENPAI.

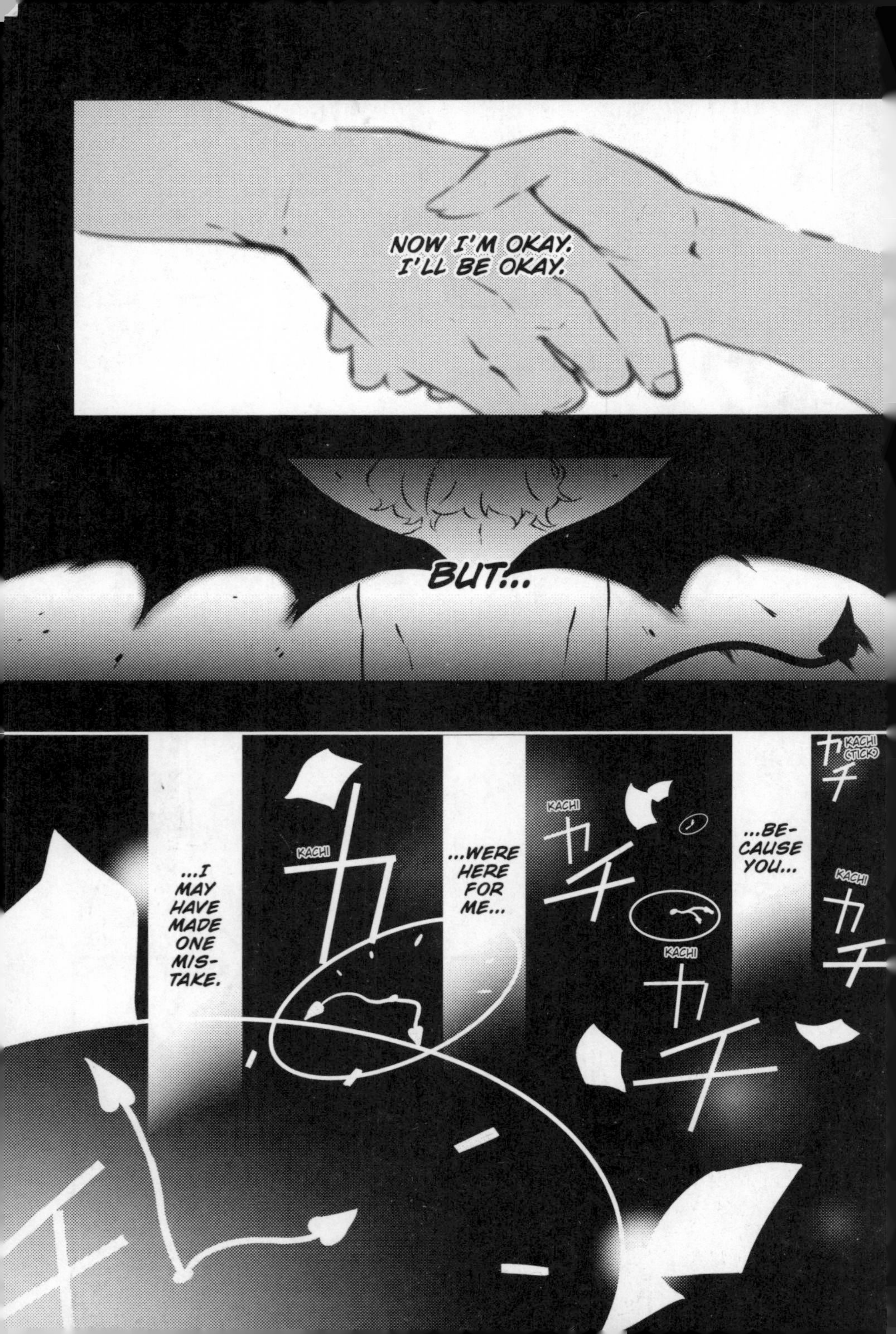
NOW I'M OKAY. I'LL BE OKAY.
BUT...
KACHI (TICK)
カチ
...BE-CAUSE YOU...
KACHI
カチ
KACHI
カチ
KACHI
カチ
...WERE HERE FOR ME...
KACHI
カチ
...I MAY HAVE MADE ONE MIS-TAKE.

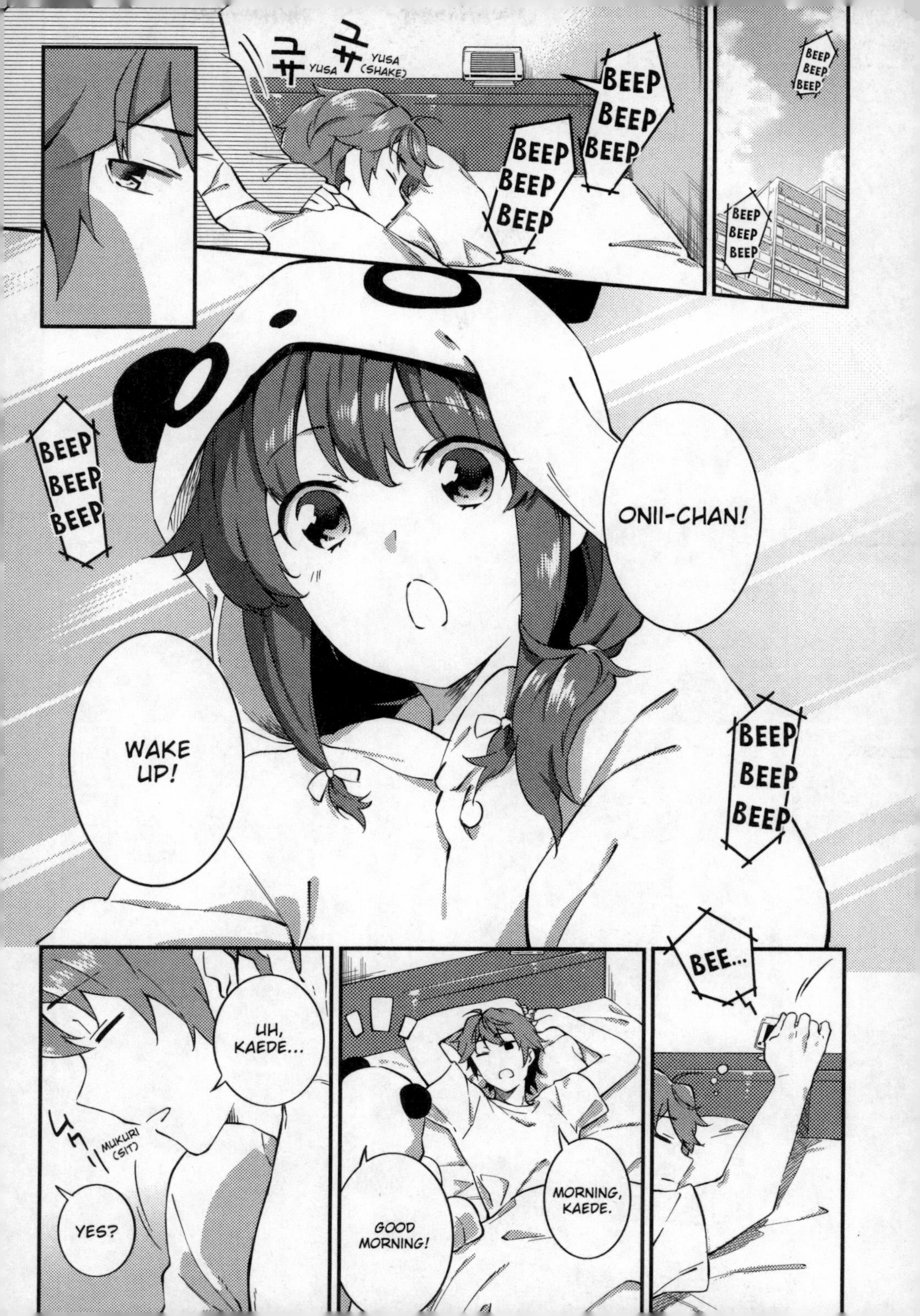
BEEP BEEP BEEP
BEEP BEEP BEEP
BEEP BEEP BEEP
YUSA YUSA (SHAKE)
ONII-CHAN!
BEEP BEEP BEEP
BEEP BEEP BEEP
WAKE UP!
BEE...
MORNING, KAEDE.
GOOD MORNING!
UH, KAEDE...
MUKURI (SIT)
YES?

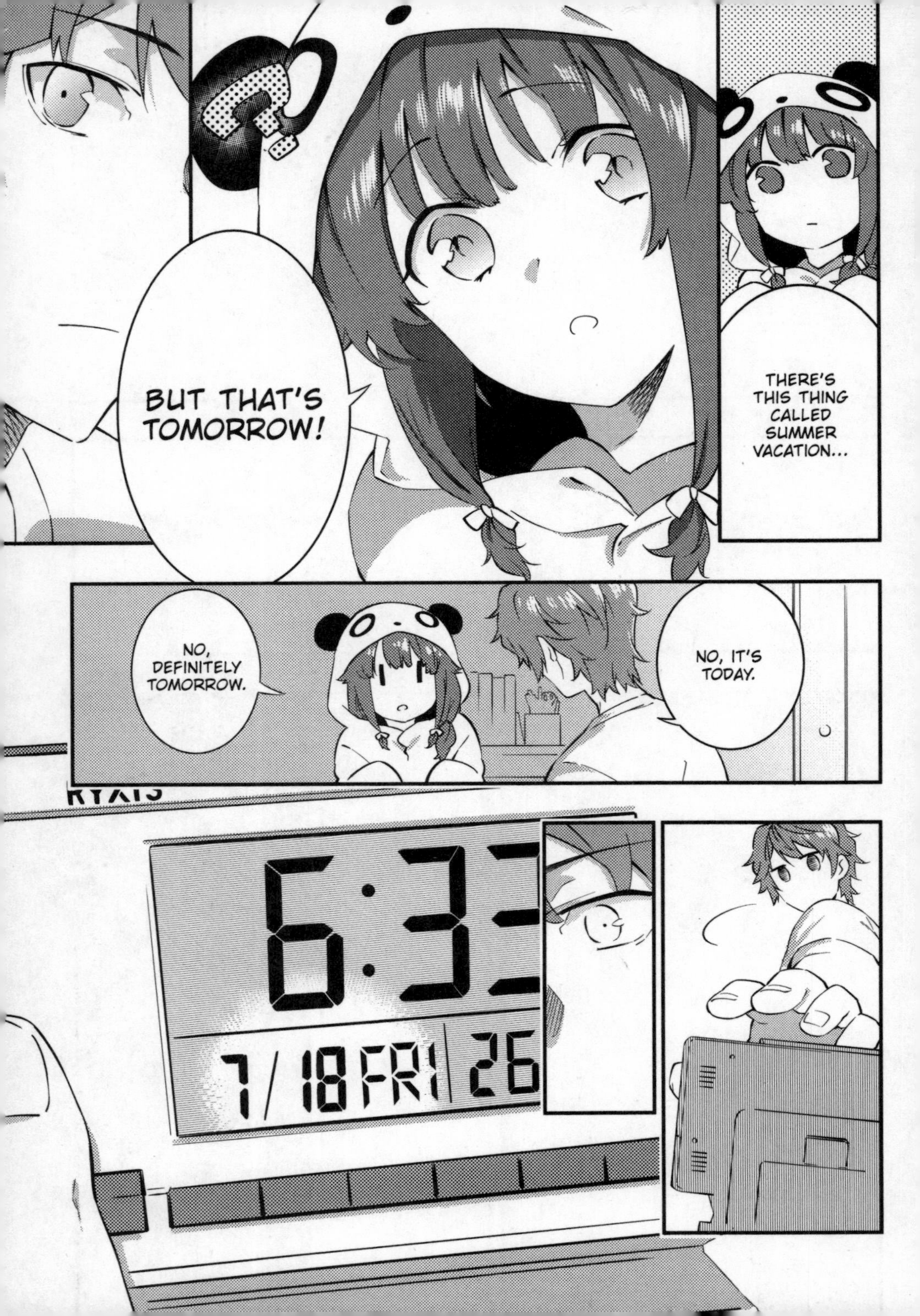
THERE'S THIS THING CALLED SUMMER VACATION...
BUT THAT'S TOMORROW!
NO, IT'S TODAY.
NO, DEFINITELY TOMORROW.
7/18 FRI 26

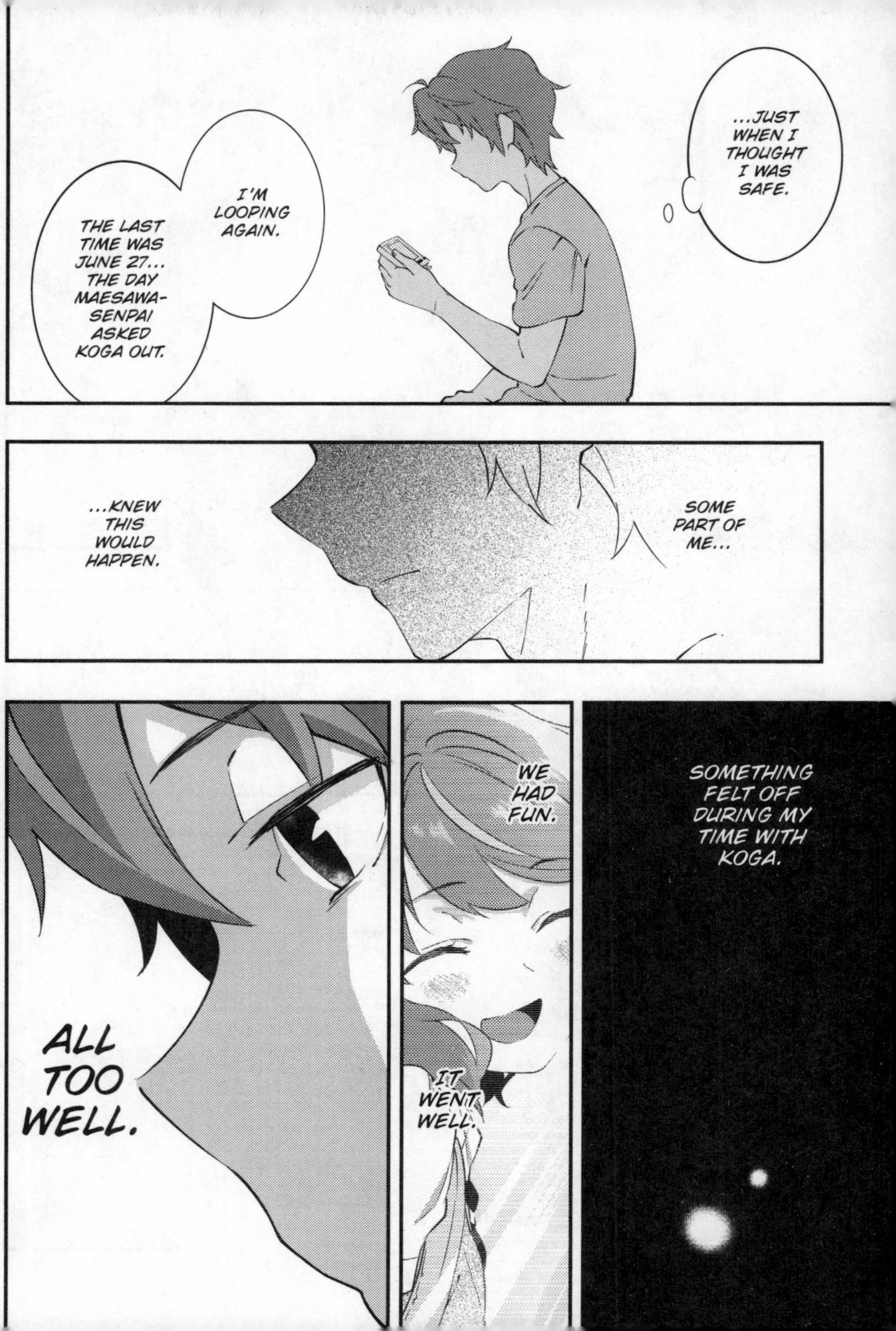
...JUST WHEN I THOUGHT I WAS SAFE.
I'M LOOPING AGAIN.
THE LAST TIME WAS JUNE 27... THE DAY MAESAWA-SENPAI ASKED KOGA OUT.
SOME PART OF ME...
...KNEW THIS WOULD HAPPEN.
SOMETHING FELT OFF DURING MY TIME WITH KOGA.
WE HAD FUN.
IT WENT WELL.
ALL TOO WELL.

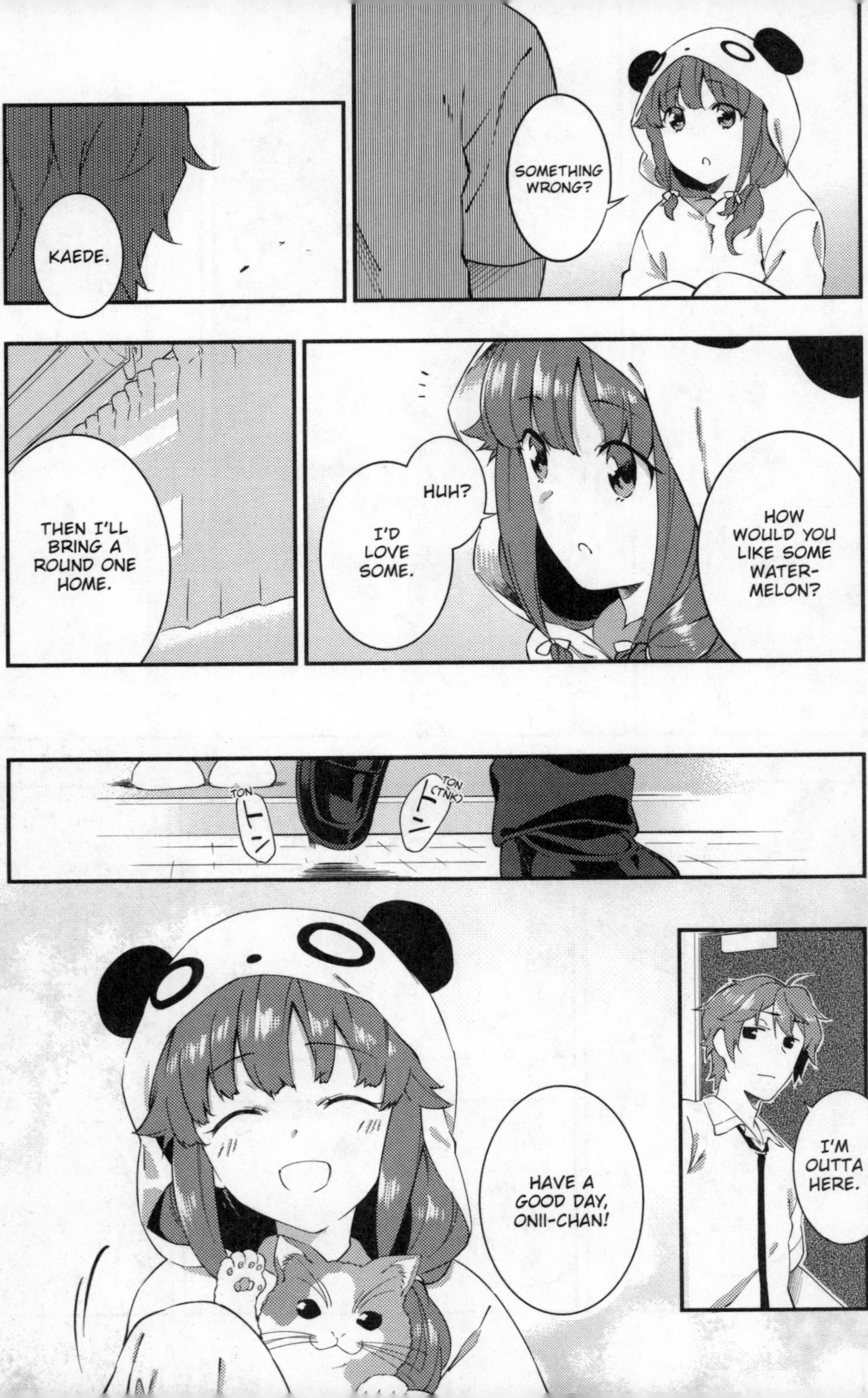
SOMETHING WRONG?
KAEDE.
HOW WOULD YOU LIKE SOME WATER-MELON?
HUH?
I'D LOVE SOME.
THEN I'LL BRING A ROUND ONE HOME.
TON (TNK)
TON
I'M OUTTA HERE.
HAVE A GOOD DAY, ONII-CHAN!

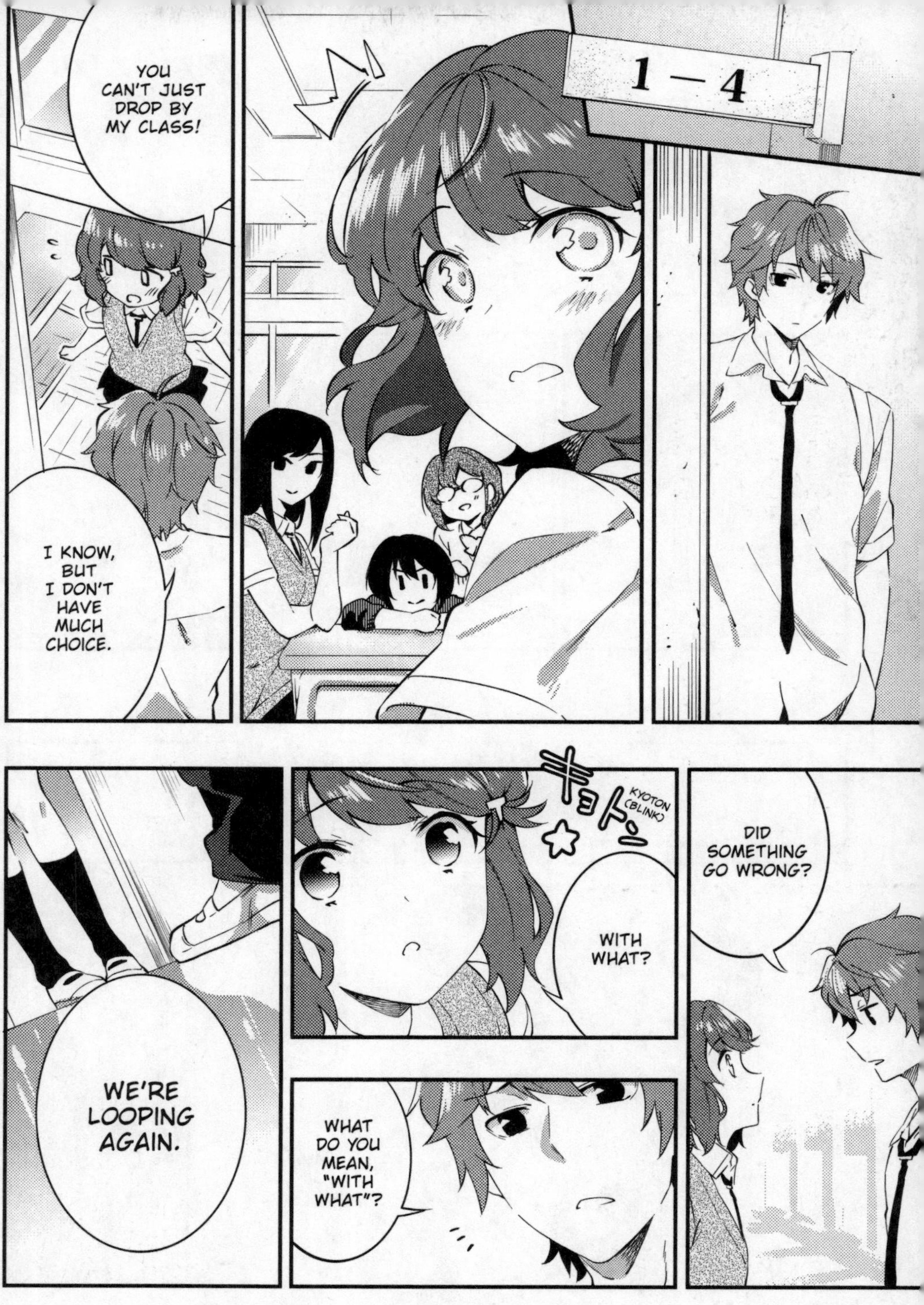
1—4
YOU CAN'T JUST DROP BY MY CLASS!
I KNOW, BUT I DON'T HAVE MUCH CHOICE.
DID SOMETHING GO WRONG?
KYOTON (BLINK)
WITH WHAT?
WHAT DO YOU MEAN, "WITH WHAT"?
WE'RE LOOPING AGAIN.

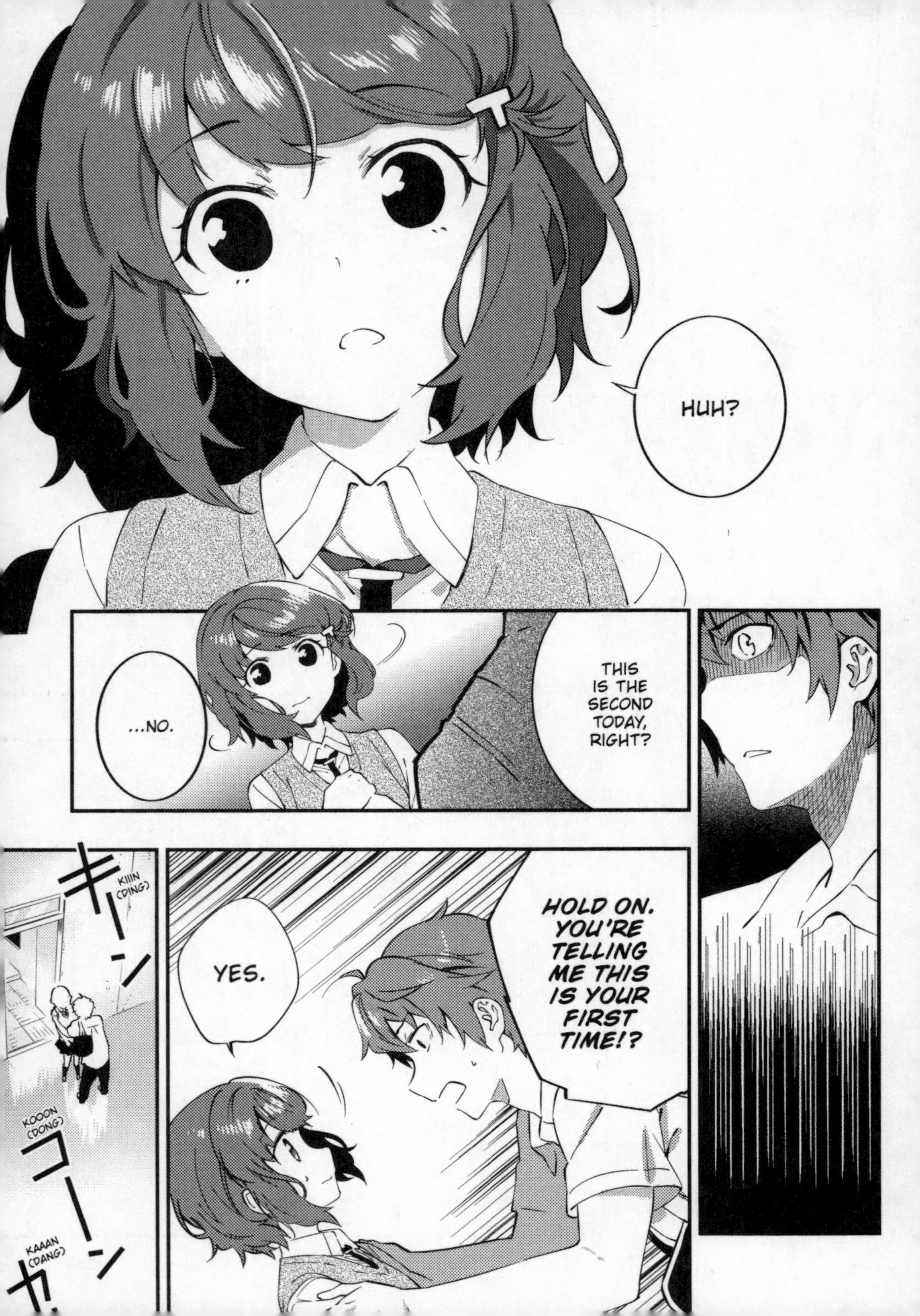
HUH?
THIS IS THE SECOND TODAY, RIGHT?
...NO.
HOLD ON. YOU'RE TELLING ME THIS IS YOUR FIRST TIME!?
YES.
KIIN (DING)
KOOON (DONG)
KAAAN (DANG)

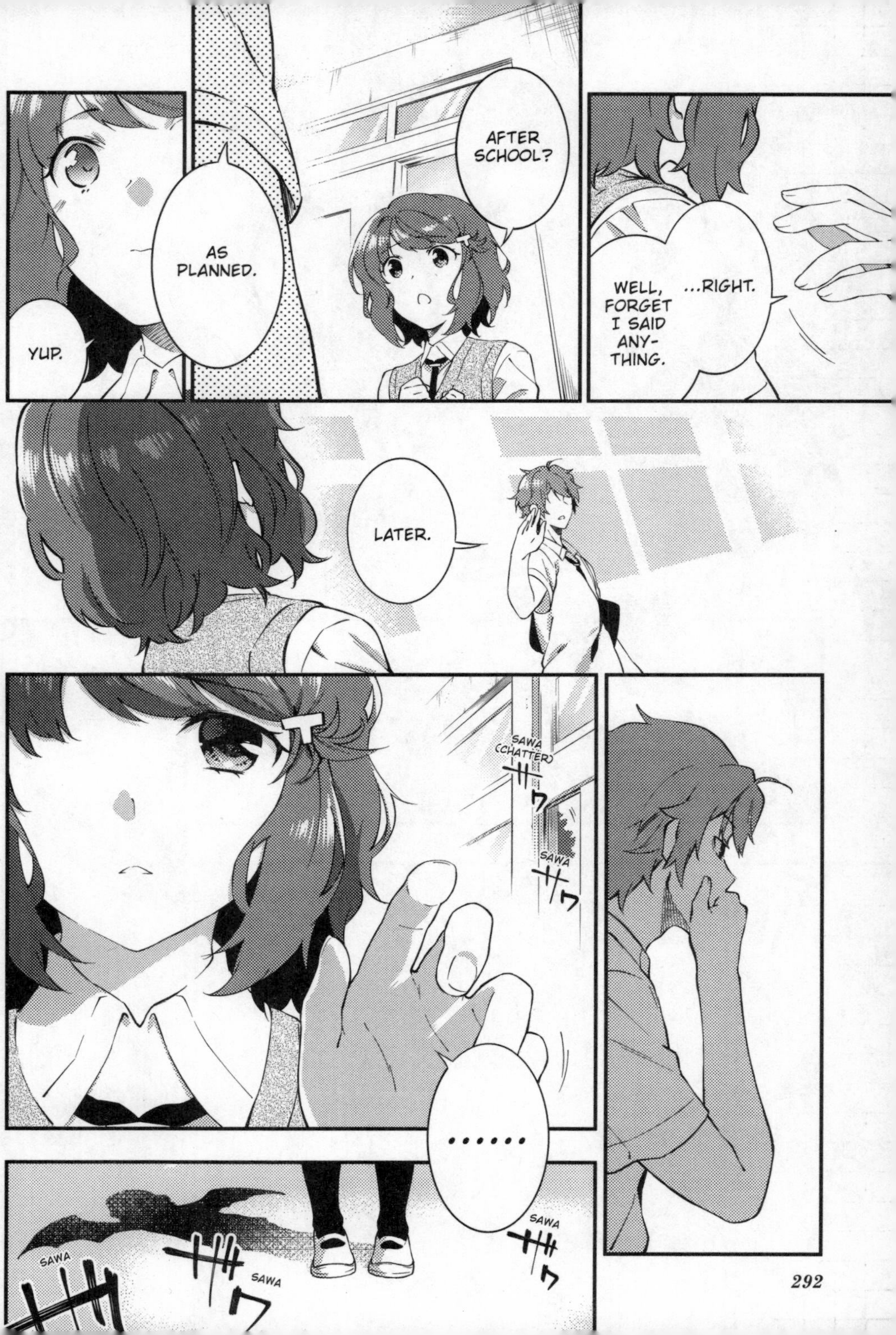
...RIGHT.
WELL, FORGET I SAID ANYTHING.
AFTER SCHOOL?
AS PLANNED.
YUP.
LATER.
SAWA (CHATTER)
SAWA
......
SAWA
SAWA
SAWA

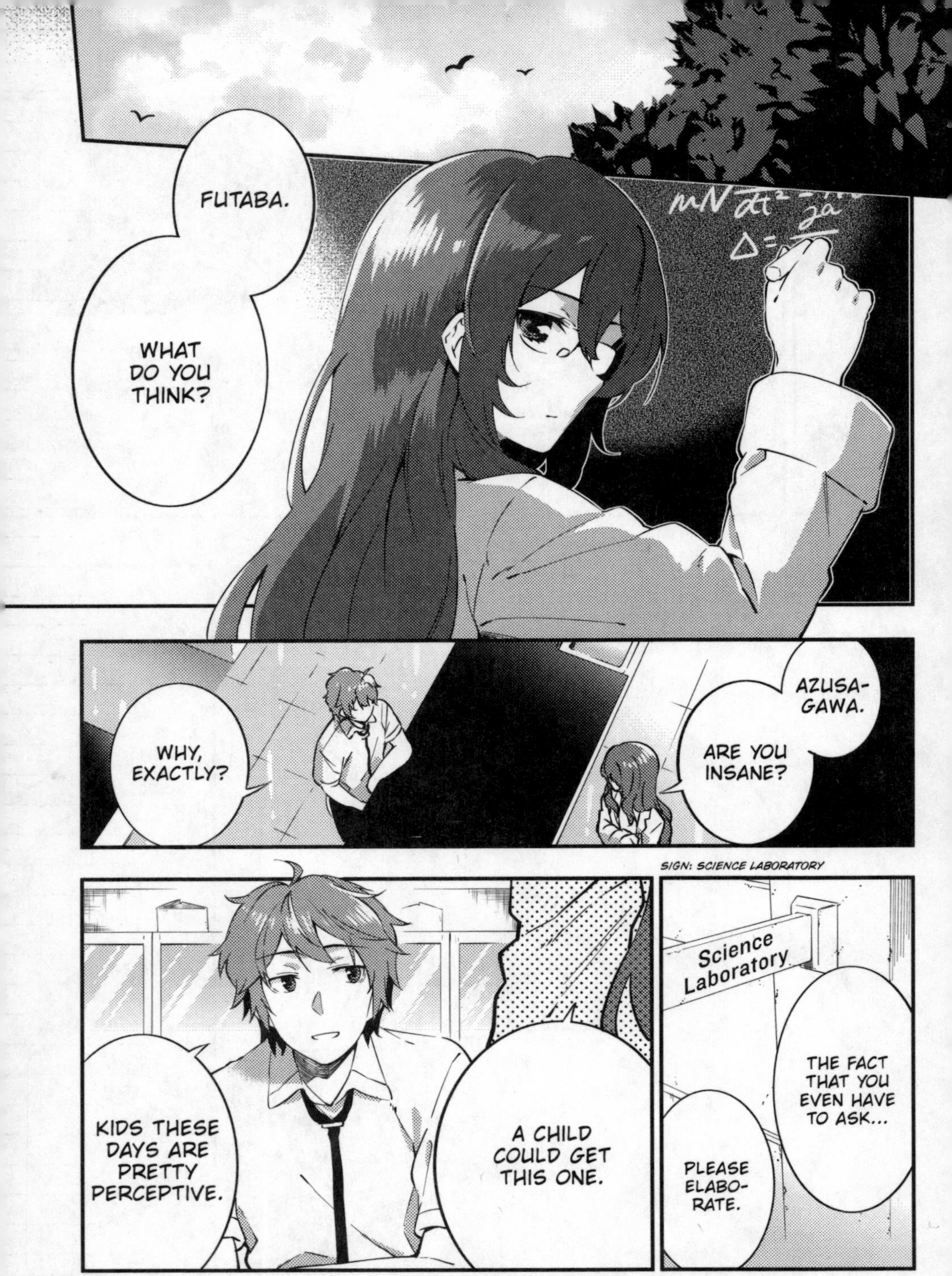
FUTABA.
WHAT DO YOU THINK?
AZUSA-GAWA.
ARE YOU INSANE?
WHY, EXACTLY?
SIGN: SCIENCE LABORATORY
Science Laboratory
THE FACT THAT YOU EVEN HAVE TO ASK...
PLEASE ELABORATE.
A CHILD COULD GET THIS ONE.
KIDS THESE DAYS ARE PRETTY PERCEPTIVE.

# #011

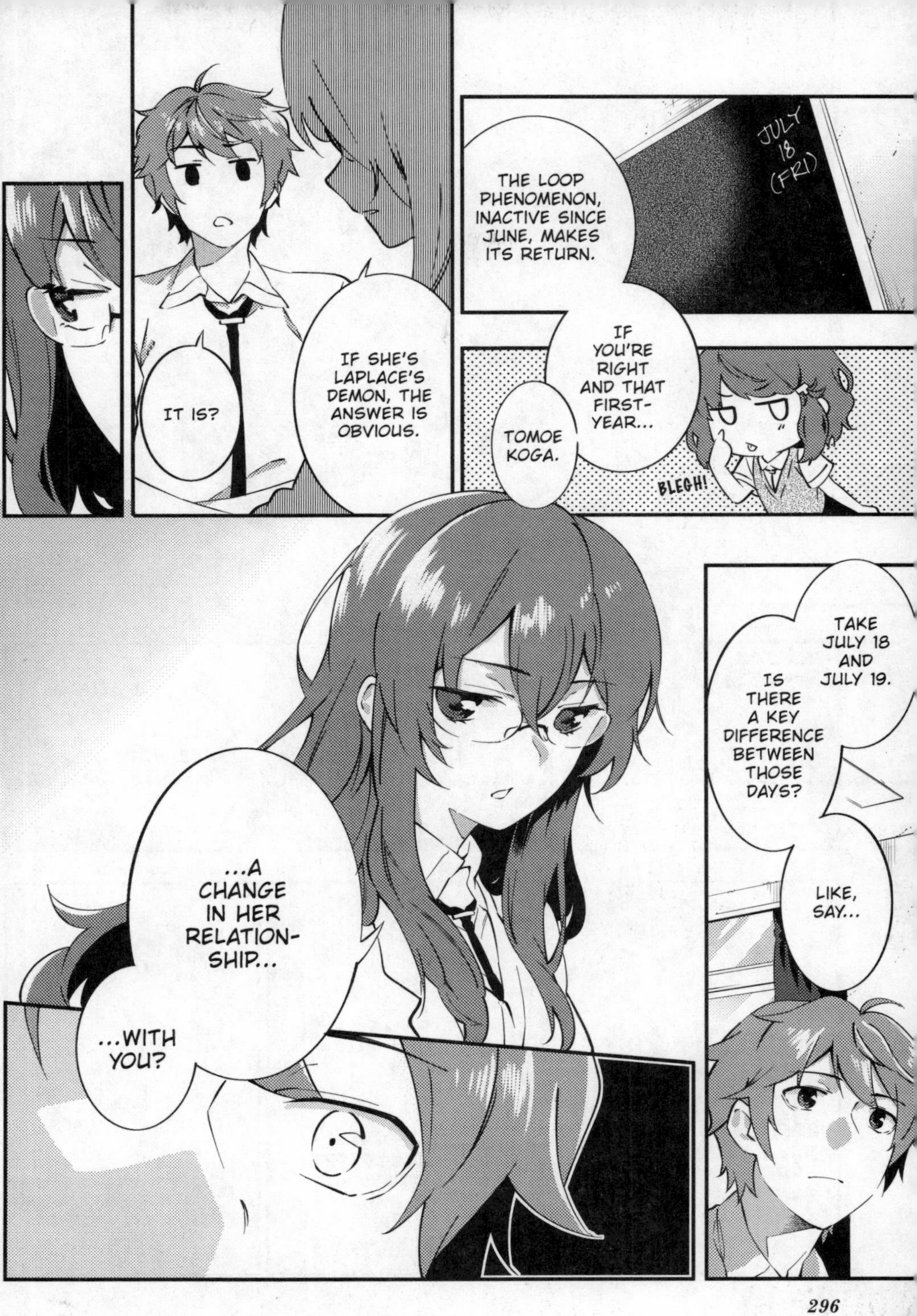
JULY 18 (FRI)
THE LOOP PHENOMENON, INACTIVE SINCE JUNE, MAKES ITS RETURN.
IF YOU'RE RIGHT AND THAT FIRST-YEAR...
TOMOE KOGA.
BLEGH!
IF SHE'S LAPLACE'S DEMON, THE ANSWER IS OBVIOUS.
IT IS?
TAKE JULY 18 AND JULY 19.
IS THERE A KEY DIFFERENCE BETWEEN THOSE DAYS?
LIKE, SAY...
...A CHANGE IN HER RELATIONSHIP...
...WITH YOU?

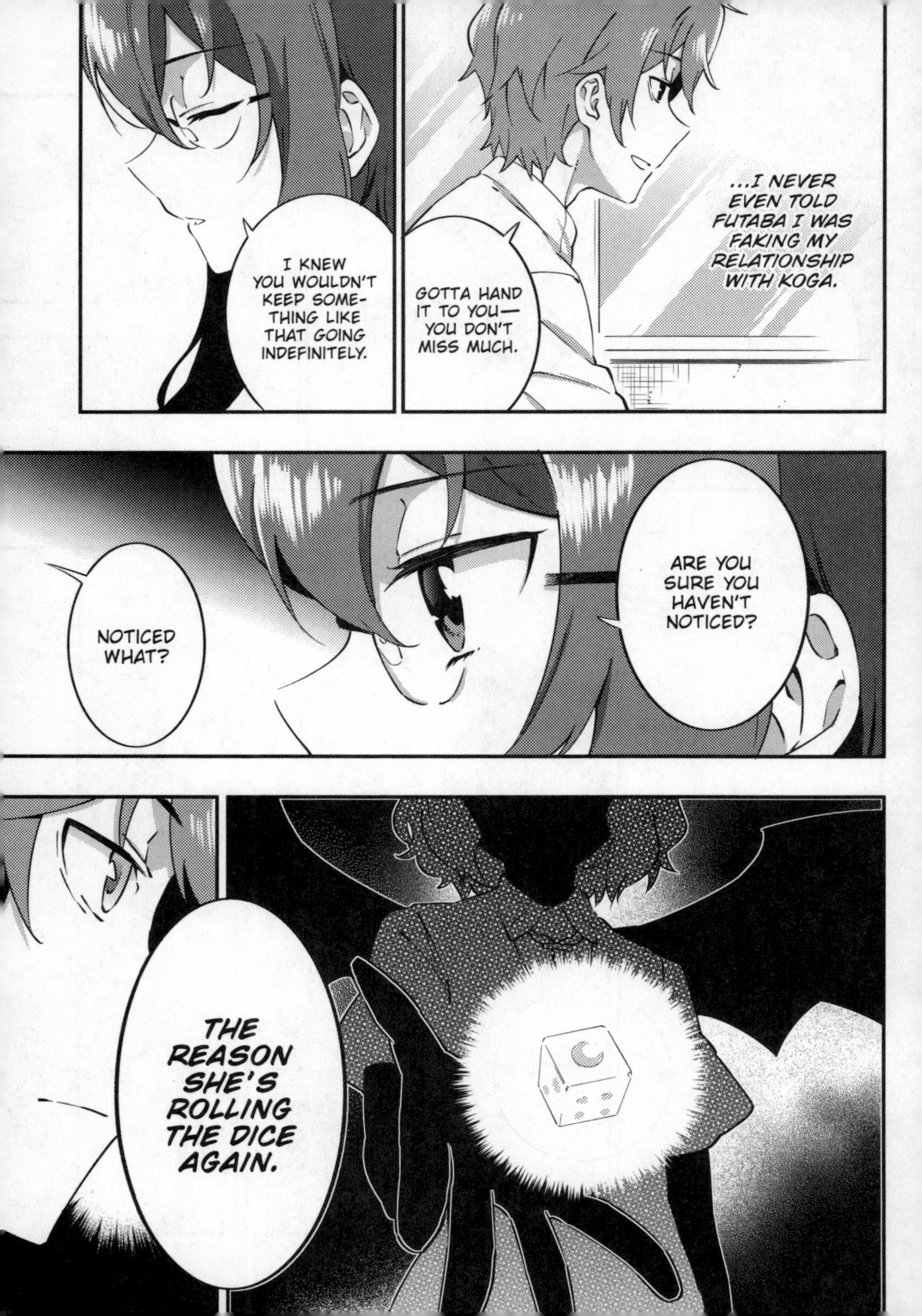
...I NEVER EVEN TOLD FUTABA I WAS FAKING MY RELATIONSHIP WITH KOGA.
GOTTA HAND IT TO YOU—YOU DON'T MISS MUCH.
I KNEW YOU WOULDN'T KEEP SOMETHING LIKE THAT GOING INDEFINITELY.
ARE YOU SURE YOU HAVEN'T NOTICED?
NOTICED WHAT?
THE REASON SHE'S ROLLING THE DICE AGAIN.
—

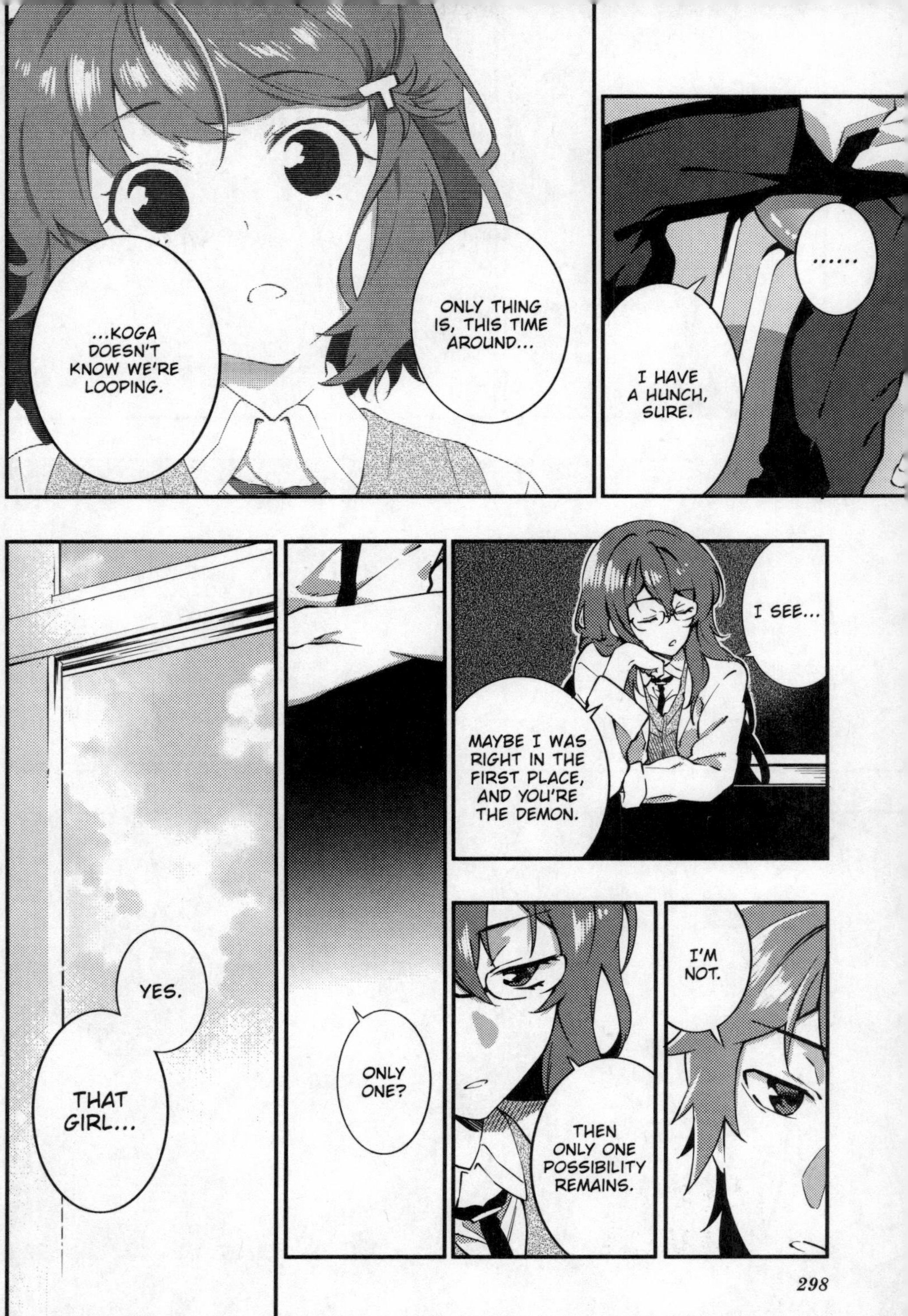
......
I HAVE A HUNCH, SURE.
ONLY THING IS, THIS TIME AROUND...
...KOGA DOESN'T KNOW WE'RE LOOPING.
I SEE...
MAYBE I WAS RIGHT IN THE FIRST PLACE, AND YOU'RE THE DEMON.
I'M NOT.
THEN ONLY ONE POSSIBILITY REMAINS.
ONLY ONE?
YES.
THAT GIRL...

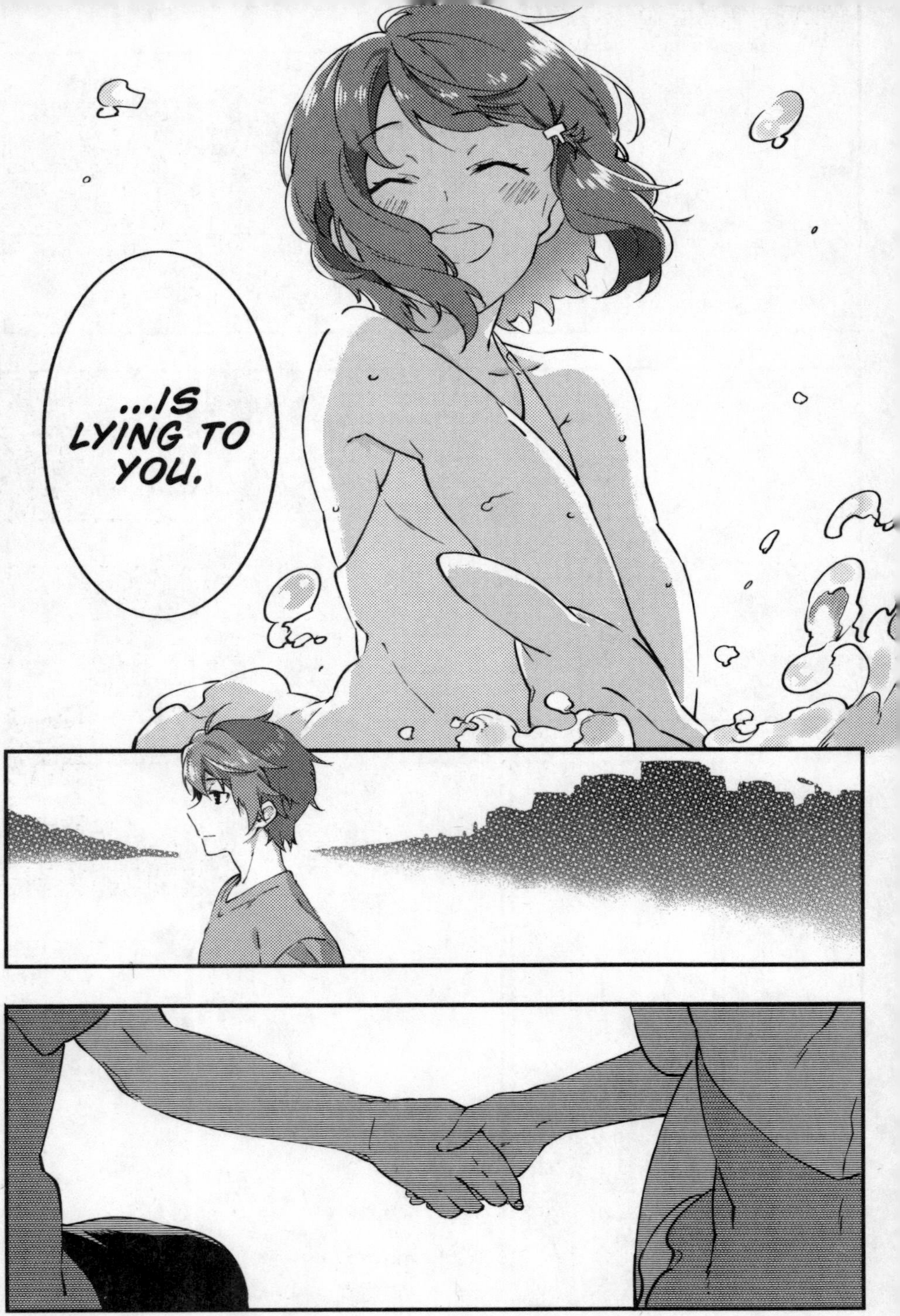
...IS
LYING TO
YOU.

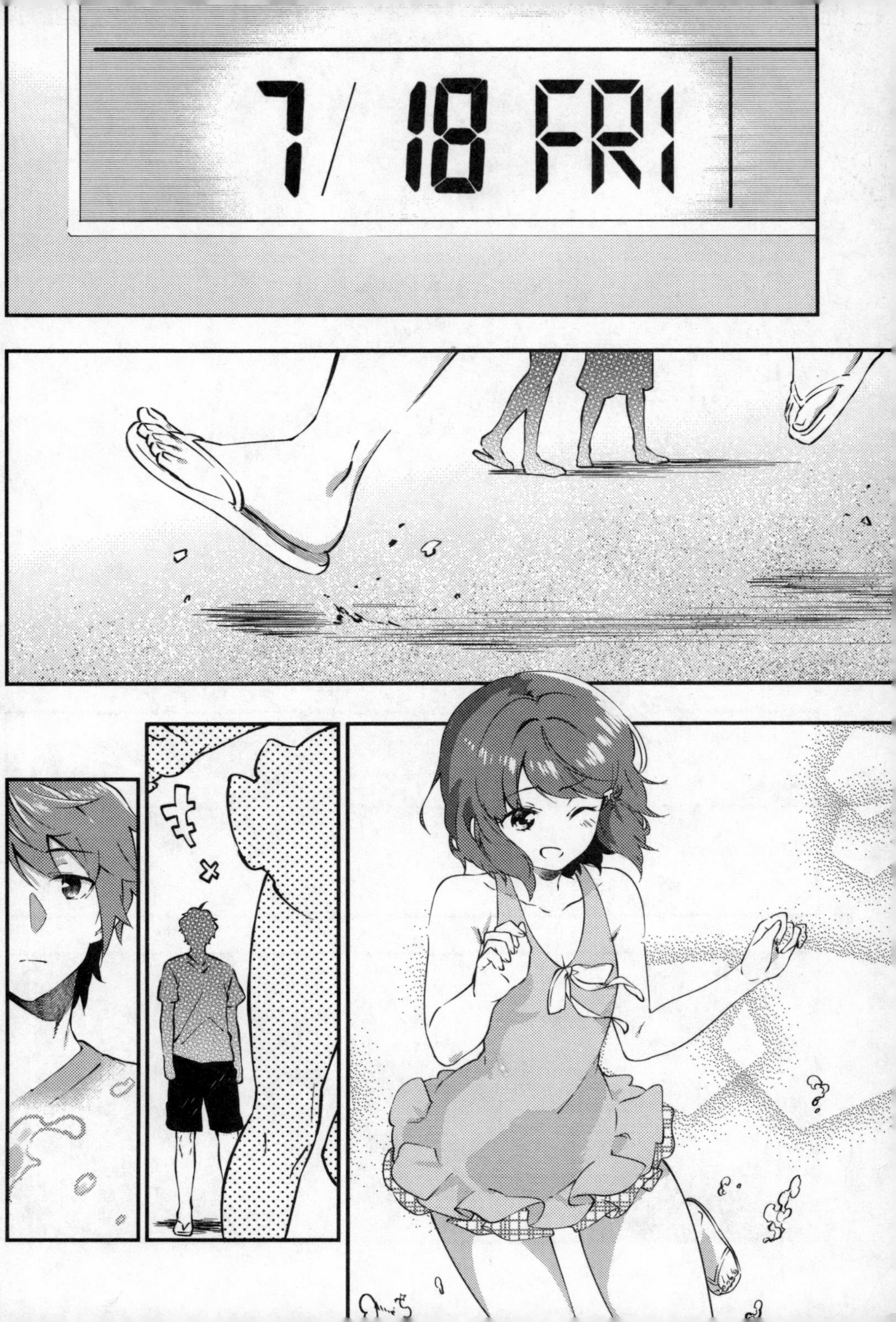
7/18 FRI

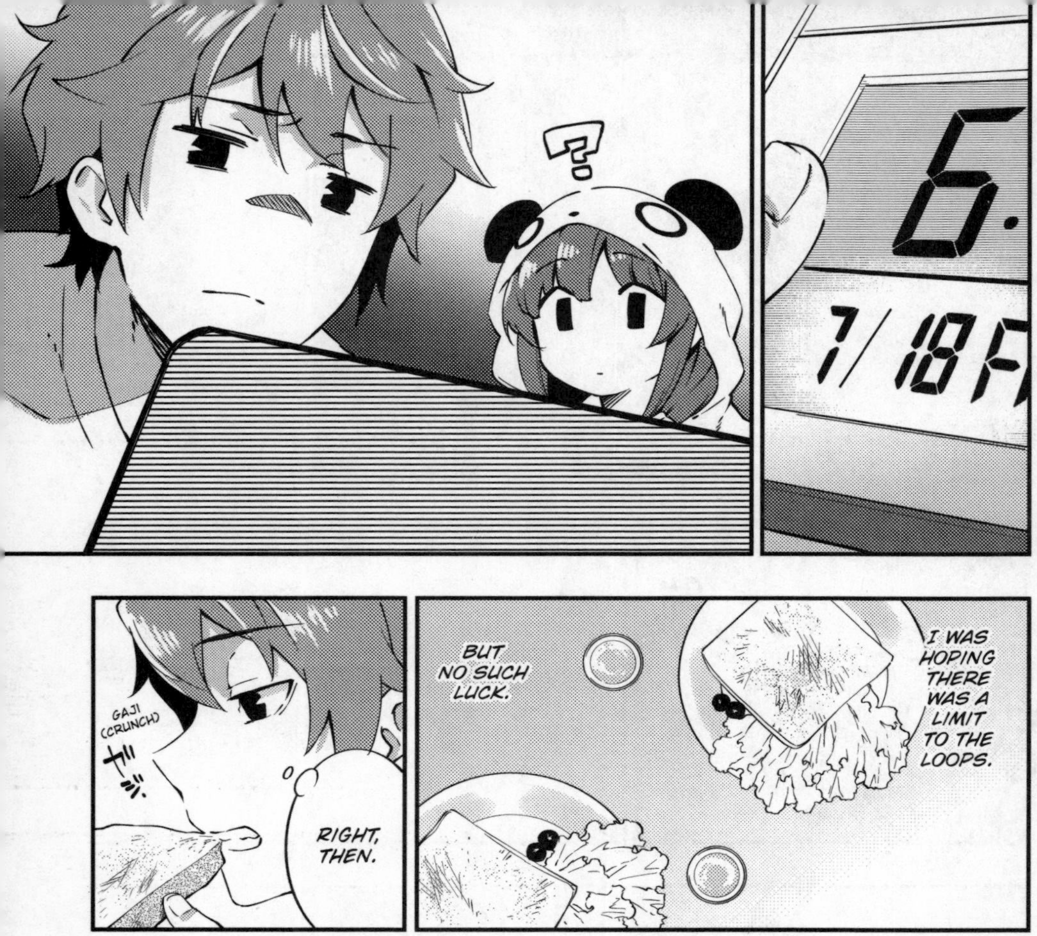
6.
7/18 F
?
I WAS HOPING THERE WAS A LIMIT TO THE LOOPS.
BUT NO SUCH LUCK.
GAJI (CRUNCH)
RIGHT, THEN.

I'LL HAVE TO BANISH LAPLACE'S DEMON.

THAT'S THE ONLY WAY OUT OF THIS MESS.

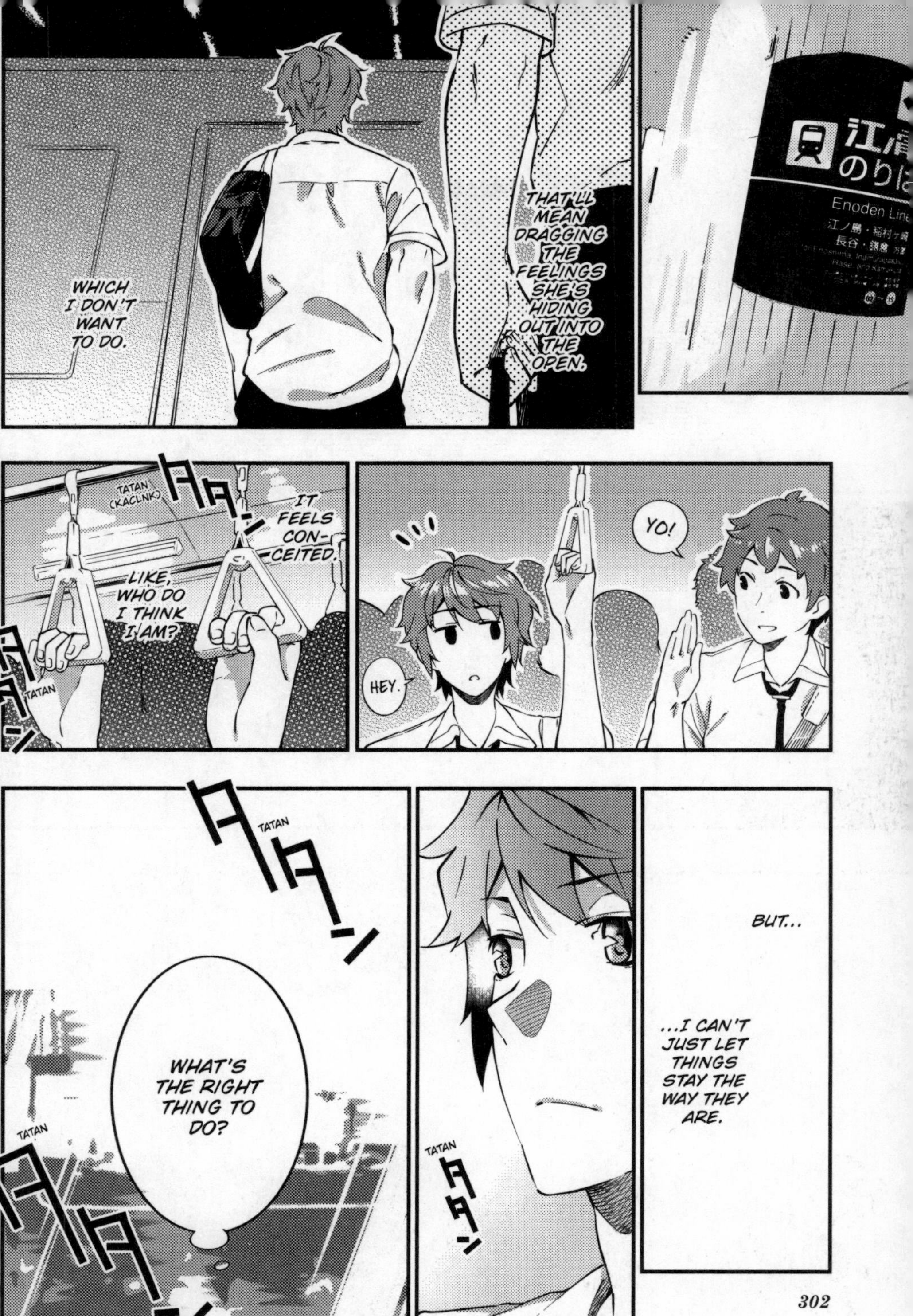
Enoden Line
THAT'LL MEAN DRAGGING THE FEELINGS SHE'S HIDING OUT INTO THE OPEN.
WHICH I DON'T WANT TO DO.
YO!
HEY.
IT FEELS CONCEITED.
LIKE, WHO DO I THINK I AM?
TATAN (KACLNK)
TATAN
BUT...
...I CAN'T JUST LET THINGS STAY THE WAY THEY ARE.
TATAN
TATAN
WHAT'S THE RIGHT THING TO DO?
TATAN

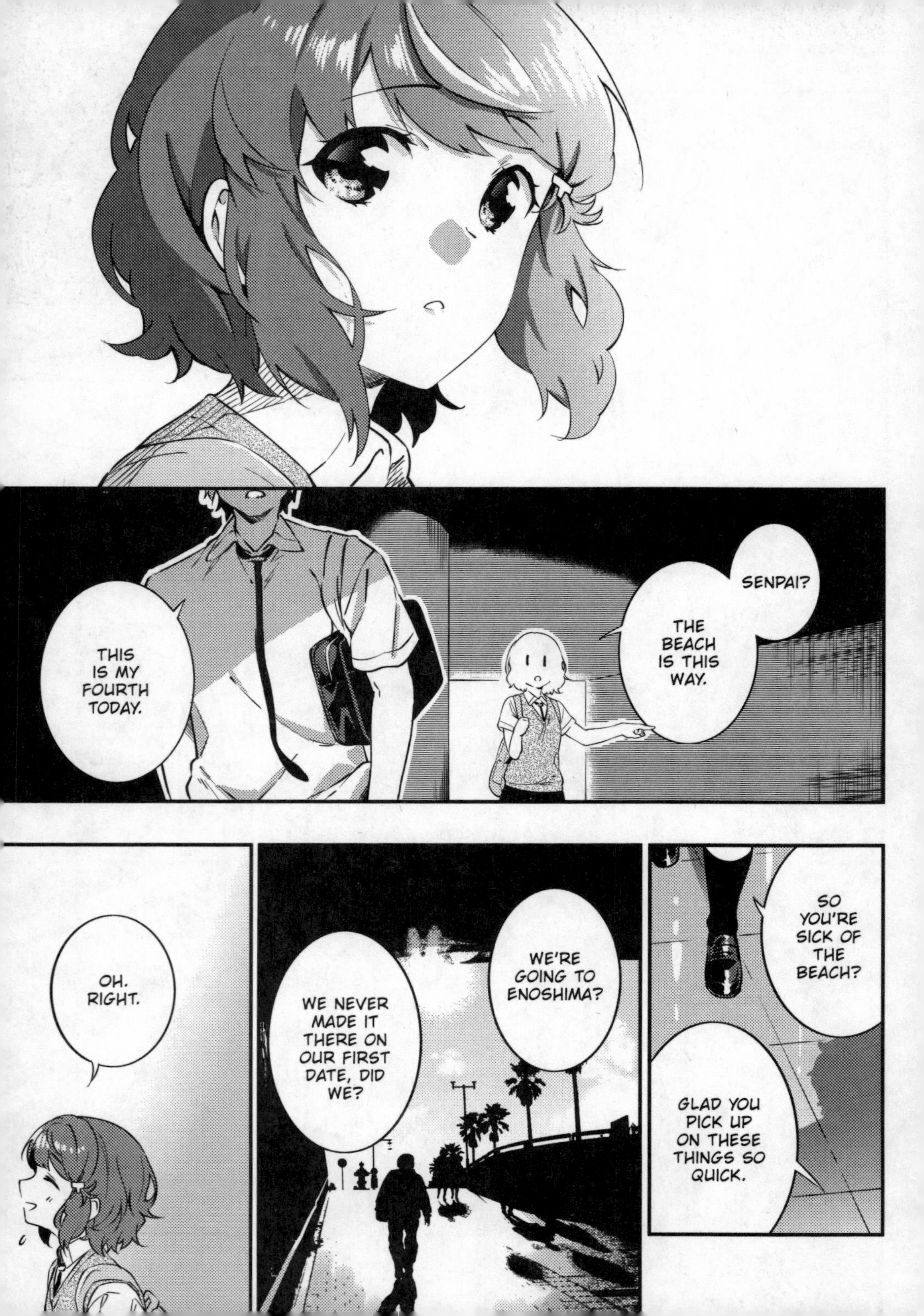
SENPAI?
THE BEACH IS THIS WAY.
THIS IS MY FOURTH TODAY.
SO YOU'RE SICK OF THE BEACH?
GLAD YOU PICK UP ON THESE THINGS SO QUICK.
WE'RE GOING TO ENOSHIMA?
WE NEVER MADE IT THERE ON OUR FIRST DATE, DID WE?
OH. RIGHT.

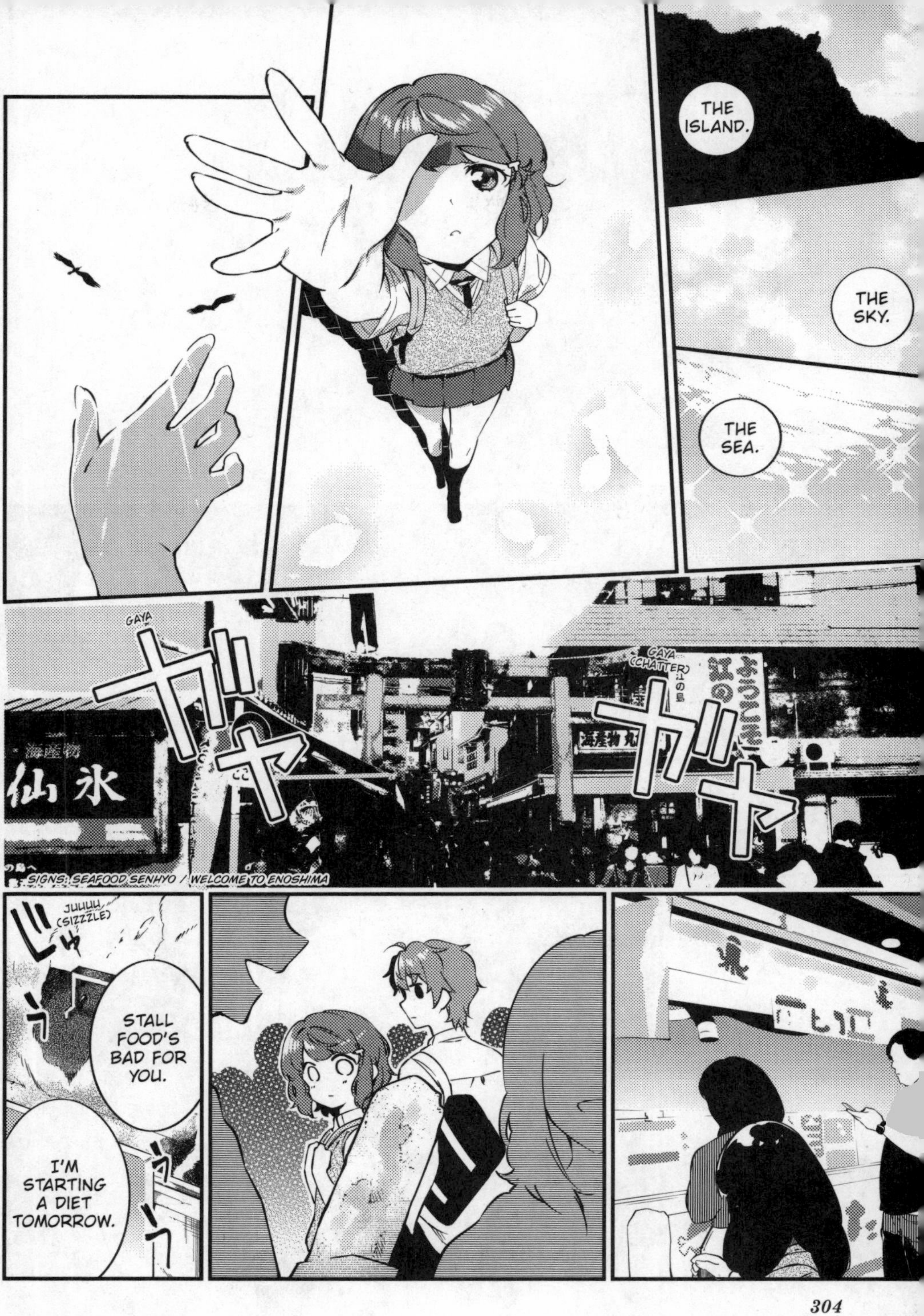
THE ISLAND.
THE SKY.
THE SEA.
GAYA (CHATTER)
GAYA
SIGNS: SEAFOOD SENHYO / WELCOME TO ENOSHIMA
JUUUU (SIZZZLE)
STALL FOOD'S BAD FOR YOU.
I'M STARTING A DIET TOMORROW.

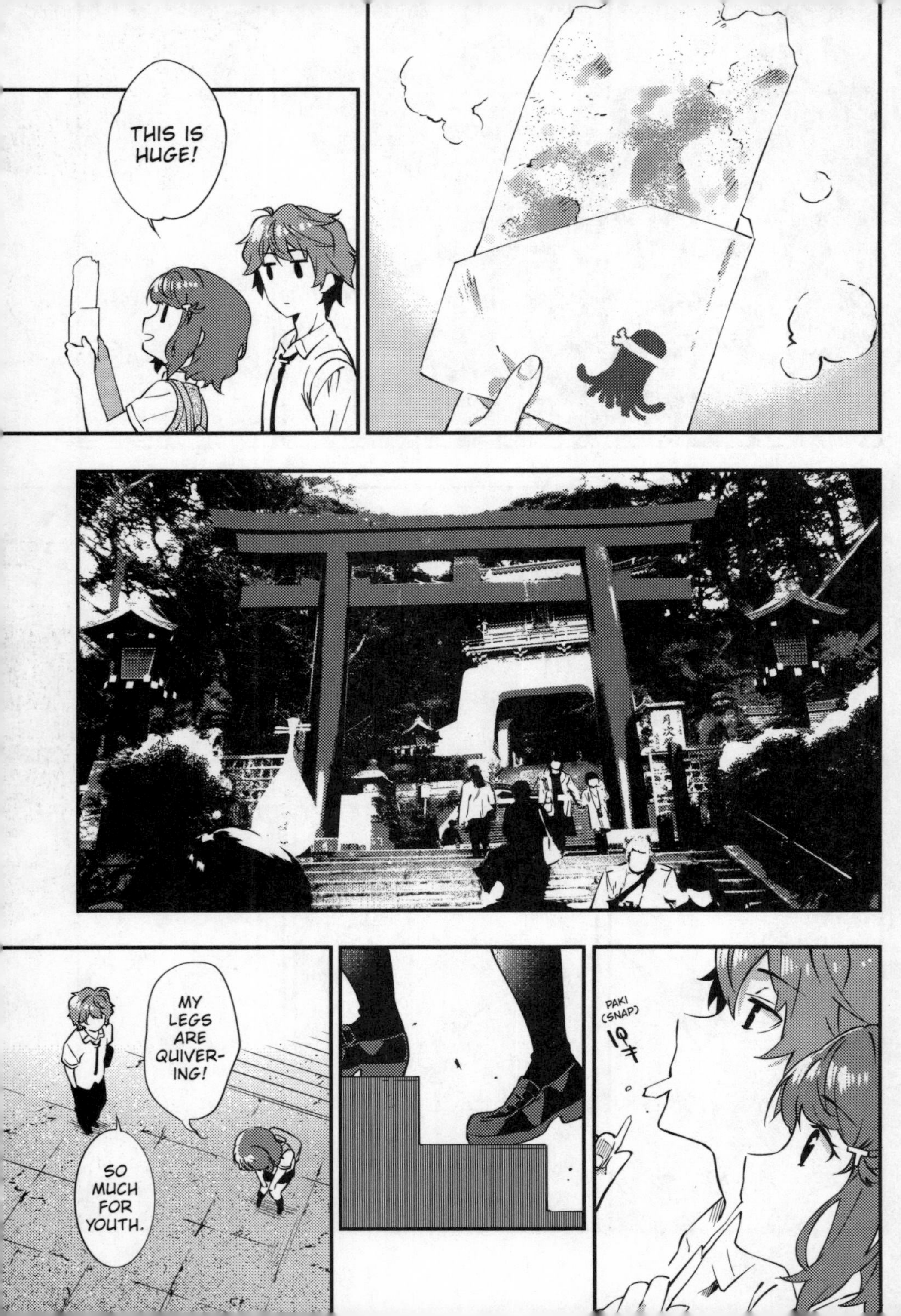
THIS IS HUGE!
PAKI (SNAP)
MY LEGS ARE QUIVERING!
SO MUCH FOR YOUTH.

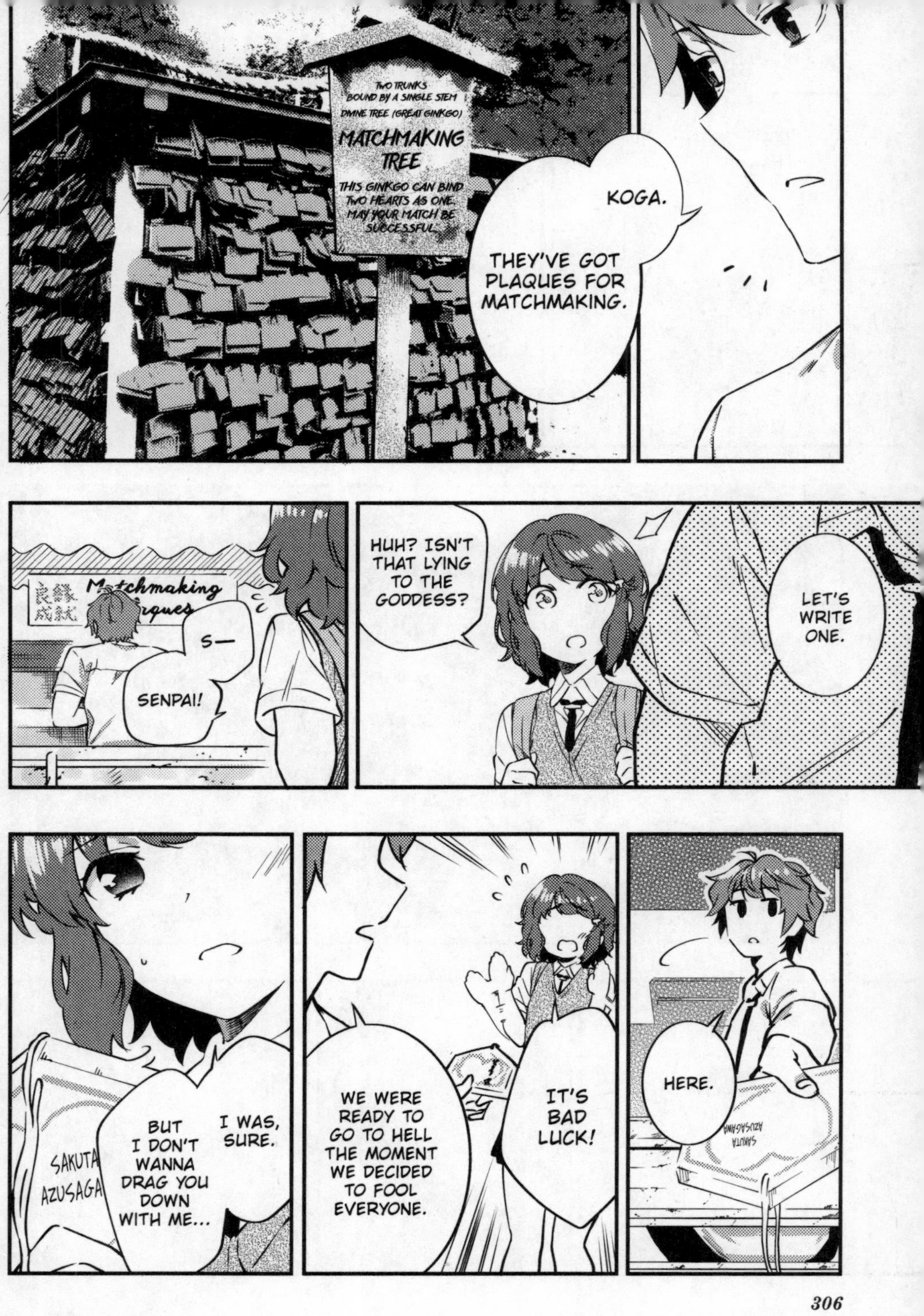
KOGA.
THEY'VE GOT PLAQUES FOR MATCHMAKING.
TWO TRUNKS BOUND BY A SINGLE STEM
DIVINE TREE (GREAT GINKGO)
MATCHMAKING TREE
THIS GINKGO CAN BIND TWO HEARTS AS ONE. MAY YOUR MATCH BE SUCCESSFUL.
LET'S WRITE ONE.
HUH? ISN'T THAT LYING TO THE GODDESS?
良縁成就
S—
SENPAI!
HERE.
SAKUTA AZUSAGAWA
IT'S BAD LUCK!
WE WERE READY TO GO TO HELL THE MOMENT WE DECIDED TO FOOL EVERYONE.
I WAS, SURE.
BUT I DON'T WANNA DRAG YOU DOWN WITH ME...
SAKUTA AZUSAGA

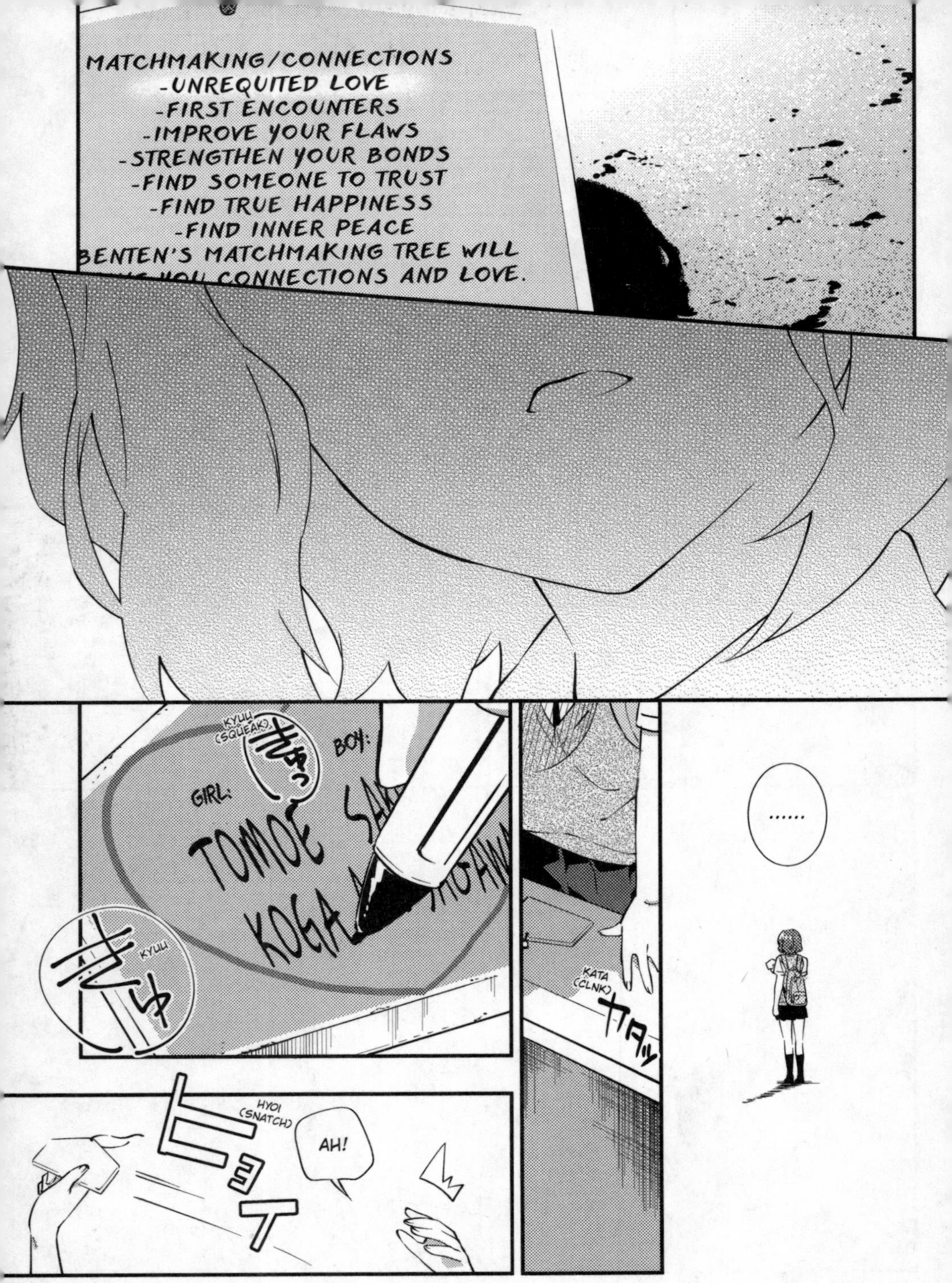
MATCHMAKING/CONNECTIONS
-UNREQUITED LOVE
-FIRST ENCOUNTERS
-IMPROVE YOUR FLAWS
-STRENGTHEN YOUR BONDS
-FIND SOMEONE TO TRUST
-FIND TRUE HAPPINESS
-FIND INNER PEACE
BENTEN'S MATCHMAKING TREE WILL
YOU CONNECTIONS AND LOVE.
......
KATA (CLNK)
KYUU (SQUEAK)
BOY:
GIRL:
TOMOE
KOGA
KYUU
HYOI (SNATCH)
AH!

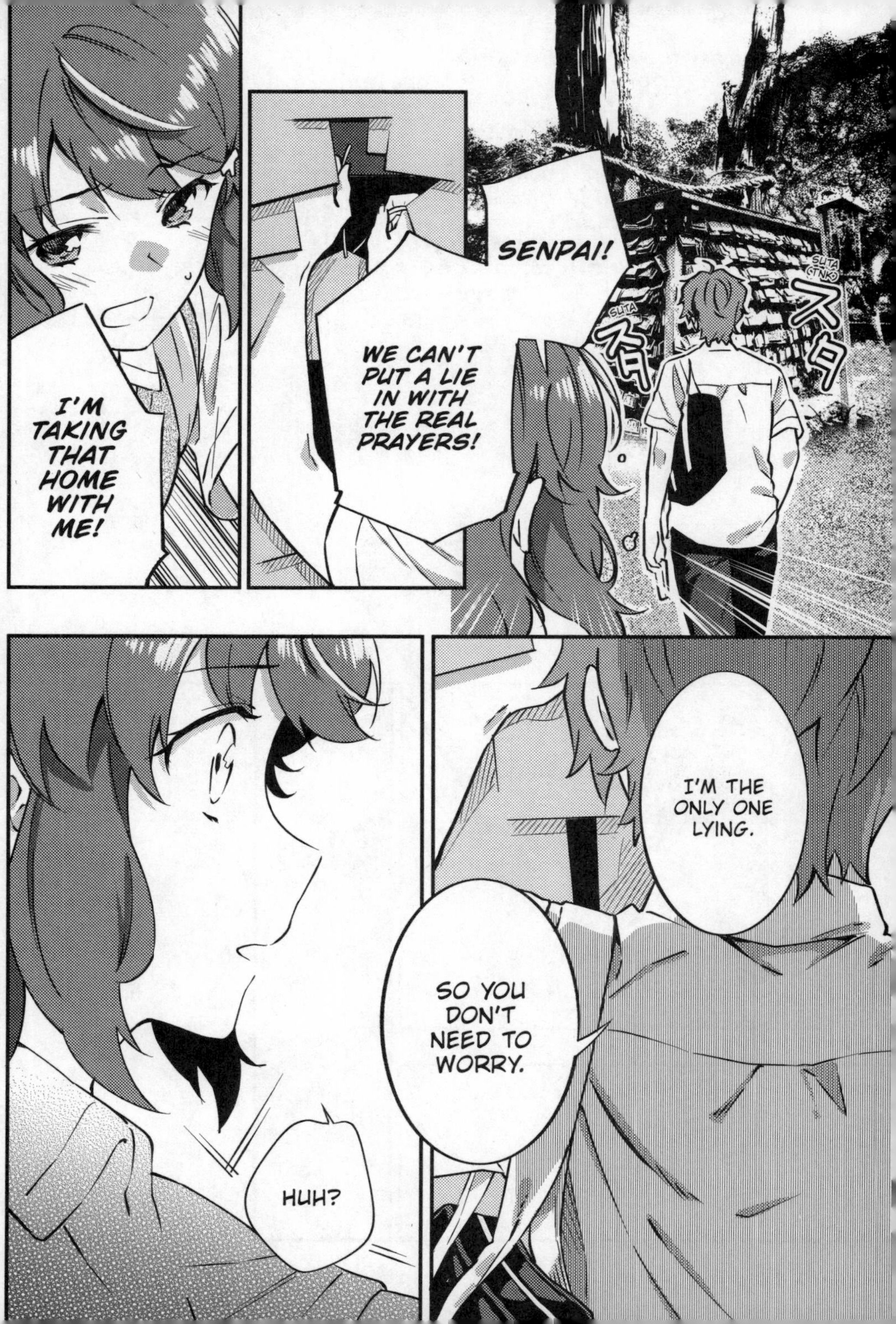
SUTA (TNK)
スタ
SENPAI!
SUTA
スタ
WE CAN'T PUT A LIE IN WITH THE REAL PRAYERS!
I'M TAKING THAT HOME WITH ME!
I'M THE ONLY ONE LYING.
SO YOU DON'T NEED TO WORRY.
HUH?

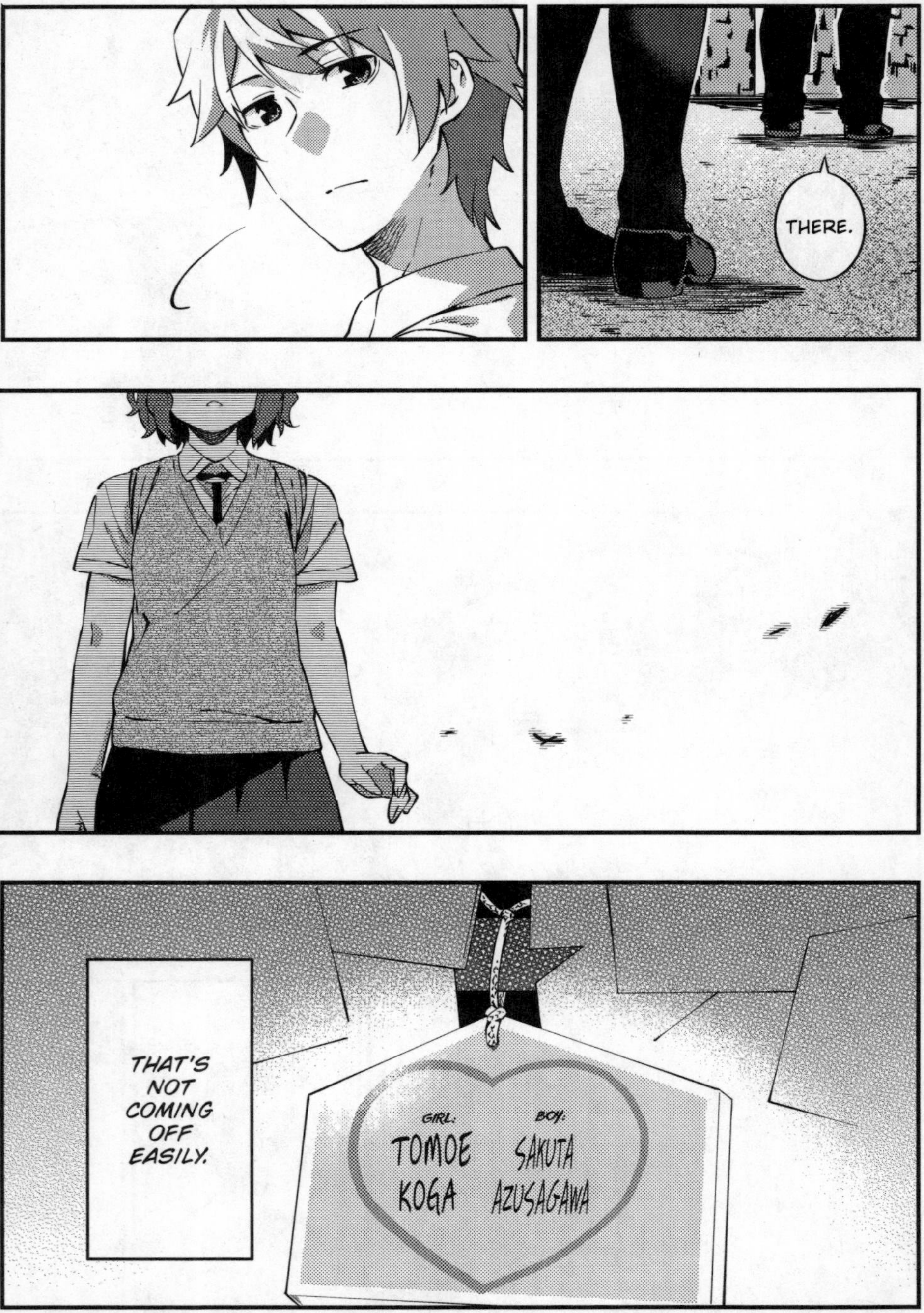
THERE.
THAT'S NOT COMING OFF EASILY.
GIRL:
TOMOE KOGA
BOY:
SAKUTA AZUSAGAWA

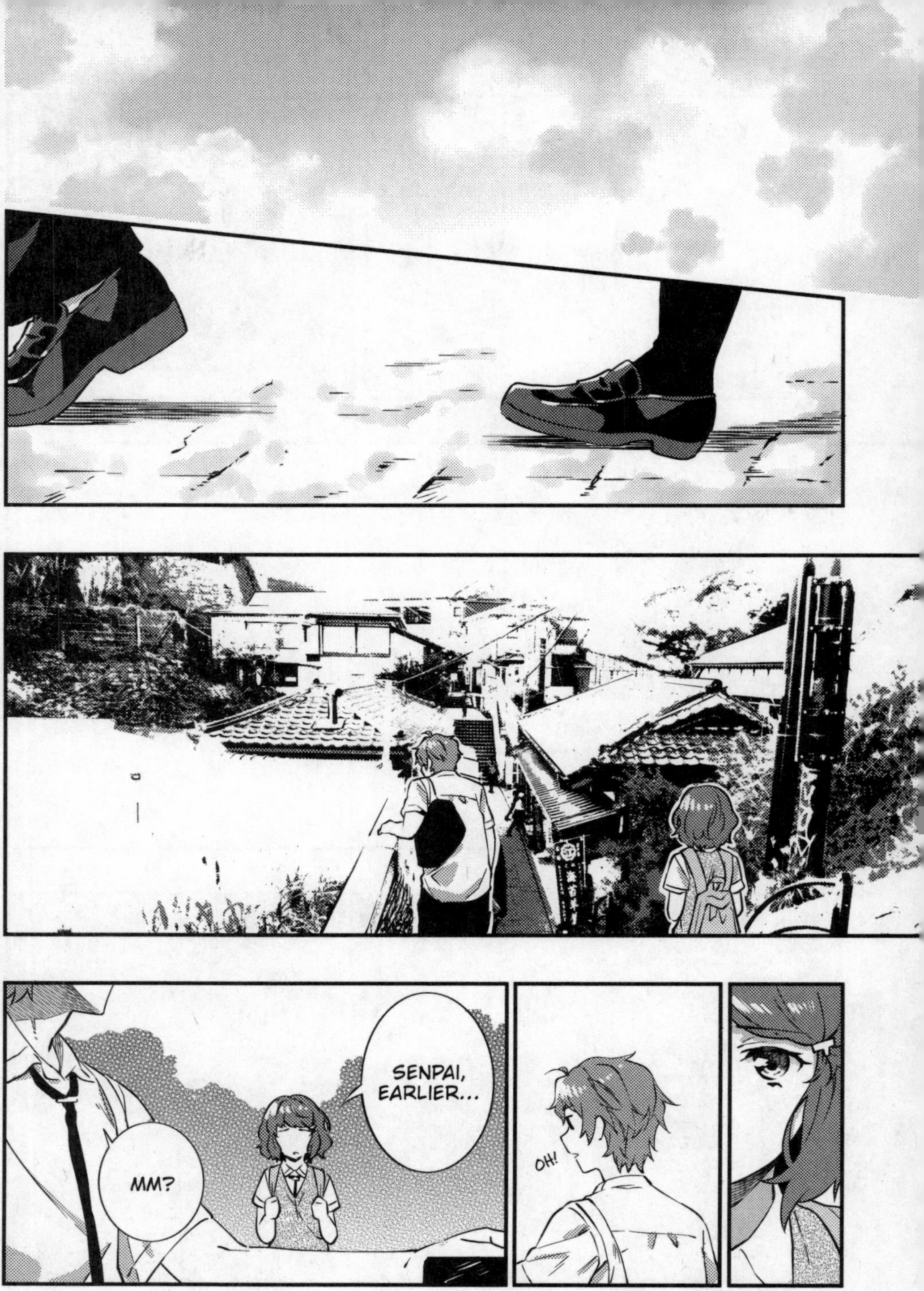
OH!
SENPAI, EARLIER...
MM?

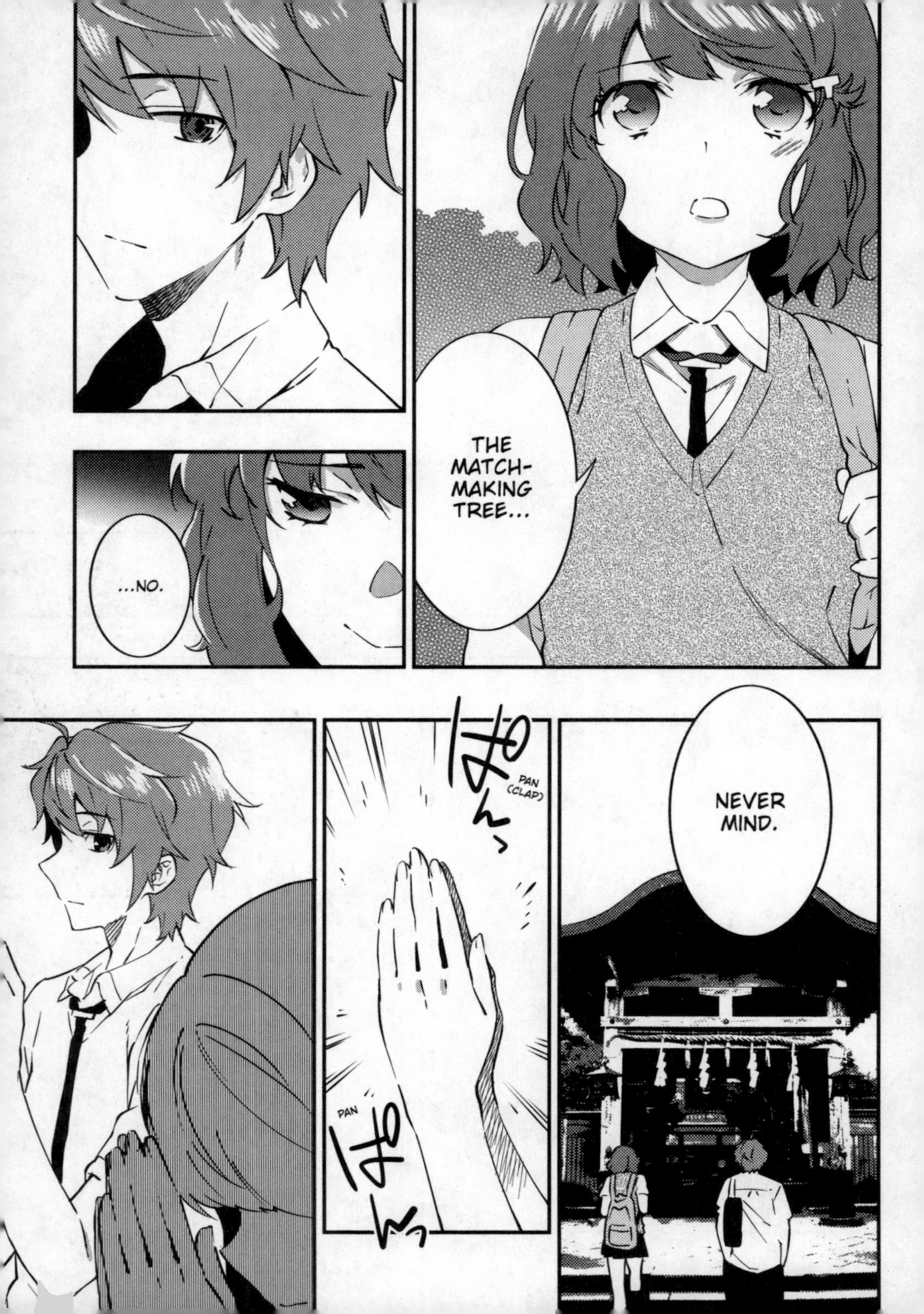
THE MATCH-MAKING TREE...
...NO.
NEVER MIND.
ぱん
PAN (CLAP)
ぱん
PAN

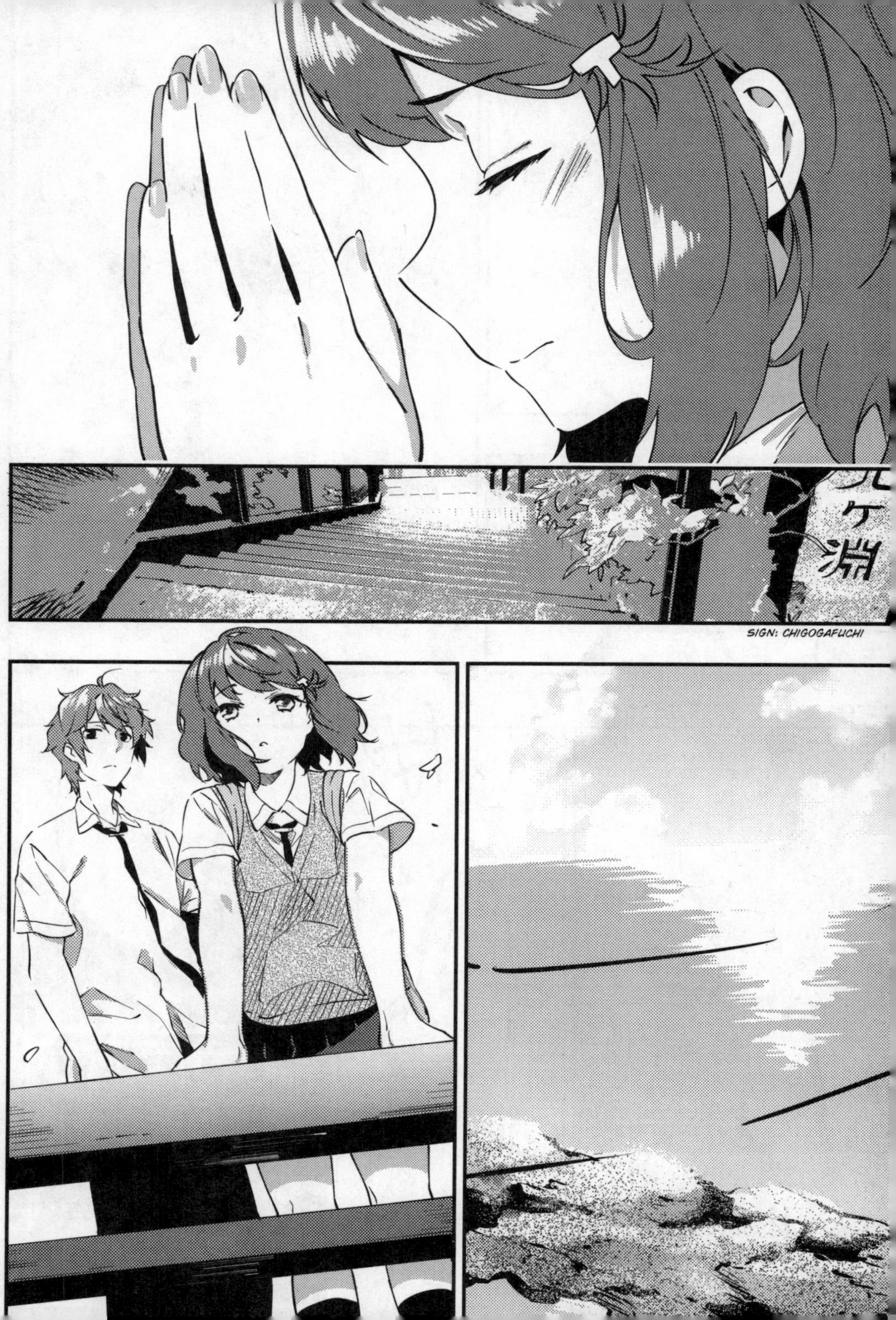
ケ淵
SIGN: CHIGOGAFUCHI

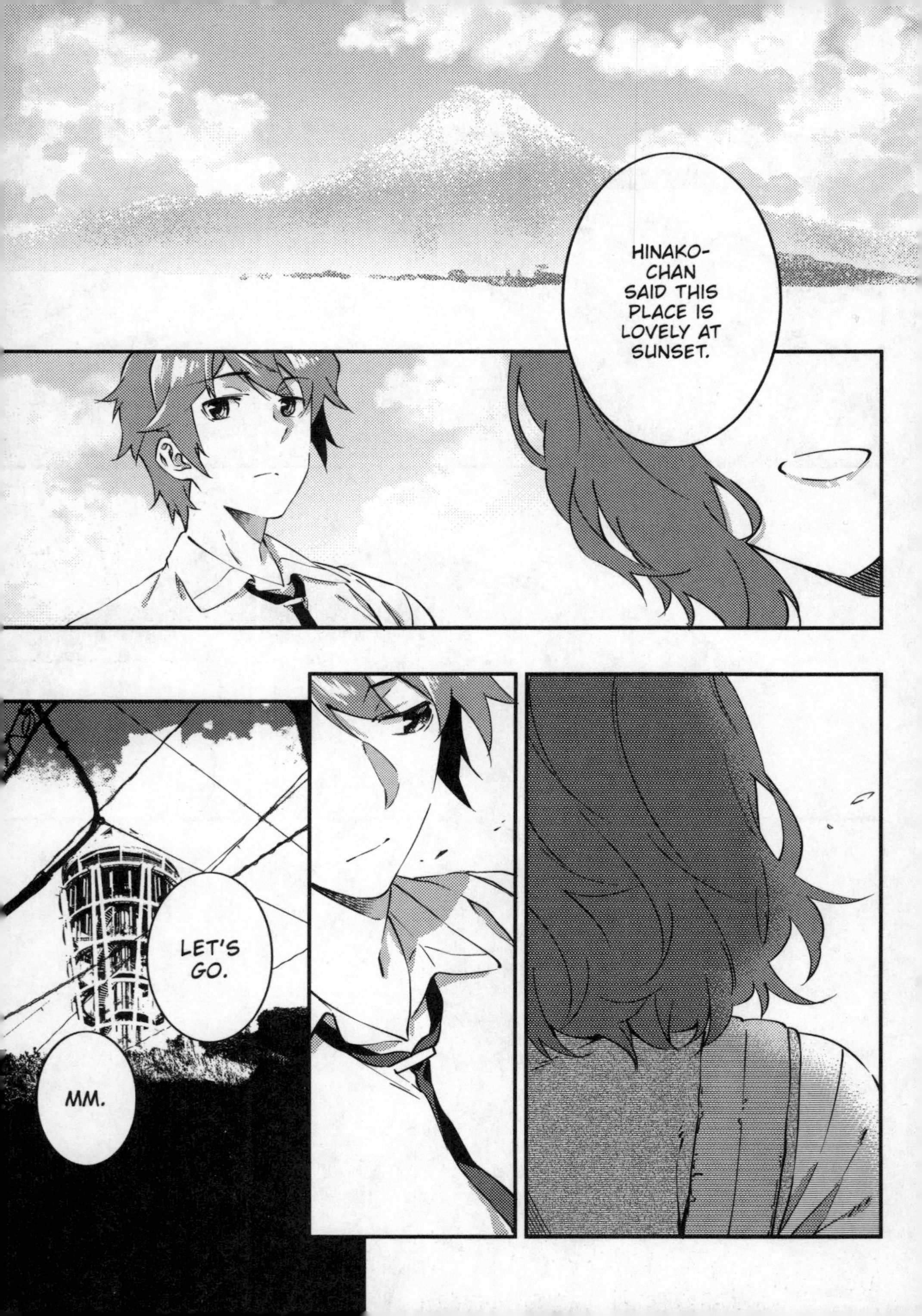
HINAKO-CHAN SAID THIS PLACE IS LOVELY AT SUNSET.
LET'S GO.
MM.

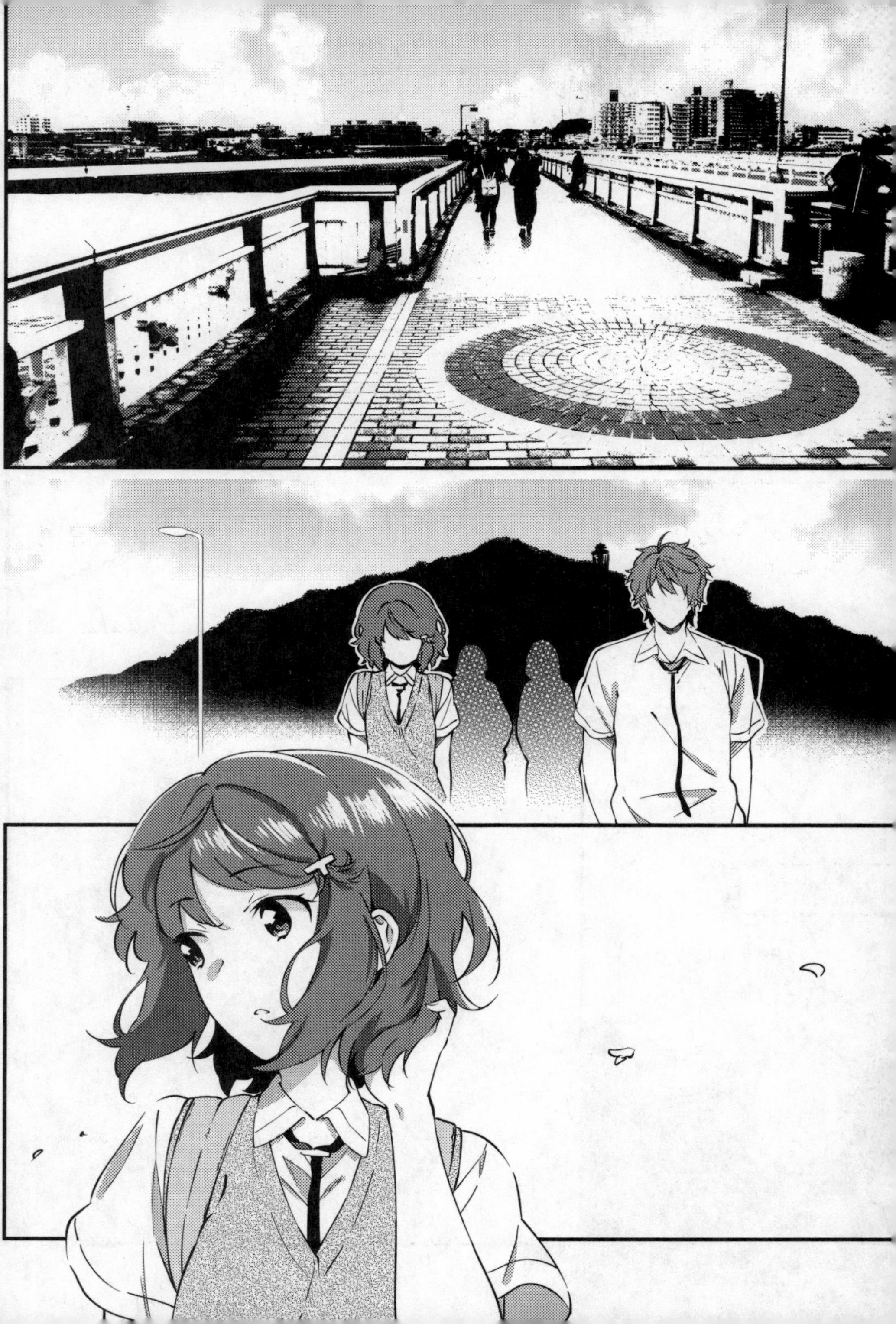

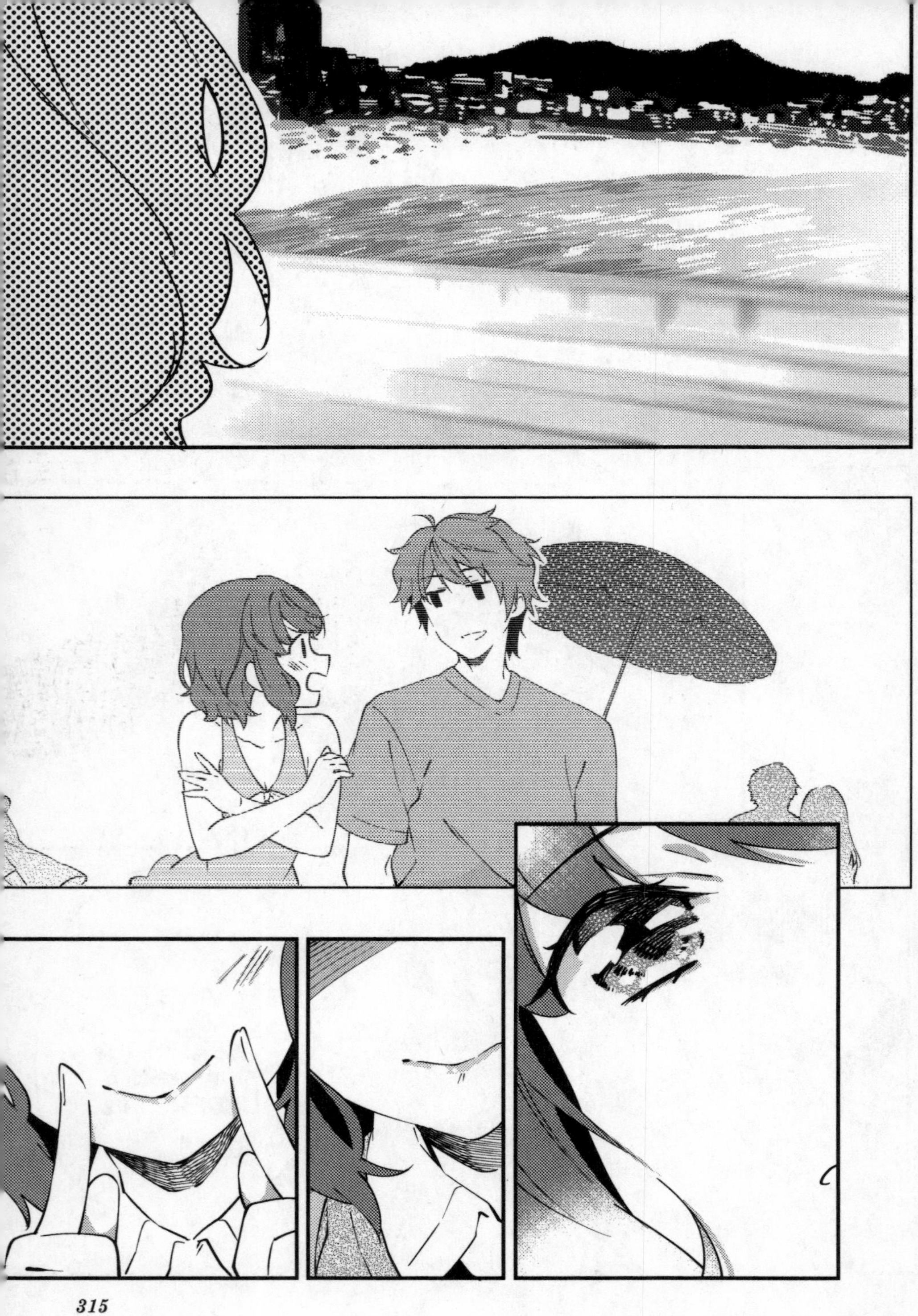

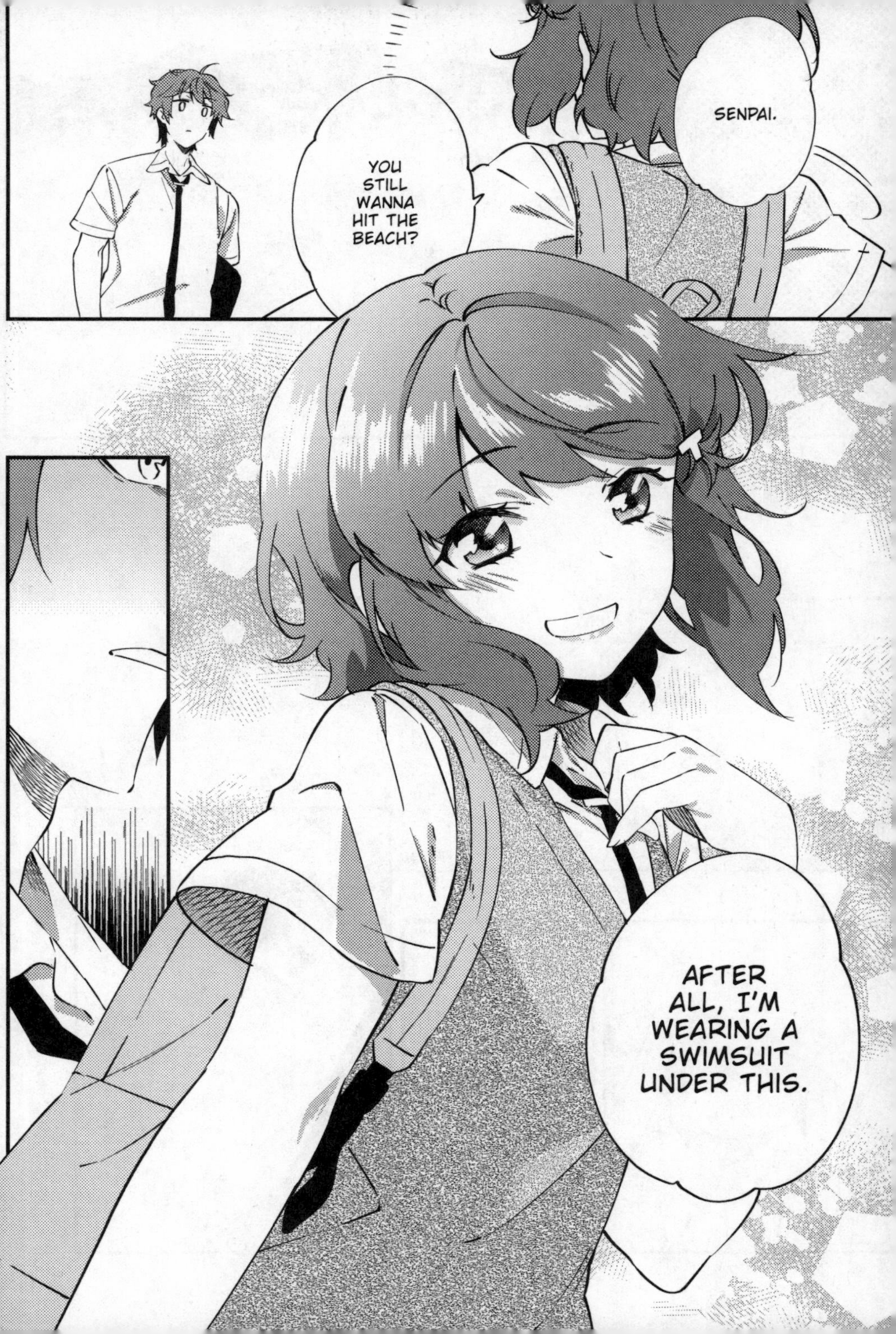
SENPAI.
YOU STILL WANNA HIT THE BEACH?
AFTER ALL, I'M WEARING A SWIMSUIT UNDER THIS.

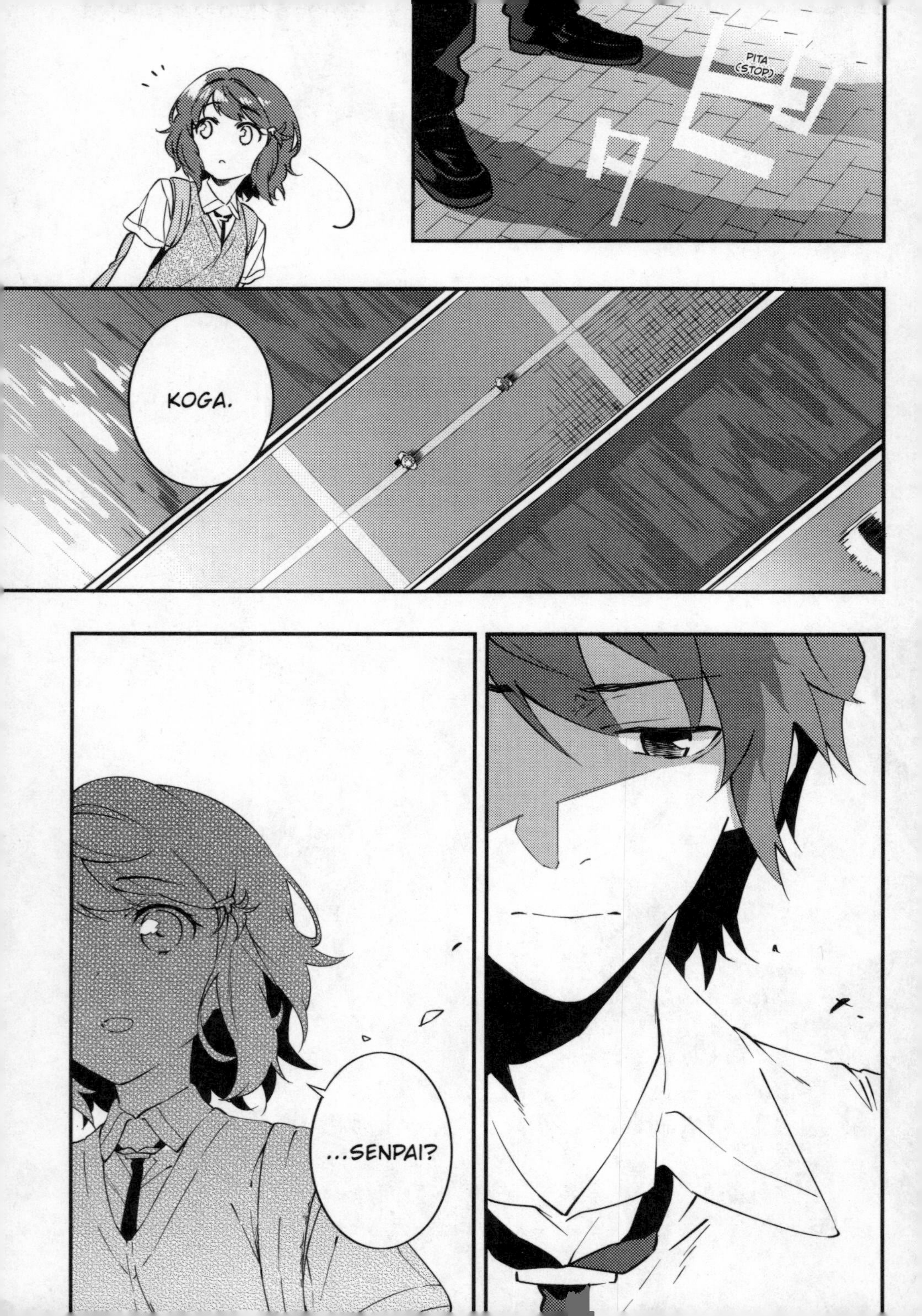
PITA
(STOP)
KOGA.
...SENPAI?

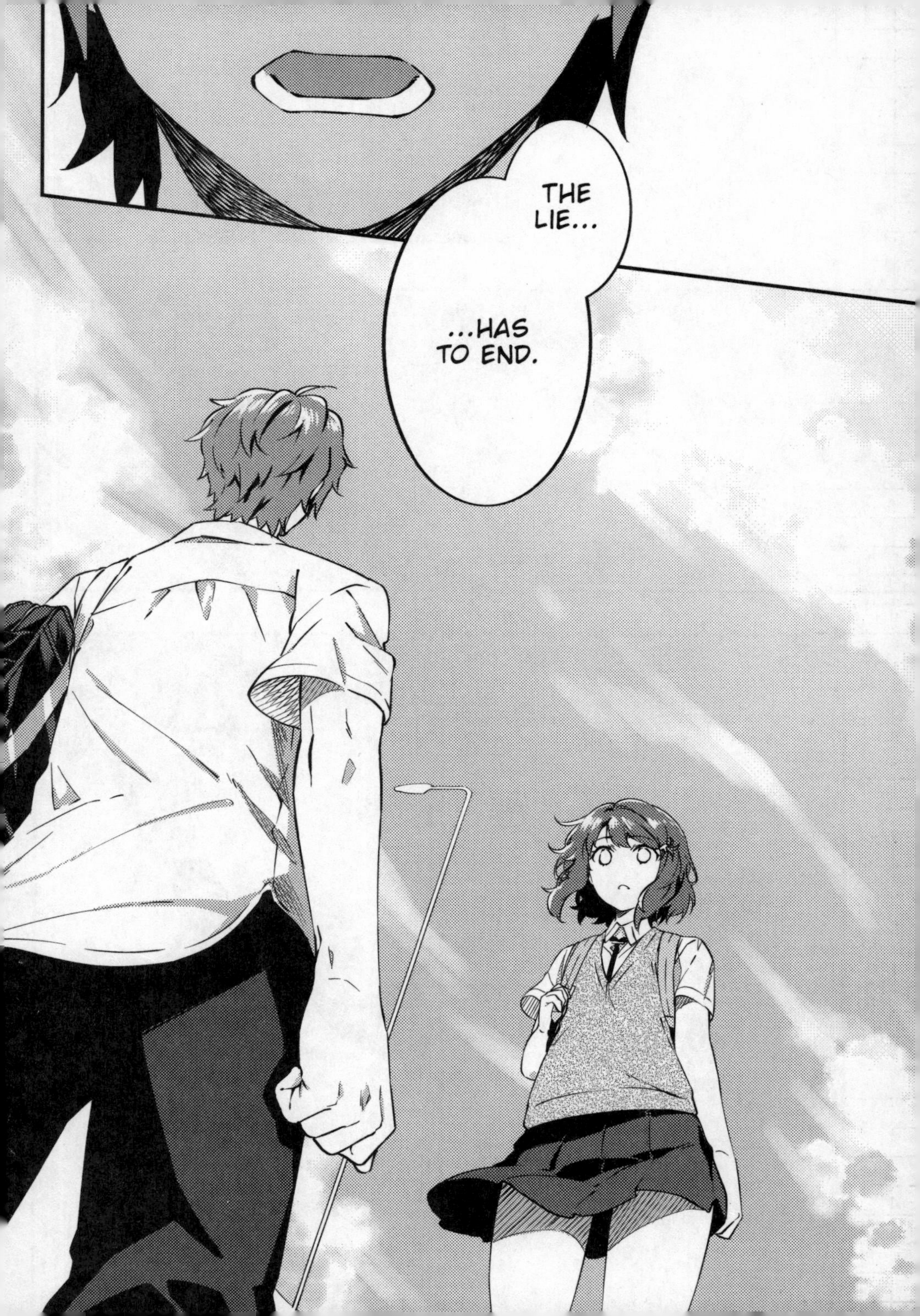
THE LIE...
...HAS TO END.

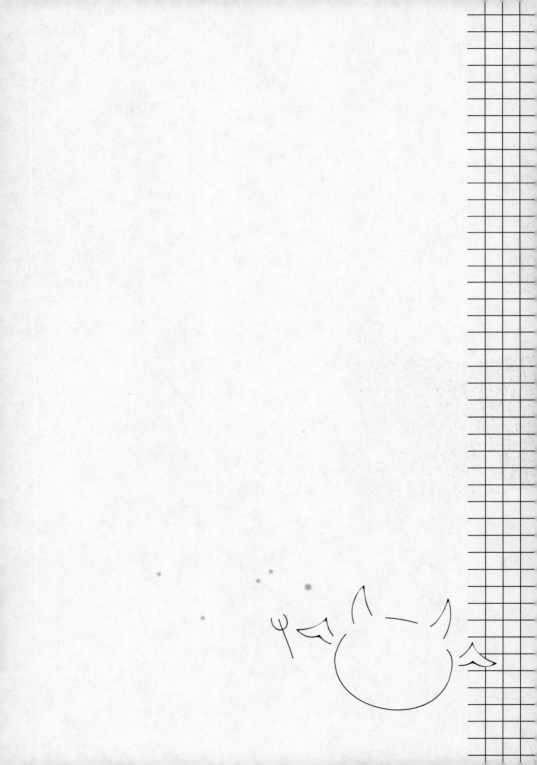

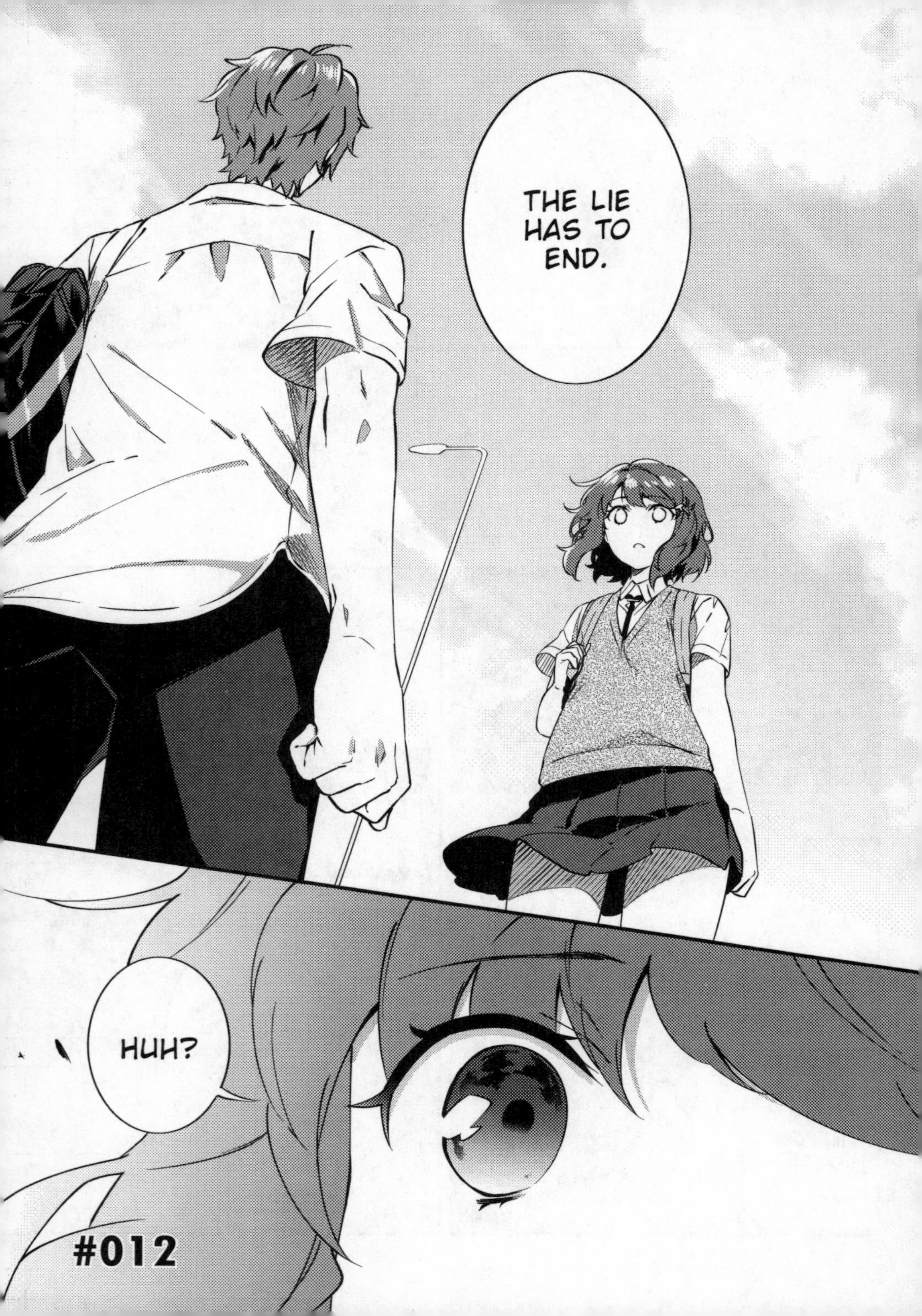
THE LIE HAS TO END.
HUH?
#012

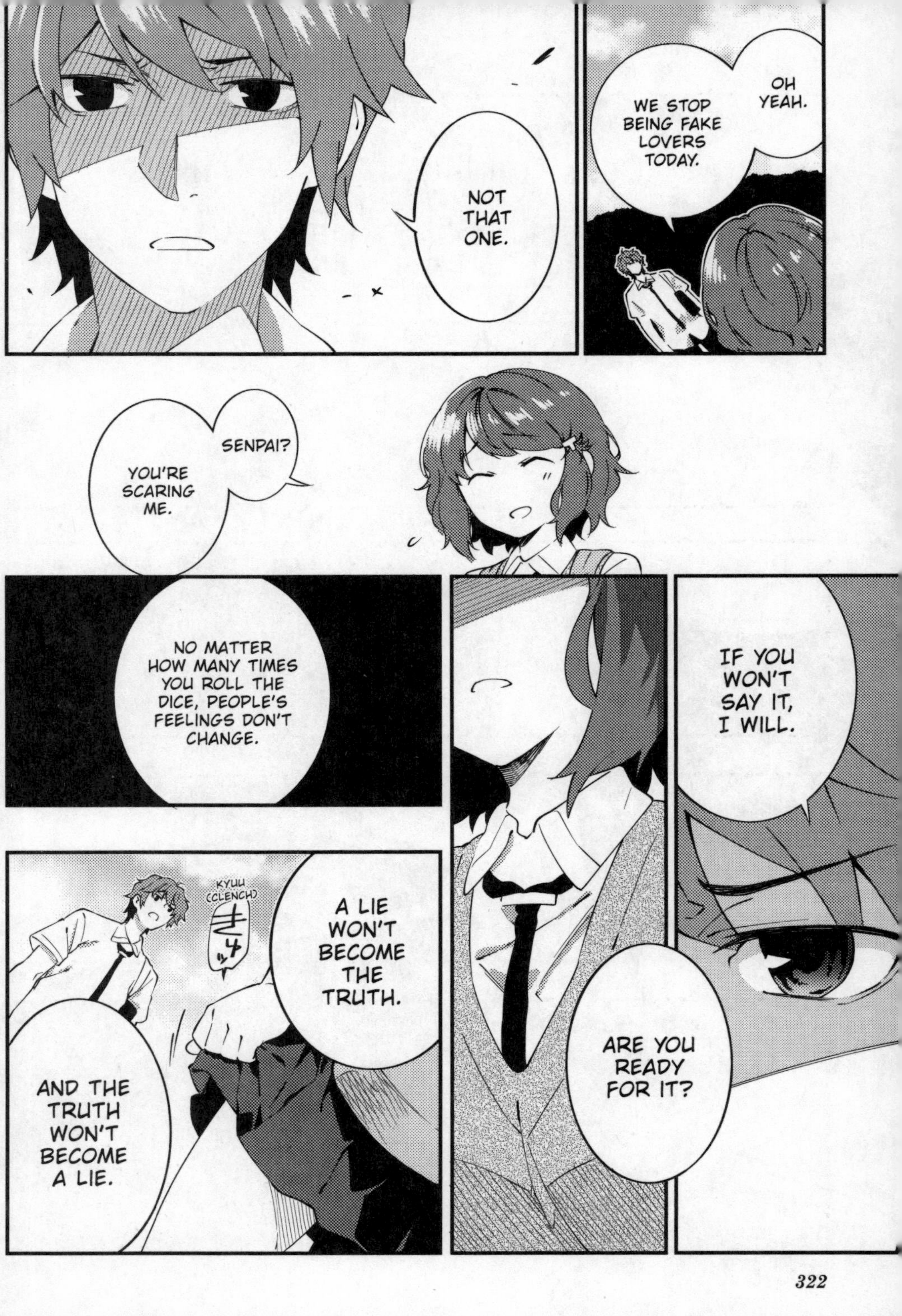
OH YEAH.
WE STOP BEING FAKE LOVERS TODAY.
NOT THAT ONE.
SENPAI?
YOU'RE SCARING ME.
IF YOU WON'T SAY IT, I WILL.
ARE YOU READY FOR IT?
NO MATTER HOW MANY TIMES YOU ROLL THE DICE, PEOPLE'S FEELINGS DON'T CHANGE.
A LIE WON'T BECOME THE TRUTH.
KYUU (CLENCH)
AND THE TRUTH WON'T BECOME A LIE.

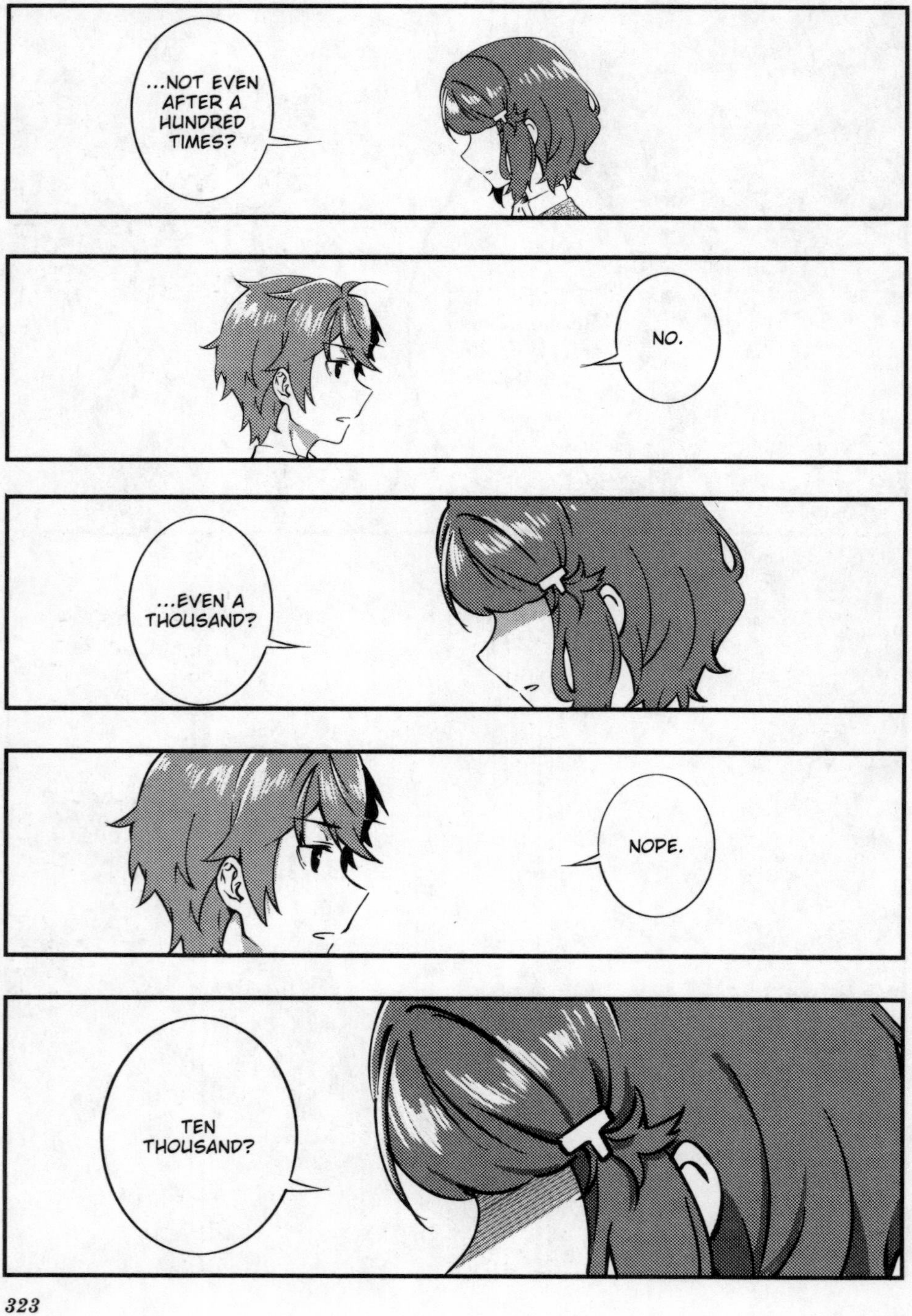

...NOT EVEN AFTER A HUNDRED TIMES?
NO.
...EVEN A THOUSAND?
NOPE.
TEN THOUSAND?

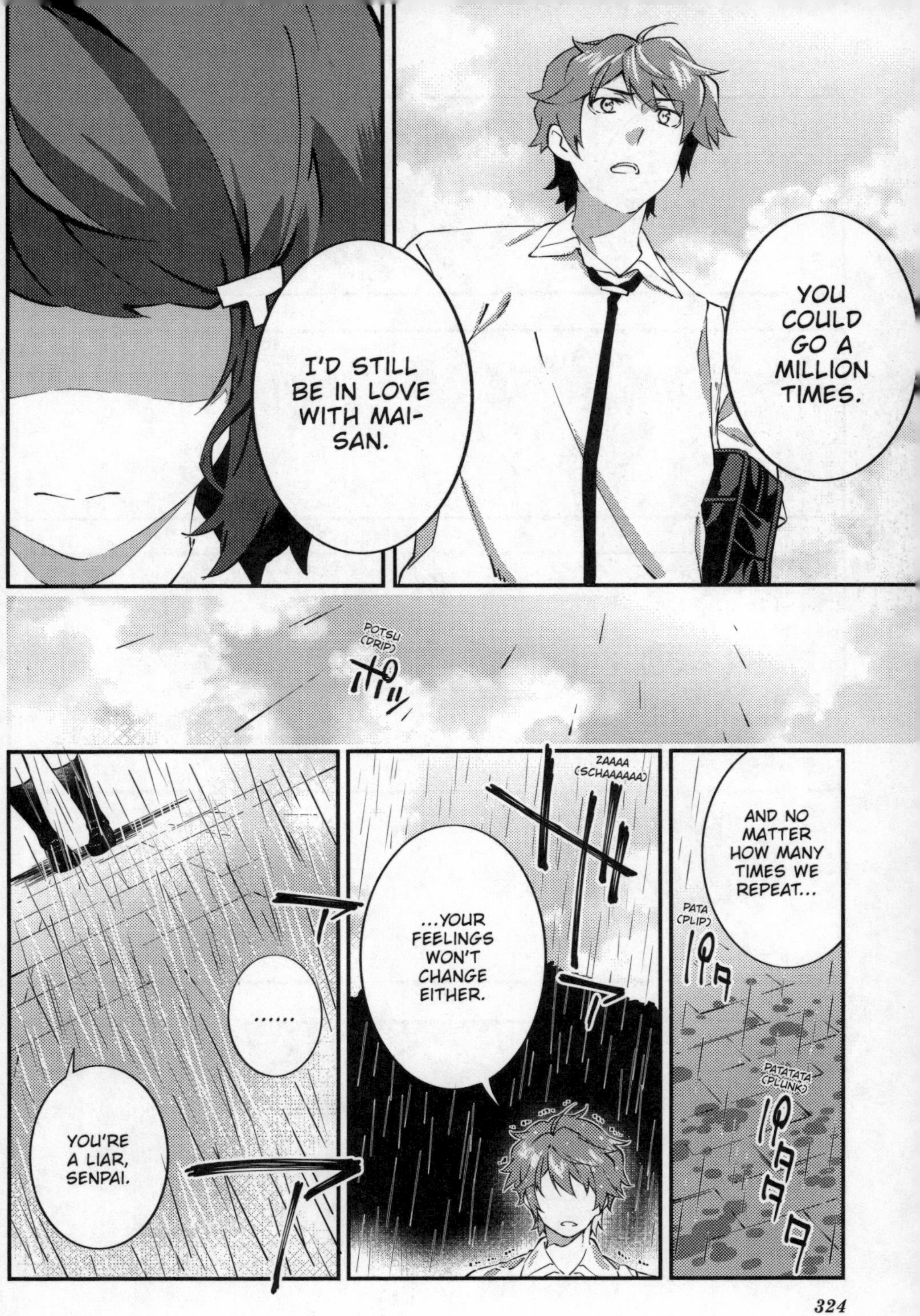
YOU COULD GO A MILLION TIMES.
I'D STILL BE IN LOVE WITH MAI-SAN.
POTSU (DRIP)
AND NO MATTER HOW MANY TIMES WE REPEAT...
PATA (PLIP)
PATATATA (PLUNK)
ZAAAA (SCHAAAAAAA)
...YOUR FEELINGS WON'T CHANGE EITHER.
......
YOU'RE A LIAR, SENPAI.

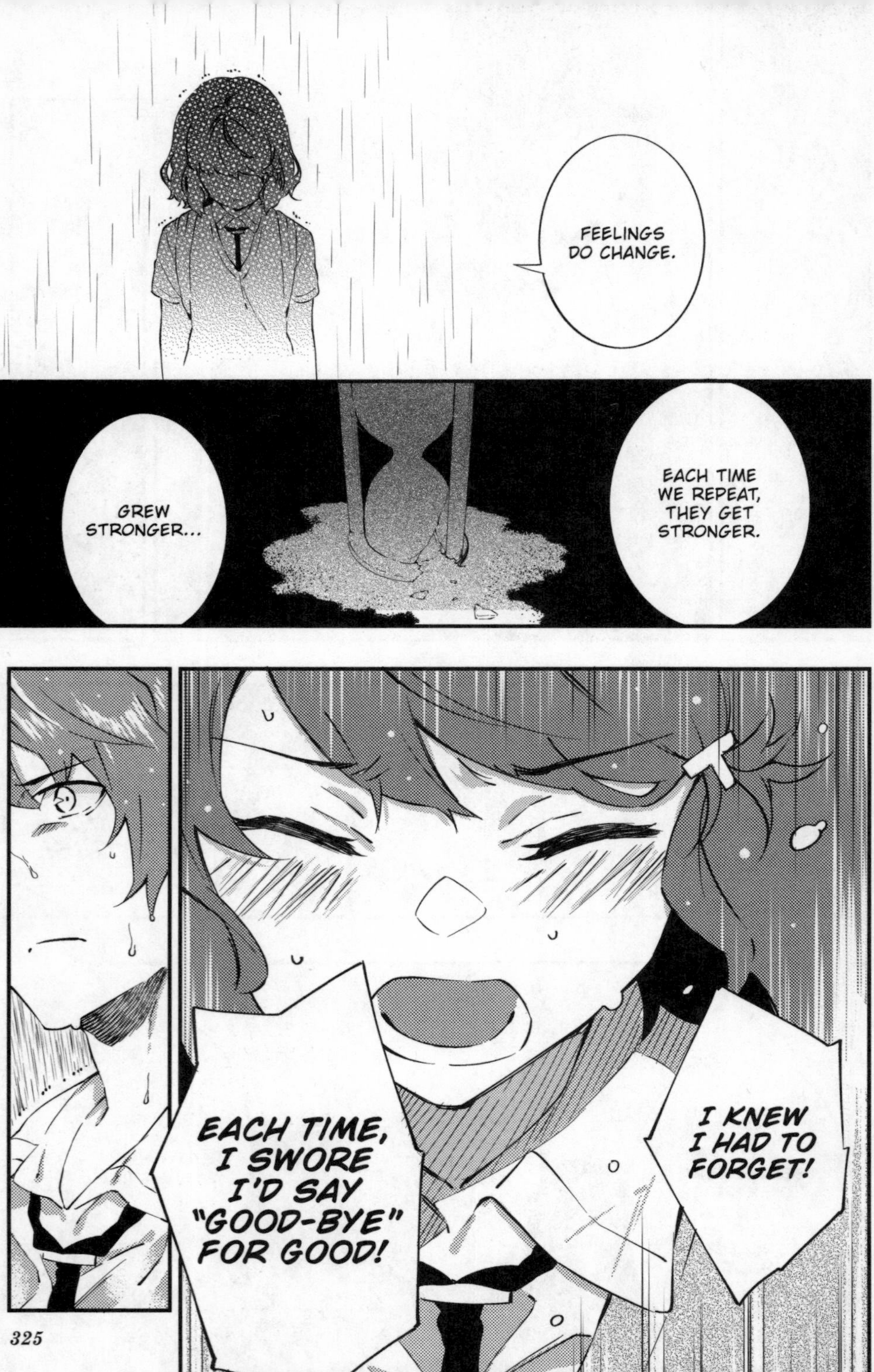
FEELINGS DO CHANGE.
EACH TIME WE REPEAT, THEY GET STRONGER.
GREW STRONGER...
I KNEW I HAD TO FORGET!
EACH TIME, I SWORE I'D SAY "GOOD-BYE" FOR GOOD!

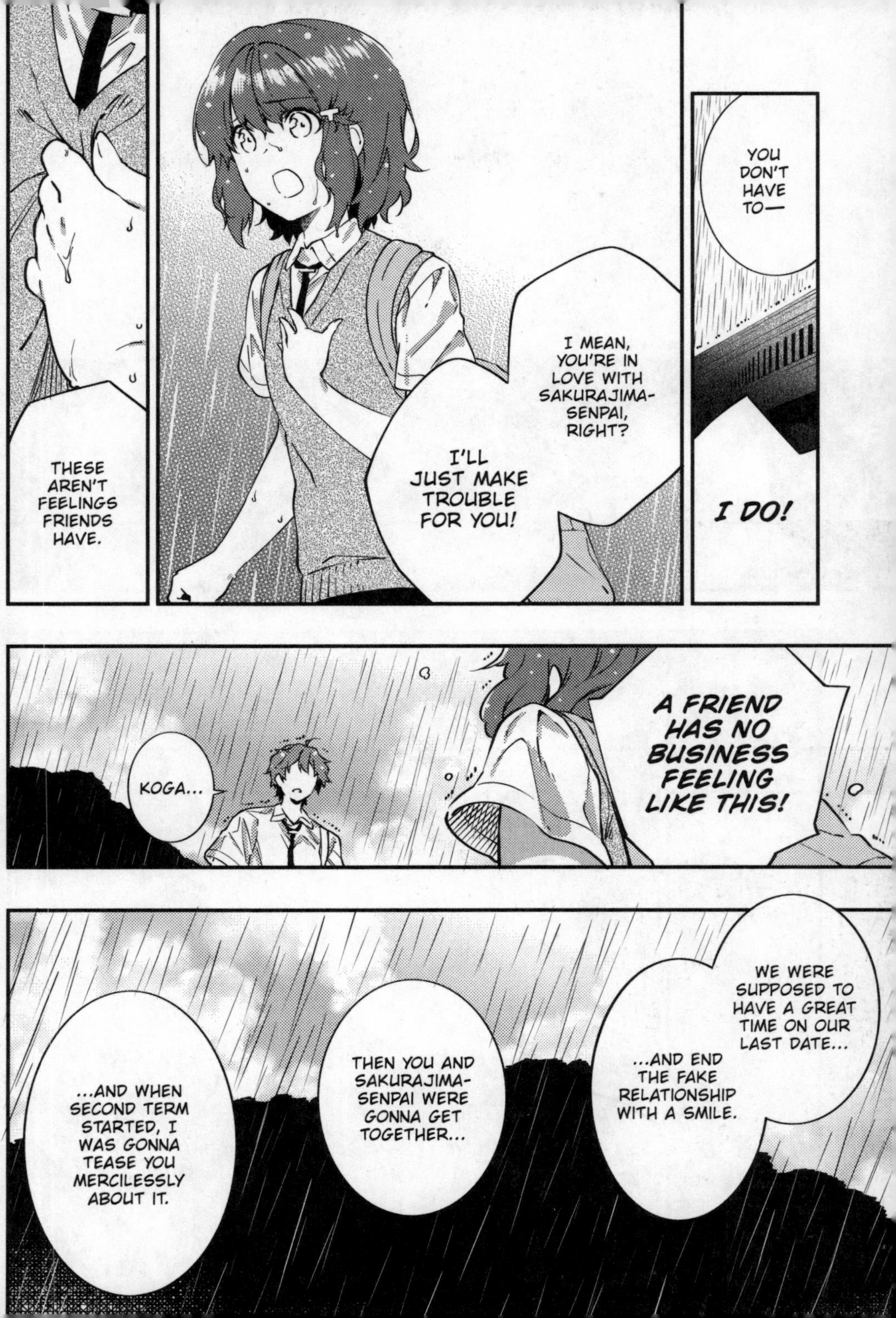
YOU DON'T HAVE TO—
I DO!
I MEAN, YOU'RE IN LOVE WITH SAKURAJIMA-SENPAI, RIGHT?
I'LL JUST MAKE TROUBLE FOR YOU!
THESE AREN'T FEELINGS FRIENDS HAVE.
A FRIEND HAS NO BUSINESS FEELING LIKE THIS!
KOGA...
WE WERE SUPPOSED TO HAVE A GREAT TIME ON OUR LAST DATE...
...AND END THE FAKE RELATIONSHIP WITH A SMILE.
THEN YOU AND SAKURAJIMA-SENPAI WERE GONNA GET TOGETHER...
...AND WHEN SECOND TERM STARTED, I WAS GONNA TEASE YOU MERCILESSLY ABOUT IT.

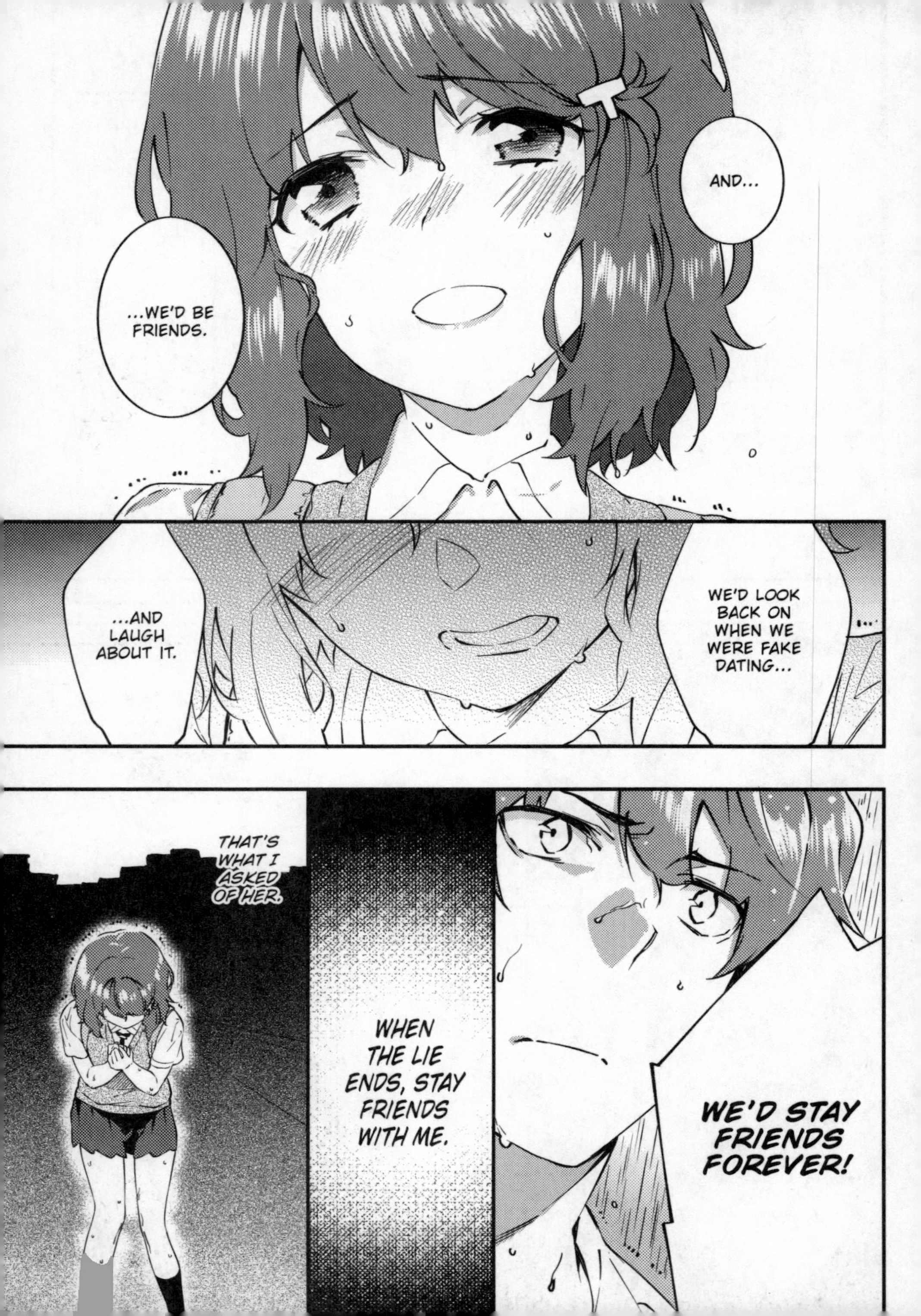
AND...
...WE'D BE FRIENDS.
WE'D LOOK BACK ON WHEN WE WERE FAKE DATING...
...AND LAUGH ABOUT IT.
WE'D STAY FRIENDS FOREVER!
WHEN THE LIE ENDS, STAY FRIENDS WITH ME.
THAT'S WHAT I ASKED OF HER.

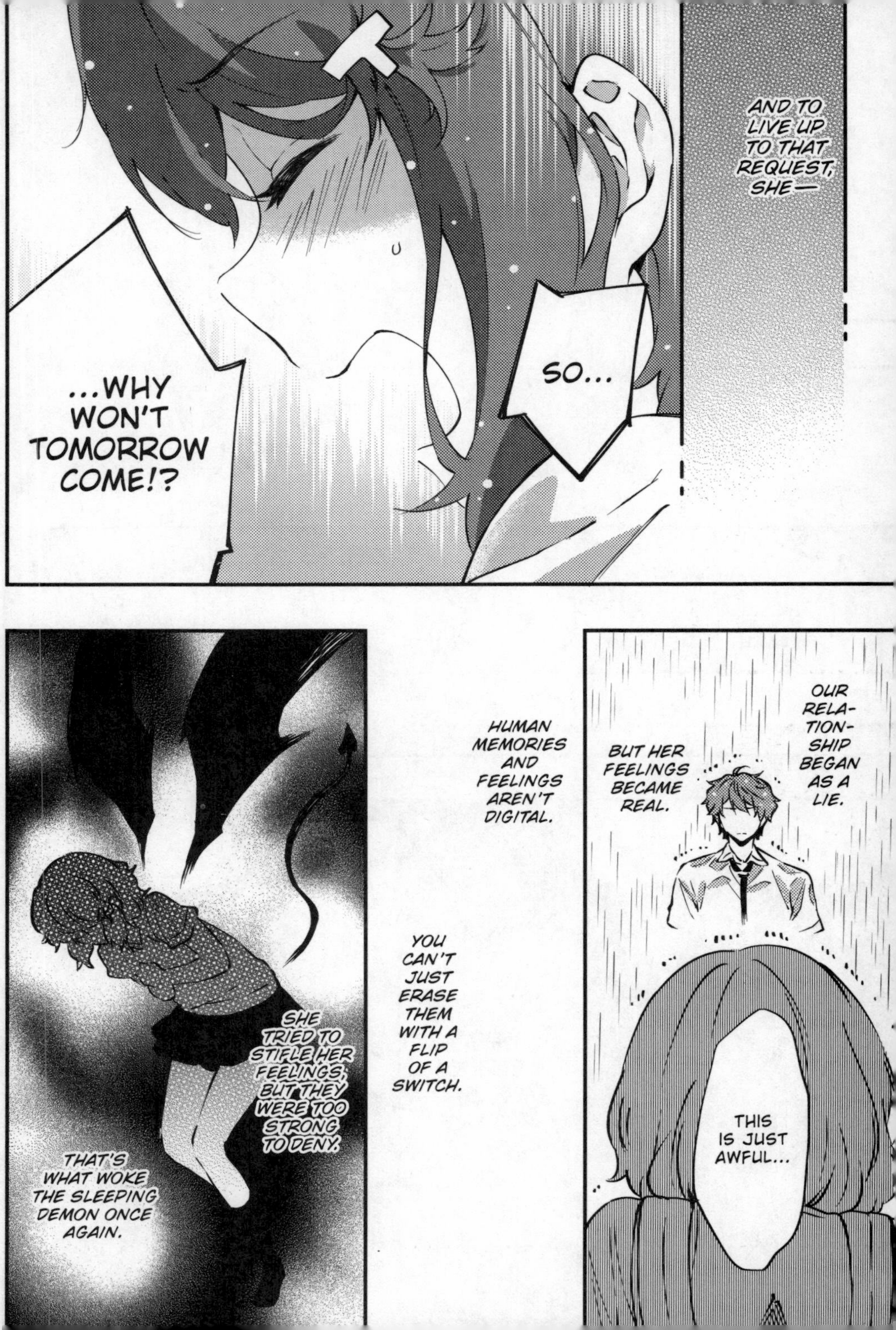
AND TO LIVE UP TO THAT REQUEST, SHE—
SO...
...WHY WON'T TOMORROW COME!?
OUR RELA-TION-SHIP BEGAN AS A LIE.
BUT HER FEELINGS BECAME REAL.
THIS IS JUST AWFUL...
HUMAN MEMORIES AND FEELINGS AREN'T DIGITAL.
YOU CAN'T JUST ERASE THEM WITH A FLIP OF A SWITCH.
SHE TRIED TO STIFLE HER FEELINGS, BUT THEY WERE TOO STRONG TO DENY.
THAT'S WHAT WOKE THE SLEEPING DEMON ONCE AGAIN.

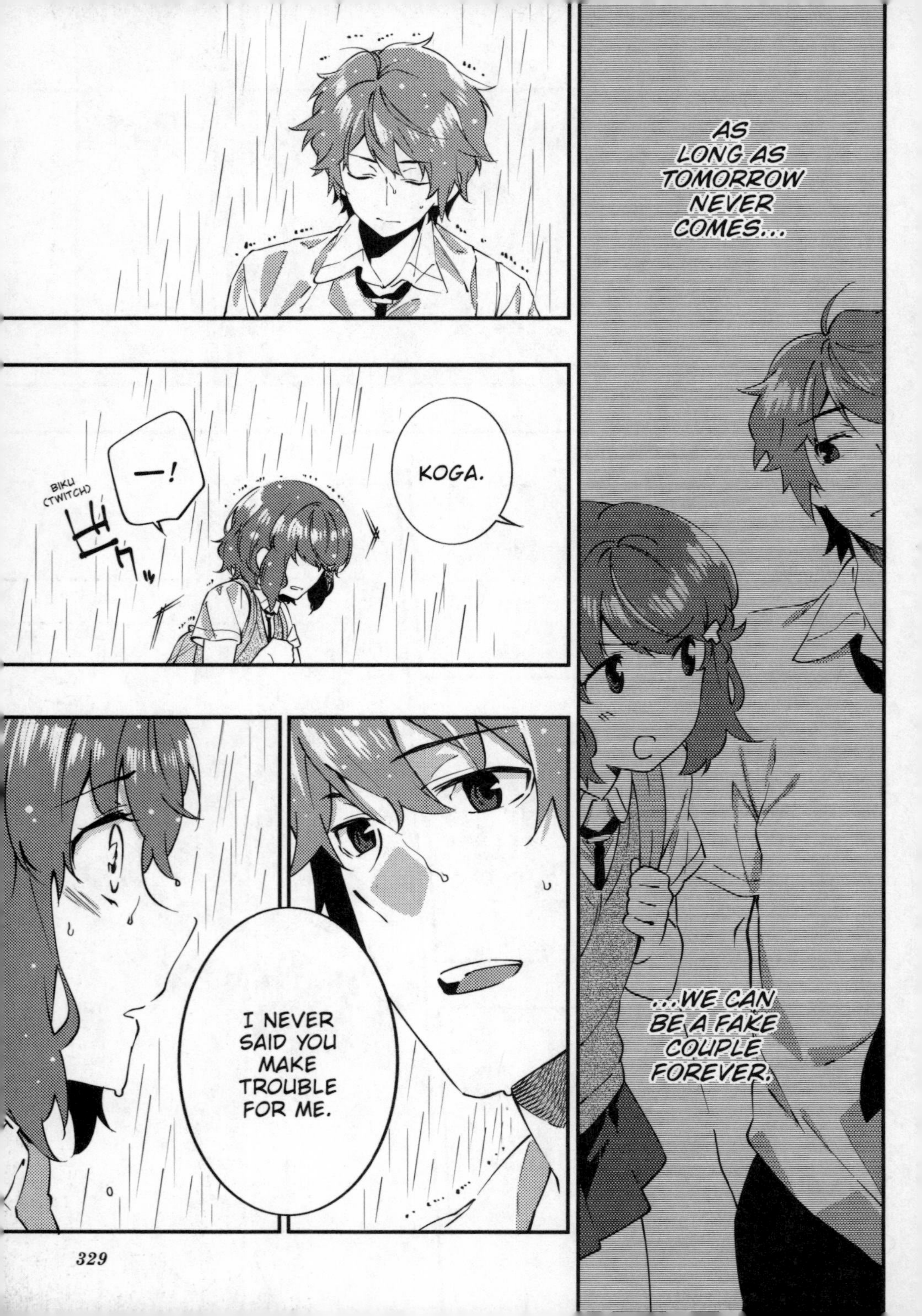
AS LONG AS TOMORROW NEVER COMES...
...WE CAN BE A FAKE COUPLE FOREVER.
KOGA.
—!
BIKU (TWITCH)
I NEVER SAID YOU MAKE TROUBLE FOR ME.

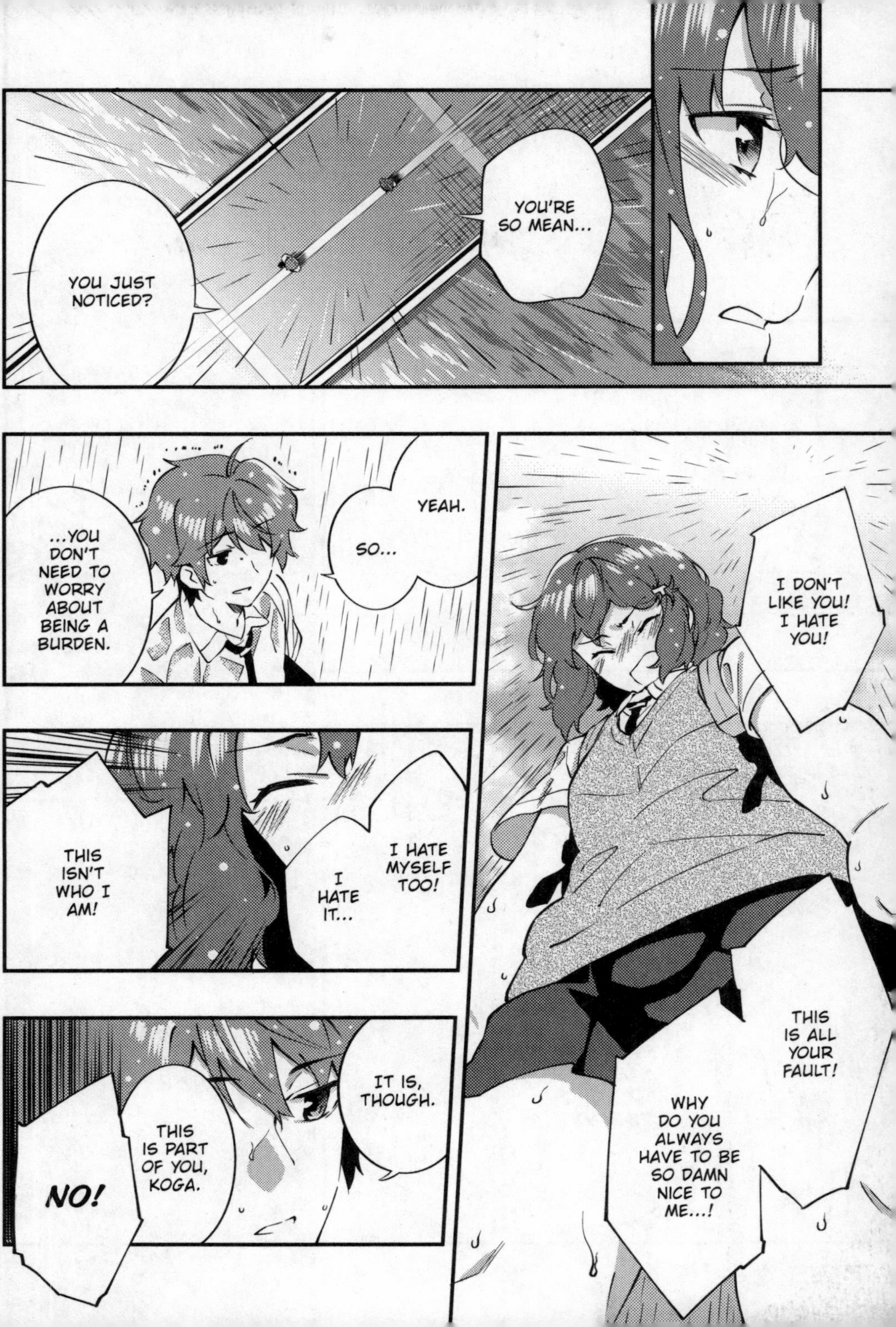
YOU'RE SO MEAN...
YOU JUST NOTICED?
I DON'T LIKE YOU! I HATE YOU!
THIS IS ALL YOUR FAULT!
WHY DO YOU ALWAYS HAVE TO BE SO DAMN NICE TO ME...!
YEAH.
SO...
...YOU DON'T NEED TO WORRY ABOUT BEING A BURDEN.
I HATE MYSELF TOO!
I HATE IT...
THIS ISN'T WHO I AM!
IT IS, THOUGH.
THIS IS PART OF YOU, KOGA.
NO!

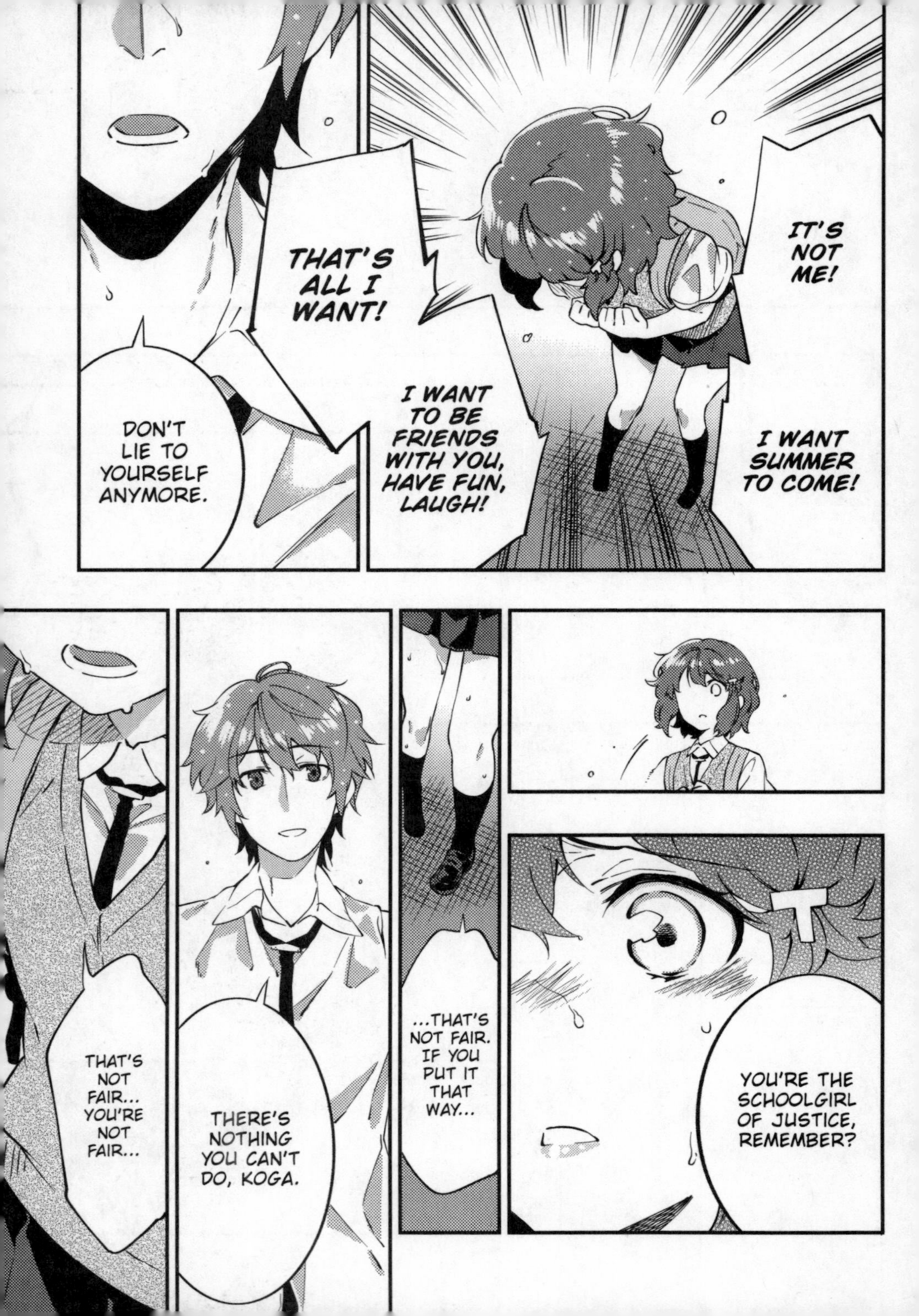
IT'S NOT ME!
I WANT SUMMER TO COME!
I WANT TO BE FRIENDS WITH YOU, HAVE FUN, LAUGH!
THAT'S ALL I WANT!
DON'T LIE TO YOURSELF ANYMORE.
YOU'RE THE SCHOOLGIRL OF JUSTICE, REMEMBER?
...THAT'S NOT FAIR. IF YOU PUT IT THAT WAY...
THERE'S NOTHING YOU CAN'T DO, KOGA.
THAT'S NOT FAIR... YOU'RE NOT FAIR...

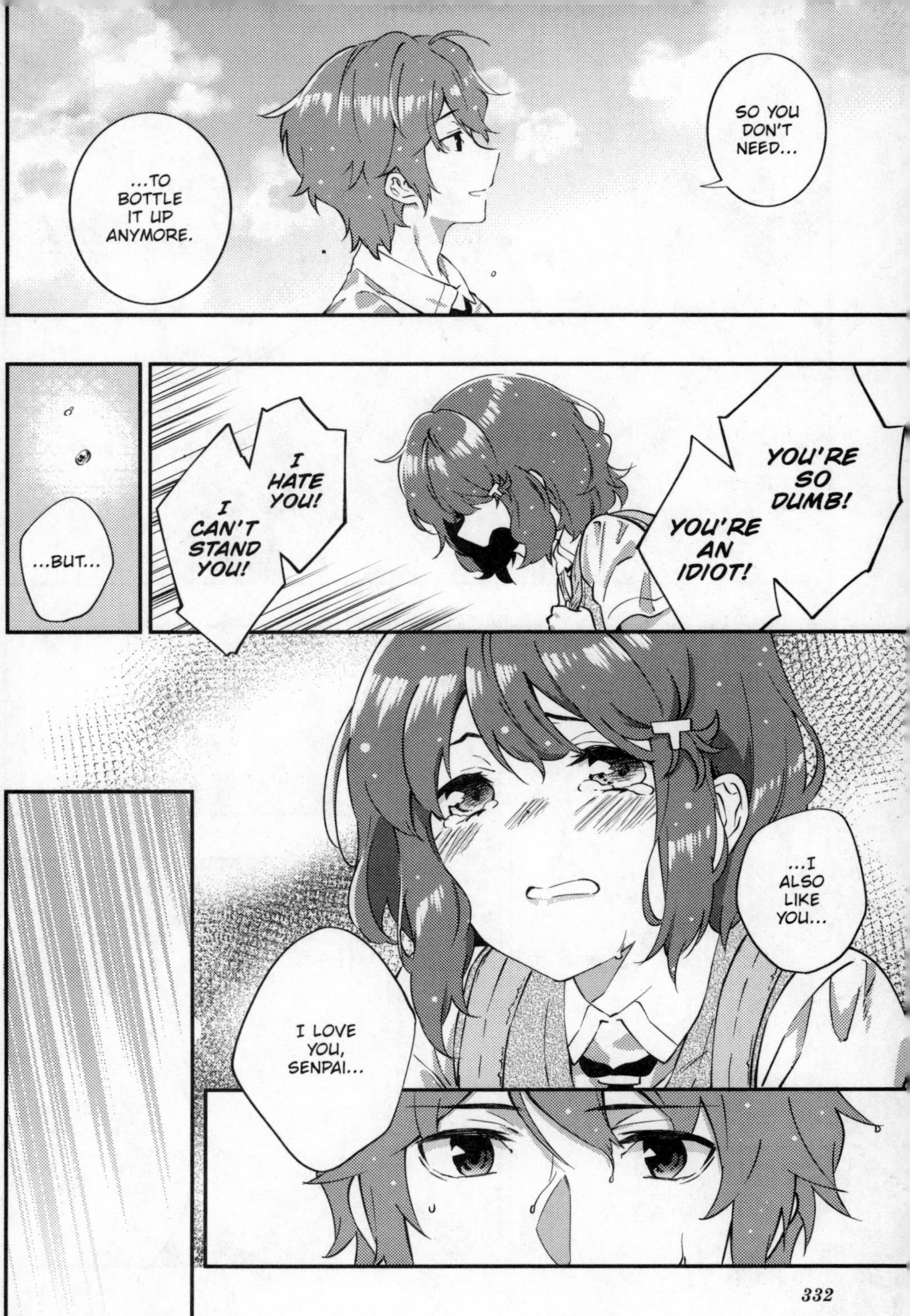
SO YOU DON'T NEED...
...TO BOTTLE IT UP ANYMORE.
YOU'RE SO DUMB!
YOU'RE AN IDIOT!
I HATE YOU!
I CAN'T STAND YOU!
...BUT...
...I ALSO LIKE YOU...
I LOVE YOU, SENPAI...

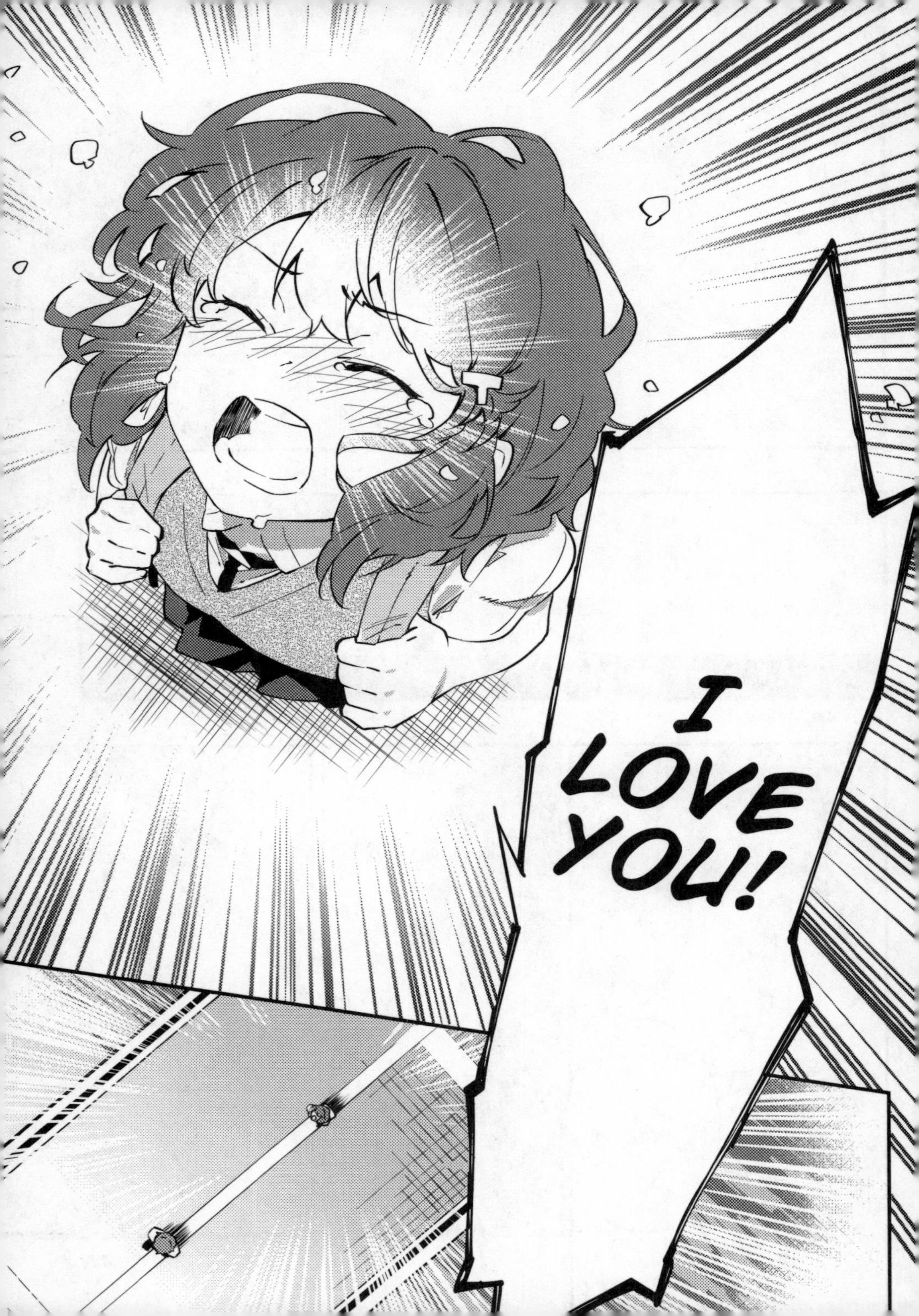
I LOVE YOU!

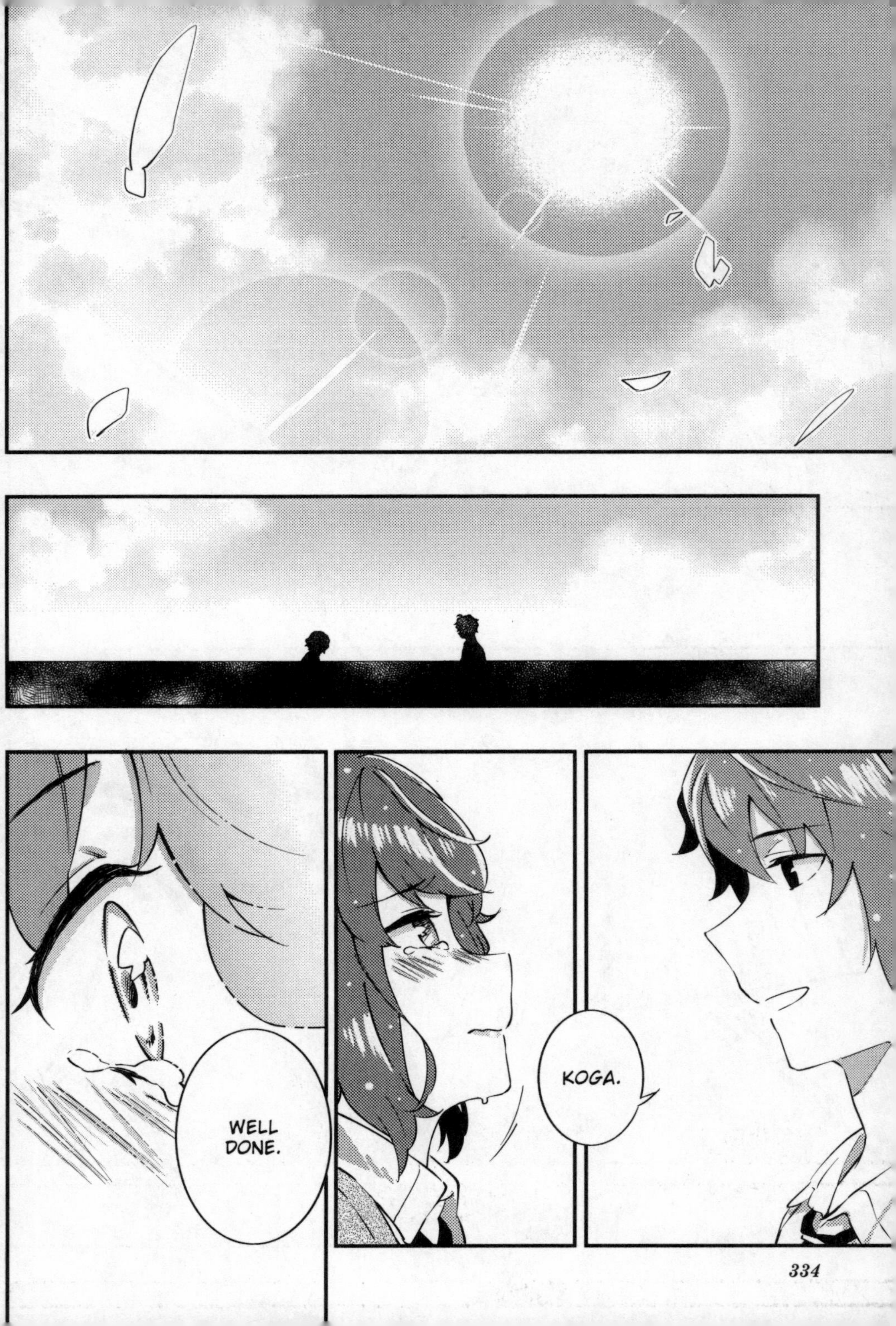
KOGA.
WELL DONE.

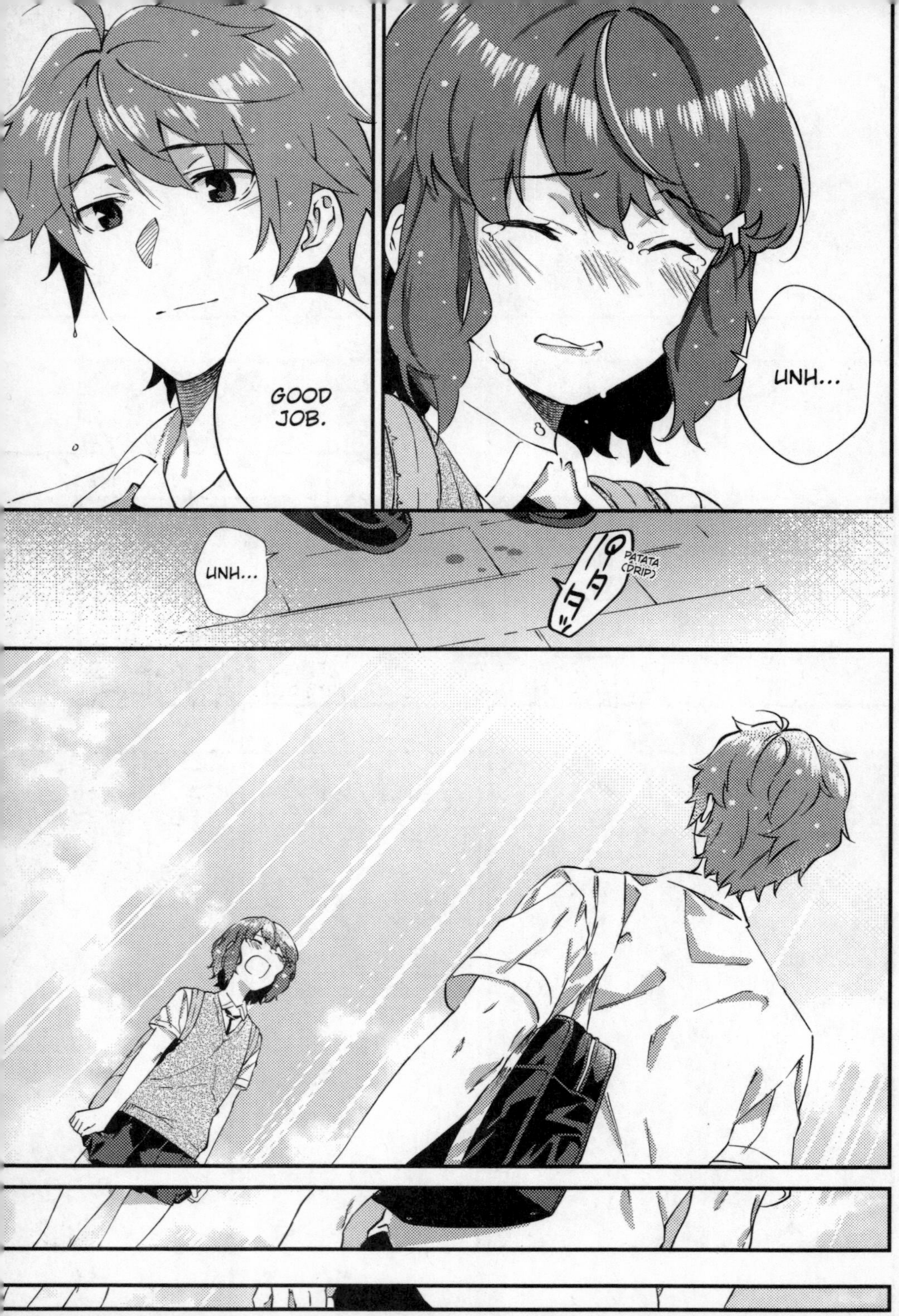
UNH...
GOOD JOB.
パタタッ
PATATA (DRIP)
UNH...

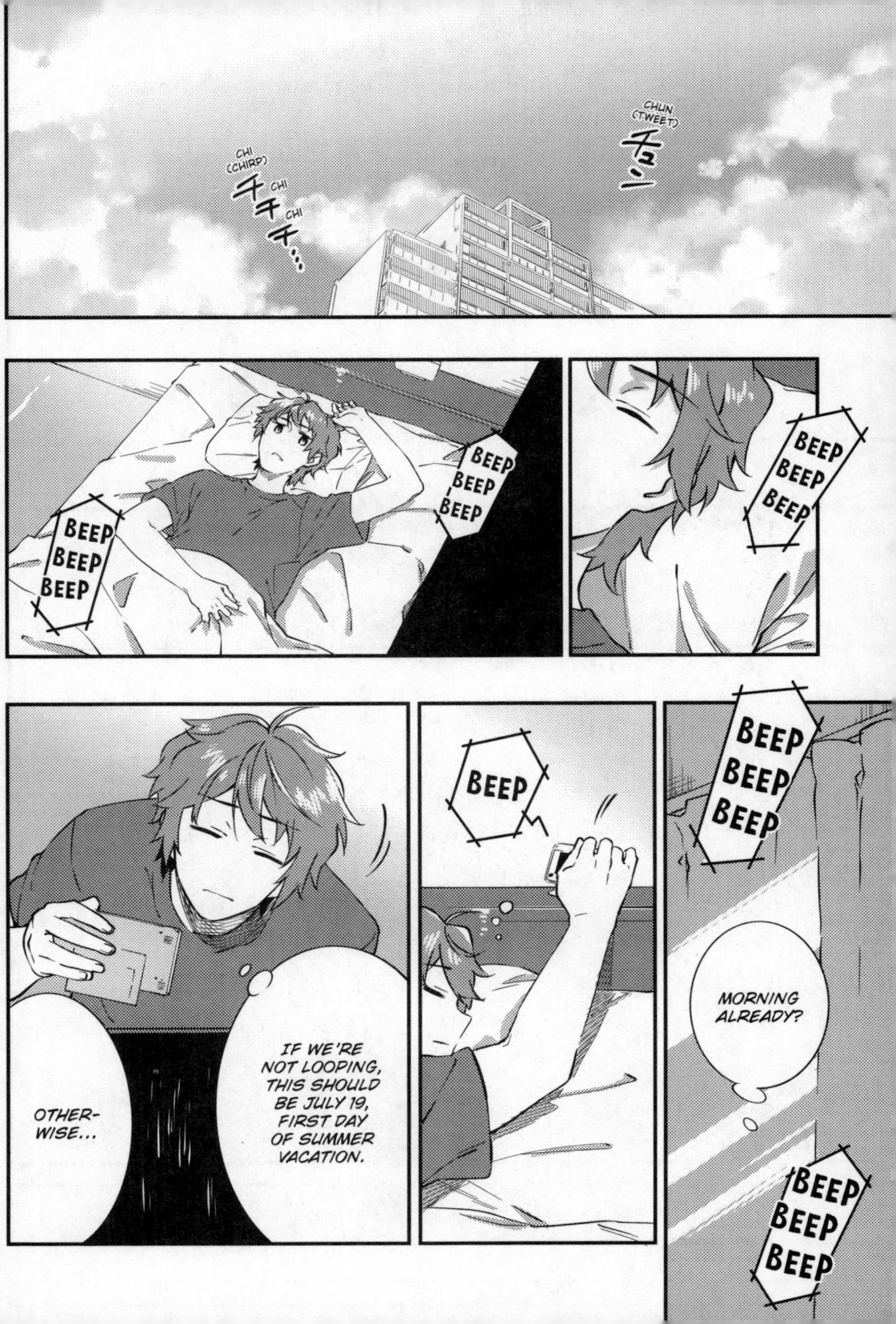
CHUN (TWEET)
チュン
CHI (CHIRP) CHI CHI
チチチ…
BEEP BEEP BEEP
BEEP BEEP BEEP
BEEP BEEP BEEP
BEEP BEEP BEEP
MORNING ALREADY?
BEEP BEEP BEEP
BEEP
IF WE'RE NOT LOOPING, THIS SHOULD BE JULY 19, FIRST DAY OF SUMMER VACATION.
OTHER-WISE...

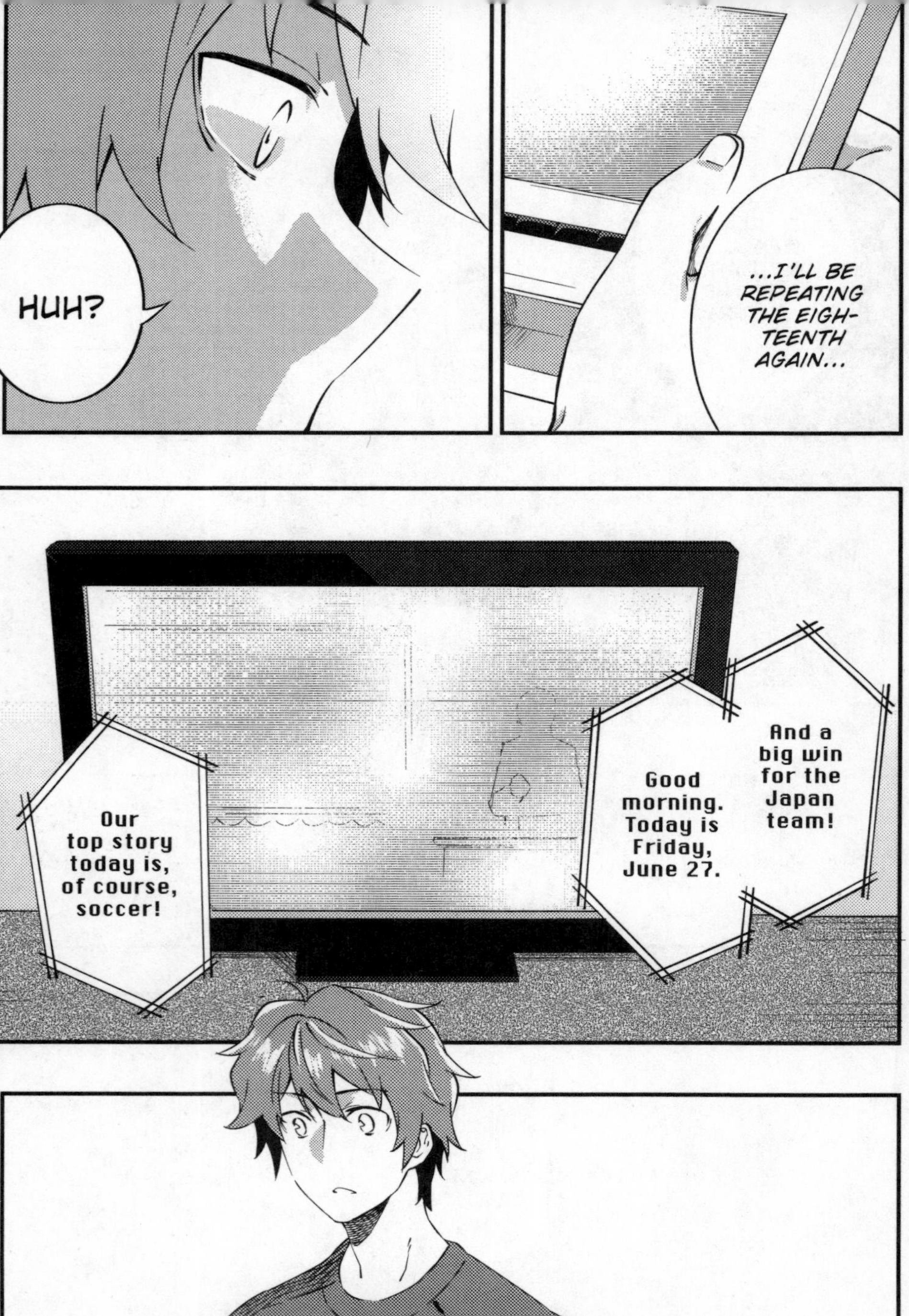
...I'LL BE REPEATING THE EIGH-TEENTH AGAIN...
HUH?
And a big win for the Japan team!
Good morning. Today is Friday, June 27.
Our top story today is, of course, soccer!

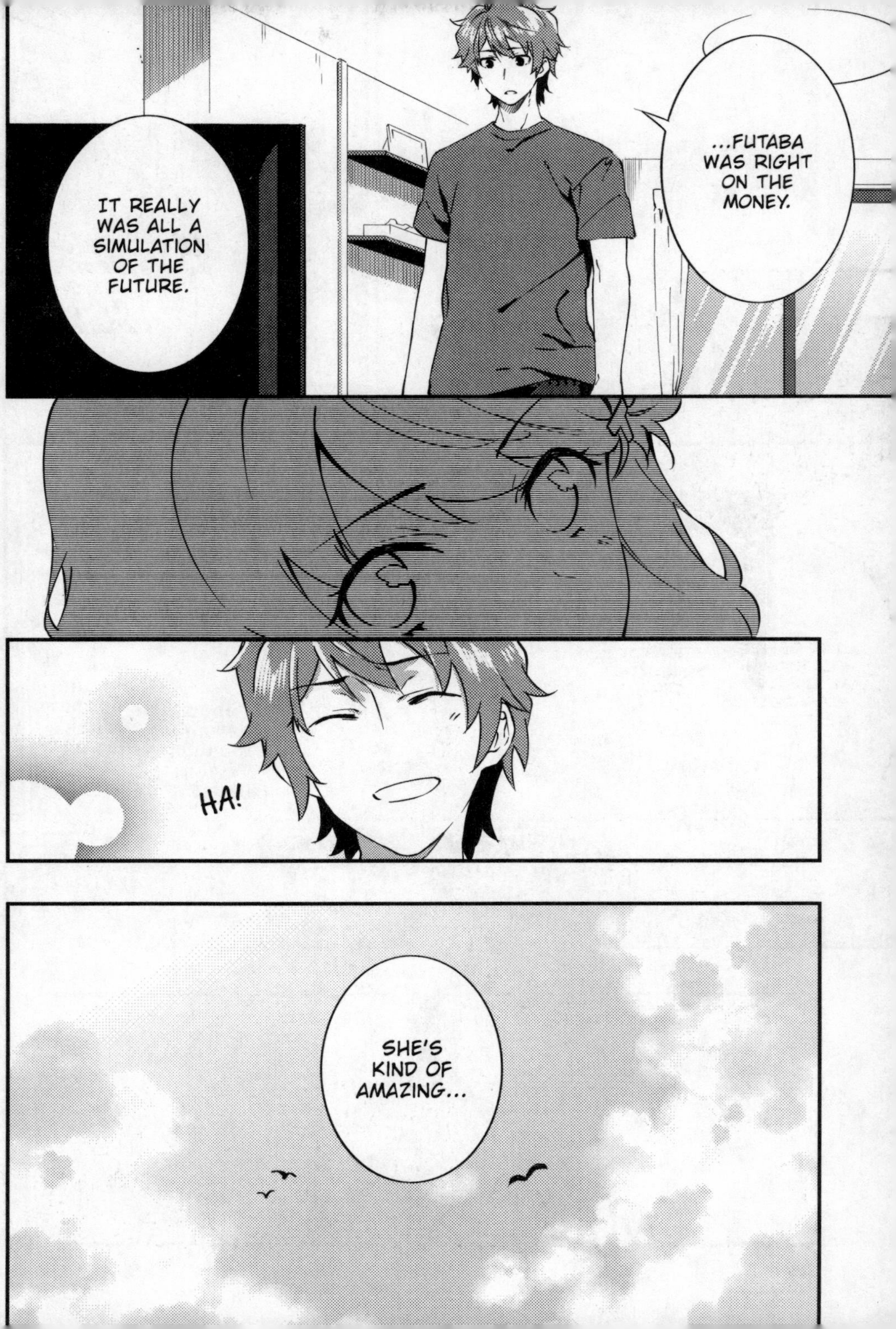
...FUTABA WAS RIGHT ON THE MONEY.
IT REALLY WAS ALL A SIMULATION OF THE FUTURE.
HA!
SHE'S KIND OF AMAZING...

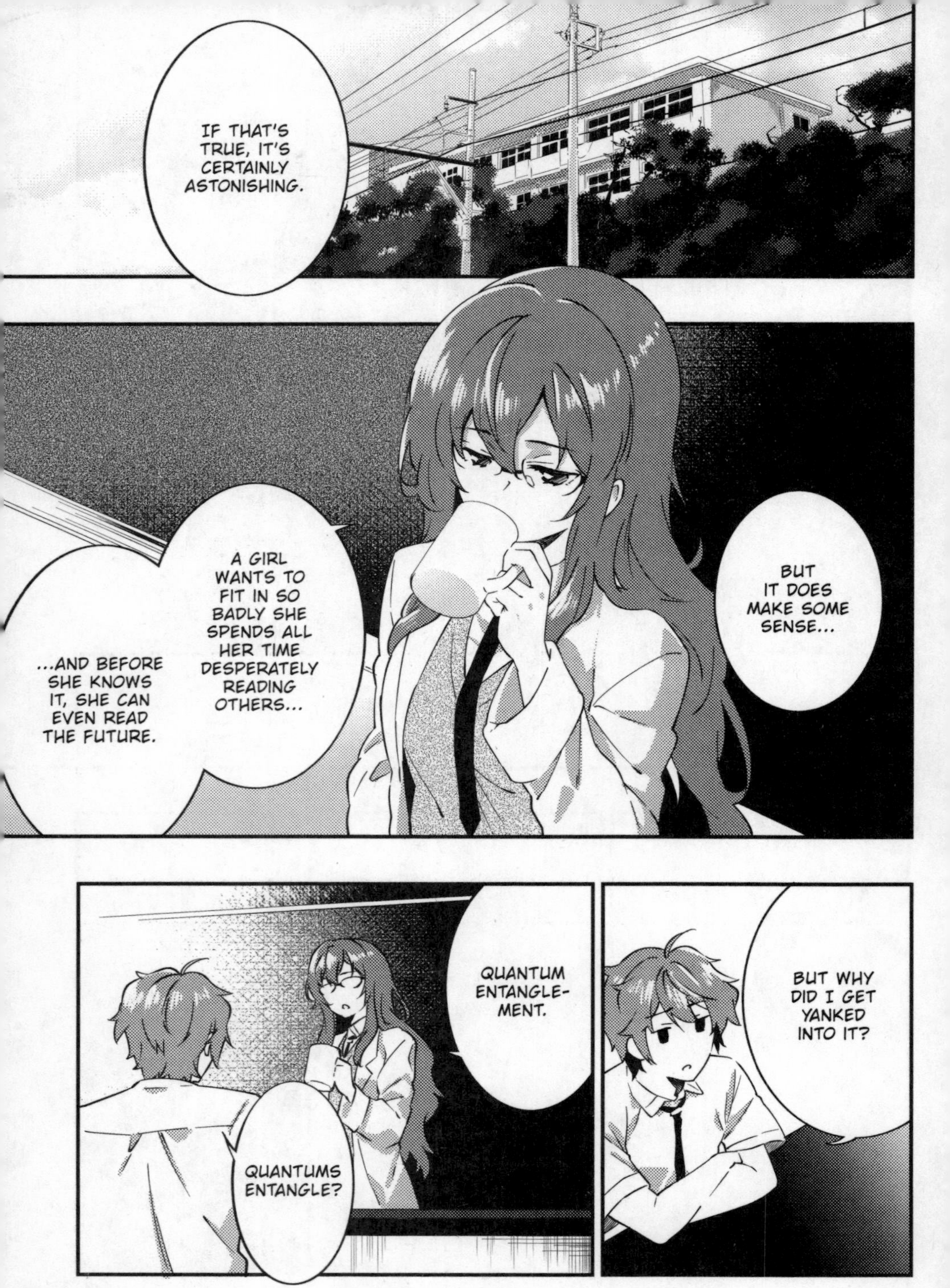
IF THAT'S TRUE, IT'S CERTAINLY ASTONISHING.
BUT IT DOES MAKE SOME SENSE...
A GIRL WANTS TO FIT IN SO BADLY SHE SPENDS ALL HER TIME DESPERATELY READING OTHERS...
...AND BEFORE SHE KNOWS IT, SHE CAN EVEN READ THE FUTURE.
BUT WHY DID I GET YANKED INTO IT?
QUANTUM ENTANGLE-MENT.
QUANTUMS ENTANGLE?

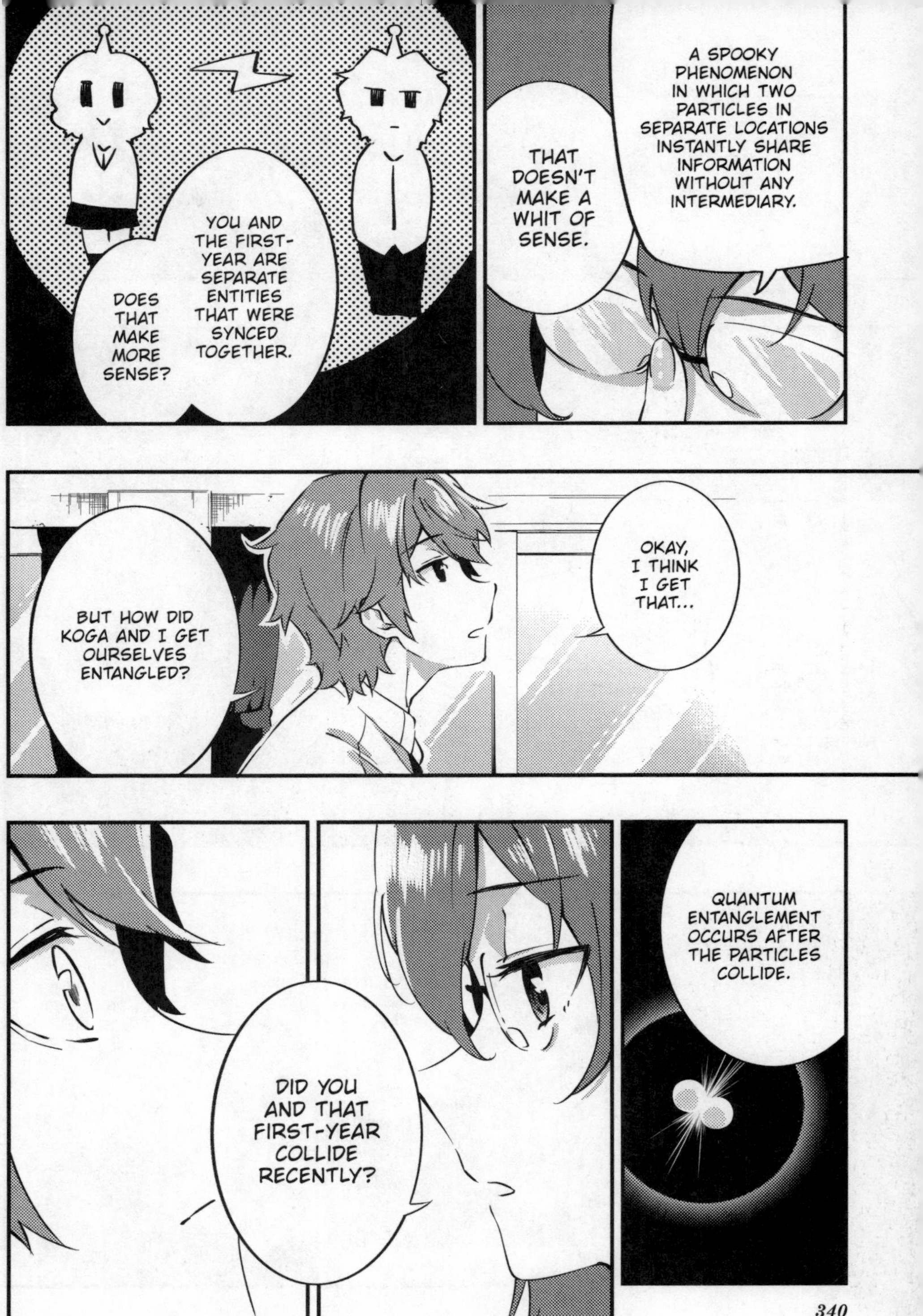
A SPOOKY PHENOMENON IN WHICH TWO PARTICLES IN SEPARATE LOCATIONS INSTANTLY SHARE INFORMATION WITHOUT ANY INTERMEDIARY.
THAT DOESN'T MAKE A WHIT OF SENSE.
YOU AND THE FIRST-YEAR ARE SEPARATE ENTITIES THAT WERE SYNCED TOGETHER.
DOES THAT MAKE MORE SENSE?
OKAY, I THINK I GET THAT...
BUT HOW DID KOGA AND I GET OURSELVES ENTANGLED?
QUANTUM ENTANGLEMENT OCCURS AFTER THE PARTICLES COLLIDE.
DID YOU AND THAT FIRST-YEAR COLLIDE RECENTLY?

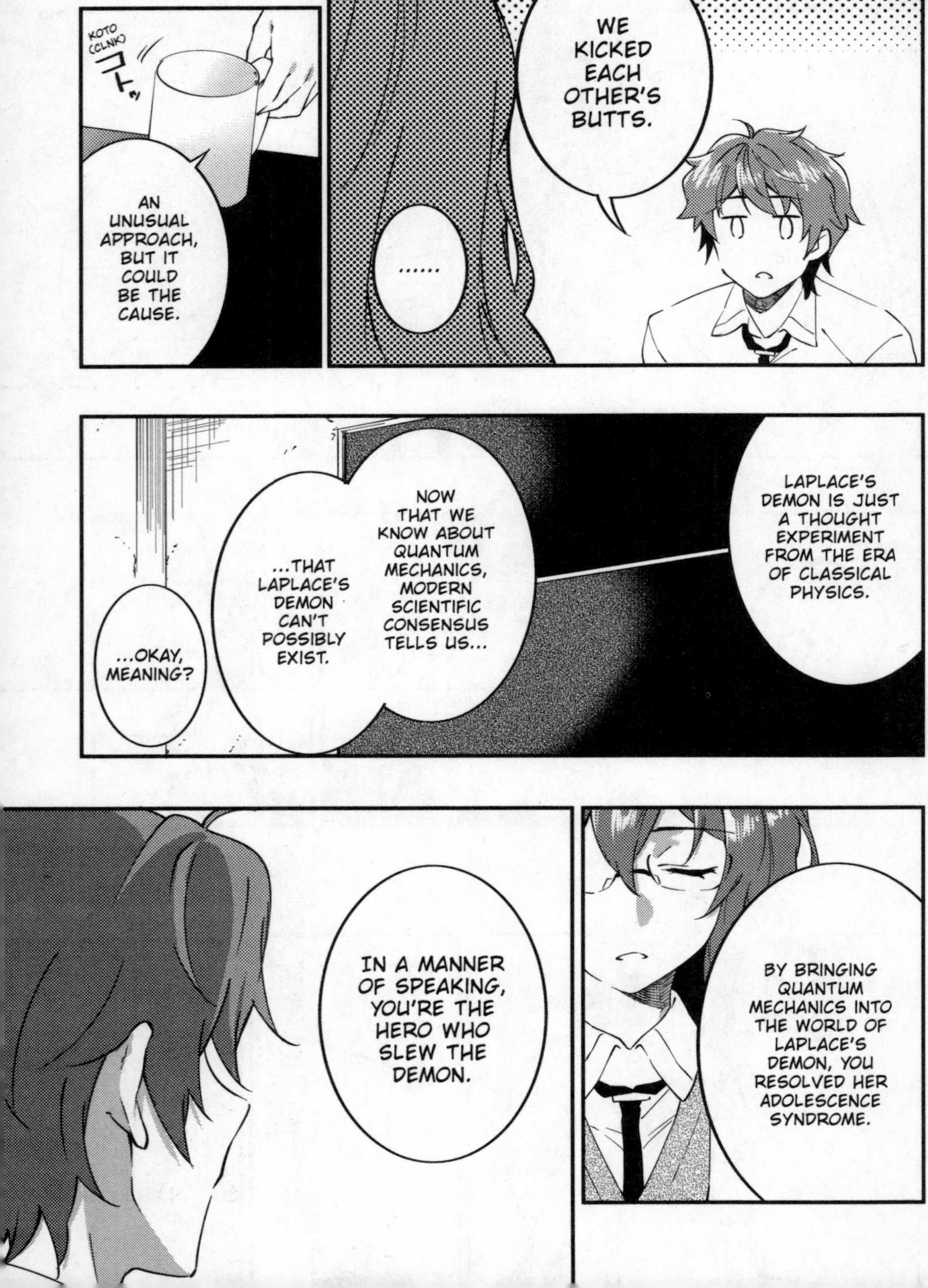
WE KICKED EACH OTHER'S BUTTS.
......
KOTO (CLNK)
コトッ
AN UNUSUAL APPROACH, BUT IT COULD BE THE CAUSE.
LAPLACE'S DEMON IS JUST A THOUGHT EXPERIMENT FROM THE ERA OF CLASSICAL PHYSICS.
NOW THAT WE KNOW ABOUT QUANTUM MECHANICS, MODERN SCIENTIFIC CONSENSUS TELLS US...
...THAT LAPLACE'S DEMON CAN'T POSSIBLY EXIST.
...OKAY, MEANING?
BY BRINGING QUANTUM MECHANICS INTO THE WORLD OF LAPLACE'S DEMON, YOU RESOLVED HER ADOLESCENCE SYNDROME.
IN A MANNER OF SPEAKING, YOU'RE THE HERO WHO SLEW THE DEMON.

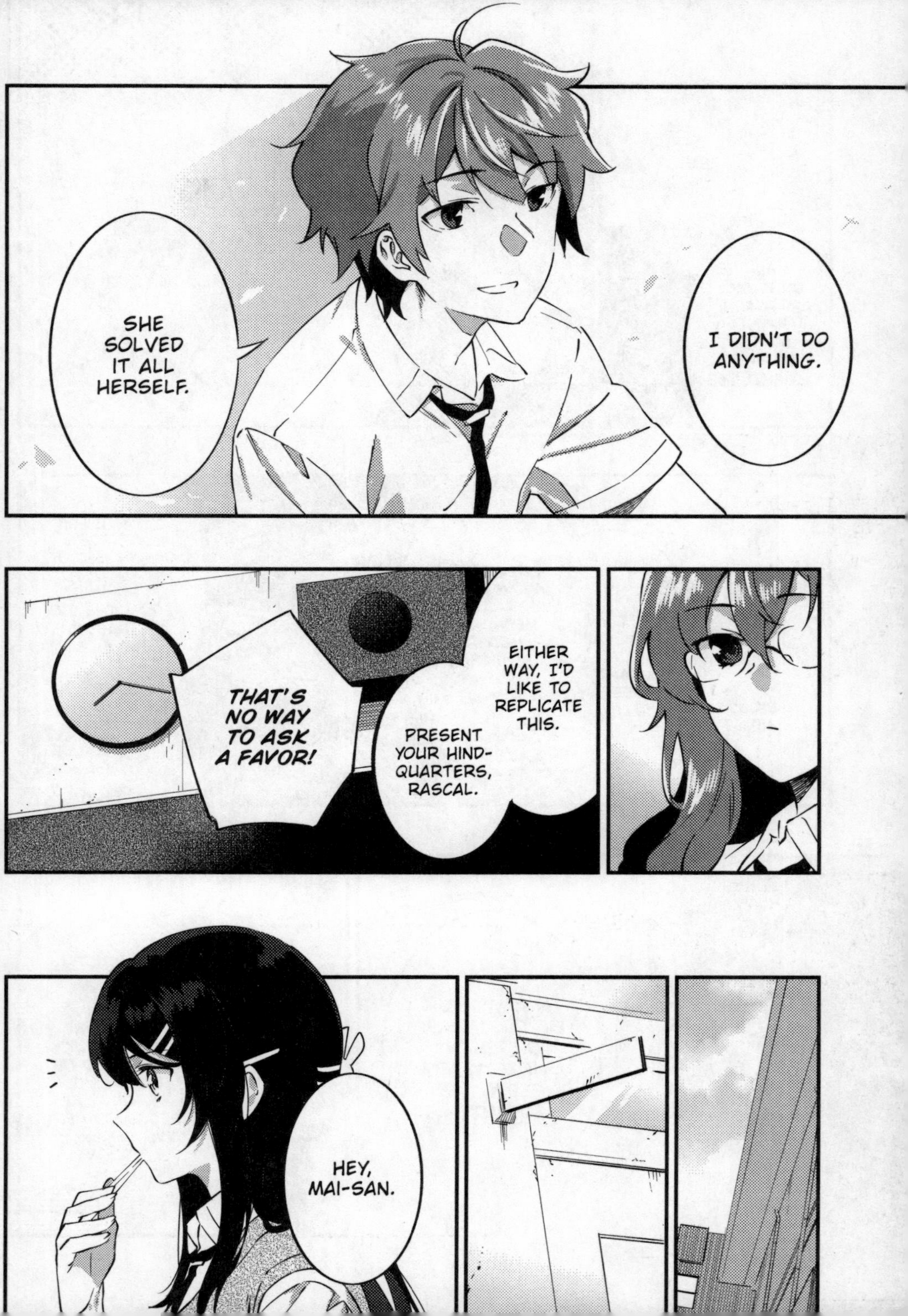
I DIDN'T DO ANYTHING.
SHE SOLVED IT ALL HERSELF.
EITHER WAY, I'D LIKE TO REPLICATE THIS.
PRESENT YOUR HIND-QUARTERS, RASCAL.
THAT'S NO WAY TO ASK A FAVOR!
HEY, MAI-SAN.

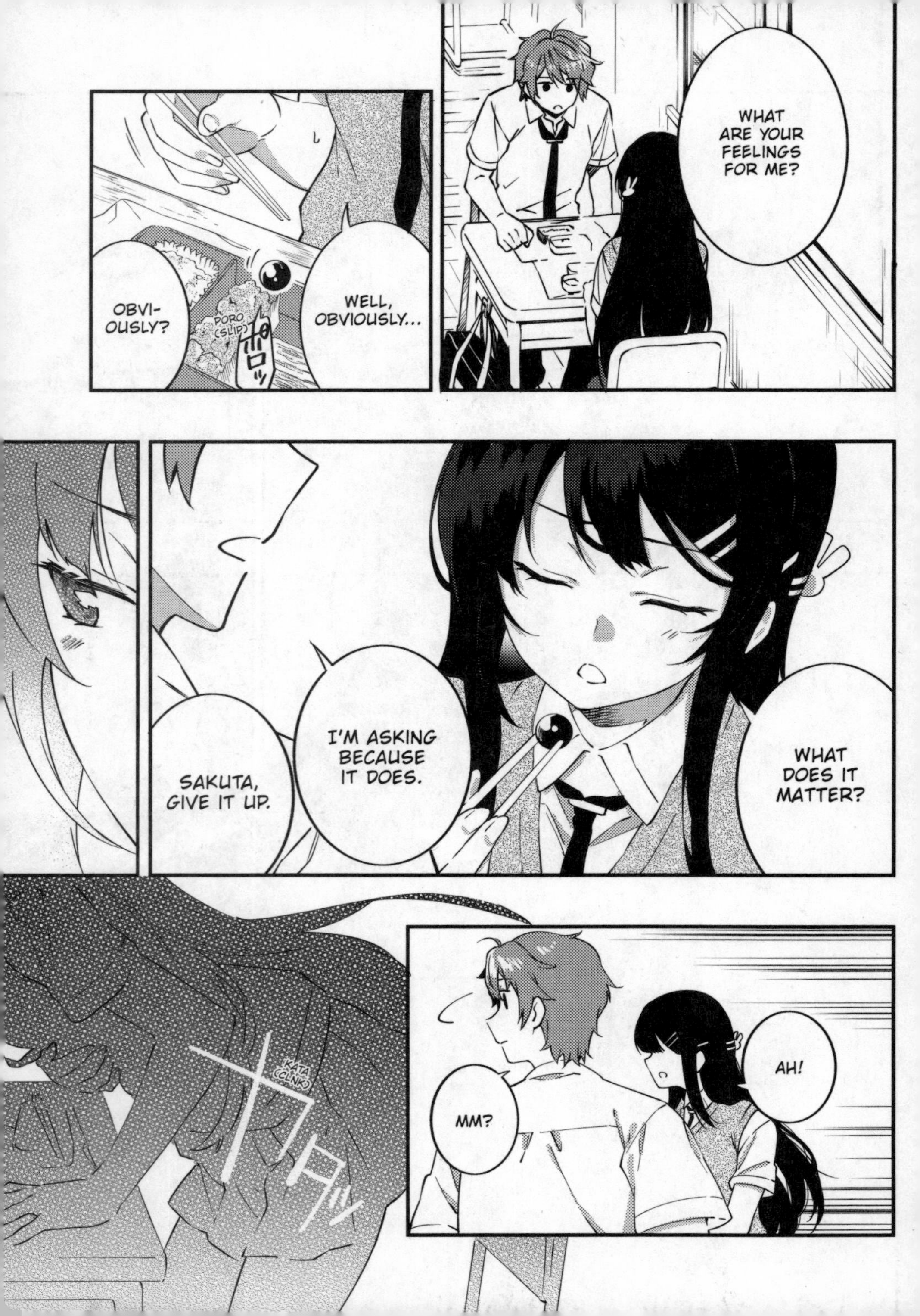
WHAT ARE YOUR FEELINGS FOR ME?
WELL, OBVIOUSLY...
PORO (SLIP)
OBVI-OUSLY?
WHAT DOES IT MATTER?
I'M ASKING BECAUSE IT DOES.
SAKUTA, GIVE IT UP.
AH!
MM?
KATA (CLNK)

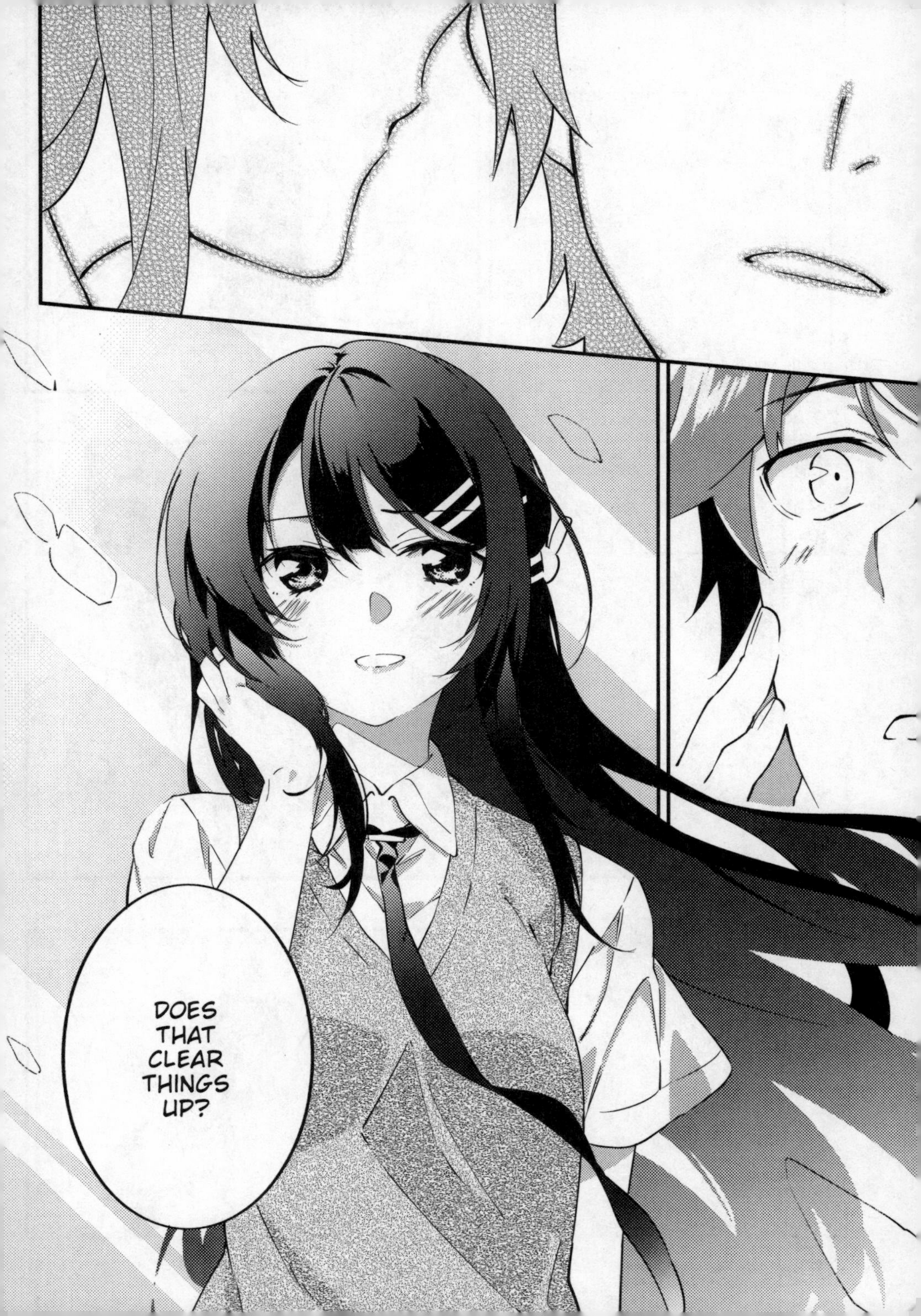
DOES THAT CLEAR THINGS UP?

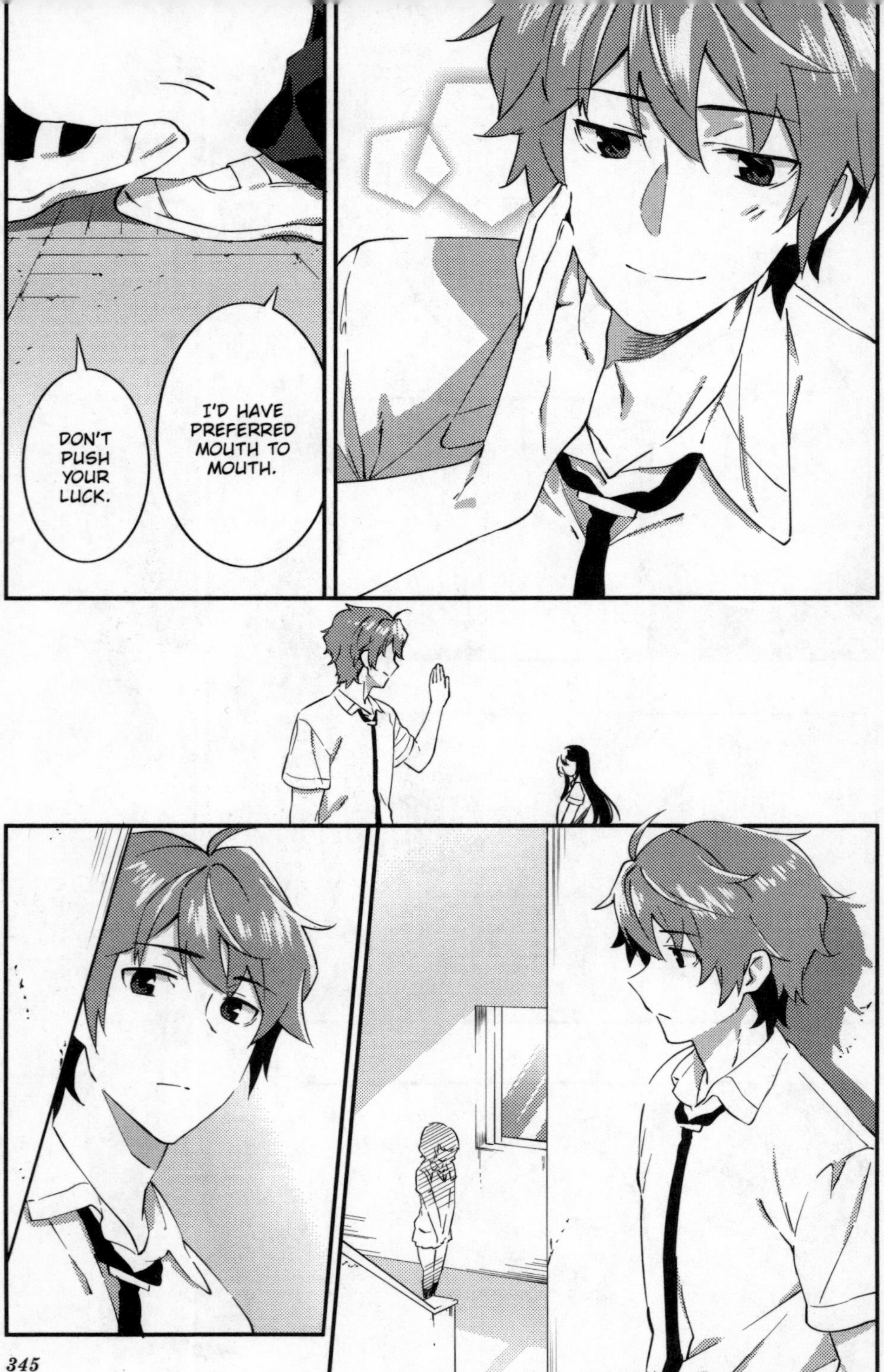
I'D HAVE PREFERRED MOUTH TO MOUTH.
DON'T PUSH YOUR LUCK.

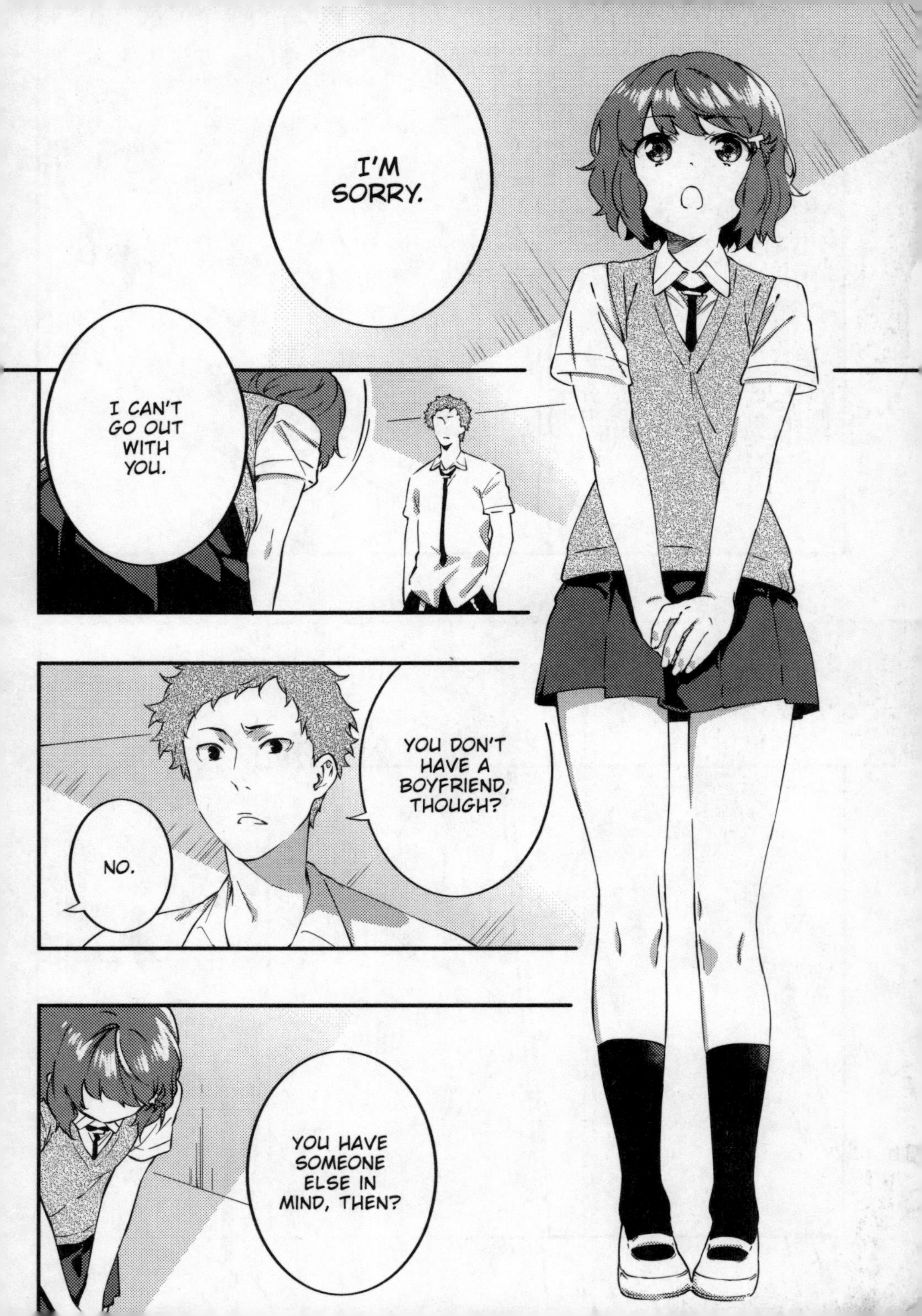
I'M SORRY.
I CAN'T GO OUT WITH YOU.
YOU DON'T HAVE A BOYFRIEND, THOUGH?
NO.
YOU HAVE SOMEONE ELSE IN MIND, THEN?

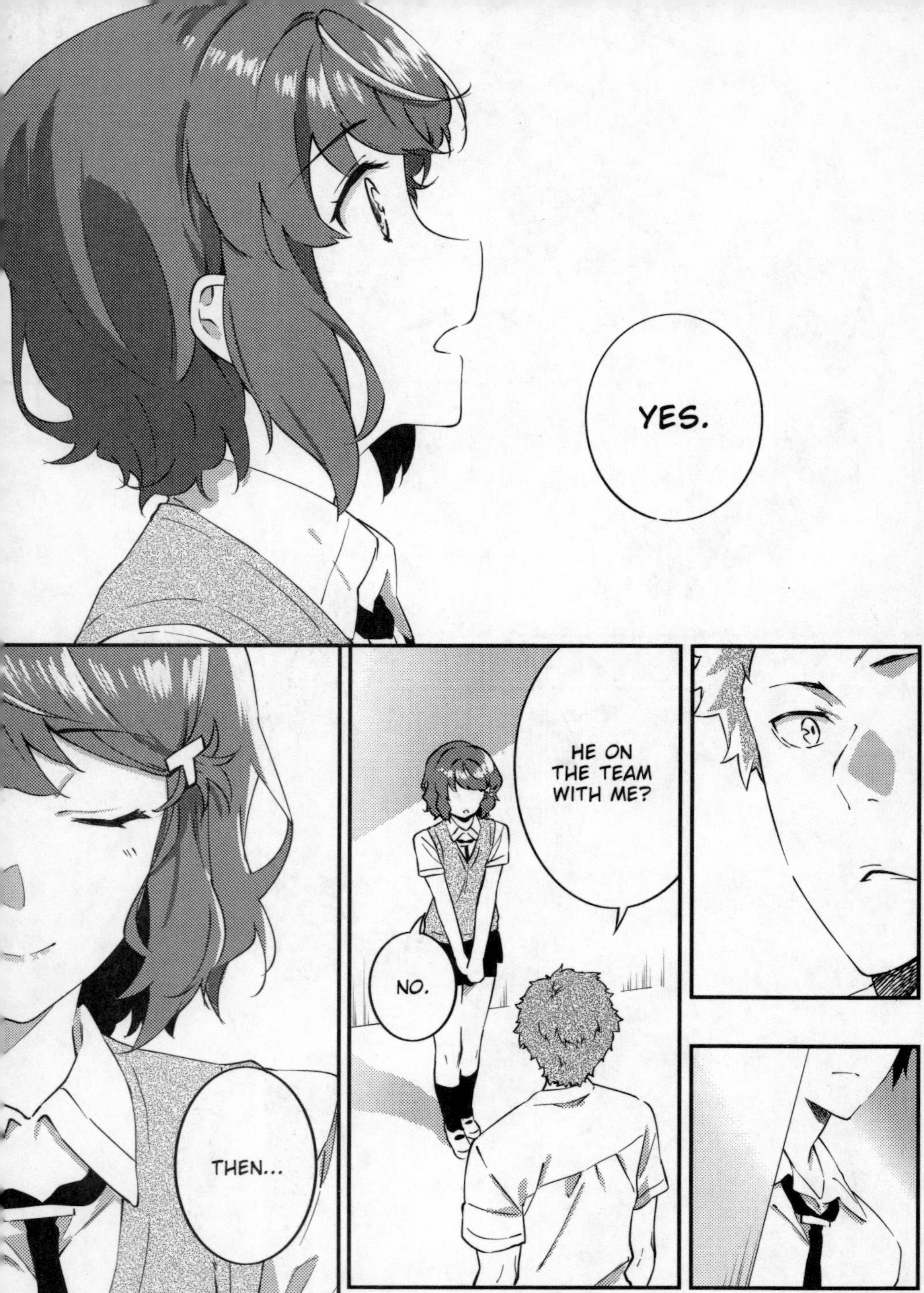
YES.
HE ON THE TEAM WITH ME?
NO.
THEN...

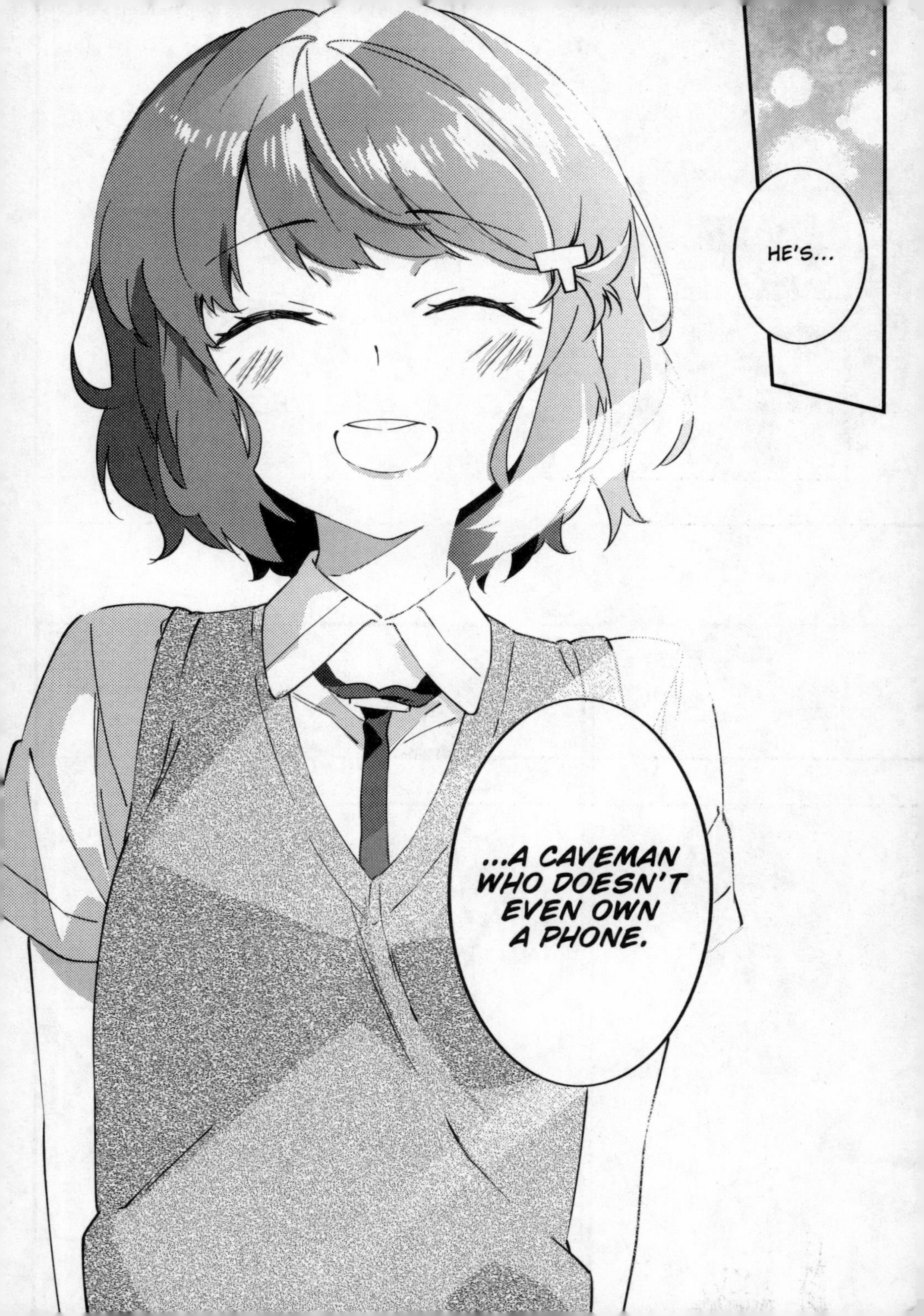
HE'S...
...A CAVEMAN WHO DOESN'T EVEN OWN A PHONE.

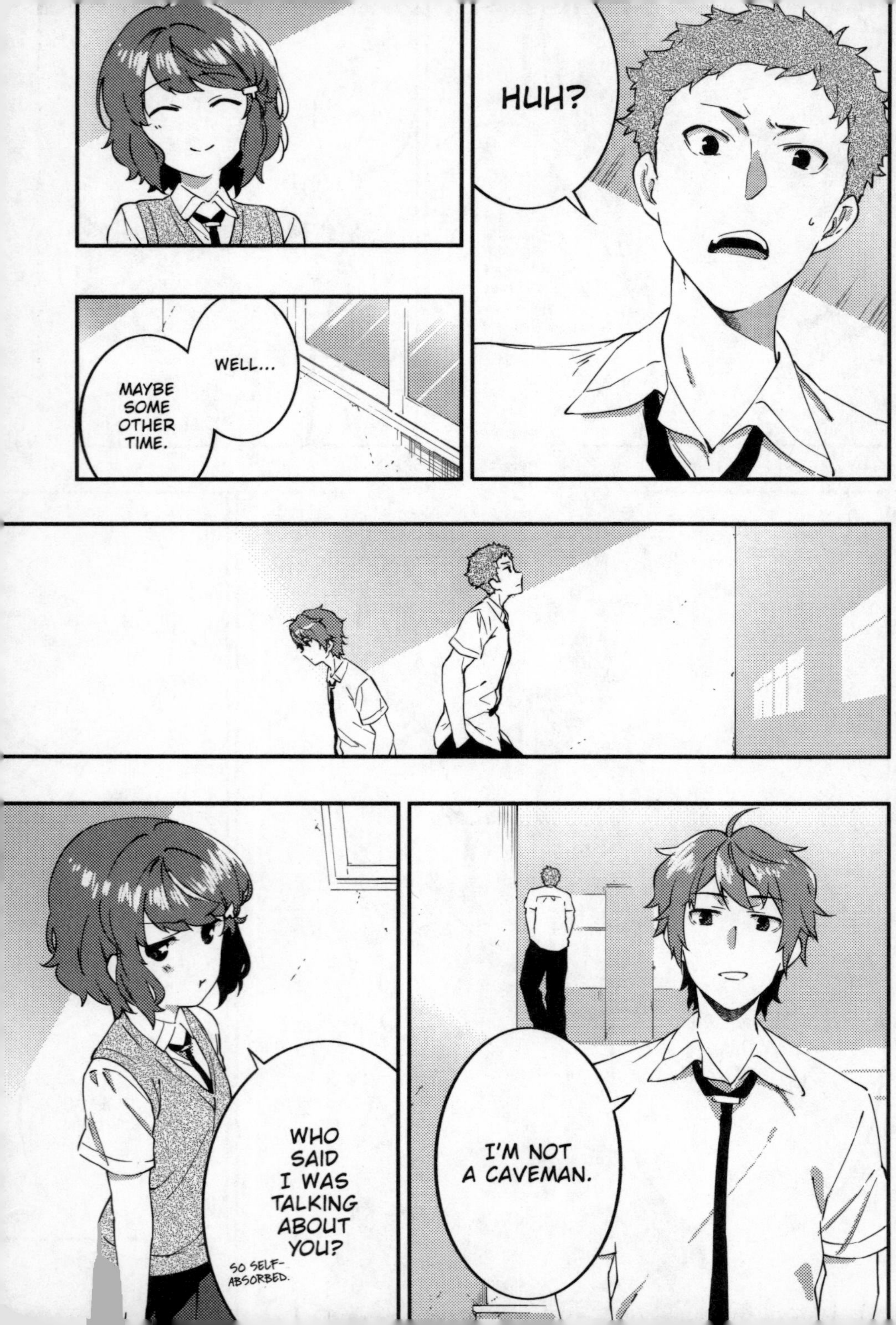
HUH?
WELL...
MAYBE SOME OTHER TIME.
I'M NOT A CAVEMAN.
WHO SAID I WAS TALKING ABOUT YOU?
SO SELF-ABSORBED.

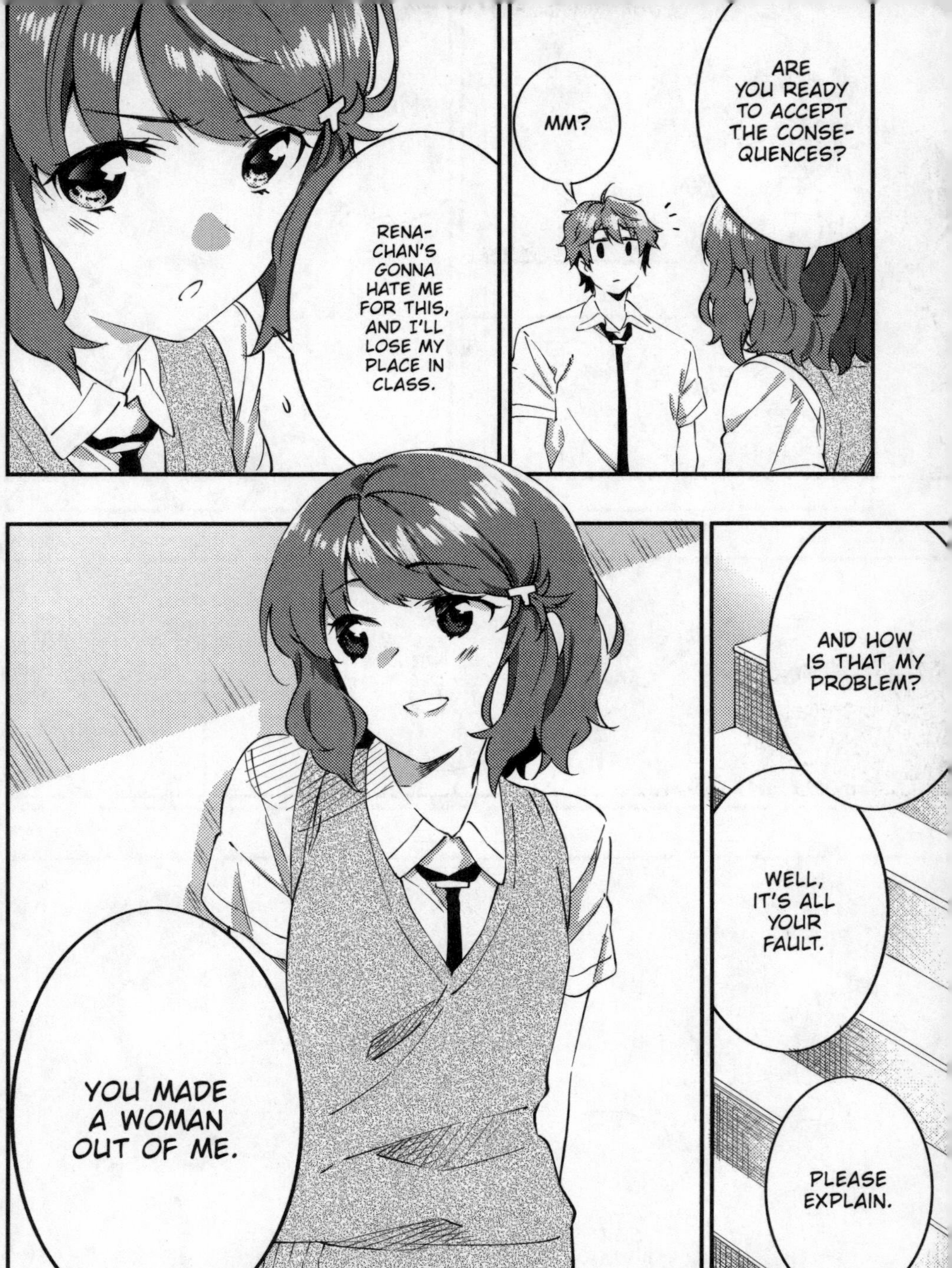
ARE YOU READY TO ACCEPT THE CONSE-QUENCES?
MM?
RENA-CHAN'S GONNA HATE ME FOR THIS, AND I'LL LOSE MY PLACE IN CLASS.
AND HOW IS THAT MY PROBLEM?
WELL, IT'S ALL YOUR FAULT.
PLEASE EXPLAIN.
YOU MADE A WOMAN OUT OF ME.

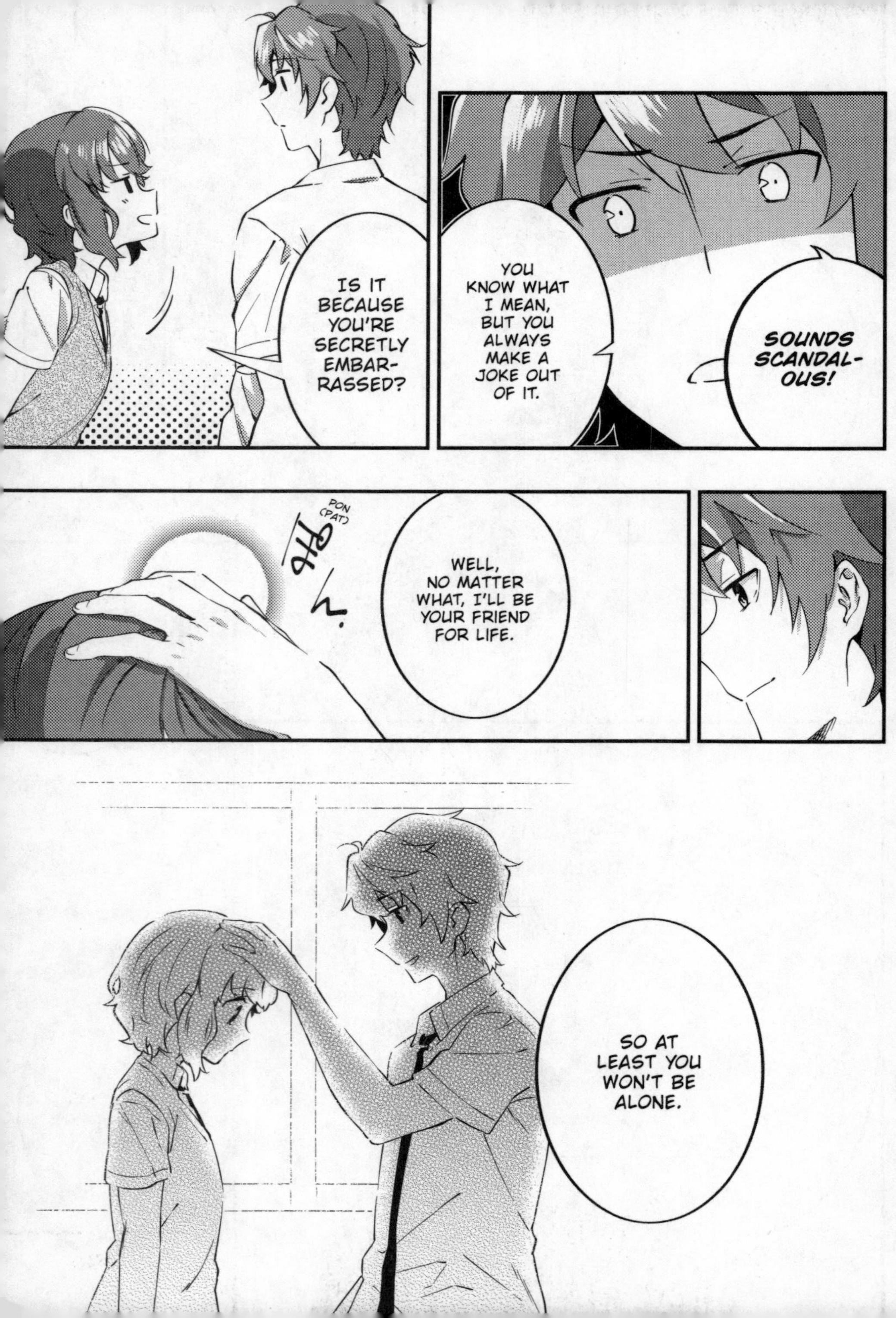
SOUNDS SCANDAL-OUS!
YOU KNOW WHAT I MEAN, BUT YOU ALWAYS MAKE A JOKE OUT OF IT.
IS IT BECAUSE YOU'RE SECRETLY EMBAR-RASSED?
WELL, NO MATTER WHAT, I'LL BE YOUR FRIEND FOR LIFE.
PON (PAT)
SO AT LEAST YOU WON'T BE ALONE.

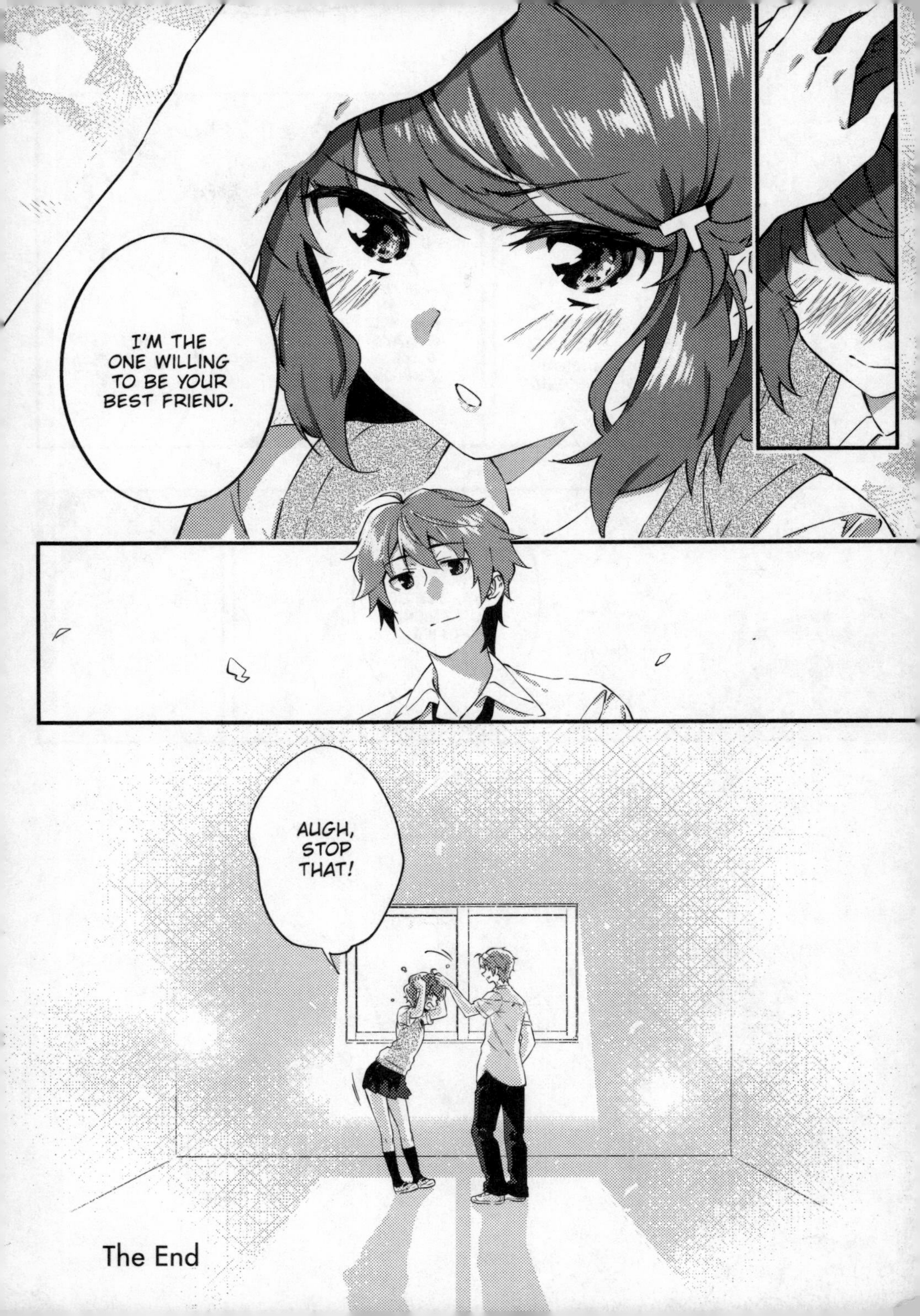
I'M THE ONE WILLING TO BE YOUR BEST FRIEND.
AUGH, STOP THAT!
The End

# Translation Notes

## Common Honorifics

no honorific: Indicates familiarity or closeness; if used without permission or reason, addressing someone in this manner would constitute an insult.

-san: The Japanese equivalent of Mr./Mrs./Miss. If a situation calls for politeness, this is the fail-safe honorific.

-kun: Used most often when referring to boys, this indicates affection or familiarity.

-chan: An affectionate honorific indicating familiarity used mostly in reference to girls; also used in reference to cute persons or animals of either gender.

-senpai: Used to address upperclassmen or more experienced coworkers.

-kohai: The inverse of senpai, used to address those who are younger or less experienced.

-sensei: A respectful term for teachers, artists, or high-level professionals.

-oniichan: A familiar, somewhat childish way to refer to one's older brother.

## Page 19

An **indirect kiss** is the act of touching one's lips to something another person has recently put to their own lips, usually in the context of sharing food or drink. While hardly risqué, it is regarded as somewhat flirtatious in Japan.

## Page 29

"Ore no misoshiru wo maiasa tsukutte kudasai," meaning "please make miso soup for me every morning," is a **classic Japanese marriage proposal** line. Since it obviously expresses rather rigid and outdated gender roles, it's seen as a bit of a cliche and isn't used often anymore, which is why Mai dates it to the Showa era (1926-1989).

## Page 53

A **"delusional middle schooler"** is someone suffering from the grave illness known as chuunibyou (eighth-grader syndrome), a common term in Japanese for the delusions of grandeur often held by middle schoolers who believe they are special and desperately want to stand out.

## Page 72

Sakuta's advice that **"squeezing them makes them bigger"** refers to the Japanese old wives' tale that touching breasts will cause them to grow.

## Page 140

**Enoshima** is a small island just off the coast of Fujisawa. It's a popular tourist location with a somewhat romantic image, featuring the matchmaking tree seen later on page 306 and the Dragon Lovers' Bell, which is said to eternally bind together couples who ring it.

## Page 182

Enoshima and Fujisawa Station (which is where they left from in the afternoon) are three and a half miles apart, so Koga had to walk at least that far in wet clothes to get home.

## Page 216

July 7 is the date of the Japanese holiday Tanabata, a celebration of the meeting of the deities **Orihime and Hikoboshi**. This legend tells the story of two lovers who were once married but were separated across the Amanogawa river (the Japanese term for the milky way) by Orihime's father, the Sky King. The Sky King allows Orihime to cross the Amanogawa only on Tanabata, and she must do so on a bridge made from the wings of a flock of magpies. It is said that the magpies cannot come if it rains on Tanabata, but based on the weatherman's prediction, it sounds like that will not be a problem on this particular July 7.

## Page 231

**Jamoke** may sound vaguely Japanese, but it's actually old-timey American slang for a stupid or clumsy person that started as a portmanteau of two words for coffee, "java" and "mocha." The actual Fukuoka dialect word Koga used is shiketou, which is slang there for "boring." It comes from the verb shikeru, meaning "to be damp/wet."

## Page 255

While Yokohama does sprawl inland, it's better known as a romantic seaside city, featuring attractions like Cosmo Clock 21, one of the largest Ferris wheels in the world.

## Page 305

In this scene, Koga is trying out a **tako senbei**, an Enoshima specialty. Senbei are usually flat, crispy rice crackers, but tako senbei are made by battering, flattening, and cooking several octopuses to produce a snack with a similar shape and consistency.

## Page 306

In Japanese shrines, visitors can purchase wooden **plaques** known as ema where one can write requests to the gods and hang them on a wall within the shrine. Various shrines and their associated gods have reputations for being good at fulfilling particular types of requests; Enoshima Shrine, dedicated to the goddess Benten, has one for matchmaking.

## Page 355

**The Pet Girl of Sakurasou**, about a male college student who comes to take care of his female classmate, a world-famous artist severely lacking in common sense, is one of Kamoshida-sensei's previous light novels.

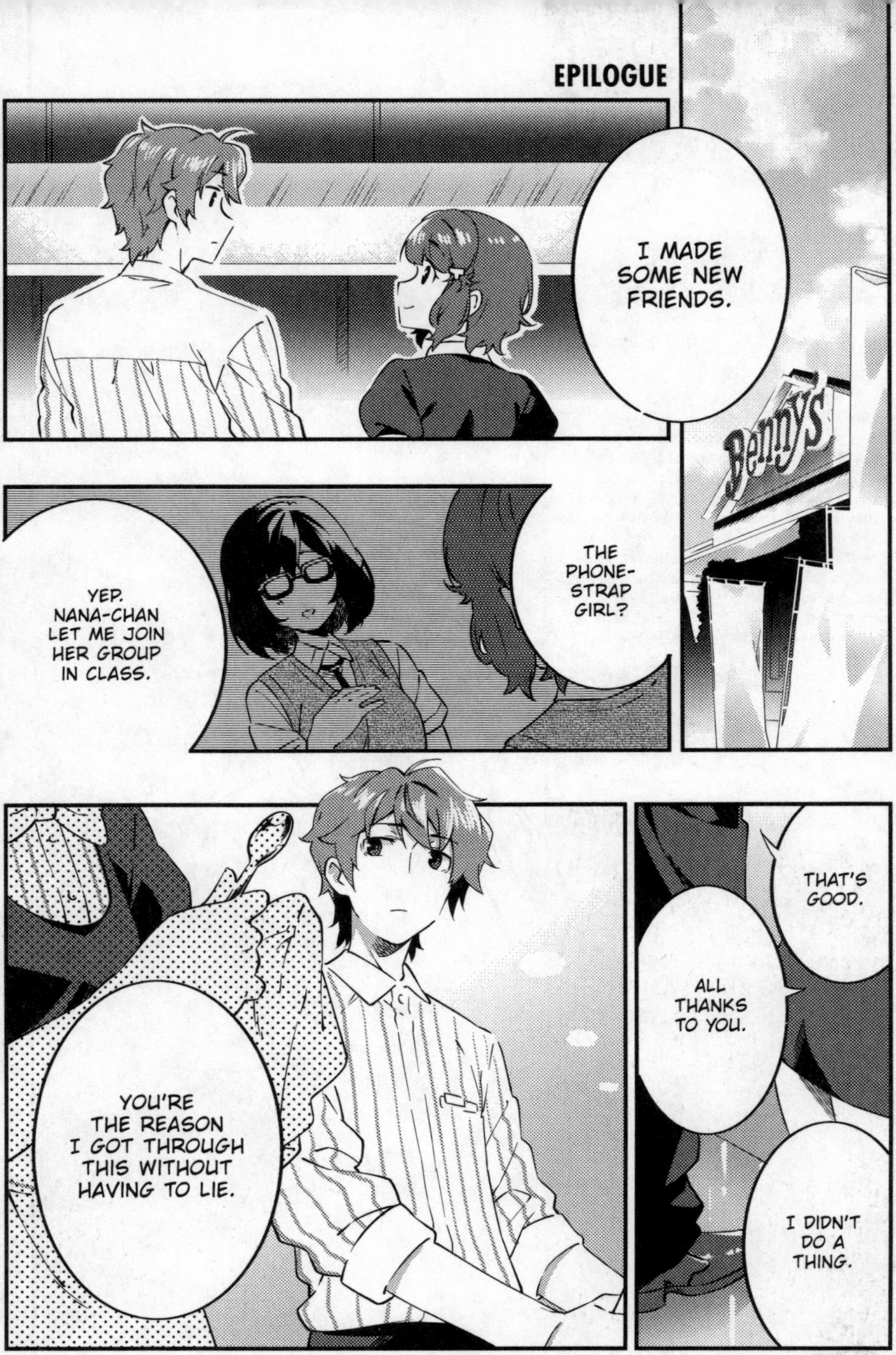
I MADE SOME NEW FRIENDS.
THE PHONE-STRAP GIRL?
YEP. NANA-CHAN LET ME JOIN HER GROUP IN CLASS.
THAT'S GOOD.
ALL THANKS TO YOU.
I DIDN'T DO A THING.
YOU'RE THE REASON I GOT THROUGH THIS WITHOUT HAVING TO LIE.

# AFTERWORD

I was first asked to adapt *Petite Devil Kohai* in July 2017.

I had read *Sakurasou* as a student but never dreamed I'd be asked to adapt a book by that writer...I still can't believe it.

Preparation went on behind the scenes, and I got a fair number of pages stockpiled. Then, in March of this year, serialization began. And it's about to be December! I wrapped up working on this manga while the anime was still airing. I'm glad to have been part of the *Rascal* series' media mix strategy.

I'm sure it has its flaws, but I feel like I found ways to show Sakuta, Tomoe, and Mai's story that the source novel and anime can't do, ones that can only be found in manga. I hope you enjoy that.

TSUKUMO ASAKUSA

2018.11

## Thanks,

HAJIME KAMOSHIDA-SENSEI

KEJI MIZOGUCHI-SENSEI

EDITOR T

PREVIOUS EDITOR A

DENGEKI BUNKO EDITORS

G'S COMICS EDITORS

DESIGNERS

...and You!

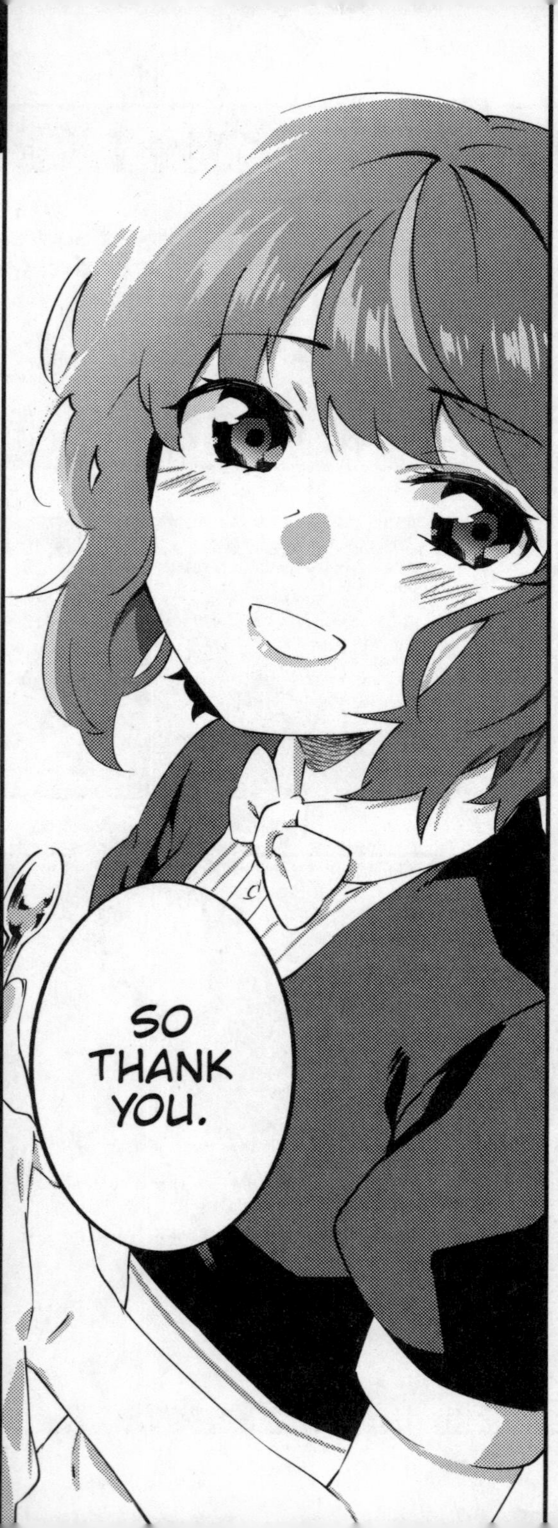
SO THANK YOU.

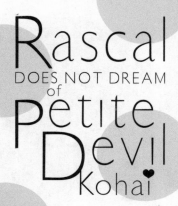

# Rascal
## DOES NOT DREAM
### of
# Petite
# Devil
## Kohai ♥

**2**

ORIGINAL STORY:
**Hajime Kamoshida**

ART:
**Tsukumo Asakusa**

CHARACTER DESIGN:
**Keji Mizoguchi**

TRANSLATION: ANDREW CUNNINGHAM

LETTERING: PHIL CHRISTIE

SEISHUN BUTA YARO WA PETITE DEVIL KOHAI NO YUME WO MINAI Vol. 1, 2
© Hajime Kamoshida, Tsukumo Asakusa 2018
First published in Japan in 2018 by KADOKAWA CORPORATION, Tokyo.
English translation rights arranged with KADOKAWA CORPORATION, Tokyo
through TUTTLE-MORI AGENCY, INC., Tokyo.

English translation © 2020 by Yen Press, LLC

Yen Press
150 West 30th Street, 19th Floor
New York, NY 10001

Visit us at yenpress.com
facebook.com/yenpress
twitter.com/yenpress
yenpress.tumblr.com
instagram.com/yenpress

First Yen Press Edition: December 2020

Yen Press is an imprint of Yen Press, LLC.
The Yen Press name and logo are trademarks of Yen Press, LLC.

The publisher is not responsible for websites (or their content) that are not owned by the publisher.

Library of Congress Control Number: 2019948598

ISBNs: 978-1-9753-1801-7 (paperback)
       978-1-9753-1802-4 (ebook)

10 9 8 7 6 5 4 3 2

WOR

Printed in the United States of America